IRRAWADDY IMPERATIVES

Reviewing India's Myanmar Strategy

IRRAWADDY IMPERATIVES

Reviewing India's Myanmar Strategy

Jaideep Chanda

Vivekananda International Foundation
New Delhi

PENTAGON PRESS LLP

Irrawaddy Imperatives: Reviewing India's Myanmar Strategy

Jaideep Chanda

ISBN 978-93-90095-34-6

First Published in 2021

Published by
PENTAGON PRESS LLP
206, Peacock Lane, Shahpur Jat,
New Delhi-110049
Phones: 011-64706243, 26491568
Telefax: 011-26490600
email: rajan@pentagonpress.in
website: www.pentagonpress.in

Printed at Aegean Offset Printers, Greater Noida, U.P.

To Baba

Late Col Jayanta Chanda

The 3rd Gorkha Rifles & The Dogra Scouts

RIMC (1953-1956), 17th NDA & 26th IMA

CONTENTS

Foreword *ix*

Acknowledgements *xiii*

Abbreviations, Acronyms and Initialisms *xvii*

Editorial Notes *xxiii*

Introduction *xxv*

1. A Geographical Study of Myanmar and the India-Myanmar Border (IMB) Region 1
2. A Historical Perspective of India-Myanmar Relations: Independence to 1989 23
3. A Historical Perspective of India-Myanmar Relations: 1989 Onwards 45
4. Myanmar Consciousness and a Blind Spot 73
5. The Kaladan Project 90
6. Myanmar and India's Northeast 115
7. The Rakhine Conflicts 132
8. The Tatmadaw: Raising the 'Standard' 165
9. Defence Diplomacy and India-Myanmar Relations 189
10. Myanmar and Sanctions 206
11. The Lady and The Law: Daw Aung San Suu Kyi and the International Court of Justice Imbroglio 232
12. Is the China-Myanmar Economic Corridor (CMEC) actually China's Myanmar Exploitation Corridor? 254

13. The Cultural Connects and Beyond 291

14. Making Sense of It All 308

Postscript 340

APPENDICES

A Agreement on International Boundary with India (10 March 1967) 345

B Detailed State-wise Physical and Demographic Description of the India-Myanmar Border 351

C Detailed Description of Chin State 359

D Detailed Description of Sagaing Region 367

E Detailed Description of Kachin State 376

F Detailed Description of Rakhine State 381

G Passport (Entry into India) Rules, 1950 386

H Land Border Crossing Agreement, 2018 389

I List of Books on Myanmar and India-Myanmar Relations by Indian Authors 394

J Dramatis Personae 397

K Treaty of Peace and Friendship, 1951 407

L MoUs Exchanged during visit of President U Win Myint of Myanmar: 26-29 Feb 2020 409

M List of Agreements, Joint Statements, Memoranda of Understanding and other Selected Documents pertaining to India-Myanmar Relations (2014–2020) 411

N Framework Agreement Between India and Myanmar on Kaladan Multi-Modal Transit Transport Project, 2008 421

O Arakan Rohingya Salvation Army 427

P First Person Account of Indian Abducted by the Arakan Army 435

Q Selected Extracts of the Republic of the Union of Myanmar Defence White Paper (2015) 438

R Summary of Current Resolutions and Reports of the UN in Relation to Myanmar 447

S Summary of Sanctions Imposed on Myanmar by Various Entities 449

T Department of Investment and Company Affairs: Investment Opportunities in Myanmar 452

U A Brief History of the Stilwell Road 461

Index 464

Foreword

On 1 February 2021, days before the President of Myanmar was to be sworn in following the 8 November 2020 elections, the Myanmar Armed Forces under the Senior General Ming Aung Hlaing did the unthinkable – they staged a coup d'état, declared an emergency and placed Daw Aung San Suu Kyi and other members of her National League for Democracy behind bars. The hopes of a democratic transition were snuffed out once again. A serious regional and international security issue has materialised.

The people of Myanmar have reacted with anger. Widespread protests against the Armed Forces have broken out across the country. The military has reacted harshly. In clashes between the civilian protestors and the army, several hundred people have been killed. Many more are missing. The masses have started fighting back. The international community has been divided in its response to the developments in Myanmar.

Myanmar is a complex country with a chequered history of a long military rule, raging ethnic insurgencies and flashes of democracy. The people are devout Buddhists and peace loving. It is surrounded by China, India and the ASEAN countries. It has a prominent location in the Bay of Bengal. To understand the country, one needs to be familiar with its culture, history and economy. Understanding Myanmar is not easy.

Why has Myanmar not been able to adopt democracy? Col Jaideep Chanda's book *Irrawaddy Imperatives: Reviewing India's Myanmar Strategy* provides the reader the necessary background to help the reader make sense of this complex country. Divided into 14 chapters and 21 appendices the book has evolved into a reference work on Myanmar. It contains a large number of documents and other information that scholars would find useful.

Col Jaideep Chanda, a serving officer in the Indian Army, was a Senior Fellow, Vivekananda International Foundation, New Delhi, during 2019-20. While writing this book, he visited Myanmar and Mizoram on study trips during which he spoke to many people as he collected relevant academic information. The book also deals with Tatmadaw and its role in the mainland politics. It has a chapter on the conflict in the Arakan region where the Arakan Army is dominant. It is in this region that India's Kaladan Multimodal Project is located. The book has a chapter on the significance of the project and how it is faring. Col Chanda delves deep into the history of the project and brings out what many people may not know; that it was late BG Verghese, a noted Indian journalist and scholar, who first conceived of the project way back in 1968 to overcome the dilemma posed by the narrow Chicken's Neck which connects mainland India with the northeast.

The close ethnic linkages between the Chins of Mizoram and their brethren (including those in the Arakan Army) across the international boundary is an important facet of India-Myanmar relations. India cannot remain unaffected by the developments in Myanmar particularly at a time when many people have started crossing the border and taking shelter in Mizoram.

It is ironic that the same Aung San Suu Kyi who defended the Tatmadaw at the International Court of Justice on the Rohingya issue, was detained by the military in February 2021. Aung San Suu Kyi was careful all these years. She tried to maintain a balanced relationship with the Tatmadaw. She made it a point not to disturb this balance. The peaceful coexistence between the military was a way out for Myanmar. However, the equation was upset with the November 2020 elections in which the military lost a large number of seats. This was unacceptable to Tatmadaw.

The author's archival research extends to the historical evolution of India-Myanmar diplomacy. He delves into the personal papers of M. A. Rauf, Y. D. Gundevia, Baleshwar Prasad and S. A. S. Tyabji, all prominent Indians of their times in Burma. The first three were India's Ambassadors to Burma at various stages. This research lends considerable depth to the book.

Myanmar has a love hate relationship with China. A chapter on China's interest in Myanmar, especially with reference to the China Myanmar Economic Corridor (CMEC), provides a welcome perspective to the study. In this chapter the author has mapped and analysed the constituents of the CMEC, from a pragmatic standpoint of both India and Myanmar.

Being a military man, Col Chanda approaches the subject from the twin perspectives of borderland studies and geographic realism. He devotes considerable time to document the geographic nuances of the India-Myanmar border region. His study brings back to pole position the centrality of India's northeast in any Indian approach to Myanmar. He argues that the conventional mainland-heartland approach to the Northeast now needs to be shed in favour of a more pragmatic policy wherein the Northeast and its people are given primacy.

I would like to congratulate the author for his painstaking research. He has produced an outstanding work on Myanmar and India-Myanmar relations. In writing this book, Col Jaideep Chanda hopes to raise Myanmar consciousness in India. The book will be beneficial to policy makers, scholars, soldiers as well as students.

15 May 2021
New Delhi

Dr. Arvind Gupta
Director
Vivekananda International Foundation

Acknowledgements

That this book saw the light of day in a short time of a year speaks volumes of the assistance and encouragement that innumerable people and well-wishers have bestowed on it, and its author.

To begin with, I am beholden to General MM Naravane, PVSM, AVSM, SM, VSM, ADC, who, as the Eastern Army Commander during the commencement of the Fellowship, took the time and effort to vet my first research proposal and provided invaluable guidance especially based on his experience as a Defence Attache to Myanmar. It was from here, really, that the research took shape and has evolved into this book.

This book would not have been possible without the support and encouragement of Dr Arvind Gupta, Director, Vivekananda International Foundation, New Delhi, who reposed total faith and confidence in my ability to deliver. The two field trips to Myanmar and Mizoram were courtesy his belief in the value of this Fellowship.

I am particularly grateful to Lt Gen Anil Chauhan PVSM, UYSM, AVSM, SM, VSM, ADC, Eastern Army Commander, who guided me during the research phase of the book and discussed different aspects over the many iterations we had. In many ways, his encouragement to me as a young Commanding Officer a decade ago put me on the path to academic pursuits.

I am particularly grateful to my colleagues, both serving and retired, in various services, who have assisted me on numerous aspects of this Fellowship. The long list includes Abhishek Yadav, Ajay Kothiyal, Anit Mukherjee, Amardeep Singh Godara, Deepinder Rathore, Harish Bahuguna, Harsh Agarwal, H. K. Jain, Ketan

Mohite, M.P. Dinesh Nair, Naval Jagota, PMS Dhillon, Pushpendra Mishra, R. Karthik, Robeen Chatterjee, Sarfraz Sanghera, Shubhankar Basu, Snehal Rathore, Vineet Agarwal, Vijeet Tomar, VS Sharda and Yogesh Kumar Sati.

I gratefully and humbly acknowledge the support of Lt Gen Ravi Sawhney (Retd), Centre Head & Senior Fellow, National Security and Strategic Studies & Internal Security Studies, VIF, who guided me through the Fellowship. I am also indebted to Ambassador Gautam Mukhopadhyay, former Ambassador to Myanmar and Distinguished Fellow at the VIF, who was my de facto mentor, and I, his tormentor!

Team VIF has been a great source of strength and support, and I must acknowledge the help provided by Lt Gen Gautam Banerjee (Retd) and Brig Vinod Anand (Retd). The brainstorming sessions with Dr Sreeradha Datta greatly added value to my understanding of the subject. Cchavi Vasisht, Alakh Ranjan and Aakriti Vinayak co-authored articles with me and have contributed to this project. Dr Arpita Mitra's contribution in explaining the cultural connect between Myanmar and India was substantial. Anjali Gupta was instrumental in helping me sort out mountains of data sourced from the MEA Website. Several maps in the book have been made by the GIS wizard, Jyothy Nair (www.getitmapped.in). On the administrative side, Anuttama Ganguly, Secretary VIF and her fantastic team comprising Abhijit Biswas, Abhinandan Rai, Alka Sahasrabudhe, Krishan Redhu, Kamal Sajwan, Manisha Bhadula and Vijender Verma, to name but a few, were a constant support.

Veteran journalist Subir Bhaumik, with his encyclopedic knowledge of the Northeast and Myanmar, helped clarify the complex issues on the subject. Constantino Xavier helped me clear my mind on the methodological aspects of the subject. Pratyush Manoj Nair and Soumyadeep Guha were a great help in sorting out the data used in the book. Many of the infographics in the book were by the talented young Rishabh Srivastava, and I would strongly recommend him to others. My heartfelt thanks to Mr Debabrata Bhattacharjee (IOCL, Yangon), who warmly hosted me during my stay at Yangon and accompanied me to several sites. I would be failing if I did not mention the assistance provided by Ankita Vinayak and Jyoti in the Manuscript section of Nehru Memorial Museum and Library.

My sincere thanks to General NC Vij (Retd) and General VP Malik (Retd) for their inputs and Ambassadors Shyam Saran and Rajiv Bhatia for their assistance and advice. I would also like to doff my hat to the Embassy of India, Yangon and all members who warmly hosted the VIF delegation during our visit there and have been in touch through the inception of this project till its completion.

I have probably missed out on many persons, but they fondly remain acknowledged. Needless to say, the shortcomings of this book are my own folly, and I must solely bear the consequences for them. Critiques are more than welcome at jaideep.chanda@protonmail.com

Finally, my family; Debalina, my wife and the wind beneath my wings, who probably believed in me more than I did in myself and encouraged me to get this going and impatiently put up with my absence; my son Jayostu put up with my hours of absence as patiently as a 14-year-old can; my sister Rittika and her husband Jyoti Parruck for warmly hosting me at Gurgaon where I wrote the bulk of this book, and last, but not the least my mother, Soma, for making me what I am today.

Abbreviations, Acronyms and Initialisms

A

AA — Arakan Army
ACARE — Advanced Centre for Agriculture Research and Education
ADC — Autonomous District Council
AEP — Act East Policy
AMM — Aqa Mul Mujahid (precursor to the ARSA)
ANC — Arakan National Congress
AR — Assam Rifles (a distinguished paramilitary force in Northeast India)
ARSA — Arakan Rohingya Salvation Army
ASEAN — Association of South East Asian Countries
ATTF — All Tripura Tiger Force

B

BCIM-EC — Bangladesh-China-India-Myanmar Economic Corridor
BECZ — Border Economic Cooperation Zones
BIMSTEC — Bay of Bengal Initiative for Multi-sectoral Technological and Economic Cooperation
BP — Border Pillar
BRI — Belt and Road Initiative (of China)
BRICS — Brazil, Russia, India, China & South Africa (an alliance)
BROUK — Burmese Rohingya Organisation of UK

C

CAPF — Central Armed Police Forces
CCCC — China Communications Construction Company Limited
C-in-C — Commander-in-Chief (used by the Myanmar Armed Forces and several EAGs)

CIPE	Centre for International Private Enterprise
CIPEC	China-Indochina-Peninsula Economic Corridor
CLMV	Cambodia, Lao PDR, Myanmar and Vietnam
COAS	Chief of Army Staff (of the Indian Army)
CORPAT	Coordinated Patrol (a Naval manoeuvre involving two or more countries)
COVID-19	CoronaVirus Disease 2019
CM	Chief Minister
CMEC	China Myanmar Economic Corridor (component of the BRI)
CNF	Chin National Front
CPEC	China Pakistan Economic Corridor
	D
DA	Defence Attache
DASSK	Daw Aung San Suu Kyi (State Counsellor of Myanmar a.k.a. The Lady)
DDSI	Directorate of Defence Services Intelligence (Myanmar)
DICA	Directorate of Investment and Company Administration, Myanmar
DMG	Development Media Group (a Myanmar based media group)
DoNER	(Ministry for the) Development of North East Region
DSA	Defence Services Academy
DSTA	Defence Services Technological Academy
	E
EAOs/EAGs	Ethnic Armed Organisations/Groups (Myanmars' indigenous insurgent groups)
EAM	External Affairs Minister
EAS	East Asia Summit
ECRL	East Coast Rail Link
EEZ	Exclusive Economic Zone
	F
FCO	Foreign Office Consultations (a bilateral mechanism between India and Myanmar)
FMCG	Fast Moving Consumer Goods
FMR	Free Movement Regime (across the India Myanmar Border)
FPNCC	Federal Political Negotiation and Consultative Committee
	G
GAIL	Gas Authority of India Limited
Gen	General

GoI	Government of India
	H
HADR	Humanitarian Assistance and Disaster Relief
HUJI-A	Harkat ul Jihad al Islami-Arakan
HUMINT	Human Intelligence
	I
ICC	International Criminal Court, The Hague
ICJ	International Court of Justice, The Hague
IED	Improvised Explosive Device
IFC-IOR	Information Fusion Centre, Indian Ocean Region, New Delhi
IFS	India Foreign Service
IIFFMM	Independent International Fact Finding Mission in Myanmar (a UN entity)
IIG	Indian Insurgent Group
IIMM	Independent Investigative Mechanism in Myanmar
IMB	India-Myanmar Border
IMNEX	India-Myanmar Naval Exercise
IMPLM	India-Myanmar Post Level Meetings
INA	Indian National Army (the original India Army raised by Netaji Subhash Bose)
IRCON	Indian Railways Construction Limited (now IRCON International Ltd)
ISI	Inter-Services Intelligence
ISP-Myanmar	Institute of Strategy and Policy-Myanmar (a Myanmar based think tank)
IWAI	Inland Waterways Authority of India
IWT	Inland Water Transport
	J
JBWG	Joint Boundary Working Group (between India and Myanmar on boundary issues)
JMB	Jamaat-ul-Mujahideen Bangladesh
JNU	Jawaharlal Nehru University
JTC	Joint Trade Committee
JWG	Joint Working Group (between India and Myanmar)
	K
KIO	Kachin Independence Organisation
KOGAS	Korea Gas Corporation
KMMTTP	Kaladan Multi-Modal Transit Transport Project

KNU	Karen National Union
	L
LBCA	Land Border Crossing Agreement (between India and Myanmar)
LDC	Least Developed Countries (A UN list of 43 countries based on per capita income and other human and economic indicators)
LET	Lashkar e Tayyaba
LIB	Light Infantry Battalion (of the Myanmar Army)
LID	Light Infantry Division (a Myanmar Army Formation)
LLP	Limited Liability Partnership
LTTE	Liberation Tigers of Tamil Eelam (a Sri Lankan Tamil insurgent group)
Lt Gen	Lieutenant General
	M
MEA	Ministry of External Affairs (of India)
MEDC	Myitkyina Economic Development Zone (a part of the BRI at the state level)
MHA	Ministry of Home Affairs (of India)
MILEX	Military Exercise
MIMU	Myanmar Information Management Unit (of the UN)
MIPS	Myanmar Institute of Peace and Security (a Myanmar based think tank)
MNDAA	Myanmar National Democratic Alliance Army (aka the Kokang Army)
MNF	Mizo National Front
MNFF	Mizo National Famine Front
MNP	Mizo National Party
MOGE	Myanmar Oil and Gas Enterprise
MOOTW	Military Operations Other Than War
MoU	Memorandum of Understanding
MTPA	Million Tonnes Per Annum
	N
NCA	Nationwide Ceasefire Agreement (Myanmar)
NDAA	National Democratic Alliance Army
NDA-K	New Democratic Army - Kachin
NE	Northeast (North East)
NLD	National League for Democracy (of Myanmar)
NLM	National Level Meetings (a bilateral mechanism between India and Myanmar)

NMML	Nehru Memorial Museum and Library
NSA	National Security Advisor
NSAZ	Naga Self-Administered Zone (in Myanmar)
NYC	New Yangon City (a proposed BRI project)
NYDC	New Yangon Development City
	O
OCEBV	ONGC CASPIAN E&P B.V.
OCMI	Office of the Chief of Military Intelligence (Myanmar)
OCMSA	Office of the Chief of Military Security Affairs (Myanmar)
OIC	Organisation of Islamic Cooperation
ONGC	Oil and Natural Gas Corporation (of India)
ORF	Observer Research Foundation (a New Delhi based independent think tank)
OVL	ONGC Videsh Limited
	P
PFR	Project Formulation Reports
PIWT	Paletwa Inland Water Terminal
PLA	People's Liberation Army (Manipur based insurgent group)
PM	Prime Minister
PMO	Prime Minister's Office (of India)
PPF	Project Preparation Facility
PRC	People's Republic of China
PSU	Public Sector Undertaking
	Q
QC	Queen's Counsel
	R
RBC	Regional Border Committee (between India and Myanmar)
RCSS	Restoration Council of Shan State (Myanmar)
RITES	Rail India Technical and Economic Service
	S
SAARC	South Asian Association for Regional Cooperation
SARDP-NE	Special Accelerated Road Development Programme in North East
SEAGP	South-East Asia Gas Pipeline Company Limited
SEAP	South East Asia Pipeline
SEZ	Special Economic Zone
SLM	Sectoral Level Meetings (MHA led Joint Secretary level bilateral mechanism between India and Myanmar)
SLORC	State Law and Order Restoration Council (Myanmar)

SPDC	State Peace and Development Council (Myanmar)
SSPP	Shan State Progressive Party (Myanmar)
	T
Tatmadaw	The Myanmar Armed Forces
TDS	Tax Deducted at Source
TECHINT	Technical Intelligence
TISS	ThayNinGa Institute for Strategic Studies (a Myanmar military sponsored think tank)
TNLA	Ta'ang National Liberation Army
	U
UCAV	Unmanned Combat Aerial Vehicle
ULA	United League of Arakan
ULFA	United Liberation Front of Asom (Assam based insurgent group)
UMFCCI	Union of Myanmar Federation of Chamber of Commerce & Industry
UNECAFE	United Nations Economic Commission for Asia and the Far East
UNFC	United Nationalities Federation Council
UPC	Union Peace Conference
USDP	Union Social and Development Party (a Tatmadaw mentored political party)
UWSA	United Wa State Army (a Myanmar insurgent group)
	V
VIF	Vivekananda International Foundation (a New Delhi based independent think tank)
VPRS	Victims Participation and Reparation Section (a part of the ICC Registry)
	W
WARDEC	Wargaming Development Centre
	Y
YTHIC	Yunnan Tengchong Heng Yong Investment Company

Editorial Notes

Nothing is easy in Myanmar, not even the name of the country. Myanmar changed its name a number of times. It started with the *Union of Burma* in 1948 and swung to the *Socialist Republic of the Union of Burma* in 1974. The next change came when vide the Adaptation of Expressions Law passed on 18 June 1989 by the Ne Win Government, the country's name was changed to the *Union of Myanmar*. Ostensibly this new name was more inclusive of minorities. Finally, after the constitutional referendum of 2010, the country settled on its current name, the *Republic of the Union of Myanmar*.

While Burma is phonetically easier than Myanmar, in this book, I have tried to use the version of the name as applicable in the context, though not very consistently. So in one sentence you may find both versions being used as they came to me naturally. Similarly there are two versions of almost all local names. Irrawaddy is presently referred to as the Ayeyarwady, however I opted for the former for alliterative convenience in naming the book. The same principle holds good for the other names e.g. Mrauk Oo is also spelt Mrauk U and even Mrauk-U. Achieving consistency in the spellings and formats was an editorial challenge.

The description of the India-Myanmar Border follows the South to North alignment which is based on the sequence of BPs which start from the south (BP 1) upwards to the north. Hence in deference to this fact, I have sequenced my study of the region, at most places, from south to north.

The list of abbreviations, acronyms and initialisms is exhaustive, though there would still be a few which have got left out.

Introduction

This book is the outcome of a one-year Research Fellowship with the Vivekananda International Foundation, New Delhi, as part of a sabbatical from the Indian Army. My interest in Myanmar had started as a result of my professional interaction with that country's uniformed counterparts. The Fellowship began as a generic proposal to study the role of the military in stabilising boundary issues, but that was felt to have too large a scope for a year-long fellowship, given the vast land borders of the country. Accordingly, it was narrowed down to the India-Myanmar context. The end result touches upon various aspects of India-Myanmar relations beyond the narrow confines of border management. What has evolved is material, which is, I believe, unique and hopefully provides a fresh approach to India-Myanmar relations. One hopes this will be of use to policy makers and scholars of the subject.

This book has two broad aims. One is that it attempts to raise 'Myanmar Consciousness' in Indian strategic thought and scholarship. I coined the term 'Myanmar Consciousness' as a generic phrase to describe the state of awareness about Myanmar in individuals and institutions in India, especially in academic and policy-making circles. There is an acute shortage of Myanmar consciousness in virtually all segments of the strategic society, academia and the media. I first used the term in an article[1] covering the visit of the President of Myanmar to India, which was largely missed out by the Indian mainstream media, which, in effect demonstrated the lack of Myanmar consciousness in the Fourth Estate. Further, during the course of the Fellowship, I realised that there was an acute paucity of Myanmar scholars in India, who could provide clarity from an Indian perspective. One relied on diplomats in general, former ambassadors in particular, military officers and a handful of scholars and experts on the Indian neighbourhood, to navigate through the labyrinth of information, often conflicting, to make sense of the situation.

Two, the book also serves as a reference for Myanmar scholars through the various appendices which contain data and documents relevant to India-Myanmar relations. Not all the data related to Myanmar is easily accessible and the Joint Statement on the occasion of the visit of President U Win Myint to India in February 2020 is a case in point. Initially, the Joint Statement was posted on the Ministry of External Affairs (MEA) Twitter account. Trying to read a 2,300-word document through tweets has its own challenges! Then it was found that the entire text was also posted on the Myanmar Ministry of Foreign Affairs' Facebook account. Not the first place one would look at from an Indian perspective. Thus, this book serves to provide, at one place, some of the documents and information that would be useful to other Myanmar scholars, in their future scholarship. I believe India-Myanmar relations and studies deserve this effort.

The problem that a professional, in my case a soldier, faces when he dives into the world of academics and research is that he ends up studying issues analytically and instinctively, without the benefit of an academic grounding in the theoretical aspects of the study. There are merits and demerits to this since the lack of conventional academic training enables fresh and unconventional work. On the demerits side, the output, without the benefit of a sound theoretical foundation, appears lacklustre.[2] Hence, a few words about the multiple approaches used in this book are in order. Firstly, this book approaches India-Myanmar relations from a borderland studies perspective. To understand the borderland perspective, I have relied on Kathleen DuVal's introduction[3] to borderland studies where she describes the borderland as both a place and a historiographic methodology, often combined. She adds that a borderland is a place where two entities (usually nations or societies) border each other. As a methodology, borderlands studies question what happens when distinct societies rub against each other or contest lands in between.

Sahana Basavapatna, succinctly applies it to the India-Myanmar borderland in her paper on Chins in Mizoram,[4] where she brings out that the idea of a nation bounded within a specific geographic space is unique to modernity and is an essential constituent of a sovereign state. What borders, and by implication sovereignty, consist of, is not simply the control of physical areas; rather the control over various elements which flow across these zones. She states that:

> *Borders and borderlands in India, in keeping with this fundamental characteristic, are fuzzy areas that, on the one hand, denote the need for the state*

> *to manifest its authority and power. On the other hand, and paradoxically, they are also spaces that call into question the state's authority and, by implication, the idea of a sovereign nation. The case of Chin migration into Mizoram across the India-Burma border is taken as a case in point to understand how our conception of nation and citizenship are played out in this border region.*

Pum Khan Pau, of Vishva Bharati University, West Bengal, India, writes[5] in his paper that the Indo-Burma borderlands are a space where one can see decay and revival of relationships among the transborder people. He argues for moving beyond state-centric conceptions of the border as rigid and static lines, and emphasises the 'duality' or 'paradoxical character' of the borderlands. He maintains that while colonial and post-colonial borders divided indigenous communities thereby creating 'difference' or 'otherness,' it also unifies and facilitates revival of relationships among the trans-border people through dialogue, interaction and exchange across the border. His, too, is a case study of the Zo people of the Indo-Burma borderlands. This borderlands approach really defines the limits of this project. The India-Myanmar Border (IMB) is the major and central theme in this work and the border zone which, in this case, extends to the Irrawaddy for reasons which we define further on in this section.

The second approach to this work is that of geographic realism. In a sense, it is about coming to terms with the ground realities; a back-to-basics kind of approach to acknowledge what is irreversible. This is something that appeals to the soldier in me. It stems from a very basic military principle of studying the 'ground,' i.e., the terrain, very well. These are the 'whites'[6] which cannot be fought and have to be heeded to.

The third concurrent approach which straddles this project is the centrality of the Northeast and its people as the principal stakeholders in India-Myanmar relations. And, by corollary, the need to have the perspectives of the Northeasterners incorporated into India's Myanmar strategy and policy. Thus, the outlook of the Northeast as a problem to India-Myanmar relations must be jettisoned in favour of the Northeast as a positive enabler in the India-Myanmar calculus. For too often now, the Northeast and Myanmar have been described as 'bridges', 'links', 'gateways' and 'an access' to ASEAN markets, to the East, and critical to the Act East Policy. This transitional space approach needs to give way to view the Northeast and Myanmar from an 'ends' perspective rather than a 'means to an end' perspective. This approach is, what I believe, will give impetus to develop the region (both the Northeast and Myanmar) and provide the boost to India's growth story.

This book begins with a geographical study of Myanmar and the IMB Region and sets the ground for this journey into the world of India-Myanmar relations. Chapter 1 goes over the geographic subdivisions of Myanmar and studies the Western Ranges, the range along which the IMB runs, in great detail. It also traces the evolution of the IMB right from the 1826 Yandaboo Treaty to the India-Burma Boundary Agreement and the on-ground demarcation in the 1960s. The chapter undertakes a physical and demographic description of the Myanmar provinces bordering the IMB and analyses the importance of each border province to India, from an investor's perspective. It dwells on the implications for both countries as also Bangladesh, which shares a critical 267 km border with Myanmar. Finally, it analyses the Free Movement Regime (FMR) and briefly dwells on the unresolved border issues between India and Myanmar. Eight appendices to this chapter add valuable data to the study. These include detailed geographic and demographic descriptions of Rakhine, Chin, Sagaing (including the Naga Self-Administered Zone) and Kachin provinces of Myanmar. This is over and above the detailed description of the IMB Region *per se*.

Chapters 2 and 3 place the geography into context and provide a historical framework to India-Myanmar diplomacy based on archival material accessed at the Nehru Memorial Museum and Library (NMML). Chapter 2 draws on the personal papers of four esteemed individuals including three ambassadors who had been associated with Burma in the early days, post-Independence. These include Y.D. Gundevia, S.A.S. Tyabji, M.A. Rauf and Baleshwar Prasad. The chapter also looks at the chronological history phased in two (out of four) parts, viz., independence till 1962 and 1962 to 1989. It relies on some possibly hitherto unpublished archival material from the Baleshwar Prasad Papers to throw light on the India-Myanmar relations in the 70s.

Chapter 3 takes on from 1989 in the balance two parts, i.e., 1989 to 2015 and from 2015 till 2020. Much outstanding scholarship is available on the historical perspectives of Myanmar and hence, rather than reproducing what has already been written by other scholars, this section focuses on the current history, i.e., of the past few decades. The past decade has seen two major changes for both India and Myanmar. For India, we have had two editions of the Modi Government at the helm since 2014 with drastic and remarkable positive changes. Equally drastic for Myanmar, the decade has seen the transition of power from the military government to that of the government of the National League for Democracy (NLD) led by 'The Lady', i.e., Daw Aung San Suu Kyi (DASSK) herself. Both these changes have permeated the realms of India-Myanmar relations and thus merit documentation. The chapter also carries two appendices, one which lists out all the books on Myanmar and India-Myanmar Relations by Indians, and a *Dramatis Personae,* i.e., an annual tabulated chart from 1946 to 2020 which lists out important decision-makers including the Indian Ambassadors to Myanmar, External Affairs Ministers, Prime Ministers, Foreign Secretaries, Defence Attaches, Defence Secretaries, Defence Ministers, Army Chiefs, Eastern Army Commanders and, for reference, the *de facto* Heads of State in Myanmar for each year. I expect both to be of use to scholars on the subject.

A pet peeve of scholars of Myanmar studies in India is that Myanmar is perpetually consigned to the 'Blind Spot' of India. Chapter 4 examines this aspect by looking at five instances where Myanmar fails to feature in the discourse. It relies extensively on interviews of Ambassadors Shyam Saran and Gautam Mukhopadhyay to come to identify the reasons for this blind spot, whether actual or perceived. It also examines whether there is a need to work on alternative alliances to offset Myanmar's segregation from South Asia. Some analysts[7] have argued that the South Asian construct is a flawed one and this skews Indian foreign policy away from the relevant neighbourhood. I have taken this debate forward and proposed a Greater South Asian alliance to offset the limitations of SAARC and BIMSTEC while combining their strengths. The chapter also takes a hard and critical look at the absence of Myanmar studies as a discipline in most Indian universities. The irony of the fact is that the premier Jawaharlal Nehru University (JNU) School of Language Literature and Culture Studies provides courses on countries with which India has no borders and are thousands of kilometres away, but does not offer Myanmar studies, the study of a country with which we share 1,643 km of crucial borders. Similarly, in Delhi University, the Department of Slavonic and Finno-Ugrian Studies offers exotic courses in Slavonic languages, namely, Bulgarian, Croatian, Czech, Polish, Russian and Hungarian from the Finno-Ugrian group of languages, but not in the Myanmar language. This soundly reinforces the hypothesis of the lack of Myanmar consciousness in the academia. This study, it is hoped, will provide the rudimentary foundations for subsequent scholarship to take forward and acknowledge the need to inculcate measures to address the problem of the paucity of Myanmar consciousness.

Chapter 5 looks at the Kaladan Multi-Modal Transit Transportation Project (KMMTTP) starting from its conceptualisation in 1968. This is based on a paper titled *'Proposal for a Road-River link from the Mizo Hills District to Akyab in Burma'* by the then Information Advisor to Prime Minister Indira Gandhi, Mr. B.G. Verghese. The chapter then moves to the present-day Kaladan Project, including the current status of the port and road components. The Kaladan Project has acquired a sort of a 'white elephant' status. There is a thought process which suggests that India should cut its losses on the venture and abandon it in view of the inordinate delay in construction and implementation. It is also argued that since the Sheikh Hasina Government in power in Bangladesh has good relations with the Indian Government and allows access to Northeast India through Bangladesh, the *raison d'être* for the Kaladan Project is nullified, adding to the voices who recommend the Kaladan Project be abandoned. The chapter strongly pitches against this and puts forth an alternative perspective on the Kaladan Project and why it complements Prime Minister Modi's vision of a five trillion dollar[8] economy. This chapter also analyses the functioning of the Arakan Army (AA), which has emerged as the most powerful local stakeholder in the region and the *de facto* representative of the people. Without taking into account the sensitivities of the Arakan people and, in effect, the AA, the final leg of the Kaladan Project is unlikely to be completed.

In Chapter 6, I look at the interplay between Myanmar and India's Northeast. Specifically, I analyse the Mizo connection with the AA and also try and assess the impact the Kaladan Project would have on Mizoram. The material I have used was collected during a field visit I had undertaken to Mizoram in early March 2020. The field visit was conducted with a number of aims, including to assess the importance of the Northeastern states in India-Myanmar relations; to assess the influence of Mizoram in the Rakhine conflict with specific reference to the AA, and *vice versa*; to assess the impact of the Kaladan Project on the Northeast, especially Mizoram; to see on ground the state of progress of the Kaladan Project in Mizoram and, finally, keeping all these in mind, generate policy recommendations for implementation. It also draws on interactions with various vendors involved in the Kaladan Project. The initial plan for the Fellowship had been to visit all the four Northeastern states on the IMB, but time constraints and COVID-19 put paid to the proposal. Hence, the scope of the first aim (to assess the importance of the Northeastern states in India-Myanmar relations) had to be reduced to assess the importance of Mizoram in India-Myanmar relations. In this chapter, I conclude that the Kaladan Project needs to be repackaged to address the negative legacy baggage attached to it and to re-envision it as the main and preferred route of transportation to the Northeast and from Myanmar to India rather than as an alternative to the Siliguri Corridor.

From the borderland perspective, the Rakhine conflict is undoubtedly the most serious and potentially devastating for the southern part of the IMB, including

Bangladesh. Chapter 7 provides an overview of the two conflicts that plague the Rakhine region, i.e., the conflict with the Arakan Rohingya Salvation Army (ARSA) and the ethnic Buddhist Rakhine insurgency being fought by the AA. It explains the background of the Arakan aspirations and dwells on the difference between confederation and federalism and documents the build-up to the present crisis. It also highlights the Tatmadaw's attempts to isolate the AA. It carries out a detailed analysis of the AA operations, funding and Chinese involvement. Finally, it looks at India's recommended approach to the AA issue. Since a vast amount of awareness and literature exists on the Rohingya crisis, the chapter is not about Rohingyas and human rights violations. Rather, it mostly confines itself to the ethnic Buddhist violence. To put things into perspective, it does however a carry a brief on the current status of the ARSA in Appendix P and the *modus vivendi* between the ARSA and the AA.

Chapter 8 is devoted to the study of the Tatmadaw and I start with a detailed examination of the Myanmar Defence White Paper 2015, selected extracts of which have been reproduced at Appendix R. Thereafter, I try and identify the components of the 'Standard Army' as proposed by the Tatmadaw. In doing so, I specifically look at the recruitment patterns, gender aspects, intelligence functions and the overall professional ethos of the Tatmadaw. The political tradition of the Tatmadaw and the implications on the polity of the nation also find mention in this chapter. Counter-insurgency operations in the context of the Rakhine conflict are analysed and finally I mull over the Senior General and his succession plans. The overall prognosis is not encouraging and the Tatmadaw is in need of a serious revamp in order to remain a credible force in this journey towards durable and definitive democracy.

India-Myanmar defence diplomacy is one of the best examples of defence diplomacy amongst India's neighbours. Why this falls into place in the overall India-Myanmar relationship is because of the unique role that the military-to-military relationship played in normalising relations between the civilian components of the two nations. Chapter 9 traces the post-independence history of India-Myanmar defence relations and highlights the role defence diplomacy has played in steering the bilateral relations of the two nations, especially in the context of the counter-insurgency operations along the India-Myanmar border. Traditionally, Myanmar has remained a closed society totally dominated by the military. In this context, the real breakthrough in India-Myanmar relations came through using defence diplomacy which effectively commenced in the early 1990s and culminated in game-changing outcomes for national security in Northeast

India in 2019. Hence, in this context, the study of defence diplomacy in India-Myanmar relations, becomes all the more relevant. Defence diplomacy in India-Myanmar relations has also succeeded in providing impetus to security and development in the Northeastern states and has the potential to develop the region further. Hence, I argue that if Myanmar is engaged diplomatically on the defence perspective more, the probability to achieve mutually beneficial security and developmental goals will be far enhanced than by confining ourselves to traditional diplomatic mechanisms.

Chapter 10 traces the entire journey from the Rohingya crisis to the kind of sanctions imposed or recommended to be imposed by the West and the UN and analyses whether or not they would be useful. It studies the build-up to the imbroglio, Pakistan's involvement and Myanmar's response to the crisis. It then studies the UN reports and looks at the shortcomings of the most important report of the Independent International Fact Finding Mission in Myanmar (IIFFMM) in specific. Certain Indian companies also find mention in the IIFFMM report for engaging with the Myanmar Armed Forces, including Infosys, which developed banking software for a military-owned bank in Myanmar. Finally it takes a holistic look at the efficacy of sanctions and makes certain recommendations for India's role in Myanmar.

Chapter 11 looks at another aspect of the same issue, viz., the international legal battle between the Organisation of Islamic Cooperation (OIC) proxy, The Gambia, and Myanmar and its implications. Noble Laureate Daw Aung San Suu Kyi, much to the consternation of her admirers and critics alike, threw the Western world into a tizzy when she opted to personally go to The Hague and defend her country at the International Court of Justice over allegations of genocide. Altogether, Myanmar faced a barrage of three international court cases processed over four days—the International Court of Justice Case; the International Criminal Case and the case in the Argentinean Federal Court. This chapter also looks at the relationship between the military and 'The Lady' and analyses the motives and machinations of her defence at The Hague. I argue that the defence at The Hague was an astute initiative by DASSK which endears her to the nationalistic Burmese as also the Tatmadaw. Eventually, it may enable her to wrangle more concessions from the Tatmadaw on the issue of constitutional amendments.

Chapter 12 looks at the China Myanmar Economic Corridor (CMEC). In this chapter, I attempt to map the entire gamut of proposals under the CMEC and analyse the impact. I come to the conclusion that Myanmar has woken up to the dangers of the debt trap while it continues to engage with China. The Chinese outlet to the Bay of Bengal through Myanmar's Deep Sea Port will fructify but over an extended time frame and can eventually be used by India as well. India needs to be pragmatic and more importantly develop its own and Myanmar's capabilities rather than trying to stymie the Chinese interests in Myanmar. I argue that India must resist the temptation to meet Chinese investments dollar for dollar and instead focus on those areas where India can genuinely contribute to the Myanmar economy. These investments I refer to as 'hearts and minds investments' which appeal to the heart of the Myanmar locals and are sound profitable ventures for investors and the invested.

Chapter 13 looks at the various cultural and other connections between India and Myanmar over the ages. It discusses the earliest cultural connections from the 15th century onwards till the reciprocal exiles of Bahadur Shah Zafar and Thibaw Min. It looks at the politics of the time and the prisoners in the freedom struggle who were imprisoned in Burma. It also dwells upon the religious connections between Hinduism and Buddhism and also the Chettiars who played an important role in establishing the colonial Burmese economy for which they were later vilified and exiled. The chapter chronicles an interesting people-to-people connect with two Indian First Ladies being from Myanmar and some eminent Myanmar persons working in or related to Indians. Lastly, the chapter makes a few policy recommendations to take forward this connect to enhance people-to-people relations.

Chapter 14 puts it all together and tries to codify a certain policy for India towards Myanmar. In this, I conclude that a strong and developed Myanmar is the best bet for India and for the development of India's Northeast. It is also the best way to hedge against Chinese influence in Myanmar and Northeast India. In this context, India's first Secretary General of the Ministry of External Affairs, Sir Girija Shankar Bajpai,[9] had postulated three circles of Indian security which are relevant to this discourse. The outermost circle was from Suez to Shanghai, the middle circle from Aden and Hormuz to Malacca Straits and the innermost from the Hindu Kush to the Irrawaddy. Similarly, General V. P. Malik (Retd), after his visit to Myanmar in 2000, postulated as such to Prime Minister Vajpayee that *'from the China border till the Irrawaddy, the Chinese influence is very strong already and there is nothing much that we can do today; but we can limit that influence to the Irrawaddy, if we develop our relationships with Myanmar today'.*

Thus, we see this extension of Indian influence up to the Irrawaddy is not a new concept and has a logical historical and geographic basis. Success in engaging Myanmar and thereby holding off the Chinese negative influence depends on the initiatives that India takes in reaching out and engaging the Tatmadaw and the Myanmar Government including the provincial governments. This book draws inspiration from this need to address the imperative to invest in the areas west of Irrawaddy, hence, the name 'Irrawaddy Imperatives.'

I was fortunate to be able to undertake two field trips for this Fellowship.

The first to Myanmar in December 2019 was of immense help in understanding first hand some of the issues which the Fellowship covered. The second to Mizoram was equally useful in understanding the impact India-Myanmar relations have on the Northeast, especially Mizoram.

Information from Myanmar is scarce, shrouded in secrecy, and needs to be contextually deciphered to make sense. Against this backdrop, one year is too little a period of time to do justice to the subject. In that sense, this remains work in progress.

NOTES

1. Jaideep Chanda, *Raising Myanmar Consciousness: Visit of the President of Myanmar to India (26–29 February 2020),* Vivekananda International Foundation, New Delhi, February 2020; https://www.vifindia.org/article/2020/february/28/raising-myanmar-consciousness-visit-of-the-president-of-myanmar-to-india (Accessed on 23 August 2020).
2. I am grateful to Dr. Kreizho Yhome, Senior Fellow, Observer Research Foundation, New Delhi, himself a Myanmar scholar, for pointing this out to me during the Fellows' Seminar for this project, where he had been invited by the Vivekananda International Foundation as a subject matter expert to review the manuscript and as a panellist.
3. Kathleen DuVal, *Borderlands: Oxford Bibliographies Online Research Guide* (Oxford Bibliographies Online Research Guides), OUP, USA, 1 June 2010, https://www.oxfordbibliographies.com/view/document/obo-9780199730414/obo-9780199730414-0010.xml (Accessed on 17 July 2020).
4. Sahana Basavapatna, *Chins in Mizoram:* 'The Case of Borders Making Brothers Illegal', *Journal of Borderlands Studies*, 2012, 27:1, 61-72, http://dx.doi.org/10.1080/08865655.2012.687209 (Accessed on 17 July 2020).
5. Pum Khan Pau, 'Transborder People, Connected History: Border and Relationships in the Indo-Burma Borderlands', *Journal of Borderlands Studies*, 2018, https://doi.org/10.1080/08865655.2018.1438914 (Accessed on 17 July 2020).
6. '*Don't fight the whites*', in military parlance means to stop resisting what cannot be changed. This originates from an age-old military practice of printing the 'setting' of an exercise or problem situation on white paper. This is distinguished from the answer to the problem, i.e., the solution, which is printed on 'pink' paper.
7. Nitin Pai of the Takshashila Institution for one.
8. Or whatever is the Covidised equivalent of the same figure.
9. As narrated by Ambassador Rajiv Sikri, former Ambassador to Kazakhstan, in a book discussion on '*The Borderlands and Boundaries of the Indian Subcontinent: Baluchistan to the Patkai Range and Arakan Yoma*' by Shri Dilip K. Chakrabarti, Professor Emeritus, University of Cambridge & Distinguished Fellow, VIF, on 18 March 2020. https://www.youtube.com/watch?v=8e8_6abcxZ8 (Accessed on 20 April 2020). Ambassador Bajpai speaks at 49:27 mins.

CHAPTER 1

A Geographical Study of Myanmar and the India-Myanmar Border (IMB) Region

The geography of Burma is important in understanding its history, its current ethnic make-up, and its possible futures.

—**Thant Myint-U**[1]

Robert D. Kaplan, author of the highly acclaimed classic, *The Revenge of Geography: What the Map Tells Us About Coming Conflicts and the Battle Against Fate,* writes[2] that geography has often been associated with fatalism and therefore stigmatized and thus apparently, to think geographically is to limit human choice. But in engaging with tools such as relief maps and population studies, he superimposes geographic layers on to foreign policy analyses to understand deeper and more powerful ways to analyse the world. He postulates that the more mankind remains preoccupied with the present, the more it seems that individuals and their choices matter; but the more we look at history, the more geography becomes relevant. And really, it is this sentiment that reigns in this study of Myanmar and the IMB Region. Thus, in a sense, this is a work of geographic realism. It acknowledges the ground realities and adopts a back-to-basics approach to the study. This is something that appeals to my military mind as it emerges from the most basic military principle of studying the terrain, very well. Thus, the geography of the IMB Region forms the *terra firma* on which the hypothesis of the Irrawaddy Imperatives rests. Also, since people form a central theme in this study, demography must therefore form part of this chapter.

The geography of the IMB Region is all about linkages—physical, ethnic, linguistic, cultural and fraternal. So much so that geographically even the northernmost mountains of the Western Range of Myanmar are linked with, unbelievably, the Andaman Islands over a thousand kilometres to the south. The Western Range runs along the IMB before it dives underground at the base of the Arakans and continues its journey undersea, resurfacing above the ocean far south, in what we now call the Andaman Islands. Physically, Myanmar encompasses fertile plains of the stately Irrawaddy River up to the forested plateaus of the Shan State, and from the majestic snowscapes of the Himalayan peaks in the northern apex of the China-India-Myanmar trijunction to the enchanting islands in the Andaman Sea.

Overview

This section looks at the geography of Myanmar in general and Western Myanmar in particular, as bordering India. Myanmar lies on the northwestern frontier of southeastern Asia. It shares maritime boundaries with the Andaman Sea and the Bay of Bengal (2,218 km) and land borders with Bangladesh (269 km), China (2,194 km), India (1,643 km), Laos (2,37 km) and Thailand (2,097 km) and has a total area of 678,500 sq km. Of this, land covers 657,740 sq km and water covers 20,760 sq km[3, 4] (see Figure 1.1).

The lie of the land in Myanmar slopes downward in elevation from the north to the south and naturally forms Upper Myanmar and Lower Myanmar. The terrain is made up of central lowlands ringed by steep, rugged highlands. Effectively, Myanmar is hemmed in from all directions by mountains, except in the south, which is a vast deltaic plain. The three mountain ranges, namely, the Arakan Yoma (i.e., Rakhine Yoma), the Bago Yoma, and the Shan Plateau, run north-to-south from the Himalayas. They form the valleys through which Myanmar's three main river systems flow. These are the Irrawaddy, the Salween or Thanlwin, and the Sittang. Myanmar's longest river, the Irrawaddy, flows nearly 2,170 km through the country and into the Gulf of Martaban. The upper courses of these rivers flow through deep gorges close to each other. Minerals and jade are mined in the northern mountains while fertile plains punctuate the valleys between the mountains. The bulk of Myanmar's population lives in the Irrawaddy valley between the Arakan Yoma and the Shan Plateau (see Figure 1.2).

Figure 1.1: Myanmar Borders

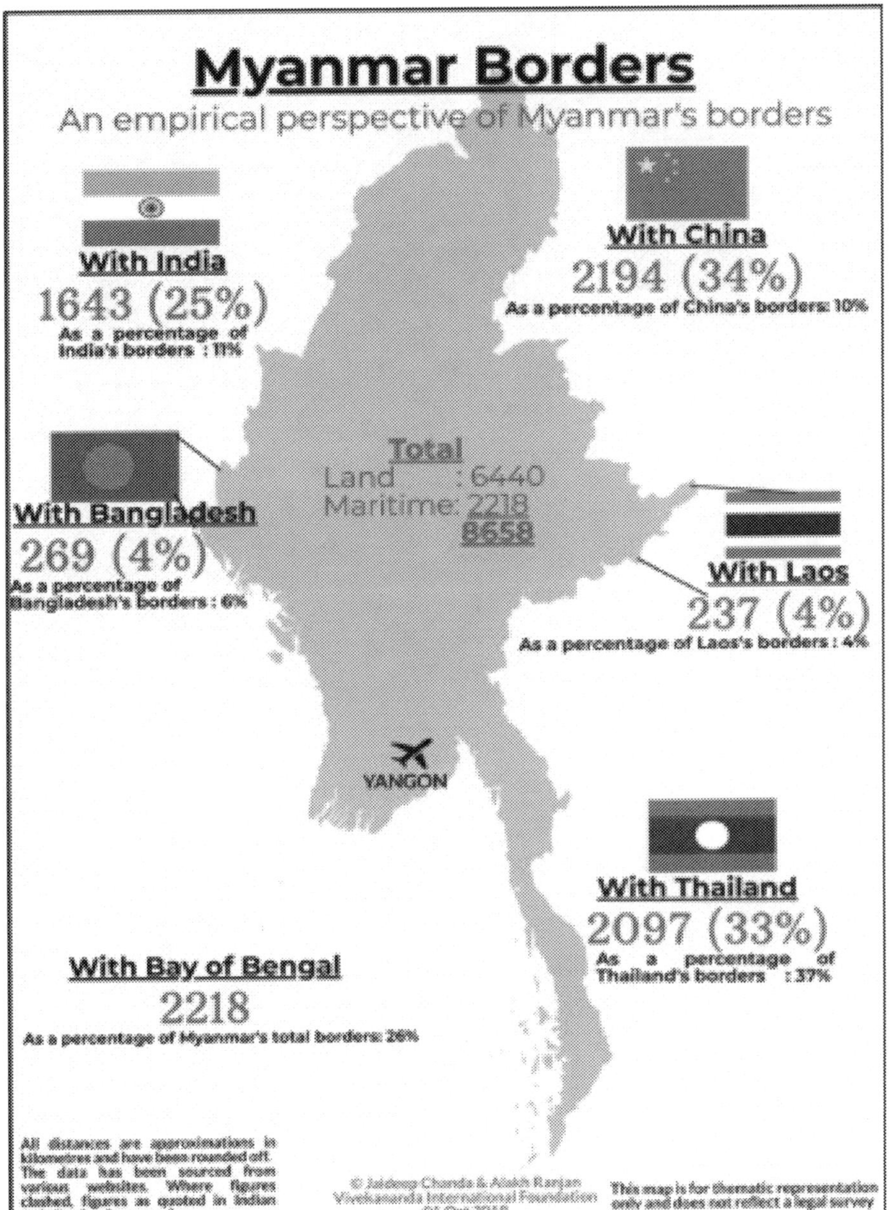

Figure 1.2: Myanmar Elevation and Major Rivers

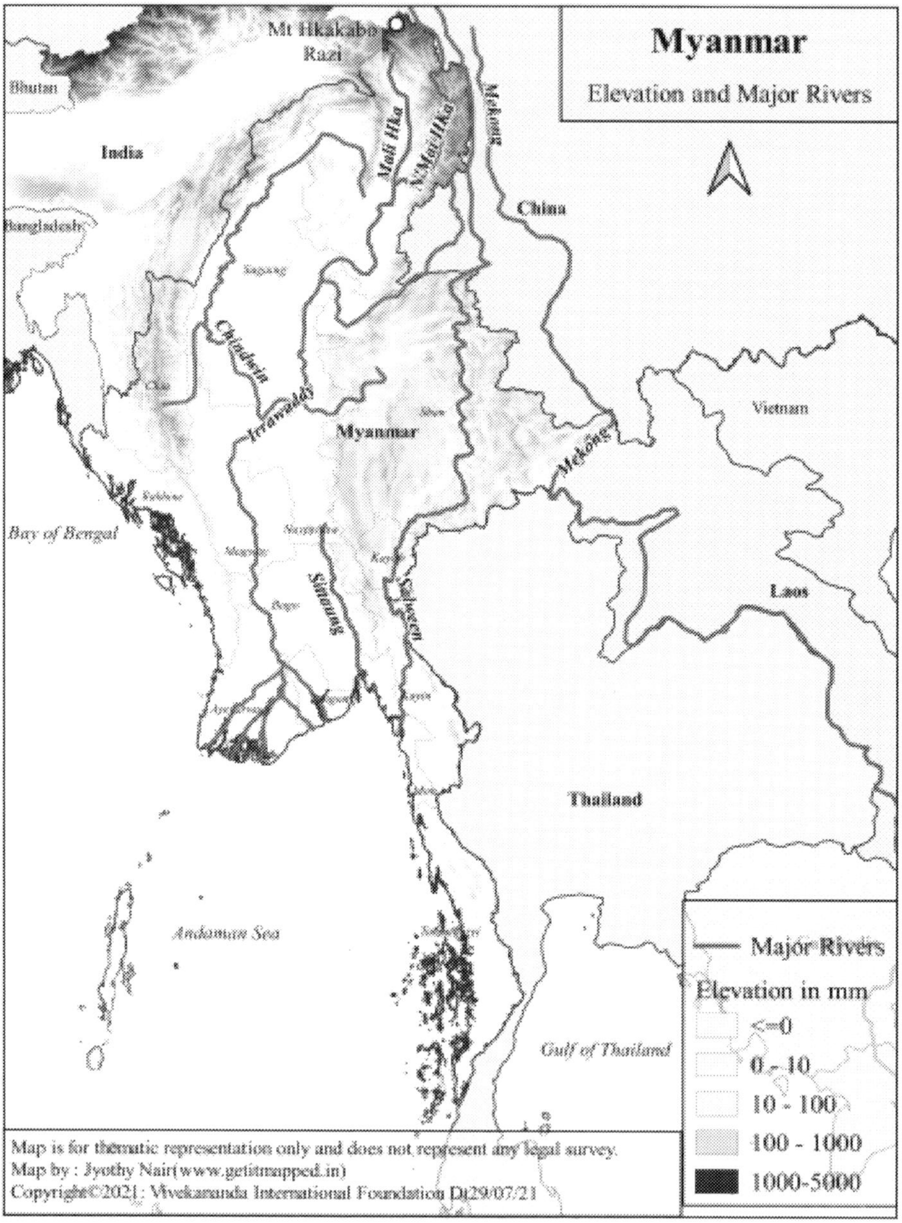

Geographic Subdivisions of Myanmar

Myanmar has five geographic regions, namely, the Northern Mountains; the Eastern Plateau; the Central Basin and Lowlands, the Coastal Plains and the Western Ranges.

Figure 1.3: Myanmar Geographic Subdivisions

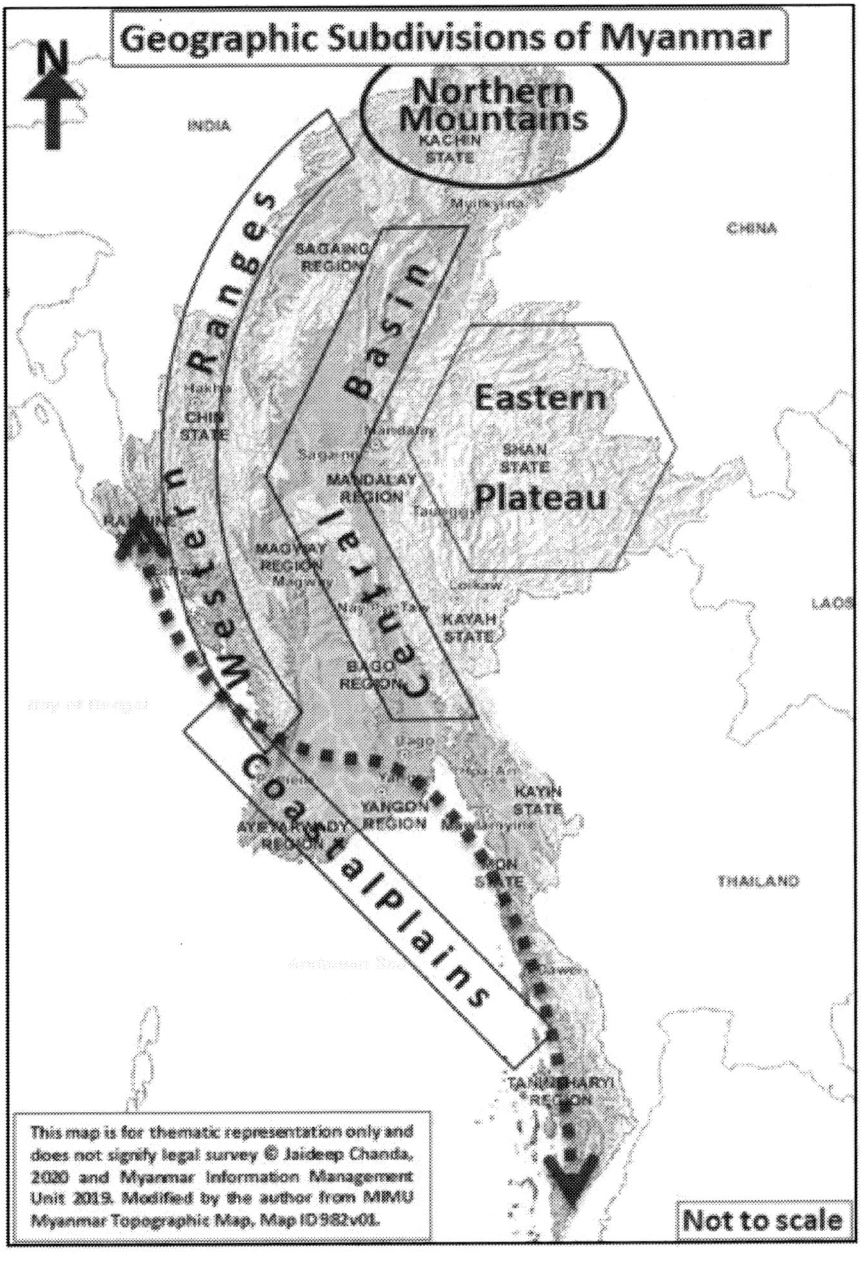

The Hengduan Shan Mountains in the northeast form the border with China. The Hengduan Mountains are primarily large north-south mountain ranges that separate the lowlands in northern Myanmar from the lowlands of the Sichuan Basin. This Northern Mountain region consists of a series of ranges that converges at Mount Hkakabo Razi (5,881 m) in Kachin State, the highest point of Myanmar.

The Eastern Plateau, i.e., the Shan Plateau, has an average height of 900 m and rises abruptly from the floor, very often in a single jump to 600 m. Its north-south oriented ranges rise to 1,800 m till 2,600 m above the plateau. To the north, it merges into the northern mountains, and southward it runs through the Dawna Range and to the Tenasserim (i.e., Tanintharyi) Mountains.

The Central Basin and Lowlands, lying between the Rakhine Mountains and the Shan Plateau, are structurally connected with the folding of the Western Ranges. Because of this geological characteristic of the region, precious and semi-precious rubies and sapphires have been mined in the northern reaches of the Shan Plateau since long. The Burmese leaders have traditionally depended on the sales of these precious stones such as sapphires, pearls and jade to fund their regime. Rubies are the biggest contributors; 90 per cent of the world's rubies come from Myanmar, whose red stones are prized for their purity and hue. Thailand is the major importer of Myanmar's gems. Myanmar's 'Valley of Rubies', 200 km north of Mandalay in the mountainous Mogok area is famous for the rare pigeon's blood rubies and blue sapphires.

The Central Basin occupies most of Myanmar and in the deltaic regions the landscape is absolutely flat except for a few blocks of erosion-resistant rocks up to 18 m high. The basin has two unequal parts, the larger being the Irrawaddy Valley and the smaller Sittang Valley. Between these valleys are the Bago Mountains. In the centre of the basin and also structurally connected with the Bago Mountains and their northern extension is a series of extinct volcanoes with small crater lakes and eroded cones. The largest of these eroded volcanic cones is Popa Hill, at 1,518 m. The Coastal Areas comprise the Rakhine and Tenasserim plains backed by the heights of the Rakhine and Tenasserim mountains. These coastal regions are fringed with numerous islands of varying sizes.

The Western Ranges are the ones that border India and are therefore covered in detail subsequently in this chapter.

Evolution of the India-Myanmar Border

The Treaty of Yandaboo[5] which was signed on 24 February 1826 between the 'Honourable' East India Company (as it was referred to in the Treaty) and the

King of Ava, is the basis of the evolution of the IMB. Articles Two and Three of the Treaty have the provisions that give out the details of the border:

ARTICLE 2

His Majesty the King of Ava renounces all claims upon, and will abstain from all future interference with, the principality of Assam and its dependencies, and also with the contiguous petty States of Cachar and Jyntia. With regard to Munnipoor it is stipulated, that should Ghumbheer Sing desire to return to that country, he shall be recognized by the King of Ava as Rajah thereof.

ARTICLE 3

To prevent all future disputes respecting the boundary line between the two great Nations, the British Government will retain the conquered Provinces of Arracan, including the four divisions of Arracan, Ramree, Cheduba, and Sandoway, and His Majesty the King of Ava cedes all right thereto. The Unnoupectoumien or Arakan Mountains (known in Arakan by the name of the Yeomatoung or Pokhingloung Range) will henceforth form the boundary between the two great Nations on that side. Any doubts regarding the said line of demarcation will be settled by Commissioners appointed by the respective governments for that purpose, such Commissioners from both powers to be of suitable and corresponding rank.

The IMB was eventually resolved 169 years after the Treaty of Yandaboo, by a Joint Border Demarcation Committee in 1969 which led to the Boundary Agreement between India and Burma (see **Appendix A**).

Vice Admiral Ram Dass Katari, independent India's first Indian Naval Chief and Ambassador to Burma from 1964 to 1969 describes how the decision came about:

The other important decision taken during Mr. Chagla's visit was to demarcate the boundary between India and Burma. Once the agreement was reached, the matter was pursued energetically. A Joint Boundary Commission was set up with Colonel Kyi Maung, Colonel GS of the Ministry of Defence, and myself as co-chairman. We got down to business without delay. Survey teams from both countries were introduced into the scheme and they had regular meetings in Rangoon as well as Delhi and Dehra Dun to work out the modalities. The sections of the border to be demarcated and the order in which it should be done were worked out. We had, of course, to leave out the tri-junctions with China and East Pakistan for the time being for obvious reasons. Of course, this was just the opportunity for opposition members in our Parliament to embarrass the government, quite unnecessarily and thoughtlessly, I felt. But I got the impression that the government fielded the onslaught quite skilfully. The work of the Joint Boundary Commission proceeded quite smoothly, by and large, and its members from both countries established welcome cordiality.[6]

S.C. Banerji recounts the progress in the border demarcation in the Baleshwar Prasad Papers as:

> *Between December 1968 to April 1969, a total of 46 border pillars were to be erected, Burma taking responsibility for 25 pillars and India 21. However, most of the work along the 240-mile sector has been completed by February, two months ahead of the schedule. The border now demarcated is understood to be the same as the one (that) existed under the British rule. The Myanma Alin said: The work progressed so well, because no problems exist between Burma and India.*[7]

However, this resolution did nothing to restore the injustice to the locals who had been split by this treaty. The British took no cognizance of local ethnic sensitivities and drew the line, thus dividing the ethnic population into two nations, leaving the regions to come to terms with this travesty on their own. This was endemic to the entire IMB, as it was to the borders on the Western front as well. Possibly the most notorious evidence of this disastrous tearing asunder of a people lies in the residence of the Village Chief of Longwa, Mon District in Nagaland. The intriguing fact of this residence is that the IMB passes through it, dividing it into two halves, one that falls in India and the other in Myanmar. This is the case with a number of such houses in the village.[8] In fact, not all villagers have romanticised notions of the partition. The COVID-19 pandemic has forced authorities to fence off the villages. Now while the Indian authorities provide provisions to its side, the same is not so with the Myanmar side which, across the IMB, is generally less developed.[9]

The hills along the IMB were never clearly demarcated between British India and British Burma since the British considered these areas harsh, inhospitable and inhabited by hostile tribes who regularly fought amongst themselves and the farmers of the plains. The British punitive military campaigns followed by Christian missions dominated the period even as British maps marked the entire areas as Independent Tribal Areas. The demographic distribution along the IMB is based on latitudinal spread and similarity of population. Thus the Nagas are spread on both sides of the IMB in Nagaland and Arunachal Pradesh. Similarly, the Kukis of Manipur, the Paites, Lushais, Lais and Maras of Mizoram share ethnicity with the Chins being from the same Zou community.

Western Ranges: The India-Myanmar Border Terrain

Of the five geographical subdivisions of Myanmar, it is the Western Range that borders India and runs from the northern mountains to the southern tip of the

Arakan Peninsula. Thereafter, it runs under the sea and then reappears above the ocean as the Andaman and Nicobar Islands of India. The Western Range has an average elevation of 1,800 m, rising above 3,000 m at some peaks. From an Indian perspective, from north to south, the Patkai Range which includes the Naga Hills, and the Arakan Yoma Range including the Chin Hills, forms the borders between India and Myanmar. While these two ranges also mark the geographic extent of the Indian subcontinent, Prof. Dilip K. Chakravarti, a noted anthropologist, goes on to state that both Upper and Lower Myanmar and the territory beyond them was "*administratively a part of British India (lower Myanmar: 1858-1937, upper Myanmar: 1886-1937) for long periods.*"[10] The Patkai Range and Naga Hills stretch up to Manipur from where the hills continue as the Arakan Yoma, which lies entirely within Myanmar and separates the coastal Arakan strip from the central Irrawaddy Basin. Prof Chakravarti describes the range thus:

> *Much lower in average height than the Himalayas, the Patkai Range, which is linked to the Himalayan node in Arunachal, harbours a world of wooded peaks and deep and narrow valleys, its highest peak, Mt. Saramati (3,826 m or 12,552 feet), being located in Tuensang in Nagaland near the Myanmar border. The highest peak of the Arakan Yoma in Myanmar is Nat Ma Taung/Mt. Victoria (3,094 m or 10,151 feet). The Arakan Hills and the Patkai Range are both pierced by routes which lead from Arakan to the Irrawaddy Valley in the case of Arakan and from Assam/Arunachal Pradesh to Myanmar in the case of the Patkai Range.*

In a more detailed description of the Arakan, Prof Dilip K. Chakravarti writes:

> *Arakan shows a long and narrow coast, continuation in a sense of the Chattagram coast of Bangladesh, separated from it by the Naaf River. It is separated from the Irrawaddy valley by the hills of Arakan Yoma range which is pierced by a number of passes: 'An' Pass which links the Arakanese township of An with Ngape in the Minbu district of upper Myanmar; Talak Pass to the northwest of An; and Taungup Pass which links Taungup with Padaung in Prome in lower Myanmar. The long Bay of Bengal coastline has ensured that Arakan did not have to depend exclusively on overland journeys to maintain cultural and other interactions. Coastal traffic, for instance, must have played a major role in keeping Andaman open to movements of people from the Chittagong area and elsewhere in Bengal.*
>
> *The Kaladan is the longest river of the Arakan, rising in hills and joining the sea at Akyab. The other rivers also flow into the Bay of Bengal. All Arakanese rivers are tidal and remain navigable throughout the year. North Arakan has deltaic plains, where the southern portion is rocky and narrow. There are at least two major islands, Ramree and Chebuda, off the coast. Because of their soil, the Mayu, Kaladan and Lemro valleys have been traditionally very important areas*

of rice cultivation. Arakan has enjoyed a solid reputation as a rice-growing area till the modern period. In addition to rice, Arakan has been known for its timber, principally teak and (a) variety called 'iron wood' (Pyinkadow), which was used principally in ship-building industry. The coast yields rich harvests of fish of all sorts.

A Political and Demographic Description of the India-Myanmar Border[11]

The IMB starts from south to north at the tri-junction Border Pillar (BP) in the Parva Salient of Mizoram. This is a unique triangular BP which marks the tri-junction of Bangladesh, India and Myanmar. It is referred to by various names such as the Tri-junction Border Pillar, Tin Mukh Pillar[12] and most commonly as BP 1 since the India-Myanmar face of the pillar is numbered BP 1. From BP 1 the border runs east up to BP 23[13] and thence north along the four states bordering Myanmar, i.e., Mizoram (up to BP 32), Manipur (BPs 32 to 130), Nagaland (BPs 130 to 154) and culminating at BP 186 in Arunachal Pradesh (BPs 154 to 186).[14] The Bangladesh-Myanmar face is numbered BP 74 and is the last border pillar between Myanmar and Bangladesh. The international border between Bangladesh and Myanmar runs south to north and culminates at this Tri-junction Border Pillar. The Bangladesh-India face bears the inscription BP 2364 and is the last border pillar between India and Bangladesh.[15] The Bangladesh-India border begins at another BP 1 in the

Figure 1.4: Border Pillar No 1

Sunderbans in 24 Parganas District of West Bengal, running clockwise bordering the Indian states of Assam, Meghalaya, Tripura and Mizoram before finally ending at this Tri-junction BP.

Proceeding from south to north in the sequence of the border pillars, the IMB traverses the Indian states of Mizoram (510 km), Manipur (398 km), Nagaland (215 km) and Arunachal Pradesh (520 km), totalling 1,643 km of some of the most isolated and pristine forests and hills in the region. Across the IMB, the corresponding provinces from south to north are Chin State (702 km), Sagaing Region (878 km) and Kachin State (199 km). The Sagaing Region and Kachin State also include the Naga Self-Administered Zone (NSAZ), an autonomous area adjoining India's Nagaland and three districts of Arunachal Pradesh bordering Myanmar, i.e., Lohit, Tirap and Changlang districts.

There are two un-demarcated portions on the IMB which are dwelt upon in detail subsequently in this Chapter.

Figure 1.5: India-Myanmar Border: From Trijunction to Trijunction

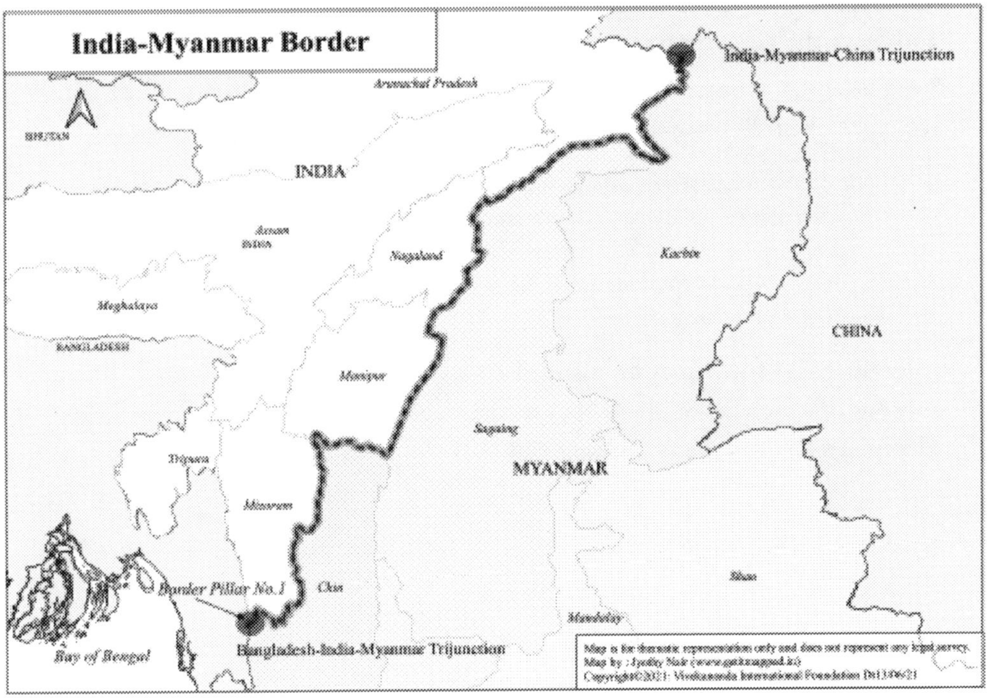

For a detailed State-wise physical and demographic description of the IMB along with maps, please see **Appendix B.**

Importance of Myanmar's Border Provinces for India

At this stage, we need to study the three provinces that border Indian states, viz., Chin State, Sagaing Region and Kachin State. The Rakhine State technically does not border India, but it is worthy of detailed study for two major reasons; it is close to and influenced by Mizoram and conversely impacts Mizoram as well and, secondly, a major portion of India's flagship Kaladan Multi Modal Transit Transport Project (Kaladan Project) is located in Rakhine State, hence events in Rakhine affect India majorly. Rakhine State has been covered separately in a chapter dedicated to the Rakhine conflict. But before we delve into the above three bordering provinces, we need to understand how the 2008 Constitution of Myanmar has structured its states.

The Republic of the Union of Myanmar consists of seven regions, seven states, one union territory (i.e., the capital of Nay Pyi Taw), five self-administered zones, and one self-administered division. Essentially states are places where mainly ethnic minorities reside while regions are where mainly a Bamar majority reside. Both have the same status.[16]

The 2008 Constitution of Myanmar, stipulates in Chapter II, on 'State Structure' the following organisation with reference to States and Regions:

> *The Union is delineated and constituted by seven Regions, seven States and the Union territories as follows: Kachin State; Kayah State; Kayin State; Chin State; Sagaing Region; Taninthayi Region; Bago Region; Magway Region; Mandalay Region; Mon State; Rakhine State; Yangon Region; Shan State; Ayeyawady Region and Union territories.*

It goes on to list five Self-Administered Zones and one Self-Administered Division, only one of which lies on the IMB, i.e., the Naga Self-Administered Zone (NSAZ). The image below depicts the zones and division:

Figure 1.6: Myanmar Self-Administered Zones and Divisions

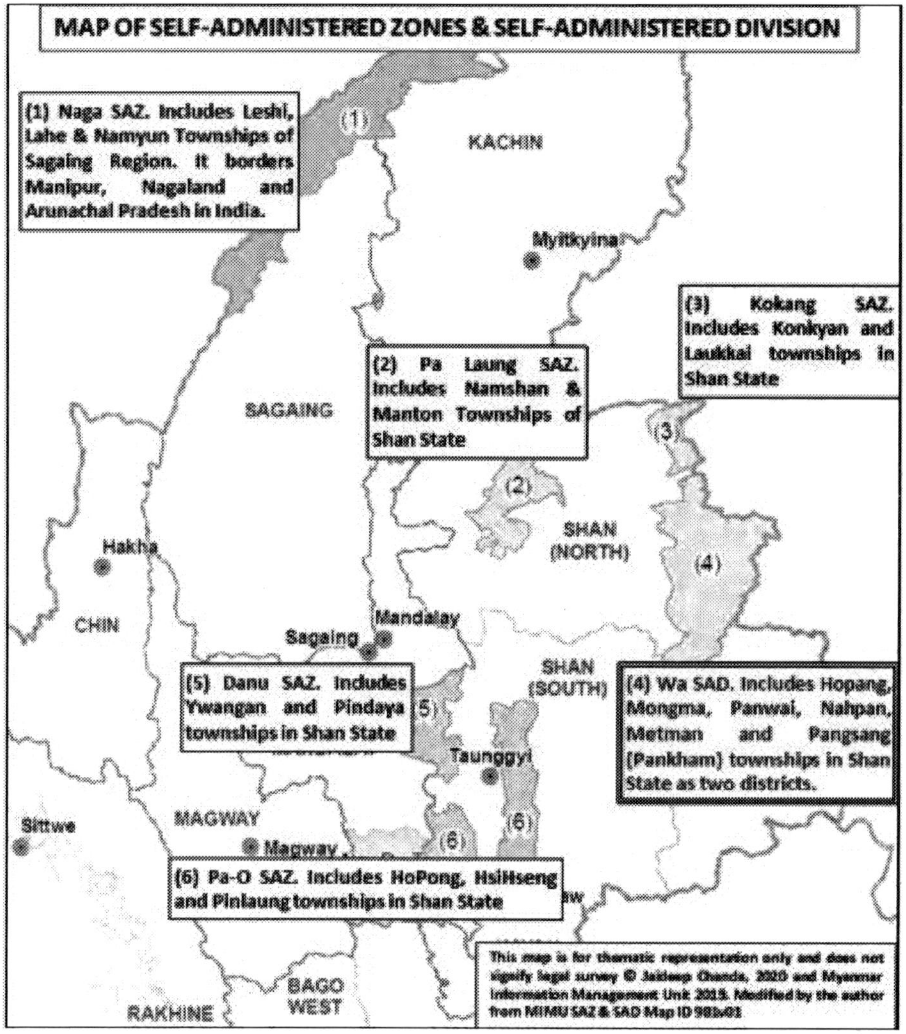

Chapter II goes on to state that:

'The Union is constituted as follows: villages are organized as village-tract; wards are organized as town or township; village-tracts and wards or towns are organized as township; townships are organized as district; districts are organized as Region or State; townships in a Self-Administered Zone are organized as Self-Administered Zone; townships in a Self-Administered Division are organized as District and such Districts are organized as Self-Administered Division; If there are Self-Administrated Zone or Self-Administered Division in a Region or a State, those Self-Administered Divisions, Self-Administered Zones and Districts

are organized as Region or State; Regions, States and Union territories are organized as the Republic.'

This is depicted below as:

Figure 1.7: State Structures of Myanmar

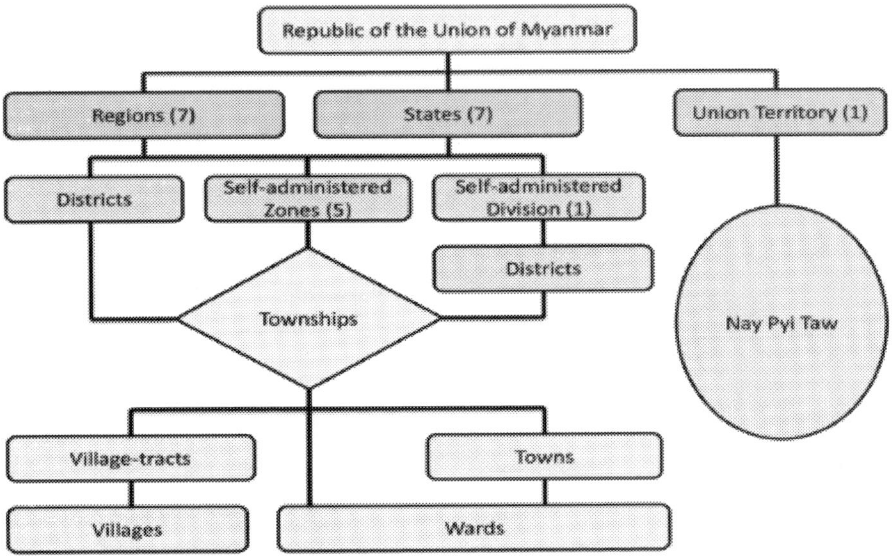

Source: Prepared by author © Jaideep Chanda, 2020.

Chin State holds critical importance for Indian interests in Myanmar. Firstly, it borders Mizoram which has an intense relationship with Chin. It is said of Mizoram that the biggest lake of Mizoram is the Rhi-Dil which is 'incidentally' in Chin State in Myanmar.[17] The present political dispensation in Mizoram has a distinctly pro-Chin orientation which was evidenced by the release of the Chin National League for Democracy (NLD) Member of Parliament (MP) held hostage by the Arakan Army (AA) at the behest of the CM of Mizoram, Pu Zoramthanga in January 2020. This affinity for the AA, though not Chin in ethnicity, harks back to the ages when the Mizo National Party (MNP) was the insurgent Mizo National Force (MNF). This is covered in detail in the chapter on the Rakhine conflict.

Secondly, the success of the Kaladan Multi Modal Transit Transport Project (KMMTTP) better known as the Kaladan Project, which runs through the Paletwa Township of Chin State and is currently held up due to violence between the AA and the Tatmadaw. This project has the potential to have a huge positive impact on Northeast India, Mizoram specifically and Chin and Rakhine states. Thirdly,

Mizoram has two established border crossing points, one at Zokhawthar and the second at Zorinpui (as and when it comes up). Both are important from the connectivity aspect and impact both Mizoram and Chin, directly and India and Myanmar overall.

From the perspective of the Indian investor, Chin State holds promise. As per the brochure of the Chin State division of the Directorate of Investment and Company Administration (DICA), the state welcomes local and international investors to invest in 10 projects of the Hotel and Tourism Sector and 28 projects of the Electricity & Energy Generation and Distribution Sector. To incentivise and facilitate this, the state will provide land, water and skilled and unskilled labour and tax benefits to the investor.[18]

Of the three provinces of Myanmar located on the IMB, Sagaing provides the maximum opportunity for Indian investors. It has a complete blend of all types of terrain, urban and rural mix of population and availability of labour and material, especially for agro-based industries. Agriculture is the predominant occupation with the major crop being rice, which occupies most of the cultivable ground. Other crops include peanut, wheat, sesame, pulses, cotton, and tobacco. Sagaing is the gateway to India for Myanmar. It is Myanmar's leading producer of wheat, contributing more than 80 per cent of the country's total production.[19] Forestry is important in the wetter upper regions along the Chindwin River, with teak and other hardwoods being the primary produce. Large-scale illegal logging is reportedly a major problem.[20] Important minerals include gold, coal, salt and small amounts of petroleum. Industry includes textiles, copper refining, gold smelting, and a diesel engine plant. The region has many rice mills, edible oil mills, saw mills, cotton mills, and mechanized weaving factories. Local industry includes earthen pots, silverware, bronzeware, ironware and lacquerware. The controversial Letpadaung copper mine in southern Sagaing Division, Monywa Township has been the site of several serious incidents relating the land and resource rights. Nationally controlled mining and forestry interests are found throughout Sagaing. Kalewa Township hosts several coalmines.[21]

From the security perspective, the Sagaing Region used to be home to bulk of Indian Insurgent Groups (IIGs) till January 2019 when in a coordinated operation named Operation Sunrise 1, the Indian and Myanmar armies launched an offensive against the IIGs in their respective sides, thereby denying space to them who till now had simply been moving across the porous border whenever one army operated against it. Operation Sunrise 1 effectively destroyed the back of the insurgent movement which was surviving on criminal intent rather than on ideology.

However, the risk of the IIGs reviving from Sagaing remains and it is for this reason that Sagaing will remain a top security concern for India. Further, being a gateway to India, this is the preferred smuggling route for trade and contraband items. The Moreh-Tamu trade link into Manipur is badly compromised by ineffective checks and balances and is a well known source for prohibited items including arms and weapons.

The links between Kachin and India are marginally developed and have the most potential for mutual benefit. The Putao Single Runway Airfield is 7,000 x 100 feet and is the closest to India being just 40 km away from the Vijaynagar salient. There is a proposal for the revival and development of the Ledo road, also known as the Stilwell road. The Ledo road connects Assam in India with Kunming in China through Myanmar. Named after Gen. Joseph Stilwell of the US Army, it was built during World War II for the Allied Powers to transport supplies to China. The major part of this road lies in Myanmar territory, passing through Shingbwiyang, Myitkyina and Bhamo in Kachin state and although it is no longer in use, upgrading the road will make it useful for Myanmar. The Indian government is wary that the road may be used by anti-India insurgents and rebels.[22]

State linkages with Kachin remain unexploited unlike in Manipur where the state interacts with the Sagaing Region frequently with friendly football matches and other cultural and people-to-people interactions. Similar interaction is required between Arunachal Pradesh and the Kachin Government to enable trade and other opportunities to be exploited.

The Rakhine State holds significance for India for a number of reasons. For one, the Kaladan Project commences here at the Sittwe Port and the success of the project depends on the security situation here. This is the closest state to the Indian mainland from the sea route with Kolkata Port being just over 500 km away. Rakhine is well endowed with mineral resources such as gas and the like. The state also produces a large amount of food items such as rice which is relevant for food security in the COVID-19 scenario. It provides access to the Chin state which is contiguous with Mizoram and critical for India. From a more geopolitical and security angle, the Chinese interest in the Kyaukphyu Deep Sea port and the Shwe Gas Fields necessitates India's countervailing presence there. It is indeed a matter of time before China decides to securitise the port and place its military presence in the region and in the Bay of Bengal. Thus, despite the fact that the state has no border contiguous with India, it holds its place in importance for India.[23]

For detailed descriptions of each of these four provinces, please see **Appendix C (Chin State), Appendix D (Sagaing Region), Appendix E (Kachin State) and Appendix F (Rakhine State).**

The Free Movement Regime (FMR)

As counter to the British blunder of having created a border through homes, villages and the people, India and Myanmar have evolved a Free Movement Regime (FMR) which allows locals residing within 16 km of the border to travel up to 16 km across the border into the other country, without the need for immigration, passport or visa. The FMR commenced as an understanding for years before it was formalised, basically to retain the socio-cultural ethos of the border areas. Over the years, a number of notifications have been issued which have institutionalised the system. These include initial notifications of 29 June 1950 and 18 January 1968 vide which indigenous tribes of both countries inhabiting up to 40 km were exempted from possessing passports and permitted entry into Myanmar up to the same distance, i.e., 40 km. In a notification of 28 June 1968, a permit system was introduced and further, in a notification of 30 October 1979, the permit was modified to include the purpose of visit and amounts of cash and merchandise being carried. Due to repeated misuse of this facility by inimical elements using the locals for smuggling contraband and human trafficking, the distance of 40 km was reduced to 16 km by the Ministry of Home Affairs Notification of 21 July 2010 (see **Appendix G**). Subsequently, a Ministry of Home Affairs Office Memorandum of 15 March 2018 by the Bangladesh and Myanmar (BM) Division added certain restrictions for prevention of unauthorised crossing of vehicles across the IMB.

The fencing of the IMB is a certainty which has already gathered steam as a fallout of the COVID-19 measures. This has traditionally been resisted on a number of grounds such as cultivable lands falling on the Myanmar side, better grazing grounds for mithun (the local buffalo) and so on.[24] The fine balance between security and connectivity is difficult to evaluate, especially when the local and central authorities tend to view things through the all-pervading prism of security. However, innovative options are available to enable the FMR, even while fencing the border. The Line of Control fencing in Kashmir where several villages are across the fence and the villagers regularly cross the innumerable manned gates several times a day at will, is just one working example. This gated fencing model is also prevalent on the India-Pakistan International Border (IB) where the gates are opened for farmers by the Border Security Force to go to tend their land which is across the fence but inside the IB.

The Myanmar Government too issued equivalent instructions initially permitting movement up to 40 km if the stay did not exceed 30 days in Myanmar, thereafter reducing it in 1971, to 16 km and duration of stay to three days. Further, the entry points were restricted to three, viz., Zokhawthar (Mizoram), Moreh (Manipur) and Pangsau Pass (Arunachal Pradesh).

In 2018, the FMR was further modified and sanctified by the signing of the Land Border Crossing Agreement (LBCA) on 11 May 2018 (**Appendix H**). The LBCA enables the movement of people from both nations across the land border with passports and visas as applicable, from two border crossing points, viz., Moreh-Tamu in Manipur and Zokhawthar-Rhikhawthar in Mizoram. In addition, vide Article 4, Paragraph 4, Indian personnel working on the Kaladan Project have been permitted to enter and exit through Zorinpui-Paletwa for the duration of the project on the basis of a work permit to be issued by Myanmar. Vide the LBCA, the FMR was modified to define the Border Pass which would then permit multiple entry with the holder permitted to stay in the other country for up to two weeks at a time. The caveat was that the Border Pass would only be issued to residents of Border Areas which was defined as 16 km on either side of the IMB. The LBCA finally came into force on August 2018.[25, 26]

Unresolved Border Alignment Issues

As has been brought out earlier, the IMB is the physical manifestation of an arbitrary and artificial line imposed on villages, tribes and peoples of a region in a hostile terrain. Since it does not follow geographical features at most places, there is adequate scope for confusion and dispute on the exact alignment of the IMB, especially when keeping in mind the sentiments of the locals vis-à-vis the respective state and central governments of India and Myanmar. Currently, there are nine unresolved border alignment issues including two stretches where the border has not been demarcated. As per the Ministry of Home Affairs Annual Report of 2017-18, out of 1,643 km, demarcation of 1,472 km has been completed leaving two un-demarcated portions along the IMB, viz., Lohit sub-sector of Arunachal Pradesh (136 km) and Kabaw valley in Manipur (35 km).[27] The former since it impacts the China-India-Myanmar Trijunction, and the latter due to the sensitivities of the locals.

The China-Myanmar international border, which totals 2,185 km, has been demarcated by a joint Sino-Burmese Boundary Commission created vide the Burma-China Boundary Treaty of October 1, 1960. The *International Boundary Study No. 42 (November 30, 1964), Burma–China Boundary*[28] published by The

Geographer Office of the Geographer Bureau of Intelligence and Research of the Department of State of the USA, records the following statement in the study:

> *The Sino-Burmese treaties did not resolve the problem of the Sino-Indian–Burmese tripoint. Chinese claims to most of the Northeast Frontier Agency of India would place the tripoint much further south than the point claimed by India. The Treaty (1960) is vague, defining the boundary only as "passing through Gamlang La to the western extremity of the Burmese Indian boundary". There are strong hints, however, that the Protocol carries the Diphu La*[29] *as the tripoint. This pass has been mentioned many times as a point on the McMahon Line as well as being on the Burmese-Indian border. Hence, according to this reasoning, the pass would be the Sino-Indian-Burmese tripoint. However, modern maps locate the Diphu La south of the Di Chhu-La Te watershed, i.e., the McMahon Line according to Indian claims. The problem appears to stem from inaccurate plotting of the Diphu Pass on earlier maps; it is quite impossible for the pass to be situated where it is shown and to be on the watershed.*

Thus, this 136 km of the IMB at the northern fringe of Arunachal Pradesh remains unresolved and given the present relations between India and China, is unlikely to see resolution in the near future.

The Kabaw Valley border includes BP 81 which is a bone of contention between the locals in Manipur and Sagaing in Myanmar. The violation of the 10 m 'NO CONSTRUCTION ZONE' on both sides gives rise to friction at the local levels. One of the issues which keep coming up from time to time is the Haolenphai issue at BP 76 wherein villagers in India complain of Myanmar Army personnel coming into India and destroying crops and houses on the basis of perception of the IMB.[30, 31]

However, none of the issues are allowed to derail overall India-Myanmar relations since adequate mechanisms are in place to handle them. These include Foreign Office Consultations, National Level Meetings (NLM), Sectoral Level Meetings (SLM), meetings of the Heads of Survey Department and Director (Survey) and Joint Working Group (JWG) meetings on boundary issues. The Foreign Office Consultations are led by the Foreign Secretary and Permanent Secretary of Myanmar. The 18th Foreign Office Consultations were held on 6 December 2019 at Delhi. The NLM is the main forum to discuss security cooperation, consular issues, drug trafficking and liaison between agencies at the level of the Home Secretary/Deputy Home Minister. The 22nd NLM was held on 25-26 October, 2018 at Delhi. It is supplemented by a Ministry of Home Affairs-led Joint Secretary-level SLM which was last held on 23-24 September, 2019.

The forum for the representatives of the armed forces to discuss counter insurgency and border security is the Regional Border Committee (RBC) meeting. The 15th RBC was held in Manipur, India, in December 2019. Boundary matters are discussed by the JBWG led by Joint Secretary (BM), MEA. The 3rd JBWG meeting was held on 26-27 August, 2018 in Yangon. Commercial issues are discussed in the Joint Trade Committee (JTC) held at Commerce Minister-level.[32]

Having seen the geographic and demographic aspects of Myanmar and the IMB, a historical overview sets the context for the rest of the study in this book.

NOTES

1. Thant Myint-U, *Where China meets India: Burma and the New Crossroads of Asia,* Farrar, Straus and Giroux, 2012, pg. 72.
2. Robert D. Kaplan, *The Revenge of Geography: What the Map Tells Us About Coming Conflicts and the Battle Against Fate,* Random House, New York, 2012, pg 14.
3. See, for example, R. Lee Hadden, "*The Geology of Burma (Myanmar): An Annotated Bibliography of Burma's Geology, Geography and Earth Science*", Topographic Engineering Centre, US Army Corps of Engineers, September 2008, Virginia, https://www.pdfdrive.com/the-geology-of-burma-myanmar-an-annotated-bibliography-of-burmas-geology-geography-and-e40832598.html (Accessed on 9 May 2020) and Luc Guo, "*Understanding Burma Myanmar: History, Geography, Economy (Oxford Historical Studies: Understanding)*", Createspace Independent Publishers, May 2013.
4. Dilip K. Chakrabarti, *The Borderlands and Boundaries of the Indian Subcontinent.* New Delhi, Aryan Books International, 2018.
5. Treaty of Yandaboo, 24 Feb 1826, from: C. U. Aitchison, ed. *A Collection of Treaties, Engagements and Sanads: Relating to India and Neighbouring Countries.* Vol. XII. Calcutta: Government of India Central Publication Branch, 1931, 230-233, https://web.archive.org/web/20081202003039/http://projectsouthasia.sdstate.edu/Docs/history/primarydocs/Treaties/Burma/002.htm (Accessed on 18 May 2020).
6. Admiral R. D. Katari. *A Sailor Remembers.* Prabhat Books. Kindle Edition.
7. Baleshwar Prasad Papers, Nehru Memorial Museum and Library,
8. Travel + Leisure India Web Article, Longwa Village: From One Country To Another Without A Visa, https://travelandleisureindia.in/longwa-village/ (Accessed on 18 May 2020).
9. Al Jazeera Web Article, Tribes along India-Myanmar border dream of a 'united Nagaland', 28 Apr 2020, https://www.aljazeera.com/news/2020/04/tribes-india-myanmar-border-dream-united-nagaland-200428052323328.html (Accessed on 18 May 2020).
10. Ibid, p. 163.
11. Bulk of the material in this section has been taken from the Assam Rifles Publication entitled *Compendium on Indo-Myanmar Border Management,* EBH Publishers India, 2018, from Chapter 2 *Demystifying Indo Myanmar Border: Peculiarities and Challenges* by Maj Gen P. C. Nair, YSM and Chapter 3 *Demographic Kaleidoscope along Indo-Myanmar Border* by Maj Gen Virendra Singh, VSM.
12. See a Youtube Video, "Tin mukh border pillar | 3 countries border meets | Bangladesh | India

| Myanmar | 2012" by BDExplorer, 27 Oct 2012, https://www.youtube.com/watch?v=pH42Cp2ucNQ (Accessed on 20 April 2020).

13. Border pillars are not equidistant and hence the number of BPs has no correlation with the length of the border on which they are erected which complicates things further in the case of the IMB.
14. For a detailed description of the India-Myanmar Border, please see Boundary Agreement between the Government of India and the Government of the Union of Burma dated 10 March 1967 at Ministry of External Affairs Website, https://mea.gov.in/bilateral-documents.htm?dtl/5886 (Accessed on 20 April 2020).
15. As inscribed on a replica memento of the Trijunction BP presented to the Vivekananda International Foundation by the Assam Rifles.
16. Ministry of Land, Infrastructure, Transport and Tourism, Japan, An Overview of Spatial Policy in Asian and European Countries, Myanmar https://www.mlit.go.jp/kokudokeikaku/international/spw/general/myanmar/index_e.html
17. Mizoram Portal, State Portal of Mizoram, Web Article, Rih Dil (Rih Lake), https://mizoram.gov.in/page/rih-dil-rih-lake (Accessed on 20 May 2020).
18. Invest Myanmar Summit 2019, Chin, 28-29 Jan 2019, Nay Pyi Taw, Myanmar, https://investmyanmar2019.com/regions/chin/ (Accessed on 2 June 2020).
19. Invest Myanmar Summit 2019, Sagaing, 28-29 Jan 2019, Nay Pyi Taw, Myanmar, https://investmyanmar2019.com/regions/sagaing/ (Accessed on 2 June 2020).
20. The Irrawaddy Web Article, Sagaing Division, https://www.irrawaddy.com/election/region/sagaing-division (Accessed on 20 May 2020).
21. United Nations Development Project (UNDP) Report, Local Governance Mapping, The State of Local Governance: Trends in Sagaing, 2015https://themimu.info/sites/themimu.info/files/documents/Report_Local_Governance_Mapping_Sagaing_UNDP_Feb2015.pdf (Accessed on 24 May 2020).
22. Observer Research Foundation, Kolkata, India-Myanmar Connectivity: Possibilities and Challenges, 2015 https://www.orfonline.org/wp-content/uploads/2015/12/IndiaMyanmar.pdf pg 85, 96 & 94 (Accessed on 26 May 2020).
23. Ashrafuzzaman Khan, The strategic importance of Rakhine State: Daily Star contributor, The Straits Times, Asian Voice, 3 Sep 2018, https://www.straitstimes.com/asia/south-asia/the-strategic-importance-of-rakhine-state-daily-star-contributor and Annabelle Heugas, The Geopolitics of Rakhine, Mizzima, 6 Nov 2017, https://www.bnionline.net/en/news/geopolitics-rakhine (Both accessed on 26 May 2020).
24. Bidhayak Das, India-Myanmar Open Border Policy: A Travesty for Sustainable, Traditional Agriculture, The Irrawaddy Web Article, 16 May 2018, https://www.irrawaddy.com/features/india-myanmar-open-border-policy-travesty-sustainable-traditional-agriculture.html (Accessed on 21 May 2020).
25. Brig K.P. Singh, 'Free Move Regime: Provisions, Applicability and Impact', Chapter 15 of *Compendium on Indo-Myanmar Border Management*, EBH Publishers, Gauhati, 2018.
26. Sujan Dutta, India and Myanmar quietly open up their border for villagers and trade, The Print Web Article, 25 Oct 218, https://theprint.in/diplomacy/india-and-myanmar-quietly-open-up-their-border-for-villagers-and-trade/139877/ (Accessed on 21 May 2020).
27. Ministry of Home Affairs, Annual Report 2017 – 2018, Indo-Myanmar Border, Para 3.19, pg 34, https://www.mha.gov.in/sites/default/files/MINISTRY%20OF%20HOME%20AFFAIR%20AR%202017-18%20FOR%20WEB.pdf (Accessed on 21 May 2020).
28. https://fall.fsulawrc.com/collection/LimitsinSeas/IBS042.pdf (Accessed on 25 May 2020).

29. Diphu Pass is a mountain pass on the McMahon Line, eight km south of the tri-junction of India, China, and Myanmar and a strategic approach to eastern Arunachal Pradesh. See https://en.wikipedia.org/wiki/Diphu_Pass (Accessed on 2 June 2020).
30. Iboyaima Laithangbam, Myanmar Armymen enter Manipur Village, The Hindu Web Article, 24 Nov 2018, https://www.thehindu.com/news/national/other-states/myanmar-army-men-enter-manipur-village/article25588357.ece (Accessed on 27 May 2020).
31. Rabi Banerjee, On Peril's Edge, The Week Web Article, 14 May 2017, https://www.theweek.in/theweek/current/india-myanmar-border.html (Accessed on 27 May 2020).
32. Ministry of External Affairs Website, https://mea.gov.in/Portal/ForeignRelation/Mynmar_may2020.pdf

CHAPTER 2

A Historical Perspective of India-Myanmar Relations: Independence to 1989

...what hurts Burma hurts us equally.

—V.K. Krishna Menon[1]

To get a sense of how India-Myanmar relations evolved is also essentially a peek into how diplomacy evolved in India *per se*. In the years preceding Independence, Burma was the happening place for a number of reasons. The Japanese onslaught during the Burma Campaign saw one of the toughest battles[2] being fought in the harshest of terrains in which fortunes changed with the seasons. During this Campaign, the freedom struggle led by India's soldier-statesman, Netaji Subhash Chandra Bose and his Indian National Army was a parallel engagement. Even the genesis of the current Rohingya crisis can be traced to this period. The Burmese freedom struggle led by Aung San and the Thakins also originates here. So, to understand how, through this turmoil and confusion, dedicated individuals worked their hearts out to provide the proverbial 'method in the madness' and create a system and put in place a process to provide substance to India-Myanmar relations, one needs to delve into the archives of history.

The author was fortunate to be able to access the papers of a number of individuals who served in Burma in the years straddling Independence and the early years of Indian diplomacy. Perusal of these documents provides a fascinating insight into India-Myanmar relations in the mid and late 1940s and subsequent years. Hence, the initial part of this chapter primarily focuses on certain facets of the history of India-Myanmar relations based on archival material accessed at the Nehru Memorial Museum and Library.

The Gundevia Papers

Yezdezard (Yezdi) Dinshaw Gundevia (1908–1988) was an Indian Civil Services officer who later became a diplomat and finally retired as the Foreign Secretary (1963-1965). He authored four books, one of which, *Outside the Archives,* gives us a glimpse of life as the Secretary to the Agent General to the Government of Burma.[3] The archives give us a sense of his apprehensions upon his posting to Burma (initially the appointment was at Shimla,[4] and later at Rangoon), from Farrukhabad where he was the officiating Magistrate and Collector, in early 1945. He was asked to report first to Delhi for training at the Department of Commonwealth Relations India, under R.N. Banerjee, Secretary of the Department, before moving to Burma. In his book he describes his battle to ensure that Indian refugees in Burma were not allowed to return to war-ravaged Burma, post the withdrawal of the Japanese, since there were no jobs forthcoming there due to the near total destruction of the industrial facilities of Rangoon, especially the harbour. It had been destroyed by the British as part of their 'denial' policy prior to evacuation from Rangoon in 1942.

Approximately 2,50,000 Indians had been registered as Burma Refugees in India from 1942 to 1945 and their return to their original jobs had been approved by the Refugee Government of Burma (in Shimla), without assessment of the ground situation in post-war Burma. This line was accordingly taken up by the Department of Commonwealth Relations, which passed instructions to its Secretary in Burma (Gundevia) to ensure that '*the Indian refugee got back and was assisted to settle down, as fast as possible, after the war.*'[5] He goes on to describe how despite being categorically ordered by the Secretary to send the refugees back, he fought his case through correspondence. Finally, he was called to India in September 1946 for consultations. He met his colleagues at the Department (there were only one Joint Secretary, one Deputy Secretary {i.e., Gundevia himself} and two Assistant Secretaries under the Secretary at that time) and failed to convince the Secretary who insisted the refugees must go back. Gundevia decided to go above the Secretary to press home his case and the next person who came to his mind was the then interim Prime Minister (PM), Jawaharlal Nehru. He called up the Private Secretary to the PM, another ICS officer, Mr. H.V.R. Iengar, for an appointment with the PM. Ienger was outraged at his temerity and that ended there. Not one to give up, he penned a note to the PM requesting for a half-hour meeting after dinner and sent it to through a bearer to the bearer of the Prime Minister's Office in North Block. The Department of Commonwealth Relations was also in North Block itself. Soon enough there was a call from one 'Mathai'[6] informing him that the PM had invited him for dinner at No. 4 York Road (the Prime Minister's residence at that time, which had been hired from noted lawyer Harish Chandra)[7] at 8.15 p.m. Elated, Gundevia went to inform his Joint Secretary, A.V. Pai, who was horrified and sent him to the Secretary. The Secretary, 'Dada' Banerjee, as he was known, was equally horrified, but wanted to know what it was that Gundevia wanted to discuss with the PM. Banerjee was further appalled to know that Gundevia wanted to impress upon the PM that Indian refugees from Burma should not be sent back and also to inform the PM that Banerjee had ordered that they be sent back. The shot having been fired, Gundevia went on to have his dinner with the Interim PM and his daughter, and post dinner conveyed his point and received an immediate favourable direction that the refugees were not to be sent back to Burma under the present conditions. Gundevia goes on to give credit to R.N. 'Dada' Banerjee for not holding his indiscretion in writing to the PM against him in future. Thus was prevented, what would have been another major humanitarian crisis in the making for India-Myanmar relations.

The S.A.S. Tyabji Papers

The management of the Indian refugees in post World War II Burma and their property was a primary concern of quasi-civil and civil servants at that time and the correspondence between S.A.S. Tyabji, the Hon'ble Advisor on Indian Affairs to His Excellency the Governor of Burma as well as Director, Welfare and Rehabilitation Department, Rangoon, reveals the chaos and confusion of those turbulent times. Son of Abbas Tyabji,[8] former Justice of Baroda, S.A.S. Tyabji assisted his father in providing support to the Rangoon University students who were protesting the University Act in 1921, vide which six letters had been committed from the Burmese script and also demanding an increase of pay for vernacular teachers. S.A.S. Tyabji's role finds mention in various records of the time for being one of the prominent members supervising the sea-borne evacuation of Rangoon alongside Swami Punyananda of Ram Krishna Mission, from 20 January to 23 February 1932.[9]

The war years, i.e., from 1943 to 1945, saw solidarity between Indian and Burmese. Post war, the old issues of vernacular education, citizenship and remittance of earnings to India, amongst other things, would swamp relations. Tyabji was appointed Honorary Advisor on Indian Affairs to the Governor after his return from India.[10] This was opposed by many people on both sides on the ground that since he had not been in Burma during the war, he had no idea of the bonhomie that existed between the Indians and the Burmese. Some went on to conjure a conspiracy of British intentions to continue divide and rule amongst Indians and Burmese.[11] However, his appointment remained and he delivered to the extent possible under the trying circumstances.

The Mohammed Abdul Rauf Papers

Dr. M.A. Rauf was India's first Ambassador to Myanmar. His papers, i.e., the M.A. Rauf Papers, include a copy of a possibly unpublished article by an unknown author, which gives a sense of the background of the legendary diplomat. The article titled 'Nehru's Envoy' sought to commemorate the birth centenary of Pandit Jawaharlal Nehru in 1989.[12] It begins with a paragraph titled '*Problematique*', in which it laments that the '*The reticence of Indian diplomats has obscured the achievements of foreign policy. The thoughts and reasoning of those involved in the making of policy has been displaced by impressionistic accounts*'. It reasons that '*Diplomats, by and large, however, have failed to record their role in history*', which is a fact true not only of diplomats but also of most services in the nation.[13] In the next paragraph titled '*Objective*', our anonymous author concludes that the birth centenary of Pandit Nehru is '*an opportune time to rectify this.*' He goes on to eloquently describe the role of Dr. M.A. Rauf on Nehruvian foreign policy and gives a detailed biography of the diplomat.

> *The triumph of Nehruvian foreign policy can be recapitulated by collecting, compiling, editing and publishing essays on the life and career of India's longest serving envoy. Dr. Rauf's was the first of a series of diplomatic appointments by Panditji. He set up free India's first embassy. Dr. Rauf served as envoy of Burma, Japan, Canada, Belgium, Luxemborg, Switzerland and the Vatican. His diplomatic career matched the entire span of Nehru's Prime Ministership. In recounting their experiences those who worked with him will be provided an opportunity to record important facts of their lives and times as well.'*

The document informs us that Mohammed Abdul Rauf was born in Rangoon on 15 November 1901. His grandfather had been imprisoned for the part he had played in the First War of Independence (1857). On his release from the Andamans, he returned to Allahabad via Burma in 1885. His eldest son, M.A. Shakoor, settled in Rangoon which was then part of British India. The family maintained close ties with India and Shakoor served as president of the All Burma Indian National Congress. He had the honour of being the first political detainee for opposition to World War I. In fact, he was in prison when his first born, Rauf, left to study in England after completing his secondary education.

Rauf studied Jurisprudence B.A. 1924 and B.C.L. 1925 at Oxford and secured an Ll.D Degree from Trinity (Dublin). On his return he practised as a barrister at the Rangoon High Court. In 1930 he married Maqsood Jahab Begum, a relative of Sir Syed Ahmed Khan. He was appointed second judge but resigned shortly afterwards. At his invitation as president of the All Burma Indian National Congress, Pandit Nehru and his daughter visited Burma in 1937. During the World War II Japanese occupation of Burma, he moved with his family to their ancestral seat at Allahabad. Towards the end of the war he was appointed Judicial Member of the Income Tax Appellate Tribunal of India. He served in this post with distinction.

> *In November 1946, at Pandit Nehru's personal request, he returned as representative of the Government of India to Burma. As ambassador he helped unravel the problem of overseas Indians and thwarted a rebel takeover of Rangoon through the deployment of Indian armed forces. After a long tour of duty in Burma (1946-52) he accepted a posting to Tokyo (1952-54) where, among other things, he investigated the fate of the I.N.A treasure and laid (the) foundation of Indo-Japanese commerce and bought the land and buildings in Tokyo that have appreciated manifold. Later as High Commissioner for Canada (1954-58) he helped secure the transfer of nuclear technology to India. And as Ambassador to Belgium he was involved in the resolution of the Belgian Congo crisis. Finally as Ambassador at Berne and concurrently to the Holy See (1962-64) he was privy to Vatican II and locating the Eucharistic Conference in Bombay. He retired, after Pandit Nehru's death, in 1964. On April 13, 1967[14] he passed away. The officers of the foreign service, in their meeting, described him as 'a great son of India'.*

Obituaries of M.A. Rauf published in *The Toronto Star* and *The Globe Mail, Toronto*,[15] describe him as the Indian High Commissioner to Canada from 1954 to 1958, who passed away in Mount Sinai Hospital at the age of 66. While in Ottawa as the Ambassador, he had worked closely with the then Canadian External Affairs Minister Lester Pearson, securing foreign aid loans for India and for construction of India's first nuclear reactor. Mr Rauf's association with Canada, harked back to the 1919-24 period at Oxford University, where he became acquainted with Roland Michener, the Governor-General of Canada.[16] The obituaries mentioned that Mr. Rauf joined the Indian diplomatic corps at the request of Prime Minister Nehru and for several years handled

Figure 2.1: Dr. M.A. Rauf

Source: Photograph sourced from Facebook Page of Dr. M. A. Rauf

India's delicate relationship with bordering Burma. Later, he served in Belgium, Japan, Switzerland and the Vatican. He lived in Toronto since his retirement in 1964 with six of his ten children who settled there. Several of his older sons graduated from the University of Toronto.

The Embassy of India, Yangon, website lists Dr. M. A. Rauf as being the first Ambassador to Myanmar from 8 November 1946 till 1953, i.e., for over six years.[17] Unknown members of the family of Ambassador M. A. Rauf now maintain a Facebook Page[18] to commemorate his achievements. As per the Facebook posts by the family, the Ambassador's residence was bought by Ambassador M. A. Rauf for the Indian External Affairs Office, possibly referring to the Embassy of India premises in Yangon. The Facebook Post rates it as one of the finest buildings along with other just as fabulous residences which Ambassador Rauf also bought for the Indian government. It goes on to state that both these buildings (the Embassy and the Ambassador's residence) reveal Ambassador Rauf's discriminating taste as well as his foresight in investment for the Indian Government as these two properties are currently prime ones.[19] The Ambassador's residence was originally Bengal House, the residence of the Manager, Imperial Bank of India,[20] Rangoon, before it became the residence of the Indian Ambassador. It was apparently purchased for a tidy sum of ₹ 4.5 lakhs in 1952 during the Ambassadorship of Dr. M.A. Rauf who would have then become its first occupant.

Figure 2.2: The Residence of the Indian Ambassador to Myanmar which was purchased by Dr. M. A. Rauf for the Government of India

Source: From Facebook Page of Dr. M. A. Rauf

During the course of the Fellowship for this book, the author had an opportunity to visit Yangon and Nay Pyi Taw as part of a delegation from the VIF to Myanmar. The delegation was hosted by the present incumbent, Ambassador Saurabh Kumar, to a dinner at this majestic building. Only then were we able to fully comprehend the grandeur of the building and the importance of the initiative taken by its first occupant, Ambassador M.A. Rauf, in procuring it.

Figure 2.3: Vivekananda International Foundation Delegation at the majestic Indian Ambassador's Residence in Myanmar (9 December 2019)

(L-R: Capt Prashant Mohanan, Naval Attache; Dr. Sumit Seth, Deputy Chief of Mission; Ambassador Gautam Mukhopadhyay (Retd), Indian Ambassador to Myanmar 2013-16; Dr. Arvind Gupta, Director, Vivekananda International Foundation, Ambassador Saurabh Kumar, Indian Ambassador to Myanmar; Mrs. Saurabh Kumar; Mrs. Sawhney; Dr. Sreeradha Datta, Centre Head & Senior Fellow, Neighbourhood Studies, VIF; Lt Gen Ravi Sawhney (Retd), Centre Head & Senior Fellow, National Security and Strategic Studies & Internal Security Studies, VIF and the author.)

An interesting trivia is that the brother of Dr. M.A. Rauf, i.e. Mr. M.A. Raschid, was the Home Minister of Burma at the time of independence.[21] It is a tribute to the family where the two brothers straddled the foreign policies of the two neighbouring states. These brothers, one as India's first Ambassador to Burma in 1946 and the other as a member of the Burmese cabinet, contributed to a very close and cooperative relationship between India and Burma for its first 10 years of Independence. Unfortunately, this relationship ended with General Ne Win taking over the government of Burma and harassing its Indian population and even putting U. Raschid in prison.[22] A book by Bilal Raschid, M.A. Raschid's son, titled *The Invisible Patriot: Reminiscences of Burma's Freedom Movement*, apparently tells this story in detail.

The Baleshwar Prasad Papers

Baleshwar Prasad, an officer of the Indian Administrative Service, was the Indian Ambassador to Burma from 9 February 1970 till 1971 and subsequently Lieutenant Governor of Delhi.[23] In a handwritten note dated 7 February 1970, he paints a vivid picture of his journey to Rangoon to take over as India's Ambassador to Burma, on an Indian Airlines chartered flight along with his wife, servant and his two Sikkimese Terriers 'Shirter' and 'Sherry' (in the hold of the aircraft). The note reveals that he was not new[24] to Burma:

> *'Twice before I happened to be with the Burmese people under very difficult and complex circumstances. In 1942 it was the Japanese Occupation in the last World War and in 1949-50 it were the days of the Karen rebellion combined with the Burmese Militant Communist insurgency which had earned the nickname of 'Rangoon Government' for the administration. Yet it was a new resurgent Burma that I come to now engaged in the great task of building up of a nation with better life for its people adopting means best suited to the genius of its people'.*

Another entry in his diary a few months[25] later revealed his frustration with the other members of the diplomatic community in Rangoon and gives out his profound understanding of the Golden Land, its people and their psyche:

> *'Diplomats went on projecting their hopes and irritations and apprehensions and proceeded to sympathise or disparage without really understanding the Burma of to-day. But many are hardly capable of being objective about Burma and once could often come across indictments, outbursts of frustration and forebodings of doom. It is not easy to be informed about another people and another country at any time and much more so in such a fast changing Burma where absolute secrecy reigns till decisions are announced to be acted upon without any kind of 'why' or 'whereof' about it becoming even known or publicised. To many all this was highly frustrating.*
>
> *It did not take me long to understand the basis for such a situation. Burma's primary and all absorbing pre-occupation is with internal affairs within the country. And this has ever remained highly complex and involved for over a quarter of century ever since 1942 when the Imperial Japanese Army came to drive the British out only to be themselves thrown out with Japan's defeat and surrender in 1945. Political Independence of Burma which emerged with the British withdrawal in 1947 which began with seriously critical home problems of revolts and rebellions has continued to be plagued with these all the time in varying intensities, necessitating strengthening of military posture and garrisoning and field operations by the armed forces of Burma.'*

Having got a sense of some of the players in the early years of India-Myanmar relations, let us now move on to the history of India-Myanmar relations *per se*.

An Overview of the History of India-Myanmar Relations

Post-independence, India-Myanmar relations had an ominous start with Burma, in effect renaming the Indian Ministry of External Affairs! Vineet Thakur, University Lecturer at Leiden University, The Netherlands, vividly describes[26] that in March 1947, the External Affairs Department and the Commonwealth Relations Department were amalgamated into a single department, named the Department of External Affairs and Commonwealth Relations. Five months later, in August 1947, the word 'Department' was replaced with 'Ministry', hence renamed the Ministry of External Affairs and Commonwealth Relations. Initially, even as the two departments were amalgamated, the two wings effectively worked as separate departments. Eventually, territorial divisions got blurred and the Commonwealth Secretary was given the charge of Southeast Asia. Burma, which had severed its Commonwealth connection, protested against being dealt with by the Commonwealth Relations wing in the Ministry. To do away with this relic of past dualism and to assuage Burma, the Ministry was once again renamed the Ministry of External Affairs in 1949, but it did not end there. Now Britain was displeased and sought clarification if the shortened name in any way reflected a change in India's Commonwealth policy!

Robert D. Kaplan, writes[27] in his book *Monsoon—The Indian Ocean and the Future of American Power* that the history of Myanmar was impacted by '*geographical fluidity on the one hand and by religious-cultural isolation on the other*'. This was since the trade routes brought the country into contact with both China and the Indian Subcontinent. However, Myanmar's Theravada Buddhism insulated it from both Hindu India and Confucian China. The outcome was '*a unique history that was, nevertheless, influenced by outsiders*'.

For a study of the Indian perspective of the various facets of the history of Myanmar and India-Myanmar Relations a number of relatively recent books by Indian authors have been published. These include those written by Dr. N. Kipgen, Dr. Lipi Ghosh, Dr. Sonu Trivedi, T.S.L. Haokip, Ambassador Rajiv Bhatia and Ambassador P.M.S. Malik. There is no justification for me to reproduce what they have already covered so well, beyond a very brief reference of the history to provide the context to this project. For a substantial, though not exhaustive, list of books on India-Myanmar Relations by Indian authors, see **Appendix I.**

In any historical review, scholars tend to group time periods based on prominent political or other landmarks in the history of that nation. One of the advantages of identifying such time periods for grouping in the India-Myanmar context is that the landmark events took part during similar periods for both nations. Thus, Myanmar gained Independence on 4 January 1948, a few months after India's Independence on 15 August 1947. The year 1962 was a watershed year for India due to the debacle with China, and 1962 was the year Gen Ne Win took over power from U Nu in a coup. The 8 August 1988 Revolution, also called the 8888 Revolution, was a landmark event in Myanmar and the next year, in 1989, PM Rajiv Gandhi was ousted from power, plunging Indian politics into a period which saw six governments in nine years till 1998. India saw a major change of guard in 2014 with the PM Narendra Modi-led National Democratic Alliance coming to power and just a year in 2015 later Myanmar made history with Daw Aung San Suu Kyi's NLD coming to power.

For the benefit of researchers, **Appendix J** (*Dramatis Personae*) contains a chronological tabulated chart from 1946 till 2020 which lists out the important decision-makers including the Ambassadors, External Affairs Ministers, Prime Ministers, Foreign Secretaries, Defence Attaches, Defence Secretaries, Defence Ministers, Army Chiefs, Eastern Army Commanders, and, for reference, the de facto Heads of State in Myanmar, for each year.

Pre-Independence till 1962

India's relations with Burma began well before the two nations gained Independence. With the assassination of Gen Aung San on 19 July 1947 by an armed team of conspirators led by former PM of British Burma, U Saw, Burma lost its most popular leader just six months before its Independence. Aung San had been in touch with Pandit Nehru in 1947, in view of India's impending independence, prior to moving to UK for talks with Atlee that eventually led to Burma's Independence in January 1948. Sadly, he did not live to see the day. Had he lived, Burma might have been very different from the one we are seeing now. The 1947 interaction had been preceded by an accidental weather-driven visit by Nehru to Rangoon on his return journey from Malay. During this stopover, he met Aung San and reiterated his assurance to oppose the use of Indian troops to enforce colonial rule in Burma.

Nehru had earlier been denied permission to visit Burma and Indonesia to meet the nationalist leaders of those countries. This denial has been documented in the Oral History Interview with Lord Mountbatten at London, England, 26 July 1967 by Shri B.R. Nanda for the Nehru Memorial Museum and Library.[28] Mountbatten recalled:

When I was staying in the Viceroy's House, on one occasion, seeing the Viceroy, Lord Wavell, in his capacity as Minister of State for South East Asia, he said that there was one thing that would give him great pleasure, which was – if I would agree to extend an invitation to Pandit Jawaharlal Nehru, in his capacity as acting Prime Minister (there was no such position legally). Because he thought it would do him (Pandit Nehru) a great deal of good to get out of India, where he had been shut up for so long, and to see something of South East Asia and how the world regarded India, and perhaps he could see some of the Indian troops and some of the Indian inhabitants. I said, "Certainly, I will extend the invitation to him to visit Singapore and Malaya, with great pleasure". He then said, "Will you also extend an invitation to him to visit Burma?" To this, I replied, "As I had transferred the government from military to civil government – he should ask permission of Sir Reginald Dorman Smith". He said, he would do so. I warned him that he would be wasting his time because I saw he wouldn't get his permission. I am speaking from memory. Reginald Dorman Smith wrote to him, it appears – (Wavell later told me) – "Well, by all means send Pandit Nehru here. We would love to have him and rush him straight to prison when he comes." This was apt to be the attitude at that time of the British governors. So he didn't go to Burma.

Post-independence, India-Burma relations commenced well with India supporting its nascent neighbour on a number of issues. At the initial stages it was India that influenced the Commonwealth to assist Burma in the battle against the rebel forces and eventually it was the Commonwealth Ambassadors that influenced the stakeholders to sue for peace, in effect saving Rangoon from falling into the hands of the Karens. The irony of this was that Burma had opted out of the Commonwealth due to pressure from the then powerful Communist Party of Burma, which would brook no truck with the British.[29] Another instance of where India supported Burma was in getting the United Nations resolution for evacuation of the Chinese nationalist army, i.e., the Kou Min Tang out of Burma. The then head of the Indian delegation at the UN, V. K. Krishna Menon, led the debate against the USA which was supporting and financing the KMT. These efforts led to the passing of two resolutions, viz., the UN General Assembly Resolution No. 707 (VII) of 23 April 1953 and No. 717 (VII) of 8 December 1953, both titled *Complaint by the Union of Burma regarding aggression against it by the Government of the Republic of China.*[30]

Ambassador Preet Malik describes the event in his book:

Again, India gave unstinted support to Burma's efforts to get the Kou Min Tang (KMT) forces, almost 12,000 strong, off its territory. U Nu wanted them out as their presence in Burma was a sore point with the PRC and was becoming an increasing source of destabilisation. India extended firm support for the UN Resolution which sought the evacuation of the KMT Chinese soldiers and their families out of Burma. The debate on the resolution at the UN once again saw the drama of a vitriolic exchange between India's Krishna Menon and the Americans. Krishna Menon spelled out the nature of the closeness of the India–Myanmar relations, when he categorically stated: '...what hurts Burma hurts us equally. We have no military alliance, but Burma is closely linked to us and it is naturally of great concern to us that she should suffer'. India's strong support at the UN was greatly appreciated by the U Nu government. Americans in those days supported the KMT to the extent of encouraging opium cultivation as a source of revenue, which resulted in a number of these Chinese settling down along the Myanmar border with China and the entrenchment of the manufacture and trade in heroin out of that region.[31]

The posting of Shri Benegal Narsing Rau,[32] an Indian constitutional expert, to Burma to assist in drafting the constitution of Burma was another example of the intimate support that India provided to Burma in the post-Independence years.[33] It was during this period that the Indo-Burma Boundary issues were negotiated and an agreement signed in Imphal when Nehru and U Nu met. However, the demarcation of the border would finally be completed only in 1969. The signing of the Treaty of Peace and Friendship between the two countries on 7 July 1951 by Ambassador M.A. Rauf and Sao Hkun Hkio, Minister for Foreign Affairs of Burma, effectively institutionalised the bilateral relations between the two neighbours (see **Appendix K**). The eight Articles of this Treaty lead to co-operation in trade, customs, cultural relations, communications, extradition, immigration or repatriation of nationals and other matters of common interest.[34]

Rice purchase by India from Burma was a regular feature of trade with a significant goodwill element. In April 1954, India purchased nine lakh tons of rice over three years at a then relatively high price of 48 sterling pounds per ton.[35] An Agreement of Trade and Commerce between India and Burma was signed at New Delhi on 5 September 1956[36] which committed India to purchase 2 million tons of rice from Burma over a five-year period. This was followed by another agreement on 30 September 1959 wherein India agreed to purchase another one and a half lakh tons of rice over the earlier commitment, as also take another three and a half lakh tons of rice from the 1960 crop as well.

Another major assistance from India to Burma was the writing off of 50 per cent of outstanding liabilities to India arising out of separation from India in 1937; this despite India itself being starved of much needed foreign exchange. Further, India went on to grant a loan of US$ 300 million to Burma on very favourable terms in 1957 even though it was short of capital itself.[37]

The engagement was not one sided and reciprocally, U Nu respected Nehru's advice and requests wholeheartedly. Ambassador Preet Malik writes:

> *The U Nu–Nehru relationship once again came into play at the Colombo Conference on Indo-China where U Nu, irritated by the Chinese support for the CPB, was inclined to lean towards the United States (US) position which was vigorously put forward by Pakistan. But he was persuaded by Nehru to support the unanimous resolution that was adopted, urging that 'Indo-China be allowed to settle its own future without intervention by the Great Powers'. Nehru managed to convince U Nu to support his views on the subject by indicating that he would take up Burma's concerns with Beijing and confirming this trust by instructing India's Ambassador to China to request Beijing to extend satisfactory assurances to Burma. However the problems confronting the relations between the PRC and Burma continued to reach critical moments as U Nu became increasingly incensed over the persistent Chinese support for the CPB and the insurgencies in Burma (which he apprehended were sure signs of China's 'imperialistic designs'); U Nu was even contemplated (sic) joining SEATO. He wrote to Nehru: 'I fear to find myself entering the SEATO alliance in spite of myself.' Nehru had to once again intervene with Zhou En Lai in order to prevent such a development which would have come in the way of his design for peace in Asia.*[38]

During this phase from Independence till 1962 there was virtually no engagement between the two militaries. The only military assistance that India provided the U Nu regime was the sale of six Dakota transport aircraft on concessional terms in 1950 when Rangoon was surrounded by rebels and needed help to maintain liaison with towns still under its control.[39, 40]

From 1962 to 1989

The previous section highlighted the close bonds that Nehru and U Nu had, even to the detriment of the Indian diaspora, from Independence till 1962. The next period from 1962 to 1989 saw fortunes dip for both the statesmen, and their states. From a purely Burmese perspective, this period should have ended in August 1988 when Burma erupted into the 8888 Revolution. From the India-Myanmar relations perspective, I have extended it to 1989, when, with the defeat of the Indian National Congress led by Rajiv Gandhi, India plunged into a cycle of political instability which saw six successive governments in nine years till 1998. From 1962 till PM Rajiv Gandhi lost the elections in 1989, India saw four Prime Ministers, viz., Nehru, Lal Bahadur Shastri, Indira Gandhi and Rajiv Gandhi. In contrast, Ne Win remained constant in Myanmar, almost during the same period.

PM Nehru's equation with Ne Win was coloured negatively due to Nehru's long and personal relationship with U Nu. The circumstances under which Ne Win deposed U Nu were such that Nehru never favoured Ne Win the way he did U Nu. This was basically his principled stand on dealing with a dictator. Plus this was 1962 and personally Nehru had taken a hit with his stand on China-India relations. Ne Win on his part tried to reach out and improve relations and visited Nehru and offered to speed up the Colombo Powers' efforts at reconciliation, but Nehru remain sceptical. Prof. L.K. Choudary writes that:

> *The chauvinistic and anti-foreigner policies of General Ne Win had strained the Indo-Burmese relations. Although Burma had been cut off from the rest of the world during the period, India with vibrant democracy was looked with jaundiced eyes by the ruling elites because of its tradition of supporting people fighting for democracy. Ne Win's mindset made Myanmar one of the world's most isolated countries with economically disastrous consequences.*[41]

One of the most devastating consequences of Ne Win's policies was on Indian businesses in Burma. In fact, it remains one of the most defining features of this period in Indo-Burma relations.

Baleshwar Prasad's papers at the Nehru Memorial Museum and Library include documents on the Indo-Burma Relations of that era. A document from his collection titled "*Indo-Burma Relations Since 1961 to to-date* (sic)" attributed to an S.C. Banerjee, dated 14 October 1970, recounts:

> *The year 1962 witnessed great upheavels (sic) in Burmese politics. The Armed Forces seized power in March 1962. Discontentments (sic) among the constituent States increased; they demanded a federal form of Government. Introduction of Buddhism as the State Religion did please neither the staunch Buddhist nor the non-Buddhist minority. The overnight nationalization of foreign trade shocked the business community. Despite drastic changes to the detriment of the Indian citizens in Burma, relations with India remained friendly. In December 1962, a three-year trade agreement with India was concluded when India stood first among Burma's customers and third as supplier. Traditionally, Indo-Burma relations have been based on trade and commerce. India has been the largest purchaser of Burma rice, and Burma of various Indian goods, particularly textiles and base metals. Relations have extended to other fields during the post-war time. We have co-operated together, but there is need for still closer co-operation for the world shrinks with the growth of technology and science.*

However, the cracks in the relationship had started appearing. The paper mentions the strained relations between Indians and the Burmese as follows:

> *Perhaps for the first time in recent memories, relations between India and Burma, which had been very friendly showed some sign of strain in the year 1964,*

particularly of the Indian nationals in Burma. Approximately 7 per cent of the urban and 1.5 per cent of the rural population were Indians in Burma. Before the war, of Burma's 14.6 million, there were one million Indians. Vice-Admiral Katari, Indian Ambassador to Burma, rightly pointed out the problem of Indians in Burma was of historic origin. Till 1963, Indians controlled 60 per cent of trade and commerce of the country – directly or indirectly. When the Burmese Government nationalized privately owned business establishments in 1963-64, Indians were the first to be hit severely. About 50,000 Indians were affected, and their assets were valued at Kyats 60 million, which were either nationalized or confiscated, for which the Government promised to pay compensation, but nothing so far materialized.

Following the nationalization of catering shops, the Indians and the Chinese, out of fear, drew large sums from the banks. In May 1964, the Government, to bring out the hoarded money, which deprived it of some monetary power, demonetized Kyats 100 and Kyats 50 currency notes. Subsequently, various nationalistic and socialistic measures adopted by the Government went against the foreigners and therefore against the Indians. Practically all Indians, even of middle and poorer classes – were dislodged from their occupations. In fear of destitution, they clamoured to go back to their homeland.

Of the total population, there were approximately 2 per cent or about 500,000 foreigners in Burma, the majority of whom are Indians. It is difficult to ascertain the number of Chinese, who have continuously been absorbed among the indigenous races of this land through intermarriages. They have advantages: both the Burmese and the Chinese have descended from the mongoloid stock with similar religion and not very unlike physical features; whereas the Indians came from Aryan stock with distinctly different physical features and customs. Though the fundamentals of both Buddhism and Hinduism are the same, in appearance they differ. The Indians, being conservative, maintained their separate identity.

Nationalization under the Burmese Way to Socialism hit hard both foreigners and nationals, particularly capitalists. Indian nationals had played an important role in the development of the Burmese economy, mainly agriculture and industry.

There were about 500,000 Indians in Burma, many of them having lived on this soil for three or four generations. By mid-September 1964, 43,623 foreigners had left the country, of which Indians were 37,165. Indian External Affairs Minister Swaran Singh paid a four-day goodwill visit to Burma from 2 to 5 September 1965. But for some obscure reason, the Indian Government never allowed the troubles of its diaspora in Burma to strain its friendly relations with Burma. Totally 152,793 Indians left Burma for good between April 1963 and December 1966.

On 27 May 1964, PM Nehru passed away and the mantle of leadership passed on to Lal Bahadur Shastri on 9 June 1964. General Ne Win paid a State visit to India from 5 to 12 February 1965 wherein he assured the new Indian PM that nationalization of private enterprises was non-discriminatory. PM Lal Bahadur Shastri's reciprocal visit to Burma in December 1965 eased the tensions that resulted from the nationalization of private businesses owned by Indians in 1964, though no succour was forthcoming for the Indians who had to flee. However Lal Bahadur Shastri's tragic demise in Tashkent on 11 January 1966 put paid to furtherance of the initiative. The paper chronicles that:

> *In March 1966, Ne Win visited India to get acquainted with the new Prime Minister of India, Indira Gandhi. The two leaders discussed the Mizo problems on the Indo-Burma borders. The Mizos and Nagas rebelled against the Indian Government. Relations with India were better in 1967. Late in January, M. C. Chagla, Indian Foreign Minister, visited Rangoon and had talks with General Ne Win and Foreign Minister U Thi Han, which were reported to be fruitful. It was said certain principles regarding payments of compensation for the nationalized Indian properties in Burma was reached, but so far no tangible results are visible.*
>
> *General Ne Win made an informal visit to India from March 15 to 23, 1968 at the invitation of Indira Gandhi. The talks covered the entire range of economic and cultural fields, particularly on trade and finance, and also on Chinese activities among dissident tribesmen—the Nagas and the Mizos of Northern Burma and Northeast India. They were receiving arms from China. In June 1968, the Mizos raided Tiddim and Falam, and looted the Treasury and trade godowns in Falam, the capital of Chin Special Division of Burma, probably as reprisal for preventing them to raid India.*

General Ne Win made another informal visit to India from 15 to 25 March 1968 at the invitation of Indira Gandhi. The talks covered the entire range of economic and cultural fields, particularly commerce and finance, and also on Chinese activities among the dissident tribesmen—the Nagas and the Mizos of Myanmar and India. The reciprocal Friendship Visit by Mrs. Indira Gandhi was carried out from 27 to 30 March 1969. The paper mentions that:

> *Shrimati Gandhi thanked General (Ne Win) for helping India with increased quantities of rice in her trying days. As to the difficulties the Indians are facing in Burma, she said: Indian citizens must see the realities in Burma: social attitudes are changing and every change entails hardship. We have to adjust to it. Indian citizens must be proud of Burma—their country of adoption. They must show loyalty and responsibility to this country.*
>
> *Following the visit of Indira Gandhi to Rangoon (March 27 to 30), an important*

announcement was made on May 7 regarding resident foreigners of Burma, which said 60,000 foreigners would be granted Burmese citizenship. This measure of the Revolutionary Government will increase friendship between India and Burma, since the majority of foreigners are Indians. The Immigration and National Registration Department was to issue National Registration Certificates (NCRs) to foreigners who have applied for them.

Vice Admiral R.D. Katari, the Indian Ambassador, recounts in his memoirs that this was one visit where even Mrs. Gandhi was left feeling stifled. He highlights that being a personal guest, no diplomatic protocol was involved and the embassy had no role to play. She was accommodated in the State House, the Chairman's official residence. Her programme included a couple of days of relaxation at their pleasant seaside resort, Sandoway, called Ngapali by the Burmese. The Ambassador and his wife were invited to join the party on this very pleasant visit. In Rangoon, Mrs. Gandhi was looked after with such personal care that she was unable to leave the State House on her own. She was not even able to get out to do some personal shopping of a few gifts for her staff and friends at home because she could not lay her hands on any Burmese currency. In sheer desperation, she made an unheralded call at the Ambassador's residence and walked straight up to his wife's room for a chat and also to borrow some Kyats with which to buy some Burmese umbrellas! On her return home, she wrote a charming and complimentary letter to Ambassador Katari's wife.

The paper continues on the 'rice diplomacy' and trade aspects of India-Myanmar relations:

Previously, Burma purchased from India Kyats 130 million worth of goods (and) sold to India Kyats 200 million worth a year on average. In 1967-68, Burma imported from India Kyats 42.6 million worth of goods, of which textiles comprised 47 per cent, and India purchased from Burma, goods to the value of Kyats 85 million of which 88 per cent was rice and rice products and 10 per cent base metals, mainly pig lead. In 1966, India took from Burma 23 per cent of Burma's total exports, rice comprising 96 per cent of this while Burma purchased Indian goods only for Kyats 23.9 million, 3 per cent of Burma's total imports.

Despite various encouraging trade talks between the two countried (sic), India's sales to Burma declined from Kyats 65.6 million in 1964-65 to Kyats 24.1 million in 1966-67 to Kyats 19.0 million in 1967-68. Whereas Burma's sales to India averaged Kyats 119 million a year from 1964-64 to 1967-68. Thus India was having adverse balance of trade with Burma continuously. From the 1969 harvest, India bought 200,000 tons of rice from Burma, and it was reported Burma has contracted to purchase Rs. 80 million worth of rails and other track materials from India.

> *The largest concentration of Indians are still to be found in Zeyewaddy and Kyauktaga, Pegu Division, the former having 35,000 Indians and the latter 25,000 approximately. Indian inhabitants of these two towns are mainly peasants, earn their living by raising crops. The forefathers of these Indians came to Burma about a century ago and settled in these places and worked as farmers. Their descendants have continued to be farmers. Many of them never took up foreigner's registration certificates, nor applied for the NRC; perhaps because they thought they were citizens of Burma by virtue of their forefathers' century-old settlement under Section 10(3) of the Burmese Constitution. But the Immigration Department of Burma did not look at (it) that way, and as a result, they had to undergo a lot of difficulties.*
>
> *Other Indians were mainly traders and industrialists. With the Government take-over of these two sectors of the economy, practically most of them left the country for good. So far, it is learnt that around 175,000 Indians left the country for good since 1962, and approximately 16,000 Pakistanis and 6,000 Chinese, according to reports.*
>
> *Following her three-day visit to Burma in March, 1969, Indira Gandhi informed the Indian Parliament that General Ne Win and his Government had agreed to look into the problems concerning Indian citizens in Burma and those of Indian origin awaiting registration as Burma citizens sympathetically and expeditiously.*

By 1970, India-Myanmar relations at the Government level were getting closer. A new Trade Agreement was concluded in May 1970, and the demarcation of the Indo-Burma boundaries was proceeding without any problems.

General Ne Win visited India again in January 1970 and secured an agreement by India to purchase 100,000 tons of rice from the 1970 crop in Myanmar. India's purchase of rice was the largest quantity bought by a single purchaser and equals around half the quantities so far sold by Burma in 1970. The paper highlighted that this purchase was made by India despite her assurances to Thailand to purchase Thai rice and thus risk incurring Thai displeasure despite Thailand importing a much larger volume of Indian goods than Burma did. This indicated India's desire to maintain closer ties with Burma.

Ne Win visited India on a number of occasions. One such informal visit recorded in the P. N. Haksar Papers mentions Lok Sabha Starred Question No. 1018 tabled by Shri Beni Shankar Sharma and Shri Himatsingka[42] answered on 3 April 1968. The question enquired of the Minister of External Affairs was "*whether General Ne Win, Burma's Head of State, visited in March 1968; if so, the nature of discussions held; and outcome thereof*". The answer endorsed was "*Chairman of the Revolutionary Council of the Union of Burma, General Ne Win, accompanied by Madame Ne Win, paid an informal visit to India from March 15 to March 22,*

1968. Opportunity was taken to have an exchange of views on matters of mutual interest. As is customary, exchange of views and conversations were done in confidence and the Hon. Members would not expect me to give the details."[43]

The Seventies saw Ne Win bring in a new constitution in 1974 which effectively transferred power from the armed forces to a single party, i.e., the Burma Socialist Programme Party (BSPP) established by Ne Win himself to remain in complete control. The decade also saw the commencement of massive protests in 1974 against corruption, inflation and food shortages, especially rice. In December 1974, the biggest anti-government protests over the denial of a state funeral to former UN Secretary-General U Thant were a manifestation of the opposition to the military regime. Over the decade these built up to a point where in 1981 Ne Win relinquished presidency to San Yu, another retired general. However he continued as Chairman of the BSPP.

The year 1982 saw the infamous Citizenship Act 1982 come into being which denied people of non-indigenous backgrounds full citizenship and therefore effectively barred them from public office. Falling commodity prices and rising debt led to an economic crisis which precipitated into the September 1987 wiping out of the savings of the vast majority of people. This eventually worked its way into the 8 August 1988 Revolution which later became known as the 8888 Revolution. General Saw Maung, staged a coup on 8 August to restore order, killing thousands in the process. The military swept aside the Constitution of 1974 in favour of martial law under the State Law and Order Restoration Council (SLORC) with Saw Maung as chairman and prime minister. The 1988 demonstrations and the ruthless manner in which they were dealt with, first by U Sein Lwin and then the SLORC, attracted immediate condemnation from India. The protests in Myanmar were already winning public and political support in India. The SLORC's suppressive actions aroused strong reaction among all Indians. The Indian Ambassador, Dr. I.P. Singh in 1988, perceived that the events would ultimately lead to a political compromise in favour of democracy that would meet the wishes of the vast majority of the people of Myanmar. Unfortunately that was not to happen.[44]

Support for the students and politicians who fled to India was institutionalised with Minister for External Affairs P.V. Narasimha Rao briefing the India Parliamentary Committee that India was doing everything possible to support the people of Myanmar and that orders had been passed to all concerned that no Burmese seeking refuge in India would be turned back from its borders.

This crisis plunged India-Myanmar relations into an abyss and it would take several years before trust could be re-established to a point where relations could be attempted to be normalised. In the next chapter, we see how India-Myanmar relations fared from 1989 till 2020.

NOTES

1. Quote is attributed to V. K. Krishna Menon during a debate in the UN in support of Burma's request for a UN Resolution seeking eviction of KMT soldiers and families from Burma, by Ambassador Preet Malik in his book "*My Myanmar Years – A Diplomat's Account of India's Relations with the Region*", pg. 41.
2. Reuters, "Britain's Greatest Battle? The 1944 Victory over Japanese in Kohima," *India Today*, April 21, 2013, https://www.indiatoday.in/india/northeast/story/britain-greatest-battle-japanese-kohima-159507-2013-04-21 (Accessed on 19 Feb 2020).
3. Gundevia, Y. D., *Outside the Archives.* Sangam Books (India) Private Limited, Delhi, 2008, https://www.amazon.in/Outside-Archives-Y-D-Gundevia-ebook/dp/B07H2CW9HC/ref=sr_1_2?qid=1582048189&refinements=p_27:Y.D.+Gundevia&s=books&sr=1-2. (Accessed on 18 Feb2020). In this book, Gundevia refers to the appointment as 'Secretary to the Representative of the Government of India to the Government of Burma'.
4. Gundevia, pg. 2. The Refugee Government of Burma was established in Simla during the war.
5. Gundevia, pg. 3.
6. Nehru's Personal Assistant from 1946 to 1959 approximately.
7. Bhushan, Shanti. *Courting Destiny: A Memoir.* Penguin Books, New Delhi, 2008.
8. Kyaw, Aye. *The Voice of Young Burma.* Cornell South East Asia Program, New York, 1993, pg. 32, https://books.google.co.in/books?id=VFpdDwAAQBAJ&pg=PA32&lpg=PA32&dq=SAS+Tyabji&source=bl&ots=GvG3Esdfzj&sig=ACfU3U1ndy9L9sZXcMHIRUulavi2MGaehg &hl=en&sa=X&ved=2a hUKEwi8z_T67tz nAhVIWH0KHVoFAPg Q6AEw Ano ECCUQAQ#v=onepage&q=SAS%20Tyabji&f=false. (Accessed on 19 Feb 2020).
9. Leigh, Michael D. *The Evacuation of Civilians from Burma: Analysing the 1942 Colonial Disaster.* Bloomsbury Academic, London, 2014, pg. 130, https://books.google.co.in/books?id=kvYqAwAAQBAJ&pg=PA130&lpg=PA130&dq=SAS+Tyabji&source=bl&ots=mc8uqL93QT&sig=ACfU3U30hehsfyhmuD7TacIAu6YX4TL1Ew&hl=en&sa=X&ved=2ahUKEwi8z_T67tznAhVIWH0KHVoFAPgQ6AEwBnoECCkQAQ#v=onepage&q=SAS%20Tyabji&f=false. (Accessed on 19 Feb 2020).
10. Reginald Dorman Smith was the Governor at that time.
11. Nilanjana Sengupta, *The Gentleman's Word: The Legacy of Subhash Chandra Bose in South East Asia* pg.137 (Singapore: Institute of South East Asia Studies, 2012), https://books.google.co.in/books?id=ZV9HuHYS3CgC&pg=PA137&lpg=PA137&dq=SAS Tyabji&source =bl&o ts=LPVkAxmEb9&sig=ACfU3U09QYuXH7e4SM4N3r06WGG6QCzhuA&hl=en&sa=X&ved=2ahUKEwi8z_T67tznAhVIWH0KHVoFAPgQ6AEwA3oECCcQAQ#v=onepage&q=SAS Tyabji&f=false) (Accessed on 19 Feb 2020).
12. M. A. Rauf Papers, Individual Collection, Writings by Others, Ser. No. 1, Undated, *An Article 'Nehru's Envoys',* Xerox Copy. Accessed at Nehru Memorial Museum and Library.
13. This author has worked on the absence of a culture of military history in the Armed Forces. The paper titled "*A Historiographic Analysis of the Military History of Post Independent India*", CLAWS Manekshaw Paper No. 64, 2016, is available at https://www.claws.in/publication/a-historiographic-analysis-of-the-military-history-of-post-independent-india/(Accessed on 15 April 2020).

14. The date of death mentioned, i.e., 13 April 1967, is possibly incorrect since both the obituaries mention the death as having taken place on a Saturday in April 1967. The closest Saturday to 13 April 1967 is 15 April and is likely to have been the date of death.
15. M. A. Rauf Papers, Press Clippings Acc. No. 1507, Extract of Canadian Obituaries, April 1967, Xerox copy of Press Clippings on M. A. Rauf, *The Toronto Star* and *The Globe Mail,* Toronto. Accessed at Nehru Memorial Museum and Library, New Delhi, India.
16. Website of the Governor Generals of Canada, The Right Honourable Daniel Roland Michener, Archives https://archive.gg.ca/gg/fgg/bios/01/michener_e.asp (Accessed on 15 Apr 2020).
17. Embassy of India, Yangon, website, Link 'Previous Ambassadors', https://embassyofindia yangon.gov.in/pages?id=eyJpdiI6ImpTXC9rem5tejVjTW9hRVwv Z0cr WXZj Zz09Iiwidm FsdWUiOiJkUHljY3NSZ1lqZHJUXC9jUVc2Qmw1Zz09IiwibW FjIjoiMjE2ODIxN2Y5 NTRkZD U1ZDY4NzY0ZmE5MmIwNmRjYzNmY2M1N2QxY2UwNmRiYWViNzE5 MzM0 MGQ4 NzE5ZGM4 NSJ9&subid=eyJpdiI6I kcyQ3dcL0hDekRGRnVITElcL25EYjZ JZz09Iiw idmFsdWUiOiJId3lZRkRRbU5qcnIxYzYyOXFcL2hNQT09IiwibWFjIjoiNzlhYm Y4Zm M1 MDAxYzNh MTIyM2NhNWY4M2MzNGY3YTNkNWY3Yzg1NzY5YTZiYz Y3MzhiYzkxOGQ0YTIyMDUxNyJ9 (Accessed on 15 April 2020).
18. Facebook Account, Ambassador MA Rauf, https://www.facebook.com/ambassadormarauf/ (Accessed on 15 April 2020).
19. Facebook Account, Ambassador MA Rauf, https://www.facebook.com/pg/ambassadormarauf/ posts/?ref=page_internal (Accessed on 15 April 2020).
20. The Imperial Bank of India was in 1955 transformed into the State Bank of India.
21. Preet Malik, '*My Myanmar Years: A Diplomat's Account of India's Relations with the Region*', Sage India, New Delhi, 2015, pg. 37.
22. Facebook Account, Ambassador MA Rauf, https://www.facebook.com/pg/ambassadormarauf/ about/?ref=page_internal (Accessed on 15 April 2020).
23. From 24 April 1972 to 3 October 1974.
24. He had earlier been appointed as the President of the Indian Independence League of Burma.
25. Probably dated around 10 March 1970.
26. Vineet Thakur, *Postscripts on Independence: Foreign Policy Discourses in India and South Africa*, Oxford University Press, New Delhi, 2018, pg. 161.
27. Robert D. Kaplan, *Monsoon – The Indian Ocean and the Future of American Power,* Random House, New York, 2012, pg. 236.
28. Oral History Transcript, Acc. No. 451, pgs. 1 & 2.
29. Preet Malik, '*My Myanmar Years: A Diplomat's Account of India's Relations with the Region*', Sage India, New Delhi, 2015, pg. 40.
30. Please see these United Nations Documents accessed at https://undocs.org/en/A/RES/707(VII) and http://www.worldlii.org/int/other/UNGA/1953/77.pdf. (Accessed on 2 May 2020).
31. Ibid, pg. 41.
32. Wangchuk, Rinchen Norbu. "*Two Civil Servants Who Built India's Democracy, But You've Never Heard of Them!*" *The Better India*, 23 Jan 2019, https://www.thebetterindia.com/170367/ias-hero-republic-day-india-first-election-democracy/ (Accessed on 2 May 2020).
33. Malik, pgs. 36 and 39.
34. Ministry of External Affairs, Treaty of Friendship between India and the Union of Burma, https://www.mea.gov.in/bilateral-documents.htm?dtl/6645/Treaty (Accessed on 2 May 2020).
35. Soe Myint, "*Burma File - a question of democracy*", India Research Press, New Delhi, 2003. pg. 504.
36. Legal Information Institute of India Web Site, Indian Treaty Series, Agreement of Trade and Commerce between the Government of the Republic of India and the Government of the Union of Burma, Sep 1956 http://www.commonlii.org/in/other/treaties/INTSer/1956/15.html (Accessed on 2 May 2020).

37. Malik, pg. 44.
38. Ibid., pgs. 44 to 46.
39. Ibid., pg. 201.
40. Vijay Sakhuja, "*India and Myanmar: Choices for Military Cooperation*", Issue Brief, Indian Council of World Affairs, New Delhi, pg. 2, https://web.archive.org/web/20150924032659/http://www.icwa.in/pdfs/IBindiamyanmar.pdf (Accessed on 2 May 2020).
41. L. K. Choudhary. "*Indo-Myanmar Relations: Retrospect and Prospect.*", *India Quarterly: A Journal of International Affairs,* 61(4), 143–168. doi:10.1177/097492840506100406 (Accessed on 4 May 2020).
42. Both were Parliamentarians of the 4th Lok Sabha from Bihar. http://164.100.47.194/loksabha/writereaddata/biodata_1_12/1492.htm and http://loksabhaph.nic.in/writereaddata/biodata_1_12/1958.htm (Accessed on 4 May 2020).
43. P. N. Haksar Papers, Instalment I, Volume II, Subject File 36, pg. 6.
44. Malik, pgs. 59-62.

CHAPTER 3

A Historical Perspective of India-Myanmar Relations: 1989 Onwards

It was decided that India would now adopt 'a two-track policy'. This implied that it would continue to extend moral and political support to the democratic forces and leaders while concurrently it would also engage the military government in order to improve and upgrade government-to-government relations.

—Ambassador Rajiv Bhatia[1]

From 1989 to 2014

For the purposes of brevity, I have resisted splitting the above period into more narrow segments. A detailed analysis of this period is available in Ambassador Rajiv Bhatia's book *India-Myanmar Relations: Changing Contours*, where he treats the years 1987 to 1992 as a transitional period in the history of India-Myanmar relations, which marked the turnaround of relations between the two nations. The initial years in this period were lost to the Indian stance on democracy and it was only when the P.V. Narasimha Rao Government took over in 1991, that realpolitik resurfaced and the graph of India-Myanmar relations halted its downward slide and commenced its journey upwards. Ambassador Bhatia writes that soon after he took over as the Joint Secretary in charge of Myanmar, a policy review exercise was undertaken wherein consultations with Foreign Secretary Dixit, Special Secretary Malik who had served as the ambassador in Yangon from 1990 to 1992, Ambassador Parthasarathy (who was the ambassador from 1992 to 1995) and others led to the formulation of a policy paper. Political direction was obtained from the Prime Minister's Office (PMO) and it was decided that India would now adopt '*a two-track policy*' to extend moral and political support to the democratic forces and leaders while concurrently engaging the military government in order to improve and upgrade government-to-government relations. He writes that '*It was a calibrated and complex initiative to balance principles, values, interests and geopolitical realities*'.[2]

The two-track policy was a welcome change from the earlier policy which was candidly acknowledged by former Foreign Secretary Shyam Saran, as having failed due to an Indian assumption that the longevity of the military regime was limited.[3] However, simply changing a policy would not yield results. The immediate spinoffs post the policy change were manifest in a slew of important visits starting in August 1992. These included visits by U Aye, director general in the Ministry of Foreign Affairs (August 1992); a Foreign Secretary J.N. Dixit-led delegation to Yangon (March 1993); a reciprocal visit by Deputy Foreign Minister U Nyunt Swe (January 1994); Home Secretary N.N. Vohra (February 1994); Army Chief General B.C. Joshi (May 1994) and Commerce Secretary Tejendra Khanna (June 1994). These visits served to remove misconceptions and created a foundation for rapprochement between the two Governments. It culminated in the signing of the Agreement on Border Trade and the Agreement on Cooperation between Civilian Border Authorities. Ambassador Bhatia concludes that Myanmar got a clear signal that while India would continue to press for restoration of democracy and release of political prisoners, it was willing to build a fresh government-level relationship that helped to enhance security and commercial cooperation. In turn, Myanmar sent a clear message that while China would remain its close and vital partner, Yangon had no desire to set up permanent foreign bases on its soil and that it was willing to extend cooperation to India in dealing with insurgent activity in the border region.[4]

However, by 1997, it was evident that the relations had not provided the traction required for engagement between the two nations and the gains, till then, had been modest. What followed was a classic example of out-of-the-box thinking on the part of the then Ambassador Shyam Saran, duly supported by PM Vajpayee and National Security Adviser Brajesh Mishra, wherein defence diplomacy was leveraged to break through the impasse. This worked and led to a quick succession of visits at all levels and it was from here really that India-Myanmar relations gained momentum. This facet of defence diplomacy in India-Myanmar relations has been covered in detail subsequently in this book in the chapter on Defence Diplomacy and India-Myanmar Relations.

The period from 2000 to 2007 saw a vast amount of engagement between India and Myanmar which included the re-establishment of the Consulate General at Mandalay. Renaud Egretau writes in his book:

> *In November 2002, India's top career diplomat, Foreign Secretary Kanwal Sibal, visited Mandalay to reopen India's Consulate-General after a gap of two decades. New Delhi intended to broaden its diplomatic influence in Burma's second city, where the only other foreign diplomatic representation was that of China. The Indian Consulate has since striven to expand its presence westward and spread a positive image of India towards the strategic—but massively underdeveloped—Sagaing region and border areas. This implicitly left the Shan State, northeast of Mandalay, to Chinese domination along the historical "Burma Road".*[5]

In October 2004, a power struggle within the SPDC led to the removal of PM Gen Khin Nyunt including from his position as Chief of Military Intelligence on grounds of smuggling. This was followed by a massive purge on the intelligence apparatus of Khin Nyunt including the release on over 14,000 prisoners apparently wrongly imprisoned by the National Intelligence Bureau.[6] In a surprise move, the Government, in November 2005, announced that it had initiated the first phase of relocation of the country's administrative capital from Yangon to Pyinmana, 400 km north, owing to its central location. It was officially named Nay Pyi Taw in March 2006.[7]

Protests against the substantial increase in fuel prices in September 2007 led to a spiral of violence and deaths. This was later to be christened the Saffron Revolution since the protests were led by Buddhist monks. On the bilateral front, further substance was added to India's relations with Myanmar with the first Head of State visit from India (since PM Rajiv Gandhi's visit in 1987) and the first ever President's visit to Myanmar by President Dr. A.P.J. Abdul Kalam in March 2006. Three projects, viz., the Framework Agreement for Mutual Cooperation in the field of Remote Sensing; the Memorandum of Understanding on Cooperation in the Petroleum Sector between the Ministry of Petroleum and Natural Gas of India and the Ministry of Energy Myanmar; and Memorandum of Understanding on Cooperation in Buddhist Studies between the Indian Council for Cultural Relations (ICCR) and Ministry of Religious Affairs of Myanmar were signed during this visit. In a boost to the IMB states improving their relations with Myanmar, a five-member delegation from the Government of Mizoram led by the Secretary, Trade & Commerce Department, visited Myanmar in May 2006 and had meetings with the Central Executive Committee members of the Union of Myanmar Federation of Chamber of Commerce & Industry (UMFCCI),

Myanmar Timber & Forests Products Merchant Association and Indian Association of Myanmar.[8] On 23 September 2007 signing of Production Sharing Contracts (PSC) by ONGC Videsh Limited with the Myanmar Oil and Gas Enterprise for three deep-sea blocks AD-2, AD-3 and AD-9 in the presence of the Minster of Petroleum & Natural Gas, Murli Deora, in the Myanmar capital Nay Pyi Taw was carried out. A Memorandum of Understanding for Establishing Indian Myanmar Centre for Enhancement of IT Skills at Yangon was also concluded in December 2007.[9] October 2007 also saw Thein Sein formally appointed PM post Soe Win's death. Soon after, Thein Sein instructed Aung Kyi, Minister of Labour, to commence talks with Aung San Suu Kyi.

The year 2008 was tumultuous for Myanmar for three reasons. One, Cyclone Nargis devastated coastal Myanmar in May 2008 leading to 84,500 deaths officially acknowledged and unofficially approximately 1,28,000 deaths. India was one of the first countries to rush emergency relief assistance to Myanmar in the aftermath of the cyclone. Two Indian Naval ships and eight Indian Air Force aircrafts delivered immediate relief material, including food grains and two self-sustained medical teams with medical supplies to Myanmar. In the rehabilitation phase, supply of corrugated steel sheets for roofing, replacement of 16 damaged transformers, delivery of 500 solar torches and lanterns, installing 20 biomass gasifiers, and 1.8 lakh bottles of IV fluids were undertaken by India. Cash assistance of US$ 200,000 (approximately 85 lakhs) for the reconstruction of the Shwedagon Pagoda complex in Yangon was also handed over to Myanmar.

Two, this was the year that the current version of its Constitution[10] was adopted. Paul Chambers, Institute of Southeast Asian Affairs, Chiang Mai University, Thailand, explained[11] that after 18 years of martial law, the State Peace and Development Council enacted Myanmar's latest constitution in 2008. The authors,[12] including military and civilian representatives, drafted a constitution for a government led by civilians, with the military retaining power behind the scenes. In May 2008, the military held a popular referendum on the constitution, and claimed that over 90 per cent of voters consented to the hybrid democracy. The constitution allows for a 75 per cent elected legislature and indirectly-elected president while mandating some increases in civil liberties, among other changes. However, the constitution mandates 25 per cent of the members of the lower and upper houses of the national legislature be in-service military personnel (Sections 109, 141). Similarly, regional and state legislatures are mandated to include security personnel (Sections 14, 17, 161, 170). In addition, legislative committees related to defence are mandated to have a majority of active duty military personnel as parliamentarians.(Sections 115, 147). Further, the President can only be selected by a Presidential College formed from the members of the legislature, including the 25 per cent active duty component of the security forces (Section 60). Finally, the President must be well acquainted with military affairs, a criterion which implies a military background (Section 59).[13]

Three, in February 2008, the SPDC announced that a constitutional referendum would be held in May, followed by multi-party elections in 2010. This, though expected, was met with wary skepticism.

Year 2008 was fruitful for India-Myanmar bilateral relations as well. The historic Framework Agreement on the Kaladan Multi-Modal Transit Transport Project including two Protocols, one on Facilitation of Transit Transport and another on Maintenance and Administration of the Kaladan Project, were signed between India and Myanmar, in addition to the Double Taxation Avoidance Agreement during the visit of Vice Senior General Maung Aye, Vice Chairman, SPDC, in April 2008. The Third Meeting of the Joint Trade Committee (JTC) was held in Myanmar from 13 to 15 October 2008 in which both countries agreed to upgrade border trade to normal trade at the border points Moreh-Tamu and Zowkhathar-Rhi, open a new border trade point at Avangkhung in the state of Nagaland in India and Robermi in Myanmar and to expand the list of commodities under the Indo-Myanmar Border Trade Agreement from 22 to 40 items. Two additional Memoranda of Understanding were signed between the two Governments, one for Intelligence Exchange Cooperation and the second for the Reciprocal Promotion and Protection of Investments in 2008.[14]

The Tamu-Keygone-Kalemyo stretch of road, built with Indian assistance, was handed over to the Government of Myanmar in October 2009. India's bilateral assistance, extended through the Indian Technical and Economic Cooperation (ITEC) Programme to 156 countries, saw participants attending training courses aimed at capacity building and human resource development. Requests for increased assistance in this area were conveyed at various bilateral meetings including at the highest level from the developing world. The programme also assumed new dimensions with regional and multilateral organizations actively associating themselves with the programme. Further progress in developing in-house expertise in project delivery with a view to maximizing cost effectiveness, expeditious delivery, and coordination, buttressed the increasing emphasis on the delivery of development projects as part of India's development cooperation programme. In the case of Myanmar, this was an extremely popular programme with 105 slots allotted for Myanmar trainees in 2008-09 which increased to 140 the next year.[15]

In March 2010, the Myanmar Government approved the new electoral laws and set the tone for the elections that year. In April 2010, PM Thein Sein resigned and registered a new political party, the USDP, of which he became the leader. Elections were scheduled for 7 November 2010. The NLD along with five other parties was dissolved due to non-registration with the Union Election Commission (UEC). The UEC had been established in March with a retired army officer in the chair. The elections, predictably, were far from free and fair and the USDP won and formed the next government. On 13 November 2010, Daw Aung San Suu Kyi was finally released from house arrest.

On the India-Myanmar relations side, with the visit to India in July 2010 of Senior General Than Shwe, Chairman of the State Peace and Development Council, six MoUs and agreements were signed including the Mutual Assistance in Criminal Matters; MoU on Information Cooperation; Agreement on Cooperation in the fields of Science and Technology; MoU on Small Developmental Projects; MoU on Conservation and Restoration of Ananda Temple in Bagan; and Agreement for Line of Credit of US$ 60 million for Railway Infrastructure Project. The ground-breaking ceremony for the Kaladan Project was held in December 2010 and the inauguration of a heavy-duty truck project under an Indian Line of Credit of US$ 20 million was held in the same month.

Defence diplomacy gained momentum through bilateral visits and various training programmes for Myanmar Armed Forces personnel. A total of 11 Indian Armed Forces delegations and three Indian Navy/Coast Guard ships visited Myanmar in 2010. A total of nine delegations from Myanmar Armed Forces visited India during 2010.[16]

In mid-January 2011, General Than Shwe appointed the 25 per cent military representatives to the Hluttaws and the provincial assemblies as per the constitutional quotas. On 1 February 2011, the Pyidaungsu Hluttaw nominated five legislators including PM Thein Sein for three vice-presidential seats. The three automatically would become presidential candidates. On 3 February, the Pyithu Hluttaw voted for Thein Sein as its presidential candidate and the Amyotha Hluttaw elected Dr. Sai Mauk Kham, a Shan USDP member while the third candidate was the military presidential candidate Tin Aung Myint Oo. Thein Sein secured 408 votes to become the President of Myanmar while Tin Aung Myint Oo with 171 votes and Sai Mauk Kham with 75 votes were confirmed as Vice Presidents.

On 30 March 2010, an era of reform in Myanmar began with the Presidency of Thein Sein. The SDPC was dissolved, signalling the formal completion of transfer of power from the military junta to an elected parliament. Than Shwe was replaced by General Ming Aung Hlaing as the Commander-in-Chief (C-in-C) of the Tatmadaw. Engagement with Suu Kyi also increased as the new regime relaxed its stance towards her. She met Thein Sein at Nay Pyi Taw following her first invitation from the Government to attend a workshop on economic development. The President received her underneath a large portrait of her father, General Aung San—a very symbolic gesture.[17]

President Thein Sein paid a State Visit to India from 12 to 15 October, 2011. This visit marked the first high-level bilateral interaction between India and Myanmar after the swearing in of a civilian government in Myanmar in March 2011. During the visit, the two sides signed an MoU for the upgradation of the Yangon Children's Hospital and Sittwe General Hospital; and a Programme of Cooperation in Science and Technology for the period of 2012 to 2015. India announced the extension of a US$ 500 million Line of Credit to Myanmar. India also undertook to set up an Advanced Centre for Agricultural Research and Education in Yezin, a Rice Bio Park in the Integrated Demonstration Farm at Nay Pyi Taw and an Information Technology Institute in Mandalay.[18]

In November 2011, the NLD re-registered itself to contest by-elections scheduled on 1 April 2012 for 45 parliamentary seats. It won 43 of the 44 seats it contested including 33 seats in the 440-member lower chamber. Ambassador Preet Malik construes[19] that the strategy behind the changes that took place leading to the Than Shwe-led SPDC transferring power to the newly elected and nominally civilian government headed by Thein Sein, was derived from a 346-page master plan evolved by a researcher at the Myanmar Defence Services Academy, Lt Colonel Aung Kyaw Hla. Malik writes:

> *According to this thesis the intent was not that the opposition led by Suu Kyi be enabled, by a changed approach, to eventually be involved within the governance system, but to utilise concessions to her and the democracy lobby to bring the USA back into a relationship that would help reduce Myanmar's dependence on China in the domestic, security and economic space. The idea behind this being that the US, once it re-emerged as a player, having a strategic interest in Myanmar, would result in a more balanced presence of China in Myanmar. It is not an attempt to reduce the importance of China in Myanmar's scheme of things but to make for a more realistic relationship that enabled Myanmar to exercise all options open to it to improve the security and the socio-economic developmental environment.*

In this entire scheme of things, the relatively low profiled position of the Tatmadaw is on account of the safeguarding of its dominant political position and the overall preservation of its economic and social bases. For now, C-in-C Hlaing has gone along with the reforms set out by Thein Sein which was seen as a victory of the moderates, which would help the continuation of the reforms and the national reconciliation process.

In 2011, The Lady, as Daw Aung San Suu Kyi is reverently referred to in Myanmar, was given a passport for the first time in 24 years and she visited a number of countries including India and Norway where she received the Nobel Peace Prize that had been awarded to her in 1991. Her willingness to leave Myanmar indicated her confidence in Thein Sein that she would be permitted to return again. In a significant development, in August 2012, the Government announced abolition of pre-publication censorship of media and a Press Council was established to monitor the strict regulations still in place. In December 2012, the Government announced that from April 2013, the publication of privately-owned newspapers would be permitted for the first time in nearly 50 years. Further, the first female cabinet minister, Dr. Daw Myat Ohn Khin, was appointed Minister of Social Welfare, Relief and Resettlement. A sign of improvement in the authority of the Parliament was when the Pyithu Hluttaw approved impeachment of all nine judges of the Constitutional Tribunal following an attempt by the Tribunal to limit the power of the parliamentary committees and commissions.[20]

PM Dr. Manmohan Singh paid a State Visit to Myanmar in May 2012 which was the first visit by an Indian PM in 25 years. During the visit, twelve Agreements and MoUs were signed. These included the Air Services Agreement and MoUs on a Line of Credit of US$ 500 million extended by India to Myanmar; Border Area Development; Establishment of the Advanced Centre for Agriculture Research and Education (ACARE); Establishment of Rice Bio Park; Setting up of Myanmar Institute of Information Technology; Establishment of Border Haats; Setting up of a Joint Trade and Investment Forum; Cultural Exchange Programme for 2012-2015; and Cooperation among Think Tanks and Universities of the two countries. The year ended with Daw Aung San Suu Kyi visiting India in November 2012 to deliver the Nehru Memorial Lecture in New Delhi.[21]

The process of political freedom gained momentum in January 2013 with the Government abolishing a 25-year-old ban on public gatherings of more than five people, enabling public mobilization and protests. The NLD's first ever congress was held in March 2013 and Daw Aung San Suu Kyi was unanimously re-elected as the party leader while the executive committee was enlarged from seven to 15 members.

On the India-Myanmar relations front, the Line of Credit sanctioned to Myanmar for Railway projects amounted to US$ 155 million. Ongoing cross-border projects as in 2013 included the Kaladan Project; the Trilateral Highway from India to Thailand via Myanmar including construction of 71 bridges in the Tamu-Kalewa-Kalemyo section and construction of a 120 km road in the Kalewa-Yagyi section; and other road projects like the Rih (India-Myanmar border)—Tiddim (Myanmar). Development cooperation with Myanmar comprised establishment of capacity building institutions in the livelihood sector including agriculture for enhancing agricultural yield and quality (Advanced Centre for Agricultural Research and Education and a Rice Bio-Park); IT (Myanmar Institute of Information Technology (MIIT) in Mandalay); Health (upgradation of Yangon Children Hospital and Sittwe General Hospital with supply of state-of-the-art medical equipment and training); and a Language and an e-resource centre in Yangon and Nay Pyi Taw. The Government of India opened a new Consulate General of India in Sittwe on 24 June 2014 to expand its footprint in Rakhine and Chin states of Myanmar.[22]

PM Dr. Manmohan Singh paid a two-day official visit to Nay Pyi Taw on 3-4 March 2014 to attend the 3rd Bay of Bengal Initiative for Multi-Sectoral Technical and Economic Cooperation (BIMSTEC) Summit. He was accompanied by External Affairs Minister Shri Salman Khurshid, NSA Shri Shivshankar Menon, Foreign Secretary Smt. Sujatha Singh and other senior officials. On the sidelines of the BIMSTEC Summit, Dr. Manmohan Singh had bilateral meetings with President of Myanmar, U Thein Sein.

From 2014 to 2020

For Indian politics, 2014 was a major year of change when the incumbent United Progressive Alliance government lost the elections and paved way for the National Democratic Alliance led by PM Narendra Modi. As in some of the past historical events in India and Myanmar, this event too would be mirrored in Myanmar in the 8 November 2015 elections with the NLD Government sweeping out the USDP and taking over the reins of the nation, heralding a new change in Myanmar. This was the first openly contested general elections since 1990 with the NLD getting an absolute majority. It won 255 out of 330 elective seats in Pyithu Hluttaw and 135 out of 168 elective seats in Amyotha Hluttaw, against the USDP's 30 and 12, respectively. The next was the Arakan National Party with 12 and 10 seats while the Shan Nationalities League for Democracy won 12 and three, respectively. On 11 November 2015, Suu Kyi called for 'national reconciliation' talks with the USDP and the military and the next day, President Thein Sein and the C-in-C announced that they had accepted the results of the polling and pledged to support the smooth and peaceful transition of power.

The process for electing a new President commenced on 11 March 2016 with the Pyithu Hluttaw voting for a long-time aide of Suu Kyi, U Htin Kyaw. The Amyotha Hluttaw voted for Henry Van Thio of the NLD while Lt Gen Myint Swe (Retd), then Chief Minister (CM) of Yangon Region, was the military candidate. Htin Kyaw secured 360 of the 652 votes and was elected President while Henry Van Thio and Lt Gen Myint Swe (Retd) received 213 and 79 votes becoming the First Vice President and Second Vice President, respectively. The first civilian Government in more than 50 years was sworn in on 30 March 2016. Suu Kyi initially joined the 18-member Cabinet as the Minister of Foreign Affairs, President's Office, Education, Energy and Electricity. However, in April 2016, a new post of State Counsellor was created at par with that of the President with the approval of both the houses less the military members. She accordingly assumed the office of the State Counsellor of Myanmar, relinquishing her Cabinet appointments except that of Foreign Affairs. With this the official resurrection of The Lady was complete and the future of Myanmar lay in her hands, though not totally since the military still had a say.[23]

Signing of the Nationwide Ceasefire Agreement (NCA) between eight ethnic armed groups and the Government of Myanmar and holding of general elections in Myanmar were the two domestic developments in Myanmar, where India, as a close and friendly neighbour, was invited to both events. As one of the few international witnesses, the NSA represented India at the NCA signing ceremony in Nay Pyi Taw, Myanmar, on 15 October 2015. The Government of India had also deputed a team of three election observers, nominated by the Election Commission of India, for elections in Myanmar.[24] Notwithstanding the NCA, violence commenced ominously with the first reported clash between the non-NCA signatory AA and Tatmadaw in Buthidaung Township, northern Rakhine State, in March 2015. Despite several subsequent bouts of fighting, however, the AA maintained a low profile in the region until late August 2017, when it ambushed a boat carrying Tatmadaw soldiers along the Kaladan River in Paletwa Township, Chin State. From this point on, violence in Rakhine and Chin States would rise manifold and in scale (quantum of incidents), scope (nature of targets and violence) and spread (i.e., geographical extent).

On the bilateral front, PM Narendra Modi made his maiden visit to Myanmar from 11 to 13 November 2014 to attend the ASEAN-India Summit and the 9th East Asia Summit. During the visit, he met President Mr. U Thein Sein and Daw Aung San Suu Kyi. This had been preceded by External Affairs Minister Smt. Sushma Swaraj's visit from 8 to 11 August 2014 to attend the 4th East Asia Summit (EAS) Foreign Ministers' Meeting and the 21st ASEAN Regional Forum.

Interaction was also held amongst the political leadership of the bordering states of India and Myanmar. The Chin State CM, Mr. Hong Ngai, accompanied by a 38-member trade and cultural delegation visited Manipur from 20 to 23 November 2014 to attend the annual Sangai festival of Manipur. The Sagaing Region CM, Mr. U Thar Aye and the Kachin State CM, Mr. U Lajon Ngan Sai led a 10-member delegation to attend the annual Hornbill festival of Nagaland. The delegation also visited Assam and Meghalaya where it had interactions with the Chief Ministers of Assam and Meghalaya besides civil society, educational institutions and businessmen. Vice President (1) Dr. Sai Mauk Kham led a 35-member delegation on an official visit to India from 19 to 23 January 2015. During his visit, he called on President Pranab Mukherjee and the PM and held bilateral discussions with Vice-President Shri M. Hamid Ansari.[25]

During the year 2014-15, India further scaled up its development cooperation assistance to Myanmar to approximately US$ 1.8 billion. Of this, US$ 750 million was in the form of a concessional loan to be utilized for projects relating to upgradation of refineries and roads; setting up a truck assembly plant; power transmission lines; agriculture, telecommunication and railway projects. The remaining amount was in the form of grant-in-aid for projects on connectivity; construction of roads; port; setting up of centres of excellence;[26] upgrading the public health services; restoration and conservation of shared cultural heritage (Ananda Temple). The Indian Government also committed to provide US$ 5 million each year for five years for the border area development cooperation projects in Chin State and the NSAZ. Under this, first year projects which were nearing completion were transferred to the Ministry of Border Affairs, Myanmar. The Government of India has also provided US$ 1 million for construction of 10 schools in Rakhine State to help the Government of Myanmar towards rehabilitation and reconciliation of the communities living in this relatively backward area. In the first half of 2014-15, bilateral trade grew significantly and stood at US$ 1.184 billion. Of the total foreign investment of US$ 46.718 billion in Myanmar, India's investment stood at US$ 382.4 million.

During the second round of onshore oil and gas block bidding, ONGC

Videsh won two onshore oil and gas blocks (B2 and EP3). In the second round for offshore blocks, Reliance won two blocks (M17 and M18) and Oil India Limited won two blocks (YEB and M4). Permission was accorded to the State Bank of India and the Punjab National Bank to open representative offices; a direct shipping service was launched by the Shipping Corporation of India between India and Myanmar and direct air connectivity between Yangon and Delhi by Air India commenced.[27]

By this time adequate banking presence was in place to support normal trade with Myanmar at the border and the Reserve Bank of India, in consultation with the Government of India, decided to do away with the barter system of trade at the India-Myanmar border and switch over completely to normal trade with effect from 1 December 2015.[28] The Duty Free Preference Scheme for the Least Developed Countries (LDC) had been improved to offer import of goods from Myanmar at zero duty for over 96.4 per cent of tariff lines. The Land Customs Station at Zawkhatar (Mizoram) was inaugurated earlier by the Commerce and Industry Minister in March 2015 to boost border trade via Mizoram to Myanmar and beyond.

President U Htin Kyaw visited India from 27 to 30 August 2016 on his first bilateral visit after the assumption of power of the NLD Government in March 2016. State Counsellor of Myanmar Daw Aung San Suu Kyi paid a bilateral visit to India from 17 to 19 October 2016, after attending the BRICS-BIMSTEC Outreach Summit on 16 October 2016. From the Indian side, Minister of State (Independent Charge) for Commerce and Industry, Smt. Nirmala Sitharaman visited Yangon leading the first high-level foreign business delegation on 18 to 20 May 2016. The NSA visited Myanmar as a Special Envoy of PM on 16 June 2016 and met the Myanmar President and State Counsellor. The External Affairs Minister visited Nay Pyi Taw on 22 August 2016 and had useful interactions with the State Counsellor and the Myanmar President. In March 2016, the State Bank of India was awarded a Commercial Banking Licence and started its operations from 3 October 2016.[29]

The year 2016 was also the one when the first manifestations of the current Rakhine conflict became visible. The first force to reveal its hand was the military wing of the United League of Arakan (ULA), the AA. Throughout the period of government changeover, fighting spread across the tri-border region with India and Bangladesh. By July 2016, the AA had had over 70 clashes with Tatmadaw in Buthidaung, Ponnagyun, Rathedaung, Kyauktaw and Mrauk-U townships in addition to the Paletwa area.[30] Almost concurrently, violence was initiated by the

Rohingya militant group, Harakah al-Yaqin, subsequently renamed the Arakan Rohingya Solidarity Army (ARSA) which had launched four attacks since 2012. The attacks on 9 October 2016 and 25 August 2017 by the ARSA were the ones which triggered the Myanmar military's response. The 9 October 2016 attack was launched by 250 militants armed with knives and hand-made guns who killed nine police officers and injured five in Maungday and Rathedaung townships. The attackers stole 50 guns and 10,000 bullets but lost eight members while two were captured alive by the Myanmar forces. They disclosed that they were members of the terrorist group called Aqa Mul Mujahid (AMM) led by Ataullah Abu Ammar Junjuni@ Hafiz Tohar which subsequently merged with the ARSA.[31]

Politically, two other major developments at this time were the 21st Century Panglong Conference and the Kofi Annan Advisory Commission on Rakhine State. Martin Smith writes[32] that:

> *Buoyed by the party's election victory, public confidence was boosted after Aung San Suu Kyi announced two new processes to address nationality concerns upon taking office: first, a "21st Century Panglong Conference" to achieve ethnic peace and reform; and second, an independent "Advisory Commission on Rakhine State", headed by former UN Secretary-General Kofi Annan, to make recommendations to help resolve the Rohingya Muslim crisis. Both processes suggested that there were finally political leaders in the country prepared to pursue peace and reconciliation in new ways.*

The Panglong Initiative ran aground with the Tatmadaw resuming operations just after the Initiative concluded. The NLD's intent for a genuine outcome was undisputed; however, the major issue was that there was very little discussion on the meat of the subject, i.e., the political resolution. The NLD and Tatmadaw were perceived as trying to resell the original Panglong initiative in a new avatar. The government narrative caused scepticism amongst the minorities as they recalled the 1950s Bamar leaders who had also promised them the world but very little actual reforms had taken place. The NLD and Tatmadaw appeared reluctant to move ahead from Thein Sein's NCA towards a more meaningful peace process. Tatmadaw propagated six non-negotiable principles based on the 2008 Constitution to counter the eight principles put forward by the EAGs. The Arakan National Congress (ANC) and the United Nationalities Federation Council (UNFC), the alliance of the EAGs, at a meeting in August 2016 wanted the eight principles to be added to the 2015 Nationwide Ceasefire Agreement before further signing. In total contrast to the spirit of the Panglong Initiative, in the following months, the Tatmadaw launched major offensives against the non-NCA signatories in the Kachin and northern Shan states. The AA also joined the KIO in forming a new "*Northern Alliance*" alongwith the Kokang group, the Myanmar National Democratic Alliance Army and Ta'ang National Liberation Army.

China's engagement in Myanmar's internal affairs, especially with regard to the peace process, also saw reorientation in 2016 as it grappled with the new NLD Government. Not only has China lost its pre-eminent international position among foreign actors, but Chinese investments have also come under frequent criticism during the revival of an increasingly vibrant media, political and civil society culture. China is Myanmar's largest foreign investor, but a litany of sensitivities plague the country where anti-Chinese sentiment reigns and manifests in issues such as the Kokang crisis, ethnic conflict, the Myitsone dam and rampant natural resource exploitation. The most complaints about Chinese investments are lack of transparency, suitability of Chinese plans, consultation with stakeholders and the resultant protests. The Chinese approach is very different from the inclusive and community-based approach prioritised by Myanmar's peoples as they seek to rebuild after decades of conflict and military-based rule. Taking into account the changes in Myanmar post the NLD Government, China's presence in the country has turned more nuanced and engaged. Doubts still persist over China's strategic intentions and though aid assistance and economic cooperation are undoubtedly appreciated, it more often than not, threatens livelihoods, the environment and local communities. The lessons are clear: projects and practices that benefit the country and the people are always welcome; those that are detrimental will always be sources of controversy and rejected.[33]

On the bilateral side, PM Narendra Modi paid his first State Visit to Myanmar from 5 to 7 September 2017 during which eleven documents were signed by the two sides in health, culture, capacity building, maritime security sectors and for collaboration between key institutions. A Joint Statement was also signed during the visit. Minister of Petroleum and Natural Gas of India Shri Dharmendra Pradhan visited Myanmar in 2017 to enhance and expand regional cooperation in the hydrocarbon sector in collaboration with Myanmar. From Myanmar, Commerce Minister Dr. Than Myint visited India in June 2017 to attend the 6th India-Myanmar Joint Trade Committee (JTC). The Myanmar Minister for Electricity and Energy, U Win Khaing, visited India from 17 to 20 December 2017 and met the Minister of Petroleum and Natural Gas and Minister of Power in India besides visiting prominent installations pertaining to power and natural gas in India.[34]

The year 2017 was really the tipping point in the current Rohingya crisis which was initiated by the 9 October 2016 attack, and exacerbated by the 25 August 2017 attack. This attack broke new ground in scale, coordination, brutality and symbolism. It took place near *simultaneously* on 30 police posts and one army base in the townships of Maungdaw, Buthidaung and Rathedaung in North Rakhine killing 10 police officers, one soldier and an immigration official against 77 insurgents killed and one captured as per reports of the International Crisis Group.[35] It was *coordinated* because on the same date the ARSA also conducted a brutal massacre of 99 Hindu children, women and men of Ah Nauk Kha Maung Seik and Ye Bauk Kyar villages in north Maungdaw Township as reported by Amnesty International.[36] This was followed up the next day on 26 August 2017 when ARSA members killed another six Hindus—two women, a man, and three children near Myo Thu Gyi village outside Maungdaw town.

Year 2017 also saw the BRI come to Myanmar. Aung San Suu Kyi attended the First Belt and Road Forum for International Cooperation in Beijing in May 2017 and a MoU on '*Cooperation within the Framework of the Silk Road Economic Belt and the 21st Century Maritime Silk Road Initiative*' was signed during this visit. Xi Jinping even mentioned Myanmar in the context of the BRI in his speech at the Forum.[37] Aung San Suu Kyi subsequently also attended the Second Belt and Road Forum in April 2019 where nine deliverables were agreed upon out of the 38 proposed by China as 'early harvest' projects. These included three bilateral proposals including an agreement on economic and technical cooperation, an MoU on a five-year economic and trade development cooperation plan (with a 1 billion Yuan, i.e., US$ 144.5 million grant), and an MoU on the China-Myanmar Economic Corridor (CMEC) spanning 2019 to 2030.[38] The 29 projects which were not agreed to is evidence that credit is due to the State Counsellor Daw Suu Kyi and her team in ensuring a conservative approach given the dubious Chinese reputation in matters of debt.[39, 40]

State Counsellor Daw Aung San Suu Kyi visited India in January 2018 for the 25th anniversary of India-ASEAN relations, thus maintaining the positive trajectory of bilateral ties. External Affairs Minister Smt. Sushma Swaraj visited Myanmar in May 2018, signing five MoUs including the LBCA. Capacity building projects continued to expand, with nearly 1,000 Myanmar officials, policemen and citizens receiving training at Indian institutions. Defence ties with Myanmar also expanded with visits by the Chief of Air Staff and the Myanmar Chief of Staff (Navy). Partnerships were also established in building defence infrastructure including a Technical Agreement to supply coastal surveillance systems.

July 2018 saw a third Panglong-21 Conference take place at Nay Pyi Taw with no substantive progress. The Rohingya crisis was again conveniently ignored in the Panglong Conference agenda. This time another 'fourteen principles' were agreed upon with the ALP and NCA signatories for inclusion in a future Union Peace Accord. But, as in the previous two meetings, ethnic nationality representatives complained that there was no real discussion of the key political and security issues that, they believe, are holding back peace and reform. The involvement of China in the peace process was omnipresent. Once again, they organised invitations for representatives for the non-ceasefire ULA, KIO, TNLA, MNDAA and other FPNCC members to attend as "guests". It was clear that all parties—the NLD, Tatmadaw and EAOs—felt bound to accede to Chinese government requests. Smith brings out that the 16 January 2018 killings[41] of Rakhine protestors in Mrauk-U was another incident which ignited Rakhine nationalist sentiment when seven civilians were killed and eight hospitalised in a clash between protestors and the security forces in the ancient Rakhine capital of Mrauk-U. The timing and location of the government crackdown was symbolic, coming after permission for a ceremony to mark the fall of the Arakan kingdom in 1784 was revoked. Two days later, the former ANP leader, Aye Maung, and the author, Wai Hin Aung, were arrested and charged with both "high treason" and "unlawful association" for speeches that they gave at a literary rally in Rathedaung. The two were accused of endorsing the ULA's bid to regain Arakan's lost sovereignty and after a year-long trial, were sentenced to 20 years' imprisonment. Smith equates the 2018 deaths in Mrauk-U symbolically equivalent to the shooting of protestors by the security forces in the 1967 "Rice-Killing Day" in Sittwe. In the aftermath of the Mrauk-U killings, the political mood darkened. The descent into civil war was accelerating with killings and counter-killings on the rise.[42]

The year also saw a change in the Presidency of Myanmar as on 21 March 2018 President U Htin Kyaw resigned due to ill health. On 30 March 2018, the Speaker and close aide to Daw Aung San Suu Kyi, U Win Myint, was elected President. President Win Myint, a geologist by education and a lawyer by profession, had served in both the High Court and the Supreme Court and had also been involved in the 8888 Revolution and was imprisoned till 1990. After winning the 2012 Pathein[43] constituency by-elections he entered the Pyithu Hluttaw (Lower House, i.e., House of Representatives). He was Speaker of the Lower House till 2018 and then selected as the NLD candidate for Presidency after incumbent U Htin Kyaw's resignation. He defeated the USDP candidate by 273 votes to 27 for Vice Presidency, and finally he was elected President on 28

March 2018, after winning 403 out of 636 votes. In one of his first major decisions post elections, he released 8,500 prisoners, including 51 foreigners and 36 political prisoners, on 17 April 2018 as a general amnesty.[44]

Bilaterally, on 8 August 2018, the landmark Agreement on Land Border Crossing was brought into effect with the opening of the two international land border exit/entry posts at Tamu-Moreh and Rihkhawdar-Zokhathwar. It will enhance people-to-people contacts enabling them to cross the land border with passport and visa, including for accessing health and education services, pilgrimage and tourism. India has provided assistance amounting to more than US$ 1.75 billion, of which projects worth nearly US$ 1 billion are completely grant-funded, and others through concessional financing. In September 2018, an MoU for handing over 15 tractors and 15 harvesting machines to Rakhine State Ministry for Agriculture, Livestock, Forest and Mines and 40 computers to the University of Computer Studies, Sittwe, was also signed.

On the defence diplomacy side, a platoon of the Myanmar Army (35 persons) participated in BIMSTEC MILEX 2018 at Pune in September 2018. This was the first time that the Myanmar Army participated in a joint or multilateral exercise. A senior observer team from the Myanmar Army and Vice Senior General Soe Win witnessed the MILEX. Four English Language labs were established by the Indian Army at the Defence Services Academy, Pyin Oo Lwin and handed over to the Myanmar Army in July 2018. The Myanmar Armed Forces employ CDR7 War-gaming Software for their training which was gifted by the Indian Chief of Army Staff (COAS) in 2013. On the request of the Myanmar Army, an upgraded version, tailor-made to meet Myanmar military requirements has been formulated by WARDEC and gifted to Vice Senior General Soe Win by the COAS during his visit to India in September 2018. An Artificial Limb Fitment Camp was organized for amputees of the Myanmar Army in August 2018 in which 102 limbs were fitted by the technical team of Bhagwan Mahaveer Viklang Sahayata Samity (BMVSS).[45]

President Ram Nath Kovind and Smt. Savita Kovind paid a State Visit to Myanmar from 10 to 14 December 2018. In Myanmar, President U Win Myint and President Kovind witnessed the signing of MoUs between the two sides in the areas of judicial and educational cooperation. India handed over the first 50 units of prefabricated houses built in Rakhine State under the Rakhine State Development Programme funded by the Indian Government. Both sides also agreed to sign the MoU for Cooperation on Combating Timber Trafficking and

Conservation of Tigers and Other Wildlife and the MoU on Bilateral Cooperation for Prevention of Trafficking in Persons; Rescue, Recovery, Repatriation and Re-integration of Victims of Trafficking, on which negotiations are nearing completion. A Joint Statement was also signed during the visit.[46]

In retrospect, the year 2019 can actually be called the year of conflicts in Myanmar. Violence transcended the region with varying intensities and peaked along the Muse-Mandalay route in August 2019 and remained at an all-time high in the Rakhine and Chin states throughout the year. The Myanmar Institute of Peace and Security (MIPS) Yangon, a reputed think tank, prepares[47] an outstanding Annual Peace and Security Review and the one for the year 2020 is insightful in the data it presents towards mapping the violence in Myanmar in 2019. The Review concludes that Myanmar saw a major rise in armed conflict in 2019, due to two conflicts involving three players, i.e., the Tatmadaw, the AA and the Ta'ang National Liberation Army (TNLA). The conflict between the Tatmadaw and AA was mostly confined to northern Rakhine State and Paletwa Township in southern Chin State, while the conflict between the Tatmadaw and TNLA took place almost exclusively in northern Shan State. In Rakhine State, severe fighting began after the AA launched coordinated attacks on police posts on 4 January 2019, prompting an angry response from both the government and Tatmadaw. The AA launched multiple large-scale attacks on Tatmadaw, while the latter fought to dislodge AA bases and dug-in positions across the theatre. Slowly, but surely, throughout the year, AA succeeded in effectively dismantling the civil administration in Rakhine. In response, Tatmadaw jumped into a phase of conflict dominated by the use of sustained air power and artillery.

The year 2019 began with optimism for stability in the northern Shan state, but bilateral ceasefire talks between the Tatmadaw and TNLA failed. TNLA, together with the AA and the MNDAA, launched a large-scale offensive along the main transportation (Muse-Mandalay) route linking Myanmar to China in August. The alliance managed to disrupt the economic corridor for nearly two weeks causing major financial losses, after which the Tatmadaw pushed the fighters back off the highway and pursued them deeper into the remote Shan hills. Sporadic clashes would continue into 2020.

Since June 2018, the KIA and Tatmadaw have maintained a tacit ceasefire across Kachin State. Despite periodic clashes in northern Shan State, both sides demonstrated a clear willingness to further de-escalate tensions in Kachin, engage in bilateral negotiations, and cooperate in areas like IDP resettlement.

The battlefield environment in 2019 was characterized by indiscriminate use of landmines, artillery and air attacks with resultant collateral damage causing a large number of civilian casualties and a sharp rise in the movement and seizure of drugs and weapons for funding and arming of the EAGs. The peace process remained a non-starter in 2019 since both the Karen National Union (KNU) and Restoration Council of Shan State (RCSS) suspended their participation in October 2018. The government could not even convene the 21st Century Panglong Union Peace Conference (UPC) this year.

At the invitation of the PM of India, President U Win Myint visited India on 29-30 May 2019 to attend the oath-taking ceremony of the new government. This was followed by a visit of the C-in-C Myanmar Defence Forces, Senior General Min Aung Hlaing to India in July 2019 during which the MoU on Defence Cooperation and an MoU on Exchange of White Shipping Information were signed. The then Defence Secretary, Shri Sanjay Mitra, visited Myanmar in May 2019. The Indian PM met the State Counsellor on 3 November 2019 on the sidelines of the India-ASEAN Summit in Bangkok. On 1 October 2019, India opened a new Liaison Office at Nay Pyi Taw,[48] the capital city of Myanmar.[49] With the opening of this office, India now has representation in four major cities of Myanmar, viz., Embassy in Yangon, two Consulates in Mandalay and Sittwe and a Liaison Office in Nay Pyi Taw.

The year 2020 saw two important visits dominate India-Myanmar equations. The first was the high profile and low substance visit of President Xi Jinping to Nay Pyi Taw in January 2020. The visit resulted in the signing of a total of 33 documents comprising Memoranda of Understanding (MoU), Handover Certificates, Exchange Letters, Letters of Intent, Protocol Documents and Implementation Agreements. An analysis of these documents revealed very little had actually been achieved and most were proposals or follow-up documents to older projects.[50] The second visit was that of President U Win Myint from 26 to 29 February 2020,[51] with a 26-member delegation. This quiet visit within a month of Xi Jinping's visit to Myanmar apparently came about as Myanmar put in place its foreign policy of strategic balance to hedge against overdependence on China. Timed as it was in the wake of the visit by Trump, the visit saw the exchange of 10 MoUs (**Appendix L**) and the issue of a very comprehensive Joint Statement[52] which revealed a number of new initiatives.

That Rakhine featured high on India's priority was signified by the presence of CM of Rakhine State, U Nyi Pu in the 26-member delegation and in fact four of the 10 MoUs were dedicated for Rakhine State alone and it is assessed that the other MoUs could also benefit it. In Rakhine, the MoUs targeted the most violent townships including Buthidaung and Mrauk Oo and certain other unnamed townships. Five townships of Rakhine would be electrified using solar power; Mrauk Oo township hospital would have an incinerator constructed; seed storage houses and water supply systems would be implemented in Gwa township; two roads would be constructed in Buthedaung, all these under the Rakhine State Development Programme. Under the Ministry of Social Welfare, Myanmar, and the Embassy of India, pre-schools would also be constructed in the State.[53]

The year 2020 is significant for another major event—the elections scheduled for 8 November 2020. This would be the third since political reforms were initiated in 2010. Over 90 political parties are expected to contest a total of 1,171 seats in both Houses of the Union Parliament and in the state/regional legislatures.

This section has covered only those major events that have taken place over the past years. However, apart from these events, there have been continuous ongoing engagements which have been categorized and summarized in the next few pages.

Summary of India-Myanmar Relations as in 2020[54]

Development Cooperation

Development cooperation is a prominent feature in India's overall bilateral cooperation with Myanmar. India has set up major connectivity infrastructure and established long-term, sustainable and relevant institutions for capacity building and human resource development in areas such as agricultural research and education, IT and skill development. These initiatives are completely grant funded, though India also extends concessional finance for projects ranging from transport and communications to agriculture and farm mechanization and highway development. The total portfolio of projects involving Indian assistance is valued at approximately US$ 1.75 billion, of which projects worth nearly US$ 1 billion are completely grant-funded.

The Port Operator for Sittwe Port under the Kaladan Project was appointed in November 2019. Work on the waterway component is complete, however, that on the road component from Zorinpuito Paletwa is underway.

The third year of the Border Area Development Programme has been completed. Twenty-eight projects for the fourth year BADP have begun in 2019.

Under the Rakhine State Development Programme, India has committed over US$ 25 million for development programmes in the state. In July 2019, about 250 prefabricated houses were handed over to Myanmar in Rakhine State. Over 20,000 relief material kits were provided to internally displaced persons in Rakhine in December 2019.

Defence Cooperation

India-Myanmar defence engagement was further strengthened with the signing of an MoU on Defence Cooperation in 2019. There were substantial high-level visits, military training programmes, capacity building and the established interaction mechanisms functioned vibrantly. Visits/symposia such as the Goa Maritime Conclave, National Defence College reciprocal visit and Higher Command Courses have aided in strengthening understanding between officers of both armed forces at mid and senior level. An Indian Air Force Meteorology Squadron team established two Meteorology Squadrons of the Myanmar Air Force and imparted training from August-November 2019. Installation of a Coastal Surveillance System in Myanmar is in progress. The 4th Army and 4th Air Force Staff talks took place between 13 and 15 March 2019 at Nay Pyi Taw and 18 and 20 September 2019 at Yangon, respectively. The 15th Regional Boundary Committee meeting took place between 9 and 12 December 2019.

Pursuant to the MoU on Exchange of White Shipping Information signed in July 2019, near real time exchange has commenced between Information Fusion Centre, Indian Ocean Region, New Delhi, and Maritime Regional Coordination Centre, Yangon, bringing in the much-needed transparency in the regional maritime environment.[55]

The first maritime security dialogue under the MoU on Maritime Security Cooperation took place in September 2019. Substantial headway was made in the field of cooperation in maritime safety, maritime domain awareness, hydrography, etc. Initiatives such as the addition of maritime patrol aircraft and increase in the frequency of coordinated patrols to twice a year has increased their efficacy. Two Myanmar Navy ships were deployed at Visakhapatnam for the second edition of INMEX from 18 to 22 October 2019. These initiatives were aimed at ensuring regional security and smooth flow of maritime trade.

Figure 3.1: Author with a VIF Delegation at IFC IOR

In the last one year, 126 trainees were deputed to various defence establishments across India under the ITEC-1 scheme. In addition to the structured courses, Indian Armed Forces Mobile Training Teams (MTT) undertook UN Peacekeeping training courses and two such courses were conducted in February and September-October 2019. Five other courses were also conducted by MTTs from the Indian Navy. Subject Matter Expert Exchange for fighter aircrew of MiG-29 with Observer Sorties was held for pilots of the Myanmar Air Force in April 2019. A Myanmar combat team was trained in October 2019. Further, training on English language, hydrography, medical aspects and Humanitarian Assistance and Disaster Relief was carried out.

Commerce

India–Myanmar bilateral trade commenced in 1970 and has grown steadily, albeit with a slight decline in the Eighties. Bilateral trade stood at US$ 1.7 billion in 2018-19, an increase of 7.53 per cent from 2017-18, while India's imports from Myanmar saw a decline of 18.47 per cent with India's exports to Myanmar witnessing 24.74 per cent growth during the same period. India is the fifth largest trading partner of Myanmar.[56] India's exports to Myanmar during 2018-19 was US$ 1205.60 million and imports from Myanmar was US$ 521.49 million. In terms of investment, India stands at the 11th position with an approved investment of US$ 768.567 million by 31 Indian enterprises (out of an estimated US$ 81.598 billion from 50 countries by 1846 enterprises) as on October 2019.

Myanmar's investment in India is US$ 8.97 million. The major import items from Myanmar are beans, pulses, wood, metal and so on. India's exports to Myanmar are agro-commodities, chemicals, fuel, pharmaceutical items and machinery. Border trade with Myanmar during 2018-19, estimated at US$ 154.04 million, took place through two land border crossing points—Moreh-Tamu in Manipur and Zowkhathar-Rhikhawdar in Mizoram. Twelve Indian Public Sector Undertakings (PSUs) have their representative offices in Myanmar. Myanmar is potentially an important partner in the energy sector as future offshore gas finds can be piped to India. India currently has a JWG on Oil and Gas and JSC and another JWG on Power Cooperation.[57]

Visit of Business Delegations

Over 25 Indian companies participated in the COMPLAST Exhibition in June 2019; 40 Indian healthcare companies participated in MEDEX 2019 in Yangon in October 2019, and about 74 Indian participants exhibited their products at MYANFOOD in November 2019 under the patronage of the Trade Promotion Council of India, ASSOCHAM and Department. of Commerce, India.

Training & Capacity Building

Under the ITEC programme in 2019-20, 240 vacancies were utilised by civilians. A new Hindi Language Course was started at Yangon University in October 2019. The EAM remotely inaugurated the e-ITEC programme on Big Data Analytics at Myanmar Institute of Information Technology (MIIT) in Mandalay on 7 October 2019. India also donated 10,000 vials of anti-rabies vaccines to Myanmar in September 2019. India continued to provide training to Myanmar officials such as administrators; town planners; election officers; police officers; parliamentarians; judiciary officers; and others in English, IT, accounting and finance.

Seven courses for the Union Election Commission of Myanmar (UECM) were conducted by the Election Commission of India in New Delhi and Nay Pyi Taw for UECM officials in 2019. Two courses were completed earlier in 2018. The first batch of 40 judges/judicial officers attended training at the National Judicial Academy of India (NJAI), Bhopal, from August 23 to29, 2019. In all, 400 officers were trained. Two Mid-Career Training Programs for 34 Township Administrators (July 15-27, 2019) and 28 Township Administrators (November 18-30, 2019) in Governance and Leadership Training were conducted at the National Centre for Good Governance (NCGG), Lal Bahadur Shastri National Academy of Administration, Mussoorie. A Special Training Programme for

Myanmar Educational Administrators was conducted by the National Institute of Educational Planning & Administration (NIEPA), New Delhi, from 1 to 23 November 2019. More than 250 Myanmar Police Officers received training in India in 2019.

A team of sportspersons in hockey, badminton and shooting were trained in India for the 30th South East Asian Games from 29 September to 28 October 2019. An MoU on Cooperation in Sports in under discussion to formalize the framework of such training in the future. India is also offering 1,000 Integrated PhD Fellowships for ASEAN students including Myanmar at 23 IITs. A delegation from IIT-Madras visited Yangon and interacted with rectors of leading universities and prospective students in October 2019. Another delegation from IIT Delhi visited Myanmar between 15 and 18 December 2019, for interacting with officials of the Ministry of Education and rectors for sharing their experiences in frontier areas in Science and Technology.

Cultural Exchange

In 2019-20, several events such as the 150th birth anniversary of Mahatma Gandhi, 550th birth anniversary of Guru Nanak Dev, and International Yoga Day were celebrated in Myanmar. A full-fledged Indian Cultural Centre will become functional in Yangon by mid-2020. The level of engagement in this field has also increased due to the deployment of a full time director in addition to teachers of Indian Culture, Hindi and Dance. The current centre conducts regular classes for Hindi, Yoga and Indian classical dance.

BIMSTEC

BIMSTEC, being a sector-driven alliance, has 14 sectors distributed amongst its seven members, with each country being a lead nation for one or more sectors and also a lead shepherd for a sub group under a sector.[58] Myanmar is the Lead Nation for the Energy and Agriculture sectors and is the Lead Shepherd for the Sub-Group on Narcotic Drugs, Psychotropic Substances and Precursor Chemicals (SGNDPSPC) under the Counter-Terrorism & Transnational Crime Sector (India). On the multilateral fronts, the first BIMSTEC Ministerial Meeting on Agriculture (1st BAMM) preceded by the first BIMSTEC Senior Official's Meeting on Agriculture (1st SOM-A) was held on 11-12 July 2019 in Nay Pyi Taw which was attended by the Indian Minister of State Shri Purshottam Rupala. India announced six Post Graduate and six PhD scholarship for BIMSTEC students in the Agriculture sector.

Project Preparation Facility

A mechanism called Project Preparation Facility (PPF) has been set up by India to assist its development partner countries towards preparation of Project Formulation Reports (PFR) for viable projects that can be considered for concessional financing under Lines of Credit in 2018. The PPF trains staff in identifying a need, conceiving a project and preparing a proper proposal. It provides consultancy support on grant basis to requesting governments for project formulation. It is a demand-responsive mechanism and a quick access facility to address priority needs of requesting governments.[59] The PFRs submitted under PPF during the financial year 2019-20 includes a state-of-the-art General Hospital at Nay Pyi Taw, Myanmar.

It is evident from the nature of engagements that India has with Myanmar that a lot of ground is being covered and on a vast range of topics. For a list of agreements, joint statements, MoUs and associated documents, please see **Appendix M**. This historical perspective was intended to place Chapter 1 (Geography) into context. Armed with this basic understanding of the historical context, we can now strive to understand why Myanmar often falls below the radar of Indian foreign policy.

NOTES

1. Rajiv Bhatia, *India-Myanmar Relations: Changing Contours,* Routledge India, 2016, pg. 101.
2. Ibid.
3. Medha Chaturvedi, *India's Strategic Interest in Myanmar: An Interview with Shyam Saran,* IPCS Special Report No. 98, 2011. http://www.ipcs.org/issue_briefs/issue_brief_pdf/SR98-ShyamSaranInterview.pdf (Accessed on 19 December 2019).
4. Rajiv Bhatia, pg. 102.
5. Renaud Egretau & Larry Jagan, *Soldiers and Diplomacy in Burma: Understanding The Foreign Relations Of The Burmese Praetorian State,* NUS Press, 2013, pg. 299.
6. This was to have far reaching implications on Tatmadaw's operations and is covered in detail in Chapter 7 of this book, *Tatmadaw: Raising the 'Standard'.*
7. Handbook of South Asia: Political Development, *Myanmar: Contemporary Political History,* Europa Publications, Routledge India, 2017, pgs. 233-271.
8. MEA Annual Report 2006-07. Available at https://mealib.nic.in/?pdf2534?000. Accessed on 8 November 2019.
9. MEA Annual Report 2007-08. Available at https://mealib.nic.in/?pdf2535?000. Accessed on 8 November 2019.
10. Myanmar Law Library, Constitution of 2008, http://myanmar-law-library.org/law-library/laws-and-regulations/constitutions/2008-constitution.html (Accessed on 18 May 2020).
11. Paul Chambers, *Constitutional Change and Security Forces in Southeast Asia: Lessons from Thailand and Myanmar, Contemporary* Southeast Asia, ISEAS—YusofIshak Institute, April 2014, Vol. 36, No. 1, pgs. 118-119.
12. For the evolution of the Constitution, see Preet Malik, '*My Myanmar Years: A Diplomat's Account of India's Relations with the Region*', Sage India, New Delhi, 2015, pg. 126.

13. Paul Chambers, Constitutional change and security forces in Southeast Asia: lessons from Thailand and Myanmar, The Free Library, 2014 Institute of Southeast Asian Studies (ISEAS), 07 Feb. 2021 https://www.thefreelibrary.com/Constitutional+change+and+security+ forces+in+Southeast+Asia%3a+lessons...-a0367547301 (Accessed on 8 Nov 2019).
14. MEA Annual Report 2008-09. Available at https://mealib.nic.in/?pdf2536?000. (Accessed on 8 Nov 2019).
15. MEA Annual Report 2009-10. Available at https://mealib.nic.in/?pdf2537?000/ (Accessed on 8 Nov 2019).
16. MEA Annual Report 2010-11. Available at http://www.mea.gov.in/Uploads/PublicationDocs/45_Annual-Report-2010-2011.pdf, Accessed on 8 November 2019.
17. Handbook of South Asia, pg. 249.
18. MEA Annual Report 2011-12. Available at http://www.mea.gov.in/Uploads/PublicationDocs/19337_annual- report-2011-2012.pdf (Accessed on 10 Nov 2019).
19. Preet Malik, pg. 177.
20. *Handbook of South Asia*, pg. 251.
21. MEA Annual Report 2012-13. Available at http://www.mea.gov.in/Uploads/PublicationDocs/21385_Annual_Report_2012-2013_English.pdf (Accessed on 10 Nov 2019).
22. Consulate General of India, Sittwe, Myanmar, https://www.cgisittwe.gov.in/page/the-consulate/ (Accessed on 18 May 2020).
23. *Handbook of South Asia*, pg. 251.
24. MEA Annual Report 2013-14. Available at http://www.mea.gov.in/Uploads/PublicationDocs/26525_26525_External_Affairs_English_AR_2015-16_Final_compressed.pdf (Accessed on 8 November 2019).
25. MEA Annual Report 2013-14. Available at http://www.mea.gov.in/Uploads/PublicationDocs/23873_EXTERNAL_AFFAIR__Eng__AR_2013-14.pdf (Accessed on 8 Nov 2019).
26. Myanmar Institute of Information Technology, Advanced Centre for Agricultural Research and Education, and a Rice Bio Park.
27. MEA Annual Report 2014-15. Available at http://www.mea.gov.in/Uploads/PublicationDocs/25009_External_Affairs_2014-2015__English_.pdf (Accessed on 8 Nov 2019).
28. One of the unintended consequences of this was the spike in smuggling due to the enhanced customs duty for popular items such as arecanut, an essential commodity in gutkha, an addictive mouth freshener.
29. MEA Annual Report 2016-17. Available at http://www.mea.gov.in/Uploads/PublicationDocs/29521_MEA_ANNUAL_REPORT_2016_17_new.pdf (Accessed on 8 November 2019).
30. Martin Smith, *Arakan (Rakhine State), A Land in Conflict on Myanmar's Western Frontier*, Transnational Institute, Amsterdam, December 2019, pg. 96.
31. For a detailed account of the Rakhine Conflicts, see Chapter 4: The Rakhine Conflicts.
32. Martin Smith, *Arakan (Rakhine State), A Land in Conflict on Myanmar's Western Frontier*, Transnational Institute, Amsterdam, December 2019, pg. 93.
33. Transnational Institute, "*China's Engagement in Myanmar: From Malacca Dilemma to Transition Dilemma*", TNI, Myanmar Policy Briefing No.19, July 2016. (Accessed on 29 Jul 2020).
34. MEA Annual Report 2017-18. Available at http://www.mea.gov.in/Uploads/PublicationDocs/29788_MEA-AR-2017-18-03-02-2018.pdf (Accessed on 8 Nov 2019).
35. International Crisis Group Statement, "*Myanmar Tips into New Crisis after Rakhine State Attacks*", 27 Aug 2017: https://d2071andvip0wj.cloudfront.net/Myanmar%20statement%2027viii17.pdf (Accessed on 10 Sep 2019).
36. Amnesty International, "Myanmar: New evidence reveals Rohingya armed group massacred scores in Rakhine State", 22 May 2018, https://www.amnesty.org/en/latest/news/2018/05/myanmar-new-evidence-reveals-rohingya-armed-group-massacred-scores-in-rakhine-state/ (Accessed on 1 September 2019)

37. For the full text of the speech, see http://www.xinhuanet.com/english/2017-05/14/c_136282982.htm (Accessed on 3 November 2019)
38. Aung Zin Phyo Thein, "The Belt and Road Initiative in Myanmar: staring down the dragon", *Frontier Myanmar,* 2 August 2019: https://frontiermyanmar.net/en/the-belt-and-road-initiative-in-myanmar-staring-down-the-dragon (Accessed 24 November 2019).
39. Thomas Kean, "Myanmar sets a slower pace for the Belt and Road", *Frontier Myanmar,* 25 May 2019, https://frontiermyanmar.net/en/myanmar-sets-a-slower-pace-for- the-belt-and-road. (Accessed on 23 November 2019).
40. https://www.irrawaddy.com/opinion/analysis/second-bri-forum-roundup-how-myanmar-fares.html (Accessed on 1 December 2019).
41. The Straits Times, 7 ethnic Rakhine killed as Myanmar police open fire at riot: Official, 17 Jan 2018, https://www.straitstimes.com/asia/se-asia/7-ethnic-rakhine-killed-as-myanmar-police-open-fire-at-riot-official (Accessed on 18 May 2020).
42. Martin Smith, *Arakan (Rakhine State), A Land in Conflict on Myanmar's Western Frontier,* Transnational Institute, Amsterdam, December 2019. pg. 109.
43. From the Indian perspective, Pathein is significant due to the large Hindi-speaking population there and the trade and business potential of Pathein Port. This port is allegedly as good as the Yangon Port, however, due to better intra land connectivity to Mandalay and the rest of Myanmar, this port suffers. Currently, due to congestion of the Yangon Port, Pathein is regaining importance.
44. Jaideep Chanda, Raising 'Myanmar Consciousness': Visit of the President of Myanmar to India, Mizzima, 7 Mar 2020, http://mizzima.com/article/raising-myanmar-consciousness-visit-president-myanmar-india (Accessed on 18 May 2020).
45. MEA Annual Report 2017-18. Available at http://www.mea.gov.in/Uploads/PublicationDocs/31719_MEA_AR18_19.pdf (Accessed on 8 November 2019).
46. India-Myanmar Bilateral Relations, https://mea.gov.in/Portal/ForeignRelation/India_Myanmar_Bilateral_Brief_Website_jan_2019.pdf
47. Myanmar Institute of Peace and Security, *Annual Peace and Security Review 2020,* MIPS, Yangon 2020: https://mips-mm.org/annual-review-2020/ (Accessed on 20 July 2020).
48. The VIF Delegation and the author were fortunate to be able to witness the new Liasion Office, run efficiently almost singlehandedly by a young IFS Officer, Ms Amrita Banerjee, at Nay Pyi Taw.
49. MEA Annual Report 2019-20. Available at http://www.mea.gov.in/Uploads/PublicationDocs/32489_AR_Spread_2020_new.pdf Accessed on 26 June 2020.
50. Details of this visit are elaborated upon in Chapter 10 of this book.
51. This was the second visit by the Myanmar President in a year, the first being from 30 to 31 May 2019 to attend the Swearing-in Ceremony of Prime Minister Modi for the second term.
52. Ministry of External Affairs Website, Bilateral Documents, https://mea.gov.in/bilateral-documents.htm?dtl/32435/IndiaMyanmar+Joint+Statement+during+the+State+Visit+of+the+President+of+Myanmar+to+India+February+2629+2020 Accessed on 26 June 2020.
53. Currently, two crises are concurrently under way in the state, the Rohingya Crisis and the ethnic Rakhine Crisis involving the Arakan Army which is causing heavy losses to the Myanmar Army and the Arakan Army, but most of all to innocent civilians who are caught in the crossfire. See Chapter 4: The Rakhine Conflicts
54. MEA Annual Report 2019-20. Available at http://www.mea.gov.in/Uploads/PublicationDocs/32489_AR_Spread_2020_new.pdf/ Accessed on 26 June 2020.
55. The author visited the Information Fusion Centre, Indian Ocean Region, New Delhi, and witnessed the state-of-the-art maritime monitoring system operational there.
56. Ministry of External Affairs BM Division *** India-Myanmar .... http://mea.gov.in/Portal/ForeignRelation/India_Myanmar_2019.pdf (Accessed on 18 May 2020).

57. Ministry of External Affairs, India-Myanmar Relations, https://www.mea.gov.in/Portal/ForeignRelation/India_Myanmar_2019.pdf (Accessed on 18 May 2020).
58. India leads four sectors, namely, Transport & Communications, Tourism, Environment & Disaster Management and Counter-Terrorism & Transnational Crime; Thailand leads three sectors, i.e., Fisheries, Public Health and People-to-People Contacts; Bangladesh and Myanmar both lead two sectors each with the former looking at Trade & Investment and Climate Change and the latter at Energy Sector and Agriculture; Bhutan, Nepal and Sri Lanka lead one sector each, namely, Cultural Cooperation, Poverty Alleviation and Technology, respectively.
59. Project Preparation Facility for Government of India (GoI ..., https://www.mea.gov.in/bilateral-documents.htm?dtl/29603

CHAPTER 4
Myanmar Consciousness and a Blind Spot

Politics is about people and people are about relationships, whether at a private or public level.

—**Daw Aung San Suu Kyi**[1]

As students, we were introduced to the 'blind spot'[2] in our eyes by way of an exercise where we focussed on a plus sign drawn on a paper, with one eye and moved our head towards it, while a dot beside the plus sign disappeared from our view when the head reached a certain distance from the paper.[3] This analogy has often been used to describe the case of India's foreign policy with relation to its perspective to Myanmar. With over a 1,600 km fragile and porous border, India-Myanmar relations are perceived to have perpetually been consigned to the blind spot of India's political and foreign policy practitioners since Independence. The 'plus sign' may well be analogous to Pakistan (and now, China) and also symptomatic of the obsession with the West, while the dark dot could well represent Myanmar, perpetually in the blind spot of the head which was frozen at a fixed distance from global affairs, unable to either take a step back for a world view, or to move forward for a detailed look. In this chapter, we look at this aspect in detail and try to understand the reasons behind this perception and ways to move forward.

I coined the term 'Myanmar consciousness' as a generic description of the state of awareness about Myanmar in individuals and institutions in India especially in the academic and policy-making circles. I first used the term in an article[4] covering the visit of the President of Myanmar to India, which was largely missed out by the Indian mainstream media, which in effect demonstrated the lack of Myanmar consciousness in the Fourth Estate. For academic discourse, there is a need to reasonably quantify this term and try and understand the degree of lack of awareness that would qualify an observer to be labelled as lacking Myanmar consciousness. Since this is a subjective concept, I draw the line at a basic understanding and knowledge of the geography, political history and rudimentary facets of India-Myanmar relations.

The lack of Myanmar consciousness is the net result of this blind spot. The former being the derivative of the latter, due to the inability of the observer to view foreign policy and geopolitical events from a detached perspective or conversely, the inability to view events sufficiently closely, thereby being stuck in the blind spot. For the sake of debate, one might be tempted to argue whether the blind spot was as a result of the dearth of Myanmar consciousness. This argument runs aground when we contextualise it in the Indian setting. In this setting, we observe an institutional and generic lack of awareness about Myanmar due to our inability to move away from the 'sweet spot', which is fixated on China, Pakistan and further west. Effectively, the blind spot has occurred due to our inability to move from the viewpoint which gives us the best perceived perspective of our chosen view, i.e., of Pakistan, China and beyond. Thus, for the purpose of this study, I move with the correlation that the blind spot results in the lack of Myanmar consciousness.

The Genesis of the Blind Spot: Five Examples

A look at five examples over the last two decades[5] drives home this hypothesis. To begin with, let us consider the speech of the then External Affairs Minister and later PM, I.K. Gujral at Chatham House on 23 September 1996 and subsequently reiterated at the Bandaranaike Centre for International Studies, Sri Lanka, on 20 January 1997.[6] This later went on to become enshrined as the Gujral Doctrine:[7]

> *The United Front Government's neighbourhood policy now stands on five basic principles: First, with the neighbours like Nepal, Bangladesh, Bhutan, Maldives and Sri Lanka, India does not ask for reciprocity but gives all that it can in good faith and trust. Secondly, no South Asian country will allow its territory to be used against the interest of another country of the region. Thirdly, none will interfere in the internal affairs of another. Fourthly, all South Asian countries must respect each other's territorial integrity and sovereignty. And finally, they will settle all their disputes through peaceful bilateral negotiations.*[8]

It is evident from the speech that Myanmar, despite being a neighbouring country, does not feature in his mind as a PM! However six years later, during an interview with Smt. Usha Prasad for the Nehru Memorial Museum and Library Oral History Project in June 2002, he does mention Myanmar in the context of the Gujral Doctrine. He clarifies that '*...my concept of neighbourhood was far wider, not confined to South Asia only, signing the Indian Ocean Rim Association, entering into new relationships with Myanmar, Thailand, Yunnan, part of China and other regional cooperation, closer association with ASEAN (Association of South-East Asian Nations) and building a new vision regarding the Indian diaspora.*'[9]

This aspect of foreign policy was not exclusive to the Gujral Government. The second example is from 2014. During the swearing-in of the first Modi Government on 26 May 2014, Myanmar was missing from the list of invitees whereas the Heads of States of Afghanistan, Bangladesh, Bhutan, Maldives, Mauritius, Nepal, Pakistan and Sri Lanka were invited.[10] Even the PM of the Tibetan Government-in-Exile attended. Ostensibly, the invitations went out exclusively to countries of the South Asian Association of Regional Cooperation (SAARC) and Mauritius, which though not a SAARC member-state,[11] is an Observer like Myanmar.[12] During the swearing-in of Modi 2.0, amends were sought to be made by including Myanmar in the list of eight countries called for the event which included Bangladesh, Bhutan, Kyrgyzstan, Mauritius, Myanmar, Nepal, Sri Lanka and Thailand. However, Ambassador Gautam Mukhopadhyaya, who was the Indian Ambassador to Myanmar from 2013 to 2016, reveals[13] that the proposal to invite Myanmar for the Modi 1.0 swearing-in was considered and eschewed, partly because:

> *While we were confident of getting SAARC leaders (Mauritius invited itself, not least because of its large Indian diaspora and leadership), we were not sure of Myanmar's reaction. Also, BIMSTEC then had been in slumber for some 17 years without any summit meeting until Myanmar hosted a Summit in, I think it was March 2014, attended by Dr. Manmohan Singh, just before the Indian elections that elected PM Modi. I inquired into this while I was there, and in the end I felt it was better that we did not do such an impulsive thing without first being sure they would respond. It would have put them in an awkward position, and it is quite possible that they would have sent a Vice President rather than Thein Sein himself. That would have been an embarrassment for us too. Also, I suspect, they may have felt a 'tributary' like quality to the invitation, of neighbouring 'kingdoms' paying courtesies to the new 'Chakravartin' that would not have gone well with the ethnocentric, nationalistic and proud Bama people.*

The third example is a more recent one from the academic world. Nilanthi Samaranayake, Director of the Strategy and Policy Analysis program at CNA, a non-profit research organisation in Washington DC, worked on case studies to analyse the foreign policies of smaller South Asian countries (i.e., Bangladesh, Nepal, Sri Lanka, Bhutan, and Maldives) towards India's rise in the region. She spoke on the same on 13 January 2020 at Brookings India, New Delhi, as part of the Foreign Policy & Security Tiffin Talk series.[14] This author attended the event and later even emailed the researcher, querying her decision not to include Myanmar amongst her sample of smaller South Asian countries. She was candid in mentioning that in her thinking "*Myanmar is not generally considered part of 'South Asia' (e.g., not in SAARC, but in ASEAN)*".[15] This example highlights how established academics anchor their perspectives onto traditionally accepted groupings. Thus, while conventionally South Asia does not include Myanmar, contextually, it could be argued that since the research was centred on the responses of smaller South Asian states relative to India's rise in the region, Myanmar should have found a place in the sample. Leaving it out at best could have been on the grounds that Myanmar was not a 'smaller' state vis-à-vis the others selected. Possibly, it is this same psychological anchoring coupled with the 'blind spot' effect, which may have led advisors to PM Modi to leave out Myanmar from the list of invitees to the 2014 swearing-in.

For a fourth example of the lack of Myanmar consciousness in the academic world in India, consider the options for Myanmar studies in various Indian colleges and universities. The Jawaharlal Nehru University (JNU) Centre for South Asian Studies goes by offering the traditional eight South Asian countries in its courses. While it has five other centres which include portions of Asia, viz., Schools of Inner Asian Studies, West Asian Studies, South Asian Studies and East Asian Studies, Myanmar studies do not form a subject at the JNU.[16] Delhi University offers courses in East Asian Studies but not in South Asian Studies.[17] Further east, only the University of Calcutta offers Myanmar studies (along with Philippines and Bangladesh) under the Centre for South and South East Asian Studies.[18] Jadavpur University in Kolkata covers South Asia studies, but does not have a dedicated centre for it. There is no mention of Myanmar or Burma on its website.[19]

On the language side, the JNU School of Language, Literature and Culture Studies covers various graduate and post-graduate programmes in Arabic, Bahasa Indonesia, Chinese, French, German, Greek, Hebrew, Italian, Japanese, Korean, Mongolian, Persian, Portuguese, Pushtu, Russian, Spanish, Turkish and Urdu.[20] The stark irony needs to be acknowledged that JNU teaches languages of countries with which India has no borders and some of these are thousands of kilometres away, but does not teach Myanmar, the language of a country with which we share 1,643 km of crucial borders. Similarly, Delhi University's Department of Slavonic and Finno-Ugrian Studies offers exotic courses in Slavonic languages, namely, Bulgarian, Croatian, Czech, Polish, Russian and Hungarian from the Finno-Ugrian group of languages, but not in Myanmar.[21] The premier Jadavpur University School of Language and Linguistics in Kolkata offers courses of varying durations and levels in Chinese, French, German, Italian, Japanese, Korean, Portuguese and Spanish, but not in Myanmar.[22]

The fifth and most recent example of the blind spot effect lies in the mainstream media coverage of the visit of the President of Myanmar to India. His Excellency U Win Myint, the tenth President of the Republic of the Union of Myanmar, came on a four-day visit to Delhi, Agra and Bodh Gaya from 26 to 29 February 2020. His 26-member delegation included, apart from the President and the First Lady, three senior Ministers, the CM of Rakhine State and several Director Generals of various departments of Myanmar. The visit was a bilateral one initiated by an invitation from Indian President Shri Ram Nath Kovind. Appallingly, there was virtually no coverage by the Indian mainstream print media. Common citizens could have been forgiven for missing out this important visit, coming in the post-mortem phase of Trump's sojourn to India (24-26 February 2020) and amidst the violence in Delhi, but one cannot condone Foreign Affairs Editors of the dailies in the national capital for this blind spot. Myanmar watchers were kept informed by regular tweets from the Embassy of India, Yangon; Rashtrapati Bhawan; Raveesh Kumar, Spokesperson, Ministry of External Affairs; reports from Press Information Bureau, Government of India[23] and Facebook updates from Ministry of Foreign Affairs, Myanmar. None of the print media physical newspapers covered the visit. In fact, there were very few web news reports prior to or immediately after the visit.[24]

The above examples, varied in time and covering different segments of society encompassing political and bureaucratic, academic and media, symbolises how our awareness of Myanmar suffers due to conventional norms of grouping (e.g., South Asia) and also due to falling into our strategic blind spots, whether actual, or perceived. It is worth looking at the possible causes for the development of this mindset.

The Absence of Myanmar Consciousness: Causes and Effects

The first and most common cause seems to be the definition of South Asia which conventionally excludes Myanmar and thereby excludes it from the consciousness of most South Asian scholars. Eight nations normally crowd under the South

Asian umbrella, viz., Afghanistan, Bangladesh, Bhutan, Maldives, Nepal, India and Sri Lanka. South Asia is sometimes used interchangeably with Southern Asia. The United Nations uses Southern Asia as a broader definition which groups, in addition to the eight nations which come under South Asia, a ninth nation, i.e., Iran. Myanmar falls under the head Southeastern Asia.[25] SAARC itself excludes Myanmar from the grouping. Ambassador Bhatia documents that Myanmar had been approached to join SAARC at the inception stage, but the response was negative. Eventually, as Than Shwe and the Myanmar Army began opening up and drafting the 2010 Constitution, they joined as Observers in 2008-9 with Indian support. Some news reports and scholarly articles suggest that Myanmar had in fact had apparently sought full membership of the organisation in 2008, but no decision has been forthcoming since then, which seems to be erroneous.[26]

Academically viewed, the debate of whether Myanmar comes under South Asia or not, is inconclusive. The Centre of South Asian Studies, University of Cambridge, includes Myanmar in its ambit,[27] whereas the Centre for South Asian Studies, University of Michigan, does not.[28] Rutgers University, New Jersey, offers a Minor in South Asian Studies, which in addition to the traditional eight countries, also includes Tibet Autonomous Region and Burma.[29] Nitin Pai, co-founder and director of the Takshashila Institution, an independent centre for research and education in public policy, identifies the *paradox of neighbourhood* as one of the five paradoxes afflicting India's neighbourhood policy. Thus Indians have been choosing the neighbourhoods for centuries with Gujaratis having been neighbours with East Africans; Keralites neighbouring the Gulf Arabs and the Tamils neighbouring Malaysia and Singapore. However, he says that New Delhi does not consider these countries neighbours. Treating them as if they are not has trapped us in a mindset of living in a troubled, unstable neighbourhood. He specifies that:

> *This is one unfortunate fallout of the faulty conceptualisation of "South Asia" as being limited to the countries of the subcontinent. Once you see the neighbourhood as what it is, and includes East Africa, the Gulf, and South East Asia, you'll find it full of opportunities, not vexed problems.*[30]

It is evident that there is no consistency in the inclusion of Myanmar in South Asia. In India, the conventional grouping seems to govern mindsets and Myanmar remains out of the South Asia purview. Thus, in the Indian mind, somewhere the term neighbourhood equates with South Asia which inevitably leaves out our eastern-most neighbour, Myanmar. This raises the question; does India need to redefine South Asia to include Myanmar? In support, Mirza Zulfiqur

Rahman quotes Mani Shankar Aiyar, then Union Minister for Development of North Eastern Region (DoNER), as having argued that Myanmar was the starting point for South Asia while Southeast Asia could be considered including Northeast India.[31] Against this motion, Ambassador Gautam Mukhopadhyaya, former Ambassador to Syria (December 2005–January 2009), Afghanistan (June 2010–May 2013) and Myanmar (June 2013–May 2016), feels[32] that SAARC as a more 'natural' geographical, economic and political entity, is older, with strong regional champions from its founding, and therefore it was able to evolve to a point where India's preponderant size and volume and Pakistan's hostility put brakes on its growth. He points out that for better or for worse, India's size also had the effect of acting as the 'glue' that held SAARC together. He goes on to add that in comparison, BIMSTEC is less cohesive and has its economic ties hampered by the securitisation of the northeast, and is less coherent in its agenda. He feels that the inclusion of security issues into what was always conceived as a 'technical and economic' association has been counter-productive and betrays an obsessively security oriented mindset and that lacks coherent thinking on the best uses of BIMSTEC.

Another reason for the blind spot which leads to the dearth of Myanmar consciousness is the 'Delhi centric' orientation of national politics. Northeast India has borne the brunt of the Delhi-centricity of Indian politics and politicians. Out of India's 15 prime ministers[33] since Independence, none were remotely from the east whereas even South India has provided more than one prime minister.[34] Integration of Northeast India into 'mainland' India and the mainland 'psyche' of our leadership, has remained a contentious issue. Unless this mindset issue is resolved, it will remain a 'troubled periphery'.[35] Objectively, this Delhi-centricity can be attributed to our relations with Pakistan. Four wars, cross-border terrorism, the Kashmir issue and other contentious aspects of the relationship dominate the mind space of our national leadership. For example, during an interaction with former Army Chief, General N.C. Vij, the author enquired about his views on India's engagement with the Myanmar Armed Forces (Tatmadaw) during his tenure as Chief. The General was candid that, as a Chief, he could devote very little time to the Eastern Front simply because events on the Western and Northern Fronts were overwhelming during his tenure from 2003 to 2005. This was just in the aftermath of the year-long standoff, i.e., Operation Parakram, against Pakistan following the 13 December 2001 Parliament attack, from December 2001 to October 2002. General Vij was also the driving force behind the construction of the game-changing Line of Control fencing which was instrumental in changing the counter-infiltration strategy and bringing down infiltration substantially.

Previously, he had been the Director General of Military Operations during the 1999 Kargil War. It was not as if nothing was happening in the East, only it was being ably handled by the respective Army and Corp Commanders under the overall guidance of the Chief. But the Western and Northern Fronts dominated.

The national-level threat perspective from the east does not construe as an existential threat for the Delhi-centric mindset. At best, it is perceived as a law and order and secessionist threat on the troubled periphery which can be managed and localised by the use of Armed Forces. Thus Myanmar too slips into the blind spot under the cover of the screen provided by the northeast. Dr. K. Yhome, Senior Fellow, Observer Research Foundation and a resident of Nagaland, concludes candidly that at the risk of sounding biased, that Delhi's neglect of Myanmar is essentially an extension of Delhi's neglect of India's northeast. He raises a valid sentiment when he asks whether Delhi would have been at all concerned about the northeast if it had not been for the Chinese threat.[36]

So is Indian foreign policy solely responsible for the situation? During an interview[37] with Ambassador Shyam Saran, I had enquired about this blind spot and he brought out a few interesting facets of this phenomenon:

> *It is very difficult to get any kind of political level attention to Myanmar or in fact any of our other neighbouring countries, except for Pakistan. This is not specific to Myanmar, it has been the problem with our neighbourhood policy for most of our time.*
>
> *Most of our attention to the Northeast and to our neighbours less Pakistan is essentially episodic. As long as nothing is happening, everyone is ok. Then some crisis occurs and everybody is very excited. You can't run neighbourhood policy like that. You need to have constant engagement and you need to have high level political engagement. We must deliver on the commitments we make. Bureaucrats can only do so much. Foreign relations need a whole of government kind of approach. An event by itself is only as good as the process. The event by itself cannot stand up on its own. You need a coherent approach wherein every arm of the Government is able to reinforce what the other is doing. So it is wrong to come to a conclusion that the 'blind spot' is due to a foreign secretary or a prime minister not being oriented towards the neighbourhood. Even as an Ambassador I had to draw on the resources of the Home Ministry, the Intelligence and the Armed Forces. For our work on the IT side in Myanmar we also had to get the private sector involved and we got Tata Consultancy involved.*

Coming from a military background where Standard Operating Procedures (SOPs), Operating Orders and Instructions are an established norm and Handing Over & Taking Over Notes are common practice to maintain continuity, I enquired from Ambassador Saran whether there was any concept of an overarching policy for a particular country. He explained that:

> *We don't have a standard practice of a master plan policy for a country. And the master plans mean nothing unless we endorse it at the political level and decisions are taken on their implementation. Ambassadors, as they come to the appointment, study the situation and come up with an action plan of what objectives they will have and they are going to achieve in the three or four years in which they will hold the post. Theoretically then that becomes the game plan after it has been vetted by the ministry and decisions are taken based on it. As Chairman of the National Security Advisory Board, we spent two years preparing a National Security Strategy, but the government has to vet it, accept it, and pass orders that it will be implemented.*

Ambassador Mukhopadhyaya attributes this 'blind spot' as an outcome of Myanmar's own policies. One reason, he concludes, originates cumulatively from the negative sentiment in India, following the Burmese reaction to massive Indian migration during colonial times. The grip of Indian business on the Myanmar economy and the colonial administrative relationship with Indians as intermediaries of British colonial rule in Burma, resulted in two reverse migrations. One, during World War II;[38] and the second after the nationalisation of the Burmese economy in the 1960s under General Ne Win. The second and possibly the most important reason was the inward turn and insularity of Myanmar and its turning its back on India as a reaction to colonial patterns of migration, rule and economy. He adds that the insular military regime took root for 40 years and till date we continue to see second class treatment to the Indians left behind. Post the mid-1960s, Burma and India had very little to do with each other. Myanmar declared itself 'neutral' and even withdrew from the NAM. The only things that kept the relationship going until the opening under Than Shwe-Thein Sein were beans, pulses, timber and the Burmese aspiration to visit the Buddhist pilgrimage site of Bodh Gaya.

He concludes that correspondingly, an Indian inward turn with the partition(s) of India; hard frontiers with East and West Pakistan, China and Myanmar; reaction to Indians returning from Burma; distaste for the Burmese military's treatment of the democratic opposition in Myanmar that saw many Burmese exiles including Daw Than Than Nu[39] taking shelter and influencing public and political opinion in India; our own autarchic policies until the 1990s shaped the contours of our policy towards Myanmar. But perhaps, most of all, securitising the entire northeast bordering China and Myanmar, in the latter case in response to insurgencies, and the general remoteness of the eastern borders, have impacted our neighbourly consciousness.

Myanmar Studies: An Absent Discipline

This study reveals an acute paucity of institutions teaching Myanmar studies in India. The typical 'Which came first—the chicken or the egg?' conundrum holds good for Myanmar studies. Is the lack of Myanmar consciousness a result of the lack of Myanmar studies in India or is it vice versa? This is of concern, as with India's double pronged approach of the Act East Policy and Neighbourhood First Policy, the 'Myanmar consciousness' quotient in India needs to increase manifold. This is unlikely to happen by itself. Without a generation of Myanmar scholars to drive home the pros and cons of policies and practice in northeast India bordering Myanmar, the decision makers will be deprived of the academic oversight and critique, which is so crucial a requirement in a healthy democracy. Thus, the lack of Myanmar studies as a subject in Indian universities and colleges emerges as a core drawback and thus a reason for the lack of Myanmar consciousness in India.

Let us also look at the state of Myanmar language in India. Bengali and Nepali are commonly spoken in India providing the access and environment for people-to-people contact with Bangladesh and Nepal, respectively. While Sinhala is not widespread in India, there is adequate connect with the Tamil population in Sri Lanka on the basis of language. Bhutan has a sizeable Nepali-speaking population, which provides a connect with India. Unlike the languages spoken in these neighbouring countries, the Myanmar language is endemic to Myanmar. Hence, barring some common dialects spoken by ethnic tribes living astride the India-Myanmar border, there is no language connect with Myanmar. This too puts a psychological burden on the effort to study Myanmar.

Greater South Asia: A Viable Alternative?

So is it time to look at a fresh alliance to offset the limitations of the present one? So should India look at BIMSTEC as the way forward over SAARC to offset the Pakistan limitations? Or should it look at a completely new grouping to offset the limitations of SAARC and BIMSTEC while combining their strengths such as a Greater South Asia? The BIMSTEC website seems to suggest[40] that this was an alliance that was supposed to offset the disadvantages of SAARC, not replace it:

> *The regional group constitutes a bridge between South and South East Asia and represents a reinforcement of relations among these countries. BIMSTEC has also established a platform for intra-regional cooperation between SAARC and ASEAN members.*

Conceptually, BIMSTEC is an alliance of seven countries in the littoral and adjacent areas of the Bay of Bengal comprising a regional continuum. It is a sector-driven cooperative organization including trade, technology, energy, transport, tourism, fisheries, agriculture, public health, poverty alleviation, counter-terrorism, environment, culture, people-to-people contacts and climate change.[41] In contrast, SAARC objectives are seemingly more generic. However, with the India-Pakistan animosity impacting the functioning of SAARC, it seems destined to be defunct. Thus, in 2004, when PM Vajpayee went to Islamabad, it was agreed to have a free trade agreement within the region. But Pakistan refused to give India a MFN (most favoured nation) status. So, SAFTA remained a pipedream. Similarly, terrorism vis-à-vis Kashmir remained another India-Pakistan contentious issue which ground the alliance to a halt.[42] In this context a Greater South Asia[43] alliance is proposed which will include all the nations of SAARC and BIMSTEC in addition to Malaysia and Singapore and, eventually, even Pakistan. One of the obvious benefits of this grouping will be to recondition the strategic mindset to look at South Asia to include Myanmar in addition to Malaysia and Singapore. The table below puts forth the proposed grouping in context:

Greater South Asia (12)	*SAARC (8) 1985*	*BIMSTEC (7) 1997*	*ASEAN (10) 1967*
Afghanistan	Afghanistan	-	-
-	-	-	Brunei
Bangladesh	Bangladesh	Bangladesh	-
Bhutan	Bhutan	Bhutan	-
-	-	-	Cambodia
India	India	India	-
-	-	-	Indonesia
-	-	-	Laos
Maldives	Maldives	-	-
Malaysia	-	-	Malaysia
Myanmar	-	Myanmar	Myanmar
Nepal	Nepal	Nepal	-
Pakistan	Pakistan	-	-
Singapore	-	-	Singapore
Sri Lanka	Sri Lanka	Sri Lanka	-
-	-	-	Philippines
Thailand	-	Thailand	Thailand
-	-	-	Vietnam

Source: Prepared by author.

Secondly, while establishing a new regional alliance requires massive diplomatic, political and financial investment, it could pay off in the long run in integrating this 'least integrated region of the world'. As per the RAND

Corporation report, intra-South Asia trade was just seven per cent of the region's global trade in 2012, compared to 25 per cent for Southeast Asia and 21 per cent for South America.[44] More recent figures suggest intraregional trade accounts for 50 per cent of total trade in East Asia but only a little more than five per cent of South Asia's total trade.[45] Finances being critical to any such alliance, relatively well-off countries such as Malaysia and Singapore could increase the availability of funds to the Greater South Asian grouping. A Venn diagram depicting the proposed Greater South Asia is shown below:

Figure 4.1

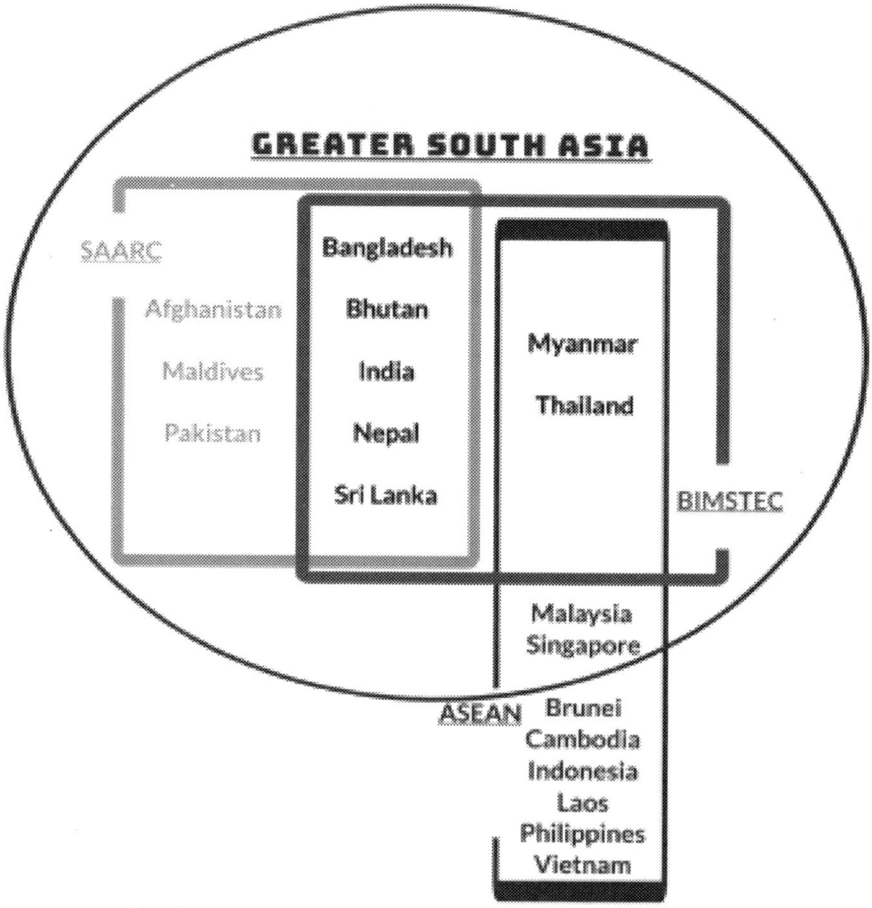

Source: Prepared by the author

Ambassador Mukhopadhyaya is less than enthusiastic about any grouping involving the combination of SAARC and BIMSTEC and points out that he does not sense a natural, organic linkage between SAARC and BIMSTEC from the west to the east. However, he has been advocating expansion of BIMSTEC to include Cambodia, Lao PDR (Laos), Myanmar and Vietnam (CLMV), i.e., the Greater Mekong Subregion which should be a natural constituency for India, linking the Ganga-Brahmaputra-Irrawaddy and Bay of Bengal with the Mekong and the South China Sea (in Vietnam). Hence, he advocates working on SAARC and the expanded BIMSTEC separately and proposes that India be the swing state between the two rather than have one more amorphous grouping.

In conclusion, the NAM experience with Myanmar provides a hint of how both Myanmar and India have approached the issue of alliances. Ambassador T.P. Sreenivasan recounts:

> *I remember the shock treatment that Burma gave to the Nonaligned Movement in Havana in 1979. Sometime in the middle of the night of the general debate, the Burmese foreign minister was invited to speak after a lengthy speech by an African leader. Normally, the rule in the Movement is that the smaller the country, the longer the speech. Delegates went out for a walk or settled down to a nap, thinking that Burma would have nothing to say. As the junior most delegate from India, I was glued to the earphone not to miss the Burmese wisdom. What shook up everybody was that the minister finished his speech in precisely three minutes. When he returned to his seat, everyone in the Indian delegation turned to me to find out what he (had) said. I told them that Burma had just left the Movement as it had ceased to be of any value to Burma. He said that Burma was too nonaligned to be in the Nonaligned Movement!*
>
> *The Movement took it in its stride and moved on till it (Myanmar) came back to a session in Bali*[46] *asking for re-entry. Under direct instructions from the prime minister, we blocked their return on the ground that the elected leader was denied power.*[47]

Ironically, in the post-Independence period, it had been Burma that was pushing India towards an alliance against China. Vineet Thakur avers[48] that in the late 1940s, U Nu had approached Y.D. Gundevia to propose to Nehru a coalition arrangement between India and Burma against China. Apparently, Nehru became visibly upset and did not respond to the suggestion. In 1950, U. Nu came up with a more concrete proposal to form a South East Asian Union comprising India, Pakistan, Sri Lanka, Indonesia, and Burma. Nehru opposed this and wrote to U Nu on 10 December 1950 that the idea was fraught with problems since all these countries were militarily weak and hence to propose a military alliance was unreal. He recommended that a better way would be to have treaties of friendship and non-aggression pacts with each other. U Nu's proposal was born out of a threat of China sending its troops into Burma. By having a military alliance with India, he was seeking to elicit Indian guarantees against China. Nehru, due to his opposition to military alliances, argued that any show of military solidarity by India with Burma would be tantamount to making China distrust India. He proposed an alternative to U Nu: a treaty of friendship between India and Burma which would be signal enough to China to know that India was not in favour of China sending its troops into Burma.

Changing mindsets takes generations. It requires a holistic approach which needs to take into account the geographic realities, geopolitical compulsions and the availability of scholarly resources. There is undeniably a need to move Indian political, bureaucratic and media mindsets out of the blind spot and work to enhance Myanmar consciousness. The process has started, but slowly. One sure way to increase political stakes in Myanmar consciousness is to increase people-to-people contacts between the rest of India and the Northeast and between India and Myanmar.

Presently, India-Myanmar relations are government-to-government driven. To insulate the relationship and make it enduring, there is a need to enhance people-to-people contacts. Once the stakes in the people-to-people relationship are enhanced to the desired levels, the leadership thereafter has to respect and pander to these stakes. This is likely what Daw Aung San Suu Kyi alluded to when she made the quote reproduced at the beginning of this chapter.

NOTES

1. Ministry of External Affairs Website, Jawaharlal Nehru Memorial Lecture, 2012 "Discovery of Nehru" by Aung San Suu Kyi, 14 Nov 2012, https://www.mea.gov.in/Speeches-Statements.htm?dtl/20812/Jawaharlal+Nehru+Memorial+Lecture+2012+ quotDiscovery+ of+ Nehruquot+by+Aung+San+Suu+Kyi (Accessed on 14 Feb 2020).
2. It is the small portion of the visual field of each eye that corresponds to the position of the optic disk (i.e., the optic nerve head) within the retina. There are no photoreceptors (i.e., rods or cones) in the optic disk and, therefore, there is no image detection in this area. With both eyes open, the blind spots are not perceived because the visual fields of the two eyes overlap, https://www.britannica.com/science/blind-spot (Accessed on 14 Feb 2020).
3. Lasik of Nevada Website, Try These 3 Fun Tests To Find Your Visual Blind Spot, https://lasikofnv.com/try-these-3-fun-tests-to-find-your-visual-blind-spot/ (Accessed on 14 Feb 2020).
4. Jaideep Chanda, Raising 'Myanmar Consciousness': Visit of the President of Myanmar to India (26–29 February 2020), Vivekananda International Foundation, New Delhi, 28 Feb 2020, https://www.vifindia.org/article/2020/february/28/raising-myanmar-consciousness-visit-of-the-president-of-myanmar-to-india (Accessed on 1 May 2020).
5. By no means does this suggest that the present situation is a product of only the last twenty years. It is the aggregate of generations of neglect. I confine this discourse to the recent past so as to reflect on the currency of the problem.
6. Inder Kumar Gujral, "*Text of 'Aspects of India's Foreign Policy,' a Speech by I. K. Gujral at the Bandaranaike Centre For International Studies in Colombo, Sri Lanka, on January 20, 1997,*"

Stimson Centre,2 February 2020, https://www.stimson.org/1997/the-gujral-doctrine (Accessed on 26 April 2020).

7. The Gujral Doctrine is a set of five principles to guide the conduct of foreign relations with India's immediate neighbours, notably Pakistan, as spelt out by Gujral when he was External Affairs Minister. The doctrine was later termed as such by journalist Bhabani Sen Gupta in his article, *India in the Twenty First Century* in *International Affairs*.
8. Inder Kumar Gujral, http://ik.gujral.tripod.com/sp1.htm (Accessed on 14 Feb 2020).
9. Shri Inder Kumar Gujral (interviewee) recorded by Smt. Usha Prasad (interviewer), 2 June 2002, pages 176-177, Nehru Memorial Museum and Library, Oral History Project, Oral History Transcript, Acc. No. 797. His only other allusion to Myanmar in the 216 pages of the transcripts is when he describes the foundation of India's foreign policy as being based on its relationship with the larger part of the world individually and culturally and in terms of religion. He describes that in several countries including Burma, the *Ramayana* is now being performed on stage as per their respective taste and culture. The interviews commenced on 2 June 2002 and the copyright declaration was signed by Shri Gujral on 1 May 2005, hence one assumes that the interviews, transcription, review and printing process of the transcript would have taken three years.
10. IndiaToday.in, "*Narendra Modi Invites All SAARC Heads to Swearing-In,*" *India Today*, May 21, 2014, https://www.indiatoday.in/india/story/narendra-modi-invites-saarc-heads-to-swearing-in-193881-2014-05-21 (Accessed on 26 April 2020).
11. SAARC Secretariat, accessed April 26, 2020, http://saarc-sec.org/about-saarc (Accessed on 26 April 2020).
12. SAARC Countries 2020, accessed April 26, 2020, https://worldpopulationreview.com/countries/saarc-countries/ (Accessed on 26 April 2020).
13. During an interaction with the author via email on 15 May 2020.
14. Soham Basu and Nidhi Varma, "*Foreign Policy & Security Tiffin Talk: Understanding the Calculus of Smaller South Asian Countries as India Rises,*" Brookings India, April 7, 2020, https://www.brookings.edu/events/understanding-the-calculus-of-smaller-south-asian-countries-as-india-rises/ (Accessed on 26 April 2020).
15. In an email to the author.
16. Jawaharlal Nehru University website, http://www.jnu.ac.in/node#school_center (Accessed on 27 April 2020).
17. Delhi University website, http://www.du.ac.in/du/index.php?page=east-asian-studies (Accessed on 27 April 2020).
18. University of Calcutta website, https://www.caluniv.ac.in/academic/department/Sseas.html (Accessed on 27 April 2020).
19. Jadavpur University website, http://www.jaduniv.edu.in/# (Accessed on 28 April 2020).
20. School of Language, Literature and Cultural Studies, Jawaharlal Nehru University, New Delhi. http://www.jnu.ac.in/sllcs. (Accessed on 26 April 2020). Italian is currently not on offer. Greek, Hebrew and Turkish are optional courses.
21. University of Delhi, Department of Slavonic and Finno-Ugrian Studies, http://www.du.ac.in/du/index.php?page=slavonic-finno-ugrian-studies (Accessed on 26 April 2020).
22. Jadavpur University, http://www.jaduniv.edu.in/ (Accessed on 28 April 2020).
23. Press Information Bureau, "*India-Myanmar Joint Statement during the State Visit of the President of Myanmar to India (*February 26-29, 2020*),*" Prime Minister's Office, Government of India, 27 February 2020, https://pib.gov.in/newsite/PrintRelease.aspx?relid=199620 (Accessed on 26 April 2020).
24. The author was in New Delhi during the visit and was surprised to see that most of the physical copies of the newspapers had given the event a miss. The websites which covered the visit were: https://www.firstpost.com/india/myanmar-president-win-myint-to-visit-india-from-

26-to-29-february-first-lady-daw-cho-cho-to-visit-agra-bodh-gaya-8070451.html; https://economictimes.indiatimes.com/news/politics-and-nation/narendra-modi-holds-talks-with-myanmar-president-u-win-myint-india-myanmar-sign-10-pacts/articleshow/74340044.cms?from=mdr; https://www.thehindubusinessline.com/news/myanmar-president-u-win-myint-to-visit-india-from-feb-26-29/article30883043.ece and https://www.hindustantimes.com/india-news/myanmar-president-visit-marked-by-signing-of-10-agreements/story-9WON0QiK0xa3freRREtiyM.html.

25. United Nations Statistics Division, "UNSD-Methodology," United Nations, https://unstats.un.org/unsd/methodology/m49/ (Accessed on 27 April 2020).
26. India-Asian News Service, "*Myanmar Seeks SAARC Membership*," *India Today*, May 20, 2008, https://www.indiatoday.in/latest-headlines/story/myanmar-seeks-saarc-membership-25443-2008-05-20 (Accessed on 26 April 2020).
27. University of Cambridge, "*The Centre of South Asian Studies*," The Centre | The Centre of South Asian Studies, https://www.s-asian.cam.ac.uk/the-centre/(Accessed on 27 April 2020).
28. University of Michigan, "*MIRS: South Asian Studies Specialization: U-M LSA Centre for South Asian Studies (CSAS),*" https://ii.umich.edu/csas/graduate-students/MIRS-south-asian-studies.html (Accessed on 27 April 2020).
29. Steve Kujan, "*Why South Asian Studies?*", https://southasia.rutgers.edu/academics-mainmenu/undergraduate/why-south-asian-studies (Accessed on 27 April 2020).
30. https://takshashila.org.in/pax-indica-five-neighbourhood-paradoxes/
31. Mirza Zulfiqur Rahman, "*Myanmar's Bid for SAARC Membership*", Institute of Peace and Conflict Studies, New Delhi, 3 Feb 2009: http://www.ipcs.org/comm_select.php? articleNo =2797 (Accessed on 16 May 2020).
32. In an email to the author on 15 May 2020.
33. Including Shri Gulzari Lal Nanda who was acting Prime Minister twice for 13 days in each term in 1964 and 1966 following the deaths of PM Jawaharlal Nehru and PM Lal Bahadur Shastri.
34. P. V. Narasimha Rao, Andhra Pradesh and H. D. Deve Gowda, Karnataka.
35. The term 'Troubled Periphery' is the name of a seminal book on Northeast India by the ex-BBC and Reuters journalist and author scholar Subir Bhaumik, https://books.google.co.in/books/about/Troubled_Periphery.html?id=MdRjDwAAQBAJ&printsec= frontcover&source =kp_read_button&redir_esc=y#v=onepage&q&f=false
36. During the Fellows' Seminar for this project, where he had been invited by the Vivekananda International Foundation, as a subject matter expert to review the manuscript and as a panellist on 13 July 2020.
37. My telephonic interview with AmbassadorShyam Saran on 4 June 2020.
38. This has been alluded to in the Gundevia Papers covered in Chapter 2.
39. She was the daughter of U Nu who worked in the All India Radio Burmese Language Service in 1988 along with U Maw Thiri. During the course of her service, she was vocally critical of the Ne Win regime through the AIR medium causing much embarrassment to both Myanmar and India and actually impacted the presenting of credentials of the then Ambassador Preet Malik to Senior General Saw Maung. For a detailed account of the episode, see Preet Malik, '*My Myanmar Years: A Diplomat's Account of India's Relations with the Region*', Sage India, New Delhi, 2015, p. 66.
40. BIMSTEC Website, About BIMSTEC, https://bimstec.org/?page_id=189 (Accessed on 14 Feb 2020).
41. The Quint Web Article, BIMSTEC: The Strategic Neighbours Who'll Attend Modi's Swearing In, 27 May 2019, https://www.thequint.com/news/india/bimstec-the-strategic-nations-wholl-attend-modis-swearing-in (Accessed on 14 Feb 2020).

42. The Hindu Web Article, SAARC a failed mission, say experts, Vishakapatnam, 31 March 2017, https://www.thehindu.com/news/cities/Visakhapatnam/saarc-a-failed-mission-say-experts/article17748997.ece (Accessed on 14 Feb 2020); and Yashwant Sinha, The SAARC experiment has failed, The Economic Times ePaper 27 June 2010, https://economictimes.indiatimes.com/special-report/the-saarc-experiment-has-failed/articleshow/6096578.cms (Accessed on 14 Feb 2020).
43. The term 'Greater South Asia' is not new, per se, but it was first used in a different context. It was used by Pakistan to project a grouping of China, Iran, Pakistan and the Central Asian Republics to counter India's clout in the SAARC which was forced to cancel its summit in Islamabad in 2016 after India pulled out. Ironically, this Greater South Asia included only one country from South Asia, viz., Pakistan! See *The New Indian Express*, "*What's a greater south asia?* 13 October 2016, https://www.newindianexpress.com/opinions/editorials/2016/oct/13/whats-a-greater-south-asia-1527320.html; Andrew Korybko, "*The Death of SAARC gave birth to 'Greater South Asia,'*" 7 November 2016, www.geopolitika.ru https://www.geopolitica.ru/en/article/death-saarc-gave-birth-greater-south-asia and N. P. Upadhyaya, "*Nepal: SAARC is dead, Greater South Asia is taking shape!*", www.telegraphnepal.comhttp://telegraphnepal.com/saarc-is-dead-greater-south-asia-is-taking-shape/ (Accessed on 29 April 2020).
44. As per RAND International Research and Analysis Projects, "*South Asia Regional Trade and Investment Policy*", https://www.rand.org/international/research/projects/south-asia-trade-and-investments.html (Accessed on 29 April 2020).
45. The World Bank, "*Realizing the Promise of Regional Trade in South Asia*" 9 October 2018, https://www.worldbank.org/en/news/feature/2018/10/09/realizing-the-promise-of-regional-trade-in-south-asia (Accessed on 29 April 2020).
46. This would have been at the XVI Ministerial Conference and Commemorative Meeting of the Non-Aligned Movement, Bali—2011.
47. T. P. Sreenivasan, *Myanmar—A mysterious country that has baffled the world,* www.rediff.com 28 Nov 2015, https://www.rediff.com/news/column/a-mysterious-country-that-has-baffled-the-world/20151128.htm (Accessed on 20 June 2020). Ambassador Sreenivasan was Deputy Chief of Mission (Ambassadorial Rank) in the Embassy of India, Washington (1997-2000), High Commissioner of India to Kenya and Permanent Representative of India to the United Nations in Nairobi (1995-1997), Ambassador and Deputy Permanent Representative of India to the United Nations, New York (1992-1995), and Ambassador to Fiji and eight other South Pacific Island States (1986-1989). He has also served in New Delhi, Tokyo, Thimphu, Moscow, New York and Yangon. He was also Governor for India of the International Atomic Energy Agency, Vienna, and Ambassador to Austria and Slovenia (2000-2004). http://www.tpsreenivasan.com/biography.php (Accessed on 16 Aug 2020).
48. Vineet Thakur, *Postscripts on Independence: Foreign Policy Discourses in India and South Africa*, Oxford University Press, New Delhi, 2018, p. 61.

CHAPTER 5
The Kaladan Project

The possibility of an outlet to the sea via Chittagong in the more distant future should not come in the way of our pursuing the possibility of an outlet via Akyab. Both links would probably justify themselves in view of our very high political stakes in the development, stability and ultimate security of the north-eastern region of India.

—B.G. Verghese[1]

No study or conversation on engagements of India in Myanmar can be complete without dwelling on the Kaladan Project. This project started in 2010 and, in keeping with the bureaucratic traditions and lack of accountability that Indian megaprojects abroad are tainted with, is yet to see the light of day even a decade later. It is the single largest investment by India in Myanmar, and hence a flagship project and a rather shaky beacon of India-Myanmar relations. But let us start at the beginning.

Historical Origins of the Kaladan Project

The first documented reference to the need for a project to connect northeast India by an alternative route to offset the vulnerability of the Siliguri Corridor possibly dates back to 18 March 1968. The Siliguri Corridor (also known as Chicken's Neck) is a narrow stretch of land of about 22 km width, located in West Bengal, which connects India's Northeast to the rest of India with Nepal and Bangladesh lying on either side of the corridor and Bhutan on the northern side. All land transportation between mainland India and the Northeastern states uses this corridor. Ankit Panda,[2] an American analyst, wrote in *The Diplomat* that:

> *The Siliguri Corridor is a terrifyingly vulnerable artery in India's geography. For Indians in the Northeast, every look at a map is a sobering reminder of just how fragile their physical and economic tether to the rest of the country remains. Unlike so many of the problems India faces, the Siliguri Corridor's vulnerability is a cruel endowment of political geography and essentially one it is stuck with.*

In a Prime Minister's Secretariat paper[3] dated 18 March 1968 and classified SECRET, B.G. Verghese[4] highlights the contours of the plan titled '*Proposal for a Road-River link from the Mizo Hills District to Akyab in Burma*'. A study of this declassified five-page document is essential to understand the genesis of this strategic venture.

Figure 5.1: B.G. Verghese

Source: Courtesy www.bgverghese.com

The paper starts by pointing out that prior to Independence, Chittagong Port was the natural outlet for the southern half of what is today[5] the Northeastern region of India. Hence, the loss of this outlet made this whole region very nearly a "landlocked" area and, together with the loss of the East Pakistan market, retarded the economy and the development of the region. The economic and political discontents of the area escalated into a security problem which needed to be tackled both on the basis of defence as well as of development. On this basis, the paper brings out that an '*outlet to the sea from the Mizo Hills District to Akyab port through Burmese territory could be very valuable*'. The distance from the southern tip of the Mizo Hills District to Akyab Port was estimated to be 120 miles along the Kolodyne (Kaladan) river through the Northern Arakan district which was then underdeveloped and '*probably lightly administered*'.

B.G. Verghese then goes on to describe that the Border Roads Organization was building a Class 9 road up to Lungleh in Mizo District and proposed that this road be extended by another 50 miles to the south till Lwangtlai. He calculated that at the rate of ₹ 12 lakh per mile, which was the cost of construction in Mizo district for a black top Class 9 road, the total cost would come to ₹ 15 crore till Akyab Port. Crossing the river at places could be achieved by ferries.

As an alternative, the paper proposed development of navigation facilities on the Kolodyne. Apparently, the Planning Commission had sanctioned a preliminary survey for this in Indian territory. As such, it was evident that the river was more amenable to navigation in Burmese territory. The overall cost of a road or river project linking Mizo District, though expensive, would, the paper surmised, '*more than recompense us for the outlay*'.

Verghese proposed that India offer to the Burmese Government that it (India) would build the road using Burmese labour and material as available and also fund the cost of construction, less the cost of acquisition of land. Post construction, the road would be handed over to the Burmese Government with an offer of five years free maintenance and the Government of India would have no rights on the road or the territory through which it passes, other than that of free and innocent passage as applicable on any international highway subject to normal Customs procedures. He writes, '*We would not have anything like a territorial lease or a "corridor" through Burma. It is necessary to state this clearly in order to allay any apprehensions in the minds of the Burmese people.*' Verghese reveals an astute understanding of the psyche of the Burmese people and leadership, who are by nature cautious on issues of sovereignty and sensitive to any perceived violation of territorial integrity.

The paper listed out six advantages that the Burmese Government would reap from this road:

(a) It would open up the northern part of Arakan district and help in the administrative control and development of the area.
(b) It would improve Burmese security in the region.
(c) It would augment the Government of Burma's revenue through normal processes of development.
(d) It would further augment the Government of Burma's revenues through such transit levies, port dues, etc., accruing on the import and export of Indian goods.
(e) It would generate employment in the area.
(f) It would stimulate trade between India and Burma and would thereby promote friendly ties among our two peoples. The development of this region would be to the mutual advantage of both countries.

Verghese took pains to highlight that the Burmese Government need have no apprehension to the proposal since it would be no different than the Raxaul-Kathmandu Road; the Sanauli-Pokhra Road or even the road to Paro in Bhutan. He even recommended that, if necessary, the project could be taken up as subsidiary to the Asian Highway scheme sponsored by the Economic Commission for Asia and Far East (ECAFE)[6] since both the nations were participants in it.

At this stage, the paper digresses from the project and dwells into '*a more attractive outlet to the sea*' from Belonia Railway Station in Tripura via Fenny to Chittagong in Pakistan as also from Demagiri in Mizo District down the Karnaphuli River to Chittagong. He informs the reader that the lake formed by the Kaptai Dam on the Karnaphuli just above Rangamati, the headquarters of the Chittagong Hill Tract, stretches back to a little beyond Demagiri. Since both these parts of the river were navigable, all it would need would be a lock to permit free passage from Mizo District to Chittagong. He then turns critical of the Government of India's inaction on the issue:

> *It is a matter of some surprise that GOI has never taken up the question of a passage to the sea through Chittagong port in the 20 years since Independence, although this is such an obvious and so vital a link for the whole of the eastern region. There is also a metre gauge railway up to Dharma Nagar in Tripura which could be extended up to Agartala or any other point to link up with the Pakistan railway system to Chittagong.*
>
> *Pakistan has in the past been anxious for Railway transit facility through India between West and East Pakistan. An agreement to this effect, in exchange for transit for Indian goods between West Bengal and Assam, was ratified by (the) Pakistani Government in 1960 but rejected by GOI in the somewhat simple and wholly erroneous belief that this arrangement would confer a major advantage on Pakistan at considerable risk to the security of India. On the contrary, the advantage to India from any such link would be far greater than the advantage to Pakistan because it is much easier and much cheaper for Pakistan to operate shipping services between Karachi and Chittagong than for India to move freight from Tripura, Mizo District, Manipur or Nagaland to Calcutta or other points in the "Indian heartland".*

He, however cautions, that the sea outlet via Chittagong '*should not come in the way of our pursuing the possibility of an outlet via Akyab. Both links would probably justify themselves in view of our very high political stakes in the development, stability and ultimate security of the north-eastern region of India.*'

The Present-Day Kaladan Project

Having understood the mindset of the original planners, let us now take stock of the project as it unfolded. The *Framework Agreement between the Government of the Republic of India and the Government of the Union of Myanmar for the Construction and Operation of a Multi-Modal Transit Transport Facility on Kaladan River connecting the Sittwe Port in Myanmar with the State of Mizoram in India*[7] was signed by the then Minister of External Affairs, Shri Pranab Mukherjee, and

Nyan Win, Minister of Foreign Affairs, Myanmar, on 2 April 2008 (**see Appendix N**). The Agreement with 21 Articles is based on the Detailed Project Report (DPR) by RITES Ltd. of April and December 2003. As per the Agreement, the project was to create an inland waterway link connecting Sittwe Port and Setpyipyin (Kaletwa) along the Kaladan and thereafter a road link till the Mizoram border, with the following components:

(a) Port & Inland Water Transport (PIWT) terminal and related infrastructure facilities at the port of Sittwe to Kaletwa for trans-shipment from ships to inland vessels and vice versa, including development of the navigation channels.

(b) Development of the Kaladan Waterway from Sittwe to Kaletwa (225 km) by dredging, removal of rock outcrops and rapids, navigation aids, etc.

(c) Construction of an IWT & Highway trans-shipment terminal and related facilities at Kaletwa.

(d) Finally, construction of a highway from Kaletwa to Mizoram border.

The land would be provided gratis by the Government of Myanmar and the project would include maintenance and management of the above facility components. The cost of upgradation of Sittwe Port and Kaladan Waterway was estimated at US$ 68.24 million while the cost for the road from Kaletwato Mizoram was US$ 49.14 million.

The Agreement also stated that the Government of India would appoint a Project Development Consultant (PDC) from India who would be responsible for preparation for selection of the construction contractors for the above mentioned four components; coordination/liaison between nodal agencies and construction contractors; and supervision of construction and project management of various works. The Government of India would also appoint the main contractor from India and, where required, different sub-contractors from both the countries could be appointed for implementing the components of the projects.

The Kaladan Project started its inception with a five-year gap between the submission of the DPR by RITES Limited in 2003 and the signing of the Framework Agreement. From available open source data of 6 July 2010[8] vintage[9] it was found that the Implementing Authority was the Ministry of External Affairs (MEA) while the Implementing Agency for the Myanmar portion was RITES Limited at an estimated cost of ₹ 545.85 crores (at the exchange rate on 31 August 2006 where 1 US$ = ₹ 46.50). For the Mizoram part of the two-way 117-km highway from Lawngtlai to the border, the Implementing Authority was the Department of Road Transport and Highways and the Implementing Agency was the Public Works Department of the Government of Mizoram at an estimated cost of ₹ 550 crores (at the same exchange rate) to be funded in Phase A of the Special Accelerated Road Development Programme for North East (SARDP-NE).[10] Two handling points were also mentioned, viz., Hmawngbu (Mobu) in Mizoram in India and Myeikwa in Myanmar.

Kolkata was envisaged as the relevant Indian port and commercial hub[11] which was sought to be connected to Mizoram and the 2003 DPR for the PIWT component was revised by the Inland Waterways Authority of India in 2009.[12] Evidently, Kaletwa was replaced by Paletwa as the IWT destination and the IWT segment reduced from 255 km to 158 km. The segments of the project, as reflected in the Ministry of Development of North East Region (MDONER), website are:

(a) Kolkata Port to Sittwe Port (by regular shipping) —539 km.
(b) Sittwe to Paletwa (by IWT on the Kaladan) —158 km.
(c) Paletwa to the India-Myanmar Border (by road) —110 km.
(d) Border to NH 54 (Lawgtlai in Mizoram by road) —100 km

The MEA appointed the Inland Waterways Authority of India (IWAI) as the PDC in March 2009 for the PIWT component and M/s Essar Projects India Limited, Mumbai, as the main contractor in April 2010 for a contract value of ₹ 342 crores. The agreement was signed in May 2010 and work finally commenced in 2010.

Figure 5.2: Configuration of the Kaladan Multi-Modal Transit Transport Project

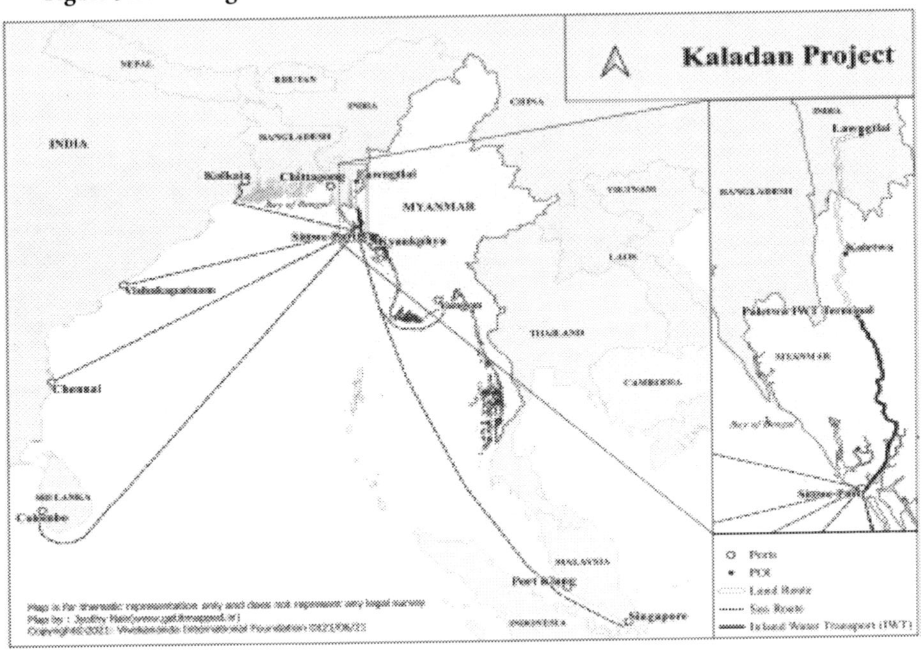

Current Status

The total project cost of the Kaladan Project would be around US$ 484 million as per an Embassy of India, Yangon, statement on 9 July 2019.[13] The quantum of funds allocated and utilised for the Kaladan Project since 2014 reveals[14] that there has been a steady increase in utilisation of funds:

Year	*Allotted (₹ Crore)*	*Utilised (₹ Crore)*	*Remarks*
2014-15	80	52.55	
2015-16	60	49.20	
2016-17	80	78.96	
2017-18	—	128.26	No specific allocation was made for Kaladan Multi Modal Transit Transport project due to mergerof Plan and Non-Plan budget heads in FY 2017-18.

Ambassador Saurabh Kumar, Indian Ambassador to Myanmar, stated in January 2020 that '*A non-optimal security environment has hampered implementation of the Kaladan Multi-Modal Transit Transport Project amid ongoing clashes in parts of Arakan and Chin states*'.[15] On that note, it is in the fitness of things that we take stock of the status of the various components of the Kaladan Project, as on 30 June 2020.

Sittwe Port and Paletwa IWT Terminal

Figure 5.3: Sittwe Port Signage at Sittwe

Source: A to Z Exim

Figure 5.4: Layout Plan of Sittwe Port

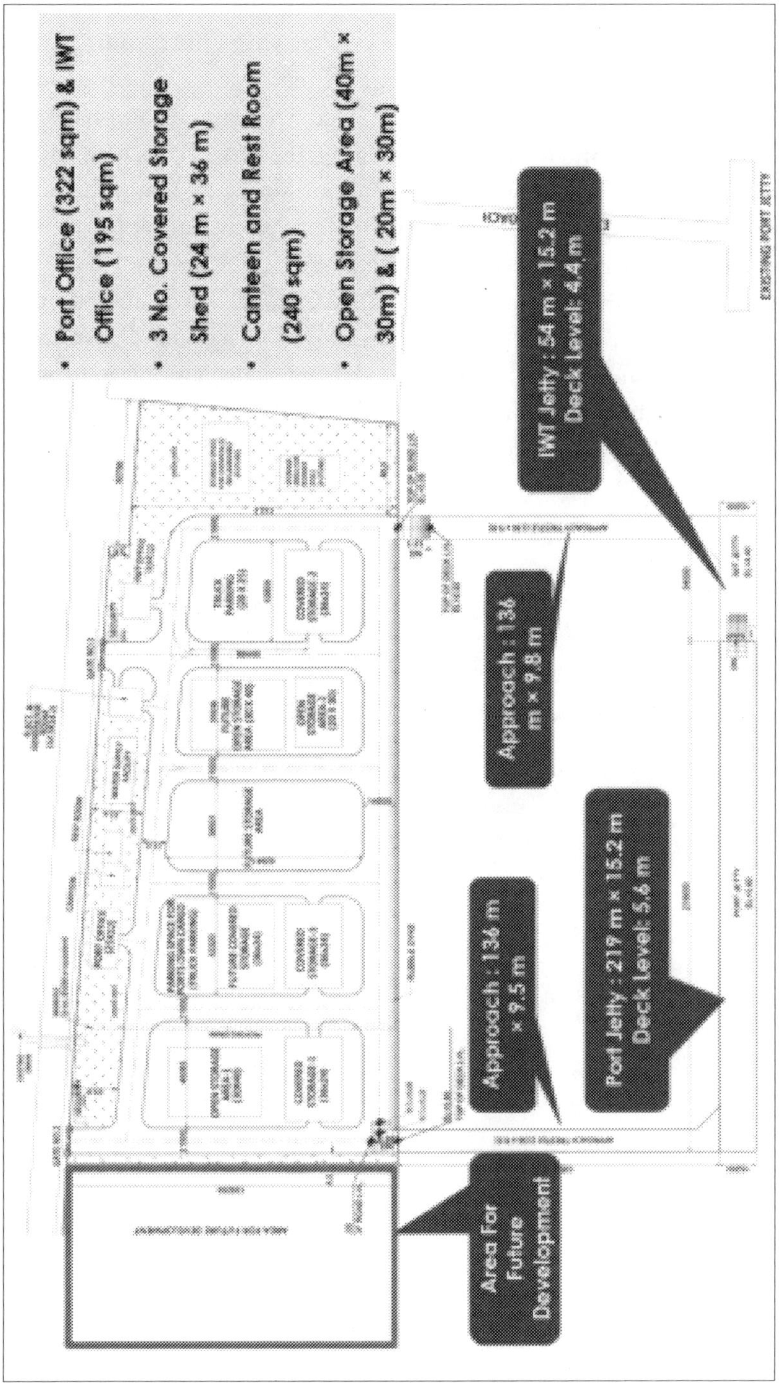

Source: A to Z Exim

The port and the IWT terminal have been completed and M/s A to Z Exim has been selected by tendering as the port operator with effect from 1 February 2020. The appointment is for three years and extendable by another two years. The work of construction of the port and IWT components is completed, which includes fairway development and sea dredging in Sittwe Port area; port and IWT terminal at Sittwe; fairway development and dredging along the Sittwe—Paletwa stretch of Kaladan River; IWT terminal at Paletwa; and procurement of six IWT vessels of capacity 300 T each. The mode of operations will see Indian origin or any other origin cargo unloaded at Sittwe, reloaded on to inland transport vessels/barges for Paletwa and thereafter transported to its inland destination in Myanmar or to Mizoram, India, by road or vice versa, i.e., any cargo originating from Mizoram or Myanmar hinterland can be transported by road to Paletwa, then to Sittwe by IWT mode, unloaded at Sittwe and reloaded on to sea-going vessels for export.

Figure 5.5: Collage of Sittwe Port

Source: A to Z Exim.

The author had extensive interaction[16] with Mr. Sohel Khazani of M/s A to Z Exim[17] who informed him that while the port is complete, the final 5 per cent of the total work is pending. This constitutes civil, electrical and mechanical work worth about ₹ 20 crores including electrical connections, construction of fuel stations with tanks, the radar, equipment, tide gauge, toilets for labourers and security gates. Apart from this, dredging worth ₹ 30 crores is pending and will be done closer to the actual commencement of operations.

The author enquired about the viability of the project in view of the inevitable delay in the completion of the road component which gives it the final connectivity with Mizoram. Mr. Khazani informed that Sittwe Port provides certain advantages with reference to the Myanmar hinterland which can be exploited by the Kaladan Project. Magway, Mandalay, Shan and Sagaing are in closer proximity to Sittwe Port than to Yangon, hence cargo from these places can be lightened at Yangon and be brought straight to Sittwe with four-metre draft, which will make the cargo more profitable and delivery more efficient. Sittwe is connected to all the major places in Western and Central Myanmar through highways which ease the transport through road than inland river. Currently, inward river channels carrying domestic cargo face year long challenges due to changes in water depths which results in more expenditure and less income. This, even though the number of cargo-carrying companies and domestic freight forwards has seen a 10-fold increase in the past few years, can be exploited in transhipment of IWT cargo to road transport.

He also highlighted that:

> *The road impacts the viability of the entire Kaladan Project. But there is enough existing potential for the port to operate independently. The entire Rakhine state is very rich in agricultural products such as rice and also fruits. A lot of the fruits, e.g., mangoes are thrown away since there are no exports. So there is a lot of rich agro content that can be taken out from there. On the other hand, there is scope for cement and steel to be sent there since there is a lot of development that is taking place in and around Sittwe. Right now Thai business persons are sending cement to the adjoining jetty at Sittwe. That jetty is just a jetty; no equipment, crane, warehouse…nothing. So ships of 2T, 3T or 4T anchor at the anchorage and the cargo is barged out by small barges of say 200-300T each, to the jetty.*
>
> *Without financial viability we would not have bid for the port. The Government was looking for bidders who had a track record of delivering. We have already delivered at Chhabahar Port in Iran where we are the operators. There we were operating seven to eight vessels a month. So we were confident we could pull it off. And we will.*
>
> *Yangon is a port where the base cargo lands in big vessels and we can get the smaller parcels from there by transhipment to Sittwe. The land route from Yangon to Rakhine State is lengthy, difficult and expensive.*

Research figures presented by Land-Marine Engineering and Port Solutions LLP during the feasibility study indicate that total pharmaceutical imports accounted for 85 per cent of the drug market and India takes the lead with a strong 40 to 45 per cent market share at present with approximately 5,000 drug varieties being imported into Myanmar. Agricultural fertilizers are in demand in several regions in Myanmar. Collectively, China and Thailand account for 80 to

90 per cent of their fertilizers entering the market with urea being the most imported fertiliser. Presently, there is 2 per cent duty on re-exports which take place via borders with neighbouring countries. Previously, only three items, sugar, betel nut, and oil, were approved for re-export but now, tyres, sesame (white and black), dried chilli, groundnut, cotton, soy beans, textiles, fresh fruit, electronic materials, cosmetics, juices and other groceries, clothes, edible oil and garlic have been included. Sugar is a major commodity with 2018 sugar exports from India to Myanmar touching a staggering high of US$ 424 million.

Thus, India has achieved a respectable share only in a few products out of the major import categories of Myanmar. India's share in other major import items of Myanmar remains marginal. This essentially highlights the potential for enhancing such exports to Myanmar, with the potential items of export including electrical machinery and equipment; machinery and mechanical appliances; plastic and its articles; articles of iron or steel; animal or vegetable fats and oils; man-made filaments; man-made staple fibres and paper and paperboard.

With regards to the future of Sittwe Port, Mr. Khazani mentioned that:

> *Right next to the existing port is the land which has been reclaimed by dumping the mud from the dredging. We propose to use this land for construction of liquid bulk petroleum products since there is a lot of demand for these products here in Myanmar. The area is suited for low draft bulk and RO-RO vessels. This can become a game changer for Sittwe. The area cannot be used for container operations due to the draft.*

As far as import potential from Myanmar is concerned, states neighbouring Rakhine, rank fifth to eighth in rice,cereal and fruits production which can translate into exports to India or Bangladesh. Similarly, only 10 per cent of total Myanmar's production of fishery and aquaculture is exported and the market has substantial outlook for growth. Millions of dollars of aid is coming to Myanmar, including infrastructure, agricultural produce, clothing, medicine and other cargo for Rohingya refugees, which currently gets transported to Rakhine from Yangon or Kyaukphyu. This can be redirected through Sittwe Port. India has proposed the development of Sittwe Industrial Park SEZ in Sittwe with cargo transportation being facilitated through the Sittwe port.

India's engagements in Myanmar have been limited so far to a few sectors. One area India could enhance its engagements with Myanmar is the Fast Moving Consumer Goods (FMCG) sector which has expanded by 15 per cent since 2014 and accounts for nearly half of a consumer's average monthly expenditure. Most of Myanmar's FMCG goods are presently imported from neighbouring countries such as China, Thailand and Singapore or from other developed countries. Another sector is cotton yarn. Myanmar imports cotton yarn from India as an input for its

Figure 5.6: Layout Plan of Paletwa IWT Terminal

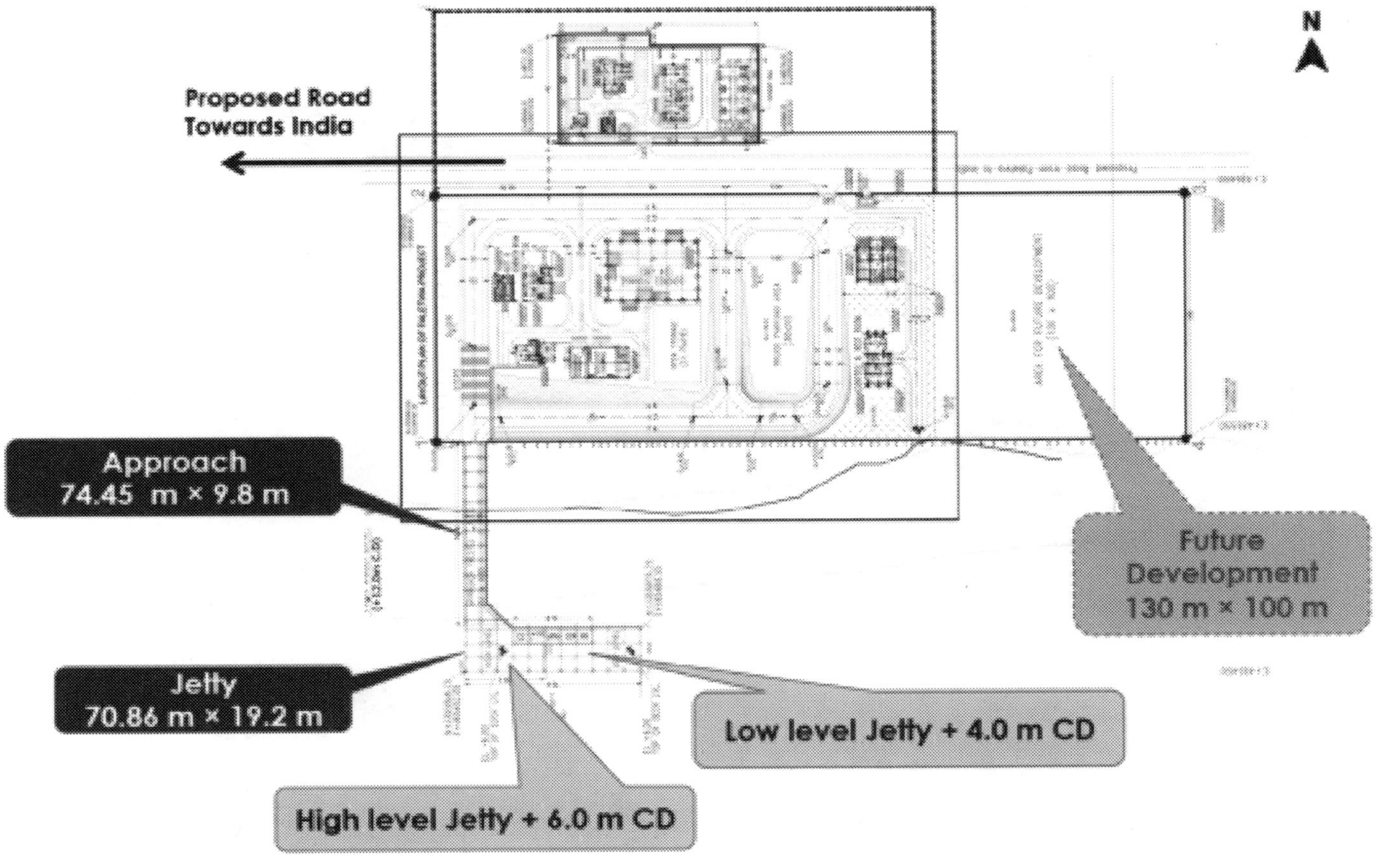

Source: A to Z Exim

garment industry, which is further exported to developed markets. Indian manufacturers can set up a part of their textile industry abroad and take advantage of the export benefits and at the same time create a value chain.

The above facts demolish the myth that for Sittwe Port to be viable, the entire project has to be completed. In fact, in a standalone mode (with reference to the Kaladan Project), Sittwe Port has the potential to bring in drastic changes to shipping in the Bay of Bengal. Khazani says that:

> *A lot of Bangladesh cargo can come and sit here at Sittwe. The Bangladesh port operational efficiency is very bad and (there are a) lot of security hazards at the port itself. So say the main vessel of 20,000 T comes to Sittwe; from here the smaller vessels could take the loads to Bangladesh as per the requirement of the importer from time to time. Today most of the vessel owners don't call on Bangladesh because they fight in (over) demurrages and detentions and they don't get the money. The ship ends up sitting for 15-30 days and the owners get fed up there. Next there is a lot material from Kolkata, Haldia and Visakhapatnam that can move to Sittwe in terms of steel and cement.*

There are some challenges which will need to be surmounted for best returns on the investments. One is security in goods transportation and at the terminals due to political unrest in Rakhine State. The infrastructure at Sittwe is manned by 26 staff (4 Indians, 22 locals) and at Paletwa by 8 staff (8 locals); total 34. All Indian nationals working on the Kaladan Project at Paletwa for maintenance have been brought back to Sittwe Port since the 22 March 2020 abduction and release 24 hours later.

Figure 5.7: Collage of Paletwa IWT Terminal

Source: A to Z Exim

Further since the majority of the work is carried out manually by labour, technical infrastructure availability is poor. Banking is a vulnerability, even though India has signed agreements with Myanmar banks but they have not been executed. Conversely, Indian bank branches of United Bank of India, Overseas Bank, EXIM Bank and State Bank of India, are all located in Yangon. There are no internationally recognized banks in Sittwe; only five local banks.

Road Components

A Ministry of External Affairs commissioned Environmental Impact Assessment Report[18] of the Detailed Project Report of the Two Laned Road from Paletwa to Zorinpui prepared by IRCON Infrastructure Services Limited outlines the specifics worthy of study. The total length of the Project Road has been estimated at 109.2 km in two packages, i.e. Package I (Paletwa to Kaletwa) is 60.7 km and Package II (Kaletwa to Zorinpui/India-Myanmar Border) is 48.5 km. There are 24 villages situated near the proposed alignment of the project road. The carriageway width of the project road is proposed to be 7 m with 2.5 m paved shoulder on both sides.

The ₹ 1,600-crore road project that passes through dense forests and hilly areas was awarded to a JV comprising Engineering Projects India Limited (EPIL), a PSU, and a Delhi-based private company, C&C Constructions, in June 2017.[19] However, this private company went into insolvency since February 2019.

Initially, the work was to commence from south to north, i.e., Paletwa to Zorinpui. Since that could not happen due to the violence, the Myanmar Government has permitted construction to commence from north to south, i.e., from Zorinpui to Paletwa. Accordingly, the other contractor, i.e., EPIL, has sub-contracted the work to RK-RPP JV and work has commenced on this stretch, i.e., Package II (km 60 to km 109.2)., This is likely to be completed by pre-monsoon season 2022. Concurrently, with the insolvency case pending with the National Company Law Tribunal (NCLT), MEA DPA II is exploring the option of handing over Package I (Paletwa to Kaletwa, i.e., km 0 to km 60) to EPIL as well since as per the JV terms and conditions, both partners are jointly and severally responsible for the project.

The author visited Zorinpui as part of a VIF-sponsored field study for this Fellowship in March 2020 and personally witnessed the fast pace of work that has commenced there. The contractor's teams had been allowed to induct into Myanmar on 5 February 2020 from Zorinpui. A camp office had been set up at Lawngtlai and a suitable camp established at Zorinpui based on containerised shelters. Full support is being provided by Assam Rifles and the Government of Mizoram. At present, two fully equipped survey teams comprising six persons each are operating from Zorinpui camp with a back support team of 20 persons. Each survey team has been assigned 25 Km +/–1 km of road, and individual contracts executed and signed for the same. Team 1 is operating from Zorinpui with an intermediary camp at village Samai at km 98. Team 2 is operating from village Samai to village Do Chaung at km 82. The present progress is approximately 750 metres daily by each team and, as on February 2020, the survey teams had already completed surveying 6 km in total with the design for approval for the first 5 km [First Phase] submitted on 25 February 2020. With both teams deployed, the expected daily progress is 2 km in the coming days with the entire survey work expected to be complete by 15 March 2020 and approval of design expected by 31 March 2020 from IRCON.

Figure 5.8: The Zero Point as on 3 March 2020. The charred portion on the right is Myanmar while the brown portion on the left with the road cutting is India. The dry nala in between is the IMB

Source: Author © Jaideep Chanda 2020

The Government, seized of the need to drive for peace in the region, and understanding that peace can only come through economic engagement, is urgently providing the stimulus to this project. Thus, since the working season in this region is only six to seven months with the remaining five to six months generally washed out due to heavy monsoon, it is providing all assistance to expedite construction. The recent launching of a bailey bridge by Army engineers across the nala at Zero Point to enable induction of plant equipment into Myanmar is a good example. The RCC bridge across the nala is yet to be constructed, pending which this bailey bridge will enable movement of heavy dozers, excavators and other equipment required for construction of the road.

Figure 5.9: Zorinpui Containerised Camp

Source: Author © Jaideep Chanda 2020.

Figure 5.10: Author at the Zorinpui Camp of the Kaladan Project

Source: Author © Jaideep Chanda 2020.

The project on the Mizoram side entails construction of a 87.19-km long two-lane highway (including three major bridges and five minor bridges) connecting Lawngtlai to Zorinpui near Zochachhuah. Zorinpui is the proposed site for a Land Customs Station on the Mizoram-Myanmar border. The DPR cost of the project was ₹ 575.65 crore as on 26.8.2010.

Expenditure as on December 2019 has escalated to ₹ 845.78 crore.[20] The project is split into three packages. The first package comprises construction of a new two-lane highway from km 0/00 (on NH 54 near Lawngtlai) to km 38/00 (37.04 km) in Mizoram to support the Kaladan Project in phase A of SARDP-NE Package-I, which is 91 per cent complete. Package 2 comprises construction of the highway from km 38/00 to km 71/00 in phase A of SARDP-NE Package-II, which is 96.80 per cent complete. The third package involves construction of a highway from km 71/00 to km 99/ 83 in Phase A of SARDP-NE Package-III which is 82.76 per cent complete. Thus, the Mizoram side of the roads connecting to the proposed Land Customs Station at Zorinpui is almost complete as on 31 March 2020. The Kaladan Project is expected to generate traffic on NH 54 by 5 per cent over the existing quantum.[21]

Social and Environmental Impacts

The Kaladan Project has the potential to provide a number of benefits for the local people such as improved transportation infrastructure; access to new markets; lower food prices and improved access to food; employment opportunities on project construction and maintenance; and economic opportunities for local small and medium-sized enterprises.

However, the Kaladan Movement, an umbrella group of civil society organizations and environmental groups,[22] is on record for its apprehension of a number of negative impacts to local communities, including land loss and forced eviction; disruption of and loss of livelihoods; increased presence of Tatmadaw troops; use of forced labour during project construction; restrictions on freedom of movement and access to river transportation; illegal taxation and extortion; violations of indigenous peoples' rights due to lack of public participation in development decisions through a process of Free, Prior and Informed Consent; and water pollution and environmental degradation.

In a June 2013 paper,[23] the Kaladan Movement documented that local people from Sittwe to Kaletwa know little about the project and perceive key phases of the project such as the Sittwe Deep Sea Port to be an "Indian" port. This is a negative in an atmosphere of top-down development that has failed to support any sense of local ownership. The location of the port was chosen against the will of the local people. Communities are already shouldering the negative environmental impacts of river dredging operations—such as the Thae Hkhun Islanders who were forcibly displaced from their homes due to the erosion of the Thae Hkhun shoreline and are yet to receive compensation from project implementers.

Similarly, local workers were paid a significantly lower salary than workers from India at the Sittwe Port construction site. An Indian worker got US$ 700-800 per month while local workers received US$ 78-137 per month.[24] However, these issues now stand resolved and the Indian companies have executed the construction of Sittwe Port.

Notwithstanding, the Indian and Myanmar Governments and the stakeholder companies must realise that the long-term success of this project depends on taking the local communities and population along. Force can only do so much.

AA and the Kaladan Project

This brings us to the question, what exactly is the AA position on the Kaladan Project? The answer to this question needs to be deduced from the various actions and statements that the AA has made over the past few years. Certain actions undertaken by the AA against the Kaladan Project, as also certain statements made by them during this period, are tabulated below for reference.

Date	*Event*	*Source*
16 Mar 2019	MV-*Yadanarwin*-7 ship carrying steel trusses worth Ks 1.072 billion weighing 286.23 tonnes left Yangon on March 10. AA attacked the ship at around 10 a.m. on March 16 near Hnamadar village in Paletwa Township in Chin State enroute Paletwa via Sittwe and Kyauktaw townships. The AA set fire to the ship and arrested the staff on board but later released them from Special Bridge-1.	https://elevenmyanmar.com/news/aa-sets-fire-to-steel-truss-loaded-ship-in-paletwa#:~:text=A%20cargo%20ship%20carryin g%20steel,spokesperson%20of%20Chin%20State%20government.
30 Mar 2019	170 AA insurgents abducted 13 Myanmar nationals working for a Myanmar-based contractor, Suu Htoo San Construction Company, involved in building the Paletwa to Mizoram road, at Twinkin Alaung village in Paletwa Township. Five persons were later released. "*We have eight persons in detention. They are spies sent by the Myanmar Army. They were working for Military Intelligence before,*" claimed Khaing Thu Kha. "*The Myanmar Army is taking advantage of the Kaladan project and sending spies in (to) the war zone. They want to create problems between the Indian Army and the AA*", he added.	https://www.hindustan times.com/india-news/myanmar-rebel-group-says-army-fuelling-trouble-along-kaladan-route/story-zg32WTFqX9l G74NJG G605O.html; https://nenow.in/top-news/arakan-army-abducts-workers-of-paletwa-mizoram-road-project-confirms-myanmar-army.html
26 Oct 2019	A group of five Indian representatives of a company were exploring the possibility of investing in the stalled Kaladan Project when	https://www.hindustan times.com/india-news/myanmar-rebel-group-releases-four-

Date	*Event*	*Source*
	they were kidnapped and released within 24 hours. Happened on the same day as the abduction of MP U Hwei Ting. One of the Indians, Mr. Vinoo Gopal, 60, construction advisor, passed away when they were climbing a mountain.	abducted-indians-fifth-dies-in-detention/story-DNgTW7v TVE9lw VX pur6m4M.html; http://mizzima.com/article/indian-engineer-died-heart-attack-chin-state-government
30 Nov 2019	Firing on Landing Craft *Marine Princess* carrying heavy machineries including bulldozers for Paletwa–Zorinpui Section of the (Kaladan project) and taking the crew hostage as also looting money and cell phones of the crew members.	https://elevenmyanmar.com/news/aa-attacks-vessel-carrying-heavy-machineries-for-paletwa-zorinpui-project
10 Dec 2019	Rakhine Tax Authority to be established to collect money from the operators of large-scale projects from "*next year*". Those failing to pay would not be allowed to do business in the area. Kaladan project operators had failed to acknowledge the group's authority in the region, and that the AA planned to collect taxes as a way of asserting itself. "*We are planning to send letters to the Indian Embassy and Indian companies. They can carry out their work, but they must inform us of their plans. And they must avoid engaging in any activities that resemble military operations. If they are only undertaking projects, they need to make sure they look like projects,*" said the AA chief. If they intend to implement any projects in Rakhine State, the AA chief insisted, *"They must negotiate with us with respect."* He said the AA would support those projects whose owners informed the group in advance of their travel plans within the region. "*If they don't inform us, we will make them,*" he said, "*for security reasons*". Maj-Gen Twan Mrat Naing promised the group would not engage in clashes near the China-Myanmar crude oil and gas pipelines, or the planned Kyaukphyu Special Economic Zone and Belt and Road Initiative projects, because Beijing acknowledged the existence of the AA. "*Sometimes China puts pressure on us in order to maintain stability at its border. That's reasonable. We are fighting the Myanmar military at home. But at the same time we have to maintain good ties with our neighbour, which (who) is much more powerful than we are.*" Chin rebels are opposing this move.	https://www.irrawaddy. com/news/burma/arakan-army-tax-large-projects-myanmars-rakhine-chin-states.html; https://www.rfa.org/english/news/myanmar/arakan-army-seizes-ferry-12312019143635.html; https://nenow.in/neighbour/myanmar/myanmar-chin-rebels-oppose-arakan-armys-paletwa-claim.html

Date	Event	Source
22 Mar 2020	AA took 15 workers from a Paletwa river port construction site in southern Chin State into their custody on 22 March 2020, before releasing them a day later. The AA alleged that the Burma Army had used the site as a point from which to attack them the day before. The workers included seven local labourers and eight Indian nationals working on the Kaladan Project.	https://www.bnionline.net/en/news/arakan-army-detains-then-releases-workers-construction-site-reportedly-used-burma-army-attack
22 Apr 2020	Spokesman Khaine Tukkha recently said, "*China recognises us while India does not*" which explains why AA does not disturb the Chinese deep sea port at Kyaukphyu but kidnaps Indian construction workers involved in the Kaladan project.	https://nenow.in/neighbour/bangladesh/chinese-weapons-for-arakan-army-through-bangladesh.html

Analysis of the incidents and statements reveals a discernible pattern. First, it is evident that the AA is not shy of targeting the Kaladan Project and infrastructure and the Tatmadaw is simply not capable or competent enough to provide the operational levels of security required for the project to function. The AA attacks are well thought out and do not target the workers per se. They are intended to bring operations to a halt. Even if the Tatmadaw provides security during the construction phase, they will not be able to provide security during the operational phase, given the spread of the force and resultant requirement of forces.

Secondly, all statements by the AA C-in-C and the spokesperson suggest that intrinsically the AA is not against the Kaladan Project. In fact, they have conceded that the project is good for the region and usable by the AA and the Arakan people as well.[25] This implies that the AA has the understanding and confidence that the project will eventually benefit its support base. This is one of the major reasons for optimism about the long-term survivability of the project.

Third, the main reason for the attacks on the Kaladan Project are not financial, even though the C-in-C has announced the formation of the taxation authority in the region. The primary reason for the attacks are to get the Indian authorities to engage with the AA, thereby seeking some official recognition, quite like the other EAGs on the East Myanmar border have, with China. India is hesitant to engage with any EAG overtly, especially one that has been declared a terrorist organisation by the legitimate government of Myanmar. But given the stakes in the Kaladan Project, and the fact that the Tatmadaw has totally alienated the local population and is unable to contain the AA, it eventually will have no other choice.

Fourth, the AA understands the geopolitics of the region and has no qualms in playing the India versus China game. Thus, announcing that they will not attack the Kyaukphyu Deep Sea Port is essentially playing to the gallery. However dependent the AA is on Chinese funds and weaponry, they have a nationalist mind and are seized of the Chinese tendency for duplicity. Thus, while China may think they have a lien on the AA, the truth is that the AA is more evolved. It remains to be seen, between the two, who exploits the other more!

Repackaging the Kaladan Project

The Kaladan Project needs to be repackaged to address negative legacy baggage attached to it. Due to the delays and cost overruns, projects such as the Kaladan Project are often viewed with cynicism and pessimism. This negative psychological perception needs to be jettisoned.

The first step is to delink it from Kolkata Port. The two ports in Kolkata and Haldia have very limited intrinsic business opportunities due to labour and draft issues. Thus, linking it exclusively to the Kolkata Port, induces a sense of negativity and pessimism. Even the Indian Ambassador, Mr. Saurabh Kumar, during a recent video conference, alluded to the project as the one which links Kolkata Port to Sittwe Port.[26] The connectivity from Kolkata to Sittwe is incidental and a legacy hangover. The MDONER website mentions this as a footnote, '*The connectivity between mainland India and Sittwe (Myanmar) could as well be with any other port on the Indian coast.*' Thus, this connectivity could as well have been from Visakhapatnam, Chennai, Colombo, Port Klang (Malaysia), Singapore or even Kyaukphyu. Large cargo ships beyond the capability of Sittwe Port could discharge at Kyaukphyu and move to the Inland Water Terminal at Sittwe by road or barges for moving subsequent bulk broken loads to Paletwa via barge and thence to Mizoram.

The second action would be to jettison the mainland (i.e., Delhi) perception to the project that it is only an alternative to the Siliguri Corridor, which will remain the primary route. It needs to be projected as the main and preferred route of goods to northeast and also from Myanmar to India. It should be seen as a measure to decongest the Corridor and provide strategic redundancy. As per an Ernst & Young report quoted by Land-Marine Engineering and Port Solutions LLP, presently the total cargo moving into and out of the northeast via the Corridor is slated to be 49 metric tonnes per annum (MPTA) in addition to 90,000 units of two and four wheelers. Additionally, around 30 MTPA of cargo moves within the northeast which essentially includes agricultural and horticultural commodities. The detailed breakdown is as under:

Movement	*Volume (in MTP)*	*Key Commodities*
Into the North-East	~ 25 MTPA + 90,000 units of automobiles (two and four wheelers)	Household goods, foodgrains, fertilizer raw material, tar coal/ bitumen, imported coal, Pharmaceuticals, iron & steel, fly ash, edible oil and other commodities
Outside the North-East	~24 MTPA	Limestone, silicon, PoL and crude, tea, fertilizers, agricultural & horticulture commodities
Within the North-East	~30 MTPA	Foodgrains, cement & clinker, PoL and crude, domestic coal, fertilizers and other miscellaneous commodities (essentially primary commodities)

Source: Land-Marine Engineering and Port Solutions LLP.

This has a potential of increasing as shown in the following table:

Volumes	*FY2017*	*FY2020*	*FY2023*	*FY2026*	*FY 2029*	*FY 2032*	*FY 2035*	*FY 2038*	*FY 2041*
Foodgrains (in MTPA)	1.55	1.56	1.58	1.59	1.61	1.63	1.65	1.67	1.69
Cement & Clinker (in MTPA)	11.35	14.85	19.4	23.77	30.76	39.4	47.4	59.36	70
Fertilizer & FRM (in MTPA)	0.37	0.41	0.46	0.52	0.57	0.64	0.7	0.77	0.85
Bitumen (in MTPA)	0.63	0.81	1.05	1.37	1.81	2.39	3.18	4.25	5.72
Fly Ash (in MTPA)	1.67	1.75	1.82	1.91	2	2.09	2.18	2.28	2.39
Edible Oil (in MTPA)	0.26	0.28	0.3	0.31	0.33	0.35	0.37	0.39	0.42
Imported Coal (in MTPA)	0.05	0.05	0.05	0.06	0.06	0.06	0.07	0.07	0.07
PoL Products (in MTPA)	0.18	0.21	0.21	0.22	0.2	0.23	0.25	0.27	0.29
Automobiles (in units)	4	5	6	9	12	16	22	30	41
Stone Chips (in MTPA)	17,220	18,007	18,829	19,689	20,589	21,529	22,512	23,541	24,616

Source: Land-Marine Engineering and Port Solutions LLP.

There is a perception amongst some sections of scholars and even government officers that this project is no longer required since it was conceived during the East Pakistan period and confirmed during the Khaleda Zia years when our relations with the Bangladesh Nationalist Party (BNP) were not cordial. Thus, now since relations with Bangladesh are good and the trade links through Bangladesh are underway, this project has lost its utility and is best scrapped to cut losses. This is a tragically myopic view of the opportunities that the project offers, even under the current circumstances. Infrastructural capabilities cannot be built overnight whereas intentions and relations can change overnight. The present crisis with Nepal is a prime example of how intentions and relations can swing adversely in a short time. Thus strategic vulnerabilities like the Siliguri Corridor need strategic redundancies, which cannot be conceived and constructed on the occurance of the crises. It has to be done well before.

In conclusion, it needs to be clearly understood that the Kaladan Project cannot succeed without a 'hearts and minds' approach involving the locals. It is evident that the extreme angst that the locals have against the Myanmar Government and the Tatmadaw, and the influence of the AA will have a massive negative impact on the locals, unless they are made stakeholders. The Tatmadaw does not have the tactical capability or strategic maturity to neutralise the AA and by its atrocities has lost all support of the locals. Thus, while construction has been completed, using the infrastructure, especially the road, will not be possible without a secure environment. A secure environment can only be achieved by involving locals rather than using the Tatmadaw to secure the road. The 268 km of waterways and roadways cannot be secured in a conventional manner without incurring prohibitive costs on security. The Tatmadaw, unfortunately, will possibly not agree to any negotiation with AA, but India will still need to engage with the group.

Ultimately, as of now, India needs the Kaladan Project more than Myanmar.

NOTES

1. B.G. Verghese, '*Proposal for a Road-River link from the Mizo Hills District to Akyab in Burma*', P. N. Haksar Papers, Individual Collection, Instalments I & II, Subject File 36, pp. 241–245. Accessed at Nehru Memorial Museum and Library, New Delhi, India.
2. For an extensive round up of what make the Siliguri Corridor a vulnerability, see Ankit Panda, Geography's Curse: India's Vulnerable 'Chicken's Neck', The Diplomat, 8 Nov 2013, https://thediplomat.com/2013/11/geographys-curse-indias-vulnerable-chickens-neck/. (Accessed on 14 Nov 2019)
3. P. N. Haksar Papers, Individual Collection, Instalments I & II, Subject File 36, pp. 241–245. Accessed at Nehru Memorial Museum and Library, New Delhi, India.
4. Boobli George Verghese was a veteran journalist who had also served in the Prime Minister's Secretariat as Information Advisor to Prime Minister Indira Gandhi (1966–1968), Inder Malhotra, "He Was A Camera," https://www.outlookindia.com/ *Outlook India Magazine*, October 24, 2010, https://www.outlookindia.com/magazine/story/he-was-a-camera/267478, K Natwar Singh, Remembering B G Verghese: Indira Gandhi's 'fine, upright man' and my faithful friend, Mail Online India, 1 Jan 2015, https://www.dailymail.co.uk/indiahome/indianews/article-2893127/Remembering-B-G-Verghese-Indira-Gandhi-s-fine-upright-man-faithful-friend.html and B. G. Verghese, Writings and Commentaries, About the Author, http://www.bgverghese.com/about.htm (Accessed on 21 Feb 2020).

5. Note this was written 21 years after Independence and three years before the liberation of Bangladesh, hence Bangladesh was still East Pakistan.
6. The Commission was first established by the United Nations Economic and Social Council on 28 March 1947 as the United Nations Economic Commission for Asia and the Far East (ECAFE) to assist in post-war economic reconstruction. Its main mandate was to "initiate and participate in measures for facilitating concerted action for the economic reconstruction and development of Asia and the Far East". On 1 August 1974, the Commission was renamed as the Economic and Social Commission for Asia and the Pacific (ESCAP) by the Economic and Social Council to reflect both the economic and social aspects of the Commission's work, as well as geographic location of its members, https://www.quora.com/What-is-the-full-name-of-ECAFE (Accessed on 22 Feb 2020).
7. Framework Agreement between the Government of the Republic of India and the Government of the Union of Myanmar for the Construction and Operation of a Multi-Modal Transit Transport Facility on Kaladan River connecting the Sittwe Port in Myanmar with the State of Mizoram in India. http://www.mea.gov.in/Portal/LegalTreatiesDoc/MM08B0360.pdf (Accessed on 24 February 2020).
8. Archival open source data from MDONER website, https://web.archive.org/web/20111205140603/http://mdoner.gov.in/writereaddata/sublink2images/KaladanMultiModal2172726384.htm (Accessed on 25 February 2020).
9. Quoting status of the information as on 17 October 2008.
10. Ministry of Road Transport and Highways has formulated SARDP—NE for enhancing road facilities in the Northeast region. The objectives of the scheme are up-gradation of national highways connecting State capitals with 2 lane or 4 lane roads; providing connectivity to 88 district headquarter towns of NER by at least a 2-lane road, providing road connectivity to backward and remote areas of NE region to boost socio-economic development; improving roads of strategic importance in border areas and improving connectivity to neighbouring countries, https://lms.indianeconomy.net/glossary/sardp-ne/ (Accessed on 25 February 2020).
11. However, no development of Kolkata was envisaged in this project, despite it being the slated start point for the project.
12. As per the Ministry of Development of the North East Region (MDONER) website which as on date reflects a Status Note of 25 April 2014, https://mdoner.gov.in/infrastructure/kaladan-multi-modal-transit-transport-project-inland (Accessed on 24 February 2020).
13. Embassy of India, Yangon, Myanmar, Press Release: Govt. of India hands over 250 pre-fabricated houses to Govt.of Myanmar (9th July, 2019), https://www.embassyofindiayangon.gov.in/index.php/whats_new?id=eyJpdiI6IjVvK24rYnJGNUhzZjFVU2NvWUU2akE9PSIsInZhbHVlIjoiZnl BcGE2a0 1ZV3pwUjlUVXZFT1J3Zz09IiwibWFjIjoiZThjNmQ3ZmZkYWQwYTZk MjkyNjNjYzU2ODY1MmZjMjlhNDk3ZThlOWIyMjkwNzAwZTFlNjQ4MGEy MjY4ZThmMSJ9 (Accessed on 24 Feb 2020).
14. Rajya Sabha Unstarred Question No. 962, https://www.mea.gov.in/rajya-sabha.htm?dtl/30180/QUESTION+NO+962+FUNDS+FOR+KALADAN+MULTI+MODAL+TRANSIT+TRANSPORT+PROJECT
15. BNI Online, Security issues hamper progress on Kaladan transport project: Indian Ambassador, 27 Jan 2020, https://www.bnionline.net/en/news/security-issues-hamper-progress-kaladan-transport-project-indian-ambassador (Accessed on 27 Jan 2020).
16. In a telephonic interview on 5 May 2020.
17. A to Z Exim, Mumbai, is a part of the Bharat Freight Group, who are also operating Chabahar Port in Iran.
18. Ministry of External Affairs, New Delhi, March 2013, Preparation of Detailed Engineering Project Report for Two Lane Road from Paletwa to Zorinpui (India-Myanmar Border) in Chin State of Myanmar, Detailed Project Report IRCON Infrastructure & Services Limited

VOLUME IV: ENVIRONMENTAL IMPACT ASSESSMENT REPORT http://mea.gov.in/Images/attach/EIA_Report.pdf (Accessed on 27 Jan 2020).

19. Pratim Ranjan Bose, India starts construction of 1,600-cr Mizoram-Myanmar Kaladan road, The Hindu Business Line, 17 Apr 2018, https://www.thehindubusinessline.com/news/india-starts-construction-of-1600-cr-mizoram-myanmar-kaladan-road/article23577107.ece (Accessed on 27 Jan 2020).
20. Government of Mizoram, Economic Survey 2019 – 2020, https://planning.mizoram.gov.in/uploads/attachments/4d6a424cb421f1fafef5c29cb0068b83/economic-survey-2019-20.pdf (Accessed on 27 Jan 2020).
21. Preparatory Study for Road Network Improvement in North-East States of India, https://www.jica.go.jp/english/our_work/social_environmental/id/asia/south/india/c8h0vm00009ijqki-att/c8h0vm00009pa853.pdf (Accessed on 27 Jan 2020).
22. Sudha Ramachandran, The Trouble With India's Projects in Myanmar, *The Diplomat*, 21 Sep 2016, https://thediplomat.com/2016/09/the-trouble-with-indias-projects-in-myanmar/ (Accessed on 27 Jan 2020).
23. Online Burma/Myanmar Library, Kaladan Movement, The Kaladan Project in India and Burma: Transparency and local benefits essential, say activists, https://www.burmalibrary.org/en/one-cannot-step-into-the-same-river-twice-making-the-kaladan-project-people-centred (Accessed on 27 Jan 2020).
24. Institute of Social Sciences & Burma Centre Delhi, India-Myanmar Relations Looking from the Border Conference Report 28 -29 September 2015 New Delhi, India, https://in.boell.org/sites/default/files/india-myanmar_relations_looking_from_the_border.pdf (Accessed on 27 Jan 2020).
25. Sadiq Naqvi, Act-East Inaction: When Will Kaladan Multi-Modal Transport Project Be Complete?, Outlook, 2 Mar 2020, https://www.outlookindia.com/magazine/story/act-east-inaction-when-will-kaladan-multi-modal-transport-project-be-complete/302827 (Accessed on 27 Jun 2020).
26. During an Interactive Video Conference on *India-Myanmar Business Promotion Challenges and Opportunities—Post COVID-19,* on 9 June 2020, organised by Punjab Haryana & Delhi (PHD) Chamber of Commerce and Industry along with the India-Myanmar Chamber of Commerce.

CHAPTER 6
Myanmar and India's Northeast

Southeast Asia begins from Northeast India, and South Asia begins in Myanmar.[1]

India's Northeastern states comprise the proverbial 'seven sisters and one brother', namely, Arunachal Pradesh, Assam, Manipur, Meghalaya, Mizoram, Nagaland, Tripura and the one brother being Sikkim. If we add West Bengal to the mix, it completes the picture despite West Bengal technically not being part of Northeast India. The eight Northeastern states are spread over an area of 262,185 sq km which is nearly 8 per cent of the total geographical area of the country. The region has a long international border of 5,182 km which is more than 99 per cent of its total geographical boundary.

The states share international borders with Bangladesh (1,596 km), Bhutan (455 km), Myanmar (1,640 km), Nepal (97 km) and China (1,395 km).[2] Geographically, with China falling to the north of the Himalayas, the rest of the areas comprise a distinct geographic entity, referred to as a compact "geo space" in Eastern South Asia.[3]

Insurgency *per se* thrives due the different terrain, porous borders, support of the local population and external support, in varying degrees. The Northeast used to provide almost all these factors, thereby propagating insurgent movements. With an improvement in governance and peace accords between insurgent groups and the government, local support to most of the insurgencies has waned. However, the terrain and the porous IMB was still a major factor in the survival of these insurgent groups. The recent coordinated operations of the Indian Army with the

Figure 6.1: Myanmar and India's Northeast

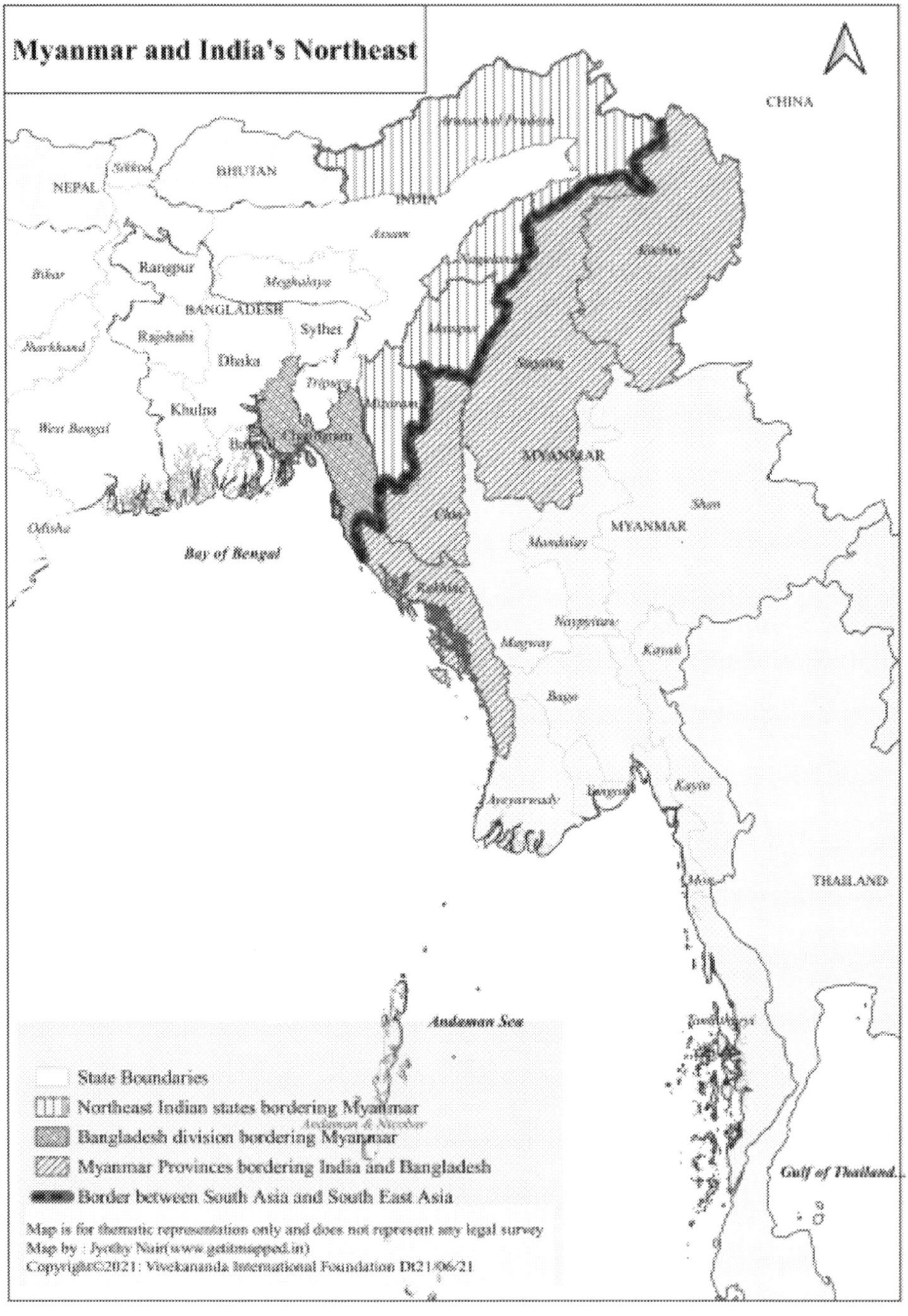

Tatmadaw called 'Operation Sunrise I and II' have also changed that constant. Since the Northeast has borders with Bangladesh, Bhutan, China and Nepal, apart from Myanmar, a quick comparison between them is called for. Bhutan used to be the chosen harbour for the ULFA and other Assam-based insurgent groups till the Bhutan Army launched 'Operation All Clear' in December 2003 and January 2004. Since then, local insurgents have moved across to Bhutan from time to time but not in the large scale it was earlier. Similarly, Bangladesh as a base for insurgents was also nullified with the improvement in Bangladesh-India relations and security cooperation. Insurgent access to the China border is limited in the Northeast due to the extremely rough and often snowbound terrain. Nepal, as a choice for a base, was also limited since there was not much support base there and India-Nepal relations precluded any major advantage to the insurgent groups. In fact, several extractions of insurgents from these countries were, in the absence of extradition treaties, simply carried out by security forces with the final apprehension of the individual being revealed as having been done in India.[4] With the present loss of the safe haven in Myanmar, the insurgent groups have been floundering. However, insurgency is only one way in which Myanmar impacts the Northeastern states. Myanmar also provides the Northeast an access to its markets and to the ASEAN markets. It provides opportunities which till date have not really been exploited, except in the negative sense. On that count, a brief state-wise analysis is in order.

Arunachal Pradesh, the northern-most of the IMB states, is also the least connected to its eastern neighbour i.e., Kachin and Sagaing provinces. Hostile terrain, lack of traditional connectivity and a longer and more volatile border with China in the north, ensures that the focus remains northbound. The opportunity to connect with Myanmar exists over two axes; one along the Stilwell Road[5] and the second along the Vijaynagar axis towards Puta-O.

Relatively, Nagaland is better connected to the Naga Self-Administered Zone (see Figure 1.6) of Sagaing Region due to similarities in ethnicity and language. However, even here there are very few institutionalised events both at the provincial and national levels from both countries. Hence, potentials remain potential and fodder for analysts and critics.

Manipur has a more active history of interactions with the Sagaing and Chin provinces, possibly due to the availability of a major axis, i.e., the Moreh-Tamu axis. Thus, there have been occasional friendly matches and visits by dignitaries on either sides. However, this relationship is yet to mature into the cooperation stage.

Mizoram has the maximum potential of engagement with Chin State with two axes, one operational (Zokhathwar–Rhi) and one under development, i.e., the Zorinpui Axis. Linkage-wise, the relationship of the present CM, Mr. Zoramthanga, with Chin and Rakhine nationals is intimate and has the potential for developing into a strong relationship.

Field Visit: Mizoram

This chapter draws upon a field visit to Mizoram[6] conducted by the author on behalf of the VIF for the purpose of this Fellowship. The field visit was conducted with a number of aims including; to assess the importance of the Northeastern States in India-Myanmar relations;[7] to assess the influence of Mizoram in the Rakhine conflict with specific reference to the AA, and vice versa; to assess the impact of the Kaladan Project on the Northeast, especially Mizoram; to see on the ground the state of progress of the Kaladan Project in Mizoram and, finally, keeping all these in mind, generate policy recommendations for implementation. It also draws on interactions with various vendors involved in the Kaladan Project. The initial plan for the Fellowship had been to visit all the four Northeastern states on the IMB, but time constraints and COVID-19 put paid to the plan. Hence, the scope of the first aim (to assess the importance of the Northeastern states in India-Myanmar relations) had to be curtailed to assess the importance of Mizoram in India-Myanmar relations.

This chapter dwells on the connect between the Northeast and Myanmar and drives home the argument that any engagement with Myanmar must take into account the genuine sentiments of the people of the Northeast. It highlights the ethnic linkages and dynamics between the AA and the Mizo people, and brings out the need for caution in India's handling of the Rakhine conflict. This chapter proposes a five-pronged strategy to handle the change that Mizoram is going to undergo with the commissioning of the Kaladan Project, to ensure optimum utilisation of the project for local and national benefits. **Firstly**, it goes without saying that peace is a primary prerequisite for long-term development of the region, and this includes the neighbouring regions of Chin and Rakhine. India must sue for peace between the belligerents, i.e., the AA and the Tatmadaw, to safeguard its interests both with reference to the Kaladan Project and also in Mizoram intrinsically. **Secondly**, the local and national thought process towards the Kaladan Project must change for the better. These changes involve making the project agnostic of the Kolkata Port. This has been covered in detail in the chapter on the Kaladan Project. **Thirdly**, development of the India-Myanmar border region on **both** sides of the border is critical for regional development. While this is already underway under the Myanmar India Border Area Development Project, this needs to be augmented and coordinated with security forces on the ground for optimal utilisation. Thus provision of Internet services to the border areas in Myanmar, banking and medical facilities, and even FM local radio stations operating from India and transmitting into Myanmar, will go a long way in ensuring psychological development of the area. **Finally**, the political environment along the IMB and in Mizoram is sensitive and comprises a large number of players such as the State Government, the political parties, the CSOs and also the Church. The sensitivities manifest in many forms and the '*Hello China, Bye Bye India*' banners incident was one such unfortunate and misplaced manifestation which found itself on display in January 2019 during a protest against the Citizenship Amendment Bill 2019. "*There is a strong feeling among us Mizos that India does not listen to us, does not care for us, and favours illegal migrants over us*," said Ricky Lalbiakmawia, the finance secretary of the Northeast Students' Organisation, an umbrella body of students' organisations in the region, which organised the protest.[8]

Out of the four IMB states, Mizoram was prioritised for the field visit since it is the one in the Bangladesh-India-Myanmar trijunction which will bear the impact of the Kaladan Project. Also, the ethnic and historical linkages of the Mizo people are closely tied to their counterparts in the violence-ridden Chin and Rakhine states. Mizoram has two international borders (with Myanmar to the east and south and Bangladesh to the west) and three borders with the other Northeastern Indian states, namely Assam, Manipur and Tripura. It first became a Union Territory in 1972 and then a full state in 1987 when peace was restored after two decades of insurgency. Kirsten McConnachie expounds[9] that like other border lands, Mizoram is simultaneously a space of international connection and of highly localized differentiation of identities and entitlements. Mizoram and Chin are small and ethnically distinct sub-states that have considerably more in common with each other than India and Myanmar. McConnachie adds that strong historical, cultural and ethnic connections between Chin and Mizo might suggest that those arriving would easily integrate into Mizoram, based on the connections between the two states. This has been true to some extent but the reception of Chin in Mizoram has also been shaped by their perception of being outsiders. They have been resented, rejected and blamed for a host of social problems, including the production and sale of alcohol and drugs. On several occasions, low-level resentment has escalated to mass push-back across the border to

Myanmar. She adds that alongside these processes of 'othering' is an understanding that recognizes the Chin as co-ethnics and kin—a discourse that, in Mizoram, is often framed around pan-ethnic identity, commonly Zo. This discourse exists as a counterpoint to prejudice and scapegoating and has arguably afforded the Chin a unique status in Mizoram, as outsiders who simultaneously have a claim to belonging.

Mizo Insurgency and the Arakan Connect

In 1955, in Mizoram, *mautam* (famine) broke out, caused by the profuse flowering of a thorny bamboo which occurs at intervals of 40 to 50 years. When the bamboo flowers, the rats gorge themselves on the bamboo seeds, multiply and then destroy all crops, thus causing famine. The fallout of the *mautam* ignited passions in the Mizo Hills in the mid-1960s against the Assam Government and the leadership of the Mizo District Council. The Mizo National Famine Front (MNFF) formed by some former Mizo soldiers of the Indian and the Burmese armies including Laldenga, became active, but after the relief operations, it dropped the word 'Famine' and became a political party: the Mizo National Front (MNF). On 28 February 1966, the MNF unleashed 'Operation Jericho'—a blitzkrieg rebellion that led to the capture of as many as 11 towns in the Mizo Hills by the rebels. The Indian Army had to organize one of the most comprehensive counter-insurgency operations it has ever undertaken to take back the towns and semi-urban townships in the Mizo Hills—an operation that took more than a month and saw some bitter fighting. As the Army regained control of the towns, eventually the leadership escaped into pre-selected locations in East Pakistan. Thus, here we find the first of the transborder linkages of Mizoram. By 1968, the MNF had allied with a 'fraternal guerrilla organisation', the Arakan National Liberation Front, which proved invaluable subsequently when the Bangladesh War of 1971 adversely affected the MNF since their bases in East Pakistan and access routes were neutralized by the Indian Army incursions into East Pakistan. This was followed up by a military coup in independent Bangladesh, which saw the Chakma Shanti Bahini in the Chittagong Hill Tracts, backed by India, keen to avenge the ill-treatment the MNF had meted out to the Chakmas in Mizoram. Subsequently, allegedly Indian intelligence maintained hideouts and arms caches in Arunachal Pradesh, Nagaland, Manipur and Mizoram for the KIA, the AA and the Chin National Front of Burma to dislodge the MNF and other rebel groups in Burmese territory.

Former insurgent and present Indian CM of Mizoram, Pu Zoramthanga himself said[10] in an interview that, "*In 1969, I became secretary to MNF president Laldenga. I was then 25 years old. We were all in Chittagong. During the war, we escaped to Arakan hills (in Myanmar) before reaching West Pakistan. It was a James Bond-type escape. The director-general of the ISI later told us in Islamabad that they couldn't imagine how we had managed to escape. Many Pakistani army personnel were killed, caught and imprisoned. We joined a group of refugees and somehow reached the Akyab (now called Sittwe), a famous port.*"

Journalist Subir Bhaumik in his book, *The Troubled Periphery*, describes the above event and says that Bangladesh's military rulers started providing shelter to the rebels from Northeast India in 1978, three years after India started training and arming the Chakma Shanti Bahini. And the MNF was the first to set up camps in the CHT after the birth of Bangladesh. In 1971, they fled after Indian troops and the Mukti Fauj swept into Bangladesh. The MNF leadership, including Laldenga, travelled down the Karnaphuli River to Burma's Arakan province, where Pakistani intelligence officials operating under consular cover in Burma provided them with false travel documents and flew them out to Karachi. Laldenga and his wife travelled under the false name of Mr. and Mrs. Zolkeps.[11] The Arakan and Mizo connect is also mentioned in another book by the same author, i.e., *Insurgent Crossfire* in which the author alludes to Laldenga's proposal of sending his ADC, Tony Tawnluia, to the MNF headquarters in Arakan to initiate talks with the Indian Government.[12]

T. S. Letkhosei Haokip corroborates Bhaumik and reveals much more when he writes:[13]

> *...it is important to state that the main Kuki Chin armed group was the Mizo National Front (MNF) led most of the time by Laldenga. MNF was not only related to Chins but was also active with Burma. In 1966 MNF troops attacked Falam. Again in 1971, MNF joined with CPB troops [and] occupied Rathedaung town. It was also active in the north Arakan, together with CPB.... The relationship of MNF and China lasted till the end of (the) 1970s. Then MNF returned to Burma because of the Liberation of Bangladesh. In 1973,...*

This suggests that MNF raids into Myanmar in conjunction with the local EAGs was a norm at that time and would have probably had reciprocal support as well. Just how thick the present ties are is evident from the AA apprehension of the Chin NLD MPU Whei Tin by the AA. He was held in captivity for 79 days and released at the behest of CM Zoramthanga. The AA said U Whei Tin was released to ensure a sustainable relationship between the Rakhine and Khumi communities and to rebuild trust and friendship. Till 10 January 2020, the AA had insisted on keeping him in detention, saying the group had security concerns if he was released. "*The Rakhine and Khumi are like brothers, living in harmony with understanding and trust. We want to rebuild trust and friendship between the two communities, and reconciliation in the long term, so we decided to release U Whei Tin at a safe place in Paletwa on Jan. 21,*" said the AA's statement. U Whei Tin had been abducted on 3 November 2020.[14] It was later revealed in an interview given by CM Zoramthanga to Subir Bhaumik, presently Director of Eastern Link, an East and Northeast India, Bangladesh and Myanmar-related news and analysis portal, that CM Zoramthanga, at the initiative of the Government of India and Myanmar, had approached the AA and secured the release of the MP. "*The Myanmar government had given him up for dead. They requested me to do something. I contacted my friends in the Arakan Army and they said we cannot refuse you*", Zoramthanga said.[15] After the release, he promptly wrote a letter thanking all "*beneficial stakeholders*" highlighting the fact that "*considering the crucial political situation of the region and the fact that he* (the NLD MP) *belongs to Khumi tribe of Chin State, Myanmar who are considered to be an integral part of the Mizo tribes*'.

Zoramthanga followed up the release with an appreciation letter which gave out valuable clues as to the extent of the Mizo connect.

Figure 6.2: MP U Hwei Ting, NLD MP from Chin State, with the letter after his release.

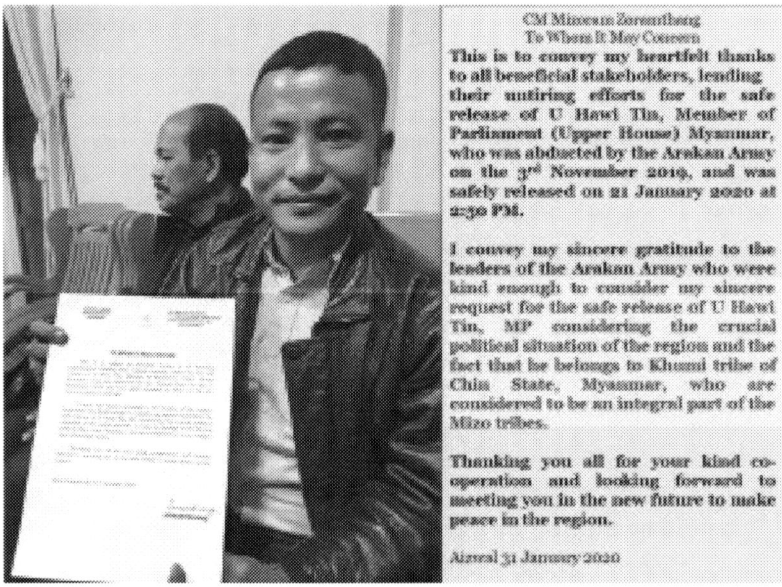

Source: Anonymous Contributor

Further, the presence of AA operatives in Mizoram working for their cause against the Myanmar Government has for long been an open secret. After what was possibly a covert operation by security forces to neutralise AA representatives in Mizoram on 7 October 2019, the AA uncharacteristically tweeted in protest "*At 1:00 am (India time), on 6 October 2019, seven armed masked persons broke down the entrance door of (a) house in Lawntlai Town, Mizoram, India and held a number of ULA/AA members under siege. The armed masked persons then abducted those ULA/AA members, and (away) took documents, a computer, some money and some phones from the house.*" The tweet was later deleted. This inadvertently gave out what everyone always knew. Currently, six AA cadres are in jail in Lawntlai.[16]

That the AA has support in Mizoram is an understatement. There seems to be institutional support as evidenced during 'Operation Sunrise II', the coordinated operation conducted by the Indian Army in collaboration with the Myanmar Armed Forces. Protests were lodged by the Mizoram State Government against the deployment of the Army and the rounding up of people by the Army, ostensibly for screening and briefing.[17] Mrinal Talukdar writes that the AA had also occupied a number of camps in Mizoram along the border to stay out of the reach of the Myanmar Army.[18]

The major conclusion that comes to the fore as a result of this study is that for any Indian intervention in the Rakhine conflict, the Mizoram angle will have to be factored in. This is especially relevant in light of the fact that certain observers have drawn comparisons with the AA and the Sri Lankan Tamil terror group, the Liberation Tigers of Tamil Eelam (LTTE). And in that light are seeing the Myanmar Army 'doing a Jayawardene' (the Sri Lankan PM) to get the Indian Army sucked into their own war. Bhaumik concludes that '*Just like Jayawardene trapped India into the Jaffna conflict by getting Rajiv Gandhi to guarantee the implementation of the Sri Lanka peace accord in 1987, the Burmese military-dominated administration of Myanmar is using India's Kaladan Multimodal project in Rakhine and Chin state to get Delhi involved in its own offensive against the Arakan Army*'. However, India must note that what Tamil Nadu was to the LTTE, in some way, is what Mizoram is to the AA. The corollary to this is that the Mizo connect provides an excellent opportunity for India to reach out to the AA on a positive note. This is likely to cause angst to the Myanmar Government, but that may have to be endured and mollified diplomatically.

Impact of the Kaladan Project on Mizoram

The Kaladan Project culminates at Mizoram or originates there, depending on whether it is seen from the perspective of an exporter or an importer. It enters

Mizoram at Zorinpui and from there moves north to Lawngtlai. Mizoram has maximum stakes and can make or break the project and hence must be incorporated into the scheme of things.

Post statehood and the signing of the Mizo Accord, most of the Mizos have by and large had it good. Apparently over 95 per cent of the entire state population is privileged, educated and used to institutionalised subsidies, being from the scheduled reserved categories. As a result, they are exempted from paying most taxes and even Tax Deducted at Source (TDS) for bank deposits are not collected since the state-wide protest organised by the locals against it in March 2019.[19] Consequently, the State Government is denied this revenue source and in fact is dependent on the Central Government for most of its budget. The 'small state mentality' results in a situation where the bulk of the working population is Government staff. Allegedly 25 per cent of this population is directly dependent on government service. In fact, as per one rather pessimistic school of thought, the recent creation of three new districts[20] is likely to create more jobs than provide any significant administrative benefits to the state.

On the income side, the three biggest contributors to the state GSDP are agriculture, public administration (i.e., government service) and infrastructure creation-related construction work. Approximately 60 per cent of the population is engaged in agriculture which contributes only 20 per cent of the GSDP. This results in a situation wherein 20 per cent of the state's staple, i.e., rice, is home-grown. The rest is imported from other states. The traditional xenophobic nature of the locals also resists developmental activity and hence industries such as tourism suffer. The annual budget of the state for the FY 2019-20 was ₹ 10,692.30 crores, of which ₹ 8,403.52 crores was spent on salaries, pensions and government establishment costs. The capital expenditure of ₹ 2,288.78 crores was towards development works and creation of infrastructure and assets. Due to unrealistic tariff regulations,[21] smuggling is a cottage industry wherein a section of the population indulges in various facets of the activity, either directly or indirectly. These include organised syndicates for transport, labour management and even warehousing of smuggled cargo.

In such a relatively secure and secluded environment, the Kaladan Project is likely to disrupt life in a big way. And thus the impact of the Kaladan Project has to be managed well so as to take all the stakeholders along, especially the impacted locals. Crystal ball gazing suggests that the Kaladan Project may end up spawning one of the largest logistics hubs in Northeast India. The Land Customs Station at Zorinpui is already sanctioned, but may need to be scaled up to include container ports, transport hubs and repair facilities. On an optimistic note, a SEZ could also be planned for South Mizoram.

While seeing everything from a security perspective is undesirable, the above-mentioned facilities would, however, have serious security constraints for which the planning and manning processes should commence now itself so as to meet the deadline. Presently, smuggling is well organised with unions and jurisdictions where several notables are stakeholders including civil society organisations. The popularity of smuggling has increased manifold ever since the December 2015 change from barter to normal trade and from border trade to normal trade. This has resulted in a duty increase from 4 per cent to 40 per cent in the case of areca nut which is the primary import into India. Compliance dropped drastically. Added to this is the complex documentation procedures. The number of documents required for import and export include multiple copies of the challan, shipping bill for export of goods, commercial invoices, packing lists, certificate of origin and consignment bill while for export it is Form TR-6 (Challan), declaration, bill of lading, invoice, packing list and bill of entry for home consumption. In all, these can run up to dozens of pages to be filled. Overall state policing is weak and the Assam Rifles, which is responsible for the IMB, does not have policing powers. Thus, seizures are handed over to the state police who ensure no convictions take place. Both issues can be addressed by policy making on tariffs and providing policing powers to Assam Rifles (after reorganising and training and them for policing duties).

Importance of the Church in Mizoram Politics

Bhaumik explains that the MNF was very serious about its Christian identity, about fostering religiosity in the rank and file. Senior leaders like Zoramthanga, then MNF vice-president (and now CM of Mizoram), personally conducted church services in the rebel camps and many MNF leaders, like Malswamma Colney, became preachers after their return to normal life. Consumption of alcohol and drugs, so easily available in the Northeast because of its proximity to Burma's infamous Golden Triangle, were strictly prohibited among the guerrillas.

MNF chief Laldenga, however, after becoming CM, snubbed the church leaders when they started pressurizing his government to enforce total prohibition. Laldenga was loath to lose one of the most important sources of revenue for his government. The Congress was quick to take advantage. To secure the support of the Church, it proclaimed in its election manifesto that it was committed to the promotion of 'Christian socialism' in Mizoram. The MNF was defeated in the ensuing elections in 1989 because the Church went against it and backed the Congress. After Laldenga's death, Zoramthanga took over as party president and repaired the MNF's relations with the Church. He assured the Church leaders of his commitment to continue with the prohibition imposed by the Congress Government. The MNF regained the support of the Church leaders and that helped it win two successive elections.[22]

Recommendations

Mizoram has the potential for developing its horticulture and services sectors as the present economy is 60 per cent dependent on the service sector, and only 21 per cent on industry (secondary sector). The potential for manufacturing is in the handloom, handicrafts and paper industries. The State has also developed a new land-use policy which will have cluster-based development. The production of rubber and palm oil can be taken up in a big way in the State. Due to its abundance of bamboo cultivation, there is a big potential for the paper industry in the State. The State also has a potential cultivation of grapes, banana, large cardamom, ginger, pineapple and other horticulture products but the marketing chain has stymied its growth.

To exploit these opportunities, there is a need to reorient national and regional thought process to the Kaladan Project. Fast-paced development in the State is necessary, but overkill has to be guarded against, especially with regard to its impact on ecology. Regional development is an essential to wean away the population from sops and freebies. However, local sentiments and stakes (Church) must be taken into account. Differences in ethnicity must be factored in, e.g., Chakma region of Parva has different dynamics and is hence presently the only BJP seat in Mizoram.[23]

The role of the Assam Rifles needs to be augmented for better border management. Thus, policing roles, if given to the Assam Rifles, needs to be supplemented with adequate preparation and restructuring of the battalions. One model would be to identify the skills lacking for the role and train additional troops and attach them as accretions or bricks to the existing units. The skill sets required would be to enable preparation and filing of charge sheets and FIRs, appointment of investigating officers to take the cases forward, dedicated attachment of magistrates to provide the necessary judicial cover for the operations being conducted and other necessary legal and administrative support. On the technical side, the units would have to be re-equipped to enable search for contraband including full-body scanners, sniffer dogs and similar assets.

Figure 6.3: Map of the three ADCs in Mizoram

Source: Chakmaland.blogspot.com[24]

Mizoram has three Autonomous District Councils (ADC) which cover the southern part of Mizoram bordering Myanmar. These include the Chakma, Lai and Mara ADCs. Southern Mizoram has very distinct features from the rest of Mizoram. Partly due to demographic differences, e. g., and the Chakma population and partly due to the isolated nature of the place, the local ethos is apparently more nationalistic than other parts of Mizoram.

This provides opportunities for better implementation of national schemes. This author was pleasantly surprised to note the implementation of a large number of Central Government schemes in the remotest villages in Mizoram. In fact all the village scapes in Mizoram are changing with the addition of mobile towers. This has been a game changer. Though at many places these are operational for only a few hours a day, depending on the availability of diesel to run the generators, those few hours provide immense utility to the locals. Given the porous nature of the border and the impracticality of trying to man every inch of it, it stands to logic that the locals are incorporated into the security structure.

Figure 6.4: Mobile towers adorn the village scape in Mizoram

Figure 6.5: Pradhan Mantri Gram Sadak Yojana at the southern tip of Mizoram

Figure 6.6: Swachh Bharat and Pradhan Mantri Sahaj Bijli Har Ghar Yojana at Bandukbanga village in Mizoram

The Bangladesh, India and Myanmar trijunction has been described in detail in Chapter 1. This is one of the remotest areas in the country and can be developed as a tourism hotspot. Presently, the trijunction can only be reached on foot and that too after a two-day walk. However, after the construction of a motorable road, the opening up of this place to international tourism would generate dividends and create local employment opportunities. The development of local industry, especially in the agricultural and food processing sectors is imperative. Pineapple farming is a local specialisation which has tremendous scope for development. At the strategic level, the extension of the railway line till Zorinpui initially and later, into Myanmar till Sittwe, can be considered for better and faster movement of good and travellers.

A major disparity is likely to occur with the development of Mizoram with their Chin cousins in Myanmar. This disparity is likely to cause inbound movement of locals, either as refugees or for access to amenities. One solution would be to work on the development of the India-Myanmar Border Region and treat the FMR limit like an extension of our own country from the development perspective to reduce the refugee problem. To this effect, the India-Myanmar Border Area Development Plan is an excellent initiative and India, in partnership with the Myanmar Ministry of Border Affairs, can implement the MOU on Border Area Development. India has extended infrastructure and micro-economic development assistance through grant-in-aid of US$ 5 million each year for five years.[25] Under this, 43 schools, 18 health centres and 51 bridges and roads have been constructed over the last three years in Chin State and Naga Self-Administered Zone of Myanmar.[26] More so, 28 additional projects[27] under the fourth year's tranche of assistance of US$ 5 million, will be implemented in 2020-21.[28] The next level of development in the region under this same head needs a large infusion of funds to be expended in consultation with the security forces on the ground on the IMB. It is for consideration that Indian Embassy staff be posted across the border in easy reach of the security forces on the ground for coordination, for example, at Tamu or Rhi or even further south. The BADP should also deploy funds and conduct development programmes astride the alignment of the Zorinpui–Paletwa Kaladan road to offset any grievance that locals may perceive due to the construction of the road say, due to loss of land.

To conclude, the bottom line would be to prepare the ground for the impact of the Kaladan Project to ensure that the interests and sensibilities of all the stakeholders are incorporated into the system. The underlying factor would be to ensure that local resentments do not give rise to resistance and, in a worst case scenario, fresh and future insurgencies. Simply assuming that the Kaladan Project is a silver bullet which will transform the Northeast would be simplistic and misleading. A well-managed project will reap dividends, but a mismanaged one can create chaos.

NOTES

1. Mirza Zulfiqur Rahman, "*Myanmar's Bid for SAARC Membership*", Institute of Peace and Conflict Studies, New Delhi, 3 Feb 2009: http://www.ipcs.org/comm_select.php?article No=2797 (Accessed on 16 May 2020).
2. Page 7, https://icrier.org/pdf/India_Myanmar_Border_Trade.pdf
3. The Asian Confluence, a Meghalaya-based think tank which "*initiates, stimulates and accelerates revival of the shared civilizational values between the peoples of India and South East and East Asia*" generated a report on Transforming Geo Spaces. Research Report: Transforming Geo Spaces, https://www.asianconfluence.org/publication-details-full/research-report-transforming-geo-spaces (Accessed on 16 May 2020).
4. Biju Kumar Deka, Returning Home after 44 years, Freed UNLF Chief RK Meghen Says He is Ready to Give His Life for Manipur, News18India, 28 Nov 2019, https://www.news18.com/news/india/will-give-my-life-for-people-of-manipur-says-freed-unlf-chief-rk-meghen-after-returning-home-2404641.html
5. Chapter 14 has a detailed analysis of the Stilwell Road.
6. The visit was conducted from 29 February to 6 March 2020 and involved visits to Aizawl, Champai, Zokhathwar, Lunglei, Lawngtlai, Zorinpui, Parva and Bandukbanga.
7. Due to Covid-19 and paucity of time, this aim had to be reduced to understand the impact of Myanmar on Mizoram.
8. Arunabh Saikia, Hello China, Bye Bye India': In Mizoram, students are protesting against Citizenship Bill, Scroll.in, 24 Jan 2019, https://scroll.in/article/910659/hello-china-bye-bye-india-in-mizoram-students-are-protesting-against-citizenship-bill (Accessed on 20 Jan 2020).
9. Kirsten McConnachie, 'Boundaries and Belonging in the Indo-Myanmar Borderlands: Chin Refugees in Mizoram, *Journal of Refugee Studies*, Oxford University Press, 2018, pg. 2, https://academic.oup.com/jrs/advance-article-abstract/doi/10.1093/jrs/fey012/4934132 (Accessed on 20 Jan 2020).
10. Shantanu Nandan Sharma, Zoramthanga: From being an insurgent to becoming Mizoram CM, Economic Times Prime, 16 Dec 2018, https://economictimes.indiatimes.com/news/elections/assembly-elections/mizoram-assembly-elections/zoramthanga-from-being-an-insurgent-to-becoming-mizoram-cm/articleshow/67109534.cms?utm_source=contentofinterest&utm_medium=text&utm_campaign=cppst (Accessed on 20 Jan 2020).
11. Subir Bhaumik, *Troubled Periphery, Crisis of India's Northeast,* Sage India, 2009, pg. 168.
12. Subir Bhaumik, *Insurgent Crossfire, North East India,* Lancer, 2008, pg. 176.
13. T. S. Letkhosei Haokip, *Ethnicity and Insurgency in Myanmar/Burma: A Comparative Study of the Kuki-Chin and Karen Insurgencies,* Educreation Publishing, New Delhi, 2018, pg. 118.
14. Zarni Mann, Arakan Army Releases Myanmar MP Held Since November, The Irrawaddy, 21 Jan 2020, https://www.irrawaddy.com/news/burma/arakan-army-releases-myanmar-mp-held-since-november.html (Accessed on 27 Jan 2020).
15. Subir Bhaumik, Zoramthanga gets National League for Democracy MP from Myanmar released from Arakan Army's captivity, 29 Jan 2020, https://nenow.in/north-east-news/mizoram/zoramthanga-got-nld-mp-released.html (Accessed on 27 Jun 2020).
16. NE Now News, 12 Myanmar nationals arrested during lockdown, over 50 foreign national

detained in Mizoram, 18 Apr 2020, https://nenow.in/north-east-news/mizoram/12-myanmar-nationals-arrested-during-lockdown-over-50-foreign-national-detained-in-mizoram.html (Accessed on 15 May 2020).

17. https://thediplomat.com/2019/03/india-deploys-the-army-to-check-rebel-refugee-influx-from-myanmar/
18. https://www.eastmojo.com/in-depth/2019/06/20/operation-sunrise-more-geopolitics-less-army-offensive
19. https://www.eastmojo.com/mizoram/2019/03/22/mizoram-sbi-reverses-decision-on-tds-deduction-from-bank-deposits and https://www.eastmojo.com/news/2019/03/18/mizo-civil-society-group-threatens-indefinite-strike-against-sbi
20. https://www.telegraphindia.com/north-east/mizoram-to-get-three-new-districts-soon/cid/1685957
21. By the year 2016-16, adequate banking presence was in place to support normal trade with Myanmar at the border and the Reserve Bank of India, in consultation with the Government of India, decided to do away with the barter system of trade at the India-Myanmar border and switch over completely to normal trade with effect from 1 December 2015.
22. *Troubled Periphery*. pp. 47-48.
23. https://en.wikipedia.org/wiki/2018_Mizoram_Legislative_Assembly_election
24. Mizoram Dist Map and ADC May, http://2.bp.blogspot.com/-P5RM8saUwt8/VNkfdXBKa_I/AAAAAAAAAAw/liHLxgfevdM/s1600/4.Mizoram%2BDistrict%2BMap%2B%26%2BADC%2BMap2.jpg (Accessed on 20 Mar 2020).
25. Ministry of External Affairs, India-Myanmar Relations, https://www.mea.gov.in/Portal/ForeignRelation/India-Myanmar_Relations.pdf
26. The Wire, India Extends $5 Million Aid to Myanmar for Border Development Projects, 27 Nov 2018, https://thewire.in/diplomacy/india-extends-5-million-aid-to-myanmar-for-border-development-projects (Accessed on 20 Mar 2020).
27. This includes 20 roads and bridges, 7 schools and 1 infrastructure project.
28. Ministry of External Affairs, India-Myanmar Joint Statement during the State Visit of the President of Myanmar to India (February 26-29, 2020), https://mea.gov.in/bilateral-documents.htm?dtl/32435/IndiaMyanmar+Joint+Statement+during+the+State+Visit+of+the+President+of+ Myanmar+to+India+February+2629+2020, Para 8 (Accessed on 20 Mar 2020).

CHAPTER 7
The Rakhine Conflicts

Arakan, the present-day Rakhine State, represents the post-colonial failures of Myanmar in microcosm: ethnic conflict, political impasse, militarisation, economic neglect and the marginalisation of local peoples.

—Martin Smith[1]

Overview

The Rakhine conflicts cumulatively comprise two distinct conflicts covering three nations, two states in Myanmar (the Rakhine and Chin states), and one each in Bangladesh (Chittagong) and India (Mizoram). The first is with the Arakan Rohingya Salvation Army (ARSA) which ostensibly triggered the well-known Rohingya crisis which was an outcome of the violent and systemic overreaction by the Tatmadaw to the ARSA attacks. The second conflict is with the ethnic Buddhist Rakhine nationalists, i.e., the Arakan people, who are being represented by the AA and its political wing, the ULA. The areas impacted by these two conflicts are adjoining and at places overlapping each other. The former afflicts three of the northern-most townships of Rakhine State, viz., Maungdaw, Buthidaung and Rathedaung townships, while the AA operates in the rest of Rakhine State till Kyaukphyu district in Central Rakhine. While both are ethnically and socially averse to each other, and protest when they are clubbed together, evidence suggests that there is a covert *modus vivendi* between them, to counter their common enemy, the Tatmadaw.[2]

Martin Smith describes[3] the '*tri-border region between Myanmar, India and Bangladesh*', as a place where a diversity of ethnic nationality movements have continued to engage in struggles on different sides of the post-colonial frontiers.

He classifies the region as a '*Regional Conflict Complex*', which identifies the concept of a regional relationship of separate conflict situations that impact each other. Thus, here conflict situations in neighbouring countries have demonstrable linkages and changes in one and can affect the other. Two possible linkages identified by Carl Turner include, firstly, a trans-border incompatibility where an ethnic group straddles an international border; and, secondly, an interaction and cooperation towards a government or group in another state.[4] He specifies:

> *Northern Rakhine State and the tri-border region with Bangladesh and India is presently one of the most conflict-divided territories in the modern world; hostility is deep between different government and nationality organisations; over a million people —or a third of the population—are refugees in Bangladesh or displaced internally from their homes; electoral politics are highly contested in the country's emergent democracy; and the contemporary humanitarian crisis bears comparison with the worst upheavals in Arakan's troubled past.*[5]

The background to the Rohingya crisis has been covered in detail in Chapter 10 (Myanmar and Sanctions) and hence is not being repeated here. However, a detailed brief on the ARSA, its resurgence in 2020 and the alliance between the ARSA and the AA is included in **Appendix O**. This chapter devotes itself to the Rakhine conflict *per se,* i.e., the conflict between the ethnic Buddhists and the Myanmar Government, i.e., essentially the Tatmadaw.

For an understanding of the Rakhine conflict, the geographical importance of the Rakhine and Chin states is relevant. The Chin State has already been covered earlier; but certain critical aspects of the Rakhine State (**Appendix F**) need to be understood. The AA, despite claiming Rakhine State and conducting operations across the state almost till the Central regions is physically operating from Chin State. Paletwa, in Chin State, is the AA stronghold. This anomaly is actually an outcome of geography. The Arakan Yoma mountain range runs along the IMB and culminates in the Arakan. Thus, the heights of the hills in Arakan are lower than in Chin, making it easier for security forces to operate. Thus, areas like Mrauk-U, which the AA is claiming for its HQ and as the capital of Arakan State, provides very little cover in terms of terrain. Paletwa, on the other hand, is broken ground and provides conditions conducive for insurgency.

From the perspective of road communications, Rakhine State is internally better connected than Chin, which is also a function of geography. For insurgency, therefore, more difficult terrain is safer since it precludes the movement of government troops by road. Myanmar has a 269-km border with Bangladesh which includes both Rakhine and Chin states. Chin State provides another tactical advantage to the AA which Rakhine does not. It borders India in addition to Bangladesh, hence providing options for external support for its sustenance. Thus, whenever the Myanmar Army increases it operational pressure on the AA, its cadres can simply slip across into India or Bangladesh. In fact, the success of 'Operation Sunrise II', the coordinated operations by India and Myanmar in Chin State, was due to the fact that the Indian Army had sealed the India-Myanmar border in South Mizoram, thereby cutting off access of AA cadres to sources of sustenance inside India.

The network of the Kaladan, Mayu and other smaller rivers in the Rakhine and Chin states provides a textbook riverine terrain in which the AA operates. This terrain has been effectively used by the AA in disrupting transport plying on these rivers by hijacking them at regular intervals. It has effectively interdicted the movement of vessels in the region thus jeopardising local inland water transportation systems. In the Rakhine and Chin states, which are infamous for poor roads, this becomes critical.[6]

Background to Arakan Aspirations

The Arakan Kingdom had reached its peak with the establishment of Mrauk-U as a capital between the 15th and 17th centuries. In the 18th century, the Konbaung King Bodawpaya overthrew Arakan King Thamada and led a violent invasion leading to massive losses for the Arakan people from 1784 to 1824. Later, the Arakan was invaded by the British (1824-1941), the Japanese (1942-45) and then again the British (1945-48). From 1948 till modern times, the region has seen various armed opposition groups active in the Rakhine territory.[7]

Cchavi Vasisht, Research Associate, VIF, describes the broad motivations of the AA when she writes[8] that:

> *The AA aims to revive the lost glory of the Arakan empire and its people, who have felt socially, politically as well as economically alienated at the hands of the Bamar people. This feeling of alienation holds merit as neglect of the state is evident from the slow growth rate of around five per cent in the period 2005 to 2013, against the State average rate of about eight per cent in the same period. The per capita State Gross Domestic Product (GDP) revealed that Rakhine, along with Chin are the most impoverished States with per capita incomes of $ 171 and $ 31, respectively. This has been reiterated by the 'Poverty Report—Myanmar Living Conditions Survey' (2017), which states that poverty is most prevalent in Chin and Rakhine States. It has been recorded that the Rakhine State (along with Chin State) have (has) been left out of the convergence process of growth and development reported in other States.*

Table 7.1: Historical Timeline: Armed Organisations in Arakan

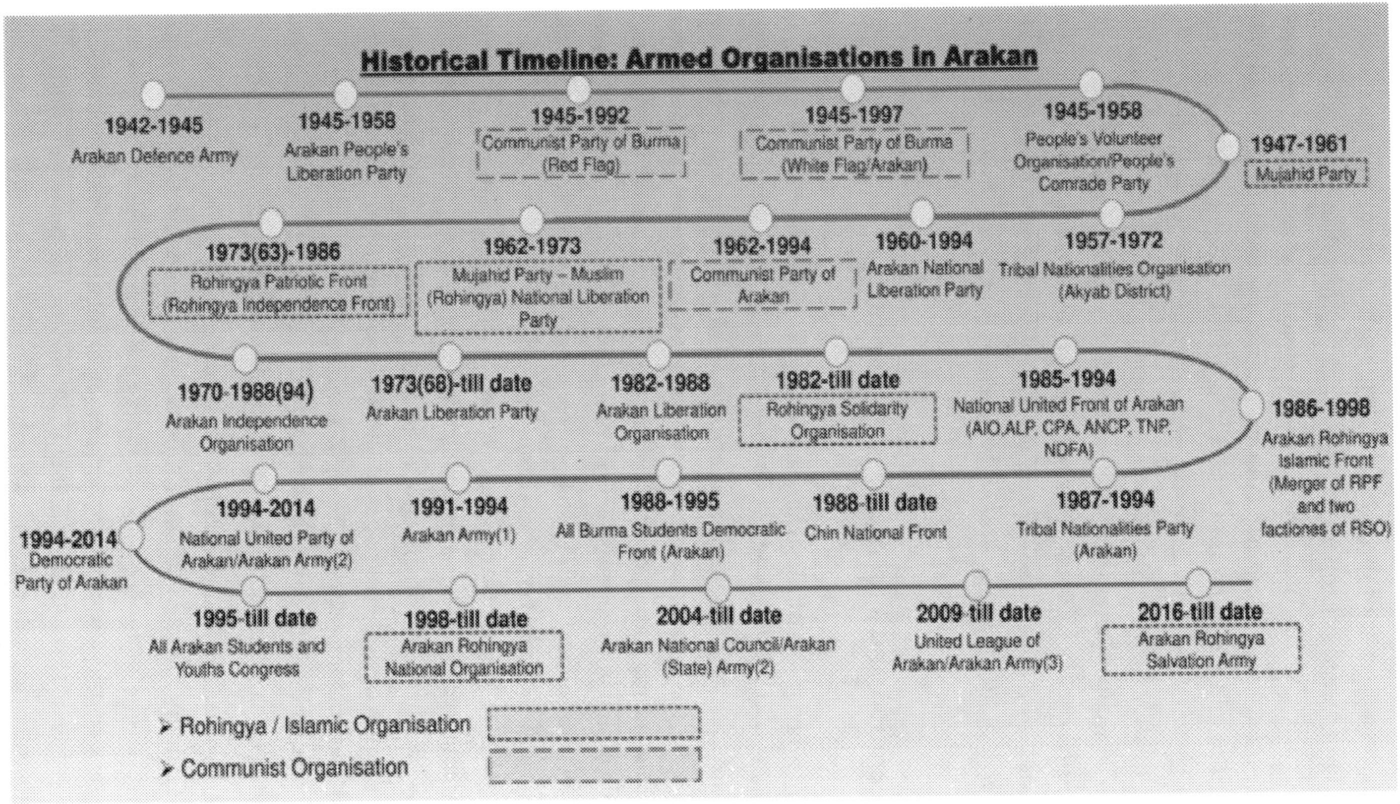

Source: Prepared by the author with data from Martin Smith's *Arakan (Rakhine State), A Land in Conflict on Myanmar's Western Frontier*, Transnational Institute, Amsterdam, December 2019.

The present avatar of the AA is the third with this name in a long series (see Table 7.1) of armed organisations which have sprouted in Rakhine State since independence. On 10 April 2009, the AA established itself as a *"revolutionary armed organisation"* in Myanmar. Politically, it is a member of the Federal Political Negotiations and Consultative Committee (FPNCC), a group of seven Ethnic Armed Organisations (EAO) in Northeast Myanmar, while militarily, it is a member of the Northern Alliance as well as the Three Brotherhood Alliance.[9] AA's official website states that "*The main objective of the Arakan Army (AA) is to defend the Fatherland of Arakan and to protect all peoples of Arakan. The presence of the Arakan Army in Arakan is to give peace, stability, security, freedom, justice and development to all peoples of Arakan irrespective of sex, race, religion and political belief.*"[10]

Confederation and Federalism

Like the other EAGs, the AA is not asking for independence from Myanmar. However, where most of the others are asking for federalism, AA is gunning for confederalism. As per Tim Mbiti,[11] a certified educator with www.enotes.com, federalism refers to a system of government in which power is split between the national or federal government and state or regional governments, with the national government having more power over the state. However, it is important to note that the regional governments have independent powers and responsibilities. In fact, federalism allows the regional governments to have their own legislative, executive, and judiciary branches through which laws can be passed, interpreted, and enforced as long as they do not contravene the constitution. The system is advantageous because it not only enables the state governments to respond more effectively to the needs of the citizens in their jurisdictions but also provides a mechanism to check the activities of the national government. Even though the national government reserves the right to make foreign policy, control imports and exports, and declare war, it works together with the state governments in such matters as civil rights, taxation, and environmental protection, among others.

On the other hand, confederalism is a system of government in which sovereign power is held by the regional governments, to which the national government is accountable. The member-states are independent and separate but give certain powers to a central authority for reasons of mutual security, convenience, and efficiency. Member-states are the ones that appoint the central authority, which can make rules that will pass as laws only after all constituent states have passed them. Currently, Belgium is a confederacy. Confederacy is not acceptable to the

Myanmar Government, which will only consider federalism as an option. However, despite the media outreach of the AA, there is a lack of clarity on what the AA is exactly looking for in concrete terms.

Build-up to the Present Crisis

The AA operated in Kachin and Shan States under the Kachin Independence Army (KIA) in Laiza. When the NLD Government came to power in 2015, it was expected that the Aung San Suu Kyi-led government would facilitate political reconciliation and recognition of the Rakhine people. However after the NLD Government appointed its own CM despite winning only nine seats, against the local Arakan National Party's (ANP), 22 out of 35 seats in the 47- member Rakhine Hluttaw, the expectations turned to dust and fuelled animosity against the Bamar majority.[12] Possibly anticipating this, the AA made its presence felt through attacks on the Tatmadaw on 29 March 2015 at Kyauktaw in Rakhine State and simultaneously at Paletwa in Chin State. In these attacks, a captain and two soldiers of the Tatmadaw were killed, and four Tatmadaw soldiers were taken prisoner.[13]

The AA gradually escalated the violence till, in 2018, an AA ambush in northern Paletwa Township on 29 August 2018 triggered a major round of fighting. In November, this fighting spread from Paletwa to neighbouring Buthidaung Township in Rakhine State. In December 2018, the Tatmadaw began attacking AA bases with artillery. In response, on 4 January 2019, Myanmar's Independence Day, simultaneous attacks by AA at four border police outposts in North Buthidaung Township, marked a significant escalation of the conflict. Retaliatory counter-insurgency (CI) operations commenced on 7 January 2019 and, since then, the clashes have intensified.[14] The Tatmadaw quickly mobilized units from multiple Light Infantry Divisions (LIDs), including the 99 LID which was partially deployed for clearance operations during the Rakhine crisis in 2017. The Tatmadaw also deployed units from 22 LID based in Kayin State. It specializes in jungle warfare, but had not been deployed to combat outside Kayin State since 2011.[15] The arrest of the ANP leader, Dr. Aye Maung, and his sentencing to 20 years imprisonment for treason in March 2019 added fuel to the fire. Cchavi Vasisht, adds that:

> *The Tatmadaw has deployed a large force and uses air and artillery strikes against the AA. The patterns depict the use of its age-old "Four Cuts" doctrine to break the AA capabilities.[15] General Ne Win, leader of 1962 military coup, inspired by Japan's "three all" ("kill all, burn all, destroy all) tactics, engineered the "Four Cuts" doctrine. The doctrine was designed to block the insurgents' access to key*

inputs: funding, food, intelligence and recruits. For the first time, the Tatmadaw used the strategy against the Karen rebellion in the 1970s and then more recently against the KIA.

The year 2019 has truly been the coming-of-age of the AA. A large number of tactical successes doubled up with a communication strategy that is better than the NLD Government and the Tatmadaw is giving them benefits. Heavy violence erupted in northern Rakhine with offensives and counter attacks by the AA and the Myanmar Army in Maungdaw District and Minbya and Mrauk-U townships of Rakhine State. The Myanmar Army promptly designated Hpon Tha Chaung of Minbya Township an active war zone. The fighting commenced in end-July 2019, and spilled into Chin State. The Deputy Commander of 105 Light Infantry Battalion (LIB), Major Win Myo Aung, was killed in action in Paletwa Township near the Bangladesh border between border posts 71 and 72. On the same day, the AA claimed it had killed about 23 soldiers in Buthidaung, Kyauktaw and Mrauk-U townships while only three of its troops were wounded. In a counter-strike, an AA camp was destroyed near Sittwe by the Myanmar Army on 3 August 2019. Towards end-August 2019, the AA retaliated hitting a camp north of Mrauk-U township killing 30 and capturing over a dozen Myanmar Army personnel including a Lt Col with apparently only two AA fatalities.[16, 17]

On 5 October 2019, the AA army attacked the Tatmadaw and police on Saitinchaung bridge in Rakhine State. A 40-mm bomb launcher was also fired at the security camp. The bridge had been previously attacked five times in the past. Khaing Thukha, spokesperson of the AA, stated on 8 October that since the Tatmadaw had equipped its armed forces with more weapons and ammunition, armed conflicts were likely to intensify. A Tatmadaw column reportedly captured a temporary camp of the AA at Kyauk Pon Taung, north of Yoe Ta Yoke village, Ponnagyun Township, Arakan State, at about 2 p.m. on 18 October, Col Win Zaw Oo told reporters. He reported that food and landmines were recovered from the site and while no Tatmadaw members were killed or injured in the clash, some fighters from AA were hurt.[18]

In December 2019, six IWT vessels were attacked by the AA in a week. The Tatmadaw and AA also clashed in Sanyin, Hinkhayaw and Tote Chaung villages in Myebon Township. According to the AA, the Tatmadaw used civilian vehicles for carrying out the attacks and killed 12 of its personnel. The army bases in Minbutaung, Nonbu and Paletwa as well as the Rarmaung bridge guard post, Yotayoke police outpost and Yaw Bridge guard column were attacked.[19]

A lady was killed and her two sisters injured by artillery shelling near Man

Wah village, Namtu Township, Shan State. In Mrauk-U Township, Rakhine State, three children and two adults were injured by shelling by the Tatmadaw. A nine-year-old boy was killed by gunfire allegedly from the Tatmadaw troops stationed at a monastery in Kyauktaw Township's Pike in Rakhine State. A third-grade student returning from school was shot by Myanmar soldiers on the road next to Shwe Kyaung Monastery. A toddler and an adult were killed and seven others injured when an artillery shell hit a passenger vessel sailing on the Kaladan River in Paletwa Township of Chin State.[20]

In January 2020, sporadic violence continued with casualties on both sides. AA fighters seized 16 bus drivers from the Transport Department from a passenger boat, *Aung Tagon*, which had stopped at a site between Sapho Kyun and Oakpho villages in Rathedaung Township while travelling from the state capital of Sittwe to Buthidaung township in northern Rakhine State. They were subsequently released without harm. Further, about 90 AA troops attacked two Myanmar units in Kyauktaw under the cover of buildings. Two civilians were wounded during the attack and some private and government buildings damaged.[21] In January 2020, sketchy reports of Unmanned Combat Aerial Vehicles (UCAVs) having been used against the AA have emerged. Using these force multiplier weapon systems in a counter-insurgency role actually crosses a red line and is open to criticism from all quarters.

February 2020 saw 81 armed clashes between the Tatmadaw and AA with maximum action in Kyauktaw and Rathedaung townships in Rakhine and Paletwa Township of Chin State. Airstrikes and heavy multiple rocket launchers were freely used by the Tatmadaw. The Myanmar Army's use of airpower to engage the AA had now become a norm. Regional Commanders were now authorized to launch airstrikes without seeking prior permission from Nay Pyi Taw. The Tatmadaw used MI-35, MI-17, and MI-2 gunships in the conflict causing casualties to civilians and even to its own troops (like during the Shwe Nadi operation). Given the difficult terrain, the slow speed and low flight pattern of the helicopters, eventually the AA will bring down one and force the Tatmadaw to change its strategy. The seizure of a Chinese-made FN-6 surface-to-air missile from the AA signifies that they are ready with a game changer. On 19 February 2020, the AA fired at a helicopter carrying Dr. Win Myat Aye, the Union Minister for Social Welfare, Relief and Resettlement, and Arakan State CM, U Nyi Pu. Though no one was injured in the attack, the AA issued a statement advising civilians in Arakan State not to use military aircraft, vehicles, and vessels when travelling in the war zones.[22]

Subsequently, on 10 March 2020, a fierce battle saw the AA maul the Tatmadaw 7 LIB which had moved from Phayagyi, Bago Region, to reinforce the Meewa post in Paletwa causing the capture of the Battalion Commander, Lieutenant Colonel Thet Naing Oo and 20 soldiers and the death of 20 other soldiers. Cchavi Vasisht and this author jointly state in a VIF Web Article that this event is a turning point in the Rakhine conflict and validates the differences in the quality of leadership, command and control, competence in tactics and the overall morale of the forces between the AA and the Tatmadaw. This kind of abject defeat of a regular infantry combat unit and the capture of its unit commander by an insurgent group reflects the nadir of any organised conventional body of troops.

This encounter deserves its place in history for another undistinguished reason, the first authentic corroborated report of use of the Myanmar Air Force, specifically fixed-wing aircraft, being used to strafe and bomb the AA, causing massive collateral damage to civilians. Reportedly, two jets of Myanmar Air Force attacked an AA occupied village on 8–9 March 2020 demolishing 62 out of the village's 66 houses. Expectedly, the AA took it upon themselves to spread the word through social media and circulated photographs such as the one at Figure 7.1.

Figure 7.1: Photo showing tail fin and parachute of bomb allegedly dropped by Myanmar Air Force jets

Source: Arakan Army.

In three days of fighting on the border of Rakhine and Chin states, 21 civilians were killed and 27 others injured. Salai Myo Htike, an Amyotha Hluttaw MP from Chin, said 12 civilians were killed and 15 injured in a military airstrike on suspected AA hideouts between Paletwa and Sami towns in Chin on 14 March 2020. Implicitly acknowledging the airstrikes on the AA, Brigadier General Zaw Min Tun, Secretary of the Tatmadaw's True News Agency, said he could not confirm or deny the military air strikes and added that since AA members were present in all villages of Paletwa Township, the Tatmadaw could not distinguish between them and villagers, sort of justifying the civilian casualties. Nearly 20 villages in Rakhine State's Kyauktaw and Chin State's Paletwa townships have been reportedly abandoned due to air strikes and artillery shelling.

On 23 March 2020, AA attacked a military training establishment, viz., No. 9 Advanced Training School, Minbya Township, Rakhine, wherein both sides suffered casualties in the fighting at the site at Kanni village. Apparently, around 300 AA fighters attacked the school from five directions and launched the attack. After the attack the military found 15 bodies of AA fighters as well as guns at the scene. Most of the dead bodies, according to the photos published online by the '*Myawady Daily*', were not in uniform, but in tracksuits. Officers and troops of the school were also killed. Allegedly, the Tatmadaw used helicopters and jet fighters during the clash leading to the death of a nine-year-old and injuring 15 civilians.

Figure 7.2: Map showing location of 7 LIB ambush on 10 March 2020, and the Mon Than Byin village which was destroyed in air strikes

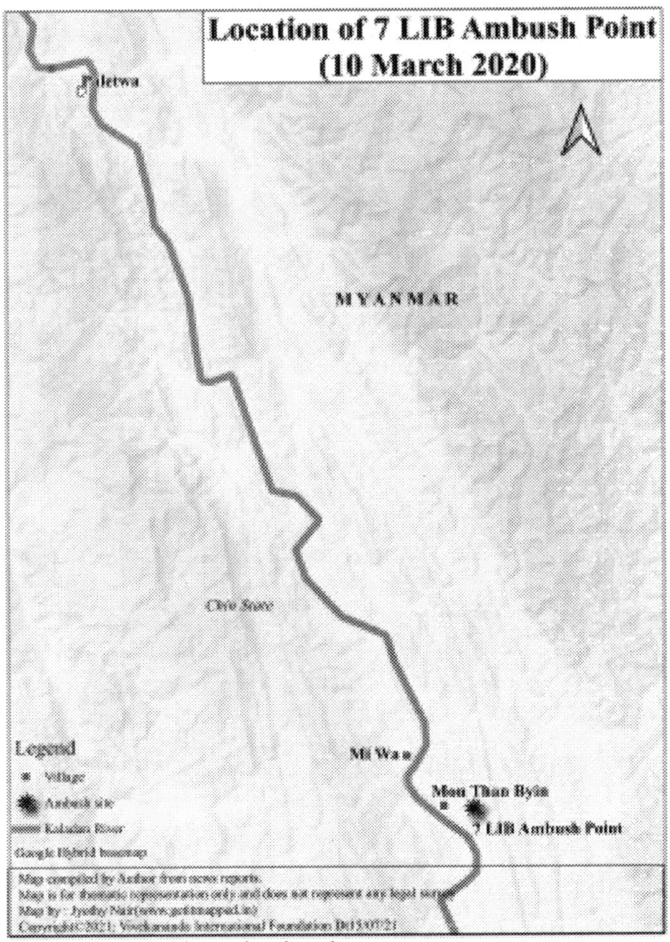

Source: Compiled by author based on news reports.

Landmine casualties plagued the region with three civilians suffering mine injuries in Rathedaung Township, Rakhine State, on 29 March 2020. Two of the injured lost their limbs in the blasts. One man stepped on a landmine while collecting fire wood. His companion phoned the villagers and asked for help. As the villagers were going to the scene, two of them who were walking ahead, stepped on another landmine and were injured.

The AA, while reputedly having a better code of conduct than the Tatmadaw, is not above ethical conduct. It looted part of a shipment of 100 sacks of rice intended for more than 1,700 displaced Chin villagers in Paletwa Township but returned most of it after media reports about the incident were published. Subsequently, it allowed 6,000 sacks of rice to be delivered to Paletwa as explained by U Kyaw Nyein, Chair of the Khumi Affairs Coordination Council.[23]

Declaration of AA as an Unlawful Association and Terrorist Organisation

The immediate reaction to 10 March 2020 setback of 7 LIB was that Myanmar President U Win Myint, on 23 March 2020, declared the AA and its political arm, the ULA, an "Unlawful Association" under Section 16 of the 1908 Unlawful Association Act. The was done on the ground that the goals of the armed group posed risks and disrupted the rule of law and national stability and the peace of its citizens. Section 16 reads:

> *If the President of the Union is of opinion that any association interferes or has for its object interference with the administration of the law or with the maintenance of law and order, or that it constitutes a danger to the public peace, the President of the Union may, by notification in the Gazette, declare such association to be unlawful.*

This declaration was followed up by the Central Committee for Counter-Terrorism declaring[24] the AA a terrorist organisation. The AA spokesperson, Khaing Thukha, promptly refuted the government statement and said this showed that the Myanmar Government was only concerned about the political issues affecting the Burmese ethnic people and not for other ethnic people in the country. However, the implications of these two developments are not clear. Prashanth Parameswaran, Senior Editor of *The Diplomat* highlights the growing reliance of the Myanmar Government on punitive measures as the AA's attacks on the government continue. He brings out that this aligns more with the Tatmadaw's preference for a military-focused approach.[25]

At this stage, it is evident that the Tatmadaw is at the lower end of the operational learning curve whilst the AA comes across as more competent, agile and confident and in all facets of warfare it chooses to fight. On the perception front, the AA is more active and provides better quality, more regular and detailed updates than the Tatmadaw. Unless the Tatmadaw gains control over its frontline troops and changes the operating culture in its counter-insurgency strategy, it is doomed to be stuck in the vicious circle of counter-insurgency. Presently, both the belligerents have not yet reached their culmination points of battle weariness, which means that both sides have the stamina to fight on for at least one to two years more. Peace efforts will take fruit only when both sides have hit certain notional levels of battle fatigue. Till then, the Rakhine region is doomed to suffer with innocent civilians caught in the crossfire suffering the most.

Tatmadaw's Attempts to Isolate AA

The Tatmadaw has taken up a three-pronged strategy to isolate the AA. Firstly, it has warned international and local non-governmental organisations (NGOs) not to support the AA; secondly, it has messaged the KIA through the Myitkyina-based Peace-talk Creation Group (PCG) not to accept any presence of the AA in KIA territory; and thirdly, it has severely restricted internet in the Rakine and Chin regions. The Three Brotherhood Alliance comprising the AA, Myanmar National Democratic Alliance Army (MNDAA) and the Ta'ang National Liberation Army (TNLA) immediately responded by declaring its support to the AA stating '*We will continue to implement military and political cooperation with the ULA/AA according to the previous practice while categorically rejecting the government of Myanmar's unfounded and unwarranted accusation against the ULA/AA.*'

The KIA however did not condemn the declaration of the AA as a terrorist group, probably since it is under pressure from the Tatmadaw to distance itself from the AA. The KIA still trains, provides ammunition and supplies food for AA soldiers, but there is a rumour of tensions between the two, with the KIA asking the AA to vacate its Laiza headquarters. Some ethnic leaders also reportedly told the AA to give up its illicit trade activities. The genesis of this tension is a December 2019 interview with *The Irrawaddy*, where AA C-in-C Maj Gen Tun Myat Naing, criticized some ethnic leaders who have been fighting in the ethnic struggle for 70 years. He lashed out at them, saying that some leaders have been enjoying lives of luxury, drinking wine, and then giving up their fight. This angered the ethnic leaders and the AA leader later relented and apologised, but this has impacted his relationship with these leaders.

Muzzling the media to isolate the AA is another tactic the Tatmadaw is using. The police arrested U Nay Myo Lin, the Chief Editor of the Mandalay-based *Voice of Myanmar* (VOM), a local Myanmar media house. He was arrested on 30 March 2020 and charged for violating sections 50(a) and 52(a) of the Anti-Terrorism Law and remanded for contacting AA spokesperson Khaing Thukha and broadcasting an interview under the title "*Peace Process has stopped*". Another senior editor from *The Irrawaddy*, Ye Ni, was charged with defamation over an April 2019 article about fighting between the Tatmadaw and the AA. The article, written by reporter Moe Myint who gave a first-person account of fighting in the ancient town of Mrauk-U that contradicted official claims made by the Tatmadaw. It was originally published in English, but it was the Myanmar translation of the article that triggered the lawsuit.

The internet ban is affecting the Myanmar Government's ability to communicate information about the deadly virus and advice on what people should and should not do to mitigate the risk of the COVID-19 pandemic. The Internet ban could have deadly consequences for residents of the nine affected townships.[26]

An Analysis of the Arakan Army Operations

Strategic Clarity

On 10 April 2020, the AA celebrated its 11th anniversary and in the commemorative speech by its C-in-C, Major General Twan Mrat Naing, he reiterated the motivations and aspirations of the AA and exhorted the Arakan people to continue their struggle for liberation and to adopt the "Way of Rakhita".[27] The "Way of Rakhita" seeks to resuscitate the erstwhile powerful Arakan kingdom, which was defeated by the Bamar Konbaung dynasty in 1784.[28] An analysis of his speech reveals a sense of strategic clarity and purpose and hence worthy of study. Certain excerpts of his speech are reproduced[29] below:

> *Our Arakan Army is resolutely fighting for the future of Arakan to write new history after transforming and rooting out current appalling situations. At the same time, we are trying to strengthen the Arakan Army. Standing with the people as a oneness, we are doing our best among the difficulties to undertake the tasks of the revolution that can be construed as "struggling by organizing; organizing by struggling, training by fighting; fighting by training." (...)*
>
> *For a successful revolution with a well-trained army, we need to try hard to be*

> *perfect. Both good leadership and good followership are required. It can't be achieved if there are no weapons but lots of people and there are no military trainings and other skills but people and weapons. What I want to mention here is a general assessment concerning solidarity, endurance, performance and capacity of each revolutionary fighter. Among these, what I want to deliver is one of the most important tasks of public relations and organizing strategies in this long struggle.*
>
> *(...)*
>
> *I want to command that revolutionary fighters of the Arakan Army always treat people with full respect whenever communicating with any member of the people of Arakan, abiding to the rules and regulations of the Army. We live with the people in unity and oneness. No army is a greater force than the people. As the Arakan Army is the defenders of the fatherland of Arakan, to protect the people is our principle. Responsible leaders and all the comrades must be cautious not to happen in the future and take actions to control misbehaviours that we have been hearing from recent reports about the misuse of the position, the misuse of power without the necessity, the use of the United League of Arakan for personal gain by some opportunists, and non-disciplinary behaviour of some troops of (ours) in some regions.*
>
> *(...)*
>
> *We can clearly see now the physical and moral collapse of the colonialist-war criminals defeated by your vigorous fighting skills. Their operations and military conducts are not like before anymore. They are adapted to the reality. Conducting indiscriminate airstrikes and artillery fire on civilians is a distinct attempt to cover up the fear and inferiority of the enemy troops. You can imagine their strategic artillery posts are becoming like the fearful homeless dogs in the darkness that are barking without any purpose whenever they hear about the breaking out of clashes.*

The centrality of 'people' in the speech reveals his understanding of revolution based on insurgency. Thus, the admonishment of his own cadres for misbehaviour and misuse of power, and the statement that no army is greater than it people, is a refreshing and hopefully positive approach to liberation which stands out in contrast to the approach of the Union and its enforcers, i.e., the Tatmadaw. This strategic maturity is reinforced by the statement that the C-in-C wants, amongst a large number of deliverables, to personally deliver, '*public relations and organizing strategies*'. This reveals a grasp of the importance of public outreach and a focus on strategic matters, i.e., the big picture. The AA is transitioning from being a small insurgency to a big one, and in this transition, the role of the C-in-C is critical. He needs to focus on the strategic outlook and hence smaller tactical level operations need to be left to the junior level commanders. This is a crucial transition for commanders, even in the armed forces, where they need to leave the minor details to junior commanders, as they focus on the larger perspective. Similarly, his reading of the mental state of the Tatmadaw based on their '*indiscriminate airstrikes and artillery fire on civilians*' seems accurate as has been covered in the chapter on the Tatmadaw (Chapter 8, The Tatmadaw: Raising the 'Standard').

Another aspect of the strategic clarity of the AA is revealed by the extent it goes to play the China versus India card. A statement by the AA on 18 July 2019 went largely unnoticed in the media. In this, the AA stated that they welcomed foreign investors including Chinese investments in the Rakhine region and would work '*hand in hand*' with all those who wanted to work for mutually beneficial multi-sectoral projects in the region. It specifically stated that it approved of governments and institutions that wanted to establish mutually beneficial projects such as the China-based deep sea port and Kyaukphyu Special Economic Zone under the BRI. AA spokesman Khine Thukha stated that "*The reason for making this announcement is to inform that we are ready to cooperate for all kinds of investments in the state which are not harmful to the public interest.*"[30, 31]

Other aspects of the strategic approach of the AA are revealed as we see other facets of the operations conducted by them.

Tactical Innovation

Abductions

Abductions are a tactical innovation and form part and parcel of the AA gamut of tactics. The overall aim of these abductions seem to be to force conversion to AA, especially from the Tatmadaw, gain intelligence, seek an upper hand in negotiations and demoralise the enemy by achieving moral ascendancy. Of the number of abductions that have been attributed to the AA in recent times, three stand out for various reasons.

The first incident is the attempted abduction of 58 persons from a passenger ferry called *Shwe Nadi* on 26 October 2019. The AA claimed that its troops received information of movement of military personnel disguised as civilians aboard the *Shwe Nadi*. Hence, they stopped the vessel for inspection and forced it to dock on the banks of the Mayu River. They then offloaded 58 passengers into* motorboats, leaving some civilians, women and elderly passengers on the boat, which was allowed to proceed upriver. The motorboats sped away on Yay Poke Creek but around midday, three military helicopters intercepted them, firing rockets and machine guns killing some AA troops and detainees while sinking two motorboats and damaging the third. The three military helicopters continued firing at the surrounding area for more than five hours, killing more AA members and detainees.[32] "*We never commit indiscriminate killing of our detainees,*" AA spokesman Khaing Thukha told the RFA's Myanmar Service.[33] The Tatmadaw was able to rescue 14 of the detainees subsequently.[34] Though technically the operation failed, it was appreciable in its scale and execution. However, in this case, the Tatmadaw's prompt reaction won it the day, despite several blue-on-blue losses. The AA subsequently released 25 of the hostages within a few days on 5 November 2019 according to Khaing Thukha, the AA spokesperson. "*Around 6 a.m. this morning, we handed over 25 civilians to the village administrator at the monastery in Ngwe Taung village. We gave them 15,000 kyats [US$ 9.85] for travel expenses and we also gave back their cell phones. We don't have any civilians left in our hands now,*" Khaing Thukha told *The Irrawaddy.*[35]

The AA subsequently released a video[36] of Capt Nyi Nyi Zaw of the 345th LIB under the 15th Military Operation Command in Buthidaung Township, who was among several persons the AA had captured on the *Shwe Nadi*. The officer claimed to have killed three Muslim men suspected of belonging to the Arakan Rohingya Salvation Army (ARSA) during the Tatmadaw's massive crackdown in northern Rakhine State in 2017. AA spokesperson Khaing Thukha denied that the AA forced the officer to make the confessions and said, "*He just told us what he experienced. We will release prisoners only if the Tatmadaw releases detained Arakan people*".[37] Another abductee, a junior engineer, who had been detained by the AA for 120 days, was released on 24 February 2019, having determined that he did not have any affiliation with the military. He was handed over to the village administrator and community leaders at Yee Pike Sone village in Rathedaung Township. As per the AA spokesperson, "*It took time to release him because the Myanmar military's attacks have been aggressive*".[38] The point being that every release was accompanied by a statement which gave out clearly why the person was released and the reason for delay in the release.

The second noteworthy abduction[39] was that of the NLD MP from Chin State, U Hwei Ting,[40] again when he was travelling by boat on the Kaladan river. This high-profile abduction was based on hardcore intelligence of the travel plan of the MP and post abduction, was well publicised. The MP, after his release, revealed that he had been looked after very well and, in fact, the abduction and safe release generated a positive image for the organisation. Good relations with Chin State stakeholders are important for the AA which actually does not have the justification for operating in Chin State, and hence cannot really afford to antagonise the Chin.

The final case study of abductions by the AA involves Indians and this coincidentally happened on the same day as the abduction of MP U Hwei Ting, i.e., on 26 October 2019, and at the same place. This group of five Indian representatives of a company exploring the possibility of investing in the stalled Kaladan Project were travelling from Paletwa to Sittwe in a speedboat on the Kaladan River when they were abducted by AA cadres who immediately took away their mobile phones and documents and started making them walk towards a hideout. During the course of the journey, the captors realised that they had apprehended Indian nationals and then they were redirected to another location on the other bank of the Kaladan. At the other side, they were again asked to walk to a hideout. After a few hours of walking, a 62-year-old gentleman collapsed due to fatigue. He was diabetic, had a heart condition and was also overweight; unfortunately, he passed away, despite the best efforts of the AA medical staff who attempted to revive him. The other captives were subsequently released and the AA apologised to them for the death of the team member. When the team offered to pay for their release, the AA were aghast and deigned to accept it as being against their principles. The total period of apprehension was less than 24 hours.

The author was fortunate to have been able to interview one of the abductees and the detailed transcript is attached at **Appendix P**. The takeaway from this experience was the sudden change in the attitude of the AA cadres when they realised that they had taken Indians captive; the utmost courtesy and the prompt release and apologetic stance at the death. These point to a high degree of self-awareness and pride in the group. The attempt at medical resuscitation suggests that battlefield medical training forms a significant part of the curriculum, possibly a result of the presence of Brig. Gen. Nyo Twan Awng, a trained surgeon and the Deputy Commander of the AA.

In addition to the above three abductions, a number of others have taken place to suggest that this form of warfare finds a major place in AA philosophy and they conduct it well. On 22 March 2020, the AA kidnapped 15 workers from the Paletwa river port before releasing them a day later. They claimed that the Tatmadaw had attacked them from the site a day earlier. The workers included seven locals and eight Indians working on the Kaladan Project.[41] The only shadow over the incident was the Chin State government spokesperson Soe Htet telling the media that the AA soldiers had taken some 5 million kyats (US$ 3,550) from the workers. However, Khaing Thukha expectedly denied this allegation.[42]

IEDs and Landmines

The next tactical innovation that the AA has successfully applied against the Tatmadaw has been the use of IEDs and land mines. While this is not unusual in any insurgency, what makes this important is the manner in which these are applied in relation to the local population and in direct contrast to the Tatmadaw which has caused more casualties to civilians than to the AA, ever since the ceasefire was broken. On 27 February 2019, the AA executed a landmine ambush on four Myanmar Police vehicles on the Yangon-Sittwe Road, killing two soldiers and injuring two in the explosion. Indiscriminate laying of mines by the Tatmadaw has rendered the region unsafe for agriculture and other civilian activities.[43] In a typical incident, three civilians were injured after stepping on landmines in Rathedaung Township of Rakhine State on 29 March 2020. One of the villagers lost a limb having stepped on a mine while collecting firewood while two villagers who went to help stepped on another landmine and were injured.[44]

Riverine Warfare

Riverine Warfare is another tactical innovation that the AA seems to have mastered at the cost of the Myanmar Navy which is now permanently stationed at the mouth of the Kaladan. Since March 2019, over six major attacks, including rocket attacks, and several minor attacks on vessels plying in the rivers in Rakhine and Chin states, have witnessed casualties on both sides. This level of competence and confidence in a relatively rare form of combat, viz., riverine warfare, complicates the movement of MA troops and vessels carrying material for the ever-elusive Kaladan Project.[45]

The author, in an web article[46] for the Kalinga International Foundation, highlighted few of the major riverine operations of the AA and their nuances:

> *Five incidents in recent months involving the AA and MA merit attention. First, was a rocket attack on a tug boat (22 June 2019), anchored near the mouth of Hsantyoe creek, east of Sittwe, killing three soldiers and damaging the rear part of the tugboat; second, firing of two rockets (22 July 19) at three government naval boats anchored near Mayu riverbank, 3 kilometres west of Yathedaung township, stationed for emergency rescue and aid operation to passenger vessels running along the coast; three, hijacking of passenger vessel Shwe Nadi (26 October 2019) sailing from Sittwe to Buthidaung, including taking 58 passengers hostage and transporting them in motor boats only to be attacked*

by MA helicopters causing unspecified number of casualties among the passengers and AA including injury to one of the helicopter pilot(s) presumably from anti-aircraft gunfire; four, abduction of 10 men travelling in two speed boats from Paletwa Township, Chin State, to Kyauktaw Township, Rakhine State (3 November 19), including a Chin Member of Parliament (MP) representing the National League for Democracy (NLD) and several Indian nationals; and five, firing at Landing Craft Marine Princess (30 November 2019) carrying heavy machineries including bulldozers for Paletwa–Zorinpui Section of the (KMMTTP) and taking the crew hostage as also looting money and cell phones of the crew members.

These incidents reveal a nuanced approach by the AA to warfare in the Rakhine region. The selection of a tug as a target was significant and highlights their understanding of the importance of tugs for manoeuvring larger vessels in constricted water bodies such as rivers. Similarly, the decision to attack Myanmar naval boats stationed for rescue operations for civilian vessels highlights a strategy to push the Myanmar Navy out of the area and gain 'riverine dominance' and influence the flow of vessels and goods to and from the region.

The attempted abduction of 58 people from the passenger ship and relocation using speed boats was a daring strategy executed with astute planning and preparation. However, it did not work in the case of the Shwe Nadi incident and that can be attributed to the MA's prompt and drastic use of helicopters. Finally, targeting of barges carrying equipment for the KMMTTP suggests adequate higher direction within the AA wherein they are willing to play the China card to extract maximum mileage for their cause.

Intelligence

The AA intelligence network is qualitatively and quantitatively of a superior order. This network, most likely based on a vast grid of sympathisers, led to the identification of the speedboat on which the Chin MP, U Hawi Ting from the NLD, was travelling, enabling his abduction. The attack on 7 LIB leading to the capture of the Commanding Officer and many soldiers is another. This edge in intelligence is expected given the local support for the AA due to the absolute disregard for humanitarian laws and brutal conduct by the Tatmadaw. A Rakhine resident who spoke to the author in December 2019 said that the draconian Sedition Law (Section 124A of the Burmese Penal Code) prevented the locals from outrightly supporting the AA. However, almost all Rakhine ethnic nationals and political parties were sympathetic towards the AA cause. The arrogant and abusive behaviour of the Tatmadaw soldiers serves to reinforce support for the AA which makes operations for the Myanmar Armed Forces difficult given that their conduct has alienated them from the locals. Effectively, the confidence which the AA exudes in the sphere of intelligence is directly proportional to the misdeeds of the Tatmadaw and the neglect of the Arakan people by the Myanmar Government. Thus, with every violent act, the Tatmadaw promotes the AA agenda in two ways.[47] One, it alienates itself from that most important source of human intelligence, the humans i.e., the local population. Andrew Selth had identified[48] five features of intelligence during Khin Nyunt'sera, and one of them was a reliance on human intelligence over technical sources. However, he opines, after the 2015 elections, "*authorities seem to be relying more on technical sources*". Herein lies an ironic dichotomy in the intelligence philosophy of the Tatmadaw.

Figure 7.3: Photo showing alleged AA yound recruits at Laiza

Source: Received from Unidentified AA Sympathiser

Internet, the best source of technical intelligence, has been cut off in the affected Rakhine and Chin regions for over a year in 2020. Thus effectively, by its conduct, the Tatmadaw has cut itself off from HUMINT; and by its internet policy, cut itself off from TECHINT, effectively making it blind. In the initial years post the 2015 elections, the Tatmadaw also sought to offset its technical disadvantages by collaborating with foreign counterparts. However, post the 2017 Rohingya crisis and the international backlash, intelligence support from Western countries looks bleak.

Two, the behaviour of the Tatmadaw pushes this aggrieved population into the arms of the only available source of physical, moral and political succour, i.e., the AA. The Rakhine are disappointed by the denial of their political rights and have lost faith in the democratic process, and justifiably so. In the general election in November 2015, the ANP won 22 of the 35 elected seats in the Rakhine Hluttaw. However, the Bamar-dominated NLD exercised its right under the Constitution to appoint one of its own as Chief Minister, despite winning only nine state Hluttaw seats.

Yun Sun of Stimson Centre writes[49] that the economic and political appeal of the AA has enabled it to recruit increasing numbers of troops. She identifies one of the most important factors in the rise of the AA as its steadily increasing popularity among the Rakhine people, who are the fundamental source of its legitimacy, strength and sustainability. She goes on to highlight the bitterness among the Rakhine over the sentencing of former ANP leader Dr Aye Maung to 20 years' imprisonment in March 2019 for high treason over a speech in which he reportedly accused the NLD of treating the Rakhine people like *"slaves"*. The long prison term eliminated any hope of a negotiated solution to ethnic reconciliation in Rakhine.

In addition, the disruption to studies, both in Rakhine[50] and Chin, due to the cancellation of exams and closure of schools in the region since the first week of February 2019 as a result of the violence, has increased the number of young recruits for the AA. There are 384 basic education schools in Paletwa, but 212 schools had already been closed since 2019 before the current clashes due to lack of teachers.[51] An unconfirmed photograph (Figure 7.3) received from sources show young children enrolled for training at Laiza for the AA.[52]

Yun Sun also states that the AA no longer feeds on the largesse of larger groups. *Au contraire*, it has become the legitimate representative of the Rakhine people. The support of the people who comprise the bulk of the state's population is the most crucial reason for the sustainability and tenacity of the AA.

To give credit where it is due, one cannot but admire the portrayal of the AA as a principled and disciplined force. Barring the occasional misconduct by its cadres, they have a reliable code of conduct which is visible in their actions. Such reliability attracts the locals which see it as the only saviour from Bamar oppression.

The AA linkages with the local population are intense and intimate. During a discussion[53] with a childhood friend of the C-in-C, the author was informed that the C-in-C's wife was also the daughter of the Speaker of the Rakhine State Government. He also brought out that most law makers covertly support the AA, though overtly, as they dare not do so openly due the draconian sedition laws in Myanmar. A lot of Rakhine MPs apparently have assisted the AA in recruitment of cadres.

Area of Operations

As brought out earlier, Rakhine State and especially the North Rakhine township such as Mrauk-U are the areas sought to be incorporated in the 'independent' Arakan State with Mrauk-U being the headquarters. The involvement of Chin

State is essentially an outcome of geography which is being resented by the Chins. The AA's plans to 'tax' big projects like the Kaldan Project scheme has been challenged by Chin rebels, threatening a turf war. The Chin National Front (CNF) insists Paletwa is part of Chin State and the AA's claim to it is 'untenable'. A senior CNF leader in Aizawl for medical treatment told veteran journalist Subir Bhaumik that Paletwa was always part of the Chin Special Division and later a part of Chin State. "*Rakhines are only fifteen per cent of Paletwa's population, the rest are Chins and smaller tribes of the Mizo-Kuki-Chin family like Khumis. The Arakan Army is pushing Khumis to accept Rakhine identity which is unfair,*" the leader said on condition of anonymity.[54]

Chin State has faced the major impact of the violence ever since the AA started using Paletwa Township as a base. Chin National Day is being celebrated since 2012, but efforts to observe it have been repeatedly foiled due to the fighting. Thantlang was chosen over Paletwa, due to the violence, as the venue for the 72nd Chin National Day on 20 February 2020.[55] The violence has now led to a situation wherein civil servants are refusing to work in Paletwa due to security concerns.

Figure 7.4: Map depicting Arakan Army ambush site

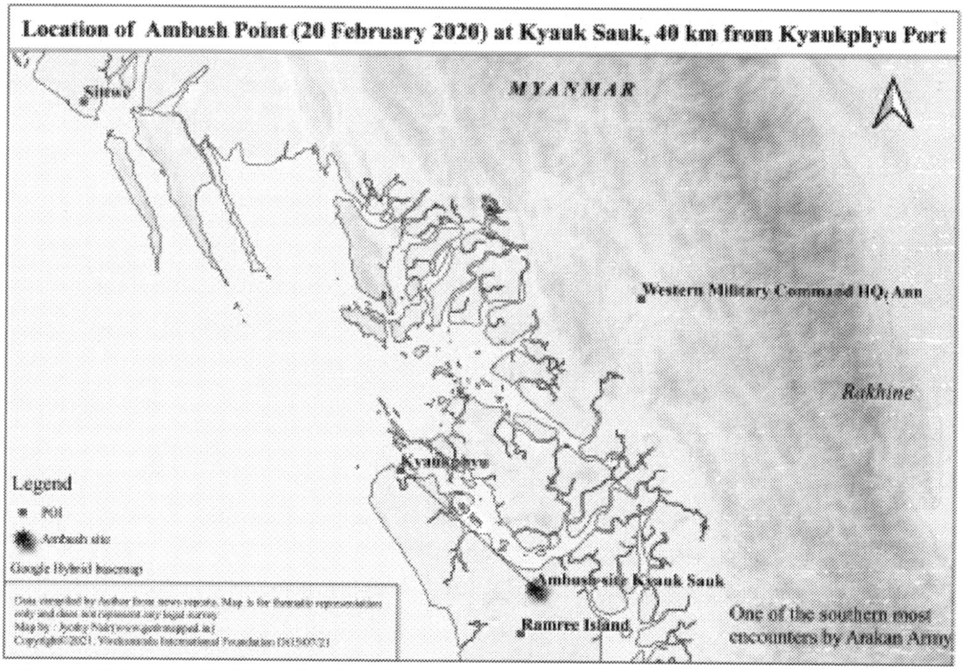

Source: Map compiled by author based on news reports © Vivekananda International Foundation, 2020

However, even while operating out of Chin State, the AA has been able to expand its operations till Kyaukphyu District in Central Rakhine State. An ambush on a Tatmadaw convoy on 20 February 2020 morning near Kyauk Sauk village in Ramree Township was a rare case of hostilities flaring up south of the heart of the conflict in northern Arakan State. Kyauk Sauk is just 40 km from the Kyaukphyu Deep Sea port. The AA attacked two military trucks with bombs here, as per the statement of the AA spokesperson.[56] This distinct southward shift in the extent of operations has two implications; it threatens the Western Regional Military Command at Ann, the highest headquarter coordinating operations against the AA, and also threatens Kyaukphyu and the associated Chinese economic infrastructure, which has major economic, diplomatic and international ramifications. This turns the wheel full circle, as the weapons supplied by the Chinese to the ethnic armed groups in Myanmar are now coming to bear on them.[57]

Motivation

One of the features of the AA cadres that make them stand out is their level of motivation. This motivation seems to be driven by the fact that the AA provides them the only hope in the face of Bamar oppression. One example worth recounting to reinforce the notion that AA cadres are immensely motivated is the case of an AA cadre who was apprehended by security forces in Mizoram during the course of 'Operation Sunrise II'. Immediately upon apprehension, the AA social media buzz started accusing the security forces and tried to pressurise them into releasing him. However, the apprehended cadre, determined not to be handed over to the Tatmadaw, attempted suicide.

This level of motivation, the tactics in vogue and the competence often compares the AA with the Sri Lankan Tamil independence group, the Liberation Tigers of Tamil Elam (LTTE).

Leadership

For an organisation of the size of the AA with over 5,000 active cadres, only three names come into the English language media. The first is of the C-in-C, Maj Gen Twan Mrat Naing; the second is Vice C-in-C, Brig Gen Dr. Nyo Twan Awng; and the third is the AA spokesperson, Mr. Khaing Thukha. *Prima facie*, this seems to be a vulnerability in the organisation which does not seem to have a sufficient second and third rung leadership.

The C-in-C, Twan Mrat Naing, was born in Sittwe, the state capital of Rakhine State. He was one of the 26 men to form the AA with support from the Kachin Independence Army. He is married to Hnin Zar Phyu and the couple have a daughter, Saw Pye Shin (11 years) and a son, Myat Lin Zan (11 months). Twan Mrat Naing's father-in-law is San Kyaw Hla, the Speaker of the Rakhine State Hluttaw and an Arakan National Party (ANP) politician. The wife and two children of the C-in-C were relocated to Switzerland on 25 March 2020 after the country agreed to accept them following a 12-week detention in Thailand after they had been detained by Thailand immigration officials in Chiang Mai on 4 December 2019 due to visa overstay by one day.[58]

In a move by the Myanmar Government, the Myanmar Police had also arrested Maj Gen Tun Myat Naing's brother-in-law, U Kyaw Naing and his wife Ma Ya Min Myat, (the AA chief's sister), when she came to Yangon International Airport to receive her husband when he arrived from Thailand in October 2019.

Vice C-in-C Nyo Tun Aung was born in 1981 in Kyaukpyu, Rakhine State, and worked in Yangon as a surgeon. He joined the AA as a founder-member and was a medical trainer in the initial years. He has a personal website[59] which has many propaganda videos but very little information about him. The high standard of medical facilities in the AA as witnessed by the five Indian abductees is probably his contribution.

Spokesperson Khaing Thukha was apparently earlier a member of the rival faction of the AA, i.e., the ALA. He then defected and joined the AA and has been spokesperson since then. He is the eldest of the three office bearers.

Social Media

The AA has learnt the importance of social media outreach a little late into the battle, but it seems to have caught up and has started using it for its benefit. During the course of this Fellowship, the author observed that other EAGs such as the KIA had a better outreach to their diaspora and this can be attributed to their competence in the English language, which in turn, would likely be a result of the advent of Christianity in those communities. The AA being a Buddhist group does not have this advantage and, as a result, the default language for their social media outreach is the Arakan language.

However, the group, during an interaction on Twitter and other social media platforms, responded positively to the author's request for translation of the posts and subsequently it became standard practice for the group to post in both languages. The group is regular in posting statements promoting itself, refuting the Myanmar Government and the Tatmadaw, or generally keeping its cadres and followers informed about its views. A well-maintained website in Arakan and the English language provides very good information. However the Chinese bias is evident with several posts being translated into Chinese as well.

Funding and Chinese Involvement

Very little is known about the source of funding of the AA and thus one has no option but to resort to deductions based on known facts. Chinese involvement in funding of all the EAGs as also the Tatmadaw, has reportedly been an established practice. The AA too has benefitted from the Chinese largesse, both in terms of money as well as arms and ammunition. In fact, during President Xi Jinping's January visit to Myanmar, this aspect was highlighted to him and he personally had to make a rare denial that "*We categorically deny allegations of supplying arms to ethnic armed organizations in Myanmar but they can acquire these arms by other means, so that we will look into this issue thoroughly to resolve it*".[60]

The interaction of the EAGs with the Chinese government is well institutionalised and accepted, albeit grudgingly, by the Myanmar Government. The Chinese Special Envoy for Asian Affairs, Sun Guoxiang, met Northern Alliance member groups including the AA and the KIO at a meeting at Laiza, on 10 January 2020. The discussions came a week before Chinese President Xi Jinping's scheduled visit to Myanmar on 17-18 January 2020. During the meeting, as per the AA spokesperson, the Special Envoy met with the leaders of the AA and urged the ethnic armed group to reduce clashes and refrain from attacks on the Tatmadaw. He also offered to help the group make peace with the Tatmadaw at the negotiating table, not on the battlefield. The media report also mentioned that although most clashes in recent months have erupted in northern Arakan State, fighting has also spread further south including in Kyaukphyu Township, where the Chinese have significant business interests. However, Khaing Thukha said the Chinese envoy did not specifically refer to hostilities in Kyaukphyu.[61]

However, the AA, unlike some other EAGs, have not kept themselves limited to Chinese funding. Alternate sources of funding have been established, including from Arakan expatriates and local businessmen. Dr. Min Zaw Oo of the Myanmar Institute of Peace and Security, brought out[62] that the insurgency in Rakhine as a route for liberation, had been visualised by the Rakhine nationalists since long. However, the reason they could not succeed was the weapons supply. But this

Figure 7.6: Maj Gen Twan Mrat Naing (L) with Chinese Special Envoy for Asian Affairs Sun Guoxiang (R) at Laizain, January 2020.

Source: DMG Media Group and The Kachin Net.

time, they managed weapons from the Bangladesh side since the Tatmadaw has tightened the movement of weapons by the land route from China and Thailand. According to him, overtly, Bangladesh policy is not to support the AA. However, during an interaction with escapees from the AA, it was evident that they had been kept in Bangladesh and they described big camps, rice mills, three hospitals and other structures endemic to Bangladesh. Dr. Min Zaw Oo suggests that even though it might not be the official Bangladesh policy to support the AA, there seems to be support possibly from the Border Guards Bangladesh (BGB). There are also reports of drug *quid pro quo* taking place between the AA and the BGB, with some drug-making chemicals coming in from India.

Bangladesh is an established supply route for weapons and was recently in the news for the supply of 500 assault rifles, 30 Universal Machine Guns, 70,000 rounds of ammunition, and a large number of grenades, transported through Chittagong Hill Tracts to Paletwa for the AA. The weapons that landed at Monakhali beach near Whaikyang on 21 February 2020 were from the TCL Company in China, and reached the AA camp at Sandak (Mro) near Thanchi on 2 March 2020. Earlier, in 2010, the same route had been used by the National Socialist Council of Nagaland (Isak-Muivah) to bring in a huge consignment of weapons. To counter this, the Tatmadaw is allegedly trying to develop links with former rebels of the Shanti Bahini in the Chittagong Hill Tracts.[63]

Figure 7.7: Route used by AA for smuggling arms on 2 March 2020

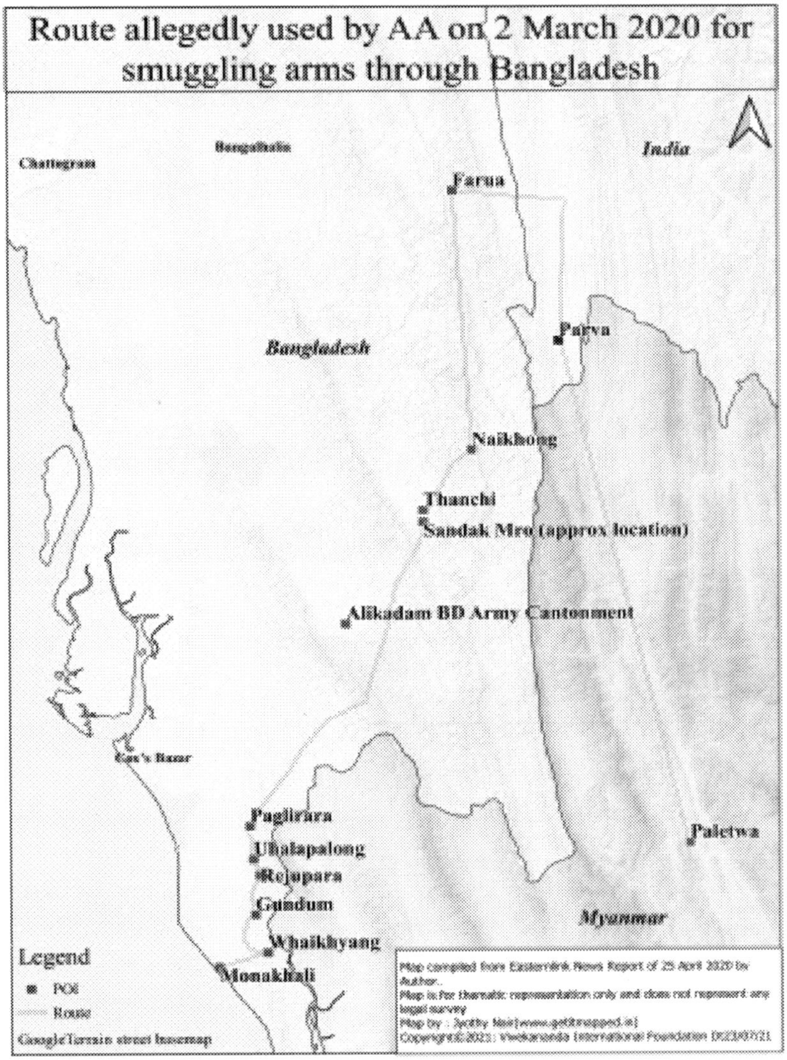

Source: Prepared by the Author based on an Easternlink report

Anders Corr, a US-based analyst with an interest in South East Asia, corroborates this input of arms supply to the AA:

> *China is providing approximately 95 per cent of the Arakan Army's funding. He said the Arakan Army has approximately 50 of the MANPADS surface-to-air missiles.(…) A diplomat in the region communicated to the author that "seven different groups (including the AA) in Myanmar received Chinese arms and support." He said that the "Chinese object has always been to keep the West away*

from Myanmar by keeping Myanmar [a] weak and closed state with a poor humanitarian record." The diplomat requested anonymity due to fear of retaliation.

A think tank analyst who also asked to remain anonymous, because he was not cleared to release the information, said that: "The Arakan Army (AA) is being supported by China as a matter of policy in line with its support to the other [ethnic militia] groups, e.g., UWSA, KIA, etc. The nature of support to the AA comprises finances, uniforms, weapons, ammunition and other war like stores including shoulder-fired SAMs (FN-6). The supply of weapons and ammunition continues till this day and so does the supply of money. AA has apparently also received money to ensure they do not stray towards [China's Kyaukphyu] Deep Sea Port." The Kyaukphyu Port is part of China's Belt & Road development project and this development seeks to compete with an Indian port project just 100 km to the north.

India's Recommended Approach to the AA

India is at the crossroads as far as the AA is concerned. The writing is on the wall that the AA has now grown too big and too competent to be taken on by the Tatmadaw. The Tatmadaw looks at assistance from the Indian Army which has so far played ball through 'Operation Sunrise II'. However, it is unlikely that India will cross the national red line and allow its troops to operate in Myanmar territory, given its experience with the Indian Peace Keeping Force in Sri Lanka. Without Indian troops operating in Myanmar, the Tatmadaw has no chance to reign in the AA. Thence, logically, India must engage the AA, which officially it cannot, being a designated terrorist organisation by a legitimate government. But there is that very narrow window of opportunity within which the Indian Government must operate and engage with the AA. Thus overtly, or covertly, India has no option but to interact with the AA and drive for peace between the belligerent sides. India has high stakes in the region due to the alignment of the Kaladan Project Thus the handling of the AA has to be with an open mind.

Presently, the road construction from the north (Zorinpui) to the south (Paletwa) has commenced under a security cover from the Tatmadaw. However, this security, and more importantly, this sense of security is transient. While it may be possible to construct a road under security cover, operating it on a long term basis will not be possible with security cover. Simply put, the quantum of security forces required to dominate the road will be too expensive to sustain on a permanent basis. Despite security, the AA or any other insurgent group would not find it difficult to interdict movement of cargo traffic on the road at a prohibitive frequency. Thus, both the Indian and Myanmar authorities would do well to exploit the stake that AA and the Arakan population have in the region and in the Kaladan Project and work out a mechanism that enables all stakeholders to benefit from the project.

This of course presupposes recognising the AA, which in the present stage, is probably not feasible by the Myanmar Government, but elections can change everything. Presently, both the AA and the Tatmadaw have not yet reached the culmination points of their offensives. Both have enough resources and stamina to continue the battle. This stage will have to be gone through. And just as well, since formation cutting of the road from Zorinpui to Kaletwa will probably be completed by post monsoon 2021 if uninterrupted. From Kaletwa to Paletwa will take another two years, i.e., till 2023. Thus, operations can, at the most optimistic, start from 2024. This gives all stakeholders (i.e., Tatmadaw and the AA) enough time to exhaust their military options and then come to the negotiating table. However, the channels of communication with the AA must remain open from the side of the Indian Government and concurrently, the Myanmar Government has to be sensitised to be open to eventual negotiations with the AA for a lasting political solution. The final end state that India must work towards is one where peace prevails in a just manner with the stakes of all the affected members, including the local population, the AA and the Myanmar Government, comprehensively addressed. In such an environment, the true potential of the Kaladan Project can be realised to generate employment, income and development in the region.

In conclusion, I cannot help but draw attention to a statement by the AA Chief, Major General Twan Mrat Naing, who stated that[64] the reason for the success of his organisation and what is essentially the key to success in the conflict thus:

> *"One of the main reasons why the Arakan Army can firmly stand up and resist full-force offensive attacks of the enemy is because the entire population of Arakan supports us. People are the main roots of the revolution."*

NOTES

1. Martin Smith, *Arakan (Rakhine State), A Land in Conflict on Myanmar's Western Frontier*, Transnational Institute, Amsterdam, December 2019.
2. Wai Mar Tun, Min Thein Aung, and Roseanne Gerin. "Myanmar's Arakan Army Denies Link to Muslim Militant Group in Rakhine State". 2018. *Radio Free Asia*, https://www.rfa.org/english/news/myanmar/myanmars-arakan-army-denies-link-01082019163459.html
3. Ibid, pg. 45.

4. Carl P. Turner, Regional Conflict Complex Theory and the Syrian War: A Conflict Analysis and Resolution Perspective, Conflict Analysis and Resolution Information Services, Working Papers 18 – 01, 27 April 2018, https://turnerconflict.files.wordpress.com/2018/04/caris-working-paper-18-01-rcct-theory-and-the-syrian-war.pdf
5. Smith, 2019, pg. 9.
6. Jaideep Chanda, *Myanmar's Rakhine Conflict Threatens Regional Peace – Analysis, Eurasia Review* Web Article, 24 March 2020, https://www.eurasiareview.com/24032020-myanmars-rakhine-conflict-threatens-regional-peace-analysis/ (Accessed on 30 June 2020).
7. Martin Smith, *Arakan (Rakhine State), A Land in Conflict on Myanmar's Western Frontier*, Transnational Institute, Amsterdam, December 2019, pg. 14.
8. Cchavi Vasisht, *Myanmar Ethnic Strife: The Rise of Arakan Army,* Vivekananda International Foundation Web Article, 30 Apr 2020: https://www.vifindia.org/article/2020/april/30/myanmar-ethnic-strife-the-rise-of-arakan-army (Accessed on 30 June 2020).
9. Northern Alliance is a group of four members, namely, Arakan Army, Kachin Independence Army (KIA), the Táang National Liberation Army (TNLA) and the Myanmar National Democratic Alliance Army (MNDAA). The Three Brotherhood Alliance consists of three members of the Northern Alliance except the KIA.
10. Arakan Army, "About Us", Available from: https://www.arakanarmy.net/about-us (Accessed on 30 June 2020).
11. enotes, *Please elaborate on Federalism vs Confederalism,* Law and Politics Q & A, https://www.enotes.com/homework-help/whats-federalism-v-s-confederalism-163973 https://www.arakanarmy.net/about-us (Accessed on 30 June 2020).
12. Of the 47 seats in the Hluttaw, 12 seats are reserved for military representatives. Thus, the electoral battle takes place for only 47 minus 12 = 35 seats.
13. Lawi Weng, 'Fighting Reported between Govt and Arakan Army', *The Irrawaddy*, 30 March, 2015, https://www.irrawaddy.com/news/burma/fighting-reported-between-govt-and-arakan-army.html (Accessed on 30 June 2020).
14. International Crises Group, 'A New Dimension of Violence in Myanmar's Rakhine State', Briefing 154/Asia, 24 January 2019, Available from: https://www.crisisgroup.org/asia/south-east-asia/myanmar/b154-new-dimension-violence-myanmars-rakhine-state (Accessed on 30 June 2020).
15. Myanmar Institute of Peace and Security, *Annual Peace and Security Review 2018,* pg. 39.
16. Jaideep Chanda, *Myanmar August 2019,* Vivekananda International Foundation Web Article, 10 September 2019: https://www.vifindia.org/print/6634 (Accessed on 16 October 2020).
17. Jaideep Chanda, *From Sanctions to Submarines: Myanmar July 2019,* Vivekananda International Foundation Web Article, 12 August 2019: https://www.vifindia.org/article/2019/august/12/from-sanctions-to-submarines-myanmar-july-2019 (Accessed on 30 June 2020).
18. Aakriti Vinayak, Alakh Ranjan & Jaideep Chanda, *Myanmar Round Up: October 2019,* Vivekananda International Foundation Web Article, 21 November 2019, https://www.vifindia.org/article/2019/november/21/myanmar-round-up-october-2019 (Accessed on 30 June 2020).
19. Aakriti Vinayak & Jaideep Chanda, *Myanmar Round Up: December 2019,* Vivekananda International Foundation Web Article, 29 January 2020, https://www.vifindia.org/print/7072?via=Azure (Accessed on 16 October 2020).
20. Ibid.
21. Jaideep Chanda, *Myanmar Round Up: January 2020,* Vivekananda International Foundation Web Article, 21 November 2019, https://www.vifindia.org/article/2020/february/14/myanmar-round-up-january-2020 (Accessed on 30 June 2020).
22. BNI Multimedia Group, *Arakan Army warns civilians to avoid using military vehicles, vessels,*

Development Media Group Web Article, 24 February 2020, https://www.bnionline.net/en/news/arakan-army-warns-civilians-avoid-using-military-vehicles-vessels (Accessed on 30 June 2020).

23. Cchavi Vasisht & Jaideep Chanda, *Myanmar Round Up: March 2020,* Vivekananda International Foundation Web Article, 21 April 2020, https://www.vifindia.org/print/7369 (Accessed on 18 October 2020).
24. Done with the approval of the Union Government in exercise of the Anti-Terrorism Law Section 6, sub-section (e) and Section 72 (b).
25. Vasisht & Chanda, note 22.
26. Vasisht & Chanda, note 22.
27. Speech by Commander-In-Chief at the 11th Anniversary Day of the Arakan Army, 10 April, 2020. Available from: https://www.arakanarmy.net/post/speech-by-commander-in-chief-at-11th-anniversary-day-of-arakan-army (Accessed on 15 April 2020).
28. Ye Mon, 'The Arakan Army and the Storm of the Revolution', Frontier Myanmar, 29 March 2019. Available from: https://frontiermyanmar.net/en/the-arakan-army-and-the-storm-of-the-revolution (Accessed on 15 April 2020).
29. Highlights in bold are by the author.
30. Mizzima Myanmar News Report, AA/ULA welcomes Chinese investment in Rakhine, 24 July 2019, http://www.mizzima.com/article/aaula-welcomes-chinese-investment-rakhine (Accessed on 4 August 2019).
31. Roseanne Grin, Arakan Army Voices Support for Big Chinese Projects in Myanmar's Rakhine State, Radio Free Asia, 23 June 2019, https://www.rfa.org/english/news/myanmar/arakan-army-voices-support-07232019152712.html (Accessed on 4 August 2019).
32. Aakriti Vinayak, Alakh Ranjan & Jaideep Chanda, *Myanmar Round Up: October 2019,* Vivekananda International Foundation Web Article, 21 November 2019, https://www.vifindia.org/print/6861 (Accessed on 18 October 2020).
33. Radio Free Asia, Myanmar Army Says it Rescued 15 Abductees From Arakan Army Custody, 28 October 2019, https://www.rfa.org/english/news/myanmar/military-rescue-10282019173126.html (Accessed on 20 June 2020).
34. Sit Thet Aung, Scores killed, 14 hostages rescued in military air assault in Rakhine, Myanmar Times, 28 October 2019, https://www.mmtimes.com/news/scores-killed-14-hostages-rescued-military-air-assault-rakhine.html (Accessed on 20 June 2020).
35. Min Aung Khine, AA Releases 25 Hostages, Blames Myanmar Military for Deadly Bombing, The Irrawaddy, 5 November 2019, https://www.irrawaddy.com/news/burma/aa-releases-25-hostages-blames-myanmar-military-deadly-bombing.html (Accessed on 20 June 2020).
36. Arakan Army, Interview with Captain Nyi Nyi Zaw, 16 Jun 2020, https://www.arakanarmy.net/post/interview-with-captain-nyi-nyi-zaw (Accessed on 20 June 2020).
37. Swe Lei Mon, AA releases interview of captive Tatmadaw officer, 18 June 2020, https://www.mmtimes.com/news/aa-releases-interview-captive-tatmadaw-officer.html (Accessed on 20 June 2020).
38. Khaing Roe La, AA releases engineer detained in Shwe Nadi ferry incident, Development Media Group, 25 February 2020, https://www.dmediag.com/news/1211-aare (Accessed on 20 June 2020).
39. Win Myat Kyaw, NLD urges for release Amyotha Hluttaw MP from detention, Development Media Group, 9 November 2019, https://www.dmediag.com/news/858-detention(Accessed on 20 June 2020).
40. In some news reports the name is spelt U Hawi Tin e.g, https://myanmar-now.org/en/news/arakan-army-detains-nld-mp-accused-of-tatmadaw-collaboration
41. Vasisht & Chanda, note 22.
42. BNI Online, *Arakan Army Detains—Then Releases—Workers From Construction Site Reportedly*

Used in Burma Army Attack, Khonumthung News, 25 March 2020, https://www.bnionline.net/en/news/arakan-army-detains-then-releases-workers-construction-site-reportedly-used-burma-army-attack (Accessed on 30 June 2020).

43. Jaideep Chanda, *Myanmar's Rakhine Conflict Threatens Regional Peace – Analysis,* Eurasia Review Web Edition, 24 March 2020, https://www.eurasiareview.com/24032020-myanmars-rakhine-conflict-threatens-regional-peace-analysis/ (Accessed on 30 June 2020).
44. Min Aung Khine, *Three Villagers Injured in Landmine Blasts in Western Myanmar's Rakhine State, The Irrawaddy* Web Article, 31 March 2020, https://www.irrawaddy.com/news/burma/three-villagers-injured-landmine-blasts-western-myanmars-rakhine-state.html (Accessed on 30 June 2020).
45. Jaideep Chanda, *Myanmar's Rakhine conflict threatens regional peace*, South Asia Monitor, Spotlight, 21 March 2020, https://southasiamonitor.org/spotlight/myanmars-rakhine-conflict-threatens-regional-peace (Accessed on 30 June 2020).
46. Jaideep Chanda, *Riverine Warfare: Emerging Trend in the Rakhine Conflict in Myanmar,* Kalinga International Foundation Web Article.
47. Chanda, note 44.
48. Andrew Selth, *Secrets and Power in Myanmar: Intelligence and the fall of General Khin Nyunt,* ISEAS Publishing, Singapore, 2019, pp. ix and x.
49. Yun Sun, *China, the Arakan Army, and a Myanmar solution,* Frontier Myanmar Web Article, 9 March 2020, https://frontiermyanmar.net/en/china-the-arakan-army-and-a-myanmar-solution (Accessed on 30 June 2020).
50. Khin Tharaphy Oo, *Class Conflict: Nearly 500 students miss exams in Kyauktaw Township*, BNIOnline.com, 2 March 2020, https://www.bnionline.net/en/news/class-conflict-nearly-500-students-miss-exams-kyauktaw-township (Accessed on 30 June 2020).
51. Lei Lei, *Fighting Closes Schools Ahead of Key Exams in Myanmar's Chin State, The Irrawaddy* Web Article, 20 February 2020, https://www.irrawaddy.com/news/burma/fighting-closes-schools-ahead-key-exams-myanmars-chin-state.html(Accessed on 30 June 2020).
52. Vasisht & Chanda, note 22.
53. During the author's visit to Myanmar in December 2019. The 'friend' who works for an NGO, preferred to remain anonymous.
54. Subir Bhaumik, Myanmar: Chin rebels oppose Arakan Army's Paletwa claim, NE Now, 27 January 2020, https://nenow.in/neighbour/myanmar/myanmar-chin-rebels-oppose-arakan-armys-paletwa-claim.html(Accessed on 30 June 2020).
55. Salai Za Uk Ling, Chin National Day: collateral damage, Frontier Myanmar, 18 February 2020, https://www.frontiermyanmar.net/en/chin-national-day-collateral-damage (Accessed on 30 June 2020).
56. BNI Online, AA attacks Tatmadaw convoy in Ramree Township, Development Multimedia Group, 24 February 2020, https://www.bnionline.net/en/news/aa-attacks-tatmadaw-convoy-ramree-township(Accessed on 13 June 2020).
57. Jaideep Chanda, note 44.
58. Nyein Nyein, Switzerland Agrees to Resettle Wife, Children of Myanmar's Rakhine Rebel Leader, The Irrawaddy, 25 February 2020, https://www.irrawaddy.com/news/burma/switzerland-agrees-resettle-wife-children-myanmars-rakhine-rebel-leader.html (Accessed on 13 June 2020).
59. Website of Dr Nyo Twan Awng https://www.drnyotwanawng.com/# (Accessed on 13 June 2020).
60. For articles on supply of arms to Myanmar from China, see the following links: http://mizzima.com/article/chinese-president-denies-supplying-arms-ethnic-armed-groups; https://www.irrawaddy.com/news/burma/chinese-presidents-claim-beijing-not-arming-eaos- met-skepticism-myanmar.html; https://www.asiatimes.com/2020/01/article/chinas- loose- arms-

still-fuel-myanmars-civil-wars/https://www.mm times.com/news/xi- says-china-never- sells-weapons-myanmar-armed-groups.html

61. Phadu Tun Aung, Chinese envoy urges AA leaders to de-escalate hostilities, Development Media Group, Sittwe, 12 January 2020, https://www.dmediag.com/news/1060-ceu (Accessed on 13 June 2020).
62. In an interaction with the Author during his visit to India for the BIMSTEC Regional Security Dialogue at VIF in November 2019.
63. Subir Bhaumik, Arakan Army Gets Chinese Weapons Through Bangladesh, *The Eastern Link*, 25 April 2020, https://theeasternlink.com/arakan-army-gets-chinese-weapons-through-bangladesh/ (Accessed on 13 June 2020).
64. Founder and Commander in Chief of the Arakan Army and the United League of Arakan. This statement was made during the 11th Anniversary Day of the Arakan Army on 10 April 2020. See https://www.arakanarmy.net/post/speech-by-commander-in-chief-at-11th-anniversary-day-of-arakan-army (Accessed on 30 June 2020).

CHAPTER 8
The Tatmadaw: Raising the 'Standard'

> *...once the Tatmadaw leadership is convinced that political stability has been established and that there is mutual trust between politicians or civilians and military personnel, then there is a possibility that it will reduce its political clout.*
>
> —**Maung Aung Myoe**[1]

In military terminology, the term 'standard' refers to a flag, usually the flag of an army or a particular regiment. The term 'raising the standard' therefore literally implies raising a flag and is figuratively used to mean raising the plane of performance at which any entity is operating, to a higher level. Contextually, in 2016, the Myanmar Armed Forces, i.e., the Tatmadaw, had formally sought to become a 'standard army'. Does this, by implication, mean that the senior leadership of the Tatmadaw has tacitly acknowledged that, in some form, the organisation was below standard? Or is it just a way of expression, similar to when any army seeks to improve its professionalism or modernise itself?

This chapter discusses the above aspects and also argues that operationally all is not well in the Tatmadaw. It comes to this conclusion through a study of the tactical level operations that the Tatmadaw has been conducting all over Myanmar, but specifically in the Rakhine conflict and the conduct of its troops in these regions. It identifies a fault line within the Tatmadaw which suggests that the vast gap in lifestyle and privileges between the bottom-rung soldiers and officers and the senior leadership is having an adverse impact on the professionalism of the force. While the religious grounding of the troops and their philosophical approach to life, guided by the principles of Theravada Buddhism, has held them in good stead, the same may not hold good for long as the country opens up to the rest of the world and exposes itself through social and other media to alternative value systems and established standards of military practices and procedures. It is particularly critical of the way it conducts its counter-insurgency operations, especially in Rakhine State. The chapter also looks at the Republic of the Union of Myanmar Defence White Paper (2015) to gain an understanding into the thought processes, whether actual or projected, of the Tatmadaw.

The Republic of the Union of Myanmar Defence White Paper (2015)

The copy of the Defence White Paper (2015) the author chanced upon was picked up during his visit to Myanmar in December 2019. This innocuous, thin, 99-page white paperback sized publication has seven chapters which provide insights into the higher defence thinking of the Tatmadaw. This is possibly the first time in recent years that such a White Paper has been published. Salient aspects of the White Paper are discussed in the succeeding paragraphs.

The importance of international acceptability to the Tatmadaw is surprisingly high, as gleaned from the White Paper. The second paragraph of the Introduction jumps straight into the need to '*...give particular emphasis to international co-operation so as to create harmony, trust, mutual understanding, and shared interests...*'[2] and then, in Chapter I itself, which is on International and Regional Security (Situation) and dedicates a five-page section on International Security Arena. This section is a global environmental scan which covers aspects such as the NATO, UN, EU, WTO, Asia Pacific and even mentions the Commonwealth of Independent States. China-India 'power rivalry' finds a mention here and again in Chapter II where the White Paper highlights that '*Myanmar is wedged between China and India which are the most populated countries in the world and also the most powerful ones in the region and has to share long borders with them.* Chapter I, Paragraph 7, gives a hint of the rationale behind the quest for international cooperation. It says that '*As non-state actors are involved in terrorism as a network, a single nation cannot afford to confront it alone by conventional means and all countries have to combine their effort to combat and eliminate these attacks*'.[3] In the run-up to this statement, it alludes to the 9/11 US attacks and concludes that they changed international relations and foreign policies. This correlation hints that the lack of success on the counter-insurgency front against the EAOs seems to be driving the pursuit for international cooperation in the possible hope that international support might assist in the battle against the EAGs. This expectation seems flawed since as long as the basics of insurgent grievances are not addressed, the counter-insurgency programme is doomed to fail.

The Tatmadaw quest for international cooperation has been the subject of study by the Tagaung Institute of Political Studies, a Myanmar-based think tank. It has brought out a fascinating paper titled *The Study of Senior General Min Hlaing Aung's Foreign Trips: Military Diplomacy and Dynamics of Tatmadaw's International Relations.* This paper analyses 46 foreign trips to 23 countries made by the Senior General from the day he assumed power (30 March 2011) till June 2018.[4] It concludes that the Senior General's foreign visits appear to have three main purposes viz. to build friendly bilateral relations; to enhance military relations; and to present to the foreign governments and militaries the Tatmadaw's willingness to cooperate both with Myanmar's civilian government, as well as with foreign governments and militaries. One constant motivation, it seems, would be to work toward strategic balance by countervailing the Chinese influence by hedging amongst all the other nations.

Chapter II devotes a section to challenges and lists globalisation as a possible challenge due to the interdependence, especially on the economic front. On the military front, it sees the '*military build-up of neighbouring countries, provision of equipment, financial assistance and encouragement by external elements to internal armed groups and unsettled boundary issues*' as the main challenges to the Union. Social media finds an oblique mention (use of soft power through technology) and neo-colonialism is described as an '*ideology that influences the mind, rather than material in a very delicate way*'. The Tatmadaw has lately, in 2019 and 2020, been seen as losing the narrative battle to the better-organised EAGs which have successfully been able to steer international opinion. The recent case against the Myanmar Government by The Gambia over the Rohingya issue is a case in point.

The chapter on National Policy and National Defence Policy (Chapter III) is essentially a textbook type list of various aspects which form National Policy, Objectives and aspects of Foreign Policy. The section on National Defence Policy lists six policies and five Defence Missions; basics of Myanmar's Defence Strategy, which is articulated as being the People's War Strategy. Chapter IV highlights the National Defence and Security Council and lists the responsibilities of the Myanmar Tatmadaw as a whole and each of the constituents, viz., Army, Navy, Air Force, Corps and Services, Defence Reserve Elements, Myanmar Police Force and the People's Militia. For the record, the National Defence and Security Council has never been called together by the NLD Government due to fears of a de facto military takeover, a fact which the Tatmadaw resents.

Chapter V, Serving Defence Duties, defines the protection of land; territorial waters including internal waters, territorial seas, contiguous zone and the EEZ and airspace. It lays down eligibility criteria for service in the Tatmadaw under two contract systems, i.e., the full term service system and the short term service system. The chapter also speaks of the existence of Sixty Codes of Conduct proclaimed for all military services, but does not list them. For internal cohesion within the Tatmadaw, it talks of Organising Committees at different levels, seemingly akin to welfare measures in other armies. These committees conduct myriad activities to include elevating the living standards of personnel, families and dependants; educational discussions; history of the Union and the Tatmadaw; implementation of eight poverty alleviation principles; social welfare services; media programmes including Tatmadaw broadcasting services, TV channels, newspapers and magazines broadcast, published and distributed. Chapter V also touches upon military equipment and organisation and makes mention of defence research and development and expenditure.

The chapter on State Building (Chapter VI) is all about the Tatmadaw's self-perception in Myanmar's politics. It brings out the number of occasions it has had to step in to preserve independence and stabilise the nation. Thus a portion of paragraph 83 reads:

> *In 1953, Myanmar Tatmadaw repelled the KMT intruders, regarding it as a nationalistic duty. Again, ignited by 1958 political splits, the tumultuous situations led the country to the brink of losing sovereignty and the Armed Forces led by General Ne Win had to step in as caretaker government.*[5]

Paragraph 85 goes on to describe the 1988 uprisings for democracy:

> *During the 1988 uprisings for democracy, Myanmar was again at the risk of disintegrating, losing sovereignty and being servitude because of the opportunistic politicians who wanted to take political power in a shortcut way amongst the people who were dissatisfied with general hardships and desire for change, and underground members of Burma Communist Party (BCP), those who want to meddle in Myanmar's politics and those who sought self-interest in the riots and the indiscriminate violence of anarchists. Under those deteriorating situations, the Tatmadaw had no alternative but to use whatever means available in restoring law and order on 18 September 1988 and had to save the Union again.*

This chapter also includes a section on State Development Activities under the Leadership of the Tatmadaw which reads more like a party manifesto listing achievements in various sectors such as the agricultural, transportation, communications, energy, education, border development and health sectors.

Another section on Participation of the Tatmadaw in HADR includes coloured photographs and records of its participation in various natural disasters such as floods, cyclones and earthquakes.

The last chapter, Chapter VII, tells us about the Tatmadaw's Security Cooperation with International Organisations over the years. The White Paper concludes with the assertion that the paper reflects the national security and defence activities of Myanmar in simple terms.

Selected extracts of the White Paper are reproduced in **Appendix M** for reference.

The Standard Army

At the inaugural Union Peace Conference from 12 to 16 January 2016, the Tatmadaw C-in-C, Senior General Min Aung Hlaing, outlined a vision to transform it into a *Standard Army*. While the term 'Standard Army' was not mentioned in the Defence White Paper (2015) published in late 2014, and no official documents on it have been released to the public, however, it has become the Tatmadaw's official stand, and one that is quoted frequently by the Chief.[6] Amara Thiha of the Myanmar Institute of Peace and Security (MIPS) has identified five features of the Standard Army as alluded to by the Chief. The first concludes that:

> *The Tatmadaw uses the English expression "Standard Army" and never a Burmese translation. It is not the same as a "professional army", although the media and international organisations often use this expression in its place. "Standard Army" is also different from "federal army", which has been proposed by ethnic armed groups during the nationwide ceasefire negotiations and political dialogue. The Tatmadaw's position is that it is already the one and only Union army, as different ethnic groups serve throughout its ranks. Through modernisation, they will transform this one and only Union army, the Tatmadaw, into a Standard Army. Although there is no official or clear rationale for not using the term "professional", it may be due to connotations with mercenaries, and with civilian control or oversight.*

The reluctance to use the word 'professional', has been elaborated upon[7] by Dr. Maung Aung Myoe, Professor, Associate Dean and Programme Director of the Graduate School of International Relations, International University of Japan, and author of *Building the Tatmadaw: Myanmar Armed Forces since 1948*. He explains that in Myanmar language the word 'professionalism' is commonly translated as *Kyesar*, which has a derogatory connotation in that the job is being undertaken for money which implies that the person would betray someone to a higher bidder or do the job with '*no social responsibility*'. Because of this negative image, the Tatmadaw shuns the term 'professional army', which translates as *Kyesar-Tat* which connotes 'mercenary army'. The senior military leadership since independence has often drawn out this difference. Aung San, father of the present-day Tatmadaw, claimed that, '*our Tatmadaw is not a mercenary army and it is unlike the one formed by the British*'. General Ne Win too has said that the Tatmadaw was formed with hard-core politicians and it was not a mercenary army. Senior General Min Aung Hlaing also echoed the sentiment when he highlighted the patriotic nature of the Tatmadaw, '*borne out of Myanmar people through the struggle for freedom*'. This conceptual differentiation between patriotic soldier [*Myochit Sitthar*] and mercenary soldier [*Kyesar Sitthar*], concludes Dr. Maung, is important for the Tatmadaw psyche.

Secondly, Thiha highlights that the process to achieve 'standardisation' is one which is integral to the Tatmadaw and would run parallel to the security sector reforms which were more relevant to the peace process. Thus, by implication, 'standardisation' was independent of the peace process and would continue, irrespective of the success or failure of the process. Third, the present Tatmadaw military doctrine dates back to 1988[8] and has been described as "*the people's war under modern conditions*", which was reiterated during the January 2016 Union Peace Conference as "*supporting the Tatmadaw through the people's war strategy for national defence*". This suggests that the people's war doctrine is still the official position, even though a transition may be in the process. Fourthly, for the Tatmadaw, achieving international recognition and transforming its image is top priority. This is one sphere in which the Tatmadaw has been courageous and opened exposure to international instructors, both with trainers coming from China, India and Japan, as well as subscribing to courses abroad, including in India. Thus, the Defence Services Technological Academy was upgraded on the lines of the Defence Services Academy in 2012-13 and it was from 2015 that foreign visitors were permitted to enter.

Finally, he concludes, though the Tatmadaw is seeking to transform into a Standard Army, its national goals and national defence policy remain unchanged. The focus of the transformation process is international engagement, modernisation and defence capability. However, it will remain embedded in national politics and international recognition may serve to legitimise the role of the Tatmadaw in politics creating a unique form of civil-military relationship. Another anonymous observer who has worked with the Tatmadaw, opines that the Tatmadaw was expected to undertake substantial structural, qualitative and inclusive reforms to become 'The Standard Army' to be accepted as a neutral Myanmar national military and remove the tag of 'Burmese/Barmar Army'.

Yan Pai of *The Irrawaddy* writes that:

> *Recruiting more non-Bamar ethnic soldiers, especially in the officer cadre, to reflect inclusiveness and represent a national union army, was another measure to transform the army. However, promotions to higher ranks remain exclusive to Barmar officers. The recent visit of Senior General Min Aung Hlaing and his wife to the grave of General Smith Dun, the first commander-in-chief of the Myanmar Armed Forces*[9] *for the first time on 14 February 2020 in Kalaw, Shan State, seems to promote acceptability of ethnic soldiers. Known as the 'four-foot Colonel', Gen Dun was a Karen who was promoted to the rank of General and appointed as the commander-in-chief of the armed forces. This was not only because of the key role he played in the early years of the country's struggle for independence, but also to foster confidence between different ethnic groups and the majority Burmans in a future union that would include all ethnic minorities. However, that confidence was shaken post the January 1949 Battle of Insein when Karen insurgents began their war for independence from Burma. From that point on, Burman leaders no longer trusted the Karens, and Dun was removed from his position, along with his fellow Karen troops. He spent his final years in Kalaw, a hill town in Shan State, where he devoted most of his time to gardening, reading and writing the book, "Memoirs of the Four-Foot Colonel," which was published a year after his death in 1979 by Cornell University.*[10]

This journey to standardisation was expected through modernisation, increasing educational standards, foreign exposure of Tatmadaw officers, interaction with foreign armies, joint training and increasing maritime capabilities. And all this was with a hidden aim to transform the Tatmadaw to be acceptable to the EAOs and the international community as the only Union army called Myanmar Standard Army. One of the measures that has been taken by the Tatmadaw to transform into a Standard Army include increasing the basic required educational level for recruits of the Tatmadaw from 6th to 8th standard in 2016. Further, in a bid to make the Tatmadaw more gender inclusive, enrolment of women officers in it commenced from 2015. Prior to this, a batch of 21 female medical officers was commissioned on 1 March 2012 after a gap of 15 years. In addition, the recruitment of female nurses, through the army scholarship programme at the Institute of Nursing, was introduced in December 2012.[11]

Dr. Prashanth Parameshwaran, Senior Columnist at *The Diplomat* and a Fellow at the Wilson Centre's Asia Program, identifies two more features of the 'Standard

Army', viz., acquisition of new weapons and trying to improve recruitment and training. On 15 December 2019, Myanmar's Air Force commemorated its 70th anniversary with a high-profile ceremony at the Air Training School at Meiktila Air Base in Mandalay. At the anniversary, Senior General Min Aung Hlaing commissioned 10 military aircraft, including six Russian Yak-130 fighter jets, two Dutch Fokker-70 and two French-Italian ATR 42-430 aircraft. During his speech, he, for the first time cast the development of the Air Force's capabilities as part of a wider transformation of the military into the Standard Army, and noted the importance of air power given the growing prominence of asymmetric warfare and the role of air operations within them. The allusion to the importance of airpower in asymmetric warfare reveals a sense of the rationale for using fighters indiscriminately in the Rakhine conflict. This is discussed in detail subsequently.[12]

Anthony Davis, a Bangkok-based *Jane's* Correspondent, writes[13] that from 3 to 5 February 2018, the military staged its largest ever air-land-sea war game,[14] 'Sinbyushin' with a very public live-fire exercise to beef up its poor image and raise its credentials as a professional war-fighting machine to an international as well as domestic audience, and display the armed forces' growing capabilities and ambitions. The scale of the drills reflects efforts to build a "standard military". The term implies a force that is both technologically modern and operationally far better trained and integrated than at present.

Figure 8.1: Army fires missiles during the combined military exercise 'Sinbyushin' in Pathein

Source: https://www.globalnewlightofmyanmar.com/tatmadaw-army-navy-air-force-conduct-sinbyushin-military-exercise/

Having seen the basics of the Standard Army, let us now take a look at various facets of the Tatmadaw, based on various interactions. Interaction of Indian Army personnel with those of the Myanmar Army takes place at regular intervals over the 1,643-km border that India and Myanmar share. At several locations on the IMB there were eight such interactions, at the last count. A monthly institutionalised interaction also takes place as part of the India-Myanmar Post Level Meeting (IMPLM). In addition, there are a number of Myanmar officers undergoing training in India and Indian officers in Myanmar. Finally, junior-level meetings, exchanges, military exercises and visits provide ample opportunity for lasting impressions to be formed on both sides. Some of these impressions have been highlighted in the following paragraphs and reasonable conclusions have been attempted to be drawn from them.

Recruitment

The White Paper quotes the Defence Services Council Order (13/73) to lay down that all eligible citizens in good health over 18 years of age can join the Tatmadaw on their own accord for serving as soldiers and other ranks. For joining as commissioned officers, the White Paper refers to the Office of the Chief of Military Appointment General's Directive, which stipulates that those who have passed the matriculation examination, are between 16 to 18 years and university degree holders not older than 23 years are eligible. The entrance process includes written tests, medical examination and personal interviews. Option also exists for serving soldiers to qualify and get commissioned as officers.

Unanimous opinion exists amongst observers that manpower management within the Tatmadaw is, in various ways, actually sub-standard. Several observers have reported manpower shortages plaguing the army, as seen from reports of under-strength battalions deployed on its various borders including the IMB. Davis also highlights that '*manpower shortages across multiple fronts mean unit rotations in combat areas are typically extended months beyond the level of military effectiveness.*' This leads to another major issue for the Tatmadaw; that of recruitment. Part of the problem, it seems, was self-inflicted. An interaction with Tatmadaw officers[15] during the author's visit to Myanmar in December 2019 reveals the existence of a 'From Quantity towards Quality'[16] policy which apparently came into effect in 2012. As per this policy, which was initiated by the present C-in-C immediately on taking over in 2011, the strength of cadets was reduced from 1,200 to 400-500 per intake. This reduction was effected by increasing the qualifying marks for the entrance exams by 50. The source also provided a sense of the selection procedure when she brought out that from 2012 onwards, candidates scoring 480 and above out of the 600 marks entrance exam[17] were sent to the medical corps; those scoring between 429 to 479 were allotted the tech institutes and those scoring from 380 to 419 were sent to the DSA to join the arms and the supporting arms. *Prima facie*, this sounds extraordinary since the assessment requirements for medical aspirants would be different from those aspiring for, say, engineering or combat arms and so on.

The recruitment problem was also brought out by Dr. Min Zaw Oo[18] who revealed that the Tatmadaw was not being able to recruit enough to fill the rank-and-file and this was a major issue. He attributed this to the other employment opportunities now available to youth and also to the political legitimacy of the Tatmadaw. Dr. Naing Swe Oo of the Thay Nin Ga Institute of Security Studies, a security-oriented think tank in Yangon, reiterated[19] the same and mentioned that this problem is specific to soldiers and not officers. He explained that the youth prefer to work in Thailand and Malaysia rather than join the Tatmadaw, and that this problem affects other sectors as well, such as agriculture.

Gender

One of the major steps taken by the Commander-in-Chief has been to include women in the armed forces. Women officers from the Tatmadaw and Yangon University were appointed in 2015. Women officers are being inducted into the Education Corps, Signals, Information Technology, Intelligence, C-in-C Office, Media (Myawady) and for administrative duties. They are trained at Officer Training School (Army) at Hmawbi, Yangon, since December 2015.

Figure 8.2: Senior General Min Aung Hlaing inspecting the Graduation Parade of Female Army Cadets of the 6th Intake at the Officer Training School (Army) in Hmawbi, Yangon Region, on 24 December 2019

Source: https://www.globalnewlightofmyanmar.com/hmawbi-officer-training-school-army-holds-6th-woman-army-cadets-graduation/

The process of induction of women into the army for commissioned posts at the rank of second lieutenant, commenced with an advertisement in the state-media in October 2013 inviting women to apply to join the ranks of the military for the first time since the recruitment of women for non-medical roles was stopped in 1961. The unmarried candidates had to be minimum 160 cm tall, weigh less than 59 kg, and be between 25 and 30 years. According to Maung Aung Myoe, the first women commissioned into the Myanmar Armed Forces were by the Air Force in 1954. A year later, the army took in its first female officers, but recruitment of women for non-medical services was stopped in 1961. In January 2014, Lieutenant Colonel Soe Soe Myint and Lieutenant Colonel San Thida Khin became the first female military officers appointed to parliament. Both joined the military in medical roles.[20]

The remarks[21] of the C-in-C at the Graduation Parade of the 6th Intake which took place on 23 December 2019, reveals the official stand of the Tatmadaw on women in the armed forces. The Senior General received the salute of the cadets on the parade ground and reviewed the military parade before addressing them. He then awarded the best graduate of the 6th intake, Cadet Yamin Inzali, and the best shot, Cadet Aye Htet Htet Hlaing and subsequently met their parents, after the parade.

In his address, the Senior General informed the cadets that the Tatmadaw had opened the women army cadet training course in order to offer inclusive opportunities for them to serve in defending the nation. He said they were being trained to have equal duties and positions with male soldiers in serving the nation and this was all part of modernizing the Tatmadaw. He added that women have always played important roles in successive generations and have caught up with men to shine in social affairs, business, politics and even astrophysics. He urged the cadets to uphold traditions and dutifully fulfil tasks assigned for the Tatmadaw and the nation. He also urged them to continually improve themselves and become a source of strength for the Tatmadaw and the country.

Given the poor gender sensitivity in the Myanmar Armed Forces, and the track record of the army in counter-insurgency operations, the aim of including women in the armed forces is laudable. However, six intakes is too short a period to be able to assess the impact of women in the Tatmadaw. It remains to be seen whether this exercise lives up to its noble expectations, or remains a public relations exercise to gain international acceptability. As brought out earlier in this chapter, 21 female medical officers were commissioned on 1 March 2012 after a gap of 15 years, followed by recruitment of female nurses, through the army scholarship programme at the Institute of Nursing, in December 2012. The enrolment of regular women officers in Tatmadaw actually commenced from 2015.

Intelligence

Extensive work has been done to analyse the intelligence apparatus of the Tatmadaw by Andrew Selth of the Griffith University. In his 2019 publication[22] titled *Secrets and Power in Myanmar: Intelligence and the fall of General Khin Nyunt*, Selth describes in great detail the evolution and function of the intelligence apparatus.

Basically, the intelligence functioning within Myanmar can be phased in three parts; from independence till 1983 when then Col. Khin Nyunt took over the organisation; from 1983 till 2004 when Khin Nyunt, who by then had become a General, was purged; and the period from 2004 till date. The official nomenclature of the Tatmadaw intelligence set up was changed from Directorate of Defence Services Intelligence (DDSI) to Office of the Chief of Military Intelligence (OCMI) in 2001 and finally to the Office of the Chief Military Security Affairs (OCMSA) in 2004:

> *The power and behaviour of DDSI/OCMI exacerbated tensions between Khin Nyunt and other members of Myanmar's military leadership, leading to his downfall in 2004. OCMI was comprehensively purged and replaced by Office of the Chief of Military Security Affairs (OCMSA). Primary responsibility for internal security shifted to the Myanmar Police Force's Special Branch. However, Myanmar's intelligence capabilities have been severely weakened. Since 2004, considerable efforts have been made to recover these capabilities, but they have still not been fully restored, contributing to a number of notable intelligence failures.*
>
> *Since the advent of Thein Sein's quasi-civilian government in 2011, and the election of Aung San Suu Kyi's National League for Democracy administration in 2015, there appears to have been few significant structural changes to the Myanmar intelligence apparatus. The organizations and practices that characterized military rule appear to have survived, although the authorities now seem to be relying more on technical sources, and semi-legal rather than extra-legal means, to exercise control. Some recent developments, however, including a series of attacks by militant groups in Rakhine State, could prompt greater attention to intelligence issues.*

Selth goes on to highlight that the renewed pariah status of Myanmar precludes intelligence cooperation with Western countries. A review of the tactical operations carried out by the Tatmadaw in the years 2017, 2018, 2019 and 2020, especially on the western Myanmar side reveal serious lacunae in operations, mostly driven by a lack of intelligence. Anthony Davis[23] highlights that field intelligence, the basis of effective operations, has been severely compromised as revealed by two parameters. One, front-line battalions were suffering unacceptably high casualties *'at a rate that in any 'standard' army would be seen as militarily unacceptable and politically toxic'.* He recounts that since 2012, campaigns in Kachin, Shan and increasingly in Rakhine states have entailed several thousand Tatmadaw fatalities. Between February and May 2015 alone, fighting in the Kokang region of Shan State set a bleak record of some 800 troops killed. Second, he highlights that combat units were 'succumbing to a culture of brutality and impunity' especially in the case of the LIDs which operate in support of regionally based forces and constitute '*the tip of the Tatmadaw's spear*'.

This is probably most evident in the Rakhine and Chin states, where, for the past years, horrendous human rights violations is alienating that very thing that the Tatmadaw needs, i.e., operational intelligence, and simultaneously takes it away from its stated goal of becoming a 'standard army'. This author had written in a commentary earlier on the VIF Website on the occasion of Tatmadaw Day 2020 (27 March 2020):

> *The recent overrunning of a Battalion and capture of the Battalion Commander by the Arakan Army is a blot on their abilities. Repeated tactical and operational losses at the hands of the Arakan Army in the Rakhine and Chin states reveal a less than competent, higher leadership at the operational and strategic levels. Rampant and inefficient use of artillery barrages and fighter jets for strafing and aerial bombing with massive collateral damage is symptomatic of a mindset which over relies on conventional asymmetries to offset un-conventional disadvantages of terrain, intelligence and training. Such actions have further alienated the Tatmadaw from the locals, depriving them of local intelligence...a sine qua non for counter insurgency. The Rohingya crisis that the Tatmadaw has foisted upon the nation is an example of how short sighted military leadership has cost the Government aplenty.*
>
> *Overall, the Tatmadaw today has been found somewhat wanting in working towards delivering national level aspirations. This is a major mismatch between capability and aspiration which the military leadership does not publicly acknowledge, either because they do not realise it, or they are do now want to highlight it at the peril of losing face and space in the national narrative.*

More about this aspect is covered in the section on Counter-Insurgency.

Professional Ethos

An impression exists that the junior ranks in the Tatmadaw have been encouraged to 'live off the land' and hence all extortional activities are in fact 'fair play'. In the pre–'Operation Sunrise' period,[24] Indian insurgent groups operating along the IMB with camps in Myanmar, e.g., at Taga, were expected to pay the local battalion and its commanding officers in lieu for permission to operate in the area of responsibility of that battalion. If these IIGs were to cultivate opium, required to be done as a source of income, the Tatmadaw local unit commander would charge for that over and above the normal payment. These payments could be in cash or kind, e.g., rations to sustain the troops. This overall culture leads to a situation where the troops 'help themselves' to resources from their own local residents during counter-insurgency operations, as is being repeatedly reported in Rakhine State. These 'resources' could vary from a chicken, eggs, rice and other edibles[25] to gold ornaments and even buffalos and mobile phones![26] This is something that goes against the ethos of counter-insurgency operations since it alienates the battleground, i.e., the local population, as we are so evidently witnessing in Rakhine.

A retired Indian Army officer who spent over two years in Myanmar brought out some interesting facets, especially when viewed from an Indian perspective. He observed that subservience to elders is a way of life and the same carries on in the Army too. Thus, officers till the rank of Captain, whether attending courses or in their units, are expected to broom and mop the classrooms and, cut grass on Saturdays. It is only from the rank of Major that they are excluded from menial labour. From the rank of Lt Col, perks and privileges abound with apparently every Lt Col being provided with a vehicle. It is considered courteous for a junior officer to serve (food) to a senior officer and the officer even witnessed Brigadiers serving Generals. During official parties, officers up to the rank of Major were not permitted to eat along with senior officers. As a result, the Liaison Officer of the Indian officer often used to remain hungry during the call ons. He also highlighted the lack of confidence of the junior leadership in interactions with Indian counterparts during border meetings due to a highly and strictly centralised command and control structure, with feudal overtones.

General V.P. Malik, in his book, writes that within the Tatmadaw, amongst junior and senior officers and families, the relationship was not only respectful, but noticeably feudal. I enquired about this aspect during my interaction[27] with the former COAS and he elaborated that while all armies have an hierarchical structure and there is usually a healthy reverence the juniors are expected to have towards seniors, in the Myanmar Armed Forces, this was of a higher degree and it percolated into the families as well as their personal lives. Thus while gestures such as lifting of a cup by a junior officer's wife for a senior officer's wife would be construed as subservient in other armies, in the Myanmar Army it was considered acceptable and even expected from the junior officer's wife. This was really an outcome of the feudal nature of that army and the fact that career progression depended almost solely on the preference of the senior officer. He added:

> *Having Commanded 8 Mountain Division on the IMB and having interacted with the Myanmar soldiers, I used to observe that they were not very well paid. Whenever they came to our side, they looked forward to goodies and freebies from our canteens which we would happily oblige in the interest of better relations. Conversely, the kind of lifestyle the senior officers maintained was lavish and ostentatious. The difference was stark.*

This observation by General Malik two decades ago reinforces the argument that all was not well with the Myanmar Army. This was surprising considering that the senior hierarchy of the Government was totally military dominated and could have easily provided better facilities to its troops if it so desired. The author's interactions with other sources who have interacted with or been in touch with the Myanmar Army in recent years confirm that the same situation exists even today. General Malik went on to describe an incident which further reinforced his views on the feudal nature of the Tatmadaw:

> *During my second visit to Myanmar, we were to travel to some place in the northern part of Myanmar by boat and were about to board the vessel when a civilian came in our way. The Liaison Officer accompanying me, just physically kicked the man out of the way in front of us! This was unthinkable in our context. I was totally taken aback. But don't forget that this was 20 years ago. Things may have improved now with the democratic systems starting to come into place.*

However, despite this severe protocol and strict hierarchy, there exists a refreshing bonhomie at the junior levels which enables an NCO to share a smoke with a Major. Junior officers and soldiers are regularly seen together in restaurants along with their families. The officer described a situation where, at a Lieutenant Colonel's wedding reception, the officer, his driver and a General were all standing in the same line for the buffet. Similarly, an NCO can be seen leading a party of junior officers in academies to shift furniture, while he cheerfully observes them while smoking.

That the Myanmar soldier is not paid as well as his Indian counterpart[28] is a mathematical fact, but it would be misleading to try and draw lessons from this comparison. However, two aspects offset this disparity; firstly, the low cost of living and the secondly the religious value systems of Theravada Buddhism which promotes simple and contented living. The author, during his visit to Myanmar, was told that the pay scales in the Tatmadaw were based on meeting basic living standards. A small military family in Myanmar can subsist reasonably comfortably between ₹ 5,000 and ₹ 10,000 a month. Thus a new soldier is paid approximately MMR 1 lakh (roughly equals ₹ 5,000)[29] while a senior NCO with 12 years' service would get double. Captains get MMK 3.30 lakh (₹ 16,500) while Majors get MMK 4 lakh (₹ 20,000). These emoluments exclude free ration, electricity and water.

From the rank of Lieutenant Colonel and above, there is a substantial enhancement of perks and privileges. A Lieutenant Colonel gets MMK 5 lakh (₹ 25,000) and in addition is entitled to a civilian pattern vehicle and 40 litres of fuel per day/equivalent. There is an exponential jump in pay and perks of Colonel (MMK 8 lakh, i.e., ₹ 40,000) and above. The ranks of Colonel and above are considered senior and are often appointed independent local authority (akin to Station Commander in India). In such appointments, the incumbent is privileged to use all the available free station land for cultivation and associated animal husbandry and in turn gets the profit. In fact, all officers are allowed to undertake other professions when they are free and many of them run small businesses or give tuitions to augment their incomes. So, many of them are into business, tuitions and some even run KTVs (karaoke music bars).

Despite hardships such as poor pay, small dwellings, irregular working hours and even the spouses expected to contribute as much as the officer,[30] resentment, if any, seems to be well concealed, subdued and accepted philosophically. This could be attributed to being part of a closed society for decades and thereby more resilient and content with small things. The influence of religion is evident when the officers and soldiers proceed on short leave and during that period devote time to go to the monastery doing menial tasks and leading an ascetic life. Despite the meagre salary, donations form an important part of their culture. The ease with which the Myanmar youth speak of death reveals a rare philosophical approach to life which enables them to weather the storms. At the same time, young officers are candid in revealing their fears of the front line and discussing the dangers of battle. The officer witnessed how stoic the families were when bodies from the frontlines reached their stations. He concludes that it is Buddhist spirituality, with its inherent concept of accepting death as a natural and inescapable phenomenon, that helps them to be resilient. He finds it common to see young men and women frequently retreating into the confines of ascetic life. He specifically recalled a vibrant young girl with beautiful hair, cutting it off without any qualms and entering a monastery. When asked about her choice, she said earning for her afterlife was more important than a few strand of hairs.

This religious mooring has created an interesting paradox amongst the officer class. While the motivation to serve the fatherland is immense, the motivation for individual ambition seemed to be philosophically lacking. Thus, career progression and self-development are not high on the individual bucket lists, even though they are by nature loyal and sincere in their relationships. An interesting conclusion to this section can be on the subject of homosexuality. Our observer reported that at the academy, one officer was publicly identified as homosexual, and openly referred to as such without an iota of malice and in good spirit on both sides. In fact even the lady instructors at the academy referred to him as '*our daughter*'. There seems to be no written policy on homosexuality in the Tatmadaw, but there seemed to be no stigma attached to alternative sexual orientation. Thus, they are found to be part of gay groups which socialise together, both within the military and outside. Apart from some comments made in lighter vein, our observer did not find them being ostracised in any manner. This community even takes the responsibility of organising the local beauty pageant which is the prelude to the Miss Myanmar contest conducted in Yangon. I quote this to highlight the breadth of social acceptance in culture in the Tatmadaw, which is otherwise an extremely secretive and closed society.

Political Tradition of the Tatmadaw

Maung Aung Myoe, in his paper[31] *The soldier and the state: the Tatmadaw and political liberalization in Myanmar since* 2011, lucidly brings out the political genesis of the Tatmadaw. During the anti-colonial struggle, nationalists and politicians formed unarmed private armies called Tats to back up their political activities. Over the years, Tats developed and eventually got armed and remained under various political, regional and individual entities. These armed bodies proved difficult to handle and, finally in 1958, Tatmadaw commanders placed all 'armed forces' constitutionally under the C-in-C's control. Further, the Tatmadaw was born out of the historical necessity of the nation for an armed independence struggle, and from its inception it was a political force. Myoe explains that:

> *The 'Thirty Comrades' who initiated the present-day Tatmadaw were mostly politicians from the leading nationalist organization of the 1930s, the Dobama Asiayone. Therefore, the genealogy of the Tatmadaw can be traced back to the national struggle for independence, and the employment of the Tatmadaw as a political force, beyond the scope of classic professional armies (in the Western sense), has become conventional wisdom and established fact. Many Myanmar politicians have joined the Tatmadaw since its inception in December 1941.*

Some have remained in the Tatmadaw and have played important political roles. Both politician-turned-soldier and soldier-turned-politician have employed the Tatmadaw to advance their careers. This political tradition of the Tatmadaw is firmly established.

Moe elaborates that the Tatmadaw, in the early 1940s, was exposed to the idea that the army exists to serve political and national causes, not to work for money. As time went by, the Tatmadaw imbibed the political orientation and this was institutionalised through indoctrination by embedded political advisors on the lines of the communist political commissars. Political indoctrination became important since it was during this period that they were battling the communist insurgents. Subsequently, the Tatmadaw formalised its political role culminating in 1958 as a national security doctrine known as the National Ideology and the Role of Defence Services (NIRDS). This was the ideological basis of the Tatmadaw's political involvement and activism and it equated internal security and national development as a coherent whole, encompassing military, political, socio-economic and ideological defences. It assigned the military the dual functions of dealing with internal security and economic development as its primary tasks. By setting internal security as a precondition for further economic development, it provided the necessary rationale for the military's political activism and domination. The NIRDS assigned the Tatmadaw a guardianship role in nation-building and state-building. Therefore, the Tatmadaw considers that it has a right and obligation to involve itself in the socio-political field in addition to its primary duty of national defence. It has enabled the Tatmadaw to assume a corporate identity as the guarantor as well as the embodiment of state authority. Various political education programmes were organized for soldiers. In a way, these programmes aimed to deal with the communist insurgents who propagated the view that the Tatmadaw was a mercenary force with no (leftist) political belief. Subsequently, the Tatmadaw continued its political indoctrination under the banner of the Three National Causes: non-disintegration of the Union, non-disintegration of national solidarity, and perpetuation of national sovereignty. Myoe concludes that:

Until and unless military officers are socialized with a new discourse of military professionalism, which focuses on external defence and on the concept of objective civilian control, this 'new professionalism' will remain with the Tatmadaw and it will be natural for the Tatmadaw to involve itself in national politics.

Dr. Naing Swe Oo, during the course of his conversation with the author, brought out that the C-in-C had stated that the Tatmadaw would move away from politics in the future; however there was no timeline.

Counter-Insurgency Operations

The Tatmadaw conduct of counter-insurgency operations, especially in the Rakhine conflict, is a deemed disaster, and tragically so because the Tatmadaw has had considerable experience in this form of operation. This verdict is an outcome of analysis of open source English media reports, Twitter handles and other social media analysis for a period of two -and-a-half year from 1 January 2018 till June 2020. Details of the operations *per se* are covered in greater detail in the chapter dedicated to the Rakhine conflict. However, it is important to highlight the major errors that the Tatmadaw is making in the counter-insurgency battle.

First, the nature of operations, the repetitive nature of casualties and the reactions of the Tatmadaw to the casualties suggest that there is no higher direction of operations. It is suggestive that the senior leadership does not have the time and initiative to put effort into this battle, and the actions are mostly being driven at the unit level with no coordination, overall direction or broad plan. Counter-insurgency operations, while being led by the armed forces, are required to be followed up by administrative mechanisms and political engagement to address the core rationale for the insurgency. Pure hard power operations may bring the situation under control for some time, but it will only buy time, not solve the problem. In the ibid case, there seems to be no presence of administrative authorities or any attempt at political engagement from the side of the Myanmar Government. This gives rise to a suspicion that this could be due to the Yangon-centricity of the Tatmadaw which reflects in lower priorities for the Western Myanmar region as a whole.

Second, the Tatmadaw seems to be intent on burning the platform on which it operates. The platform on which counter-insurgency is fought is the local population. Whichever side can sway the population, wins the tactical and operational-level battles. The Tatmadaw, with its outrageous conduct with the civilian population has effectively alienated it and cut off its source of intelligence. Already strained by over-reliance on technical intelligence, this action spells disaster for its counter-insurgency campaign in Rakhine. Further, it has cemented the cause for the AA, provided them with sympathisers and enabled them to increase their ranks with members of the disgruntled population.

Thirdly, the excessive use of artillery and air power smacks of overdependence on these two modes of assault which are conventionally rarely used for counter-insurgency operations. The collateral damage to civilian life and property has been substantial and uncompensated. Over-reliance on these weapon systems fuels the impression that the planners are being unimaginative, unconcerned about the efficacy and the collateral damage and under-confident about the capability of their troops in foot soldiering.

Finally, on a higher plane, the Tatmadaw and Myanmar Government approach to counter-insurgency, especially in the case of the AA does not seem to be based on a careful consideration of its capabilities. Rather, it seems driven by Bamar ego and arrogance. This approach, when clubbed with the Rohingya crisis and the operations of ARSA, make the region the most conflict-ridden region in recent times.

The Senior General and Succession Plans

The Senior General in the Tatmadaw is a highly revered father figure about whom even joking is not considered in good humour. He is the *de facto* leader and the alternate power centre to DASSK. There have been cases when senior officers have jumped the fence and crossed over to the NLD, but mostly, the armed forces have been able to keep their flock together. The loyalty to the Senior General, whether forced or spontaneous, is of a very high level. In military training establishment debates, he has been heard as being referred to as the leader of Myanmar doing wonderful work and so on. Mentioning the name of DASSK is almost a sin in military establishments.

The display of loyalty, whether forced or spontaneous, is important in Tatmadaw culture and extends even to the senior lot. Officers who inadvertently crossed the path of his cavalcade have known to be physically punished by confinement in the Quarter Guard. Even the Army Chief, who is also the Defence Minister, Vice Senior General Soe Win, has been heard profusely expressing his gratitude to the Senior General for permitting him to travel to India. As a practice, apparently senior officers of the Tatmadaw do not leave the HQ premises without the permission of the Senior General. To that extent, the power, authority and decision-making is highly centralised.

However, this loyalty is a two-way street. Thus, Lt Gen Aung Kyaw Zaw, Commander of Bureau of Special Operations No. 2 and Maj Gen Maung Maung Soe, Western Regional Military Commander, were allowed to resign and removed from command after being sanctioned by the European Union for the campaign against the Rohingyas and the removal was done without any reference to any wrongdoing.[32] And in all probability, they would have been adequately compensated in the various quasi-military appointments in the myriad industries run by the Tatmadaw.

Senior General Ming Aung Hlaing became the new C-in-C of the Armed Forces of Myanmar, replacing the outgoing head of state and junta chief, Senior General Than Shwe on 30 March 2011.[33] He was promoted to the rank of Senior General in 2013 and was due to retire in 2016, but received a five-year extension.[34] Born on 3 July 1956, Senior General Min Aung Hlaing is past the Tatmadaw's mandatory retirement age of 60, but he was able to continue because of a 2014 directive by the Department of Defence Council that said he could serve until he was 65, which he will become on 3 July 2021, or four months into the term of the new government.[35] There is a general consensus that while he will not fade away into the sunset like some of his predecessors, he is unlikely to resign to fight the November 2020 elections. He could take the military route and use the military MPs who constitute 25 per cent of Parliament and are entitled to choose a Vice President, to become a Vice President. However there is widespread speculation that Min Aung Hlaing has higher political aspirations and aspires for the Presidency after the next general elections.[36] The results of the elections will define whether the Senior General will achieve Presidency, since under the Myanmar constitution, the president is chosen from among the three vice-presidents by Myanmar's 664-member national legislature, the Pyidaungsu Hluttaw, sitting as an electoral college. The Amyotha Hluttaw (Upper House), Pyithu Hluttaw (Lower House) and the 25 per cent un-elected military MPs each get to choose one presidential candidate; the candidate who attracts the most electoral college votes becomes the president and the other two hold the post of vice presidents. The party with the most seats decides the outcome, as the NLD demonstrated after the 2015 election. It won 390 seats in the Lower House well above the 333-seat threshold required to ensure the party could select its preferred candidate (though in practice, the threshold was lower due to the cancellation of voting in some constituencies because of armed conflict). For the Senior General to win, a large number of seats would need to change hands from the NLD to parties that would support his candidacy, e.g., the Union Solidarity and Development Party (USDP), which won just 41 seats in 2015.

Regardless of whether he remains C-in-C, retires completely or seeks a political position after the election, Ming Aung Hlaing would want insulate himself from possible prosecution, both in Myanmar and abroad, and for that he has to ensure he has the support of senior officers of the Tatmadaw. Hence, the May 2020 reshuffle has strengthened the position of those perceived as loyal to Min Aung Hlaing, in keeping with the traditions of self-preservation.

Lieutenant General Moe Myint Tun, commander of Bureau of Special

Operations 6 at Nay Pyi Taw is, expected to become the next Tatmadaw C-in-C, with Lieutenant General Kyaw Swar Lin as his Deputy C-in-C. Lieutenant General Moe Myint Tun had earlier served as personal assistant to Vice Senior General Maung Aye when the country was under junta rule. The May 2020 reshuffle by the Tatmadaw also saw the rise of another star of the next generation of Tatmadaw senior leadership, Maj Gen Kyaw Swar Lin.[37] At 49, he is commander of the Central Command, promoted to become the military's youngest lieutenant-general and take over as quartermaster general, the sixth highest position in the Tatmadaw.[38]

Conclusion

The Tatmadaw is a unique force with intrinsic strengths and character. It has behind it, a vast experience of counter-insurgency operations. However, the independence with which it operates, suggests there are no internal or external checks and balances or oversight mechanisms. Over-centralised command and control, a culture of reverence and subservience often crossing the thin line into sycophancy and no evidence of a 'professional' culture indicates that the Tatmadaw has its task cut out for it. An analysis of the Tatmadaw's tactical operations over the past few years suggest that there is no effective institutional memory or system of battle zone specific training. Further, repeated losses and captures by the AA lead to the feeling that the Tatmadaw troops operating in the Rakhine conflict, have been severely demoralised.

This is one sphere where the Indian Armed Forces can provide invaluable assistance to the Tatmadaw, given its vast experience in operations especially while operating under human rights laws and in the media glare. Specific recommendations for the same are included in the chapter on Defence Diplomacy.

NOTES

1. Myoe, M. A. (2014). *The Soldier and the State: The Tatmadaw and Political Liberalization in Myanmar since 2011.* South East Asia Research, 22(2), 233–249, pg. 241. doi:10.5367/sear.2014.0205 https://www.jstor.org/stable/43818522?seq=1 (Accessed on 15 June 2020).
2. The Republic of the Union of Myanmar Defence White Paper (2015), Para 2, pg. 1.
3. Ibid., Para 7, pg. 4.
4. He visited Thailand 10 times; China four times; India, Singapore and Malaysia three times; Vietnam, Russia, Laos, Philippines and Japan twice each; Indonesia, South Korea, Nepal, Belarus, Pakistan, Serbia, Israel, Brunei, Belgium, Italy, Cambodia, Austria, and Germany once each.
5. Ibid., Para 83, pg. 47.
6. Thu, Myint Myat. "*Understanding the Tatmadaw's 'Standard Army' Reforms.*" *Frontier Myanmar*, 3 July 2020: https://frontiermyanmar.net/en/understanding-the-tatmadaws-standard-army-reforms (Accessed on 3 July 2020).

7. Myoe, pg. 242.
8. This is its third doctrine since 1950.
9. "Myanmar Military Asks NLD Patron to Join Armed Forces Day Celebration." *The Irrawaddy*, February 21, 2020, https://www.irrawaddy.com/news/burma/myanmar-military-asks-nld-patron-join-armed-forces-day-celebration.html (Accessed on 25 February 2020).
10. Yan Pai, "*The Forgotten General of Burma's Army*", *The Irrawaddy*, August 20, 2016, https://www.irrawaddy.com/news/burma/forgotten-general-burmas-army.html (Accessed on 25 February 2020).
11. Myoe, pg. 244.
12. Parameswaran, Prashanth. "Myanmar Military Modernization in the Spotlight Amid Air Force Anniversary." *The Diplomat*, December 19, 2017, https://thediplomat.com/2017/12/myanmar-military-modernization-in-the-spotlight-amid-air-force-anniversary/(Accessed on 25 February 2020).
13. Davis, Anthony. "Myanmar's Military Just Wants to Be Normal." *Asia Times*, February 18, 2020, https://asiatimes.com/2018/02/myanmars-military-just-wants-normal/ (Accessed on 25 February 2020).
14. Apparently this is only the second time that such an exercise has taken place with the first about two decades ago.
15. They understandably preferred to remain anonymous.
16. This also finds mention in the Defence White Paper, Paragraph 74, Page 38, under the section on Training.
17. The entrance exam for regular officers is common for the three services for all the three streams, viz., medical, technical and combat.
18. Founder-director of Myanmar Institute of Peace and Security, a Yangon-based think tank which maintains one of the best conflict monitoring databases in Myanmar.
19. During an interaction with the author during his visit to the Vivekananda International Foundation, New Delhi, for the BIMSTEC Security Dialogue in November 2019.
20. "First Women Graduate from Officer Training." *The Myanmar Times*, August 30, 2014, https://www.mmtimes.com/national-news/11487-first-women-graduate-from-officer-training-school.html (Accessed on 25 February 2020).
21. Agency, Myanmar News. "Hmawbi Officer Training School (Army) Holds 6th Woman Army Cadets Graduation." Global New Light Of Myanmar, December 23, 2019, https://www.globalnewlightofmyanmar.com/hmawbi-officer-training-school-army-holds-6th-woman-army-cadets-graduation/ (Accessed on 25 February 2020).
22. Andrew Selth, *Secrets and Power in Myanmar: Intelligence and the fall of General Khin Nyunt*, ISEAS Publishing, Singapore, 2019.
23. Davis 2018.
24. Operation Sunrise I (January-February 2019) and Operation Sunrise II (June 2019) were game-changing coordinated operations conducted by the Indian and Myanmar authorities against IIGs and EAGs along the IMB. These operations effectively broke the back of insurgency in Northeast India.
25. https://www.hrw.org/reports/2005/burma0605/burma0605.pdf, pg. 33.
26. See for example, "Tatmadaw Attacks Destroy Civilian Property and Displace Villages in Northern Papun District". Online Burma/Myanmar Library, February 27, 2012, https://www.burmalibrary.org/en/tatmadaw-attacks-destroy-civilian-property-and-displace-villages-in-northern-papun-district ;"Tatmadaw Soldier Arrested for Raping 70-Year-Old Woman, Stealing Gold Earrings in Monghpyauk". *Burma News International*, April 8, 2018, https://www.bnionline.net/en/news/tatmadaw-soldier-arrested-raping-70-year-old-woman-stealing-gold-earrings-monghpyauk ; "Dooplaya Incident Report: Tatmadaw Soldiers Steal Two Buffalos Belonging to a Local Farmer, December 2018." Karen Human Rights Group, September 17,

2019, https://khrg.org/2019/05/19-34-i1/dooplaya-incident-report-tatmadaw-soldiers-steal-two-buffalos-belonging-local. (All accessed on 25 February 2020).

27. In an interview with the author at the India International Centre, New Delhi, on 20 February 2020.
28. For reference, very roughly, a new soldier in the Indian Army receives 25,000; a senior NCO receives 40,000; a Captain gets 75,000; a Major gets 1,00,000; a Lieutenant Colonel gets 1,12,000and a Colonel gets 1,30,000. These figures comprise basic salary, grade pay and military service pay, https://www.ssbcrack.com/2013/02/indian-army-officers-pay-scale.html
29. The Myanmar Kyat (MMK) is the currency of Myanmar and roughly INR 1 equals MMK 20.
30. Interestingly, families are also trained in firing and, in fact, women of a unit repulsed an attack on their base by a rebel group near the eastern border with China. The rebel group that attacked was part of the Northern Alliance and led to casualties in the failed attack.
31. Myoe, M. A. (2014), pg. 241.
32. See "Myanmar Military Sacks Top Army Officer Accused of Human Rights Violations against Rohingyas". Scroll.in, June 26, 2018, https://scroll.in/latest/884218/myanmar-military-sacks-top-army-officer-accused-of-human-rights-violations-against-rohingyas; https://www.washingtonpost.com/world/asia_pacific/myanmar-fires-general-who-led-campaign-against-rohingya/2018/06/25/9781d7c0-7567-11e8-b4b7-308400242c2e_story.html; (Accessed on 25 February 2020).
33. https://web.archive.org/web/20180112154939/http://www.altsean.org/Research/Regime%20Watch/Executive/CIC.php (Accessed on 25 February 2020).
34. "Myanmar Army Chief to Get Five Year Extension as Talks with Suu Kyi Continue - Media." Reuters. Thomson Reuters, February 13, 2016, https://in.reuters.com/article/myanmar-army-chief-five-year-extension/myanmar-army-chief-to-get-five-year-extension-as-talks-with-suu-kyi-continue-media-idINKCN0VM06O (Accessed on 25 February 2020).
35. "The Game of Myanmar's Senior General." *The Myanmar Times*, February 19, 2020, https://www.mmtimes.com/news/game-myanmars-senior-general.html
36. Zwa Moe, Kyaw. "Opinion: How Myanmar's Military Chief Could Become President." *The Irrawaddy*, September 23, 2019, https://www.irrawaddy.com/opinion/commentary/myanmars-military-chief-become-president.html (Accessed on 25 February 2020).
37. He is a graduate of the 35th batch of the elite Defence Services Academy and served as a staff officer with the rank of brigadier-general before being appointed to head the Mandalay-based Central Command in 2018.
38. Nanda, "*Min Aung Hlaing Reshuffles Senior Military Ranks Ahead of Election,*" *Frontier Myanmar*, June 3, 2020, https://frontiermyanmar.net/en/min-aung-hlaing-reshuffles-senior-military-ranks-ahead-of-election (Accessed on 25 February 2020).

CHAPTER 9

Defence Diplomacy and India-Myanmar Relations

The foreign policy agenda of the new government should also incorporate defence diplomacy in the overall diplomacy. This requires a fundamental overhaul of the internal mechanisms to improve coordination between the ministries of defence and external affairs and the armed forces. Such coordination so far has been ad hoc and inadequate.

—Dr. Arvind Gupta[1]

Diplomacy has various tools of engagement and defence diplomacy is one such tool. Given the kinship of soldiers, especially when soldiers of both India and Myanmar have operationally rubbed shoulders with each other, it is natural that defence diplomacy, as a tool, holds pride of place in India-Myanmar relations. Soldiers from Myanmar and India have worked with each other under various regional operational circumstances beyond joint training and exercises. Since bilateral relations driven by traditional diplomacy are generally subject to political equations, defence diplomacy has often been found to be an alternative channel for testing the waters and ice breaking with new governments or renewing relations after a freeze. The aim of this chapter is to analyse the role of defence diplomacy in India-Myanmar bilateral relations and identify the next generation of initiatives required to be taken through defence diplomacy to support India's Act East Policy.

Genesis of Defence Diplomacy

The term 'defence diplomacy' took birth in the post-Cold War period and was first alluded to in the 1990s in British writing. It was considered an important tool for military statecraft and with an overarching aim to move past the use of force as the last instrument of foreign policy. Former US Secretary of State, Robert Gates,[2] highlighted how important it was to use all possible means to avoid imposing one's will, forcibly or otherwise, on any entity in the pursuit of national interests when he said, "*Success will be less a matter of imposing one's will and more a function of shaping behaviour—of friends, adversaries, and most importantly, the people in between.*" This is especially relevant to India's neighbourhood in these disturbed times today.

A definition by Gregory Winger of the University of Cincinnati is particularly appealing and states that defence diplomacy is the '*nonviolent use of a state's defence apparatus to advance the strategic aims of a government through cooperation with other countries*'.[3] Brig K.A. Muthanna adds[4] a rider to the debate when he says that '*While the aims and objectives of nations participating in military diplomacy or cooperation could differ, the crux is that they work together to develop an environment of peace and trust.*'

These definitions leave open to debate whether '*coordinated operations*' or even '*joint operations*' against a common, usually non-state actor, fall under the category of defence diplomacy. For the purpose of clarity, there is a need to make some assumptions. Thus, coordinated operations are ones in which both armies operate in synchronisation to complement each other's manoeuvres, however, by operating on their own side of their common border. Joint operations on the other hand would imply either mixed bodies of troops or troops of both nations operating in very close proximity on a common terrain, which could be in either country. The presence of one force in the country of the other force, operating jointly with the host nation force, would be the operating rider and would move the operation across the line from 'coordinated' to 'joint'.

Finally, there is always a question as to how the terms 'security diplomacy', 'defence[5] diplomacy' and 'defence cooperation', relate to each other and what each constitutes. Again, for functional reasons, there is a need to correlate them. Thus, at the top of the pyramid, security diplomacy is the all-encompassing term which includes all forms of security. Security diplomacy comprises defence, non-military law enforcement, human rights, and humanitarian crisis response initiatives that meet the mutual needs of the nations. It brings to bear the comprehensive security power of a nation-state's security prowess to support another's security organizations. This can include but is not limited to military exchanges, military cooperation, joint exercises, rule-of-law training, human rights training, and humanitarian disasters response training.[6]

Defence diplomacy, which is essentially a subset of security diplomacy, is used as an overarching term to cover the entire gamut of bilateral and multilateral mutual defence cooperation and engagement including joint and coordinated operations. Col Arvind Dutta, former Research Fellow, IDSA, identified[7] defence cooperation as a subset of defence diplomacy and referred to the text of the Keynote Address by the Hon'ble Raksha Mantri during a seminar[8] which defined defence cooperation as "*any arrangement between two or more nations where their armed forces work together to achieve mutual aims and objectives*". He elaborated that defence cooperation is but one arrow in the quiver of defence diplomacy which "*aims at sharing of operational and doctrinal expertise, training and capability enhancement of one's own military, strengthening of ties with other countries and sales of weapons and military technologies. It also allows for the examination and imbibing of 'best practices', creates ability to operate alongside and enhances Maritime Domain Awareness, through a variety of information-sharing mechanisms.*

The frontline defence diplomats of nations are the Defence Attaches (DAs). The Vienna Convention on Diplomatic Relations of 18 April 1961 provides immunity to persons according to their rank in a diplomatic mission. Thereby, Defence Attaché Officers have the same rights and legal status as other diplomats as defined by Article 7:

> *Subject to the provisions of articles 5, 8, 9 and 11, the sending State may freely appoint the members of the staff of the mission. In the case of military, naval or air attachés, the receiving State may require their names to be submitted beforehand, for its approval.*[9]

Hence, under the Convention, DAs are considered members of the diplomatic staff enjoying full immunity. Though Defence Attaches have had diplomatic status for long, defence diplomacy gained recognition following the fall of the Iron Curtain, when the roles of DAs drastically shifted from information collection and monitoring to more of a diplomatic content.

The Myanmar Context

Myanmar had been a closed society, totally dominated by the military for over four decades. The bulk of the political appointments were for many years held by serving and retired military men. As of date, three key ministerial appointments are still appointed by the C-in-C of the Tatmadaw, those of the defence minister, the minister for border affairs and the home minister. While this is considered less than desirable in the context of democracy, however, it gave a fillip to defence diplomacy.

The initial years (till 1962) saw only one act of defence cooperation on record. This was the 1950s sale of six Dakota aircraft to the beleaguered U Nu Government which was almost at siege in Rangoon itself. The U Nu regime was surrounded by rebels; hence, it needed help to maintain liaison with towns still under its control.[10]

The Indira Gandhi–Ne Win years, i.e., 1966 to 1977 saw a few important defence-related developments. These included joint patrolling featuring for the first time, to include allowing hot pursuit as well. It also saw the institutionalisation of bilateral meetings at local commander level. The Myanmar Armed Forces successfully intercepted 1,000 Naga insurgents who were exfiltrating to East Pakistan for training, and sent them back to India. India and Myanmar signed the Boundary Agreement (1969) and interactions at Border Post level enabled physical demarcation of boundaries and erection of border pillars (1968-69). The Baleshwar Prasad Papers at the Nehru Memorial Museum and Library include a document from his collection titled "*Indo-Burma Relations Since 1961 to to-date* (sic)" attributed to a S.C. Banerjee. It records:

> *A 12-man Burmese Delegation headed by Colonel Kyi Maung with his Indian counterpart considered a draft treaty for delineation of the 950-mile border between the two countries under the Agreement signed in March 1967. The boundary was never formally demarcated. The demarcation would help prevent the Nagas crossings into China through Burma for arms. (About) 990 more Indians left Burma on June 1, 1968.*
>
> *A Joint Boundary Commission of the Government of India and Burma held the third round of discussions from March 30 to June 4, 1969. It was decided that a further 250 miles of the border may be demarcated during the 1969-7 field session. Demarcation of the borders between the two countries is but part of the process of strengthening friendship and peace.*
>
> *The Indo-Burma boundary demarcation has been proceeding with mutual goodwill and understanding without any problems. The armed Naga movement for an independent Nagaland begun (sic) in 1965, and some 2,000 Nagas were known to have been trained in China and infiltrated into India via Burma: Indian Defence Minister Swaran Singh told the Parliament in May last. The Joint demarcation of boundary work by the Indian and Burmese teams commenced in 1968-69, during which 240 miles of the borders were demarcated, and a further stretch of 250 miles in 1967-70; it was agreed that 225 miles would be demarcated in 1970-71. Total length of Indo-Burma borders is 950 miles.*

Vice Admiral Ram Dass Katari, India's first Indian Naval Chief and Ambassador to Burma from 1964 to 1969 describes how the decision came about:

> *The other important decision taken during Mr. Chagla's visit was to demarcate the boundary between India and Burma. Once the agreement was reached, the matter was pursued energetically. A Joint Boundary Commission was set up with Colonel Kyi Maung, Colonel GS of the Ministry of Defence, and myself as co-chairmen. We got down to business without delay. Survey teams from both countries were introduced into the scheme and they had regular meetings in Rangoon as well as (in) Delhi and Dehra Dun to work out the modalities. The sections of the border to be demarcated and the order in which it should be done were worked out. We had, of course, to leave out the tri-junctions with China and East Pakistan for the time being for obvious reasons. Of course, this was just the opportunity for opposition members in our Parliament to embarrass the government, quite unnecessarily and thoughtlessly, I felt. But I got the impression that the government fielded the onslaught quite skilfully. The work of the Joint Boundary Commission proceeded quite smoothly, by and large, and its members from both countries established welcome cordiality.*[11]

S.C. Banerji recounts the progress in the border demarcation in the Baleshwar Prasad Papers as:

> *Between December 1968 to (and) April 1969, a total of 46 border pillars were to be erected, Burma taking responsibility for 25 pillars and India 21. However, most of the work along the 240-mile sector has been completed by February, two months ahead of the schedule. The border now demarcated is understood to be the same as the one (that) existed under the British rule. The Myanma Alin said: The work progressed so well, because no problems exist between Burma and India.*[12]

The period 1988 to 1999 was turbulent in India in that India saw eight governments in power. The notable security engagements included the 1991 incident when Ambassador Preet Malik was directed by the then Foreign Secretary to interact with the Myanmar Government to intercept militant groups entering from Bangladesh into India via Myanmar. General Khin Nyunt, the Chief of Military Intelligence, assured all help. This thus become the first instance of security engagement under the new regime in India. In March 1993, a bilateral agreement was signed by J. N. Dixit in Yangon to control drug trafficking and border trade. But the most significant event was the conduct of the 1995 'Operation Golden Bird'—the first major joint military operation possibly after WWII—in which 40 insurgents were killed and major arms recovered.

Defence Diplomacy as Foreign Policy: The Breakthrough Years

In this context, the real breakthrough in India-Myanmar relations came through using defence diplomacy which effectively commenced in the late 1990s and culminated in game-changing outcomes for national security in Northeast India in 2019 and 2020. Hence, if Myanmar is engaged diplomatically on the defence perspective more, the probability to achieve long-lasting mutually beneficial security and developmental goals will be far enhanced than by confining ourselves to traditional diplomatic mechanisms.

For an understanding of how defence diplomacy was leveraged to engage Myanmar in the year 2000, the author interviewed the then Ambassador and later Foreign Secretary, Mr. Shyam Saran. Mr. Saran was the Indian Ambassador to Myanmar from 1997 to 2001 and has extensively elaborated[13] on the circumstances of this strategic push in using the Armed Forces to catalyse the relationship. He stated that while in 1992, India reached out to Myanmar and restarted the Foreign Secretary-level talks, however it was during this period that there were a number of instances when the relationship was put under pressure. Ambassador Saran identifies three specific pressure points which strained the relationship. These included firstly, the award of the Jawaharlal Nehru Prize for International Understanding to Suu Kyi in 1995 which created a lot of resentment on the Myanmar side; and secondly the movement of Chin State residents into Mizoram as a fallout of the ethnic strife in Myanmar which was frowned upon by the Tatmadaw. The third pressure point was the enthusiastic sloganeering (*Bharat Mata ki Jai*) by the Indian Diaspora in response to the visit by the veterans of the Indian National Army (INA) who were on a semi-official tour revisiting their erstwhile battlefields of World War II. This display of mass fervour, innocent though it may have been with no anti-Burmese connotations, so unnerved the Tatmadaw that it promptly withdrew permission to the veterans to continue the tour and return to India by road as hitherto planned, and forced them to fly back to India. These instances stacked up and were weighing against the relationship.

The award of the Jawaharlal Nehru Prize, which happened when an India-Myanmar joint operation was underway, resulted in the operation being abandoned by the Myanmar Armed Forces halfway through. Brig Rumel Dahiya, former Deputy Director General of IDSA from October 2010 to October 2016, was also one of the commanders on the ground during the joint operation. He has documented the details of the operation and the impact of the award. 'Operation Golden Bird', the joint operation targeting Indian Insurgent Groups (IIGs) operating out of Myanmar soil was conducted along the IMB in Mizoram in April–May 1995. The operation was launched following intelligence reports that about 200 Indian insurgents, later identified as from the United Liberation Front of Assam (ULFA), the People's Liberation Army (PLA), and the All Tripura Tiger

Force (ATTF), were planning to enter Manipur with a huge consignment of arms and ammunition from Bangladesh. This group was intercepted at various locations in coordination with the Myanmar Army over an extended period of time. Brigadier Rumel Dahiya writes:

> *In the meantime, on 4 May 1995, the Jawaharlal Nehru Award for International Understanding for the year 1993 was announced for Aung San Suu Kyi, following which our own troops observed through binoculars the Myanmarese Army personnel shaking hands with the insurgents across the border and waving them off.*[14]

It was under these circumstances that Ambassador Shyam Saran reached out to the Tatmadaw through the Directorate of Defence Services Intelligence (DDSI) which was then headed by the famous General Khin Nyunt. His point of contact was the second-in-command of the DDSI, Major General Kyaw Win, who was sufficiently powerful to enable the Ambassador's word to reach the highest levels. Concurrently, the Embassy of India was also prevailing upon Delhi to accept that while India would continue to support Aung San Suu Kyi and the democratic movement, but by not having a strong countervailing presence in Myanmar, it would leave the door open for increasing Chinese influence. The Myanmar side had also made it very clear to the Embassy that they were extremely uncomfortable with their over-dependence on China. Thus, it was incumbent on the Embassy to convince Delhi that notwithstanding the military Government in Myanmar, it was essential to engage with them so as to have a bulwark against Chinese influence. Concurrently, options were being explored to get the Tatmadaw to operate against the IIGs and their camps in Myanmar to regain some control on the insurgency situation in Northeast India. The location of the camps inside Myanmar territory also exposed them to Chinese influence and support. The presence of these camps and the IIGs was consistently being denied by the Tatmadaw. Thus, the purpose of this engagement with the military was to get them to operate against the IIGs and also to evolve a method to be able work along with the Myanmar government of the day.

The year 1997 provided Myanmar a break from the Chinese bear hug when it joined ASEAN[15] on 23 July 1997 and, at the behest of India, BIMSTEC in December 1997. However, the July 1997 Asian financial crisis came to the fore and stalled all hope of any investment, aid or cooperation from these quarters thereby forcing Myanmar to continue its dependence on China.

The first opportunity to engage the Tatmadaw came when they wanted 105-mm artillery guns and other military equipment which was already almost obsolete in India. This was a good opportunity to wean them away from China and accordingly Delhi was worked upon to enable this. Expectedly, this supply of equipment was required to be done with utmost secrecy since they did not want to let the Chinese become aware of this. To execute this procurement, Maj Gen Kyaw Win, the second in command of the DDSI, came on a secret visit to India, interacted with the DG MI and the Defence Secretary and conveyed his wish list of military hardware. However this visit and the list of equipment sought by Myanmar got leaked and was extensively covered in *The Pioneer* newspaper. This made headlines in India and Myanmar and the immediate backlash was that the Chinese came down heavily on Myanmar and the relationship between the Embassy and the DDSI disintegrated. The Embassy now had to restart the whole process of re-engaging with the Tatmadaw.

The next opportunity available to the Ambassador came during the Annual Army Day Reception[16] where President Than Shwe and Vice President Maung Aye, who was also the Army Chief, interacted with the invitees. This was considered one of the rare opportunities during the year where one came into contact with the top leadership. During this meeting in 1999, Ambassador Shyam Saran interacted with General Maung Aye who happened to mention that he had a very good relationship with the earlier Indian Army Chief General B. C. Joshi. General Maung Aye continued and said that even though there was an issue of protocol between them since he (Maung Aye) was the Vice President, they had agreed that as the Chiefs of their respective Armies, they could meet perhaps at the border (IMB). However, due to the sudden and untimely death[17] of General Joshi, this could not be taken forward. Ambassador Saran seized the opportunity and on the spur of the moment enquired of General Maung Aye that in case he was still interested, the present Indian Army Chief could invite him and they could have the meeting at the border as had been proposed initially. General Maung Aye was noncommittal and Ambassador Saran pressed on to suggest that if the General allowed, he would take this forward with Delhi. The interaction ended there, but the next morning the Minister of Science and Technology, U Thaung[18] called the Ambassador over urgently to discuss the proposal. U Thaung was considered close to General Maung Aye and was also very well known to the Ambassador. He spoke on behalf of General Maung Aye and conveyed to the Ambassador that General Maung Aye was interested in the revival of the proposal that they had discussed the previous evening. However, he cautioned that the General had directed that the Ministry of Foreign Affairs (MoFA) or the DDSI[19] were not to be informed and that this was to be discussed only with General Maung Aye through U Thaung, directly. Only, once the visit was confirmed, would the details be announced to the other departments. The Ambassador immediately took this forward and this fructified in the back-to-back meetings of the Chiefs in January 2000 at Mandalay and Shillong.

General V.P. Malik, then Chief of Army Staff, has deftly chronicled[20] the meetings and the process by which, in effect, defence diplomacy was used to catalyse traditional civilian diplomatic interaction between the two nations. During the reciprocal meeting, the Myanmar delegation, including ministers, were able to meet our Union Ministers and senior counterparts. On 6 January 2000, the Indian delegation reached Mandalay where a red carpet welcome by almost the entire cabinet awaited them. Several one-on-one discussions between the Chiefs took place wherein General Maung Aye reassured General Malik that he would not allow anti-Indian forces in Myanmar. The delegations also discussed the need for greater cooperation between the two sides; ways to improve communication between respective Command HQs; additional vacancies in Indian flying academies and civil-military training establishments and an invitation for the Myanmar Navy[21] to participate in Exercise Milan. In a rare instance of back-to-back reciprocal visits, on 7 January 2000, both delegations flew to Shillong where India got an opportunity to host the Myanmar delegation.

Ambassador Saran recalls that this was essentially the most crucial part of the interaction—the meeting of the civilian counterparts—and in effect the first high-level meeting between the two governments. Then Indian Minister of Commerce and Industry, Murasoli Maran and the Minister of Power, P. R. Kumaramangalam led the delegation which had eight Cabinet Ministers, secretaries from Ministry of External Affairs, Ministry of Home Affairs, Chief Secretaries from border states and the DG BRO. General Maung Aye's delegation had a similar number of ministers. They were able to meet their respective counterparts to discuss details of their various projects. These discussions covered myriad topics such as hydropower development on the Myanmar side; methods to increase the export of pulses from Myanmar to India; development of IT assistance in Myanmar and so on.

On the military side, General Malik recalls that General Maung Aye was pro-Indian, had authority and was decisive. He mentions that on 8 January 2000, a marked map was presented to him with locations of Indian insurgent groups. General Maung Aye accepted the map without comment. Ambassador Saran recalls that a week after the delegation returned to Myanmar, he was urgently summoned to the office of the Quarter Master General of the Tatmadaw, Lt Gen

Tin Hla.[22] In his office, Lt Gen Tin Hla spread out a map of the IMB with the IIG camps marked on it and informed the Ambassador that, on the instructions of General Maung Aye, and as a follow up to his interaction with General Malik, a major offensive was going to be launched to clear the camps on a particular date and time. Lt Gen Tin Hla informed that the Indian troops be alerted since the insurgents would in all probability run across the border back into India to avoid elimination, and could then be apprehended. He also told the Ambassador that this was being done as a goodwill gesture on the part of Myanmar. Ambassador Saran promptly informed the Indian Home Secretary since the Assam Rifles manning the IMB was a Home Ministry force. On the due date, which was within a fortnight of the meeting at Shillong, the camps were raided by the Myanmar Armed Forces which was a major milestone and signalled Myanmar's willingness to engage. In the course of the operation, approximately 12 to 14 Myanmar soldiers lost their lives. The Myanmar Army debriefed the Indians that these camps had a large number of families, especially of the ULFA. Further, they were guarded by insurgents equipped with modern high-quality communication equipment, sniper rifles and other arms which resulted in the casualties to the Myanmar side. The Myanmar Army also handed over a boxful of material and literature confiscated from the camps which were then sent to Delhi for scrutiny by the concerned agencies.

In July the same year, General Malik was invited to Yangon where the Chiefs reviewed the progress of points discussed in January 2000. This time, the discussions included foreign cooperation and other developmental issues; the Myanmar Navy confirmation in participation in Ex Milan and the International Fleet Review; inputs about recovery of ₹ 1.8 million stolen from a bank in Mizoram; requests for seats in Indian technical institutes and extensive discussion on management of insurgencies. Finally, General Malik called on Senior General Than Shwe, Chairman SPDC. Now the ball had started rolling with the Government of India inviting General Maung Aye to Delhi and Bodh Gaya in November 2000. Exactly a year later, in November 2001, the Myanmar Army raided rebel bases on a large scale.

Speaking to the author in an interview,[23] General Malik shared some insights on the India-Myanmar January 2000 interaction:

> *Initially, the MEA said that the meeting (between Gen Maung Aye and Gen Malik) was to take place at the India-Myanmar Border itself. I told the NSA that Chiefs do not meet at the borders. The Army Commander or Corps Commander can meet there. I suggested that the meeting take place at Kolkata*

from our side and from their side it could be Yangon or Mandalay. It was finally decided that it would be at Shillong and Mandalay. I flew quietly in the Avro to Mandalay and there the whole cabinet was lined up to receive me with red carpet and all. There was a tri-services Guard of Honour. Gen Maung Aye received me and took me to the guest room and right up to my room where I was to stay. I was taken aback at the warmth and hospitality and we too reciprocated in a befitting measure. I found him to be a quiet, soft-spoken and very friendly person.

On our reciprocal leg of the interaction, we flew down together from Mandalay to Guwahati and from there to Shillong by our helicopters. Immediately upon landing at Shillong, he was given a Guard of Honour. Now he and I were staying at one bungalow together. When the talks were going on, I had no role to play since it was being done by the ministerial delegation which had come from Delhi. So he and I would have long chats together in the bungalow. This was the time I handed over the map of the insurgent camps to him and within two weeks they had raided the camps. When I met the PM subsequently, I told him in detail what had happened and I said that they mean business and they want to be friendly with us; now it's up to us to reciprocate.

Later, when Gen Maung Aye visited India on an official trip as a Vice President, the first thing that he conveyed was that he wanted to meet me. I had retired by then, but I went there with my wife and we met up and spent over an hour with them. This is what I mean that we, in the military, have a very different relationship, even across armies.

Present Levels of Engagement

The Border Cooperation MoU (8 May 2014) marked a significant development in bilateral relations on the security front. The MoU includes a framework for security cooperation and exchange of information between Indian and Myanmar security agencies; institutionalises conduct of coordinated patrols on their respective sides of the international border and the maritime boundary; enables info exchange—insurgency, arms smuggling and drugs, human and wildlife trafficking; prevents illegal cross-border activities; spells out the level and frequency of meetings between the Armed Forces, Drug Control Agencies and Wildlife Crime Control agencies; institutionalises National and Sectoral annual meetings and biannual Border Meetings.[24] This was followed up by the India-Myanmar Bilateral Military Exercise in November 2017 wherein 31 officers participated in the six-day UN training exercise. The India-Myanmar Coordinated Patrol (CORPAT) and India-Myanmar Naval Exercise (IMNEX–18) have also matured into regular scheduled events.

India-Myanmar relations really stand out as a positive example of what can be achieved in the field of defence diplomacy. Two events of 2019–2020 are evidence that India-Myanmar relations in the field of security have excelled due to the defence diplomatic initiatives. One is the conduct of 'Operation Sunrise' series of operations, i.e., 'Operation Sunrise' I and II. The second is the handing over of the 22 insurgents of IIGs apprehended by Myanmar in the recent past. Cumulatively, these two developments have had game-changing consequences for Northeast India. These were not achieved overnight but were a culmination of engagements covering the entire spectrum of defence diplomacy starting from information exchange, joint and coordinated patrols right up to reciprocal coordinated operations. The importance of these events cannot be understated. Specifically, after several decades of insurgency, the operations by Myanmar have denied the Northeast insurgents a crucial element of insurgency...the safe haven in a neighbouring country. This vastly increases the probability of restoring normalcy in the Northeast. The handing over of the 22 insurgents complements this as it signals to the IIGs that a *modus vivendi* with the Myanmar Armed Forces is no longer a given, and they must therefore fall in line with the government.

Insurgency apart, defence engagement with Myanmar has increased at strategic levels as well. On the naval cooperation front, India handed over Bharat Dynamics Limited (BDL)-manufactured Shyena Advanced Light Torpedoes to Myanmar as part of a defence deal. Further, India is also refitting INS *Sindhuvir*, a 1980-Kilo class Russian submarine, at the Hindustan Shipyard Ltd., Vishakapatnam, for handing over to the Myanmar Navy.[25] The deal also includes a training package for Myanmar as it aspires to have its own submarine fleet, as have Bangladesh, Thailand, Singapore, Vietnam and Indonesia. Notably, INS *Sindhuvir*, in service with the Indian Navy since 1988 and having undergone a deep refit in 1999, is considered far superior to the Ming class submarines being peddled by China to other navies in the region. The 3,000-tonne INS *Sindhuvir* may be 31 years old but it has undergone regular refits in India and Russia over the years, with the latest modernization work being undertaken on the diesel-electric boat at Hindustan Shipyard Limited in Visakhapatnam.[26]

The MoU on Defence Cooperation signed on 29 July 2019 by Senior General Min Aung Hlaing, C-in-C of Defence Services (CDS), Myanmar, during his visit to India[27] was a significant continuation of India's engagement with Myanmar. It is reported that the MoU would cover enhancing military training, joint surveillance, and maritime security. India's engagement with Myanmar is maturing, though yet to take off on the scale desired to meet Myanmar's aspirations vis-à-vis the one-sided economic development that it is forced to accept under the present global geopolitical environment, from China.[28]

The other engagements with Myanmar include Foreign Office Consultations, National Level Meetings (NLM), Sectoral Level Meetings (SLM), meetings of the Heads of Survey Department and Director (Survey) and Joint Working Group (JWG) meetings on boundary issues. The Foreign Office Consultations are led by the Foreign Secretary of India and the Permanent Secretary of Myanmar. The most recent 18th Foreign Office consultation was held on 6 December 2019 at Delhi. The main forum to discuss security cooperation, consular issues, drug trafficking and liaison between agencies is the NLM at Home Secretary/Dy. Home Minister level. The 22nd NLM was held on 25-26 October 2018 at Delhi. The NLM is supplemented by a Joint Secretary-level SLM, also led by the Ministry of Home Affairs. The 24th SLM was held on 23-24 September 2019. The main forum for the representatives of the armed forces to discuss counter-insurgency and border security is the Regional Border Committee Meeting (RBCs). The 15th RBC was held in Manipur, India, in December 2019. Boundary matters are discussed by the JBWG led by Joint Secretary (BM), Ministry of External Affairs. The 3rd JBWG meeting was held on 26-27 August, 2018 in Yangon. Commercial issues are discussed in the Joint Trade Committee (JTC) held at Commerce Minister-level.[29] For the purposes of people-to-people interaction, junior level interactions of officers and soldiers with families have also begun with extremely positive feedback. These add up to considerable goodwill generated bilaterally.

Criticisms to Defence Diplomacy

A question that comes to mind when using defence diplomacy, is whether there is a danger of overdoing it? Ambassador Preet Malik strikes a note of caution when he says that India must never allow its military to become the key dominant factor in its foreign policy decisions related to Myanmar. General V.P. Malik however rules out[30] any such apprehension since he maintains that the entire function of defence diplomacy really had nothing to do with the military *per se*; rather it had everything to do with diplomacy. Other criticisms in defence diplomacy include the fact that it is not being used to promote democracy in Myanmar. While this is true, the counter that defence diplomacy is not a tool to promote democracy may be justified. Another perspective over defence diplomacy privileges the function and purpose of "diplomacy" in its classical definition of "the management of international relations by negotiation" whilst transforming the role of its agent, the military, into a reductionist one.

Figure 9.1: India-Myanmar Relationship Matrix

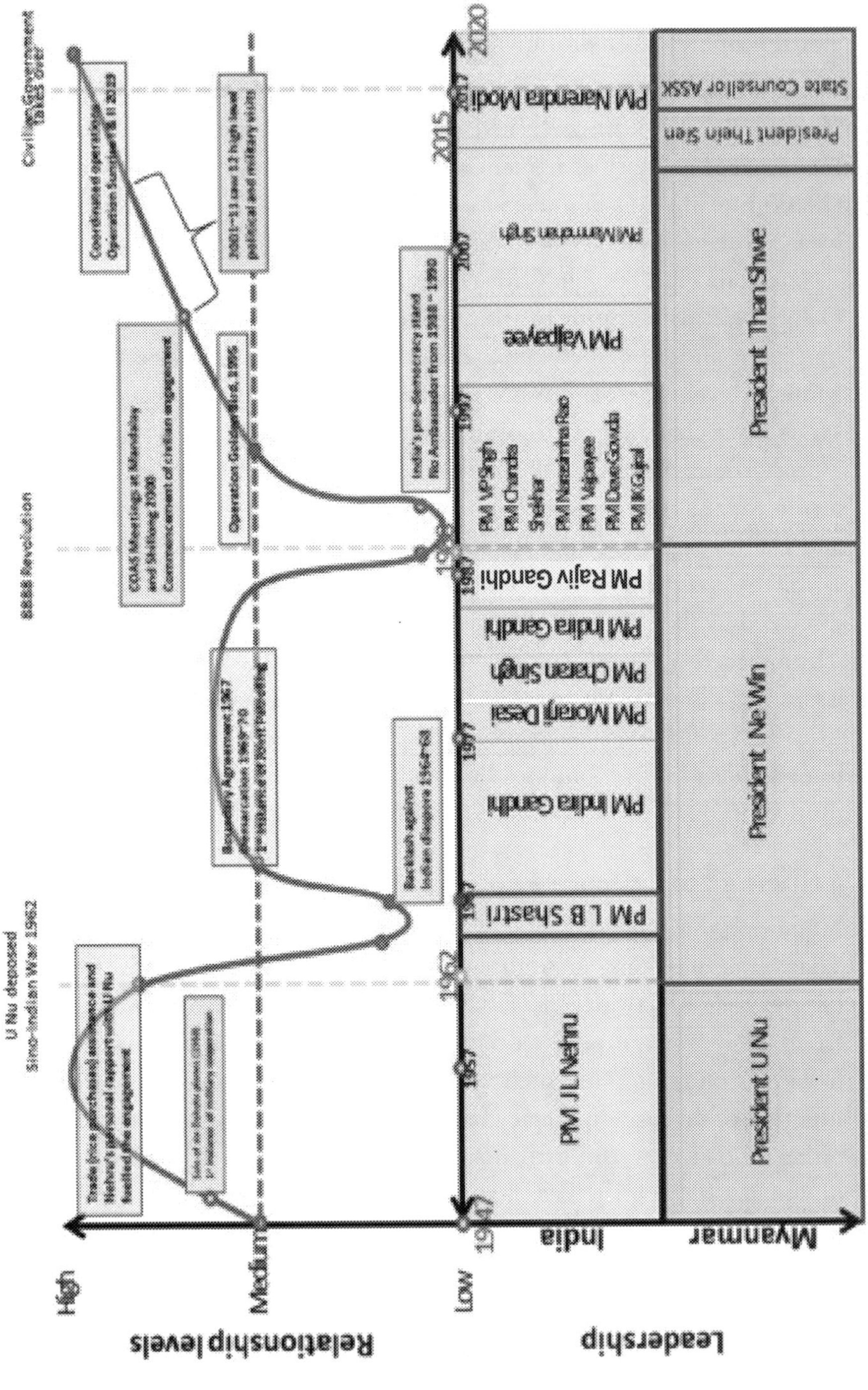

NOT TO SCALE

Source: Compiled by author

Conclusion

Defence diplomacy in India-Myanmar relations has succeeded in improving security and stability along the India-Myanmar border and providing impetus to improving relations between the two countries. Hence, the greater the diplomatic engagement with Myanmar through defence diplomacy, the higher the probability of achieving mutually beneficial security and developmental goals than only by traditional diplomatic mechanisms.

India-Myanmar bilateral relations have been driven essentially by common direct and indirect security concerns and hence diplomatically the best dividends were generated by defence diplomacy. India's connectivity objectives with Myanmar depend on a stable cross-border security context and are leading to more confident and better coordinated military-to-military relations between both the countries.

Of the various connectivity dimensions to the Act East Policy, viz., economic, infrastructure, cultural, diasporic, developmental and defence connectivity, amongst others, it is the last one that holds the key to laying the ground for the others. Notwithstanding the advent of democracy in Myanmar, the constitutional provisions of Myanmar mandate adequate military presence and participation in the government and hence the 'comfort level' for military engagement is greater than perceived in other regional countries.

The next decade of intercourse on this subject has the scope to metamorphose the northeast into a vibrant economy and is a strategic imperative to India's overall growth and stature in the world. I conclude with a statement made by John F. Kennedy, way back on 16 November 1961 wherein he said "*Diplomacy and defence are not substitutes for one another. Either alone would fail.*"[31]

NOTES

1. Arvind Gupta, New govt's foreign policy agenda needs comprehensive approach, The Economic Times Epaper, 3 June 2019, https://economictimes.indiatimes.com/news/politics-and-nation/new-govts-foreign-policy-agenda-needs-comprehensive-approach/articleshow/69626240.cms?from=mdr (Accessed on 15 May 2020).
2. Gregory Winger, The Velvet Gauntlet: A Theory of Defense Diplomacy, IWM Post 126, Institute for Human Sciences, 2014, https://www.iwm.at/publications/5-junior-visiting-fellows-conferences/vol-xxxiii/the-velvet-gauntlet/ (Accessed on 15 May 2020).
3. Gregory Winger, The Velvet Gauntlet: A Theory of Defense Diplomacy. In: What Do Ideas Do?, ed. A. Lisiak, N. Smolenski, Vienna: IWM Junior Visiting Fellows' Conferences, Vol. 33, 2014, https://www.iwm.at/publications/5-junior-visiting-fellows-conferences/vol-xxxiii/the-velvet-gauntlet/#_ednref1 (Accessed on 15 May 2020).
4. K.A. Muthanna, *Military Diplomacy*, Journal of Defence Studies, Vol 5, No 1, January 2011, https://idsa.in/system/files/jds_5_1_kamuthanna.pdf (Accessed on 15 May 2020).
5. In this chapter, defence and military are used interchangeably. It can be argued, albeit debatably,

that defence has a wider scope than military since it includes aspects beyond the scope of pure military, e.g., defence production.

6. Nicholas D. Kron, *Security Diplomacy: Beyond Defence,* Thesis submitted to Johns Hopkins University in conformity with the requirements for the degree of Master of Arts in Global Security Studies, Baltimore, Maryland, May 2015.
7. Col Arvind Dutta, *Role of India's Defence Cooperation Initiatives in Meeting the Foreign Policy Goals,* Journal of Defence Studies, Vol 3. No 3. July 2009,https://idsa.in/system/files/jds_3_3_adutta.pdf (Accessed on 15 May 2020).
8. At the Centre for Land Warfare Studies (CLAWS), New Delhi, 18 February 2008, on *Defence Cooperation as a Tool for Enhancing National Interest,*
9. Geneva Centre for the Democratic Control of Armed Forces (DCAF), *Defence Attachés,* DCAF Backgrounder, July 2007, https://www.files.ethz.ch/isn/38583/dcaf-backgrounder-defence-attaches.pdf (Accessed on 15 May 2020).
10. Indian Council of World Affairs, https://icwa.in/pdfs/IBindiamyanmar.pdf (Accessed on 15 May 2020).
11. Admiral R.D. Katari, *A Sailor Remembers.* Prabhat Books. Kindle Edition.
12. Baleshwar Prasad Papers, Nehru Memorial Museum and Library.
13. In a telephonic interview with the author on 4 June 2020.
14. Rumel Dahiya, 'Operation Golden Bird: Revisiting Counter-Insurgency on the India-Myanmar Border', *Journal of Defence Studies,* Vol. 10, No. 3 July-September 2016, pp. 5-20. http://idsa.in/jds/jds_10_3_2016_operation-golden-bird (Accessed on 10 November 2019)
15. Myanmar joined ASEAN 30 years after it was formed in 1967.
16. This event is held on 27 March every year and includes a grand parade.
17. Gen B.C. Joshi had visited Myanmar in May 1994 but tragically passed away on 18 November 1994, while in harness—the only Chief of the Indian Army to do so. He had been the Chief since 1 July 1993.
18. U Thaung served as Minister for Science and Technology of Myanmar from 1 November 1998 to 30 March 2011. He was a MP in the House of Representatives for Kyaukse Township constituency in the 2010 elections.
19. This was a logical manifestation of the Gen Maung Aye vs Gen Khin Nyunt rivalry. The latter, as Chief of Intelligence, was *de facto* the third senior-most in the hierarchy while Maung Aye was second. See Andrew Selth, *Secrets and Power in Myanmar: Intelligence and the fall of General Khin Nyunt,* ISEAS Publishing, 2019, pp. 56–81.
20. Gen V.P. Malik, *India's Military Conflicts and Diplomacy: An Inside View of Decision Making,* Harper Collins Publishers, Noida, 2013.
21. However, it was only during Ex Milan 2006 that for the first time a Myanmar ship '*Anawratha*' sailed out of Myanmar territorial waters in 40 years. See Bilveer Singh, *Southeast Asia-India Defence Relations in the Changing Regional Security Landscape,* IDSA Monograph Series No 4, May 2011, pg. 37, https://idsa.in/system/files/MonographNo4.pdf (Accessed on 20 May 2020).
22. Lt Gen Tin Hla was Deputy Prime Minister and Military Affairs Minister and also the Quarter Master General until November 2001. He was forced to retire in 2001, accused of corruption, believed to be initiated by Gen Khin Nyunt. Being a graduate of the Defence Services Academy at Pyin Oo Lwin,Tin Hla was considered to be from Maung Aye's camp as against Khin Nyunt who was from the Defence Services (Army) Officers' Training School.
23. In an interview at the India International Centre, New Delhi, on 20 February 2020.
24. Ministry of External Affairs, Government of India, India and Myanmar sign Memorandum of Understanding on Border Cooperation, Press Release, 10 May 2014, https://www.mea.gov.in/press-releases.htm?dtl/23315/India+and+Myanmar+sign+Memorandum+of+Understanding+on+ Border+Cooperation (Accessed on 4 August 2019).

25. Manu Pubby, Taking it to next level, India readies submarine for Myanmar, *The Economic Times*, E-Paper, 30 July 2019, https://economictimes.indiatimes.com/news/defence/taking-it-to-next-level-india-readies-submarine-for-myanmar/articleshow/70442448.cms?from=mdr (Accessed on 4 August 2019).
26. Aakriti Vinayak & Jaideep Chanda, Myanmar Round Up: December 2020, Vivekananda International Foundation, New Delhi, 29 January 2020, https://www.vifindia.org/article/2020/january/29/myanmar-round-up-december-2019 (Accessed on 4 August 2029).
27. Press Release, Indian Embassy, Yangon, http://www.pib.nic.in/PressReleasePage.aspx?PRID=1580637 (Accessed on 4 August 2019).
28. https://www.vifindia.org/article/2019/august/12/from-sanctions-to-submarines-myanmar-july-2019
29. Ministry of External Affairs, Government of India, India-Myanmar Bilateral Brief, May 2020, https://mea.gov.in/Portal/ForeignRelation/Mynmar_may2020.pdf (Accessed on 4 August 2020).
30. In an interview with the author at the India International Centre, New Delhi, on 20 February 2020.
31. Greg Lange, President Kennedy delivers major policy speech at UW on November 16, 1961, History Link, 16 March 1999, https://www.historylink.org/File/968 (Accessed on 4 August 2020).

CHAPTER 10

Myanmar and Sanctions

(This Chapter has been adapted from a Vivekananda International Foundation Paper written by this author, titled, *Counterproductive Effects of Sanctions – The Myanmar Case Study,* published on 28 Oct 2019)[1]

> *There's a myth that sanctions led to the political opening in 2011. At a personal level, many in the army establishment and their friends in business did far better under sanctions than after 2011. For the generals, a Burma more integrated into the rest of the world is the risky proposition, not a return to more isolation.*
>
> **—Thant Myint-U[2]**

This chapter seeks to analyse the circumstances leading to the United Nations (UN) recommendations on imposition of sanctions[3] on Myanmar and the efficacy of the sanctions as a whole. Presently, certain bans have already been imposed or recommended to be imposed by Israel, the USA and the UN on officials of Myanmar in the aftermath of the Rohingya crisis. But this chapter is not about Rohingyas and human rights violations. As such, it neither concurs nor dispels the allegations made against the Myanmar Government. It argues for the need to ensure that the democratic discourse in Myanmar does not get subsumed by the Rohingya rhetoric and that sanctions in effect subvert the larger democratic process that is currently underway there. Sanctions are counterproductive to the overall scheme of development and democratisation of Myanmar and therefore ethnic minorities themselves. Finally, it looks at the way ahead and India's role in supporting Myanmar through this crisis.

Build Up to the Imbroglio

The current discourse on sanctions was originally triggered by the Israeli and US bans on Myanmar military personnel[4] due to the Rohingya crisis. But before we get there, a deep dive into history is essential. A British Second World War strategy was to arm pro-British Muslims including Rohingyas in Arakan to create a rear-guard-cum-intelligence gathering guerrilla force called the 'V' Force to slow down the Japanese during the retreat from Burma in 1942.[5] In return, they were apparently promised a '*Muslim National Area*'[6] in northwest Arakan but the British eventually reneged on their promise. This strategy effectively pitched the Arakan Muslim Rohingyas against their Buddhist brethren who had sided with the Japanese against the colonial British.[7, 8] These Arakan Buddhists were armed by Aung San's Burma Independence Army, who ended up clashing with this same 'V' Force. It was under these circumstances in 1942 that the first large-scale massacre of Rohingyas by Arakan Buddhists took place claiming over one lakh lives,[9] and set the tone for continued persecution of Rohingyas.

The actions by the Rohingya militant group, *Harakah al-Yaqin*,[10] subsequently renamed as the Arakan Rohingya Solidarity Army (ARSA) which had launched four attacks since 2012 led to the current crisis. Two of these attacks on 9 October 2016 and 25 August 2017 were the ones which triggered the Myanmar military's response. The 9 October 2016 attack was launched by 250 militants armed with knives and hand-made guns and killed nine police officers and injured five in Maungday and Rathedaung townships. The attackers stole 50 guns and 10,000 bullets but lost eight members while two were captured alive by the Myanmar forces. They disclosed that they were members of the terrorist group called Aqa Mul Mujahid (AMM) led by Ataullah Abu Ammar Junjuni@ Hafiz Tohar[11] which subsequently merged with the ARSA.

The 25 August 2017 attack took place *simultaneously* on 30 police posts and one army base in the townships of Maungdaw, Buthidaung and Rathedaung in North Rakhine killing ten police officers, one soldier and an immigration official while 77 insurgents were killed and one captured as per reports of the International Crisis Group.[12] *On the same date* the ARSA massacred 99 Hindu children, women and men of Ah Nauk Kha Maung Seik and Ye Bauk Kyar villages in north Maungdaw Township as reported by Amnesty International.[14] This was followed the next day, on 26 August 2017, when ARSA members killed another six Hindus—two women, a man, and three children near Myo Thu Gyi village outside Maungdaw town. For a detailed analysis of the ARSA actions, see **Appendix O.**

Myanmar Response

The Myanmar response to the ARSA attacks of August 2017, has as always, been violent, brutal, grossly disproportionate to the scale of the violence perpetrated by the ARSA, and totally indiscriminate. On this occasion, the Tatmadaw acted to a plan to evict the Rohingyas for good under the euphemism of '*clearance operations*', duly funded by Tatmadaw-solicited donations. Effectively, what has been alleged by the UN-delegated International Independent Fact-Finding Mission on Myanmar (IIFFMM) on clearance operations[14] falls into a typical pattern with Tatmadaw troops attacking villages, indiscriminate firing leading to deaths, looting, targeted killing of civilians, arson, murder and rape.

The IIFFMM concluded on reasonable grounds that gross human rights violations and serious violations of international humanitarian law had been committed in Myanmar and that many of these violations undoubtedly amount to the gravest crimes under international law. The human rights violations and abuses stemmed from deep fractures in society and structural problems that have been apparent and unaddressed for decades. They were shocking for the level of denial, normalcy and impunity that is attached to them. Hence, the actions of the Tatmadaw in the context of the "clearance operations" in northern Rakhine State in 2016 and 2017 had so seriously violated international law that any engagement in any form with the Tatmadaw, its current leadership, and its businesses, would be indefensible. Engagement would only be considered when a complete restructuring of the Tatmadaw has commenced; its current leadership is replaced and extensive reform is undertaken to place the Tatmadaw under full elected civilian control and oversight and to remove the Tatmadaw from Myanmar's political and economic life. This was in effect, an utopian wish list.

United Nations Initiatives

In addressing the human rights situation in Myanmar, the UN took three steps. In the first instance, the United Nations Human Rights Council (UNHRC), vide Para No. 11 of Resolution No. A/HRC/RES/34/22 passed during the 34th Session of the Human Rights Council on 24 March 2017, decided to establish the above-mentioned IIFFMM. The IIFFMM submitted a number of reports which have been tabulated and summarised at Table 10.1. A detailed version of this table is in **Appendix R.** These included three generic reports and two thematic reports.

Table 10.1: Summary of Reports of the IIFFMM

Document No. (Date)	*Name*	*Gist of Contents*
A/HRC/39/64 (12 Sep 2018)	Report of the IIFFMM	A 21-pg document which gives out the gist of the detailed report submitted subsequently.
A/HRC/39/CRP.2 (17 Sep 2018)	Report of the detailed findings of the IIFFMM	A 441-pg document which should be read in conjunction with the report of the Independent International Fact-Finding Mission on Myanmar (A/HRC/39/64) above.
A/HRC/42/50 (8 Aug 2019)	Report of the IIFFMM	A 20-pg document which contains the findings of the Independent International Fact-Finding Mission on Myanmar since its previous report (A/HRC/39/64).
A/HRC/42/CRP.3 (5 Aug 2019)	The economic interests of the Myanmar military	A 111-pg thematic supplementary report of the IIFFMM
A/HRC/42/CRP.4 (22 Aug 2019)	Sexual and gender-based violence in Myanmar and the gendered impact of its ethnic conflicts	A 61-pg thematic supplementary report of the IIFFMM.
A/HRC/42/CRP.5 (16 Sep 2019)	Detailed findings of the IIFFMM	A 190-pg document which contains information complementary to that contained in the official report (A/HRC/42/50), submitted to the Human Rights Council pursuant to Resolution 39/2.
A/HRC/42/CRP.6 (16 Sep 2019)	Compilation of all recommendations made by the IIFFMM	A 20-pg summary of recommendations that have appeared in most of the above-mentioned documents.

Source: Compiled by the author from www.ohchr.org

After analysing the findings of the IIFFMM, it was felt that there was enough substance and gravity of offence for the matter to be taken to its logical legal conclusion. Thus, in the second instance, another UNHRC Resolution No. 39/2 was adopted on 27 September 2018, which essentially expressed '*grave concern at the findings of the independent international fact-finding mission that there is sufficient information to warrant the investigation and prosecution of senior officials in the Tatmadaw*', to empower a competent court to try them for genocide. The Resolution called for a full and independent investigation and an Independent Investigative Mechanism in Myanmar (IIMM) '*to collect, consolidate, preserve and analyse evidence*' of the most serious international crimes committed in Myanmar since 2011, to '*prepare files in order to facilitate and expedite fair and independent criminal proceedings*'. Finally, Resolution 39/2 also extended the mandate of the IIFFMM, until the new mechanism became operational to ensure that the large amount of evidence of human rights violations and abuses was fully documented, verified, consolidated and preserved in order for the material to be transferred to the new mechanism for further legal processing.[15]

The third and astutely introspective step taken by the UN was to call for an independent inquiry into the involvement of the United Nations in Myanmar from 2010 to 2018. This was based on a recommendation in the Report of the Independent International Fact-Finding Mission on Myanmar (A/HRC/39/64) of 12 September 2018 and supported by Resolution 39/2 (Para 32) which stated:

> *'As a matter of urgency, a comprehensive, independent inquiry should be conducted into the involvement of the United Nations in Myanmar since 2011, with a view to establishing whether everything possible to prevent or mitigate the unfolding crises was done, identifying lessons learned and good practices, making recommendations as appropriate, including on accountability, and enabling more effective work in future.'*

The report titled "*A Brief and Independent Inquiry into the Involvement of the United Nations in Myanmar from 2010 to 2018*" was conducted by former Guatemalan Foreign Affairs Minister, Gert Rosenthal, who was also a former UN Ambassador and top executive at the UN's Economic Commission for Latin America and the Caribbean.[16] To better understand the issue, it behoves that we delve a little more into the output and outcomes of these three initiatives and also the thematic report on the Economic Interests of the Myanmar Military.

The IIFFMM Reports: Exhaustive but Exhausted

The outcome of the first initiative was the establishment of the IIFFMM. The President of the UNHRC appointed Marzuki Darusman (lawyer, human rights campaigner and former Attorney-General of Indonesia) as chair, Radhika Coomaraswamy (lawyer and former UN Special Rapporteur on Violence against Women and UN Special Representative for Children and Armed Conflict, Sri Lanka) and Christopher Sidoti (international human rights lawyer and former Human Rights Commissioner, Australia) as members of the IIFFMM. The Mission was created *to establish facts and circumstances of the alleged recent human rights violations by military and security forces and abuses in Myanmar in particular in Rakhine State* as also *to ensure full accountability for perpetrators and justice for victims.* The Mission submitted its 441-page primary report titled "*Report of the detailed findings of the IIFFMoM*" (A/HRC/39/CRP.2) in the 39th Session (hereafter referred to as the September 18 Detailed Report). It subsequently compiled 20 pages of exhaustive recommendations for stakeholders including the Government of Myanmar; the United Nations itself and the international community; non-State armed groups in Myanmar; Myanmar civil society, including religious leaders and organisations; business enterprises operating in Myanmar and Facebook and other social media platforms operating in Myanmar from the multiple reports that it generated.

The Mission also delivered thematic reports which supplemented the recommendations of the September 18 Detailed Report and covered the "*Economic Interests of the Myanmar Military*" and "*Sexual and gender-based violence in Myanmar*" and the gendered impact of its ethnic conflicts. Essentials of the former are covered in a subsequent portion of this chapter since it has reference of Indian companies. The IIFFMM reports were thorough, detailed and accurately highlighted the scale and spread of the human rights violations that the Tatmadaw had indulged in. It essentially met the requirements of the charter that it mandated. However, where it fell grossly short was in the quality of recommendations. The criticisms of the same are covered in a subsequent section of this chapter.

The First IIMM Report: Work in Progress

While the IIFFMM can be criticised on the nature of recommendations, it would be premature to pass a verdict on the functioning of the IIMM. The IIMM was established on 27 September 2018 but effectively started functioning with effect from 1 July 2019 when the Head of the IIM was appointed. The Head of the Mechanism is US international criminal justice lawyer, Nicholas Koumjian, who has 35 years of experience as a prosecutor, including almost 20 years of experience in the field of international criminal justice. However his appointment is not without controversy. Min Lwin Oo, a legal advisor at the Asian Human Rights Commission, Norway, opined that a non-US prosecutor would have been better for an investigation without bias. He recommended the names of Brazilian legal scholar Paulo Sérgio Pinheiro or human rights attorney Tomás Ojae Quintana, currently the U.N.'s special rapporteur on human rights in North Korea.[17] The first report of the IIM has concluded realistically that without the support of the States in the region and the international community, investigations such as this one, are complex, and that it can take time for such information, documentation and evidence to be shaped into strong case files ready for prosecution.[18]

Nailing It: The Independent Inquiry on UN Role in Myanmar

Out of the three initiatives of the UN mentioned above, the "Brief and Independent Inquiry into the Involvement of the United Nations in Myanmar from 2010 to 2018" by Gert Rosenthal is the least known and possibly the most nuanced and best grounded in the environmental realities. The paper has identified systemic and structural obstacles in the UN which has affected the performance in Myanmar.

It touches upon the core contradictory trend in Myanmar wherein the fledgling imperfect democracy totters along the path to a full democracy while negotiating through minefields of human rights violations of the most extreme kind. The paper argues that:

> *'In fact, although the Rohingya crisis affected a relatively small percentage of Myanmar's population (estimated at approximately 1.4 million people in 2014) and a limited geographical area (Rakhine State), the sheer scale and brutality of human rights violations inflicted on this minority immediately mobilised international attention, monopolising media coverage of the events taking place in Rakhine State in the over-all reporting concerning Myanmar, especially in Western societies. This, even though events in Rakhine State were not limited to the plight of the Rohingyas: the communal dimension was further complicated by long-standing grievances of the "Arakan" or Rakhine Buddhists towards the Bamar majority and the central government, while conflicts also persisted in other states such as Shan and Kachin.'*

Rosenthal further writes that '*It is noteworthy that these events were occurring simultaneously with the political process, and increasingly undermining it—actually, taking it as hostage—at least as perceived by Western observers.*'

The paper lists three aspects which have adversely affected the functioning of the UN:

- *Firstly*, the criticism of the perceived leadership deficit on the part of Aung San Suu Kyi which was driven by her concerns of not wanting to derail the whole process by alienating the military. We will return to this subsequently.
- *Secondly*, the upcoming elections of 2020 would be high on the minds of both the civilian and military populations.
- *Thirdly*, the fact that the UN is **not** the most important external agency and it has come into the region after Norway, the IMF and the World Bank for economic priority, since the borders opened up. Hence, the first port of call for the Myanmar Government for guidance were these entities and therefore the UN does not feature as high on the list of the international entities as it (the UN), would perhaps like to be, in the Myanmar consciousness both on the Tatmadaw as well as on the civilian side.

The other major conflict that Rosenthal has documented, and possibly the one which has prevented the UN from achieving the efficacy it should have, was within the UN. This was the one between the "*quiet diplomacy*" proponents and the advocates of "*outspoken advocacy*". The former focuses on applying major effort in the available political space so as to remain relevant with the Myanmar Government, while attempting to address human rights issues through gradual, non-intrusive methods for the overall long-term good of the nation and its people. It requires active engagement with the host nation while driving home the need for addressing human rights and international humanitarian law in private, discreet and informal interactions. The latter attempts to coerce host nations into action by firm and hard advocacy and implementing international obligations using methods which may seem intrusive and abrasive. These include public denunciations, bilateral punitive sanctions, touting the negative impacts of the country's actions on access to international finance, aid, investments, tourism and economic assistance. Rosenthal deigns to prefer one strategy over the other, but describes the former as a more pragmatic approach. He goes on to acknowledge that in practice the strategies are not watertight compartments but must necessarily have overlapping areas and are in no way mutually exclusive.

When seen through the prism of the three pillars of UN activities, viz., peace and security; human rights and development, Rosenthal identifies that UN staff working in the 'development pillar' tend to favour 'quiet diplomacy', and leave out human rights for other pillars to handle. The staff working in the 'human rights pillar' naturally align better with 'robust advocacy' whilst the 'peace and security pillar' staff follow a middle path. Finally, he recommends the need to have a central arbitrator to promote a common overall strategy between these two approaches to ensure they mutually support each other rather than subvert the process; an organisational structure to converge the divergent perspectives onto a common achievable platform; ensure decisions are communicated to the field operators and monitored and feedback and analysis of the ground inputs filed to ensure that Headquarters have an accurate assessment of ground realities.

Specific to the Myanmar experience, Rosenthal dwells upon problems of interaction with the host government as another reason for UN inefficacy. Specifically, the dual system of governance within Myanmar, where both the civilian and military jostle for space, causes confusion with their often conflicting mindsets. Thus, engagement with both sides of the same government is the order of the day with attendant complexities. Similarly, the Myanmar sense of ardent nationalism and consequently a colonial-era deep-rooted distrust towards external entities persists and permeates interactions with the UN staff. This trust deficit manifested in scrutiny and harassment of the staff, often transcending to intimidation. These assumed forms such as denial of authorisation for internal movement within the country or delay and even denial of visas.

Myanmar Government officials were apparently perceptive to the differences within the UN staff and played it to suit their interest. Under this situational environment, many officials of the UN apparently preferred 'quiet diplomacy' over 'robust advocacy'. However, the sheer scale of human rights violations against the Rohingya community became the centre of attention of member-states, human rights advocates and international media and thereby it unwittingly hijacked the discourse and overran those practising quiet diplomacy.

The initial euphoria amongst the international community on the opening up of Myanmar has been partly attributed to the status of Aung San Suu Kyi. However, the criticism of the State Counsellor in desisting from commenting on the Rohingyas is seen as having fallen from grace and thus to be shunned. In the long run, the hype of the robust advocates have effectively weakened the relative position of the State Counsellor within the Government vis-à-vis the military and has eventually jeopardised the fragile political and democratic process.

Insufficient inter-governmental support is also cited as a reason for the limited success of the UN initiatives in Myanmar. Specifically, the Chinese interest in Myanmar was crucial. Geo-politically, China has no choice but to engage Myanmar since the two share a 2,194-km boundary which translates to 34 per cent of Myanmar's boundaries and over 9 per cent of China's land borders. Further, even at the UN Headquarters, the Security Council's sluggish reaction[19] to the Secretary General's letter of 2 September 2017 is symptomatic of the UN and the member–states' failures to address the situation.

Thematic Report: The Economic Interests of the Myanmar Military

The 111-page report mapping the economic interests of the Myanmar military is innovative and successfully documents the economic interests of the Myanmar military, though not without weaknesses. It concludes that the '*ability of the Tatmadaw to draw upon alternate sources of revenue, outside the official military budget, contributes towards it operating without civilian oversight*'. In essence, the Myanmar military has an effective parallel military budget from illegal and unaccounted sources that is being used in an unauthorised manner without any civilian checks and balances. The report has therefore recommended economic isolation of the Tatmadaw:

- To encourage transformation of the Tatmadaw as a prerequisite for human rights compliance.
- To deter continued and future violations of the human rights laws and international humanitarian laws.
- To promote accountability for violations committed in the past.

The recommended modus operandi for achieving this isolation is to ensure '*no business enterprise active in Myanmar or trading with or investing in businesses in Myanmar should enter into an economic or financial relationship with the security forces of Myanmar, in particular the Tatmadaw, or any enterprise owned or controlled by them or their individual members, until and unless they are re-structured and transformed as recommended by the Mission*'.[20] The report identifies two approaches to this task. The *negative approach* is that which has been highlighted above, while the *positive approach* works on encouraging economic ties and engagement with non-Tatmadaw companies and businesses in Myanmar as a means of building and strengthening the non-Tatmadaw sector of the economy. At the functional level, it involves targeting individual sanctions, asset freezes and travel bans, amongst other things.

It has identified the two conglomerates in Myanmar that are essentially holding companies, i.e., Myanmar Economic Holdings Limited (MEHL) and Myanmar Economic Corporation (MEC) as being owned and influenced by senior Tatmadaw leaders who have also been identified as responsible for gross human rights violations. Their family members are also said to be involved in these companies. These two organisations exercise control over 147 other companies which straddle diverse sectors of the economy. Further, it has also identified 45 companies which have donated US$ 10.2 million to the Tatmadaw as solicited by them, for the infamous clearance operations against the Rohingyas.

On the other side, the paper has identified and named 59 foreign firms which have either joint ventures or other commercial ties with businesses involved with the Tatmadaw. Further, it has listed 14 foreign companies, 12 of which are state-owned enterprises, which have supplied and provided arms and related equipment to the Tatmadaw since 2016, i.e., after the Tatmadaw's dismal human rights record was widely and publicly known.

Indian companies feature in both the lists. These are tabulated below in Table 10.2:

Table 10.2: Indian Companies Operating in Myanmar as Mentioned in the IIFFMM Report "Economic Interests of the Myanmar Military"

Company	*Nature of Engagement*	*Remarks*
Adani Yangon International Terminal Company owned by Adani Ports and Special Economic Zone Ltd	Leasing Ahlone International Port Terminal 2 for 50 years in association with MEC.	Private Enterprise
Bharat Dynamics Ltd	Supply of 10 Advanced Light Torpedos 'Shyena' worth USD 38 million	State owned enterprises
Hindustan Aeronautics Ltd.	1 × HJT-16 Kiran-1 trainer aircraft as aid	
Infosys India	Contractor to Myawaddy Bank, a MEHL subsidiary and the second-largest tax payer in Myanmar	• According to the German development agency, Deutsche Gesellschaftfür Internationale Zusammenarbeit (GIZ) GmbH, in May 2018, Infosys partnered with Myawaddy Bank to provide digital banking software. • Private Enterprise

Source: Compiled by author from the IIFFMM Report "Economic Interests of the Myanmar Military"

The actual number of Indian companies operating in Myanmar and mentioned in the report pales in comparison to the number of companies from China, Hongkong, Japan, Singapore and South Korea. The details are as depicted in Figure 10.1.

Figure 10.1: Analysis of Country-wise Spread of Companies Operating in Myanmar as mentioned in the IIFFMM Report "Economic Interests of the Myanmar Military"

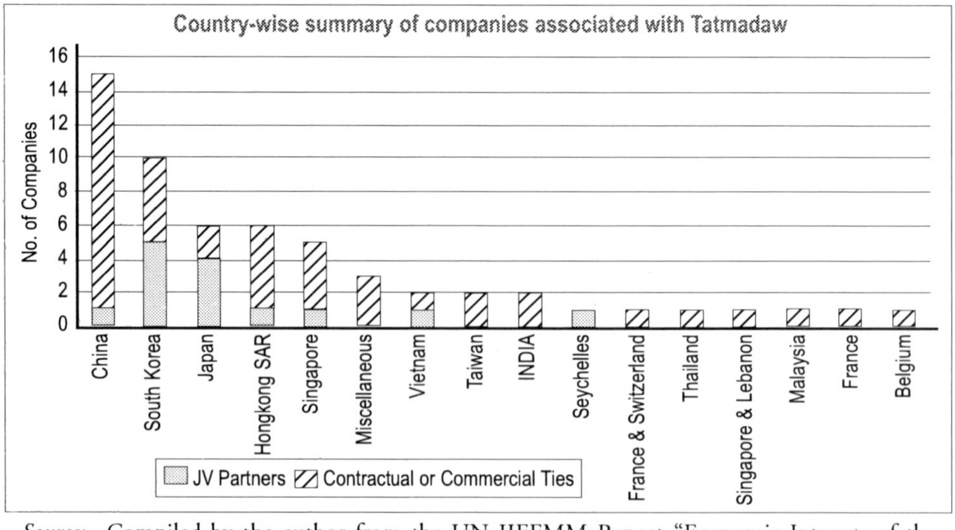

Source: Compiled by the author from the UN IIFFMM Report "Economic Interests of the Myanmar Military"

The actual participation of Indian companies in Myanmar is not significant to merit concern. However, the fact that these reputed companies now find mention in a UN-endorsed document and that the document expects the companies to ensure that they should not enter into or remain in a business relationship of any kind with the Tatmadaw or any enterprise owned or controlled by them, puts potential Indian investors in Myanmar on the caution. Theoretically the paper is sound and breaks new ground. However, contextual applicability and implementation remains a grey area which brings us to the criticism of the recommendations.

Criticisms on the Quality of Recommendations by IIFFMM

The crux of the issue lies in the fact that the recommendations[21] put forth by the IIFFMM are counterproductive and will not solve the problems but only aggravate them. An analytical approach is needed to understand the import of the recommendations. A basic empirical analysis of the quantum of recommendations vis-à-vis the implementing agencies shows an understandable tilt towards the Government of Myanmar having the maximum deliverables. Figure 10.2 below highlights the same.

Figure 10.2: Segment-wise Analysis of Recommendations made by the IIFFMM

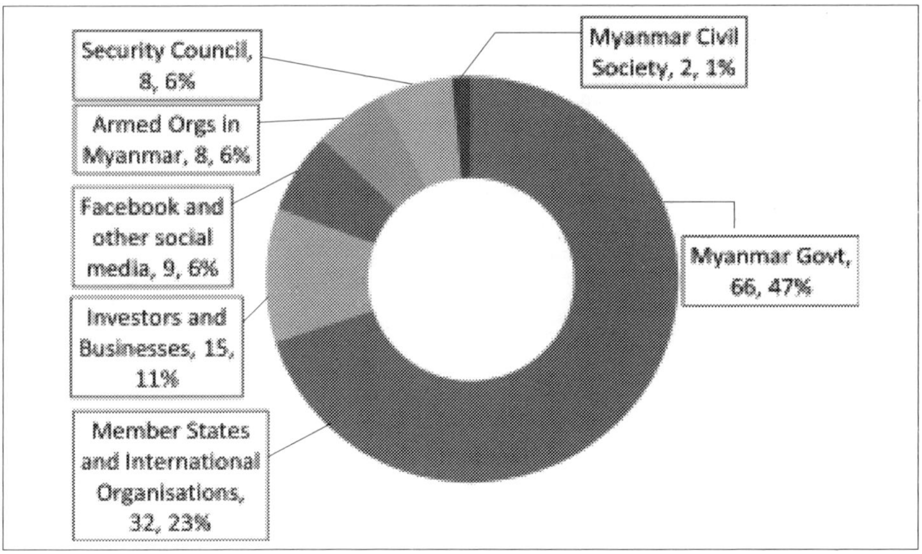

Source: Compiled by the author from "Compilation of all recommendations made by the IIFFMM" A/HRC/42/CRP.6 (16 September 2019)

The IIFFMM cumulatively made 140 recommendations with 66 (47 per cent) directed at the Myanmar Government and 32 (23 per cent) directed at the member-states and international organisations. The least recommendations, two, were reserved for Myanmar civil society amounting to just one per cent. This straightaway implies that the major onus of responsibility lies on the Myanmar Government for action. This nascent quasi-civilian government, dependent on the Tatmadaw for its existence, was now expected to bell the cat against its own benefactor and risk a coup and push the country back into a dictatorship. Instead of placing more onus on the member-states and the Security Council, the IIFFMM was focussed on directing the Government to implement what it could not.

Consider the first recommendation:

> *'The Government of Myanmar, including the civilian authorities and the Tatmadaw as relevant, should act without delay to re-structure the Tatmadaw and transform its role. That should begin with replacing the current leadership of the Tatmadaw. Through a constitutional amendment process, the Government should further pursue the removal of the Tatmadaw from Myanmar's political life'.*

The Myanmar military has been in power since 1962 and the above-mentioned recommendation is an oft-repeated one for all the ills that ail Myanmar. However, the report is silent on how to proceed to achieve this recommendation and this is the case with the other recommendations too.

Under the head "Security sector reform", the document lists seven major recommendations which directly and adversely affect the Tatmadaw and includes abolishing the quotas for military seats in the legislature; appointment of vice-presidents and ministers; control of ministries including abolishing the Commander-in-Chief's role in relation to military justice amongst others. These templated recommendations devoid of contextual applicability rob the otherwise exhaustive document of its value. Currently, the political need of the hour in Myanmar is constitutional reform; and to give credit to the civilian lawmakers there, the process for the same to reduce the role of the military in the parliamentary process has been under way for the past year. It will be unlikely to succeed given the resistance by the Tatmadaw; however, it will build up the necessary momentum within Myanmar for eventual constitutional reform, possibly years later. The IIFFMM report ignores this aspect and approaches the situation with a blinkered vision.

Certain aspects of the recommendations were found to be subjective, e.g., "*halt all current military and security operations that are unlawful, unnecessary or disproportionate...*" (Para 6). The concept of necessity or lack of necessity of a military or security operation takes the debate into a totally nebulous sphere. Other facets of the recommendations were not implementable under the present ground realities and not enforceable, e.g., "*Issue clear, public and unequivocal instructions to all branches of the Tatmadaw and other security forces that torture, rape....and other human rights violations are prohibited absolutely*" (Para 7). Similarly, the recommendation to "*permit and facilitate free and unfettered access to all parts of Myanmar, especially Kachin, Rakhine and Shan states and all other conflict or crisis areas, for national and international humanitarian actors...journalists and national and international human rights monitors to investigate and report on human rights compliance*" (Para 9) can at best be described as a pipe dream.

Some recommendations such as suspending the citizenship verification process based on the 1982 Citizenship Law (Para 12) are unrealistic and go against the will of the majority. The recommendation that is totally divorced from the ground realities are the ones related to the welfare of the Rohingyas (Para 13). Turning a blind eye to the Buddhist majoritarian view while addressing the issue is a legalistic approach to a problem that is essentially political.

Myanmar on the 'Banned Wagon': A Legacy of Sanctions

Having mapped the UN initiatives, it is imperative to logically analyse the impact of sanctions in general, and on Myanmar in specific. Myanmar is no stranger to bans. Since 1990, the USA, EU, Japan, Canada and Australia have imposed sanctions of various kinds on Myanmar. A consolidated list of sanctions imposed on Myanmar over the ages is summarised in **Appendix S**. This should be evidence enough that sanctions do not work, especially in the context of Myanmar. The most recent instances of sanctions in Myanmar are those by the USA on the Myanmar senior military hierarchy followed by the Israeli ban on Myanmar officials from attending military exhibitions. The ban on the generals was responded to by Myanmar with a suitably contrite statement stating that the ban had affected the dignity of the leaders.[22] There was no response to the Israeli action. Yanghee Lee, UN Special Rapporteur to Myanmar, said that it was not enough and more was needed to be done.[23] The USA has banned visits to the USA by Myanmar's army chief, Senior General Min Aung Hlaing, Deputy C-in-C Soe Win, Brigadier General Than Oo and Brigadier General Aung Aung and their families because of their role in the human rights violations of the Rohingyas. It hopes that this will strengthen the hands of the civilian government to further delegitimise the current military leadership.

The Israeli action too seems to be directed to meet the requirements of the USA and EU domestic politics. An EU arms embargo is currently in force until 30 April 2020.[24] It seems unlikely that Israeli realpolitik policies would jeopardise the military business opportunities that either the EU or Myanmar offers and hence would have to balance the need to be seen as going along with the rest of the world while continuing business[25] on the quiet.[26]

On the US sanctions, Erin Murphy, a former State Department official and founder-principal of the Inle Advisory Group which specialises on Myanmar, said the ban would not affect the generals too much directly, but their children or grandchildren who want to come to the USA as tourists or students would be impacted. While saying the travel ban provided a tool to encourage change, she doubted it would change attitudes toward the Rohingyas, who are "*almost a universally despised population*".[27] Similarly, the Economist Intelligence Unit[28] does not expect the UN recommendations to have any sizeable financial impact on the Tatmadaw. According to it, formal sanctions will not be adopted by the UN body, owing to likely vetoes by key Security Council members.

So, Do Sanctions Work?

At this stage it is imperative to see how sanctions have worked globally in the past. Enormous literature on this topic is available in open sources and by and large there is an understanding that sanctions, while being the preferred foreign policy tool as an alternative to military action, have limited success. The success varies depending upon a number of factors, some of which are discussed in this section. Maarten Smeets, of the Institute for Training and Technical Co-operation (ITTC), WTO, Geneva, in his paper "*Can Economic Sanctions be Effective?*" argues:

> *Economic sanctions generally inflict economic costs to all countries involved in the sanction episodes, including those taking the sanctions, thus shooting themselves in the foot. The country facing the sanctions is likely to develop trade relations with third parties that are not part of the sanction coalition. It is observed that sanctions are mostly taken in complement of diplomatic and other forms of pressure. The type of sanctions is also evolving, with countries increasingly using 'smart' sanctions, targeting financial transactions, business activities and individuals there were it hurts most and limiting their freedom of movement. It is the combination of various interventions that could eventually make the sanction episodes effective, if at all, and not the economic sanctions per se. Despite such shortcomings and lack of evidence of their effectiveness, it can safely be said that they are the preferred option compared to military intervention. At the same time, and regrettably, sanctions do not necessarily prevent armed conflict adding to the economic cost (and) the tragic cost of human life.*[29]

Smeets goes on to state that sanctions are generally recognised to be a more powerful expression of disagreement than pure political declarations and are meant to give teeth to these declarations, especially where leaders want to shows the domestic electorate that they are responsible and not just watching 'evil' taking place without acting. He concludes that generally third parties take advantage of the situation and break the sanctions and this may lead to a change in trade partners and the creation of new alliances.

The UN Security Council has imposed sanctions more than 20 times since the end of the Cold War whereas the EU has levied sanctions more than 30 times, in addition to those mandated by the UN as per the Council on Foreign Relations, a New York think tank.[30] In a comprehensive study titled *Economic Sanctions Reconsidered,* four scholars reviewed 174 instances of sanctions commencing from World War I till 2000 and concluded that sanctions were only partially successful in 34 per cent of the cases. However, this success rate was found to be heavily influenced by the nature of policy change being sought. In modest cases, e.g., the release of political prisoners, the success rate was about 50 per cent whereas where the aim was regime change or efforts to prevent a military misadventure, the success rate was far lower. Notable examples where sanctions failed to bring about the desired changes include North Korea, India (for the 1998 nuclear tests), Cuba and Russia (for the 2014 accession of Crimea).

Let us take Cuba in slightly greater detail. When the Soviet Union collapsed in 1991 ending subsidies for the Castro regime, many believed that Cuban communism was doomed. In 1994, John Sweeney of the Heritage Foundation stated that '*embargo remains the only effective instrument available to the U.S. government in trying to force the economic and democratic concessions it has been demanding of Castro for over three decades. Maintaining the embargo will help end the Castro regime more quickly*'.[31] However, the communist regime espoused by Castro lives on till date. Similarly, the North Korean regime has clung to power despite being subject to severe economic sanctions due to Chinese support which possibly fears a united Korea on its border.

Successful sanction-based interventions which are touted are of South Africa, Iran and Iraq. South Africa was sanctioned to end its apartheid regime which discriminated the black majority at the hands of the white minority. While sanctions were imposed, what really played on the sentiments of the stakeholders, apart from a strong international consensus, was the cultural impact of the sanctions, rather than the economic ones. Sports is a major cultural event in South Africa, especially rugby. Hence, not being able to participate in rugby, cricket and similar world events was considered more impactful on the psyche of the people rather than the economic consequence. Myanmar relies primarily on its regional neighbours to maintain its identity, with the vast majority of its sporting and cultural exchanges occurring with other ASEAN countries and hence is not affected similarly.

Often, sanctions serve to strengthen the resolve of those very stakeholders who are being targeted, thereby defeating the very cause of the sanctions. David Cohen, who worked in the Treasury Department during the Obama Presidency, writes:

> *'By their nature, sanctions impose costs on innocent third parties, and the more complex the sanctions, the greater the cost and the more likely they are to result in unintended harm. U.S. sanctions on Venezuela and Iran are extraordinarily complex: primary sanctions prohibit parties within the United States from engaging in a range of business and financial activities with entities in both countries. Secondary sanctions, meanwhile, prevent American individuals, banks, and other businesses from transacting with foreign entities that do business with Iran. Such sanctions impose significant compliance costs and legal risks on both U.S. and foreign businesses'.*[32]

He goes on to opine that the logic of coercive sanctions does not hold, however, when the objective of sanctions is regime change. Put simply, because the cost of relinquishing power will always exceed the benefit of sanctions relief, a targeted state cannot conceivably accede to a demand for regime change. And this takes us on to analyse the effects that sanctions are likely to have on Myanmar.

Fundamentally, sanctions on Myanmar have not worked in the past and will not work even now for reasons unique to Myanmar. Rather, sanctions will actually be counter-productive to the democratic process in Myanmar. A study by Manmeet Ajmani, P.K. Joshi, Avinash Kishore, and Devesh Roy of the *International Food Policy Research Institute*[33] reveals that historically, sanctions by the USA have been enforced asymmetrically. Thus, while Myanmar's exports to the USA dropped to zero, the USA continued to export its products to Myanmar. Further, even though sanctions were broad-based, the study shows that at the aggregate level, the impact of sanctions on Myanmar's trade was insignificant. In pre-sanction 2001, Myanmar's total trade stood at US$ 6.28 billion, which increased to US$ 6.54 billion in 2003. The total trade of Myanmar increased without interruption even after the sanctions. In 2004, its overall trade rose to US$ 7.1 billion and further increased to US$ 8.57 billion in 2006. Myanmar diversified both its products and its trading partners to tide over the sanctions. It imported an estimated total US$ 24.2 billion worth of goods in 2018, a 48.9 per cent increase since 2014 and a 25.5 per cent gain from 2017 to 2018. Top suppliers accounting for 88.1 per cent of Myanmar's international purchases were: China (31.8

per cent), Singapore (15.2 per cent), Thailand (11.3 per cent), Japan (5.5 per cent), Malaysia (5.2 per cent), India (5.1 per cent), Indonesia (4.8 per cent), USA (3.6 per cent), Vietnam (3 per cent) and South Korea (2.7 per cent). Thus, what emerges is that 87.9 per cent of Myanmar's imports in 2017 were purchased from Asian countries. European countries supplied 5.1 per cent of imports by Myanmar while goods worth 4 per cent were purchased from North America.[34] Though the textile industry of Myanmar, one of its principal exports, took a hit from the sanctions, the ASEAN+6 became a significant shock absorber for this industry. This leads us on to the importance of regional geo-political and economic dynamics as a prism through which to view sanctions. The importance of sharing a substantial border with a P-5 nation (China), favourably disposed towards Myanmar, in negating sanctions, is an invaluable asset of geography.

Andrew Thomson,[35] an Australian researcher, has identified pertinent reasons for the inefficacy of sanctions. Firstly, there is a total lack of consensus within the country and even in the neighbourhood on the sanctions. While earlier sanctions for democracy may have been acceptable to the people of Myanmar, the sanctions for human rights violations against Rohingyas will not be welcomed. And herein lies the fact that in the Bamar majoritarian psyche, the Rohingyas are unwelcome and hated. Hence, sanctioning the Myanmar generals may actually help them to play the victim card and get far greater support than they would have had in the normal course of time. In regional terms, Myanmar shares five borders with Bangladesh, China, India, Laos and Thailand. China shares 2,194 km of Myanmar's borders and a large diaspora astride this area which comprises 36 per cent of Myanmar's total borders. The language spoken and the currency generally used in this area is Chinese. With such stakes, there is likely to be no support for or compliance with any UN or regional-level sanctions. Similarly India, Laos and Thailand have too much at stake to overtly or covertly back such sanctions. Unfortunately, Bangladesh, which has just a 269-km boundary with Myanmar, has had to bear the brunt of the Rohingya crisis and has effectively been left in the lurch.

Secondly, the Myanmar economy, notwithstanding the opening up of the country, is yet to be sufficiently globalised to feel the pinch of sanctions. Hence, this largely agrarian population will never fall below subsistence levels despite cash crunches. Thomson states that '*in cases where sanctions have been successful, the countries have mostly been those deeply integrated into the global economy, with their elites reliant on such integration to maintain their standard of living. Foreign investment and trade in these countries were crucial for their governments to maintain the wealth and prosperity of their main supporters.*' Thirdly, the Tatmadaw has no electoral compulsions since they are not elected but self-appointed. By contrast, say, in the South African example, the ruling elites were elected and hence accountable. Thus, their actions were to a large degree influenced by public opinion.

Fourthly, with elections round the corner in 2020, the NLD will not like to antagonise the Tatmadaw over the Rohingya issue given the national sentiment against the Rohingyas. Against this backdrop, sanctions will only serve to insulate the Tatmadaw against international opinion, despite their overall unpopularity. Fifthly, Thomson also brings out that whenever sanctions have succeeded, it was because they supplemented and reinforced an inherent internal desire for political change. In South Africa, the pressure of Western sanctions was a factor in the South African government's decision to negotiate with the African National Congress and other groups. Presently, there is no equivalent lobby in Myanmar that can exert the desired internal pressure on the military to change its Rohingya policy.[36]

Myanmar's self-imposed isolation has shaped its security ideology which influences the military's actions in Rakhine State. The primary objective of the military is to maintain national sovereignty and unity. Sanctions will simply turn the country back towards isolation, compromising the democratic processes underway. Michael F. Martin, author of a 2012 US Congressional Research Service Report titled *U.S. Sanctions on Burma,* states that it is unclear whether the imposition of sanctions has had any effect on the government and it is equally unclear whether the absence of U.S. sanctions on Myanmar would lead to an improvement in the political situation in Myanmar.[37]

India's Support to Myanmar

Five major facets need to guide India's engagement of Myanmar against the backdrop of international sanctions. *First,* if India aspires to be the regional leader, it has to be seen to be more proactive and engage Myanmar on the Rohingya issue. Since the Rohingya issue has effectively hyphenated the diplomatic relationship between Bangladesh and Myanmar, India's engagements with these nations could be bilateral with each, trilateral or even multilateral, as shown below.

Currently this role is being fulfilled by China which is engaging both Bangladesh and Myanmar diligently and has even taken the case to be discussed in the UN. This is despite China not having any land border with Bangladesh or any ethnic linkages with the Rohingyas, unlike other ethnic groups on the China-Myanmar border. The Chinese endeavour is unlikely to succeed, but the leverage it would have gained with both the countries would be at the expense of India which seems to have ceded diplomatic space to China. India should be seen to be more energetic in the approach to the problem. Over nine lakh Rohingyas in Bangladesh with whom we have a porous 4,000-plus km border is a security issue with the potential to create major law and order problems in addition to problems of Islamic fundamentalism. A constant trickle of illegal Rohingya migrants into the country[28] and the surprise discovery of an illegal Rohingya camp on the Gurram Cheruvu lake bed at Hyderabad are cases in point.[39]

A second option would be to address the problem through a regional approach. It could do so under the ASEAN+ or the BIMSTEC umbrellas. This has benefits of being more regionally democratic and therefore in line with India's portrayal as a soft power. K. Yhome, Senior Fellow with the Observer Research Foundation, a New Delhi-based think tank, opines[40] "*Both* (ASEAN and India) *believe that constructive engagement is more practical in finding a solution rather than megaphone diplomacy. The constructive approach of India and ASEAN is based on the belief that isolating Myanmar will not solve the problem. Nudging the Myanmar government through engagement has produced positive results in the past and it remains the most pragmatic option in dealing with the current crisis. Beyond their similar approaches, the stakes are high for both India and ASEAN...the reputation and global standing of India has come under inspection.*" The efficacy of ASEAN as a regional body is also under question. Both India and ASEAN are aware that they will be the first to face the consequences of any terror activities emanating from radicalisation among the Rohingyas.

Yhome proposes an alternative to the traditional regional groupings by recommending a dedicated regional grouping to address the issue. He identifies two ASEAN members (Singapore[41] and Indonesia) and two BIMSTEC members (Bangladesh and Thailand) as critical to this effort. Bangladesh, as a victim of the crisis, will need to be a party to finding solutions. Thailand shares a long land boundary with Myanmar and as a Buddhist majority nation, has taken the lead in finding a solution to the Rohingya migration crisis in the past. Indonesia too has been actively involved in extending assistance in Rakhine State, and as the largest Muslim nation in ASEAN, Indonesia's role is significant. Singapore was mentioned for its role as the Chair in 2018.

The ASEAN experience in handling this crisis has been dismal. Ilmi Dwaistuti of the Centre for Strategic and International Studies, Jakarta,[42] takes it further to say that Myanmar's violence against 'an ethnic minority' in Rakhine State might have been due to ASEAN's negligence of its role as a regional power. This negligence, she surmises, could have resulted in its member-states' poor response to the crisis. Only Indonesia and Malaysia, out of the ten-member alliance have actively attempted to resolve the issue probably since non-interference has been an important principle guiding relationships in these states and groupings. Ironically though, this is probably the reason why Yhome writes that '*it is one of the very few organisations that enjoys the confidence of Myanmar*'. Nattapat Limsiritong, a law student from Assumption University, concludes that *ASEAN is designed to protect the principle of non-interference more than the human rights protection and the decision-making mode of ASEAN under Article 20(1) of the ASEAN Charter cannot apply in the Rohingya situation in practice because there is a lock of law, making ASEAN to respect and rely on (the) principle of non-interference which plays the key role to keep ASEAN together*'.[43]

Secondly, India's engagement with Bangladesh has effectively got hyphenated with Myanmar. Bangladesh is rightly miffed with Indian inaction on the Rohingya issue. This needs deliberate engagement and India needs to dispel the notion that it favours Myanmar over Bangladesh. This needs diplomacy and tact. Today, Myanmar is as critical to the security calculus of India as Bangladesh. 'Operation Sunrise' coordinated operations with the Myanmar Army targeted Indian Insurgent Groups in Myanmar and were very successful in decimating groups like ULFA(I) by destroying their headquarters in Sagaing Division. This is a culmination of years of defence diplomacy. Whatever India does with Myanmar, it cannot be seen to be at the cost of Bangladesh...and vice versa.

Thirdly, India's support to Myanmar should be unequivocal and, despite sanctions, as and when they come. Certain Indian scholars[44] are of the view that India needs to shed '*moral ambiguity*' and use its geo-economic leverage with Myanmar to book the perpetrators of human rights violations against the Rohingyas. This perspective is premature and likely to be rejected by one and all given the ground realities on the Rohingyas. To its credit, India has by and large stood by its neighbour. Resolutions as and when they come up in the UN General Assembly and the UN HRC against Myanmar are generally diplomatically sidestepped by abstaining from voting.

In the latest case, India's Permanent Representative to the UN in Geneva, Rajiv Chander, announced that '*Supporting extensive recommendations regarding legislative and policy actions and threatening Myanmar with punitive action, including at the International Criminal Court, to which that State is not a signatory, will only be counter-productive*'. India's argument that an investigation by the ICC could backfire was not just made at the passage of the resolution, but also during an informal interaction with the special rapporteur on Myanmar earlier during the Council's 40th session.[45]

Fourth, India's soft power quotient needs to be metamorphosed into a soft **and efficient** power. India's diplomatic deliverables fall woefully short of the needs of Myanmar and thus lose relevance in contrast to the shock and awe caused by diplomatic and commercial manoeuvres of other players in the region. India remains the first port of call for most regional countries seeking aid, infrastructure development or economic assistance. However, invariably our delivery inefficiencies grudgingly drive them away to China and make them vulnerable to debt trap diplomacy. A case in point is the bureaucratic delays leading to delays in implementation of projects as in the case of the Kaladan Project which was conceived in the 1990s and is yet to be completed. These delays are symptomatic of most Indian diplomatic ventures. Identification of these hurdles and structural solutions are the need of the hour. Hence, a soft and efficient India will have more relevant clout with Myanmar and thus be able to better influence it to migrate towards a more globally acceptable nature of conduct in dealing with the ethnic crises and a significantly improved democratic process.

Finally, defence diplomacy remains, in the geo-political context in Myanmar, the most effective diplomatic tool for engaging the military and thus must be scaled up to reach out to the Tatmadaw and the Myanmar Government. As mentioned earlier, the conduct of coordinated operations along the India-Myanmar border since early 2019 signifies a high in India-Myanmar relations. This has now got to be taken forward. Unfortunately, the defence industry in India is not in a position to take the lead in defence diplomacy and hence the engagement is bound by the limits of training, cooperation and people-to-people contacts within the military. The rumours of Senior General Aung Ming Hlaing planning to run for the Presidency in the 2020 elections add significance to the need to engage.

India needs to proactively counter the damaging discourse emerging from the West using engagement at Track 1, Track 1.5 and Track 2 levels. It is sometimes suggested that the discourse be ignored in favour of quiet diplomacy. However, often such discourse snowballs into major media hype and the resultant momentum triggers unexpected consequences which can backfire on Indian interests in Myanmar. Thus, it happens that despite being regarded as the world's third best company,[46] India's Infosys now finds mention as a defaulter in a UN document.

The Tatmadaw finds itself painted into a corner by human rights violations. However, it controls the parliament. The NLD is keen to address the need for constitutional reform...the core prerequisite for democratic reform. Assistance, if any, should only come from the ASEAN+ or the BIMSTEC nations which have cultural affinity and sensitivities.

Finally, away from analysts, international experts, NGOs, scholars and peace pundits, the people of Myanmar will have to find and work out their own peace processes. The solutions lie within the community and the neighbourhood. Western templates, perspectives and systems have been tried and have had limited enduring success. The long and arduous path to peace and democracy will need ideas which come from within.

For the long-term benefit of Myanmar and its people, including the ethnic minorities, the need of the hour is to support and not sanction Myanmar.

NOTES

1. Jaideep Chanda, '*Counterproductive Effects of Sanctions - The Myanmar Case Study*', VIF Paper, 28 October 2019, https://www.vifindia.org/paper/2019/october/28/counterproductive-effects-of-sanctions-the-myanmar-case-study (Accessed on 9 May 2021).
2. As quoted by Aung Zaw, founding Editor-in-Chief of *The Irrawady* in the web article "US Visa Ban Unlikely to See Military Change Course", 23 July 2019: https://www.irrawaddy.com/opinion/commentary/us-visa-ban-unlikely-see-military-change-course.html (Accessed on 15 August 2019). Thant Myint U is a Burmese historian, writer, a past fellow of Trinity College, Cambridge; a former Adviser to the President of Myanmar, and the founder and chairman of the Yangon Heritage Trust. He is the author of four books, including the bestselling and critically acclaimed *The River of Lost Footsteps: A Personal History of Burma* and *Where China Meets India: Burma and the New Crossroads of Asia.* He is the grandson of U Thant, the third Secretary-General of the United Nations who served from 1961 to 1971.
3. The term 'sanction' has a broader connotation while a 'ban' is one of the methods of imposing sanctions. For a better understanding of the terms, the Council of the European Union website may be referred to https://www.consilium.europa.eu/en/policies/sanctions/different-types/. Gary Clyde Hufbauer and Barbara Oegg of the Peterson Institute for International Economics (PIIE), in their February 2000 article titled *Targeted Sanctions: A Policy Alternative?* https://www.piie.com/commentary/speeches-papers/targeted-sanctions-policy-alternative has brought out nuances of types of bans.
4. *Asia Times* news report, https://www.asiatimes.com/2019/07/article/us-bans-myanmar-army-chief-over-rohingya-rights-abuses/ (Accessed on 31 July 2019).
   News report on the *Middle East Monitor* website, https://www.middleeastmonitor.com/20190717-israel-bans-myanmar-officials-from-arms-fairs/, (Accessed on 31 July 2019).
5. Jayita Sarkar, "Rohingyas and the Unfinished Business of Partition", *The Diplomat,* 16 January 2018, https://thediplomat.com/2018/01/rohingyas-and-the-unfinished-business-of-partition/ (Accessed on 11 September 2019)
6. The Australian, 'Britain's Role in Rohingya Tragedy', https://www.theaustralian.com.au/world/the-times/britains-role-in-the-rohingya-tragedy/news-story/d84285fbc330b4615997b3e4e62d9933 (Accessed on 16 September 2019).
7. Tathagata Dutta, "The Rohingya Crisis Is Another Colonial Legacy", *The Wire,* 16 September 2019: https://thewire.in/south-asia/rohingya-crisis-colonoialsm-second-world-war (Accessed on 16 September 2019).
8. Jayita Sarkar writes: '*By late 1944, the pro-Japanese Burmese military units had grown disillusioned with the Japanese and Tokyo's promise of Burmese independence. Aung San, the military leader of the Burma National Army and father of Aung San Suu Kyi, decided to switch loyalty to the British, leading to the 1945 Kandy Conference at the Allied headquarters of the South East Asia Command*

in present-day Sri Lanka.' https://thediplomat.com/2018/01/rohingyas-and-the-unfinished-business-of-partition/. (Accessed on 11 September 2019)

9. The Stateless, 'The Muslim massacre of Arakan in 1942, https://www.thestateless.com/2016/09/the-muslim-massacre-of-arakan-in-1942.html (Accessed on 11 September 2019).
10. The Faith Movement.
11. For a complete picture of the involvement of the ARSA with Islamic terrorist organisations, a study of the Background Paper on Rakhine State by the Myanmar Institute of Strategic and International Studies, May 2018, is highly recommended.
12. International Crisis Group Statement, "Myanmar Tips into New Crisis after Rakhine State Attacks", 27 August 2017: https://d2071andvip0wj.cloudfront.net/Myanmar%20statement%2027viii17.pdf (Accessed on 10 September 2019).
13. Amnesty International, "Myanmar: New evidence reveals Rohingya armed group massacred scores in Rakhine State", 22 May 2018, https://www.amnesty.org/en/latest/news/2018/05/myanmar-new-evidence-reveals-rohingya-armed-group-massacred-scores-in-rakhine-state/ (Accessed on 1 September 2019).
14. Human Rights Council, "Report of the detailed findings of the Independent International Fact-Finding Mission on Myanmar", *United Nations,* September 2018, pg. 177, https://www.ohchr.org/Documents/HRBodies/HRCouncil/FFM-Myanmar/A_HRC_39_CRP.2.pdf (Accessed on 19 September 2019).
15. The Human Rights Council comprises 47elected Member-States. Council seats are allocated to the five regional groups as follows: African States, 13 seats; Asia-Pacific States, 13 seats; Eastern European States, 6 seats; Latin American and Caribbean States, 8 seats; and Western European and other States, 7 seats. All elected members serve three-year terms. India was elected on 1 January 2019. Resolution 39/2 was adopted by a record vote of 35 to 3, with 7 abstentions. Expectedly, the three who voted against the resolution included China, apart from Burundi and the Philippines. Angola, Ethiopia, Japan, Kenya, Mongolia, Nepal, South Africa abstained from voting. India was not a member of the Human Rights Council at that time.
16. UN News, "UN chief accepts independent report on Myanmar, highlighting 'systemic' failure surrounding Rohingya crisis", 17 June 2019: https://news.un.org/en/story/2019/06/1040681 (Accessed on 30 August 2019).
17. Radio Free Asia, "Myanmar Signals It Will Give Cold Shoulder to New UN Rights Investigator on Rohingya", 3 April 2019: https://www.rfa.org/english/news/myanmar/myanmar-signals-it-will-give-cold-shoulder-04032019172944.html (Accessed on 20 August 2019).
18. Human Rights Council, "Report of the Independent Investigative Mechanism for Myanmar", *United Nations,* 7 August 2019, Para 57: https://reliefweb.int/sites/reliefweb.int/files/resources/G1923511.pdf (Accessed on 20 August 2019).
19. The Security Council took two weeks to convene a formal meeting to address the matter, and an additional 38 days to issue a perfunctory Presidential Statement.
20. Human Rights Council, "The economic interests of the Myanmar military" *United Nations,* 5 August 2019, pg. 3: https://www.ohchr.org/Documents/HRBodies/HRCouncil/FFM-Myanmar/EconomicInterestsMyanmarMilitary /A_HRC_42_CRP 3.pdf (Accessed on 20 August 2019).
21. While all the reports filed by the IIFFMM have recommendations, a consolidated report compiling all the recommendations has been published. See "Compilation of all recommendations made by the Independent International Fact-Finding Mission on Myanmar to the Government of Myanmar, armed organisations, the UN Security Council, Member-States, UN agencies, the business community and others", *UN HRC Conference Room Paper No 6,* 16 Sep 2019, https://www.ohchr.org/Documents/HRBodies/HRCouncil/FFM-

Myanmar/20190916/ A_HRC_42_CRP.6.pdf (Accessed on 1 October 2019). All recommendations being alluded to are from the compiled recommendations.

22. *Frontier Myanmar* Report, "Myanmar says military 'dignity' harmed by US ban on army chief", 17 July 2019: https://frontiermyanmar.net/en/myanmar-says-military-dignity-harmed-by-us-ban-on-army-chief (Accessed on 4 August 2019).
23. News Report by *Business Standard,* "US ban on Myanmar army chief not enough, says UN," 18 July 2019: https://www.business-standard.com/article/pti-stories/us-ban-on-myanmar-army-chief-not-enough-says-un-119071801021_1.html (Accessed on 4 August 2019).
24. Stockholm International Peace Research Institute, "EU arms embargo on Myanmar (Burma)", 19 May 2019: https://www.sipri.org/databases/embargoes/eu_arms_embargoes/myanmar (Accessed on 5 August 2019).
25. News report on the *Middle East Monitor* website, "Amnesty: Israel arms human rights violators UAE, Myanmar", 17 May 2019: https://www.middleeastmonitor.com/20190517-amnesty-israel-arms-human-rights-violators-uae-myanmar/ (Accessed on 14 August 2019).
26. Jaideep Chanda, "From Sanctions to Submarines: Myanmar July 2019", Commentary, Vivekananda International Foundation, July 2019: https://www.vifindia.org/article/2019/august/12/from-sanctions-to-submarines-myanmar-july-2019 (Accessed on 15 August 2019).
27. *Asia Times* news report, https://www.asiatimes.com/2019/07/article/us-bans-myanmar-army-chief-over-rohingya-rights-abuses/ (Accessed on 31 July. 2019).
28. *The Economist,* Economist Intelligence Unit, Country Brief, Myanmar: http://country.eiu.com/article.aspxarticleid=347706018&Country=Myanmar&topic=Economy&oid= 1417571925 &flid= 4 28062626 (Accessed on 15 August 2019).
29. Maarten Smeets, "Can Economic Sanctions Be Effective?" *World Trade Organization, Staff Working Paper ERSD-2018-03,* 15 March 2019: https://www.wto.org/english/res_e/reser_e/ersd201803_e.pdf (Accessed on 15 August 2019).
30. *The Week,* 24 June 2019, "Do economic sanctions actually work?":https://www.theweek.co.uk/88349/ fact-check-do-economic-sanctions-actually-work (Accessed on 30 September 2019).
31. Doug Bandow, "End U.S. Embargo After Fidel Castro's Death: Continued Sanctions Won't Free Cuba", *Forbes, Opinion,* 30 November 2016:https://www.forbes.com/sites/dougbandow/2016/11/30/end-u-s-embargo-after-fidel-castros-death-continued-sanctions-wont-free-cuba/#f664eb232fe9 (Accessed on 30 September 2019).
32. David S. Cohen and Zoe A. Y. Weinberg, "Sanctions Can't Spark Regime Change", 29 April 2019, https://www.foreignaffairs.com/articles/united-states/2019-04-29/sanctions-cant-spark-regime-change (Accessed on 30 September 2019).
33. Manmeet Ajmani, P. K. Joshi, Avinash Kishore and Devesh Roy, "How Did Sanctions Impact Myanmar?" *Asean Beat,* 6 January 2018: https://thediplomat.com/2018/01/how-did-sanctions-impact-myanmar/ (Accessed on 30 September 2019).
34. Daniel Workman, "Myanmar's Top 10 Imports", *World's Top Exports,* 27 April 2019: http://www.worldstopexports.com/myanmars-top-10-imports/ (Accessed on 30 September 2019).
35. Andrew Thomson, "Why Economic Sanctions won't help the Rohingya", *Tea Circle Oxford,* 26 June 2018: https://teacircleoxford.com/2018/06/26/why-economic-sanctions-wont-help-the-Rohingya/ (Accessed on 30 September 2019).
36. Ibid.
37. Michael F. Martin, "U. S. Sanctions on Burma", *Congressional Research Service Report for Congress,* 12 October 2012:https://fas.org/sgp/crs/row/R41336.pdf (Accessed on 1 October 2019).
38. For an understanding of the extent of the Rohingya spread in India, please see Yermi Brenner's, "Rohingya migration to India: patterns, drivers and experiences", *Mixed Migration Centre, Briefing Paper,* April 2019, Geneva: http://www.mixedmigration.org/wp-content/uploads/2019/04/063_briefing-paper_Rohingya_India.pdf **and** "Rohingyas in India, Birth of Stateless

Community", *Calcutta Research Group, Policies and Practices,* September 2015: http://www.mcrg.ac.in/PP71.pdf (Both accessed on 25 August 2019).

39. U. Sudhakar Reddy, "Rohingya camp on Hyderabad lake bed, PMO seeks probe", *Times of India, Hyderabad,* 26 September 2019: https://timesofindia.indiatimes.com/city/hyderabad/rohingya-camp-on-lake-bed-pmo-seeks-probe/articleshow/71301742.cms (Accessed on 30 September 2019).
40. K. Yhome, "Examining India's Stance on Rohingya Crisis", *Observer Research Foundation,* Issue Brief No. 247, July 2018: https://www.orfonline.org/wp-content/uploads/2018/07/ORF_IssueBrief_247_Rohingya_FinalFor Upload.pdf (Accessed 25 August 2019).
41. Singapore, since at the time of writing the paper in 2018, it was the Chair of the ASEAN. Currently, Thailand is the Chair for 2019. The chairmanship of ASEAN is by annual rotation based on alphabetical order of the English names of Member-States. Next year (2020) Brunei will assume the chairmanship.
42. Ilmi Dwaistuti, "Why Does the Rohingya Issue Matter to ASEAN?," *Centre for Strategic and International Studies,* Jakarta, October 2017.
43. Nattapat Limsiritong, "Why ASEAN Fails to Play Role in the Rohingya Situation from the Perspective of ASEAN Charter", *Asian Political Science Review,* Vol. 1, No. 2, 2017: https://papers.ssrn.com/sol3/papers.cfm?abstract_id=3180718&download=yes (Accessed on 1 October 2019).
44. Angshuman Choudhury, "Moral ambiguity on the Rohingya", *The Hindu,* 21 May 2019: https://www.thehindu.com/opinion/op-ed/moral-ambiguity-on-the-rohingya/article27189539.ece (Accessed on 30 September 2019).
45. Devirupa Mitra, "Explained: India's Opposition to ICC Probe on Myanmar's Rohingya Crisis", https://thewire.in/diplomacy/myanmar-rohingya-icc-bangladesh-india (Accessed on 30 September 2019).
46. Andrea Murphy, The World's Best Regarded Companies, Forbes Billionaires, 18 September 2019, https://www.forbes.com/lists/best-regarded-companies/#49da1e62124d (Accessed on 11 October 2019).

CHAPTER 11

The Lady and The Law: Daw Aung San Suu Kyi and the International Court of Justice Imbroglio

We are with her, win or lose.

—Prof. Daw Kyi Kyi Hla[1]

In the previous chapter, we saw the build-up to the current Rohingya crisis, i.e., the historical context, the ARSA attacks, the disproportionate and indiscriminate response by the Tatmadaw leading to the Rohingya exodus to Bangladesh and the reactions by the international community, primarily Israel, the USA and the UN. However, this Rohingya crisis also hit the headlines when, in a unique, unprecedented and well-organised move, The Gambia, a small West African nation, ostensibly motivated by the Organisation of Islamic Cooperation[2] (OIC), filed a case against Myanmar for genocide in the International Court of Justice (ICJ). The scale of the action was evident when it was found that three cases had been processed in a span of four days in three different courts, all of which had international jurisdiction, viz., the ICJ, the Federal Court of Argentina and the International Criminal Court (ICC).[3] What was equally unique and unprecedented from the Myanmar side was the direct involvement of the State Counsellor, Daw Aung San Suu Kyi, a Nobel Laureate, in defending her nation and its Tatmadaw against the charges of genocide. In this chapter, I analyse the organised diplomatic and judicial offensive against Myanmar wherein the three international court suits were filed against it, and their implications and probable outcomes. I also try and put forth the reasons for Daw Suu's unusual action to personally defend the Tatmadaw in such a high-profile and polarised battle, even in the face of intense Western criticism.

It was coincidental that a delegation from the VIF visited Myanmar from 9 to 12 December 2019, and was able to experience, at least in Yangon, the vibes of support for the State Counsellor who at that time was at The Hague to fight the ICJ case being the Foreign Minister of her nation. The capital was awash with hoardings and banners idolising 'The Lady' and her battle and even though one understood that a lot of the display was stage managed, this effort by her was seen as defending the honour and prestige of Myanmar, appealed directly to the Bamar psyche. Her spirited visit to The Hague, to defend her nation, its armed forces and its conduct leading to the Rohingya crisis, made history in Myanmar and in the world, but for different reasons.

Figure 11.1

However, during the unofficial dinner interactions with members of a think tank, at least one of them, was candid to disclose that there is a feeling that the ICJ case is a welcome fallout of the actions of the Tatmadaw and that they '*deserved it*'. Beneath the nationalism, there is an underlying hatred for the Tatmadaw amongst civil society which is gleeful of the situation the Tatmadaw has got itself into. The Senior General is apparently feeling the heat since he has become globally identified as the person actually carrying out the '*genocide*', unlike Daw Suu, who is being vilified for her silence. With sanctions on him and his family, it has apparently become a personal issue and hence embarrassing, even though the sanctions may not mean anything substantial, at least in Myanmar. He now needs the support of the Myanmar Government to ensure he is untouched, which now gives an opportunity to the Government to bargain for democratic reforms in return for his safety.

Triple Whammy: The Legal Ambush

In an obviously coordinated strategy to put pressure on Myanmar over the Rohingyas, three cases were processed against Myanmar in four days. The first was on 11 November 2019 when The Gambia filed a case against the Republic of the Union of Myanmar in the ICJ urging the United Nations court to order Myanmar to take measures to stop atrocities and genocide against its own Rohingya people. The Gambia has accused Myanmar of violating the Convention on the Prevention and Punishment of the Crime of Genocide, 1948.[4] This was the case that has gained global attention and the one that the State Counsellor, Daw Aung San Suu Kyi, personally defended. The major part of this chapter pertains to this case.

The second was on 13 November 2019 when a UK-based NGO, the Burmese Rohingya Organisation of UK (BROUK) filed a case against select individuals in Myanmar including President U Win Myint, State Counsellor Suu Kyi, Tatmadaw Chief Senior General Min Aung Hlaing, and former presidents Thein Sein and Htin Kyaw, in the Federal Court in Buenos Aires, Argentina, for incidents in Rakhine from 2012 to 2018. Argentina has the jurisdiction to try the case on the basis of the legal principle of Universal Jurisdiction as enshrined in Article 118 of the Argentine Constitution and Law 26200.[5]

Finally, on 14 November 2019, based on a request filed on 4 July 2019 by ICC's Chief Prosecutor Fatou Bensouda, a Gambian lawyer and international criminal law prosecutor, the the third case was authorised for investigation by a Pre-Trial Chamber for the alleged crimes within the ICC's jurisdiction over the *Situation in the People's Republic of Bangladesh/Republic of the Union of Myanmar.*[6]

Since the latter two cases are not being fought by Myanmar on the ground that those laws do not apply and Myanmar is not a signatory to the Roman Statute, these cases will be analysed first to draw a better understanding of the overall situation before moving on to the main ICJ Case. This ICJ case is being seen as a heroic fight to retain the national honour of Myanmar.

The Case in the Federal Court, Buenos Aires, Argentina

As mentioned above, this case has been filed[7] by an organisation called BROUK. A basic web search of this entity reveals a London address, two twitter handles, a defunct web address and the name of Maung Tun Khin alias Ziaul Ghaffar as the founder.[8] The case has been filed against Aung San Suu Kyi; former president Thein Sein; former president Htin Kyaw; current president Win Myint, and top military brass deemed responsible for the atrocities, including Senior General Min Aung Hlaing, C-in-C of Myanmar's armed forces. It seeks criminal sanction of the perpetrators, accomplices and cover-ups of the alleged genocide in Myanmar.[9]

The Online Burma/Myanmar Library informs us that the BROUK was founded on 2 January 2005 with seven executive committee members and is a member of Burma stake holder listed by the Foreign and Commonwealth Office UK and European Burma Network (EBN). It advocates within the UK and Europe spreading the message of the plight of the Rohingya people and human right violations in Burma. It works with Rohingya organisations around the world, Burma Campaign UK, Christian Solidarity Worldwide, Burmese Democratic groups, Burmese ethnic groups in the UK, Euro Burma Office in Brussels and other NGOs.[10] *Al Jazeera* profiles Tun Khin as born and brought up in Buthidaung, Rakhine State, Myanmar. His grandfather, during the pre-1962 democratic phase of Burma served as a Parliamentary Secretary. Tun Khin was rendered stateless by the 1982 Citizenship Act making him ineligible for Burmese nationality. *Al Jazeera* describes him as the President of the BROUK that has briefed officials on the human rights violations committed against Rohingyas at the US Congress and State Department, the British Parliament and various other international and national organisations and media. He has published articles in British independent newspapers, *Democratic Voice* of Burma, *Mizzima*, and *Huffington Post*. He has been awarded by Refugees International, Washington DC, in April 2015 for his work.[11]

For an entity and an individual which has filed a case of this magnitude, surprisingly little information is available on him on the Internet. However, the surprise emergence of a recent (June 2020) YouTube video by Rick Heizman, a San Francisco-based American ethnomusicologist[12] and Myanmar enthusiast, puts the BROUK and Tun Khin in a negative perspective. It needs to be placed on record that Rick Heizman's online presence seems to suggest that he is labelled '*anti-Rohingya*' and '*anti-Muslim*'.[13] The 15-minute video[14] is allegedly a summary of the contents of a computer, hard drives and mobile phones seized[15] from captured ARSA leader Rashed Ullah, No. 2 Commander in the ARSA and the elder brother of Atta Ullah, Commander in Chief of the ARSA. The video claims that Tun Khin is in fact a front man for the ARSA and other mujahidin groups in the UK and shows photographs of him with a Thai Muslim MP, Smarak, apparently known to support mujahidin groups; with Mathew Smith, CEO and founder of a human rights NGO; Muhammad Anwar, allegedly a lead mujahidin front man; Habibullah, a Pakistani founder of the Rohingya Mujahidin and Sheikh Abu Anas, a Saudi founder of the Rohingya Mujahidin. This seems to suggest that notwithstanding the genuine atrocities against the Rohingya, for which he seems to have done a lot, he has now crossed the line by supporting terrorist organisations like the ARSA.

Figure 11.2

Source: Screen grab from Rick Heizman's YouTube Video

The case *per se* holds legal validity since Argentina ratified the Rome Statute of the ICC in November 2000 and the implementing legislation was adopted by Law 26200 on 13 December 2006. This law adopts into domestic legislation the crimes that fall under the jurisdiction of the ICC through the application of *renvoi*[16] to the provisions of the Rome Statute.[17] The law allows for criminal sanctions including imprisonment but excludes reparation or rehabilitation of victims. It does include provisions on cooperation with the ICC regarding arrests, surrender, and judicial assistance in general. Cases based on these principles have been filed on other charges against Spain but have not fructified due to rejection by the Spanish authorities.[18] Initially the case had been rejected by the Federal Court itself on 9 December 2019.[19] However, on 29 May 2020, the Federal

Appeals Court in Buenos Aires had overruled the earlier judgement and ruled that it was necessary to approach the ICC for more information about its case against Myanmar through a formal diplomatic note, before making a final decision on whether to open an investigation in Argentina to avoid duplication of effort.[20]

Myanmar has maintained a studious silence on the matter and the overall prognosis is that this case is unlikely to see much progress. However, for the purpose of raising awareness towards the Rohingya cause and pressurising the Myanmar Government, it has met the needs. On a very optimistic note for the Rohingya lobby, some legal scholars see that the universal jurisdiction of the Argentine case complements the limited scope of the ICC's jurisdiction by focusing on crimes and incidents committed entirely on Myanmar territory, including genocide.[21]

The ICC Case

Since this case has been filed by Ms Fatau Bensouda, a Gambian lawyer, international criminal law prosecutor and ICC's Chief Prosecutor since 2012, it behoves that we are familiarised with her and her motives. The ICC website informs readers that on 12 December 2011, Ms Fatou Bensouda of The Gambia was elected[22] by consensus as the Prosecutor of the ICC by the Assembly of States Parties. Ms Fatou was sworn in on 15 June 2012 for her nine-year term which will end on 15 June 2021. She was earlier elected ICC Deputy Prosecutor (Prosecutions) by the Assembly of States Parties on 8 August 2004 and served till May 2012. She has also worked as Legal Adviser and Trial Attorney at the International Criminal Tribunal for Rwanda (ICTR) in Arusha, Tanzania, were she was promoted to Senior Legal Advisor and Head of the Legal Advisory Unit. Earlier, she had been the general manager of a bank in The Gambia. From 1987 till 2000, she was consecutively the Senior State Counsel, Principal State Counsel, Deputy Director of Public Prosecutions, Solicitor General and Legal Secretary of the Republic, and Attorney General and Minister of Justice. It was in this capacity that she served as the Chief Legal Advisor to the President and Cabinet of The Republic of The Gambia. She holds a Master's degree in International Maritime Law and Law of The Sea and is the first international maritime law expert of The Gambia.[23]

As ICC's Chief Prosecutor, Ms Bensouda heads the Office of the Prosecutor (OTP) which is an independent unit of the Court. It examines genocide; crimes against humanity, war crimes and aggression and investigates and prosecutes individuals who are responsible for such crimes. It is mandated to independently and impartially select areas for investigation where these crimes have been committed on their territories or by their nationals. Under Article 13 of the Rome Statute by which the ICC came into existence, one of the three ways the exercise of the Court's jurisdiction[24] can be initiated includes that the Prosecutor may open an investigation on her own initiative after the authorisation of the judges, as was the case for Kenya, Côte d'Ivoire, Georgia and Bangladesh/Myanmar. On the issue of jurisdiction over states that are non-signatories, the ICC states that '*the Prosecutor cannot, on her own motion, initiate investigations with respect to States not Party to the Rome Statute unless the matter involves nationals of States Parties allegedly involved in committing Rome Statute crimes on the territory of the non-State Party in question.*'[25]

Based on the above, on 14 November 2019, Pre-Trial Chamber III of the ICC authorised[26] the Prosecutor to investigate the situation in Bangladesh and Myanmar in keeping with the principle that the ICC has jurisdiction over crimes where a portion of the crime takes place on the territory of a State Party. In the Rohingya crisis, though Myanmar is not a State Party, Bangladesh is and this gives the ICC territorial jurisdiction. Myanmar, being a non-signatory, has not commented on these developments. The ICC document highlights that State Parties to the Rome Statute have a legal obligation to cooperate with the ICC. *Other non-party States, such as Myanmar, may be invited to cooperate with the ICC and may decide to do so on a voluntary basis.*[27]

Between August and November 2019, the Victims Participation and Reparations Section (VPRS) of the ICC Registry conveyed reports and representations of the victims to the Chamber, based on which it had authorised the commencement of the investigations. In continuation, the ICC, vide its Order dated 20 January 2020, also directed the Registry to ensure that two-way communication between the ICC and the victims continue. It advised the Registry to establish, in consultation and collaboration with the Prosecutor, a system of public information and outreach activities with the affected communities and particularly with the victims of the Bangladesh/Myanmar situation.[28] In April 2020, the process for establishment of a field office in Bangladesh was broached with the Registry and on 4 August 2020, it was formally filed for submission to initiate the process of assessing the feasibility of the Court sitting in a State other than The Netherlands to hear a case in whole or in part. This would enable closing the gap between Cox's Bazar and The Hague for the benefits of localised justice and the logistical considerations associated with hearings outside The Hague.[29]

The details of the victims listed in the case were also highlighted in this document and are summarised as below:

Sl.No.	*Nomenclature*	*Victims*	*Lawyer*
1	**Tula Toli Victims**	10	Megan Hirst
2	**Northern Rakhine Victims** (Comprises some of the members of eight civil society associations in Cox's Bazar: the Arakan Rohingya Society for Peace and Human Rights (ARSPH), Rohingya Women Empowerment and Advocacy Network (RWEAN), Rohingya Refugee Committee (RRC), Rohingya Women for Justice and Peace (RWJP), Voice of Rohingya (VOR), Rohingya Youth for Legal Action (RYLA), Bangladesh Rohingya Student Union (BRSU) and Rohingya Peace Innovation Unity (RPIU).	68	Kate Gibson
3	**SGBV[30] Victims** (The 14 individuals are a representative sample of a larger group of 151 individuals and two civil society groups, Shanti Mohila ('Peace Women'), a network of more than 400 women and girls located in the Rohingya refugee camps in Cox's Bazar and a group of male Rohingya 'survivor advocates,' also located in the camps.	14	Peter Haynes, Queen's Counsel (QC)

This is where the ICC case presently stands and the Chamber has advised the Registry to file six-monthly reports commencing 6 July 2020, giving details of the progress in the case. However, a question remains unanswered. Is it a coincidence that the ICJ case is being driven by The Gambia and the ICC case by the Chief Prosecutor, is also a Gambian national, or is there more to it especially considering the fact that both the cases were processed a few days apart? The former is alleged to have been motivated by the OIC. Various theories abound on this aspect in various informal discussion platforms. One suggests that the ICC case too has been motivated by the same lobby which pushed for the ICJ case. Another suggests that jumping onto the Rohingya bandwagon is a politically astute move for someone politically inclined. Others simply point out that her intrinsic concern and an illustrious legal career compelled her to try and make a difference to the Rohingyas. But the question which is often asked is why this selective singling out of Myanmar, when the Chinese Uighyur Muslims have faced systematic, organised genocide as a state policy? The jury is out on this.

The ICJ Case

The ICJ Press Release No. 2019/47 of 11 November 2019 revealed[31] to the world that The Republic of The Gambia had instituted proceedings against the Republic of the Union of Myanmar before the ICJ alleging violations of the Convention on the Prevention and Punishment of the Crime of Genocide through '*acts adopted, taken and condoned by the Government of Myanmar against members of the Rohingya group*'. This was the first time that Myanmar authorities were formally being accused of the crime of genocide. The Gambia had elaborated that from October 2016 onwards, the Tatmadaw and other Myanmar security forces began widespread and systematic 'clearance operations' against the Rohingya group. Allegedly, during these operations, and genocidal acts were committed to eliminate the Rohingyas as a group using mass murder, rape and other forms of sexual violence, including the systematic setting fire to their villages, often, apparently with inhabitants locked inside burning houses.

The Gambian Application

The violations mentioned above pertained to the Genocide Convention for which The Gambia requested the Court to declare that Myanmar has breached and continues to breach its obligations under the Genocide Convention and must cease any such ongoing act. It goes on to state that Myanmar must fully respect its obligations under the Genocide Convention and ensure that perpetrators of genocide are punished and that they must carry out reparations and guarantee non-recurrence of violations of the Genocide Convention. The case had been filed for The Gambia by Mr. Abubacarr Marie Tambadou, Attorney General and Minister of Justice of the Republic of The Gambia.[32]

The Gambia had also requested for the '*indication of provisional measures, seeking to protect the rights of the Rohingya group and those of The Gambia under the Genocide Convention and to prevent the aggravation or extension of the dispute pending the final judgment of the Court*'. The Gambia thus asked the Court to indicate provisional measures to Myanmar to prevent *extrajudicial killings or physical abuse; rape or other forms of sexual violence; burning of homes or villages; destruction of lands and livestock, deprivation of food and other necessities of life, or any other deliberate infliction of conditions of life calculated to bring about the physical destruction of the Rohingya group in whole or in part*; by its military, paramilitary or irregular armed units including any other organisation or persons under its control. Finally, it wanted the Court to indicate to Myanmar not to destroy or render inaccessible any evidence related to the events described in the application.

Why The Gambia?

The Republic of The Gambia is the smallest country in Africa, i.e., excluding the island countries like Seychelles. It is entirely surrounded by Senegal, barring the short coastline. The country is sub-tropical and comprises a narrow strip of land astride the Gambia River and is just 48 km at its widest. The Gambia River is completely navigable and hence the country's chief transport route. The Gambia gained its independence in 1965 after 200 years of British rule. In 1994, a military coup overthrew the president and banned political activity, but a 1996 constitution and presidential elections, followed by parliamentary elections in 1997, completed a return to civilian rule. Yahya A. J. J. Jammeh, the leader of the coup, has been elected president in all subsequent elections since 2002. Presidential elections held on 1 December 2016 saw opposition candidate Adama Barrow defeat long-term incumbent Yahya Jammeh.[33]

Contextually, the distance from the eastern edge of The Gambia to the western edge of Myanmar is approximately 11,140 km. So why did a country over 11,000 km away from Myanmar, and having a history of dictatorial rule, suddenly wake up on hearing the clarion call for the Rohingyas? In fact, this was the issue raised by the Myanmar counsel, Mr. Christopher Staker, who opined that The Gambia was actually a proxy or organ of an international organisation, the OIC, rather than a State party to the Genocide Convention. He stated that The Gambia had been tasked by the OIC, in its capacity as an OIC Member-State and chair of an OIC organ, its ad hoc committee, post the May 2018 OIC resolution establishing an ad hoc Ministerial Committee on Accountability for human rights violations against the Rohingya, to be chaired by The Gambia.[34] The proceedings are financed by a fund supervised by the OIC, i.e., funded by voluntary donations from OIC Member-States and requested from the Islamic Development Bank and the Islamic Solidarity Fund. Fund management is entrusted to the Chair of the ad hoc Ministerial Committee and the OIC Secretary General. Thus, while it is evident that The Gambia is backed by the OIC, the choice of The Gambia as a nation to lead this effort remains unclear. Unless those making the decision were confused between the ICC and the ICJ, and were of the opinion that the presence of The Gambian Chief Prosecutor at the ICC would prove beneficial for the case. Incidentally, the Myanmar counsel does point out that the 31 May Final Communiqué of the 14th Islamic Summit Conference is referred to in an undated item on the website of the Office of the President of The Gambia, '...*except that the second paragraph of this page mistakenly refers to the International Criminal Court rather than the International Court of Justice. The Office of the President of The Gambia was possibly not clear on the details of this proposed court case.*'[35]

The Schedule of Oral Hearings for Indication of Provisional Measures Only Based on the application, the ICJ issued instructions[36] on 18 November 2019 stating that public hearings devoted to the request for indication of provisional measures only would be heard from 10 to 12 December 2019, at the Peace Palace, The Hague. Under Article 74 of the Rules of Court, a request for the indication of provisional measures has priority over all other cases and hence was scheduled on

Figure 11.3: Relative Location of The Gambia

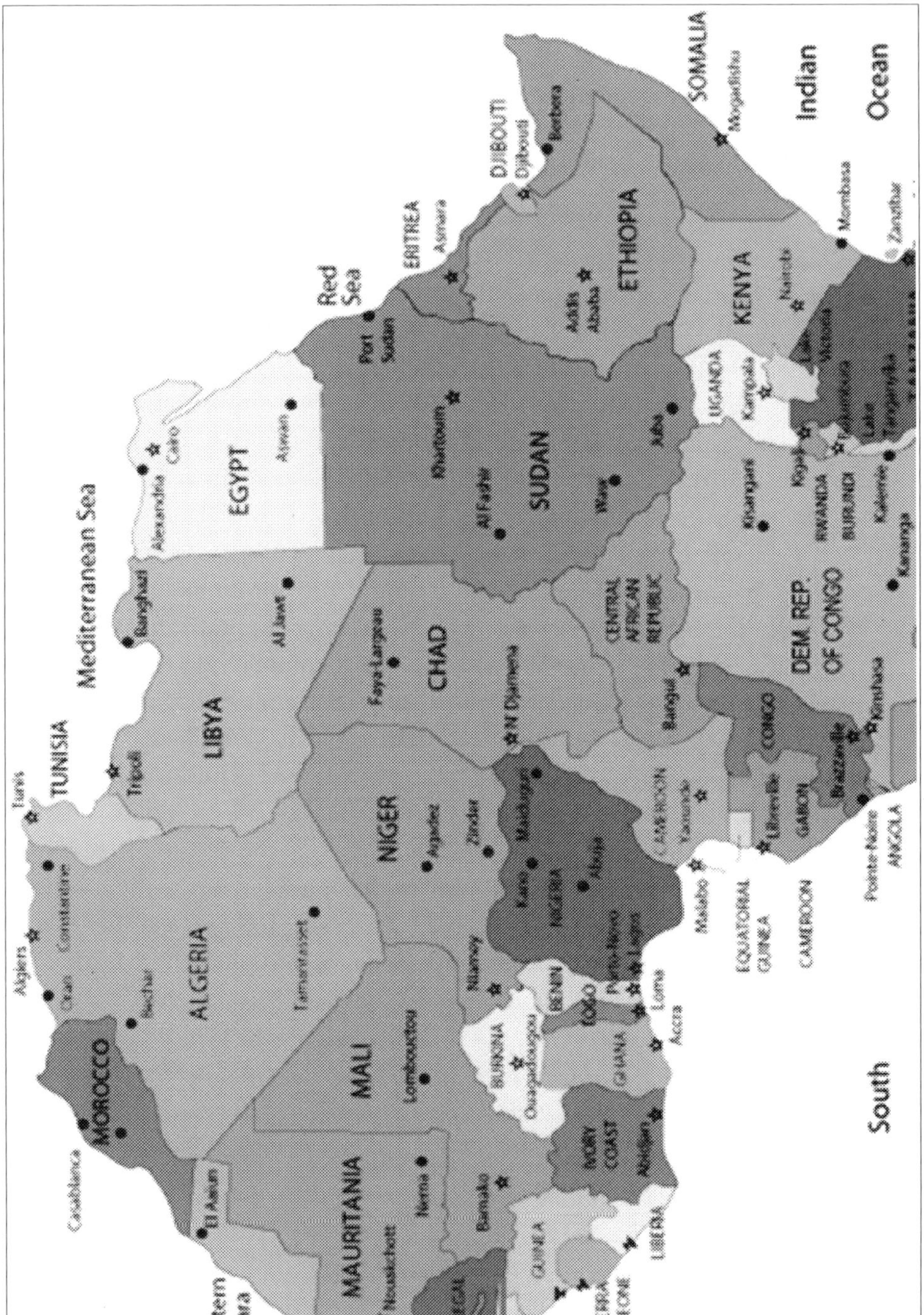

priority. The schedule was that on 10 December 2020, from 10 a.m. to 1 p.m., The Gambia would present its oral observations. On 11 December 2020, Myanmar would present its oral observations in the morning from 10 a.m. till 1 p.m. On 12 December 2020, The Gambia would again present its oral observations from 10 a.m. till 11:30 a.m. after which Myanmar would respond from 4:30 p.m. till 6 p.m.

The Lady leads the Myanmar Defence

Myanmar retained international lawyers to contest the case and also let it be known that their Nobel Laureate for Peace and State Counsellor, in her capacity as Union Minister for Foreign Affairs, would lead the team to The Hague, Netherlands, to defend the national interest of Myanmar at the ICJ.[37] Daw Suu's stand at The Hague took place on 11 December 2019 when she valiantly rose to defend her nation against an onslaught from effectively, 57 Islamic States allied under the OIC umbrella, fronted by The Gambia.

Her speech invoked the origins of the 1948 Genocide Convention, viz., the killing of six million Jews and went on to specify cases where genocide was identified as a crime, i.e., killing of Tutsis in Rwanda, and cases where it was not, i.e., Serbs in Croatia in 1995 and residents of Kosovo in Yugoslavia 1999. She identified ***intent*** as the most important factor in distinguishing whether or not genocide had occurred. She then went on to expose how The Gambia's application was misleading since it was pitched devoid of context. She explained the context of the situation in Rakhine including the ethnic Buddhist violence leading up to the Arakan conflict. She denounced the selective dissemination of facts by The Gambia as it did not present the facts in the correct context. Daw Suu then went on to explain the term 'clearance operation', a term in use since 1950.

To her credit and her political acumen, Daw Suu conceded some interesting aspects. She acknowledged the use of disproportionate force by the Tatmadaw including violations of International Humanitarian Law. She was brutally candid in admitting that '*It is never easy for armed forces to recognise self-interest in accountability for their members, and to implement a will to accountability through actual investigations and prosecutions*'. In fact, she even took a dig at her own armed forces and described how a court martial that found 10 Muslim men summarily executed in Inn Din village and accordingly sentenced seven officers and soldiers each to 10 years in prison with hard labour, only to have them receive a military pardon after serving a part of their sentence. She bluntly stated that '*Many of us in Myanmar were unhappy with this pardon*'. However, her moot point was that under the 2008 Constitution, there was a military justice system functioning in Myanmar for crimes by uniformed forces, under the Office of the Judge Advocate General and this system should be allowed to function first. Courts martial were already underway to investigate the cases. This in itself defeats the '*genocidal intent*' being sought to be projected by The Gambia. She also mentioned the Independent Commission of Enquiry headed by Kofi Annan which had collected large amounts of evidence without establishing the '*genocidal intent*'. Finally, she dwelt on the aim of the OIC to externalise the justice system without first allowing the internal justice mechanisms to deliver. She brought out that:

> *Accountability through domestic criminal justice is the norm. Only if domestic accountability fails may international justice come into play. It would be inconsistent with complementarity to require that domestic criminal justice should proceed much faster than international criminal justice. A rush to externalise accountability may undermine professionals in domestic criminal justice agencies. What does the appearance of competition between domestic and international accountability do to the public's trust in the intentions of impatient international actors?*

The Lady again very candidly highlighted the dangers of undermining the '*painstaking domestic efforts relevant to the establishing of co-operation between the military and the civilian government in Myanmar in the context of a Constitution that needs to be amended to complete the process of democratisation*'.[37] She concluded by describing a number of initiatives being taken by Myanmar to develop Rakhine State and address the issues at hand. However, before that, she also went on to highlight that leaders of States and relevant inter-governmental and non-governmental organisations should also be cognizant of their responsibility to express and affirm fundamental values. She averred that:

> *Feeding the flames of an extreme polarisation in the context of Rakhine, for example, can harm the values of peace and harmony in Myanmar. Aggravating the wounds of conflict can undermine unity in Rakhine. Hate narratives are not simply confined to hate speech language that contributes to extreme polarisation also amounts to hate narratives.*

Thus concluded the high-profile defence by 'The Lady'. She was followed by her team of lawyers who touched upon various points including the lack of a plausible claim of genocide; lack of jurisdiction of the Court; lack of standing of The Gambia; inappropriateness of the provisional measures requested; lack of real and imminent risk of irreparable prejudice to the rights in dispute and the lack of real risk of irreparable prejudice to specific rights and lack of urgency. Since this chapter is not about the merits of the case *per se*, the details are not being gone into. In sum, the Myanmar team sought to counter The Gambian demand by asking that the case be removed from listing and, if not delisted, asked for the Court to reject the request for the indication of provisional measures submitted by The Gambia. The Gambian delegation refuted the charges on the next oral hearing on 12 December 2020 morning and these were accordingly countered by the Myanmar delegation in the post-noon session on the same day, though this time exclusively by the legal team.

The Judgement

The ICJ delivered its '*Order on the Request for the indication of provisional measures submitted by the Republic of The Gambia in the case concerning Application of the Convention on the Prevention and Punishment of the Crime of Genocide (The Gambia v. Myanmar)*' on 23 January 2020.[39] It directed Myanmar to prevent genocide and report within four months from the date of the Order, i.e., 23 January 2020, and thereafter every six months, with the first four-monthly report due in the last week of May 2020. This was adhered to by Myanmar on 22 May 2020, though the contents of the report were not disclosed either by Myanmar or the ICJ, being confidential.[40]

What was notable was that the Judgement, though unanimous, was not without debate. Of the 15 judges and two ad hoc judges nominated by the litigant states, three judges (including one ad hoc judge) gave separate opinions worth noting. The Vice President of the Court, Judge Xue Hanqin,[41] a Chinese national, expressed serious reservations with regard to the plausibility of the case under the Genocide Convention. She opined[42] that:

> *For the genocide offence to be distinguished from other most serious international crimes, e.g., crimes against humanity, war crimes, genocidal intent constitutes a decisive element. Even accepting that, for the purpose of indication of provisional measures, a determination of the existence of such intent is not necessarily required, the alleged acts and the relevant circumstances should, prima facie, demonstrate that the nature and extent of the alleged acts have reached the level where a pattern of conduct might be considered as genocidal conduct. In other words, there should be a minimum standard to be applied at this early stage.*

Similarly, Judge *ad hoc*[43] Claus Kress, the Myanmar nominee, added observations[44] regarding the 'plausibility standard' of its connection with the questions of genocidal intent and protected groups under the Genocide Convention, despite having voted in favour of all points. Finally, Judge Cançado Trindade also put forth a comprehensive 22-page separate opinion wherein he made the case for the indication of provisional measures in a 13-point argument.

Reactions

Predictably, the English-language Western media hailed the judgement as historic, while others were sceptical of the capability of the ICJ to implement its ruling and also highlighted that the ruling was an interim one. Now the onus was on The Gambia to prove the charges. Prima facie, the verdict put Myanmar on the defensive and caused embarrassment to the secretive military and the leadership. A segment of the media questioned this selective activism by the OIC and The Gambia wherein equally repressive measures by China on the Uighyur Muslims have not been fought for. Predictably, Myanmar rejected the judgement and said it presents a '*distorted picture of the situation*'.[45] In response, Zaw Htay, spokesman of the Myanmar Government, while rejecting the decision of the ICC, stated that Myanmar's image has been '*severely damaged internationally*'.[46]

The Ta'ang National Liberation Army (TNLA), AA and the Myanmar National Democratic Alliance Army (MNDAA), collectively members of the 'Northern Alliance,' displayed their solidarity through a joint statement endorsing the action against the Tatmadaw at the ICJ by Gambia and at the ICC by Bangladesh and also Argentina's move to sue Myanmar leaders. In a predictable outcome, the AA spokesman said that '*the move to take appropriate legal action against guilty war criminals is a must. Only when action would be taken against war criminals, will justice and peace be achieved.*'[47]

The Next Steps

Within a week after the ruling, the ICJ announced that The Gambia must submit its initial pleading (Memorial) in the case by 23 July 2020, and that Myanmar must respond by 25 January 2021 to file the Counter Memorial.[48] The deadlines are earlier than the nine months sought by both sides to prepare their pleadings. The ICJ announced the order effective 23 January 2020 thereby granting just six months' preparation time to each party, "*taking into account the exceptional circumstances of the case and its gravity*".[49] However, the Agent of The Gambia, on 24 April 2020, requested the Court to grant at least a three-month extension due to the COVID-19 pandemic and the Court, on 18 May 2020, accordingly extended the date of filing of the Memorial to 23 October 2020. Similarly, the time-limit for the filing of the Counter Memorial by Myanmar was extended to 23 July 2021.[50]

The Lady and The Law

Suu Kyi, who was revered in the West as a big proponent of human rights, today finds herself at the receiving end of the international judicial system. She is in uncharted waters owing to her government's counter-insurgency operations due to which thousands of Rohingyas are unaccounted for and are fleeing the State *en masse*.[51] Besides defending the army, her Government has rejected cooperation with the international community to investigate crimes and hold individuals responsible for the murder and forced displacement of almost a million Rohingyas from the country. She has been accused of becoming more authoritarian and less tolerant of dissent.[52] Further, in her closing arguments at the three-day hearing at the ICJ, Myanmar's *de facto* civilian leader cautioned judges that allowing The Gambia's case against Myanmar to go ahead could undermine reconciliation.[53] The Gambia had raised the sceptre of another genocide unfolding referring to the 1994 Rwandan genocide.[54] This effort is also being criticised as selective, since no similar efforts are on to address the Chinese incarceration of lakhs of Uyghurs in Xingiang, China.

Daw Suu received tremendous support from ordinary citizens and also a few ethnic rebel groups based in Shan State such as the USWA, NDAA, SSPP and RCSS. Her loyalists had organised a series of rallies in Yangon and several other major cities in support of Suu Kyi, ahead of her visit to The Hague for the first hearing at ICJ on 10 December 2019.[55] Suu Kyi, upon returning from The Hague, made a speech on national television addressing the nation. She used her speech to play to Buddhist nationalist sensibilities. The common masses of Myanmar believe that the Western powers, under instructions from the oil-rich Islamic world, are ganging up on a poor little Buddhist country. Suu Kyi has capitalised on this very sentiment by assuring her listeners that '*we will overcome every challenge with our seamless unity, solidarity and bonds of blood.*'[56]

An objective analysis of her conduct throws light on the nature of her conduct. Firstly, she seems to be acutely aware of her limitations as the leader of a nation, just stepping out of the shadows of dictatorship, with the threat of a powerful military looming large. And, as such, she is aware of the overall negative sentiments that both the military and the Bamar majority carry over the Rohingyas. In such a situation, her priority, and rightly so, would be to focus on the big picture, the democratic reforms, rather than upset the apple cart by trying to rein in the military and risk losing the limited gains till date. In fact, without democratic reforms, she will not be able to help the Rohingyas on a long-term basis. Secondly, her transition from an activist to a mature politician is still underway. She unwittingly compromised her stand on Rakhine politics by choosing to impose a NLD CM on the ANP state parliament, thereby antagonising and politically isolating the very people who could have helped her manage the situation. Thirdly, her silence on the subject, at the cost of antagonising the Western world, is a calculated move to reassure the Tatmadaw of her grudging support. On its part, the Western media has reacted in a typical knee-jerk fashion, jumping at the symptoms of the issue, rather than on the root causes. Further, as this well-coordinated three-pronged legal attack on Myanmar reveals, the Western media has been overwhelmed by the Rohingya rhetoric and this self-induced myopia blinds it from seeing the bigger and more serious picture. Hence, she has no option but to insulate herself from the noise and focus on the core issues at hand.

Hunter Marston, a Ph.D scholar at the Australian National University researching on great power competition in Southeast Asia, has been astute in his observations that it will take generations of educated Burmese to resolve the ethnic strife and come to a solution to co-exist.[57] *Prima facie*, Myanmar is a case of trying to achieve too much too soon. The triple transition from war to peace, from autocracy to democracy, and from a still relatively closed to a more open economy has given rise to unrealistic expectations, especially amongst Western observers. Hence, when the course has deviated from the desired script, knee-jerk reactions such as sanctions and vilification of Aung San Suu Kyi have erupted.

Disastrous as the Rohingya crisis is, it should not be allowed to disrupt the core requirement: that of firming up the democratic process. Attempting to create accountability for human rights without a sound democratic structure in place is like placing the cart before the horse. Further, notwithstanding the scale of the tragedy, the Rohingya Crisis should not be allowed to become the proverbial tail that wags the dog. It is for the long-term benefit of the Rohingyas, amongst others, that the democratic discourse cannot be allowed to get hijacked by the Rohingya rhetoric.

Tagaung Institute of Political Studies analyst Soe Myint Aung[58] states the difficulties sanctions will create for the NLD Government in which three key Cabinet ministers are military officers. Further, among other things, Ms Suu Kyi's government needs the military's cooperation if it wants to work out the terms and conditions of a lasting peace with ethnic armed groups pan Myanmar. Sanctions, even if targeted at the military, may end up impacting the civilian administration.

On the other end of the scale, Kensuke Yamaguchi,[59] assistant professor at Policy Alternatives Research Institute, University of Tokyo, has recommended economic support instead of sanctions to help the Myanmar Government to deal with the issue:

'Infrastructure development needs resources that the Myanmar government cannot finance on its own. If the international community does not support local development, China will. In either case, the hope is that the Myanmar government, with accountability toward multiple ethnicities, will properly deal with the brutal violations of human and labour rights. This positive outcome is more likely if Myanmar does not rely primarily on China. Economic support, rather than economic sanctions, is needed to increase accountability'.

India's stature in Myanmar is unique. It is a trusted ally, an all-weather friend who has come a long way and sanctions notwithstanding, engages Myanmar in all spheres. In contrast, China is not trusted, but engaged purely for economic benefits. The renegotiation of a Chinese-led port project in Rakhine from the initial price of US$ 7.2 billion to US$ 1.3 billion over concerns about excessive debt, is symptomatic of this.[60] The xenophobic Tatmadaw is very conscious of the perils of engaging China and hence exercises caution in all deals. India, on its part, has been engaged in quiet diplomacy and substantial developmental work in Rakhine State.

Lastly, both the ICJ and ICC lack the mandate to enforce their judgments. In the case of the ICJ, action can only be taken through resolutions at the UN Security Council. Thus far, China has vetoed all UNSC resolutions against Myanmar and a similar fate can be expected for ICJ-related resolutions. Furthermore, Beijing and Naypyitaw are bilaterally closer than ever before in recent history, thanks to the alienation by the West.[61]

NOTES

1. Prof. Daw Kyi Kyi Hla, Professor of Philosophy, Yangon University, was a member of the delegation of the Myanmar Institute of Strategic and International Studies (MISIS) during its interaction with the VIF Delegation from India. She emphatically made the statement during the discussion with the VIF Delegation during its visit to MISIS on 10 December 2020. Coincidentally, during the visit of the VIF Delegation, the State Counsellor had left for The Hague to attend the ICJ trial and the atmosphere in Yangon was charged with patriotism and excitement.
2. The Organisation of Islamic Cooperation (OIC) is the second largest organisation after the United Nations with a membership of 57 states spread over four continents. The Organization is the collective voice of the Muslim world. It endeavours to safeguard and protect the interests of the Muslim world in the spirit of promoting international peace and harmony among various people of the world. The Organization was established in 1969. https://www.oic-oci.org/page/?p_id=52&p_ref=26&lan=en (Accessed on 8 August 2020).
3. The major difference between the two being that the ICJ settles civil disputes between nations, whereas the ICC has a penal function for criminal cases, i.e., it awards punishments for individuals. For a comprehensive understanding of the differences, see https://blog.ipleaders.in/functional-differences-icc-icj/ and http://lawdefine.blogspot.com/2017/11/difference-between-icj-and-icc.html (Accessed on 8 August 2020).
4. Aakriti Vinayak and Jaideep Chanda, *Myanmar Round Up: November 2019*, Vivekananda

International Foundation, New Delhi, 10 December 2019 https://www.vifindia.org/article/2019/december/10/myanmar-round-up-november-2019 (Accessed on 8 August 2020).

5. Constitution of the Argentine Nation, 22 August 1994, http://www.biblioteca.jus.gov.ar/argentina-constitution.pdf Myanmar Round Up: November 2019 | Vivekananda .... https://www.vifindia.org/article/2019/december/10/myanmar-round-up-november-2019.
6. Thus technically the ICC case had been filed earlier, but since the authorisation to proceed on the investigation was given on 14 November 2010 and came out in the news alongside the ICJ case and the case in the Argentinean court, the overwhelming perception was that the cases were filed almost simultaneously.
7. For the text of the complaint, see Burma Campaign UK Website at https://burmacampaign.org.uk/media/Complaint-File.pdf (Accessed on 2 August 2020).
8. Please see Burmese Rohingya Organisation UK (BROUK) Situation Update November 2013 at https://www.ohchr.org/Documents/HRBodies/HRCouncil/MinorityIssues/Session6/AgendaItem4/Mr%20Tun%20Khin.pdf (for address and web site) (Accessed on 2 August 2020). http://www.brouk.co.uk (for the defunct website) (Accessed on 2 August 2020). @tunkhin80, Rohingya *activist & genocide survivor. Forced to flee my country. Now President of Burmese Rohingya Organisation UK. Recipient of 2015 Richard Holbrooke Award.* Joined February 2013. (Accessed on 2 August 2020).

   @brouklondon, *For the rights of #Rohingya in Myanmar.* Joined January 2019. (Accessed on 2 August 2020).
9. Myanmar News Gazette, Argentina Lawsuit Seeks to Hold Aung San Suu Kyi Accountable For Atrocities Against Rohingya, 14 November 2019, https://myanmarnewsgazette.com/argentina-lawsuit-seeks-to-hold-aung-san-suu-kyi-accountable-for-atrocities-against-rohingya/ (Accessed on 2 August 2020).
10. Online Burma/Myanmar Library, https://www.burmalibrary.org/en/burmese-rohingya-organisation-uk-brouk (Accessed on 2 August 2020).
11. For details about Tun Khin, see https://www.aljazeera.com/profile/tun-khin.html and http://www.rohingyablogger.com/2013/01/interview-with-brouk-president-tun-khin.html (Accessed 2 August 2020).
12. Ethnomusicology is the study of music in its social and cultural contexts. It examines music as a social process in order to understand not only what music is but what it means to its practitioners and audiences. https://www.ethnomusicology.org/page/AboutEthnomusicol#:~:text= Ethnomusicology%20is%20 the%20study%20of, Ethnomusicology%20is%20 highly%20interdisciplinary. (Accessed 2 August 2020).
13. See http://thingsasian.com/story/strings-and-things-burmese-interview-musicologist-rick-heizman, https://www.frontiermyanmar.net/en/yangon-region-minister-hosts-american-anti-rohingya-activist/, https://www.lowyinstitute.org/the-interpreter/myanmar-press-freedom-mirage and https://www.achtzaamheid.nl/en/rakhine-arakan-2/(Accessed 2 August 2020).
14. Rick Heizman, Seized ARSA Computer Intel (minor correction), 23 June 2020, https://www.youtube.com/watch?v=PhfrCKXZHa4&t=181s (Accessed 2 August 2020).
15. The narrator, probably Rick Heizman, states that due to the fact that this is an ongoing operation, he has to be vague about where, how and when the computer was seized.
16. Renvoi is the action or process of referring a case or dispute to the jurisdiction of another country. https://www.lexico.com/definition/renvoi (Accessed on 8 August 2020).
17. See http://www.infoleg.gov.ar /infolegInternet/anexos/120000-124999/123921/ norma.htm; https://www.loc.gov/law/help/crimes-against-humanity/index.php#argentina and https://www.aba-icc.org/country/argentina/ (Accessed on 8 August 2020).
18. See http://blog.ucall.nl/index.php/2019/06/challenges-of-universal-jurisdiction-the-argentinian-complaint-against-franco-era-crimes-and-the-lack-of-cooperation-of-the-spanish-judicial-authorities/ and https://www.justiceinfo.net/en/justiceinfo-comment-and-debate/opinion/430-argentina-the-right-to-intervene-in-spain.html (Accessed on 2 August 2020).

19. Md. Kamruzzaman, Argentinian court decision brings hope for Rohingya, Anadolu Agency, 2 June 2020, https://www.aa.com.tr/en/americas/argentinian-court-decision-brings-hope-for-rohingya/1861967# (Accessed on 2 August 2020).
20. See https://www.thedailystar.net/rohingya-crisis/news/rohingya-genocide-argentine-court-moves-closer-opening-case-against-myanmar-1907933 and https://www.rohingyatoday.com/en/brouk-press-release-argentinean-judiciary-moves-closer-opening-case-against-myanmar-over (Accessed on 8 August 2020).
21. Marta Bo, Crimes against the Rohingya: ICC Jurisdiction, Universal Jurisdiction in Argentina, and the Principle of Complementarity, 23 December 2019, http://opiniojuris.org/2019/12/23/crimes-against-the-rohingya-icc-jurisdiction-universal-jurisdiction-in-argentina-and-the-principle-of-complementarity/ (Accessed on 30 June 2020).
22. Farouk Chothia, Africa's Fatou Bensouda is new ICC chief prosecutor, *BBC Africa*, 12 December 2011, https://www.bbc.com/news/world-africa-16029121 (Accessed on 30 June 2020).
23. International Criminal Court, *Who's Who: Mr Fatou Bensouda, Prosecutor,* https://www.icc-cpi.int/about/otp/who-s-who/Pages/Fatou-Bensouda.aspx (Accessed on 30 June 2020).
24. The ICC investigates and tries individuals charged with four broad types of the gravest crimes of concern to the international community, viz., genocide, war crimes, crimes against humanity and the crime of aggression. https://www.icc-cpi.int/about
25. International Criminal Court, *Office of The Prosecutor,* https://www.icc-cpi.int/about/otp (Accessed on 30 June2020).
26. International Criminal Court, *Decision Pursuant to Article 15 of the Rome Statute on the Authorisation of an Investigation into the Situation in the People's Republic of Bangladesh/Republic of the Union of Myanmar,* 14 November 2019,https://www.icc-cpi.int/Pages/record.aspx?docNo=ICC-01/19-27 (Accessed on 30 June 2020).
27. International Criminal Court, *Questions and Answers Situation in the People's Republic of Bangladesh/Republic of the Union of Myanmar,* Update: 14 November 2019, https://www.icc-cpi.int/itemsDocuments/QandA-bangladesh-myanmar-eng.pdf (Accessed on 30 June 2020).
28. International Criminal Court, *Situation in Bangladesh/Myanmar: Order on information and outreach for the victims of the situation,* 20 January 2020, https://www.legal-tools.org/doc/9zp6xl/pdf/ (Accessed on 30 June 2020).
29. International Criminal Court, *Situation in Bangladesh/Myanmar: Victims' joint request concerning hearings outside the host State,* https://www.icc-cpi.int/CourtRecords/CR2020_04736.PDF (Accessed on 30 June 2020).
30. Sexual and Gender Based Violence (SGBV).
31. International Court of Justice Press Release No. 2019/47, The Republic of The Gambia institutes proceedings against the Republic of the Union of Myanmar and asks the Court to indicate provisional measures, 11 November 2019, https://www.icj-cij.org/public/files/case-related/178/178-20191111-PRE-01-00-EN.pdf (Accessed on 30 November 2020).
32. Dhaka Tribune, Gambia set to sue Myanmar in the ICJ for Rohingya genocide, 20 October 2019, https://www.dhakatribune.com/bangladesh/rohingya-crisis/2019/10/20/gambia-set-to-sue-myanmar-in-the-icj-for-rohingya-genocide (Accessed on 20 June 2020).
33. See https://www.bbc.com/news/world-africa-13376517; https://www.britannica.com/place/The-Gambia and https://www.nationsonline.org/oneworld/gambia.htm. (Accessed on 20 June 2020).
34. Organisation of Islamic Cooperation, Resolutions on Political Affairs Adopted to the 45th Session of the Council of Foreign Ministers Dhaka, People's Republic of Bangladesh, 5-6 May 2018, Resolution No. 59/45-POL, The Establishment of an OIC Ad hoc Ministerial Committee on Accountability for Human Rights Violations Against the Rohingyas,pg. 164., https://www.oic-oci.org/docdown/?docID=1868&refID=1078 (Accessed on 20 June 2020).
35. International Court of Justice, *Verbatim Record of Public Sitting held on Wednesday 11 December*

2019, 11 December 2019, pg. 43. https://www.icj-cij.org/public/files/case-related/178/178-20191211-ORA-01-00-BI.pdf (Accessed on 20 June 2020).

36. International Court of Justice, *Press Release No. 2019/49, Request for the indication of provisional measures; The Court to hold public hearings from Tuesday 10 to Thursday 12 December 2019*, 18 November 2019, https://www.icj-cij.org/files/case-related/178/178-20191118-PRE-01-00-EN.pdf (Accessed on 20 June 2020).
37. Tara John, Aung San Suu Kyi to defend Myanmar in Rohingya genocide case, CNN, 20 November 2019, https://edition.cnn.com/2019/11/20/asia/aung-san-suu-kyi-rohingya-icj-intl/index.html (Accessed on 30 June 2020).
38. International Court of Justice, *Public sitting held on Wednesday 11 December 2019, at 10 a.m., at the Peace Palace, Verbatim Record,* https://www.icj-cij.org/public/files/case-related/178/178-20191211-ORA-01-00-BI.pdf, pp. 16-17. (Accessed on 30 June 2020).
39. International Court of Justice, *Order on the Request for the indication of provisional measures submitted by the Republic of The Gambia in the case concerning Application of the Convention on the Prevention and Punishment of the Crime of Genocide (The Gambia v. Myanmar),* https://www.icj-cij.org/public/files/case-related/178/178-20200123-ORD-01-00-EN.pdf (Accessed on 30 June 2020).
40. Kyaw Phyo Tha, Myanmar Submits First Report to World Court on Provisional Measures to Protect Rohingya, The Irrawaddy Web Article, 26 May 2020, https://www.irrawaddy.com/news/burma/myanmar-submits-first-report-world-court-provisional-measures-protect-rohingya.html (Accessed on 30 June 2020).
41. Biography of Judge Xue Hanqin, https://www.icj-cij.org/public/files/members-of-the-court-biographies/xue_en.pdf (Accessed on 30 June 2020).
42. International Court of Justice, *Summary 2020/1, Application of the Convention on the Prevention and Punishment of the Crime of Genocide (The Gambia v. Myanmar): Request for the indication of provisional measures,* 23 January 2020, https://www.icj-cij.org/public/files/case-related/178/178-20200123-SUM-01-00-EN.pdf (Accessed on 30 June 2020).
43. Under Article 31, paragraphs 2 and 3, of the Statute of the Court, a State party to a case before the International Court of Justice which does not have a judge of its nationality on the Bench may choose a person to sit as judge *ad hoc* in that specific case under the conditions laid down in Articles 35 to 37 of the Rules of Court. Before taking up their duties, a judge *ad hoc* are required to make the same solemn declaration as an elected Member of the Court. They do not necessarily have to be (and often are not) nationals of the State that designates them. https://www.icj-cij.org/en/judges-ad-hoc
44. International Court of Justice, *Public sitting held on Tuesday 10 December 2019,* 10 December 2020, https://www.icj-cij.org/public/files/case-related/178/178-20191210-ORA-01-00-BI.pdf (Accessed on 30 June 2020).
45. For ICJ related news, see the following links:
https://www.newagebd.net/article/97752/a-case- of-myanmars-defiant-response-to-icj-ruling
https://nenow.in/neighbour/myanmar/icj-ruling-on-rohingya-left-myanmar-red-faced.html
https://thewire.in/law/icj-ruling-rohingya-myanmar-caa-refugees
https://www.theguardian.com/commentisfree/2020/jan/24/rohingya-legal-protection-icj-ruling-myanmar
https://frontiermyanmar.net/en/myanmars-military-justice-system
https://www.bbc.com/news/world-asia-51229796
https://www.nytimes.com/2020/01/23/world/asia/myanmar-rohingya-genocide.html
https://www.alaraby.co.uk/english/comment/2020/1/29/justice-for-rohingya-requires-more-than-an-icj-ruling
46. *New Age* World Web Article, *Image severely damaged, says Myanmar,* 18 November 2019, http://www.newagebd.net/article/90955/image-severely-damaged-says-myanmar (Accessed on 30 June 2020).

47. BNI Multimedia Group, *Northern Alliance trio endorses legal action against Tatmadaw at ICJ*, 2 December 2019, https://www.bnionline.net/en/news/northern-alliance-trio-endorses-legal-action-against-tatmadaw-icj (Accessed on 30 June 2020).
48. International Court of Justice, *Order of 23 January 2020: Fixing of time-limits: Memorial and Counter-Memorial,* 23 January 2020, https://www.icj-cij.org/public/files/case-related/178/178-20200123-ORD-02-00-EN.pdf (Accessed on 30 June 2020).
49. Kyaw Phyo Tha, *ICJ Gives The Gambia, Myanmar Just Six Months to Prepare Pleadings in Genocide Case*, *The Irrawaddy* Web Article, 29 January 2020, https://www.irrawaddy.com/news/burma/icj-gives-gambia-myanmar-just-six-months-prepare-pleadings-genocide-case.html (Accessed on 30 June 2020).
50. International Court of Justice, *Order of 18 May 2020:Extension of time-limits: Memorial and Counter-Memorial* 23 January 2020, https://www.icj-cij.org/public/files/case-related/178/178-20200518-ORD-01-00-EN.pdf (Accessed on 30 June 2020).
51. Maung Zarni, *Why Myanmar's genocide denial will come back to haunt it, The Washington Post* Web Edition, 15 January 2020, https://www.washingtonpost.com/opinions/2020/01/15/aung-san-suu-kyi-must-be-held-account/ (Accessed on 30 June 2020).
52. Saw Greh Moo, *Choosing to defend the military against charge of genocide, aung san suu kyi is going for broke*, BNI online, 3 December 2019: https://www.bnionline.net/en/news/choosing-defend-military-against-charge-genocide-aung-san-suu-kyi-going-broke (Accessed on 30 June 2020).
53. *The Asian Post* Web Article, *Suu Kyi warns UN not to reignite Rohingya crisis*, Spotlight, 15 December 2019, https://theaseanpost.com/article/suu-kyi-warns-un-not-reignite-rohingya-crisis (Accessed on 30 June 2020).
54. *The Mint* e paper, *Myanmar's Suu Kyi told to 'stop the genocide' of Rohingya Muslims in UN court,* 10 December 2019, https://www.livemint.com/news/world/myanmar-s-suu-kyi-told-to-stop-the-genocide-of-rohingya-muslims-in-un-court-11575983062553.html (Accessed on 30 June 2020).
55. Kyaw Ye Lynn, *Genocide lawsuits prompt mixed reactions in Myanmar,* AA Web Article, 6 December 2019, https://www.aa.com.tr/en/asia-pacific/genocide-lawsuits-prompt-mixed-reactions-in-myanmar/1665573 (Accessed on 30 June 2020).
56. Zarni, note 51.
57. Hunter Marston, "The Long View on Burma" *Foreign Policy,* 29 November 2016: https://foreignpolicy.com/2016/11/29/the-long-view-on-burma-rohingya-rakhine-buddhist-muslim/ (Accessed on 30 September 2019).
58. Tan Hui Yee, "Why sanctions may not work on Myanmar's military", *The Straits Times,* 3 November 2017: https://www.straitstimes.com/asia/se-asia/why-sanctions-may-not-work-on-myanmars-military (Accessed on 30 September 2019).
59. Kensuke Yamaguchi, *Why Economic Sanctions In Myanmar Is A Bad Idea, Pacific Forum*, Honolulu, 10 January 2019: https://www.pacforum.org/sites/default/files/ 190110_PacNet_4.pdf (Accessed on 30 September 2019).
60. Yuichi Nitta, *Myanmar cuts cost of China-funded port project by 80%, Nikkei Asian Review,* 28 September 2018, https://asia.nikkei.com/Spotlight/Belt-and-Road/Myanmar-cuts-cost-of-China-funded-port-project-by-80 (Accessed on 30 September 2019).
61. Angshuman Choudhury, *What Does the ICJ Preliminary Ruling Really Mean for the Rohingya? The Diplomat* Web Edition, 4 February 2020, https://thediplomat.com/2020/02/what-does-the-icj-preliminary-ruling-really-mean-for-the-rohingya/ (Accessed on 30 June 2020).

CHAPTER 12

Is the China-Myanmar Economic Corridor (CMEC) actually China's Myanmar Exploitation Corridor?

China, especially, desires Burma as a vassal state for the construction of deepwater ports, highways, and energy pipelines that will provide China's landlocked south and west access to the sea, from where China's ever-burgeoning middle class can receive deliveries of oil from the Persian Gulf.[1]

—Robert D. Kaplan

This chapter seeks to analyse the Myanmar *avatar* of the Belt and Road Initiative (BRI), i.e., the China-Myanmar Economic Corridor (CMEC), and evaluate implications for the two direct stakeholders, viz., China and Myanmar and also for India. Geography dictates that India be a major player in any development in Myanmar, especially Western Myanmar including those that have an impact in the Bay of Bengal. In this chapter, I trace the evolution of the CMEC and identify the deliverables, as gleaned from the BRI Forum, and compile the components of the CMEC from newspaper reports, documents signed and statements made, especially during Xi Jinping's January 2020 visit to Myanmar and other open sources to understand the scope of the CMEC. This chapter also looks at the status of the Myanmar-China Oil and Gas Pipelines which predate the BRI but now have got subsumed into it. The chapter carries out an assessment of the current status of the CMEC and attempts to identify issues it has created in Myanmar.

The chapter also dwells on the Chinese concept of '*guanxi*' and the reciprocal Myanmar concept of '*ah nar de*' to understand how China seeks to obligate Myanmar into providing access to the Bay of Bengal. It analyses how the Chinese strategy in Myanmar has changed post the Myitsone project debacle and how China is re-packaging the BRI to make it more acceptable. The paper then takes into account three recent events likely to influence outcomes in Myanmar, viz., Xi Jinping's visit to Myanmar in January 2020; the corona virus outbreak and Myanmar President U Win Myint's visit to India in February 2020. Lastly, it looks at India's options in such circumstances and identifies a three-pronged strategy to enable India evolve into a preferred partner in Myanmar's journey towards development, thereby securing its own flanks.

The Belt and Road Initiative

When Chinese Premier Xi Jinping made the first mention of an "*economic belt along the Silk Road*", on 7 September 2013 at Nazarbayev University, Kazakhstan,[2] and later when the National Development and Reform Commission (NDRC) of the Chinese Ministry of Foreign Affairs and the Ministry of Commerce formally issued the '*Vision and Actions on Jointly Building Silk Road Economic Belt and 21st-Century Maritime Silk Road*' on 28 March 2015, there was no mention of the CMEC.[3] This NDRC document clearly articulated the six corridors[4] which had been planned, and out of these, the two[5] which impacted Myanmar were the Bangladesh-China-India-Myanmar Economic Corridor (BCIM-EC) and the China-Indochina-Peninsula Economic Corridor (CIPEC).[6]

The former aimed to connect Kunming, the capital of Yunnan province in China, with Kolkata, via Mu-Se, Mandalay and Lashio in Myanmar; Moreh (Manipur) and Silchar (Assam) in India; into Bangladesh through Sylhet to Dhaka, Jessore and finally re-entering India and terminating in Kolkata. This remained a non-starter due to India's security and economic concerns.[7, 8] However, during the 13th BCIM Regional Cooperation Forum in June 2019, which also marked the 20th anniversary of the establishment of the BCIM, a fresh impetus has been given to the initiative. It remains to be seen if this push leads to implementation of the initiative.[9]

Figure 12.1: Proposed Alignment of the BCIM EC

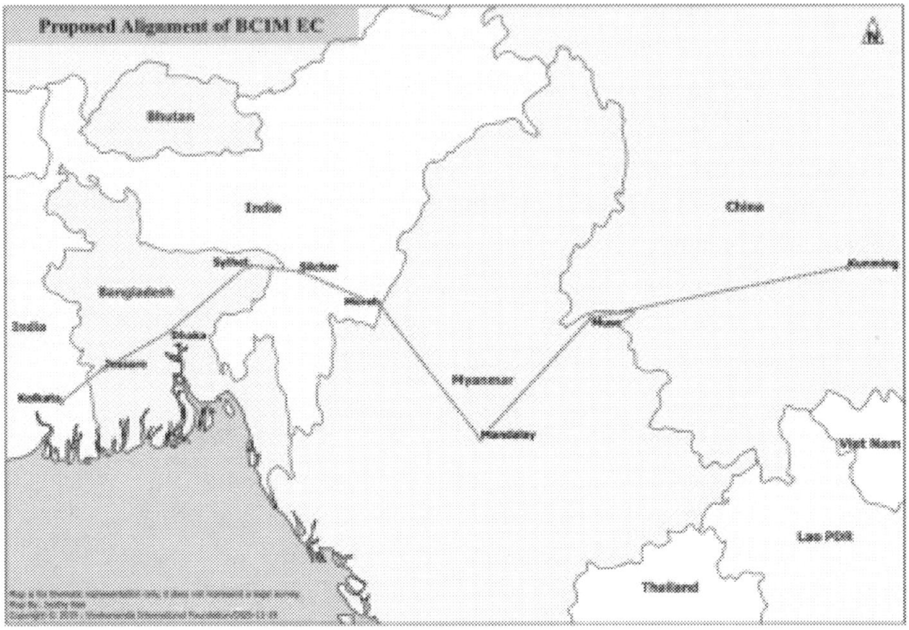

Source: Prepared by Jyothy Nair © VIF India.

The latter, i.e., the CIPEC, was to connect China to the Indochina Peninsula through the land bridge formed by the two provinces of Yunnan and Guangxi (shaded in dark brown in Figure 12.2).

The CIPEC *per se* extends from China's Pearl River Delta westward via Nanning and Pingxiang to Hanoi and Singapore, the green portion in the map above. This connects China with Vietnam, Lao, Cambodia, Thailand, Myanmar and Malaysia and is expected to boost China's cooperation with the ASEAN countries. The CIPEC alignment is depicted by the red line network.[10]

The only project that has seen the light of the day in this corridor[11] is the 688-km East Coast Rail Link (ECRL), connecting Thailand to Kuala Lumpur and Port Klang (on Malacca Straits) via Kuantan on the East Coast, thereby connecting the East Coast to the better developed region around the capital of Kuala Lumpur. The strategic significance of Port Klang to the Chinese is immense as it directly impinges on its strategic vulnerability of overdependence on the Malacca Straits for energy supplies.[12] The ECRL construction began in August 2017 but on 3 July 2018, the newly-elected Malaysian PM Mahathir Mohammed suspended all work as he followed through on his pledge to renegotiate the 'unfair' deal approved by his predecessor Najib Razak. The suspension was lifted a year

Figure 12.2: The China-Indochina Peninsular Region and the CIPEC Alignment

later on 25 July 2019 after a supplementary agreement between the two sides brought down the cost by nearly 30 per cent and a marginal reduction of the scope of the project.[13] The progress of the ECRL is symptomatic of the BRI projects around the world as we shall see subsequently in this chapter.

Figure 12.3: East Coast Rail Link

Source: New Straits Times, Malaysia

Evolution of the CMEC

When Myanmar President U Htin Kyaw attended the 70th anniversary celebrations of the founding of the PRC in October 2019, a joint China-Myanmar news release was issued which also included a mention of the BRI: "*Under the cooperation framework of the 'Belt and Road' initiatives and the Bangladesh-China-India-Myanmar Economic Corridor, the two countries will make coordinated promotion of cooperation in infrastructure connectivity such as ports, roads and railways.*"[14] A similarly worded joint press release marked the bilateral visit of Aung San Suu Kyi to Beijing in August 2016 wherein it read: "*Myanmar welcomes China's 'Belt and Road' initiative and the cooperation initiative on the Bangladesh-China-India-Myanmar Economic Corridor.*"[15]

However Myanmar effectively boarded the BRI when Aung San Suu Kyi attended the First Belt and Road Forum for International Cooperation in Beijing in May 2017 and a Memorandum of Understanding on '*Cooperation within the Framework of the Silk Road Economic Belt and the 21st Century Maritime Silk Road Initiative*' was signed during the visit. Xi Jinping even mentioned Myanmar in the context of the BRI in his speech at the Forum.[16] The State Counsellor also attended the Second Belt and Road Forum in April 2019 and it was here that nine projects, including three bilateral projects, were actually signed. These were out of the 38 proposed by China as 'early harvest' projects, and credit is due to The Lady and her team in ensuring a conservative approach given the dubious Chinese reputation in matters of debt. The three bilaterals included an agreement on economic and technical cooperation, an MoU on a five-year economic and trade development cooperation plan (with a 1 billion Yuan, i.e., US$ 144.5 million grant), and an MoU on the CMEC Plan spanning 2019 to 2030.[17, 18, 19]

The Chinese strategy is the epitome of opportunism at its best, to woo Myanmar at a time when Myanmar is increasingly under international pressure owning to its mismanagement of the Rohingya crisis. Myanmar needs Chinese diplomatic support to resist the global scrutiny and sanctions and gain investments[20] whilst China needs access to the Indian Ocean. Hence, it has pushed for the CMEC as Myanmar remains the shortest route for China to reach the Bay of Bengal, the Indian Ocean and beyond; which is an inescapable requirement for creating the redundancies and capacities to augment its strategic vulnerability in the chokepoints of the Malacca Straits.

List of Deliverables for Myanmar

The overall list of deliverables as compiled from the reports of the two Belt and Road Forums[21] is shown in Table 12.1. This list is a macro-level compilation of the strategic deliverables articulated during the First and Second Belt and Road Forums. This list simply gives a sense of the big picture that China is painting as part of the BRI for Myanmar. A large number of these deliverables are generic and common with other countries.

Table 12.1: List of Deliverables for Myanmar

Generic Deliverables	*Specific Projects*
	1ST B&R FORUM (MAY 2017)
Synergize Connectivity of Development Policies and Strategies	The Chinese government signed memoranda of understanding on **Belt and Road cooperation** with the Government of Myanmar and other countries.
Deepen Project Cooperation for Infrastructure Connectivity	Ministry of Transport of China signed the memorandum of understanding on **transport cooperation** with the relevant government departments of Myanmar.
	The Export-Import Bank of China signed a loan agreement on the airport development project with **Yangon Aerodrome** Company of Myanmar
Expand Industrial Investment, Enhance Trade Connectivity	The Chinese government signed the **economic and trade cooperation agreement** with the Government of Myanmar
	Ministry of Commerce of China signed the Memorandum of Understanding on the Establishment of **China-Myanmar Border Economic Cooperation Zone** with the Ministry of Commerce of Myanmar.
	2ND B&R FORUM (APRIL 2019)
Bilateral and Multilateral Projects Signed during or immediately before the Second BRF	The National Development and Reform Commission of China signed a **cooperation plan on China-Myanmar Economic Corridor** with the Ministry of Planning and Finance of Myanmar.
	The Ministry of Agriculture and Rural Affairs of China and the Ministry of Agriculture, Livestock and Irrigation of Myanmar jointly released the Statement of Intent for Cooperation on **Promoting Specification-setting for Pesticide Quality under the Belt and Road** Initiative, along with several other countries.
	The Ministry of Commerce of China signed the MOU on the Formulation of the Five-Year Development Plan for **Economic and Trade Cooperation** with the Ministry of Investment and Foreign Economic Relations of Myanmar.
Multilateral Cooperation Mechanisms under the BRF Framework	The Ministry of Ecology and Environment of China jointly launched the BRI International Green Development Coalition with the **environmental departments** of 25 countries including Myanmar, international organizations, research institutions and businesses.
	The China Council for the Promotion of International Trade, China Chamber of International Commerce, together with the industrial and commercial organizations and legal service agencies from over 30 countries and regions including Myanmar jointly established **the International Commercial Dispute Prevention and Settlement Organization** (ICDPASO).

Generic Deliverables	*Specific Projects*
Investment Projects and Project Lists	The National Development and Reform Commission of China signed the document on the early harvest projects list of **China-Myanmar Economic Corridor** with the Ministry of Plan and Finance of Myanmar.
	The China Railway Group Limited handed over the Feasibility Study Report (Technical Part) of the **Muse-Mandalay Railway** to the Ministry of Transport and Communications of Myanmar.
Projects by Local Authorities and Enterprises	Local authorities and enterprises upgraded and constructed the Project of Chan Mya Shwe Pyi **Bus Terminal** in Mandalay, Myanmar

Note: A large number of other non-country specific, generic deliverables have been listed in the List of Deliverables of both the 1st and 2nd Belt and Road Fora which will impact Myanmar. This list is only of those deliverables where Myanmar is directly affected.

Source: Compiled by the author from the complete List of Deliverables of the 1st and 2nd Belt and Road Fora for International Cooperation accessed at https://eng.yidaiyilu.gov.cn/qwyw/rdxw/ 13698.htm and https://eng.yidaiyilu.gov.cn/qwyw/rdxw/88228.htm on 3 November 2019.

Deciphering the CMEC

While the macro level deliverables (Table 12.1) have been articulated by the Belt and Road Forum, the details of the CMEC projects however have been kept vague, both by China and Myanmar, either deliberately or out of habit. This traditional lack of transparency with regard to the CMEC prevents us from getting a consolidated picture of the projects that would comprise the Corridor. Various open source reports were examined to try and decipher the components of the CMEC. Xi Jinping's visit to Myanmar on 17-18 January 2020 revealed some aspects[22] and hence it is important to analyse the visit from the perspective of the BRI.

The first clue of the components comprising the BRI was received from Xi's signed article preceding the visit to Myanmar, in which he wrote, "*Our two sides need to deepen result-oriented Belt and Road cooperation and move from a conceptual stage to concrete planning and implementation in building the CMEC. Efforts need to be made to promote the* ***three pillars of the CMEC****, namely, the* ***Kyaukphyu Special Economic Zone****, the* ***China-Myanmar Border Economic Cooperation Zone*** *and the* ***New Yangon City Project****. We also need to deepen practical and mutually beneficial cooperation in such areas as connectivity, electricity, energy, transportation, agriculture, finance and livelihood to deliver more benefits to both peoples.*"[23] This effectively identifies the Kyaukphyu Special Economic Zone, the Border Economic Zone and the New Yangon City project as the three pillars and hence undisputed components of the CMEC. Ironically, the Kyaukphyu Deep Sea Port does not find mention here, while that is the only project in which agreements have actually been signed. One wonders whether this is a deliberate move to keep the Deep Sea Port, without which the viability of the Special Economic Zone is suspect, out of the public gaze given the military importance of the port. Some reports suggest that in fact the Deep Sea Port is, in fact, a part of the Special Economic Zone.[24] Further, researchers have alluded to the CMEC as being the 'signature project' of the BRI, seeming to suggest that there are more projects under the BRI in Myanmar, which fall outside the ambit of the CMEC.[25] U Myint, Economic Advisor to the Union of Myanmar Federation of Chambers of Commerce and Industry (UMFCCI) associates the Kyaukphyu Special Economic Zone with the CMEC and states that the agreement to develop the Deep Sea Port is '*related*' to the Special Economic Zone.[26] Let us examine the details of the projects as available from open sources.

Open sources have revealed that there are six to seven agreements which are required to be signed for commencement of the work on the Kyaukphyu Deep Sea Port. The first agreement was the Framework Agreement signed on 8 November 2018 at Nya Pyi Taw, Myanmar[27] between the CITIC[28] Consortium[29] and Kyaukphyu Special Economic Zone Management Committee. The agreement was signed by Myanmar's Deputy Minister of Planning and Finance and Chairperson of the Management Committee of the Kyaukphyu Special Economic Zone, U Set Aung, and the President of CITIC Group, Chang Zhenming. This was followed up in January 2020 during Xi Jinping's visit to Myanmar, when two more agreements, viz., the Shareholder's Agreement and the Concession Agreement, were signed.[30] Another few agreements, including possibly an agreement for provision of land, are also required to be signed before the work starts. Notably, the Deep Sea Port has been renegotiated from US$ 7 billion to US$ 1.3 billion. Dr. Sean Turnell, Special Economic Consultant to the Myanmar State Counsellor and director of research at the Myanmar Development Institute (MDI), had stated in an interview that projects of the nature of the Kyaukphyu Deep Sea Port or any large-scale infrastructure projects with large financial, environmental, social, human rights, and other complexities have to be put through strict procedures and such "backbone" schemes must be properly assessed before they are approved.[31] During the interview on the strategic implications of the Deep Sea Port, Dr. Turnell skilfully sidestepped the question stating '*Chinese projects are approached, via the Project Bank and other procedures, in the context of the broadest consideration of Myanmar's national interest, including the strategic*'. Dr. Turnell is the person credited with having called out the Chinese attempt to hoodwink Myanmar and effected the renegotiation of the Deep Sea Port resulting in massive savings for Myanmar.

The Myanmar-China Border Economic Cooperation Zones (BECZ) alluded to by Xi Jinping refer to three locations approved by the Myanmar Government[32] and include Kanpiketi near Myitkyina, Kachin State, Chinshwehaw in Laukkai Township of Kokang Self-Administered Zone and Muse in Shan State.

Figure 12.4: Mandalay-Muse Axis and Myanmar-China BECZs

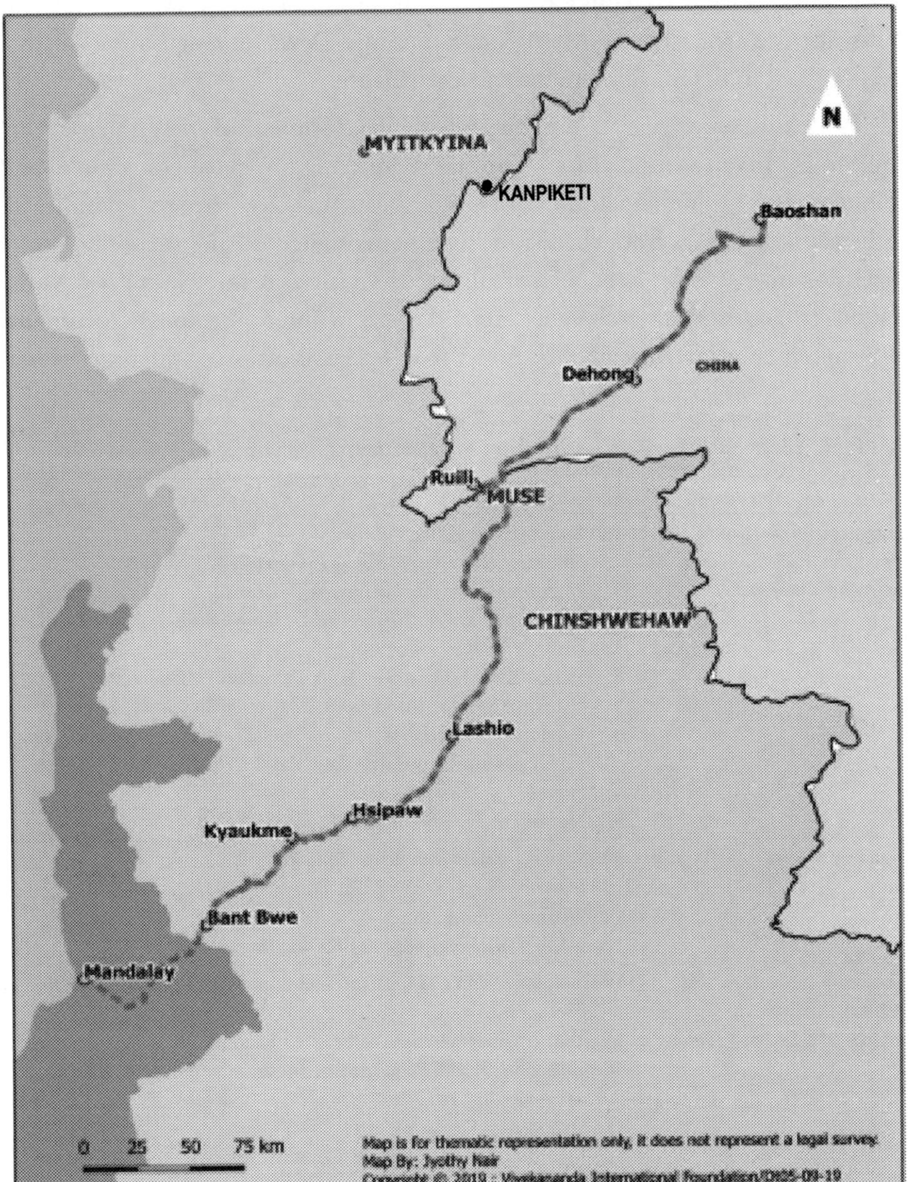

Muse and Chinshwehaw are existing major trade hubs. However, Kanpiketi, which was also a trading point with China, was to receive US$ 5 million for development. The proposed BECZ for Muse possibly aims to legitimise and organise the humongous existing legal and illegal trade on the route to Mandalay. Incidentally, apart from the BCEZ in Myitkyina, there is another major China-driven initiative, with dubious terms and conditions[33] in the region which threatens to disrupt the area, i.e., the Myitkyina Economic Development Zone. This has been covered in detail, subsequently in this chapter.

The Chinese interest in Yangon and the development of New Yangon City seems to be driven as much by a Myanmar requirement to decongest Yangon and a Chinese desire to remain at the controls in the capital city. The second indicator of the projects comes from the list of documents signed during the visit. A total of 33 documents have been signed during the visit and these comprise MoU, Handover Certificates, Exchange Letters, Letters of Intent, Protocol Documents and Implementation Agreements. A sector-wise classification of the projects is as under:

Table 12.2: Sector-wise Classification of Documents Exchanged in January 2020

Nature of Document	*Pertains To*
Equipment/Infrastructure Hand Over, Exchange Letter, Implementation Agreement, MoUs	1. ***Yangon Police Command Centre*** 2. ***Six Patrol Boats for Myanmar Police Force*** 3. 28 Passenger Coaches via Interest Free Loans 4. ***Upgradation of No. 2 Industrial Training Centre*** 5. Kunlong Bridge Project 6. Yangon River Estuary West Bank Protection Project 7. Handover of Muse-Mandalay Railway Feasibility Study Report[34] 8. Handover and Receipt of Detailed Feasibility Study Reports of Mandalay-Tigyaing-Muse Expressway and Kyaukphyu–Nya Pyi Taw Highway Project 9. Mutual Provision of Embassy Lands and Buildings
Feasibility Studies MoUs	10. Myanmar-China Power Interconnection Project 11. Mandalay-Bagan Railway Line Project 12. Watalone Tunnel Project 13. ***3-Year Development Plan of Border Areas***
Agriculture, Sericulture and Livestock Protocols and Exchange Letters	14. Plant Inspection and Quarantine Requirements for Rice Export to China 15. Head Processed Cocoons to be exported to China 16. Quarantine Health Requirements for Slaughtered Bovines to be exported to China 17. Hybrid-Rice Research Centre 18. Agricultural Product Quality Control Centre
Media MoUs and Agreements	19. Cooperation between National Radio Television Administration of China and Ministry of Information, Myanmar

Nature of Document	*Pertains To*
	20. MoU on Co-ordinating the Myanmar Day 2020 Lacang-Mekong TV Week under the Framework of the Asia Film and TV Exchanges and Cooperation Initiative
Trade & Economic Infrastructure Agreements, MoUs	21. ***Accelerating Negotiation on the Framework Agreement on the China Myanmar Muse-Ruili Cross-Border Economic Zone***
	22. Establishment of Working Group for Promotion of Smooth Trade
	23. Promoting Production Capacity and Investment Cooperation
	24. Enhancing Infrastructure Development Cooperation
Human Resource Development MoUs	25. Human Resources Development Cooperation
	26. Feasibility Study for Resettlement Project for IDPs in Kachin State
	27. Establishment of Friendship Province/Region Relationship
	28. Cooperation between Football Associations of both countries
	29. Strengthening Cooperation
Major Projects MoU, Letters of Intent and Concession and Shareholders Agreements	30. Concession and Shareholder's Agreements on Kyaukphyu Special Economic Zone Deep Sea Port Project
	31. New Urban Development of Yangon City
	32. Local Cooperation under the Framework of Joint Building China Myanmar Economic Cooperation (CMEC)
	33. Acceleration of Meel-in-gyaing integrated LNG to Power Project

Source: Compiled by the author from open sources. Serials 1, 2, 4, 13 and 21–23 have been made bold and italicised by the author to depict projects, the exchange of documents for which were witnessed by Xi Jinping and Daw Aung San Suu Kyi during the former's visit to Myanmar in January 2020.

Here too, Kyaukphyu emerges as the dominant hub of activity with other projects essentially building up to Kyaukphyu such as the Handover and Receipt of Detailed Feasibility Study Report of the Kyaukphyu–Nay Pyi Taw Highway Project. One needs to see the connectivity to China's Yunnan Province in two parts, i.e., firstly from Kyaukphyu to Nay Pyi Taw and in the second part from Nay Pyi Taw to Ruili (possibly via Mandalay) in Yunnan and beyond. The Mandalay-Nay Pyi Taw vertical alignment is also the place from where the Yangon branch of the Corridor is expected to peel off to Yangon. Presently, due to trade influx from Muse, the connectivity between Yunnan and Mandalay is of a high order and sustains high volumes of traffic where *daily trade* is estimated to touch US$ 5 million. However, on the axis from Mandalay to Kyaukphyu, apart from the alignment of the gas and oil pipelines, there is no major connectivity. This is now going to be a priority for China for access to the Bay of Bengal.

The third inkling of the relative sense of priority given to the projects can be drawn from the optics given to them. Thus, there were only seven projects, the document exchange of which was witnessed by Xi Jinping and Daw Aung San Syu Kyi. These are in bold and italicised in the list above. Three of the seven were relatively minor and not really worthy of summit-level optics, e.g., construction of the Yangon Police Command Centre, handing over of six patrol boats and upgradation of an Industrial Training Centre. Three others were macro level and included a Three-Year Development Plan for Border Areas, the Establishment of Working Group for Promotion of Smooth Trade and Promoting Production Capacity and Investment Cooperation. The seventh one was a specific one keeping in line with Xi's statement on Border Economic Zones. This was the agreement on Accelerating Negotiation on the Framework Agreement on the China Myanmar Muse-Ruili Cross-Border Economic Zone. Thus, one can assess that the development of Yangon; the Cross-Border Economic Zones; the overall development of border areas and greater institutionalised cooperation in trade, emerge as major focus areas.

From a study of other open source media, one gets a hint of other projects which could possibly be part of the BRI, but not necessarily part of the CMEC. Thus, an attempt was made to piece together details from open sources and news reports, especially those pertaining to the visit by Xi Jinping. The details have been tabulated in Table 12.3.[35, 36, 37]

Table 12.3: Other BRI Projects in Myanmar (not mentioned in the 33 agreements signed during Xi Jinping's January 2020 visit)

Sl.No.	*Project*	*Available Details*
1	Mandalay Yida Economic and Trade Cooperation Zone	$ 4 billion project
2	Irrigation Systems	Ministry of Livestock, Agriculture and Irrigation amounting to $ 400 million
3	Letpadaung copper mine project	$ 1 billion
4	Tagaung Taung (Dagongshan) Nickel Industry Development Project	$ 820 million
5	Pathein Industrial City	Project signed with the China Textile City Network to build garment factories in Pathein. This would be one of the largest foreign direct investments in the Ayeyarwady delta area in decades
6	Pathein Industrial Seaport	NK
7	Roads in Shan (1)	NK
8	Roads in Shan (2)	NK
9	Airports	NK
10	Inland Ports	NK
11	Urban Development Projects	NK
12	Resorts	NK
13	Business Districts	NK
14	Industrial Parks	NK

Sl.No.	*Project*	*Available Details*
15	Myitsone Hydropower Project	The Chinese Ambassador had pushed for resumption being essential for BRI. This $ 3.6 billion-project was suspended by President U Thein Sein in 2011 post protests since it was expected to displace 10,000-plus people and submerge area equivalent to that of Singapore. It goes against the national sentiment towards the Irrawaddy River. **Note, technically the project is suspended but *not cancelled* which leads to speculation that it may be revived.**

Source: Compiled by the author from open sources.[38] This list is not exhaustive.

What emerges is a myriad hotchpotch of ambitious projects mired in suspicion and opacity with a high probability of getting stalled due to various issues such as land acquisition problems and ethnic violence ironically fuelled by decades of Chinese duplicity in trying to play both the sides, i.e., the Myanmar Government as well as the ethnic armed organisations.[39]

The Myanmar-China Oil & Gas Pipelines

The Myanmar-China Oil & Gas Pipelines predate Myanmar joining the BRI, but is now likely to provide a pre-existing framework along which the economic corridor will run. The transport components of the CMEC are slated to run astride these pipelines. A look at these pipelines provides us with an understanding of how the proposed corridor will unfold.

The crude oil[40] and gas pipeline[41] projects starting in Kyaukphyu Township in Myanmar's Rakhine State run parallel to each other and carry supplies to Ruili in south-western Yunnan.[42] The oil pipeline can carry up to 22 million tons of oil annually, which is equivalent to 6 per cent of China's total imports in 2016. The gas pipeline draws from Myanmar's offshore fields and possesses an annual capacity of up to 12 billion cubic metres (bcm) of natural gas, of which Myanmar receives

2.5 bcm a year. China's gas import in 2018 was 123.4 bcm[43] and hence the 10 bcm piped into China from Myanmar would thus equal almost 6.56 per cent of China's 2018 gas imports which stood at 45.3 per cent of China's overall gas demand.[44, 45] The Myanmar-China Gas Pipeline Project is a joint investment between South East Asia Pipeline (SEAP) Company, Myanmar Oil and Gas Enterprise (MOGE), POSCO DAEWOO, ONGC CASPIAN E&P B.V. (OCEBV), Gas Authority of India Limited (GAIL) and Korea Gas Corporation (KOGAS). The South-East Asia Gas Pipeline Company Limited (SEAGP) is responsible for its operation and management.[46]

Thus we see that the gas pipeline is a multinational entity in which India is also a stakeholder. But all is not well here as now protests have also arisen as people astride the route are seeking fair compensation from the Chinese for the negative impact on their livelihoods due to loss of land. Additional land is now being sought by the Chinese for the transportation corridor to be constructed astride these pipelines, adding fuel to the fire. To assuage their grievances, the SEAGP has now donated over US$ 25 million for construction of schools, clinics and water supply systems for rural communities along the pipeline route.[47] A study of the Corporate Social Responsibility brochure reveals a carefully-worded Corporate Citizenship Philosophy and an International Cooperation Principle. It would not be amiss to conclude that the presence of the other international stakeholders in the SEAGP would be having a substantial say in the relatively and uncharacteristically ethical nature of the functioning of the SEAGP, despite it being run by the China National Petroleum Corporation.[48]

Current Status of CMEC Projects

By August 2020, i.e., three years after Aung San Suu Kyi signed the first MoU and after two Belt and Road Forums, a laundry list of non-binding MoUs, a few projects which predate the BRI, the signing of agreements for the Kyaukphyu Special Economic Zone are all that Myanmar has seen. A few projects are also being driven at the State Government levels, but these too have developed credibility issues. Take, for example, the Kachin State Government agreement proposed to establish a China-backed economic zone under the CMEC, based on a May 2018 MoU with Yunnan Tengchong Heng Yong Investment Company (YTHIC) for implementation of the Myitkyina Economic Development Zone (MEDZ).[49] The Namjim Industrial Zone, valued at US$ 400 million, is 25 km from the Kachin capital of Myitkyina, and comprises nearly 5,000 buildings and 500 factories over 19 sq km astride the Ledo Road. Nan Lwin, Senior Reporter, *The Irrawaddy,* wrote that the development zone is one of the lesser-known Chinese-backed projects in Kachin State and has received criticism over lack of transparency.[50] According to the MoU, YTHIC and the Kachin State Government had agreed on the following:

- To establish a **joint-venture** company to implement the zone.
- Government to **transfer the land rights within 90 days** of the company's establishment.
- The joint-venture company will **get a 50-year lease** for the land.
- **No similar project will be allowed near Myitkyina for 15 years.**
- The Chinese company has **full authority to invite third-party investors.**

- YTHIC would **loan the money** to pay for feasibility studies and the environmental impact assessment.
- Joint Venture Company must **repay YTHIC for the expenses.**
- Form investment organizations for the zone.
- Secure official permission for the project and apply for tax exemptions.

Land acquisition for the project is fraught with danger since land-grabbing by the state is rampant in Waingmaw Township, Myitkyina, Kachin, where Chinese-operated banana plantations are the major perpetrators. The Kachin Parliament's Complaints Committee had received 345 complaints since the NLD took office in 2016, including 179 complaints over land seizures. The landowners' associations had negotiated over 2.6 sq km inside the site but had been kept in the dark by the Government about compensation.[51] As on 27 February 2020, the Kachin Government had given approval for the project, but without any clarity on the final terms. The area is controlled by the New Democratic Army-Kachin (NDA-K) militia, which is allied with the Myanmar military. This was being perceived as a project for the elites and by the elites on both sides, with the locals unlikely to get any benefit from this. The project was being developed by Myanmar Heng Ya Investment Development Company Ltd., a joint venture of Myanmar's Kampaiti Development Company Ltd. and China's Yunnan Tengying Trading Company Ltd. It was no surprise that the sons of NDA-K militia founder, Zahkung Ting Ying, were directors in the Kampaiti Development Company Ltd.[52]

While economists would make better sense of the terms, a basic perusal of the MoU terms made it profusely clear that this project would be an economic disaster for Myanmar with the exception that the Kachin elites and the Chinese businesses would be laughing their way to the bank at the expense of the Kachin locals. The deadline for land transfer within 90 days when locals had not even been consulted, raised suspicions and this could well sow the seeds for a micro-insurgency in the area. This would ensure that the economic zone, even after construction, remains hostage to violence as is being seen along the Muse-Mandalay road in August 2019 when the total trade value through the Muse border trade zone between the two countries declined approximately 90 per cent from around US$ 5 million (7.6 billion Kyats) per day to around US$ 700,000 per day since hostilities began.[53] In a positive development, as per latest reports, the Myanmar authorities have rallied and held out against this attempt at economic colonialism by China. Journalist Dipanjan Roy Chaudhury reported[54] that the MEDZ has run into rough weather following reservations from both government and local residents in recent weeks. Serious differences have erupted between the Myanmar

Government and the Chinese firm over land acquisition and compensation package. Roy Chaudhury reports that clauses in the MoU were later tweaked to favour the Chinese developer and its strict condition about MEDZ being the sole economic zone in Myanmar's Kachin State for 70 years raised suspicion. Effectively, the Chinese company allotted the MEDZ would enjoy highly favourable terms at the expense of the public. Khine Win, Executive Director of the Sandhi Governance Institute, an organization that monitors the joint ventures between the Government and private groups in Myanmar wrote the MEDZ monitoring report[55] in collaboration with an international NGO, The Centre for International Private Enterprise (CIPE). He informed the journalist that ironically other investment companies would not be able to operate *even if the MEDZ project was delayed or not implemented.* The monitoring report concludes that:

> *The MEDZ is exposed to a high-degree development and construction risk because the Chinese investor, YTHIC, lacks a clear track record and suffers from opaque governance. Operation and maintenance risks are also significant as YTHIC is conflicted in its interests, and because of rampant smuggling along the Chinese border area.*
>
> *While total costs are publicly known, the MEDZ lacks estimates related to return on investment and commercial viability—exposing the Kachin government and locals to a high level of financial risk. Legal and environmental risks are also significant, in part, because Myanmar's Vacant, Fallow and Virgin Land Management Law (VFV Law) does not adequately protect indigenous communities from land seizures. Finally, the MEDZ PPP suffer(s) from political risks stemming from its location in a conflict zone.*

Another report, *Public-Private Partnership Monitoring in Myanmar: The New Yangon City Project March 2020,* also by the Sandhi Governance Institute, covering the New Yangon City (NYC) and touted by Xi Jinping as one of the pillars of the CMEC, finds that the NYC project is subject to a high degree of construction, development and environmental risk because its low-lying topography is prone to flooding. It states[56] without mincing words that:

> *Uncertainties regarding water supply, the poor reputation of CCCC, and the need to import large numbers of Chinese labourers heighten operation and maintenance risks. Lack of clarity regarding regional government oversight, and potential conflicts between agreements signed between NYDC and CCCC and the Yangon City Development Committee (YCDC) and CCCC, add financial and political risks. To mitigate the NYC project's risks, the Sandhi Governance Institute recommends that the Myanmar government and relevant authorities mandate greater transparency and clarity regarding the roles and responsibilities*

of various oversight bodies. Myanmar should ensure that contracts, project plans and agreements are available for public scrutiny, and that the NYC PPP be added to the Project Bank database. The NYC project should be subject to parliamentary approval. Finally, multi-lateral development banks, such as the World Bank, should play a role in the development of the NYC.

As if on cue, on 29 July 2020, Myanmar split up the US$ 1.5-billion project due to the sheer scale of the mega-investment required, making it possible for other companies to join the Swiss Challenge.[57] The Yangon regional government-backed New Yangon Development Company (NYDC) had initially signed a US$ 1.5-billion (2.03-trillion Kyat) framework agreement in 2018 with Beijing-based China Communications Construction Company, Ltd. (CCCC) to draw up a proposal for the infrastructure project. The 20,000-acre project included five resettlement areas, two bridges, one industrial estate and commercial and residential areas including related infrastructure. The Yangon Government's 2019 Yangon Project Bank estimates the project's total cost at US$ 8 billion. The unbundled project is valued at US$ 800 million and tentatively includes an industrial zone of three square kilometres[58] (reduced from the 13 sq km planned earlier) with supporting infrastructure; one bridge across the river connecting the new city with Kyimyindine Township on the Yangon side; five resettlement areas; commercial and residential areas measuring nine square kilometres. Six international consultancy firms have been shortlisted by a Union Government tender committee out of which three have responded to the terms of interest to ensure transparency of the Swiss Challenge process and for scrutiny of the project proposals by various bidders.[59] Journalist Dipanjan Roy Chaudhury also writes about the NYC project and states that the project had got mired by CCCC's involvement. This Hong Kong-listed, Chinese state-owned company has been accused of corruption relating to development deals in at least 10 countries in Africa and Asia and is a party to a major corruption scandal in Malaysia involving a former PM.

Thus, from the available inputs, it can be seen that not many projects under the CMEC have fructified as a result of the due diligence exhibited by the NLD Government, which could be an outcome of the impending elections in November 2020. Chinese projects justifiably carry the burden of being debt traps and cause untold suffering to locals. Even in the case of the China Pakistan Economic Corridor, corruption reigns supreme and only 32 out of the 122 announced projects have been completed while the bulk of the SEZs are underutilised.[60]

The Hambantota Effect[61]

The Chinese machinery has long been trying to depict the BRI in Myanmar as a 'win-win' deal for both.[62] Myanmar-based scholars wryly comment that both the 'wins' in the deal are for China! Objectively, benefits have accrued to the locals at least in the case of the gas pipeline project. But this was a project which predates the BRI and is a multinational one sans the typical Chinese characteristics.[63] However, as was seen in the very symptomatic ECRL deal renegotiation, realisation is emerging for the need to guard against debt trap to prevent a Hambantota type of situation. In August 2018, Myanmar deputy finance minister Set Aung negotiated an 80 per cent cost reduction to the proposed Kyaukphyu Deep Seaport, trimming the project from over US$ 7 billion to US$ 1.3 billion, baulked by the risk of an excessive debt burden.[64] Myanmar has also proposed five-year plans to ensure better implementation.[65] The table below lists some BRI projects which did not run as planned, thereby revealing the underlying core intent of the Chinese government.

The Hambantota Effect runs both ways. It affects China as well as the host nation. In Hambantota, the basic economic viability of the port had long been questioned. Now that China has the port on lease for 99 years, it will have no economic advantage...only a strategic asset in which there is no scope for basing troops as per the agreements, and the world's emptiest international airport![66] But the recently-elected Sri Lankan President, Gotabaya Rajapaksa, has now stated that he will take the port back after renegotiating with the Chinese.[67] With the current slowdown, even China has started slowing down on BRI investments.[68] Tabulated below are some of the beleaguered BRI projects which have either been scrapped, re-negotiated, re-oriented or, in the worst case situation for the host nation, even debt trapped.

Table 12.4: Beleaguered BRI Projects

Sl.No.	*Country*	*Project*	*Remarks*	*Source*
1	Bangladesh	Highway	Scrapped (For attempting to bribe a government Official)	https://www.cnbc.com/2019/01/18/countries-are-reducing-belt-and-road-investments-over-financing-fears.html
2	Kenya	Mombasa Port	Expected to get debt trapped shortly	https://economictimes.indiatimes.com/industry/transportation/shipping-/-transport/kenya-risks-losing-port-to-china-casting-shadow-over-indias-outreach-in-eastern-africa/articleshow/72136046.cms

Sl.No.	*Country*	*Project*	*Remarks*	*Source*
3	Malaysia	East Coast Rail Link	Renegotiated	https://www.channelnewsasia.com/news/asia/china-malaysia-restart-belt-road-east-coast-rail-link-11752570
4	Malaysia	Multi-Product Pipeline (372-mile pipeline connecting Melaka and Port Dickson to Jitra in Kedah State)	Scrapped	https://thediplomat.com/2018/08/malaysias-canceled-belt-and-road-initiative-projects-and-the-implications-for-china/
5	Malaysia	Trans-Sabah Gas Pipeline (411-mile gas pipeline from the Kimanis Gas Terminal to Sandakan and Tawau)	Scrapped	
6	Myanmar	Kyaukphyu Deep Sea Port	Renegotiated	https://www.scmp.com/news/asia/southeast-asia/article/2158015/myanmar-scales-back-china-funded-kyauk-pyu-port-project
7	Myanmar	New Yangon City Project	Being scaled down for renegotiation	https://economictimes.indiatimes.com/ne ws/international/world-ne ws/myanmar-continues-pushback-against-bri-chinese-eco-development-zone-faces-turbulence/articleshow/77364893.cms?UTM_Source=Google_Newsstand & UTM_Campaign=RSS_Feed&UTM_Medium=Referral
8	Myanmar	Myitkyina Economic Development Zone	Being renegotiated	
9	Nepal	$ 2.5 billion 1,200-MW Budhi Gandaki hydropower	Scrapped	https://www.hydroreview.com/2017/11/13/nepal-cancels-current-construction-plans-for-1-200-mw-budhi-gandaki-hydropower-project/
10	Pakistan	$ 2 billion coal power project	Scrapped	https://www.cnbc.com/2019/01/18/countries-are-reducing-belt-and-road-investments-over-financing-fears.html
11	Pakistan	Rail projects from $ 8.2 bn to $ 6.2 bn	Renegotiated	https://www.theweek.in/news/world/2018/10/02/imran-khan-stands-up-to-china—cuts-investment-in-railways-by—2.html
12	Pakistan	Huaneng Shandong Ruyi (Pakistan) Energy and Port Qasim Electric Power Company	Being renegotiated	https://www.ft.com/content/4af8101b-599c-407d-8850-3fd27cd9b31c
13	Sri Lanka	Hambantota Port	Debt trapped	https://www.nytimes.com/2018/06/25/world/asia/china-sri-lanka-port.html

Sl.No.	Country	Project	Remarks	Source
14	Sierra Leone	China-funded $ 318-million airport outside the capital, Freetown	Scrapped (First by an African nation)	https://economictimes.indiatimes.com/news/international/world-news/africa-cancels-a-bri-project-for-the-first-time/articleshow/66363312.cms?from=mdr
15	Tanzania	$11 billion port	Renegotiated	https://www.cnbc.com/2019/01/18/countries-are-reducing-belt-and-road-investments-over-financing-fears.html

Source: Compiled by the author from open sources. This list is not exhaustive.

'*Guanxi*' versus '*Ah nar de*': An Overview of the Chinese Strategy Post-Myitsone

The Myitsone Dam Project Agreement of 2006 had been signed by Vice Senior-General Maung Aye and the then Chinese Vice President Xi Jinping costing US$ 3.6 billion. Construction of the 6,000-MW dam began in 2009 below the confluence of the Maykha and Malika rivers 42 km north of Myitkyina. However, the Myitsone Dam became highly unpopular since the people were unanimous that it would harm Myanmar in many respects and that it should be terminated. In response, President U Thein Sein suspended the dam project in September 2011 saying it was "*against the will of the people*". Environmentalist Dr. Myint Zaw pointed out that based on international examples and local surveys, Myitsone Dam would:

> *...kill the Irrawaddy, and destroy the social security of millions of people who live along the river. A river flows not just to convey water, but also to preserve the balance of nature. Its ecological balance sustains the lives of the majority of farmers and fishermen in the country. The blocking of the natural flow of the river will cause huge changes in the flow of the entire river downstream. This will affect the agriculture and livestock farming of millions of people, not to mention changes in the waterway, river temperature, and erosion of riverbanks. The changes will be felt right down to the Delta. It has become clearer, according to recent international surveys, that the middle part of the river and the Delta areas will be hit hardest by the downstream impact.*[69]

Khin Khin Kyaw Kyee, Executive Director, Institute for Strategy and Policy, Myanmar, has identified significant changes in the Chinese strategy of engagement with Myanmar post the suspension of the Myitsone Dam project in 2011.[70] She calls the new strategy 'multi-layered' and characterised by the shift from a single track government-to-government relation to one which targets the entire spectrum of stakeholders in society. This soft power approach involves multi-faceted cultural, social, educational exchange programmes; art exhibitions; media campaigns;

scholarships for students and civil servants to study in Myanmar and targets military and government officials, politicians, civil society organisations, NGOs, community and religious leaders and academics. Similarly, a social media blitz has complemented this push resulting in a peculiar situation where a Xinhua-created Facebook page on Myanmar has garnered over 30 million 'likes' since 2014, in process outranking popular local media. Further, China has also cultivated its relations with the NLD even as it continues engaging the Tatmadaw.

The theory behind this outreach is the Chinese social behavioural concept of "***Guanxi***". Guanxi is created when one party provides a favour to another party with the expectation of reciprocity. The ultimate aim is to put the beneficiary under an obligation to return the favour in the future. The reciprocal social concept in Myanmar is "***ah nar de***" which *prima facie* means not wanting to impose or cause loss of face to the other. At a more intense level, it implies that the recipient of the benefits '*feels obliged to reciprocate similarly, failing which he experiences social discomfort when unable to meet a request*'. Khin Khin Kyaw Kyee has identified three objectives of this exercise. Firstly, to generate local support for China's economic and geo-strategic interests in Myanmar; secondly, to promote a Chinese model of governance and economic development and lastly to generate support for the Communist Party of China and its territorial claims in the South China Sea. It remains to be seen how successful these will be.

Visit of President of Myanmar to India (26-29 February 2020)

President U Win Myint paid a quiet visit to India within a month of Xi Jinping's visit to Myanmar. Apparently it came about as Myanmar put in place its foreign policy of strategic balance to hedge against overdependence on China. Timed as it was in the wake of the visit by Trump, the visit saw the signing of 10 MoUs and the issue of a very comprehensive Joint Statement which revealed a number of new initiatives.

That Rakhine features high on India's priority was signified by the presence of the CM of Rakhine State, U Nyi Pu, in the 26-member delegation which included three ministers, namely, U Kyaw Tin, Union Minister for International Cooperation, Thura U Aung Ko, Union Minister for Religious Affairs and Culture, U Thant Sin Maung and Union Minister for Transportation and Communication, U Nyi Pu. In fact four of the 10 MoUs were dedicated for Rakhine State alone and it is assessed that the other MoUs could also benefit Rakhine State. In Rakhine, the MoUs targeted the most violent townships including Buthidaung and Mrauk-U and certain other unnamed townships. Five townships of Rakhine would be electrified using solar power; Mraukk-U Township hospital would have an incinerator constructed; seed storage houses and water supply systems would be implemented in Gwa Township; two roads would be constructed in

Figure 12.5: Townships of Rakhine where Indian MoUs will impact

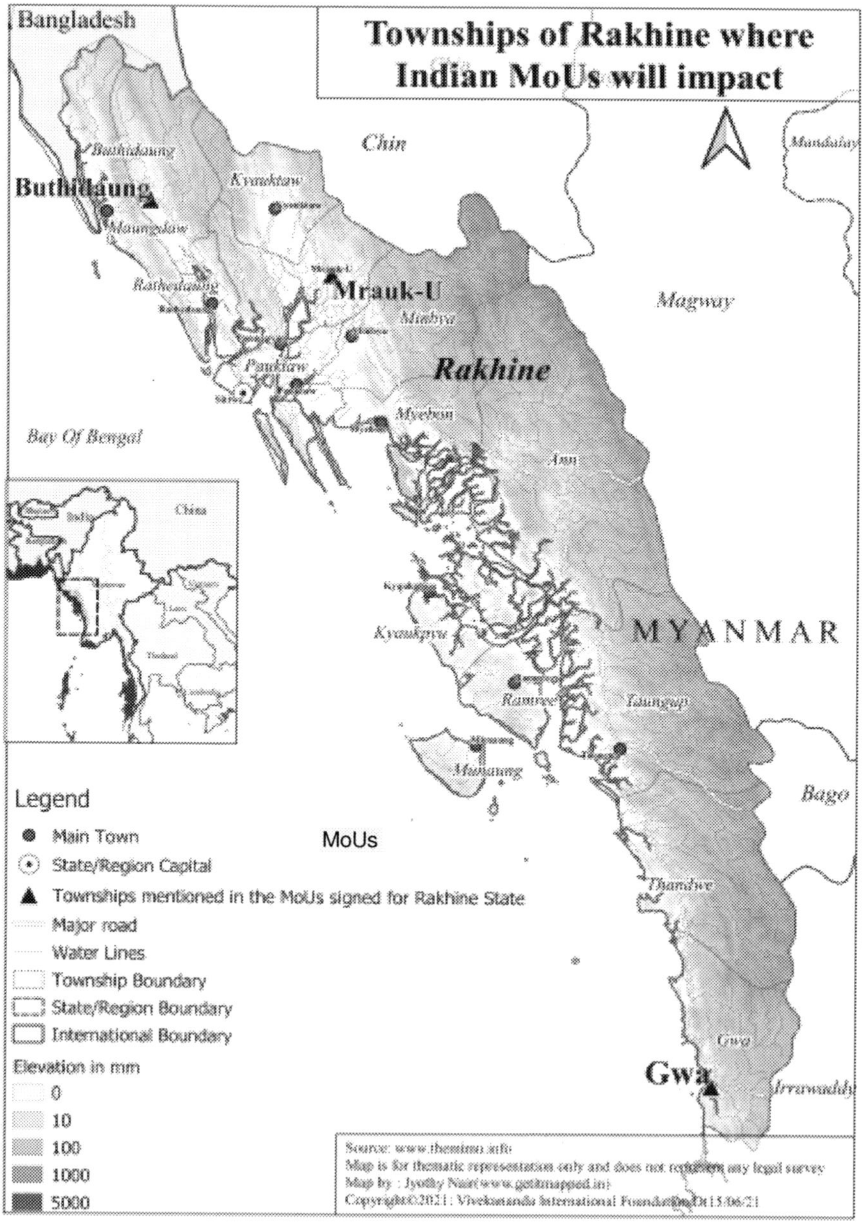

Buthedaung...all these under the Rakhine State Development Programme. Under the Ministry of Social Welfare, Myanmar and the Embassy of India, pre-schools would also be constructed in the State. Currently, two crises are concurrently under way in the state; the Rohingya crisis and the ethnic Rakhine crisis involving the AA which is causing heavy losses to the Myanmar Army and the AA, but most of all to innocent civilians in the crossfire.

Details of all the MoUs are tabulated below:

Table 12.5: MoUs Signed during the Visit of President U Win Myint

Sl.No.	*Nature of Document*	*MoU For*	*Remarks*
		PERTAINING TO RAKHINE STATE	
1.	Project Agreement	Construction of • Incinerator in Mrauk Oo Township hospital • Seed storage houses and water supply systems in Gwa Township	Project Agreements between Rakhine State Government and Embassy of India, Yangon, under Rakhine State Development Programme
2.	Project Agreement	• Distribution of electricity by solar power in five townships of Rakhine State	
3.	Project Agreement	Construction of • Kyawlyaung-Ohlphyu road, • Kyaung Taung-Kyaw Paung road, both in Buthedaung Township	
4.	Project Agreement	Construction of pre-schools in Rakhine State	Project Agreement between Ministry of Social Welfare, Relief and Resettlement and Embassy of India,Yangon
		OTHER PROJECTS	
5.	MoU	Cooperation for Prevention of Trafficking in Persons; Rescue, Recovery, Repatriation and Re-Integration of Victims of Trafficking	
6.	Agreement	Indian Grant Assistance for Implementation of Quick Impact Projects (QIP)	Agreement between the Government of the Republic of India and the Government of the Republic of the Union of Myanmar
7.	MoU	Cooperation on Combating Timber Trafficking, and Conservation of Tigers and other Wildlife	
8.	MoU	Cooperation in the field of Petroleum Products	MoU between India (MoPNG) and Myanmar (Ministry ofElectricity & Energy)

Sl.No.	*Nature of Document*	*MoU For*	*Remarks*
9.	MoU	Cooperation in the field of Communication	MoU between the Ministry of Communications of the Republic of India and the Ministry of Transport & Communications of Myanmar
10.	MoU	Cooperation in the field of Health Research	MoU between Indian Council of Medical Research (ICMR) and Department of Medical Research (DMR), M/o Health & Sports of Myanmar

Source: Embassy of India, Yangon (reorganised by the author).

The Joint Statement revealed a number of initiatives, hitherto unknown. Under the connectivity schemes, the Statement called for early conclusion of the Motor Vehicles Agreement and lauded the launch of the Imphal–Mandalay Bus Service from 1 April 2020; the appointment of a Port Operator for Sittwe Port with effect from 1 February 2020; early completion of the Zorinpui–Paletwa axis was alluded to and Myanmar was thanked for allowing access to the area from Mizoram for induction of labour, plant and material and early completion of the Kaleywa–Yargi segment of the Trilateral Highway. The India-Myanmar Border Area Development Programme was appreciated for development of schools, health centres, bridges and roads. Rakhine too found special mention in the Statement with India dodging the disputed 'Rohingya' word in deference to Myanmar's sentiments, but pushing for repatriation of displaced persons from the Rakhine region, presently located in Cox's Bazaar, thereby leaving no doubt on the intent. The Rakhine State Development Programme was alluded to in the Statement as also in the MoUs. A number of educational projects were mentioned including the Myanmar Institute of Information and Technology (MIIT); the Advanced Centre for Agricultural Research and Education (ACARE); Myanmar-India Industrial Training Centres at Pakokku and Myingyan and establishment of two new ones at Monywa and Thaton and upgradation of the Women's Police Training Centre at Yamethin. In an effort to improve bilateral trade, the launch of the Indian RuPay Card in Myanmar and the creation of an India-Myanmar digital payment gateway for cross-border remittance between the two countries was agreed upon. The Statement also made a mention of the regional sub-groupings, such as BIMSTEC, and called for cooperation on the same. In addition, the Statement touched upon provision of medical radiation equipment "Bhabhatron-2" for treatment of cancer patients; capacity building programmes, exposure visits and lecture series by India for Myanmar civil servants, sportsmen, parliamentarians, judicial and electoral officers and security personnel; the extension of its National

Knowledge Network (NKN) to Myanmar universities; support for the establishment of the Myanmar Diplomatic Academy; provision of technical assistance to the national ID project of Myanmar, based on India's "Aadhaar"; restoration and repair of 12 pagodas in Bagan and cooperation on Solar Power and enhancement of Disaster Resilience. This is not an exhaustive list but only highlights those aspects the author perceives to be lesser known.[71]

Analysis of the Joint Statement between India and Myanmar invariably lends itself to comparison with the Chinese initiatives in Myanmar and the usual off-the-cuff remarks on the stark difference between the two are highlighted in a derogatory manner. This needs to be curbed and there is a lot of sense and merit in the nature of the projects being engaged and their location. Unlike Chinese projects which are all about massive investments and large scales...the Indian initiatives touch the hearts and minds of the locals. This matters, since, for once, they are reassured about the genuine intent of the initiatives, they are targeted at sectors and locations where they are most needed and, most importantly, they do not involve more upheavals or displacement for the locals. The initiatives pitch India's strengths where it matters and it avoids the 'dollar-for-dollar' trap. It works on the basic premise that what is good for the neighbour is good for India. This is especially so since a stable Myanmar means a stable Northeast, which is an essential pre-requisite for a US$ 5 trillion economy that India aspires to be.

Corona Virus

The corona virus has affected Myanmar in five ways. It has cut off Myanmar from China and India with the borders now being sealed; it has caused a paucity of raw material from and finished goods to China, Thailand and India; the closure of markets has resulted in bankruptcy and layoffs, especially in the textile industry; and lastly, the perishable goods industry has been badly affected with surplus stocks rotting, unable to reach the markets.[72]

Overall, while the virus will have a massive negative effect on the economy, the impact on the local population, the bulk of whom have a rural background, will be minimal. This is because subsistence farming is a norm in Myanmar and hence it is unlikely that there will be any starvation-related deaths. Secondly, with the fishery industry faring better than agriculture, the overall impact on the economy may be marginally mitigated by this. The job losses and factory closures is unlikely to be long term, and given that the local population is by and large used to insulation and isolation, they will fare better than their counterparts in the Western countries. India has time and again included Myanmar students in the evacuation from Wuhan and other places which does well for bilateral relations.

India's Options[73]

India remains a safe and preferred alternative to China, in the Myanmar psyche. The reason for this lies in the historical difference between the Indian and Chinese approaches to Myanmar. China's stance has traditionally been aggressive and all-consuming as seen in the way the Chinese Mongols conquered and destroyed the Pagan Kingdom which represented the Golden Age of the Burmese Kingdom. The tributary system that the Chinese emperors imposed on the Burmese kings effectively relegated them to a secondary status within China's Middle Kingdom. This is further reinforced by the way the Nanchao Kingdom destroyed the Pyu city state that led to the eradication of the Pyu as a separate Burmese identity.[74]

This aggression remains an undercurrent even today, as seen in the statements of Ambassador Hong Liang of the Chinese Embassy in Yangon published in the Embassy's Facebook page. He contended that the Myitsone project occupied an important part of the BRI and that any further delay could hamper bilateral relations. He also warned that if the Myitsone issue is not resolved, it would seriously hurt the confidence of Chinese entrepreneurs. Similarly, Mr. Ding Gang, a Senior Editor of *People's Daily* newspaper, noted that though the reasons behind the dam's suspension were very complicated, however, since the deal was signed, Myanmar would be in breach of the contract if it decided to scrap the project and compensation payments would be required. He added that if there were new public demands or environmental concerns, talks should be held and stoking nationalism was not a solution. Hence, how the stalled project is dealt in accordance with international practices would determine Myanmar's investment environment, the government's credibility and the long-term development of the country.[75] Highhandedness and disdain for locals thus forms the hallmark of Chinese investments in Myanmar.

By the above logic, Myanmar should be turning to India and not China to meet its requirements. This has not happened due to India's inability to provide the much-needed investment in Myanmar. The reasons range from lack of political will, an unenviable track record of not fulfilling commitments made due bureaucratic processes and approaches, lack of corporations capable of taking on mega-projects and lack of funds. However, the most important reason is a psychological lack of '*Myanmar consciousness*'. In a nation which needs a dedicated policy to make it look and act 'East', the next step, i.e., to look beyond the eastern borders needs effort. The national psyche is steeped with Pakistan-centricity and now China focus. The latest example of our lack of Myanmar consciousness was displayed by the Fourth Estate, when they completely missed out on the visit of the President of Myanmar to India in the aftermath of Trump's visit amidst the political violence in Delhi. Not that those are not needed; however, they need not be at the cost of Myanmar consciousness. Even without empirical evidence, one can safely say that while there are a large number of China, Pakistan, Afghanistan and other scholars and experts, Myanmar scholars are a mere handful.

Under these circumstances, what then, should be India's vision for Myanmar and what should be the strategy to achieve that vision. Since India's vision for Myanmar is a direct fallout of Myanmar's geo-strategic location, a brief look at the geo-strategic importance of Myanmar for India is called for. Located at the Bangladesh, China and India tri-junction and on the Bay of Bengal rim straddling India's south-eastern land and sea routes, Myanmar shares a 1,643-km border with India touching the four sensitive states of Arunachal Pradesh, Nagaland, Manipur and Mizoram. This translates into India forming 25 per cent (third longest border after China and Thailand) of Myanmar's borders and Myanmar forming 11 per cent (fifth longest border[76] after Bangladesh, China, Pakistan and Nepal) of India's borders. Myanmar, in effect, also acts as a buffer state against China even as its Mergui Archipelago extends from the Malacca Straits into the Andaman Sea close to the Andaman Islands. Myanmar provides access to the South-East Asian landmass from India's Northeast. Economically, natural resources, gas and oil are the major potential areas for cooperation.

India sees Myanmar in the same way as a responsible country looks at its neighbour, i.e., with mutual respect and a sense of cooperation. A stable Myanmar is essential for a stable Northeast India. The security situation in the Northeast is closely linked to the security situation in Myanmar, especially Western Myanmar. Thus the genuine development of Myanmar is a primary vision and the corollary that emerges is that assisting Myanmar will enable it to stand on its feet and reduce dependence on the Chinese thereby improving India's security posture. With this as the broad concept of the vision, the strategy that evolves is documented in the succeeding paragraphs.

Firstly, it should be understood and acknowledged that India's support to Myanmar cannot match the Chinese investments dollar for dollar, neither should it try to. However, given the Indian goodwill in Myanmar, its investments and engagements need to be carried out through the prism of 'hearts and minds'. The concept of 'hearts and minds investments' involves reaching out to the locations and sectors which need investment of smaller scales but in greater numbers. The 'hearts' component involves identifying those areas and fields where investment is scarce and would have maximum impact on the locals without uprooting them from their traditional ways of life. The 'minds' component is to ensure that while meeting the requirements of the heart, the financial viability of projects is not compromised. Thus low but consistent and long-term profits, smaller scales of operations with lesser bureaucratic hurdles would take precedence over mega-projects and provide investment in geographical locations which are otherwise neglected. These investments are those that touch and benefit the common man and not just the local elites and investors.[77]

Ironically, the Chinese approach is also evolving as they execute their OODA loop[78] and come up with solutions to tackle the global wariness towards the BRI. Writes Yun Sun, a Senior Fellow and Co-Director of the East Asia Program and Director of the China Program at the Stimson Centre:

> *The traditional Chinese approach to major infrastructure projects—the provision of Chinese loans and contracts for Chinese companies—faces many obstacles in Myanmar. These obstacles include the bureaucratic setups and public scrutiny to which all foreign investment is subject to, as well as deeply entrenched historical factors and emotional reactions, and long-lasting perceptions and suspicions that are unique to Chinese investment.*
>
> *Contrary to the common perception that the CMEC will bring in massive Chinese financing for infrastructure, the level of investment, the lack of major projects and the incremental nature of project negotiations all suggest that CMEC (either willingly or reluctantly for the Chinese) represents a different type of BRI campaign—one that is based on genuine mutual consultation and Chinese adaptation. Reining in Chinese ambitions so that they align more closely with Myanmar's more moderate aspirations and capacity appears to be a key theme of the CMEC. Ironically, perhaps, this scaled-down version—a kind of "BRI-lite"—may not only better serve the goals of Myanmar's government and people, but also prove to be a model for Chinese-funded development elsewhere.*[79]

Implicit in this statement is that hitherto, Chinese investments in BRI campaigns were NOT based on genuine mutual consultation! Recently, delegates of a think tank in New Delhi heard with amusement and disbelief, their Chinese counterparts from Fudan University frantically and emphatically throw around words like 'soft power' and 'use of local labour' in a discussion on the BRI.[80] This seems to be based on a new strategy where "*development-oriented approach towards conflict resolution has resulted in northern Myanmar's conflicts becoming intrinsic components of China's ambitious Belt and Road Initiative*".[81]

Secondly, the possibility of multi-national joint ventures needs to be considered and pushed by Myanmar and accepted by both China and India rather than traditional bilateral ventures especially between China and Myanmar. A good example runs astride the proposed China Myanmar Economic Corridor, viz., the Myanmar-China Gas Pipeline Project which is jointly invested and constructed by South East Asia Pipeline (SEAP) Company, Myanmar Oil and Gas Enterprise (MOGE), POSCO DAEWOO, ONGC CASPIAN E&P B.V. (OCEBV), Gas Authority of India Limited (GAIL) and Korea Gas Corporation (KOGAS). The South-East Asia Gas Pipeline Company Limited (SEAGP) is responsible for its operation and management.[82] Involvement of multi-national entities brings expertise to the fore and by default induces checks and balances into the systems which tend to neutralize Chinese monopoly and brings objectivity into the projects. In this way Indian investors too have a stake in the activities and the presence of Indian and other investors increases the confidence of Myanmar investors and people. India-driven alliances may provide a reliable alternative source of 'heart and minds investments' using groupings involving BIMSTEC, the India ASEAN networks or even as an alliance with Japan.[83]

Finally, India has no option but to evolve systems to deliver projects on timelines and within the budgeted costs. The implementation of the Kaladaan Multi-Modal Transit Transportation Project is a case in point in that despite over two decades since its commencement, it has not yet been completed. The loss of credibility that India faces across the globe of being unable to deliver on its promises is greatly affecting its stature and aspirations for regional leadership.[84]

In conclusion, the CMEC is far from fructification. Notwithstanding China's protestations, the fact is that hard negotiations, re-negotiations and rescinding of contracts where required will be the new normal in the BRI circuits as has been the case in Myanmar. Chinese strategic concerns cannot take precedence over the strategic concerns of the host nation, despite the volume of investments. It is a strategic imperative for Myanmar to balance development with security and in a traditionally xenophobic country, any perceived affront to sovereignty will raise the hackles of the locals and the Government. Analysts in Myanmar are clear when they say that the CMEC is effectively held in abeyance till the elections, which have been announced[85] to be conducted on 6 November 2020, are completed. This is because Chinese projects are associated with anti-people outcomes such as loss of land, low compensation, loss of employment opportunities and ill treatment by Chinese nationals in Myanmar. Thus, no political organisation in Myanmar, least of all the NLD, would want to touch such a sensitive topic such as this before the elections. It would be electoral fodder for the opposition parties.

India has to implement 'hearts and minds investment' to offset the Chinese impact in Myanmar. It has to ensure that every rupee invested makes a positive impact to the common man especially along the India-Myanmar border. Then, India has to bring in more money to the table by engaging multiple partners from the neighbourhood like the ASEAN, Japan, Korea and even China if required. Thirdly, notwithstanding anything, India has to deliver, and be known to deliver, every time. Only then can it expect to have the credibility of an aspiring regional leader.

But we now need to answer the question that forms the title of this chapter, i.e., *Is the China-Myanmar Economic Corridor actually China's Myanmar Exploitation Corridor?* Like most things in the sphere of international relations, there are no clear and easy answers. The CMEC in the current form provides more benefit to China than it does to Myanmar.[86] Notwithstanding this, Myanmar has shown remarkable spine and appreciably held out against the Chinese debt trap. It has to continue this stand to ensure that the China-Myanmar Economic Corridor does not metamorphose itself into China's Myanmar Exploitation Corridor. The jury is still out on the verdict. What is clear is that the CMEC and the BRI will have to re-invent itself to appear humane and financially and socially viable for the locals. Unless that is done, it remains doomed to stumble along the path of history, possibly into oblivion.

NOTES

1. Robert D. Kaplan, *Monsoon – The Indian Ocean and the Future of American Power,* Random House, New York, 2010, pg. 221.
2. For the full text of the speech, see: https://www.fmprc.gov.cn/mfa_eng/wjdt_665385/zyjh_665391 /t1078088.shtml (Accessed on 3 November 2019).
3. The entire document is available at: http://en.ndrc.gov.cn/newsrelease/201503/t20150330_669367.html (Accessed on 3 November 2019).
4. The six corridors were *The New Eurasia Land Bridge Economic Corridor; The China-Mongolia-Russia Economic Corridor; China-Central Asia-West Asia Economic Corridor; China-Pakistan Economic Corridor; China-Indochina Peninsula Economic Corridor* and the *Bangladesh-China-India-Myanmar Economic Corridor.* http://china-trade-research.hktdc.com/business-news/article/One-Belt-One-Road/The-Belt-and-Road-Initiative/obor/en/1/1X3CGF6L/1X0A36B7.htm (Accessed on 1 December 2019)
5. Organisation for Economic Co-operation and Development, "The Belt and Road Initiative in the global trade, investment and finance landscape", *OECD Business and Finance Outlook 2018,* Pg. 10, Paris: https://www.oecd.org/finance/Chinas-Belt-and-Road-Initiative-in-the-global-trade-investment-and-finance-landscape.pdf (Accessed 3 November 2019).
6. Mainland Southeast Asia, or the Indochina peninsula, is connected to China by land. The transnational transport network of the Greater Mekong Sub-region (GMS), of which Guangxi and Yunnan provinces are members, in combination with the proposed maritime Silk Road that will link major sea ports along the coasts of Vietnam, Cambodia, Thailand and Myanmar, will intensify China-ASEAN trade and industrial co-operation. It will also extend the economic

benefits further afield to South Asia and Western Asia when the new multimodal transportation networks are in place. A detailed report of the CIP EC corridor is available at: https://hkmb.hktdc.com/en/1X0A3UUO/hktdc-research/The-ASEAN-Link-in-China%E2%80%99s-Belt-and-Road-Initiative (Accessed on 3 November 2019).

7. A detailed analysis of India's security considerations have been documented by K. Yhome at "The BCIM economic corridor: Prospects and challenges", *Observer Research Foundation, Commentaries,* February 2017: https://www.orfonline.org/research/the-bcim-economic-corridor-prospects-and-challenges/ (Accessed on 3 November 2019).
8. Mohd. Aminul Karim and Faria Islam, "Bangladesh–China–India–Myanmar (BCIM) Economic Corridor: Challenges and Prospects", *Korean Journal of Defence Analysis* Vol. 30, No. 2, June 2018, 283-302: http://pubs.iclarm.net/resource_centre/ 4258.pdf (Accessed on 3 November 2019).
9. Dr. Puyam Rakesh Singh, "BCIM Economic Corridor and China's New Transportation Channel", *e-pao.net,* 21 September 2019: http://epao.net/epSubPageExtractor.asp?src= leisure.Essays.BCIM_Economic_Corridor_and_China_New_Transportation_ Channel_ By_ Puyam_ Rakesh (Accessed on 1 December 2019).
10. *Global Times* web article, "Backgrounder: Economic corridors under Belt and Road Initiative": http://www.globaltimes.cn/content/1046027.shtml (Accessed on 3 November 2019).
11. Interestingly, the concept of economic corridors first broke ground in the Indochina Peninsula in the 1980s and 1990s through an Asian Development Bank (ADB) project to develop the Greater Mekong Sub-region (GMS) in Southeast Asia. The concept hinged on geographically oriented development by connecting cities, industrial and economic centres using transportation infrastructure supplemented by supporting policies with the aim to transform transportation corridors into economic corridors. Jonathan Hillman, "China's Belt and Road Is Full of Holes", *Centre for Strategic and International Studies Briefs,* September 2018, Washington: http://www.iberchina.org/files/2018-2/bri_holes_csis.pdf (Accessed on 3 November 2019); Stephanie Petrella, "What is An Economic Corridor", *Reconnecting Asia, Analysis, Critical Connections,* 27 March 2018: https://reconnectingasia.csis.org/analysis/entries/what-economic- corridor/ (Accessed on 3 November 2019).
12. Xinhua News Agency, "China-built railway gives new lease of life to East Coast of Peninsula Malaysia", 23 August 2017: https://eng.yidaiyilu.gov.cn/qwyw/rdxw/24494.htm (Accessed on 3 November 2019).
13. Channel News Asia, "China, Malaysia restart East Coast Rail Link project after year-long suspension", 25 July 2019: https://www.channelnewsasia.com/news/asia/china-malaysia-restart-belt-road-east-coast-rail-link-11752570 (Accessed on 3 November 2019).
14. Joint News Release of the People's Republic of China and the Republic of the Union of Myanmar, https://www.fmprc.gov.cn/mfa_eng/topics_665678/jnkzsl70zn/t1294751.shtml (Accessed on 3 November 2019).
15. Joint Press Release Between the People's Republic of China and the Republic of the Union of Myanmar https://www.moi.gov.mm/moi:eng/?q=news/14/11/2018/id-8194 (Accessed on 3 November 2019).
16. For the full text of the speech, see http://www.xinhuanet.com/english/2017-05/14/c_136282982.htm (Accessed on 3 November 2019)
17. Aung Zin Phyo Thein, "The Belt and Road Initiative in Myanmar: staring down the dragon", *Frontier Myanmar,* 2 August 2019: https://frontiermyanmar.net/en/the-belt-and-road-initiative-in-myanmar-staring-down-the-dragon (Accessed 24 November 2019).
18. Thomas Kean, "Myanmar sets a slower pace for the Belt and Road", *Frontier Myanmar,* 25 May 2019: https://frontiermyanmar.net/en/myanmar-sets-a-slower-pace-for- the-belt-and-road. (Accessed on 23 November 2019).

19. https://www.irrawaddy.com/opinion/analysis/second-bri-forum-roundup-how-myanmar-fares.html (Accessed on 1 December 2019).
20. Liu Zhen, "Myanmar eyes China's trade plan for much-needed infrastructure, as crisis in Rakhine goes on", *South China Morning Post,* 6 October 2017: https://www.scmp.com/news/china/diplomacy-defence/article/2114217/myanmar-eyes-belt-and-road-potential- urgent-race (Accessed on 26 November 2019).
21. The 1st Belt and Road Forum was held from 14-15 May 2017 while the 2nd Belt and Road Forum was held on 27 April 2019, both in Beijing. List of Deliverables of the 1st and 2nd Belt and Road Fora for International Cooperation accessed at https://eng.yidaiyilu.gov.cn/qwyw/rdxw/13698.htm and https://eng.yidaiyilu.gov.cn/qwyw/rdxw/88228.htm on 3 November 2019.
22. Jaideep Chanda, "Xi Hajoor! Old Wine in the 'New Era' for Myanmar", *VIF Article,* Vivekananda International Foundation, New Delhi, 22 January 2020. https://www.vifindia.org/article/2020/january/22/xi-hajoor-old-wine-in-the-new-era-for-myanmar (Accessed on 25 February 2020).
23. China.org.cn web article, 'Full text of Xi's signed article on Myanmese (sic) newspapers', 16 January 2020: http://www.china.org.cn/world/2020-01/16/content_75619897.htm (Accessed on 18 January 2020).
24. http://www.xinhuanet.com/english/2018-11/08/c_137592850.htm (Accessed on 13 March 2020).
25. For example, Khin Khin Kyaw Kyee in "Finding Peace along the China Myanmar Economic Corridor: Between Short-term Interests and Long-lasting Peace", *Institute for Strategy and Policy – Myanmar, China Research Project,* Working Paper No. 3, December 2018.
26. U Myint, "Myanmar: Going from Pause to Fast Forward with China's Belt and Road Initiative (BRI)", *Republic of the Union of Myanmar Federation of Chambers of Commerce and Industry (UMFCCI), Centennial Magazine,* 30 July 2019:https://myanmarcesd.org/myanmar-going-from-pause-to-fast-forward-with-chinas-belt-and-road-initiative/ pg. 1. (Accessed on 1 December 2019).
27. Sutirtho Patranobis, "Too close for comfort: China to build port in Myanmar, 3rd in India's vicinity", *Hindustan Times,* 9 November 2018, New Delhi: https://www.hindustantimes.com/india-news/china-myanmar-ink-deal-for-port-on-bay-of-bengal-third-in-india-s-vicinity/story-Lbm4IwOMuqrNvXGv4ewuYJ.html (Accessed on 13 March 2020).
28. CITIC Group Corporation Ltd. was formerly the China International Trust Investment Corporation and is a state-owned investment company of the People's Republic of China. Headquartered at Chaoyang District, Beijing, it was established in 1979 with the approval of Deng Xiaoping.
29. The Consortium comprises China Harbour Engineering Company (CHEC), China Merchants Holdings (International) Company (CMHI), TEDA Investment Holding (TEDA), Yunnan Construction Engineering Group (YNJG) and Charoen Pokphand Group Company Limited (CP Group) from Thailand.
30. Jaideep Chanda, "Myanmar Round Up: January 2020", *VIF Article,* Vivekananda International Foundation, New Delhi, 14 February 2020. https://www.vifindia.org/article/2020/february/14/myanmar-round-up-january-2020 (Accessed on 13 March 2020).
31. Interview of Sean Turnell by Nan Lwin, "Suu Kyi Economic Adviser: National Interest Must Come First When Deciding Large Chinese Investments in Myanmar", The *Irrawaddy,* In Person, 20 January 2020: https://www.irrawaddy.com/in-person/suu-kyi-economic-adviser-national-interest-must-come-first-when-deciding-large-chinese-investments-in-myanmar.html (Accessed on 12 March 2020).
32. The initial MoUs had been signed on 9 September 2018. https://www.irrawaddy.com/news/myanmar-set-ink-pact-china-border-cooperation-zones.html and https://www.irrawaddy.com/

business/govt-approves-sites-3-new-economic-zones-along-china-border.html (Accessed on 13 March 2020).

33. https://www.vifindia.org/article/2019/november/21/myanmar-round-up-october-2019 (Accessed on 15 March 2020).
34. For a detailed analysis of the Muse-Mandalay project and the Kyaukphyu Special Economic Zone Deep Sea Port, see the Sandhi Governance Institute Report, *Monitoring Report of Selected PPPs in Myanmar,* August 2019, https://sandhimyanmar.org/index.php/2019/09/10/monitoring-report-of-selected-ppps-in-myanmar/(Accessed on 1 August 2020).
35. Amara Thiha, "Can Myanmar Afford China's Belt and Road?", *The Diplomat, ASEAN Beat,* 29 August 2018: https://thediplomat.com/2018/08/can-myanmar-afford-chinas-belt-and-road/ (Accessed on 23 November 2019).
36. Nan Lwin, "China's Six Belt and Road Projects in Myanmar to Watch in 2019", *The Irrawaddy,* 24 January 2019: https://www.irrawaddy.com/specials/chinas-six-belt-road-projects-myanmar-watch-2019.html (Accessed on 25 November 2019).
37. The lack of details of the projects comprising the CMEC and other BRI projects in Myanmar even plagues established researchers of noted think tanks in Myanmar. Seepages 2 & 5 of Khin Khin Kyaw Kyee's "Finding Peace along the China Myanmar Economic Corridor: Between Short-term Interests and Long-lasting Peace", *Institute for Strategy and Policy – Myanmar, China Research Project, Working Paper No. 3,* December 2018.
38. These include: https://www.irrawaddy.com/specials/chinas-six-belt-road-projects-myanmar-watch-2019.html, https://www.sundayguardianlive.com/opinion/watch-kyaukpyu-port-china-myanmar-economic-corridor,https://thediplomat.com/2018/08/can-myanmar-afford-chinas-belt-and-road/; https://thediplomat.com/2018/12/myanmar-speeds-up-progress-on-chinas-belt-and-road/amongst others. (All accessed on 15 March 2020).
39. See page 7 of Khin Khin Kyaw Kyee's "Finding Peace along the China Myanmar Economic Corridor: Between Short-term Interests and Long-lasting Peace", *Institute for Strategy and Policy – Myanmar, China Research Project,* Working Paper No. 3, December 2018.
40. The 771-kilometre long pipeline extends from Madè Island on the west coast of Myanmar to Ruili in the south-western Chinese province of Yunnan, running through Rakhine State, Magwe Region, Mandalay Region, and Shan State. The pipeline is 813 mm in diameter and is able to deliver 12Mt/a upon completion of Phase I and 22Mt/a upon completion of Phase II, with a total annual delivery of 2 million tons to Myanmar. A 300,000-ton crude oil terminal has been built with an annual capacity of 22 million tons. On April 10, 2017, the Myanmar-China Crude Pipeline project was officially put into operation.
41. The Myanmar-China Gas Pipeline starts at Ramree Island on the western coast of Myanmar and ends at Ruili in China's Yunnan Province Running parallel to the Myanmar-China Crude Oil Pipeline, the crude pipeline is 1,016 mm in diameter with a distance of 793 km in Myanmar. It can deliver 5.2 billion m3 per year upon completion of Phase I, and 12 billion m3 per year upon completion of Phase II. Pursuant to the cooperation agreement, four gas off-take stations (Kyaukphyu, Yenangyaung, Taungtha and Mandalay) were established to unload less than 20% of the pipeline's total delivery in Myanmar. On July 28, 2013, the Myanmar-China Gas Pipeline became operational and started to deliver natural gas to the Myanmar market through its off-take stations.
42. For a detailed understanding of the controlling hierarchy of the pipelines, see China National Petroleum Corporation web article "Overview of the Myanmar-China Oil and Gas Pipelines", at https://www.cnpc.com.cn/en/myanmarcsr/201407/f115a1cc6cdb4700b55def91a0d11d03/files/dec09c5452ec4d2ba36ee33a8efd4314.pdf (Accessed on 3 November 2019).
43. CEIC Data, "China Natural Gas: Imports": https://www.ceicdata.com/en/indicator/china/natural-gas-imports (Accessed on 3 November 2019).
44. Erica Downs, Mikkal E. Herberg, Michael Kugelman, Christopher Len and Kaho Yu, "Asia's

energy security and China's Belt and Road Initiative", *The National Bureau of Asian Research*, NBR Special Report #68, November 2017, Washington: https://www.nbr.org/publication/asias-energy-security-and-chinas-belt-and-road-initiative/ (Accessed on 3 November 2017).

45. China Oil and Gas, web article on Export.gov, https://www.export.gov/article?id=China-Oil-and-Gas (Accessed on 3 November 2019). (Accessed on 23 November 2019).
46. https://www.rfa.org/english/news/myanmar/pipeline-04052019141852.html (Accessed on 26 November 2019).
47. Nicholas Lo, "China builds in Myanmar's conflict areas", *www.thethirdpole.net,* 26 November 2019: https://www.thethirdpole.net/en/2019/11/26/china-builds-in-myanmars-conflict-areas/ (Accessed on 26 November 2019).
48. Myanmar-China Oil & Gas Pipeline Project (Myanmar Section) "Special Report on Social Responsibility": http://csr.cnpc.com.cn/cnpccsr/xhtml/PageAssets/mdbg2016-en.pdf (Accessed on 3 November 2019).
49. Nan Lwin, 'Deal to Be Signed for BRI-Related Economic Zone in Myanmar's Kachin State', *The Irrawaddy* Web Article, 7 October 2019,https://www.irrawaddy.com/news/burma/deal-signed-bri-related-economic-zone-myanmars-kachin-state.html (Accessed on 30 June 2020).
50. Aakriti Vinayak, Alakh Ranjan & Jaideep Chanda, *Myanmar Round Up:* October 2019, Vivekananda International Foundation Web Article, 21, November 2019, https://www.vifindia.org/article/2019/november/21/myanmar-round-up-october-2019(Accessed on 30 June 2020).
51. Nan Lwin, 'Kachin Locals in the Dark Over China-Backed Industrial Zone Plan', *The Irrawaddy* Web Article, 9 April 2019, https://www.irrawaddy.com/news/burma/kachin-locals-dark-china-backed-industrial-zone-plan.html (Accessed on 30 June 2020).
52. https://www.irrawaddy.com/news/burma/kachin-state-approves-chinese-backed-business-park-border-town.html (Accessed on 15 March 2020).
53. Myo Pa Pa San, "Ongoing Fighting Decimates Myanmar-China Border Trade", *The Irrawaddy,* 28 August 2019: https://www.irrawaddy.com/news/burma/ongoing-fighting-decimates-myanmar-china-border-trade.html (Accessed on 1 December 2019).
54. https://economictimes.indiatimes.com/news/international/world-news/myanmar-continues-pushback-against-bri-chinese-eco-development-zone-faces-turbulence/articleshow/77364893.cms?UTM_Source=Google_Newsstand&UTM_Campaign=RSS_Feed&UTM_Medium=Referral (Accessed on 7 August 2020).
55. Sandhi Governance Institute, *Public Private Partnership Monitor: Case Study of the Myitkyina Economic Development Zone Project,* Yangon, November 2019: https://sandhimyanmar.org/index.php/2020/03/23/ppp-monitoring-report/ (Accessed on 7 August 2020).
56. Sandhi Governance Institute, *Public-Private Partnership Monitoring in Myanmar: The New Yangon City Project,* March 2020,https://sandhimyanmar.org/index.php/2020/06/25/3rd-ppp-monitoring-in-myanmar-the-new-yangon-city-project/ (Accessed on 7 August 2020).
57. A Swiss Challenge method of bidding is often used in public projects in which a government initiates a proposal for a bid for a project. The government publishes the bid in the public domain and invites proposals from others interested in executing it. On receipt of these bids, the original contractor gets an opportunity to match the best bid. The advantage over the conventional method of bidding is that it encourages private sector participation in government projects and obviates frivolous bids which are unrealistically low. See https://www.adb.org/sites/default/files/institutional-document/31313/ppp-swiss-challenge-route.pdf and https://www.ikigailaw.com/swiss-challenge-model-an-overview/#acceptLicense (Accessed on 15 August 2020).
58. The 3-square-kilometre industrial zone is part of the government's urgent plan to create job opportunities for migrant labourers who have returned home from overseas amid the COVID-19 pandemic.

59. https://www.irrawaddy.com/news/burma/myanmars-union-govt-splits-huge-china-backed-new-yangon-city-project.html
60. See https://www.csis.org/analysis/china-pakistan-economic-corridor-five and https://theprint.in/opinion/cpec-is-china-pakistan-corruption-corridor-this-challenges-indian-security-in-new-ways/437329/ (Accessed on 15 August 2020).
61. "The Hambantota Port fiasco is considered the best example of the end result of the Chinese debt trap. A detailed report on how it unfolded is available at Maria Abi-Habib's "How China Got Sri Lanka to Cough Up a Port", *The New York Times,* 25 June 2018: https://www.nytimes.com/2018/06/25/world/asia/china-sri-lanka-port.html (Accessed on 30 November 2019). The long-term effects of public debt in the case of Sri Lanka is covered in detail in Panos Mourdoukoutas's, "China Could Spoil Sri Lanka's Chance To Become A Breakout Nation Again", *Forbes,* 20 September 2018, https://www.forbes.com/sites/panosmourdoukoutas/2018/09/20/china-could-spoil-sri-lankas-chance-to-become-a-break-out-nation-again/#72b567b85889 (Accessed on 30 November 2019).
62. *Global Times* web article, "China, Myanmar to sign MOU on Economic Corridor in 2018", 26 June 2018: http://www.globaltimes.cn/content/1108472.shtml (Accessed on 3 November 2019).
63. Xinhua Net, "Spotlight: China-Myanmar oil, gas project benefits both", 10 May 2017: http://www.xinhuanet.com/english/2017-05/10/c_136272395.htm. (Accessed on 23 November 2019).
64. "Myanmar scales back China-funded Kyauk Pyu port project in Rakhine state due to debt concerns", *South China Morning Post,* 2 August 2018: https://www.scmp.com/news/asia/southeast-asia/article/2158015/myanmar-scales-back-china-funded-kyauk-pyu-port-project (Accessed on 30 November 2019).
65. Chan Mya Twe, "Five-year plan for BRI projects in Myanmar", *Myanmar Times,* 27 September 2019: https://www.mmtimes.com/news/five-year-plan-bri-projects-myanmar.html. (Accessed on 23 November 2019).
66. Brook Larmer, "What the World's Emptiest International Airport Says About China's Influence", *The New York Times Magazine,* 13 September 2019, https://www.nytimes.com/2017/09/13/magazine/what-the-worlds-emptiest-international-airport-says-about-chinas-influence.html?smid=tw-share (Accessed on 1 December 2019).
67. *News First,* Lanka "Hambantota port deal will be renegotiated – President Gotabaya Rajapaksa" https://www.newsfirst.lk/2019/11/25/hambantota-port-deal-was-a-mistake-president-gotabaya-rajapaksa/ (Accessed on 1 December 2019).
68. Cissy Zhou, "China slimming down Belt and Road Initiative as new project value plunges in last 18 months, report shows", *South China Morning Post,* 10 October 2019: https://www.scmp.com/economy/global-economy/article/3032375/china-slimming-down-belt-and-road-initiative-new-project (Accessed on 1 December 2019).
69. U Myint, pg. 3.
70. Khin Khin Kyaw Kyee, "China's Multi-layered Engagement Strategy and Myanmar's Reality: The Best Fit for Beijing's Preferences", *Institute for Strategy and Policy – Myanmar, China Research Project,* Working Paper No. 1, February 2018: https://www.ispmyanmar.com/2018/02/28/chinas-multi-layered-engagement-strategy-and-myanmars-realities-the-best-fit-for-beijing-policy-preferences/ (Accessed on 23 November 2019).
71. For details of the Joint Statement, see 'Raising Myanmar Consciousness: Visit of the President of Myanmar to India (26-29 February 2020), by this author. https://www.vifindia.org/article/2020/february/28/raising-myanmar-consciousness-visit-of-the-president-of-myanmar-to-india (Accessed on 15 March 2020).
72. Please see,

https://www.thestar.com.my/news/regional/2020/03/12/covid-19-india-cancels-almost-all-visas-closes-myanmar-border,
https://www.mmtimes.com/news/muses-melon-exports-severely-hit-virus-outbreak.html
https://www.mmtimes.com/news/fisheries-exports-not-badly-hit-agriculture-virus.html
https://www.mmtimes.com/news/chinese-garment-factory-yangon-goes-bankrupt.html
https://elevenmyanmar.com/news/more-than-1000-garment-workers-out-of-job-due-to-factory-closure
http://www.mizzima.com/article/coronavirus-affecting-myanmar-factory-production
https://www.irrawaddy.com/news/burma/11-factories-myanmar-close-due-lack-orders-raw-materials.html
(All accessed on 15 March 2020).

73. Parts of this portion have been published by the author in his article on the visit of Xi Jinping to Myanmar, on the VIF Website: https://www.vifindia.org/article/2020/january/22/xi-hajoor-old-wine-in-the-new-era-for-myanmar.
74. Preet Malik, "My Myanmar Years: A Diplomat's Account of India's Relations with the Region', pg. 27, *Sage Publications* 2016, India.
75. U Myint, pg. 3.
76. https://mha.gov.in/sites/default/files/BMIntro-1011.pdf
77. https://www.vifindia.org/article/2020/january/22/xi-hajoor-old-wine-in-the-new-era-for-myanmar
78. The OODA Loop (Observe, Orient, Decide, Act) is a four-step approach to decision-making that focuses on filtering available information, putting it in context and quickly making the most appropriate decision while also understanding that changes can be made as more data becomes available. https://searchcio.techtarget.com/definition/OODA-loop (Accessed on 1 December 2019).
79. Yun Sun, "Slower, smaller, cheaper: the reality of the China-Myanmar Economic Corridor", *Frontier Myanmar,* 26 September 2019: https://www.frontiermyanmar.net/en/slower-smaller-cheaper-the-reality-of-the-china-myanmar-economic-corridor (Accessed 1 December 2019).
80. During a Round Table Discussion at the Vivekananda International Foundation.
81. Yun Sun, "Peace through development: China's experiment in Myanmar", *Frontier Myanmar,* 15 October 2019, https://frontiermyanmar.net/en/peace-through-development-chinas-experiment-in-myanmar (Accessed on 1 December 2019).
82. Myanmar-China Oil & Gas Pipeline Project (Myanmar Section) "Special Report on Social Responsibility": http://csr.cnpc.com.cn/cnpccsr/xhtml/PageAssets/mdbg2016-en.pdf (Accessed on 3 November 2019).
83. For a comprehensive paper on India's options for response to the BRI, see Darshana Barua's "India's Answer to the Belt and Road: A Road Map for South Asia", Carnegie India Working Paper, August 2018: https://carnegieendowment.org/files/WP_Darshana_Baruah_ Belt_ Road_ FINAL.pdf (Accessed on 1 December 2019).
84. Chanda, Footnote 22.
85. Al Jazeera News, *Myanmar sets November 8 date for general election,* https://www.aljazeera.com/news/2020/07/myanmar-sets-november-8-date-general-election-200702033020917.html (Accessed on 12 July 2020).
86. Soe Myint, "Level Playing Field?", *Mizzima Weekly,* 5 December 2019.

CHAPTER 13

The Cultural Connects and Beyond[1]

Some of the finest post-Gupta art specimens have been located in Arakan.

—**Prof. Dilip K. Chakravarti**[2]

The lines of the nostalgic song *Mere Pia Gaye Rangoon*[3] draws instant recall of a bygone era which connected Burma to the then romantic Himalayan foothills of Dehra Doon:

Hum Burma ki galiyon main,
Aur tum ho Dehra Doon,
Tumhari yaad satati hain,
Tumhari yaad satati hain,
Jiya main aag lagati hain!

This song lives on in a remixed avatar for the younger generations to identify with. However, India-Myanmar relations have connections that include the cultural and those that go beyond an occasional song in an old movie. The colonial years saw the advent of the Chettiars and other Indians into Burma and slowly dominate society before finally being victimised out of the country *en masse* at great detriment to both the community and the country. It also saw the banishment of their respective leaders, viz., Bahadur Shah Zafar and Thibaw to Rangoon and Ratnagiri, respectively. The linkages continued through the struggle for Independence and till much after. The presence of Bodh Gaya and other Buddhist pilgrimage sites in India makes India a vital link for Buddhist Myanmar. This chapter looks at these connections and pushes for exploiting these linkages to enhance people-to-people interactions between the two nations.

Dr. Arpita Mitra, Research Fellow at the VIF and an expert on Swami Vivekananda, Sister Nivedita and Indian history and culture writes[4] that Myanmar, whose appellations have been numerous in ancient India,[5] was always a civilizational ally of *Bharatavarsha*, despite the fact that it was geographically and ethnically closer to Indonesia and other Southeast Asian countries. Right from the spread of Buddhism and also Hinduism to Myanmar in ancient times, to the annexation of Burma into the British Indian Empire in modern times, the two countries have had a thriving relationship.

Early Connections

Prof. Dilip Chakravarti[6] describes the early connections with Myanmar when he writes:

> *The evidence of historic settlements comes from the Kaladan and Lemro river valleys of north Arakan, where the strip of land containing old settlements is said to be about 60 km long (north-south) and 15-35 km (east-west) wide. There is a delta criss-crossed by inlets and estuaries, with the port of Akyab (Sittwe) occupying a position in the corner. Another point to remember about the Arakan is that it is basically an extended part of the Chittagong coast. Considering the proximity of the Kaladan and Lemro valleys near Chittagong; one considers it unlikely that the history of Arakan was ever separate from the history of the area on the Chittagong side. The encouragement which the Bengali language and literature received from the kings of Arakan in the Islamic period is one the testimonies in this direction.*

He thereafter goes on to describe how Narameikhla, an Arakanese king, sought shelter in the court of the Bengal sultans in their capital, Gaur,[7] in the 1430s and regained control of his capital, Mrauk-U, with military assistance from the Bengal Sultan. For a century post this event, the Arakan remained a vassal of the Bengali Sultanate. Chittagong was under Arakan rule in approximately the mid-16th century.

The second son of Shah Jahan, Mughal Prince Shuja, fled to Arakan around 1660 after being defeated in the succession battle to the Mughal throne. He apparently sought refuge with the King of Arakan, better known as the Pirate King, King Sanda Thudama. During his escape he stayed at Dhaka before taking a ship to Chittagong, and then by road to Mrohaung (present-day Mrauk-U) south of the Naf River which was the court of the king. The entourage from Chittagong to Mrohaung was said to include 1,000 palanquins which carried the ladies of his court. The road to Cox's Bazar and Teknaf is still referred to as Shuja Road, and the area behind Kolatoli Beach in Cox's Bazar is known as "Palongki Beach", as this was where the thousand palanquins encamped.[8]

Two Bengali literary figures, Pandit Kabi Syed Alaol (1607-1673) and Daulat Qazi (approximately 1600–1638) were based in the Arakan court even as Bengali language and culture was very much in vogue during that time in Arakan. This further reinforces the connect that the Arakan region had with Bengal, i.e., Bangladesh.

Arakan came under Indic influences from the ancient kingdoms of the Ganges delta in the Indian subcontinent. It was one of the first regions in Southeast Asia to adopt Dharmic religions and became an Indianized kingdoms in Southeast Asia. Buddhism in the Mauryan Empire spread through Arakan to other regions of Southeast Asia. Based on the evidence of Sanskrit inscriptions found in the region, historians believe that the founders of the first Arakanese state were Indian.[9]

The Reciprocal Exiles

Possibly the most symbolic example of the colonial connects is that of Bahadur Shah Zafar, the last Mughal Emperor and the last sovereign Burmese king, Thibaw Min, who were in a sense reciprocally exiled to each other's country. Emperor Bahadur Shah Zafar (also known as Aboo Zafar) ascended to the Mughal throne in 1837 at the age of 62. He succeeded his father, Emperor Akbar Shah II. He was known for his poetry, artistry and as a patron of art, language and poetry and the two most revered personalities in his court, in the field of art and poetry were Ibrahim Zauq and Mirza Ghalib. He had been Emperor for 20 years when the First War of Independence of 1857 took place, culminating in the final British clampdown on Mughal rule. Red Fort was captured on 19 September 1857, and on 21September, Bahadur Shah Zafar surrendered on the condition that his life and that of his wife, Zinat Mahal, be spared. His two sons, Mirza Mughal, Mirza Khizr Sultan and his grandson, Mirza Abu Bakr, were shot in cold blood by the British for having participated in the insurrection. On 27 January 1858, the trial of Bahadur Shah Zafar on charges of rebellion, treason and murder, commenced at the Red Fort. Two months later, he was convicted and sentenced to be exiled to a place to be decided by the Governor General in Council. Bahadur Shah Zafar was first sent to Allahabad and then to Calcutta accompanied by his wife, Zinat Mahal, and their two other sons, Mirza Jawan Bakht and Mirza Shah Abbas. On 4 December 1858 Zafar, along with his family, was transported from Diamond Harbour to Rangoon onboard the '*Magoera*,' and reached there on 10 December 1858. Initially housed in tents and later shifted to a building, the old ruler generally sat in the veranda in the upper storey gazing at passers-by and the ships. Pen, ink and paper were prohibited and even the public was not allowed to meet them.

Servants could enter using a daily pass issued by the European staff in charge. Bahadur Shah Zafar was 83 years old when he arrived in Rangoon and 87 when he developed paralysis in the throat region and finally succumbed to it on 7 November 1862.[10] He was buried in an anonymous grave which was accidentally discovered in February 1991 when workers were digging for a drain and chanced upon a inscribed brick structure. This helped revive his place in history as an Urdu poet and a Sufi saint. The grave was later renovated with the help of public donations. and eventually upgraded to a dargah and inaugurated on 15 December 1994.[11]

Figure 13.1: Plaque describing the discovery of the tomb of Bahadur Shah Zafar at his Dargah

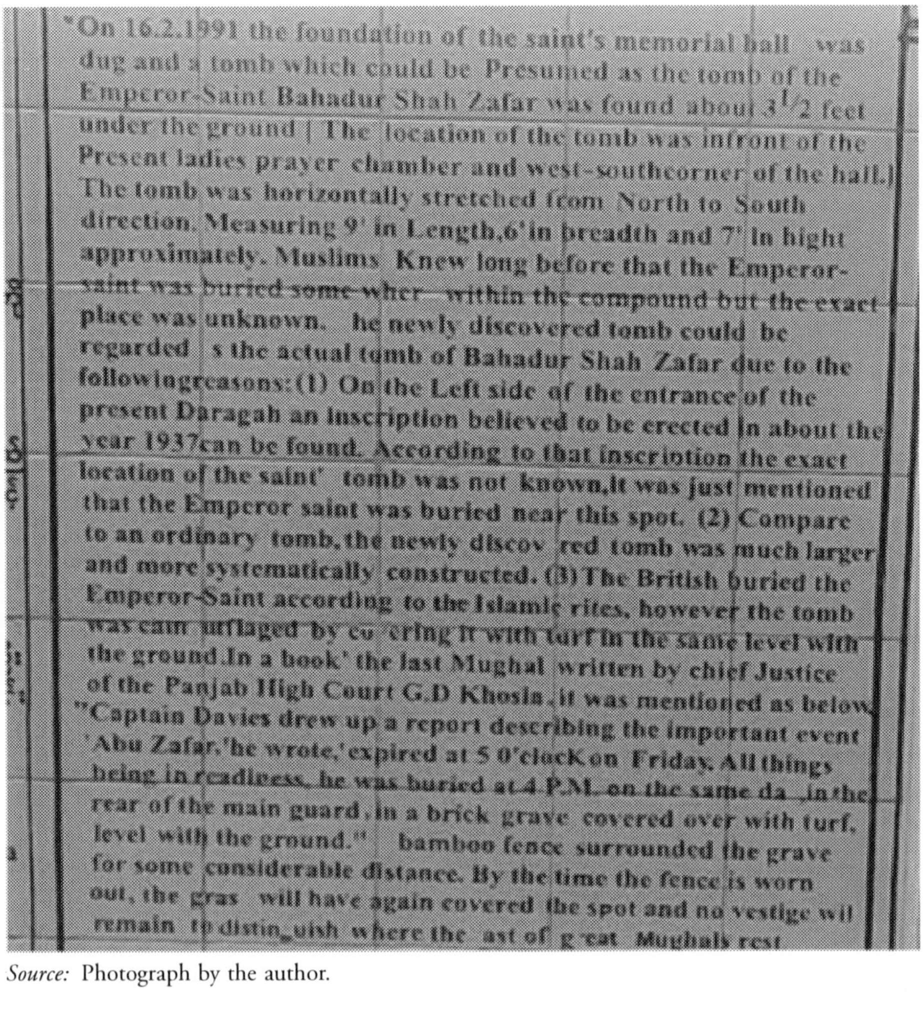

"On 16.2.1991 the foundation of the saint's memorial hall was dug and a tomb which could be Presumed as the tomb of the Emperor-Saint Bahadur Shah Zafar was found about 3 1/2 feet under the ground [The location of the tomb was infront of the Present ladies prayer chamber and west-southcorner of the hall.] The tomb was horizontally stretched from North to South direction. Measuring 9' in Length,6'in breadth and 7' In hight approximately. Muslims Knew long before that the Emperor-saint was buried some wher within the compound but the exact place was unknown. he newly discovered tomb could be regarded s the actual tomb of Bahadur Shah Zafar due to the followingreasons:(1) On the Left side of the entrance of the present Daragah an inscription believed to be erected in about the year 1937can be found. According to that inscriotion the exact location of the saint' tomb was not known,it was just mentioned that the Emperor saint was buried near this spot. (2) Compare to an ordinary tomb,the newly discov red tomb was much larger and more systematically constructed. (3) The British buried the Emperor-Saint according to the Islamic rites, however the tomb was cam urflaged by co ering it with turf in the same level with the ground.In a book' the last Mughal written by chief Justice of the Panjab High Court G.D Khosla ,it was mentioned as below "Captain Davies drew up a report describing the important event 'Abu Zafar,'he wrote,'expired at 5 0'clocK on Friday. All things being in readiness, he was buried at 4 P.M. on the same da ,in the rear of the main guard, in a brick grave covered over with turf, level with the ground." bamboo fence surrounded the grave for some considerable distance. By the time the fence is worn out, the gras will have again covered the spot and no vestige wil remain to distin uish where the ast of g eat Mughals rest

Source: Photograph by the author.

King Thibaw Min of the Konbaung Dynasty was the last Burmese king who reigned from 1878 to 1885 before he was ousted by the British following his defeat in the Third Anglo-Burmese War on 29 November 1885. Born in the then capital, Mandalay, on 1 January 1859 to King Mindon and his consort, Laungshe Mibaya, Thibaw, the 41st son of King Mindon, was married to his half-sister Supayalat. After the defeat, the question of what to do with the King and Queen who were still very popular arose. Exile was the preferred option for the British as the last king of Sri Lanka had been exiled to Vellore and Bahadur Shah Zafar to Rangoon. Accordingly King Thibaw, Queen Supalayat and their four daughters were exiled to Ratnagiri, coastal Maharashtra, in April 1886.

A 30 room palace was built by the British Government in 1910 to keep the former king of '*Brahmadesh*' under house arrest. The palace was a beautifully constructed three-storied structure with sloping roofs. Semi-circular wooden windows with beautiful carvings were the main attraction of this structure. There was a dancing hall with a marble floor on the first floor. Under dire financial constraints, King Thibaw apparently had to sell his Burmese rubies to subsist. He died a sad and lonely death on 19 December 1916 at the age of 58, possibly due to the grief over the loss of his kingdom and the strain of exile. Post his demise, the surviving family returned to Burma in 1919 with the exception of one daughter who had married a palace staff.

Presently, the palace has been converted into a museum where some of the things used by King Thibaw are still preserved. An idol of Buddha brought to India by King Thibaw is installed behind the palace. One gets a view of Someshwar Creek, Bhatye Bridge and the Arabian Sea from the palace as also beautiful sunsets.[12] Myanmar for the first time acknowledged its former king only in 2012 after democratic rule was established and President Thein Sein visited Ratnagiri to pay his tribute at King Thibaw's grave.[13] Sudha Shah has meticulously researched the King's 30 years in exile and published a book '*The King in Exile: The Fall of the Royal Family of Burma*' for which she was awarded a medal by the Commander-in-Chief of the Myanmar Armed Forces.[14]

Politics and Prisoners

Ratnagiri, home to King Thibaw till his death, has another Myanmar connect. Its most famous son, Keshav Gangadhar Tilak, better known as Lokmanya Bal Gangadhar Tilak, who gave the clarion call for *Swarajya* (Self Rule), was incarcerated in Mandalay Jail for six years from 1908 to 1914 by the British. It was here that he penned the 400-page classic *Shrimadh Bhagvad Gita Rahasya*, a commentary on *Karma Yoga,* as alluded to in the *Bhagvad Gita.* On 1 August 2020, the Consulate General of India in Mandalay organized an event to mark the 100th death anniversary of Lokmanya Bal Gangadhar Tilak. H.E. U Sai Pang Saing, Hon'ble Minister for Shan Ethnic Affairs, Mandalay Region Government, and Consul General Neeraj Kumar jointly inaugurated a portrait of Lokmanya Tilak and a marble plaque dedicated to his time in the Mandalay prison.[15] From the 1920s onwards, Burma had become the site of radical political activities of the Bengali revolutionaries including in the Burmese jails, where many Indian freedom fighters had been incarcerated. Netaji Subhash Chandra Bose was incarcerated here[16] from 1924 to 1927 and his contracting tuberculosis is attributed to his stay here.

Bengalis seemed to have a strong affinity with Burma. The Nobel Laureate Guru Rabindranath Thakur visited Burma in 1916, 1924 and 1927 and was always accorded a warm reception in the country. Thakin Ba Tin, a founding member of the Communist Party of Burma, was in fact Harinarayan Ghoshal, a Burmese of Bengali origin. He was followed by Dr. Amar Nag, alias Yebaw Tun Maung or U Hla. The former was a towering personality and the author of the Ghoshal Doctrine which led the Communist Party of Burma into armed struggle.[17] Both eventually died violent deaths with Ghoshal being assassinated in an intra-party rivalry and Nag killed in an ambush. Even the Cultural Centre at the Embassy of India is called the Swami Vivekananda Cultural Centre which conducts classes in yoga, Hindi and Bharata Natyam (Kalakshetra style), Indian folk dance and Carnatic vocal.

Tatmadaw too has a historic Indian connection. The family home of Wunna Kyaw Htin aka Mr. Dina Nath, Chairman of the Indian Independence Army for Burma and his wife, Caroline Nath, was used as the first headquarters of the Burmese Independence Army.[18] Dina Nath offered General Aung San the use of a room upstairs and that room still contains some of his original artefacts. He also helped organize secret meetings between Aung San and various Burmese and Indian leaders at his house during the independence struggle. Netaji Subhash Chandra Bose also stayed at the Nath Villa when he visited Rangoon to hold talks with Aung San.[19] The property is now better known as a heritage restaurant, The House of Memories.[20]

The India-Myanmar connect has an unlikely heroine in Dr. S. I. Padmavati, India's first female cardiologist. Dr. Padmavati was born in Rangoon in 1917 and completed her MBBS degree from Rangoon Medical College. Her family moved to India to escape the Japanese invasion of Burma and she then went to the UK

Figure 13.2: The room which General Aung San used as his first headquarters

Source: Author.

for higher studies and became a Fellow of both the Royal College of Physicians in London and Edinburgh. She is still a practising cardiologist at the age of 103. For her immense contribution to cardiology, Dr. Padmavati was awarded a Padma Bhushan in 1967 and a Padma Vibhushan in 1992.[21]

Cultural Connects

Close to 90 per cent of the people in Myanmar today are Buddhists. Myanmar is one of the major countries following Theravada Buddhism (the other two being Sri Lanka and Thailand), the older form of Buddhism, which gradually disappeared from India due to the later rise of Mahayana and Vajrayana Buddhism. Myanmar was the host for the Sixth Buddhist Council held in Yangon between 1954 and 1956. Theravada Buddhism is as central to the Burmese identity as it is to Sinhalese national identity. Burma has a national chronicle, the *Sasanavamsa*[22] which presents the history of Burma as the history of a Buddhist kingdom. It claims that the Buddha himself visited the country—this is most probably not true—and foretold its future as a stronghold of his *sasana* or rule. Dr. Arpita Mitra writes:[23]

> It is difficult to ascertain when Buddhism reached Burma, but it was quite early. Emperor Asoka has been the model for rulers all over the Buddhist world. In Myanmar, Asoka's example has been constantly invoked by kings. Even in modern times, U Nu, for example, modelled himself on Asoka, and set up innumerable small stupas. Buddhism is inextricably connected with Burmese nationalism and Burman identity.

Burma was avowedly Buddhist from very early times, but Hinduism also had a place in Burma as is attested by the popularity of the Vishnu cult and a number of Hindu sculptural images of Vishnu, Shiva, Brahma and other minor Hindu gods.[24]

India-Myanmar linkages transcend conventional aspects. For example, the Rashtriya Swayamsevak Sangh (RSS) is represented in Myanmar by the Sanatan Dharm Swayamseva Sangh. Pandit Ram Niwas, an Indian-origin Myanmar national, interacted with the author and briefed him about the role the RSS played in providing relief to the displaced Hindu community in Rakhine state following the Rohingya crisis. The organisation plays an important role in promoting India-Myanmar cultural linkages. One instance is the Raksha Bandhan festival which was organised by them (virtually due to COVID constraints) on 4 August 2020. This was attended by the Myanmar Union Minister, U Thura Aung Ko, and a recorded message by the State Counsellor Daw Aung San Suu Kyi was broadcast on the occasion. From the Indian side, Ambassador Saurabh Kumar attended the celebrations.[25]

Dr. Arpita brings out that other instances of cultural linkages include Vipassana, which is now a very popular form of non-sectarian meditation practice originating from Buddhism that was brought to India from Burma by the late Padma Bhushan Shri S. N. Goenka, who was born to Indian parents in Burma. In recent times, musicologist Kalamandalam Piyal Bhattacharya has made efforts to bring back the Burmese harp to India, which he thinks is the precursor to the Indian *veena*.[26] This clearly attests to a now obscure history of music that binds India and the Southeast and Far East Asia. The Burma connect with Indian revolutionary movement has been memorialized in the classic novel of Sarat Chandra Chattopadhyay, *Pather Dabi* (*Demands of the Road*, 1926) that has Sabyasachi, an ideal revolutionary, as the central character, set in Burma. The story was popularised in a Bengali film, *Sabyasachi*, that was made in 1977 with noted actor Uttam Kumar in the lead.[27] Incidentally, Sarat Chandra Chattopadhyay lived at Botataung in downtown Yangon. The area was later converted into a military camp.[28]

For another popular example, one would also recall the legendary Shamshad Begum and C Ramachandra song *'Mere piya gaye Rangoon'* written by Rajendra Krishan and composed by C. Ramachandra, in the black-and-white film *Patanga* (1949). This superhit song clearly attests the substantial existence of the Indian Diaspora in Burma, as the two countries were in reality politically unified for more than a century under the British Empire. During the visit of the VIF Delegation to the Ministry of Foreign Affairs, Nay Pyi Taw, U Kyaw Tin Shein,

Figure 13.3

THE GLOBAL NEW LIGHT OF MYANMAR

2 NATIONAL

4 AUGUST 2020

"People are the key"

Hindu organization holds cultural festival 'Raksha Bandhan' online

Deputy Director General, Consular and Legal Affairs Department, began his discourse on India-Myanmar relations with a nostalgic reminiscence of the love for Indian movies such as *Sholay* and *Qurbani* and actors like Amitabh Bachhan and Mithun Chakravarty, '*…even though we did not understand the language*'. He went on to give a wider scope to the relations, '*We loved alu, chapatti, paratha and other Indian food. When we see Indians, we don't feel that they are like foreigners. We*

have common dresses like the loungyi (lungi).' Conversely, in India, the 2015 Tamil movie *Anek (Anegan)*[29] picturises a discordant aspect of the relationship, that of the 1962 takeover by Ne Win and the subsequent nationalisation and eviction of Indians from Myanmar. The very short clip of the eviction seems rather well researched and uncannily accurate.

One of the more recent examples of the linkages between the citizens of Myanmar and India is evident from the evolution of the Mizzima Media Group. The author was fortunate to be able to visit the Mizzima Media Group and interact with the owner, Mr. Soe Myint to understand how the group developed in Myanmar. The group owes its roots to India where it operated from its debut in 1998 till it became the first exile media house to return to Myanmar in January 2012. How the media group started is the subject for another project, but it all commenced with the 10 November 1990 hijacking of TG305 Thai Airways Airbus A300[30] flying from Bangkok to Rangoon and Calcutta, all for a press conference to highlight the plight of Burmese citizens.[31] Released on bail and eventually acquitted since neither any passenger nor the airlines had ever pressed charges, Soe went on to stay in India and start a news network in 1998. Supported by veteran journalists such as Subir Bhaumik and human rights lawyer Nandita Haksar, he carved out a media network and eventually returned to Myanmar in 2012.[32] During an interaction with the author, he highlighted the importance of cultural linkages between both the countries and the popularity of Indian cinema in Myanmar. He explained that such was the popularity the subscription model of *Mizzima* had placed Indian movies for the 8:30 p.m. prime time slot at the

Figure 13.4

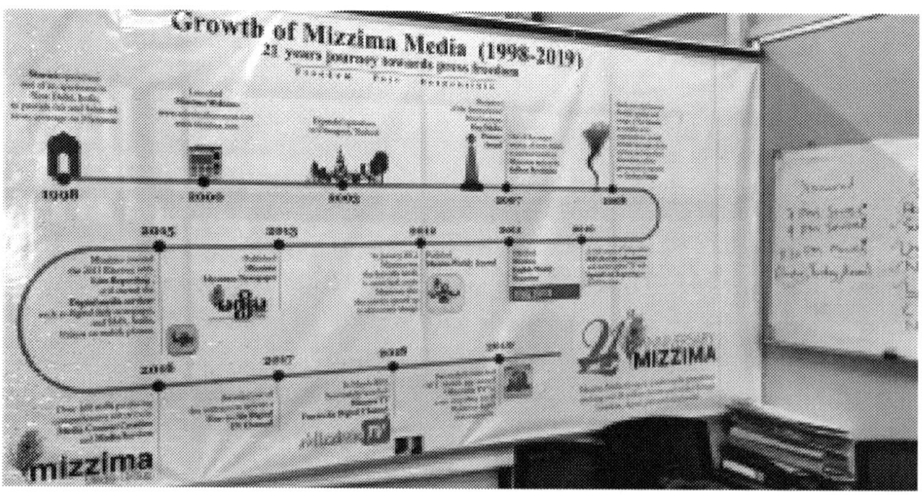

Source: Author

highest paid level, i.e., Diamond Subscription (see the inscription on the whiteboard at the right hand of Figure 13.4).

Relatively Speaking

Early India-Myanmar connections transcended families. Dr. M.A. Rauf, the first Indian Ambassador to Burma, was the brother of the Burmese Home Minister, M.A. Raschid.[33] His son, Bilal Raschid, has apparently penned a book on him called *The Invisible Patriot: Reminiscences of Burma's Freedom Movement*. M.A. Raschid was later incarcerated during the Ne Win regime. He had been one of the activists of the 1936 students' strike in Rangoon University.[34] Dr. Mohammed Abdul Rauf was born in Rangoon after his father M. A. Shakoor had settled there. Shakoor served as president of the All Burma Indian National Congress. Rauf after completing his secondary education, left to study in England where he studied Jurisprudence BA 1924 and BCL. 1925 at Oxford and enrolled in the Middle Temple. He also secured the LLD Degree from Trinity (Dublin). On his return, he practiced as a barrister at the Rangoon High Court. At his invitation as president of the All Burma Indian National Congress, Pandit Nehru and his daughter visited Burma in 1937. During the World War II Japanese occupation of Burma, he moved with his family to their ancestral seat at Allahabad.

President U Nu's daughter, Than Than Nu, worked for the All India Radio (AIR) Burmese Language Service in 1988 along with U Maw Thiri, and her hatred for Ne Win who had deposed her father was manifest in AIR Burmese Language transmissions. This turned into a major diplomatic issue for the new Ambassador to Myanmar, Mr. P.M.S. Malik in 1991. He describes[35] how the issue was raised by Senior General Saw Maung at the time of presentation of credentials by Ambassador Malik to him. He complained against the Burmese language service of the AIR which was being handled by U Nu's daughter, Than Than Nu, and brought out that she was using the broadcasting space to air her own views on developments in Myanmar including personalised attacks on Ne Win without adhering to the official Indian position. Thus, that morning's edition of news and views, in Burmese, over the AIR mentioned that India did not intend to have diplomatic relations with the SLORC which was, in fact, in direct contradiction to the fact since on the same very morning the new Indian Ambassador, i.e. Ambassador Malik was presenting his credentials.

Saw Maung clearly brought out that these damaging personalised attacks broadcast by AIR were attempting to encourage the people to rise against the government. He hoped that these hurtful and subversive broadcasts would be stopped and followed it up by giving Ambassador Malik a translated copy of that morning's broadcast. Ambassador Malik, after working to mitigate the damage, set to stop this irresponsible reporting and the use of personalised attacks by Than Than Nu who was understandably biased. Eventually, the Cabinet Secretary and the Secretary in the Ministry of Information and Broadcasting attempted to reduce the damage by closely monitoring the content and finally, since the damage continued, removed the two broadcasters, including U Nu's daughter.[36]

But the matter did not end there. India is unique in that two of its Presidents had wives of Myanmar origin. President K. R. Narayanan was the tenth President of India from 1997 to 2002. His wife, Tint Tint, (Usha Narayanan) was of Myanmar origin and the President, when posted in Myanmar as an IFS Officer, had met and married her.[37] She was fully involved with the Myanmar students, politicians and others who had taken refuge in India and was providing support from public platforms in India to the democratic movement. She turned her wrath on the Ambassador personally for stopping the AIR broadcasts. It took two meetings by the Ambassador with Narayanan and later, even his wife, before she realised the damage her tirade was doing to India-Myanmar relations.

President R. Ventakraman's wife, Janaki Venkatraman, was born in Bago, Myanmar, where her father was posted. Mrs Janaki was born to an Iyer family—Kamala and Krishna Iyer. President Venkatraman was the eighth President of India from 1984 to 1987.[38]

On the other side, Daw Khin Kyi, General Aung San's wife and DASSK's mother served as the Burmese Ambassador to India from 1960 to 1967. Nehru took special interest in her welfare which left a strong impression on Suu Kyi in her teens and she fondly recalled it in her acceptance speech during the presentation of the 1993 Nehru Memorial Prize for International Understanding.[39]

Chettiars

No discussion on India-Myanmar linkages can be complete without a reference to the Chettiars.[40] Sean Turnell explains[41] in his paper that the Chettiars were celebrated as the vital link between Burma and international finance, and as the providers of the capital that turned the country into the 'rice-bowl' of the British Empire. However, concurrently they were vilified as unscrupulous and predatory moneylenders. They were indeed the primary providers of capital to Burmese cultivators through much of the colonial period. However, the collapse of paddy prices in the Great Depression combined with the Chettiar insistence of land as collateral and the imposition of British land-title laws brought about a substantial transfer of Burma's cultivable land into their hands. Turnell concludes that:

> *The Japanese invasion of Burma in 1942 brought with it many harrowing scenes, but few would match that of the flight of the Diaspora of Indian merchants, workers, administrators and financiers who had done much to transform Burma in the colonial era. How many of these died on the long march out of Burma—most on the road from Rangoon to Assam—remains a topic of lively controversy, but it is likely that no less than 80,000 people succumbed to disease, starvation and the other dissipations of war. Prominent amongst those fleeing the onslaught of the Japanese, just as they had been prominent in the transformational role played by Indians in Burma beforehand, were the Chettiars of Tamil Nadu. Scapegoats then and now for the misfortunes that heralded the breakdown of Burma's colonial economy, the Chettiars were not allowed to return to their lives and livelihoods following the granting of Burma's independence in 1948. Portrayed by British colonial officials and Burmese nationalist politicians alike as almost pantomime villains in Burma's 20th-century dramas, they left the stage as unambiguous victims. The property they had acquired in roughly a century of money-lending in Burma was effectively nationalised by successive Burmese governments after 1948, and dissipated by the same.*

Recommendations

Dr. Arpita recommends a five-pronged approach to address the need to enhance people-to-people connections based on cultural linkages. First is the need to fund new research by Indian scholars on India-Myanmar cultural linkages. Works by Niharranjan Ray, B. C. Law and other stalwart scholars have taken place between the 1930s and the 1950s. This is a field to which Indian scholars had made seminal contributions at one point of time, but it is now commented upon only by foreign scholars and that too as part of the larger history and trajectory of Buddhism in Asian countries. Unfortunately, there is an acute paucity of Indian researchers undertaking work on the subject. Promoting research on the subject by Indian scholars will help in an intensive engagement and knowledge production on the subject, many aspects of which are still not known. This also involves setting up courses and chairs in Myanmar studies in Indian universities.[42] Second, there is a crying need to disseminate the existing pool of knowledge on India-Myanmar relations. Existing knowledge about India-Myanmar cultural linkages need to be showcased and made available to the wider public in a popular way as part of an extensive engagement with the subject. Public exhibitions organized by museums can go a long way in this respect. This history has to be made a part of public discourse in more tangible ways. A collaborative seminar also needs to be organized by an Indian institute in partnership with a Burmese one. The seminar will chart the different dimensions of India's linkages with Myanmar through the ages.

Thirdly, cultural exchange programmes between the two countries have to be promoted. It has to be done in a way that Myanmar is an equally active participant in the process and it should not be a one-sided Indian affair. This should not be confined to central government initiatives only. The IMB states should similarly carry out parallel interactions, e.g., Mizoram with Chin State, Manipur and Nagaland with Sagaing and Naga Self Administered Zone and Arunachal Pradesh with Kachin. Fourthly, in order to engage Myanmar more meaningfully, Indian cultural centres or universities should adopt a comparative studies approach. For instance, if a program is organized in Myanmar on Kalidasa, there should also be a section on a comparable Burmese poet. The Indian Government cultural centres in Myanmar need to address the local Burmese population, instead of the Indian population. Finally, India also needs to take the initiative to re-establish the Tagore College at Yangon. This college had earlier been affiliated with Calcutta University, but was nationalised in 1964 and the premises eventually housed myriad government departments.

In conclusion, India's civilizational linkages with Myanmar go deep into history, yet have disappeared from public discourse today. Our connection with Myanmar was part of the public consciousness well into the 1950s. However, for a number of reasons, from 1960 till 2000, a period of 40 years, India-Myanmar relations seem to have swept into the footnotes of history. It is time both the nations seize the opportunity to pull out the footnotes and reinstate them to the place of pride that they originally had by re-establishing institutes and rebuilding the capacity for educational, cultural and social connections.

NOTES

1. For this chapter I am indebted to Dr. Arpita Mitra, Research Fellow, VIF, who convinced me that without adequate focus on the cultural connections, I would be missing out a vital link, and in that essence the book would be incomplete. She went on to assist me in compiling and collating the material for this chapter.
2. During a book discussion on *'The Borderlands and Boundaries of the Indian Subcontinent: Baluchistan to the Patkai Range and Arakan Yoma'* by Shri Dilip K. Chakrabarti, Professor Emeritus, University of Cambridge & Distinguished Fellow, VIF, on 18 March 2020. https:/ /www.youtube.com/watch?v=8e8_6abcxZ8 (At 22:40 mins) (Accessed on 20 April 2020).
3. The translated phrase means *'I am in the streets of Burma, whilst you are in Dehradun. Your memories torment me. Your memories torment me. They warm my heart'.* The song *Mere pia gaye Rangoon (My beloved has gone to Rangoon)* was a superhit song in 1949 from the black-and-

white movie *Patanga*. For the remixed version by DZ Sheizwood and Shashwati, see https://www.youtube.com/watch?v=rqJi63LOUtM.

4. In an email interaction with the author dated 27 July 2020.
5. For details, see Chapter 1 of Niharranjan Ray, *Theravada Buddhism in Burma*, University of Calcutta, 1946.
6. Dilip K. Chakrabarti, *The Borderlands and Boundaries of the Indian Subcontinent*. New Delhi, Aryan Books International, 2018.
7. Gaur was a historic city of Bengal and one of the most populous cities in the world and most prominent capitals in the classical and medieval Indian subcontinent. This former city now straddles the international border and is divided between Malda district of West Bengal and Chapai Nawabganj district of Rajshahi Division.
8. Dhaka Tribune, The treasure of Shah Shuja, 21 November 2013, https://www.dhakatribune.com/uncategorized/2013/11/21/the-treasure-of-shah-shuja (Accessed on 20 June 2020).
9. Wikipedia, The Free Encyclopedia, Arakan, https://en.wikipedia.org/wiki/Arakan (Accessed on 20 June 2020).
10. Government of India, Indian Culture, Bahadur Shah Zafar, https://indianculture.gov.in/stories/bahadur-shah-zafar (Accessed on 2 August 2020).
11. See Anbarasan Ethirajan, Remembering the last Mughal, BBC News, Yangon, 8 November 2017, https://www.bbc.com/news/world-asia-41884390 and Revati Krishnan, Bahadur Shah Zafar, the last Mughal who would rather have been a poet, The Print, 7 November 2019, https://theprint.in/theprint-profile/bahadur-shah-zafar-the-last-mughal-who-would-rather-have-been-a-poet/316114/ (Both accessed on 2 August 2020).
12. Ratnagiri District Website, Tourist Places, Thibaw Palace, https://ratnagiri.gov.in/tourist-place/thibaw-palace/ (Accessed on 2 August 2020).
13. For more details, see https://www.livehistoryindia.com/snapshort-histories/2018/05/29/ratnagiri-and-the-last-king-of-burma, (Accessed on 6 August 2020).
14. Namita Kohli, In search of princess Phaya: Looking for Myanmar's forgotten royals in Ratnagiri, Hindustan Times 26 February 2017, https://www.hindustantimes.com/weekend/in-search-of-princess-phaya-looking-for-myanmar-s-forgotten-royals-in-ratnagiri/story-dWhy94FbPMq4sTQNaPM4RK.html and Manu S. Pillai, Opinion: A Burmese king in an Indian exile, Mint, Medium Rare, 31 May 2019, https://www.livemint.com/mint-lounge/features/opinion-a-burmese-king-in-an-indian-exile-1559272036233.html (Both accessed on 6 August 2020).
15. India in Mandalay, Twitter Handle @indiainmandalay #TilakdayinMandalay, 1 August 2020, https://twitter.com/cgimandalay/status/1289451924580777984 (Accessed on 6 August 2020).
16. Deccan Herald, The Enigma of Bose, 15 October 2011, https://www.deccanherald.com/content/198117/enigma-bose.html and K. Natwar Singh, Burma's long night may finally be over, India Today, 18 December 2011, https://www.indiatoday.in/india/north/story/democracy-in-burma-forthcoming-burmese-elections-suu-kyi-149126-2011-12-18 (Both accessed on 6 August 2020).
17. Bertil Lintner, *The Rise and Fall of the Communist Party of Burma (CPB)*. Southeast Asia Program Series, No. 6, Cornell University, 1990. pg. 58
18. Yangon Life, House of Memories, https://yangonlife.com.mm/en/directory/house%20of%20memories (Accessed on 6 August 2020).
19. Zarni Mann, A Visit to Rangoon's House of Memories, The Irrawaddy, 21 September 2013, https://www.irrawaddy.com/photo-essay/visit-rangoons-house-memories.html (Accessed on 6 August 2020).
20. Zuzakar Kalaung, House of Memories, Myanmar Times, 10 November 2017, https://www.mmtimes.com/news/house-memories.html (Accessed on 6 August 2020).

21. Shobita Dhar, At 103, India's first female cardiologist is still fixing, and winning hearts, Times of India, 29 July 2020, http://timesofindia.indiatimes.com/articleshow/77232744.cms? utm_source=contentofinterest&utm_medium=text&utm_campaign=cppst (Accessed on 6 August 2020).
22. For details, see Bimul Churn Law, *The History of the Buddha's Religion (Sasanavamsa)*, 1953.
23. Email. Ref Footnote 2.
24. For details, see Niharranjan Ray, *Brahmanical Gods in Burma: Chapter of Indian Art and Iconography*, University of Calcutta, 1932; Upendra Thakur, 'A Historical Survey of the Elements of Hindu Culture in Burma', in *India's Contribution to World Thought and Culture*, Vivekananda Kendra Prakashan, 1970; Usha R. Bhise, 'A Temple of Visnu in Burma' in *India's Contribution to World Thought and Culture.*
25. India in Myanmar, Twitter Handle @indiainmyanmar, 4 August 2020, https://twitter.com/IndiainMyanmar/status/1290645586228785154 (Accessed on 6 August 2020).
26. Yogesh Pawar, Quest to bring back Burmese harp, a precursor to veena, DNA, 26 February 2017, https://www.dnaindia.com/lifestyle/report-quest-to-bring-back-burmese-harp-a-precursor-to-veena-2334702 (Accessed on 6 August 2020).
27. Sanghamitra Mazumdar, Remembering Sarat Chandra Chattopadhyay, the 'Awara Masiha', The Indian Express, 15 September 2015, https://indianexpress.com/article/india/remembering-sarat-chandra-chattopadhyay-the-awara-masiha-on-his-139th-birth-anniversary/ (Accessed on 6 August 2020).
28. Pratim Ranjan Bose, For Bengalis in Yangon, memories of a long-gone era, The Hindu Business Line, 21 September 2017, https://www.thehindubusinessline.com/news/variety/for-bengalis-in-yangon-memories-of-a-longgone-era/article9867795.ece#(Accessed on 6 August 2020).
29. I humbly thank Noothan Venkatesh, Young Professional, at VIF for having drawn my attention to this movie by Dhanush, Amyra Dastur and Karthik. The Hindi dubbed version of the movie was released in 2016 and is available at https://www.youtube.com/watch?v=I8hhgc4dQsY&feature=youtu.be.(Accessed on 5 August 2020).
30. New York Times, 2 Burmese Hijack Jet and Give Up in Calcutta, 11 November 1990, https://www.nytimes.com/1990/11/11/world/2-burmese-hijack-jet-and-give-up-in-calcutta.html (Accessed on 6 August 2020).and Dr Jane M Ferguson, The Perfect Hijack, Australian National University College of Asia & The Pacific, https://asiapacific.anu.edu.au/perfection/perfect-hijack (Accessed on 6 August 2020).
31. See Soe Myint's TedX Diliman talk at https://www.youtube.com/watch?v=wUg_ihfgtAo and *Burma File: A Question of Democracy.*
32. Tom Nagorski, In Myanmar, a Former Hijacker Finds His Own 'Middle Path,' Without Regrets, Asia Society, 23 February 2015, https://asiasociety.org/blog/asia/myanmar-former-hijacker-finds-his-own-middle-path-without-regrets (Accessed on 6 August 2020).
33. Preet Malik, '*My Myanmar Years: A Diplomat's Account of India's Relations with the Region*', Sage India, New Delhi, 2015, pg. 37.
34. http://www.ide.go.jp/English/Publish/Periodicals/De/pdf/74_04_03.pdf
35. Ibid., pg. 66.
36. Ibid., pg. 72.
37. He had joined the Congress party following his retirement from the IFS after serving as India's envoy to Washington and he had also served as a Minister of State in the Congress government headed by Indira Gandhi and subsequently by Rajiv Gandhi.
38. *Soldiers and Diplomacy in Burma: Understanding the Foreign Relations of the Burmese Praetorian State*, pg. 151, https://books.google.co.in/books?id=bvbwBgAAQBAJ&pg=PA151 &lpg=PA151&dq= Burmese+wife+of+Indian+President&source=bl&ots=vCQYpy_Qpe&sig=ACfU3 U3hf9aU1vK8LxttMXzViE-hTUT2TQ&hl=en&sa=X&ved=2ahUKEwit05HI--zmAhVcwzg

GHeUbB0YQ6AEwEHoECBUQAQ#v=onepage&q=Burmese%20wife%20of%20Indian%20 President&f=false

39. Rajiv Bhatia, *India-Myanmar Relations: Changing Contours,* Routledge India, 2016, pg. 108.
40. Chettiar is the honorific plural for the caste variously referred to as Chetti, Chetty, and Shetty.
41. Sean Turnell, *The Chettiars in Burma*, Research Papers 0512, Macquarie University, Department of Economics, 2005, https://ideas.repec.org/p/mac/wpaper/0512.html
42. Also see chapters 4 and 14 of this book.

CHAPTER 14
Making Sense of It All

> *Our deficit as far as our relationship with Myanmar is not on the policy front; it is not due (to) the lack of desire or intention; it is not on account of certain impediments as far as implementation of the policy is concerned; it is only on account of the fact that there ought to be more interest, and both ways, not only from the Indian side in Myanmar and the Myanmar side in India, and* ***this is on the business side.*** *I would like to see more Indian businesses coming to Myanmar for exploratory visits for seeing the opportunities out here and vice versa.*
>
> **—Saurabh Kumar, Indian Ambassador to Myanmar**[1]

This chapter attempts to put together all the issues covered in the preceding chapters and tries to make some sense of the events in Myanmar so as to articulate a coherent philosophy which would help decision makers in developing policy. If one was to single out one aspect of India-Myanmar relations, which impact the overall relationship, it would be the need for greater, more meaningful and fruitful people-to-people relations based on viable commercial interests. A lot in this chapter essentially hinges around facets of this factor. This is reflected in the quotation above, where the Indian Ambassador emphasises the need for businesses to interact, thereby focussing on a durable facet of people-to-people relations.

The long-term stability and development of Northeast India is a strategic imperative to India's overall growth and stature in the world. Given the geographic configuration of the Northeastern states and their intimate association with the neighbouring countries in cultural, ethnic and linguistic terms, **regional stability of these countries** is central to the stability and development being sought in

Northeast India. For a journey to a US$ 5 trillion economy, this is crucial. Amongst neighbouring countries, Myanmar stands out as critical to Northeast India for reasons very well articulated by the Ministry of External Affairs[2] as under:

> *'India shares a long land border of over 1600 km with Myanmar as well as a maritime boundary in the Bay of Bengal. Four north-eastern states, viz., Arunachal Pradesh, Nagaland, Manipur and Mizoram, have a boundary with Myanmar. Both countries share a heritage of religious, linguistic and ethnic ties. Myanmar is the only ASEAN country adjoining India and, therefore, our gateway to South East Asia, with which we are seeking greater economic integration through the 'Act East' policy. Business opportunities that are latent in the potential of the last large and unexploited market in South East Asia also provide new vistas for engagement.'*

Thus, effectively, a stable Myanmar is essential for a stable Northeast India. Here, I put forth a caveat: Myanmar (and, for that matter, even the Northeast) should not be viewed as a means to an end, with the end being the ASEAN market. Myanmar in itself is an end, with a stable, prosperous and economically-engaged Myanmar leading to a stable and prosperous Northeast which thus provides the boost that the Indian growth engine is seeking. Looking at the ASEAN markets without first engaging the Northeast and Myanmar would be tantamount to placing the cart before the horse. Thus, the Northeast and Myanmar should not be viewed solely as transit areas or land bridges. They are much more integral to the overall geopolitical and geo-economic calculus of India.

Therefore, in such a situation, what should be India's vision for Myanmar and what should be India's strategy to achieve that vision? Since India's Myanmar strategy is directly dependent on Myanmar's geo-strategic location and because India-Myanmar relations are tied by the much-quoted shared heritage of religious, linguistic and ethnic ties, the strategy that evolves is centred around these features. This is documented in the following paragraphs.

Three Fundamentals for India-Myanmar Relations

While broad and prescriptive recommendations are best suited to academic and scholarly pursuits, however, they do serve to provide an anchor to policymakers and practitioners to peg their policies on; and it is in this spirit that I have documented three fundamental principles on which I place the edifice of India-Myanmar relations.

The first, seemingly obvious fundamental, is that a **developed and democratic Myanmar is good for India and Myanmar.** Thus, a relationship with India and

Myanmar needs to be seen on the strength of this philosophy and not only through the prism of an India-versus-China competition in Myanmar. Given the nationalistic pride and fervour of the people of Myanmar, a developed Myanmar automatically negates Chinese or Indian or any other external influence in the region which is intrinsically good for India. Hence, all Indian engagement in Myanmar must not been seen as an indirect or direct effort to contain China or any other nation.

Now the corollary to this principle is that while India need not worry about the Chinese influence in Myanmar *per se*, it needs to ensure that its own influence in Myanmar is not stymied by any actual Chinese influence. Thus, the ***genuine development of Myanmar*** is a primary vision and by implication assisting Myanmar will enable it to stand on its own feet and reduce dependence on China, thereby improving India's security posture. This almost sounds contradictory to the statement in the previous paragraph. The difference is subtle and lies in the intent of the nations. India does not need to counter Chinese influence in Myanmar and hence anything it does in Myanmar does not need to be couched in an anti-Chinese perspective. However, India does need to engage Myanmar in various spheres and for various reasons intrinsic to India-Myanmar relations. Thus, India's engagement in Myanmar should be for the right reasons as relevant to India-Myanmar relations, and China should not feature in them. But given China's economic blitzkrieg with the associated security threats; Myanmar's inherent inability to ward off Chinese influence and the vulnerability of the India's Northeast to Chinese weapons and contraband, India has no choice but to be on guard. Post COVID-19 and post the violent clash at Galwan in East Ladakh in 2020, both India and China have upped the ante even as India bans Chinese apps, investments and products in India. In such an environment of mistrust, one cannot but help looking across the IMB at the approaching Chinese influence and take appropriate action.

The question then arises, up to where and how does India retain or extend its influence in Myanmar. The Irrawaddy seems to be the most logical extent of India's influence. A look at our historical and geographical legacy provides guidance. Ambassador Rajiv Sikri, former Ambassador to Kazakhstan, in a book discussion at the VIF, New Delhi,[3] on 18 March 2020, recounted the first Secretary General of the MEA, Sir Girija Shankar Bajpai, as having postulated three circles of Indian security (see Figure 14.1). The outer-most circle was from the Suez to Shangai, the middle circle from Aden and Hormuz to the Malacca Straits and the inner-most was from the Hindu Kush to the Irrawaddy. Thus, we see this extension

Figure 14.1: India's Three Circles of Security

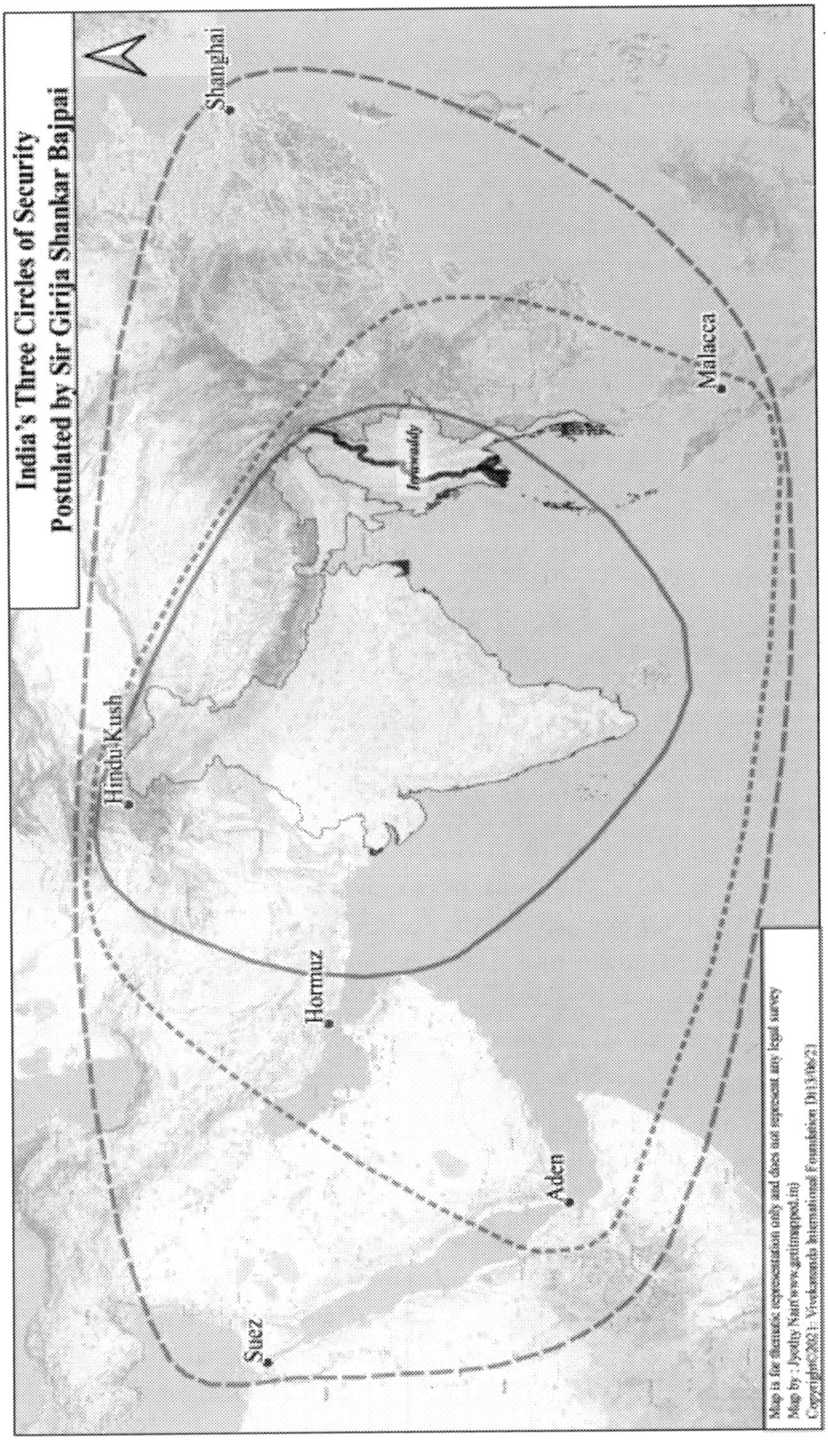

of Indian influence up to the Irrawaddy is not a new concept but a logical historical and geographic outcome.

Figure 14.2

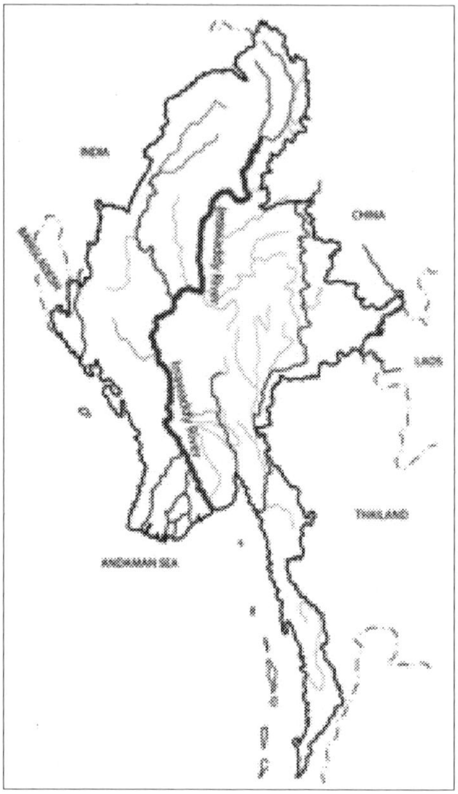

General V.P. Malik, after his visit to Myanmar in 2000, echoed the same sentiments to PM Vajpayee that '*from the China border till the Irrawaddy, the Chinese influence is very strong already, but we can limit that influence to the Irrawaddy if we develope our relationship with Myanmar today*'.

A close look at the way the Irrawaddy flows, in relation to the IMB, reinforces this view of India's security interests being till the Irrawaddy. The river originates at the confluence of two Himalayan rivers viz, the Mali Hka and N'Mai Hka in north Kachin. The N'Mai rises in the Languela Glacier north of Putao. The confluence is 45 km north of the Kachin State capital of Myitkyina. Irrawaddy flows north to south, almost parallel to the IMB. Having emanated in the Kachin Region, it flows along the boundary of Sagaing and Mandalay provinces, south into Magwe, Pegu and Ayeyerawaddy provinces, into the Andaman Sea. All along this path, it mirrors the IMB on its west, forming a natural buffer zone to the IMB.

This buffer zone is formed by the three provinces on the IMB as also the Rakhine in the south. Thus from a security perspective, this buffer zone needs to be invested in, to insulate the IMB from security vulnerabilities likely from the Chinese economic offensives in the regions. These would range from proliferation of cheap and unreliable Chinese goods pandering to the consumer psyche of the locals; smuggling of goods; movement of drugs and contraband including Chinese weapons, two wheelers leading to the Kenbo[4] effect and culminating in a Kenbo economy where Chinese currency becomes acceptable even on the Indian side of the IMB with disastrous consequences on the Indian economy in the Northeast in a worst-case scenario.

That India's support to Myanmar need not match Chinese investments dollar for dollar, needs to be clearly understood. Also, Indian investments and engagements need to be carried out through the prism of 'hearts and minds' to sustain the Indian goodwill in Myanmar. So the second fundamental that emerges is that **Indian engagement in Myanmar therefore must be based on 'hearts and mind investments'.** This evolves from a steady and justified clamour for more proactive action by India in Myanmar has dominated the discourse.[5] The idea of a hearts and minds investment revolves around touching those places and industries which crave smaller investments across a vast population. The 'hearts' side of the investment calls for touching those areas where investment is scarce and would have maximum positive impact for the locals without forcing them to abandon their traditional ways of life. Three of the most obvious sectors that emerge in this context are agriculture, fisheries and forestry based industries. When applied contextually, these sectors make for good business opportunities for the provinces adjoining the IMB, i.e., in Chin, Sagaing and Kachin provinces. Other attractive sectors for investment include extractive industries (minerals/ oil and gas), manufacturing, infrastructure, power, urbanisation, tourism and hospitality. The hospitality industry is symptomatic of the investment opportunities along the IMB:

Table 14.1: Available Capacity of Hotels, Motels, Inns/Guesthouses along IMB (FY 2016-2017)[6]

Province	*Hotels, Motels & Inns*		*Rooms*	
Sagaing Region	27	108 (7.3 %)*	1098	3514 (6%)*
Kachin State	27		751	
Chin State	5		127	
Rakhine State	49		1538	
Total in Myanmar (all provinces)	1479		58249	

*Percentage of the Myanmar national total.

This appallingly low availability capacity of hotels and rooms along the IMB states provides an excellent opportunity to Indian investors to utilise the pull cycle, i.e., more hotels provide more incentives to travellers to visit which, in turn, encourages hoteliers to invest. In the case of urbanisation, Myanmar's level of urbanisation remains lower than the Southeast Asian average; around 13 per cent of the nation's population of 52.45 million resides in cities, while in Southeast Asia the figure is 37 per cent. Thirty of Myanmar's cities have populations of more than 100,000 and are expected to become major growth hubs in the coming years.

For a compilation of investment opportunities in Myanmar from the Department of Investment and Company Administration (DICA) website and the Socio-Economic Atlas of Myanmar, see **Appendix P**.

This author, in a VIF web article covering the visit of President Xi Jinping to Myanmar in January 2020,[7] described the 'minds' component in detail. He highlighted that the 'minds' component ensures that while meeting the requirements of the 'heart', the financial viability of projects is not compromised. Thus, low but consistent and long-term profits, smaller scales of operations with lesser bureaucratic hurdles would take precedence over mega-projects and provide investment in geographical locations which are otherwise neglected. These investments are those that touch and benefit the common man and not just the local elites and investors. Here, volume would take precedence over value. These operations hold tremendous value in remote places like Kachin and Arunachal Pradesh. The aspect of 'hearts and minds' investments has been covered in detail in Pg 281 in Chapter 12 on the CMEC.

This author further brought out that this does not mean top-driven (G2G) initiatives should not be undertaken. The possibility of multi-national joint ventures needs to be considered by Myanmar and accepted by both China and India rather than traditional bilateral ventures especially between China and Myanmar. A good example is the Myanmar-China Gas Pipeline Project which is jointly invested and constructed by South East Asia Pipeline (SEAP) Company, Myanmar Oil and Gas Enterprise (MOGE), POSCO DAEWOO, ONGC CASPIAN E&P B.V. (OCEBV), Gas Authority of India Limited (GAIL) and Korea Gas Corporation (KOGAS). The South-East Asia Gas Pipeline Company Limited (SEAGP) is responsible for its operation and management.[8] Involvement of multi-national entities brings expertise to the fore and by default induces checks and balances into the systems which tend to neutralize Chinese monopoly and brings objectivity into the projects. In this way, Indian investors too have a stake in the activities and the presence of Indian and other investors increases the confidence of Myanmar investors and people. India-driven alliances may provide the reliable alternative source of 'heart and minds investments' using groupings involving BIMSTEC or the India-ASEAN networks or even as an alliance with Japan.[9] India, however, has no option but to evolve systems to deliver projects on timelines and within the budgeted costs. The implementation of the Kaladan Project is a case in point in that, despite over two decades since commencement, it has not been completed. This is a result of a systemic culture of bureaucratic indifference and total lack of accountability. The negative reputation that India has garnered across the neighbourhood of being unable to deliver on its promises is greatly affecting its stature and aspirations for regional leadership.

The third fundamental is **that India-Myanmar relations need to be taken to**

the people-to-people level to insulate it from the vagaries of international relations and domestic politics. In the post-Independence period, the India-Myanmar relations have been dependent on the personalities of the leaders and how they got along. Thus, while Nehru and U Nu were close, Nehru and Ne Win did not get along as well as Indira Gandhi and Ne Win did. Reportedly, when Indira Gandhi was assassinated, Ne Win was so struck by grief that he disappeared to an island for days of meditation.[10] Currently, the India-Myanmar relationship is better institutionalised but still overly top driven and vulnerable to the vagaries of changing foreign policies of both the nations. To insulate the relationship and make it enduring, there is a need to enhance people-to-people contact. Once the stakes in the people are enhanced to the desired levels, the leadership thereafter has to respect and pander to the requirements of the people. Herein lies the need to penetrate the constituencies which sustain the leaders. Ashley Tellis postulates that success in Indian foreign policy does not simply devolve from Indian positive influence on the societies and economies of the neighbourhood states such as Bangladesh, Nepal or Sri Lanka, which might make their populations rely on Indian goodwill for their prosperity. The politics in these countries is highly polarised and India's influence rises and falls depending on when the leadership friendly to New Delhi takes up office.[11] The imperative is thus for people-to-people contact to make the engagement a truly multi-dimensional and irreversible one. For this, increasing awareness of the Golden Land on our immediate East, is critical. And to increase awareness, the media must play its part in exposing the population to the neighbourhood, including Myanmar. [12]

As brought out by this author in a VIF Web Article and in Chapter IV on *Myanmar Consciousness and a Blind Spot*, by obsessively focussing on the West, the media reveals a colonial mindset which is best ejected in favour of a pragmatic and considered approach to promoting the Northeast by which Myanmar automatically becomes a logical extension of our east.

A number of measures are available to enhance people-to-people relations, some of which, relevant to this discourse are elaborated in the following section.

Language

Language is an obstacle in the pursuit of Myanmar studies. In the case of the rest of the neighbourhood, Bengali and Nepali are commonly spoken in India enabling people-to-people contact with Bangladesh and Nepal, respectively. While Sinhala is not widespread in India, the Tamil population in Sri Lanka connects with southern India on the basis of language. Bhutan has a sizeable Nepali-speaking population which provides a connect. However, the Burmese language is endemic to Myanmar with no links in India except for the bordering regions where the local tribal languages transcend the IMB.

Unfortunately there is a near total absence of Myanmar language resources in India. Possibly, the only place providing formal training in Myanmar language is the Centre for Myanmar Studies of Manipur University, Imphal. As per its website, the centre is an autonomous entity in Manipur University funded by the University Grants Commission (UGC) since 2005. The centre offers a six-month certificate course in Myanmar Language for young students who would like to study Myanmar in addition to their own subjects and also to young entrepreneurs and tourists for a working knowledge of Myanmar language. To be eligible, one must complete at least XII standard. The Manipur University website states that the centre offers an India-Myanmar research programme in select areas under an MoU signed between the governments of India and Myanmar with financial assistance to the tune of 12,000 Kyats per month and other perks and facilities from the Myanmar Government. The centre has a staff of four persons, including a Director, a Coordinator and two language instructors.[13] The website lists 45 students registered for 2019 and 53 students registered for 2018.[14] The only other institutionalised body teaching Myanmar in India, is the School of Foreign Languages (SFL), New Delhi, run by the Ministry of Defence. The SFL is mandated to conduct interpreter and other courses in Chinese, Arabic, Russian, Tibetan, Persian, Sinhala, German, French, Spanish, Bahasha Indonesia, Japanese and Burmese. However, due to non-availability of certain permanent faculty, interpreter courses are presently being conducted only in Chinese, Arabic, Russian, Persian, Tibetan and Sinhala.[15]

Figure 14.3: Centre for Myanmar Studies, Manipur University

Source: Manipur University Website

In Myanmar, the majority and official language is Burmese, though the minority ethnic groups have their own languages, as distinct from dialects. Burmese is spoken in the plains, and as a second language, by most people in the hills. During the British times, English became the official language, but Burmese continued as the primary language. Both English and Burmese were taught in schools and colleges, but Burmese, Chinese and Hindi were the commercial *lingua franca*. Post-independence, English ceased to be the official language, and post the 1962 military coup it lost its importance. Burmese and most of the other languages in Myanmar belong to the Tibeto-Burman subfamily of Sino- Tibetan languages. The Shan language falls in the Tai family. The south Myanmar Mon people and the Wa and Palaung of the Shan Plateau speak a dialect which falls in the Mon-Khmer subfamily of Austro-Asiatic languages. A distinct dialect of Burmese is used by the residents of Rakhine and Tenasserim coastal plains. The mountain regions in Myanmar are inhabited by Shan, Kachin, Chin speakers amongst myriad other languages. In the plains the ancient north south divide Myanmar was based on geographic and linguistic differences. The Mon lived in southern Myanmar, while the majority Bamar lived in the northern arid zone. Until the British period, only Burmese, Mon, Shan and the languages of the ancient Pyu kingdom of northern Burma had scripts. Scripts for the Karen, Kachin and Chin languages were developed later.[16]

Connectivity

Connectivity is a basic prerequisite for people-to-people interaction. India-Myanmar connectivity is not commensurate with the size of the borders we share, or with the cultural and historical linkages. This is another reason for and the outcome of the lack of Myanmar consciousness. A common, though flawed, parameter for comparison is with China. Simply put, the number of crossing points, flights to and from (pre COVID-19 figures) and tourist inflows is far less than China and possibly even Thailand. There is a need to improve the crossing points on the IMB to encourage interaction and business opportunities. In keeping with the requirement of saturating the buffer zone with meaningful 'hearts and minds' investments, and since these investments would be by *bona fide* business persons, the Indian Government needs to create enabling facilities such as roads and communication infrastructure.

Taking stock of the existing roads reveals a distinct southward orientation of the available axes which neglects the development of the northern portions of the IMB. Thus, the Moreh-Tamu axis in Manipur, the Rhi-Tiddim and the Zorinpui-

Figure 14.4

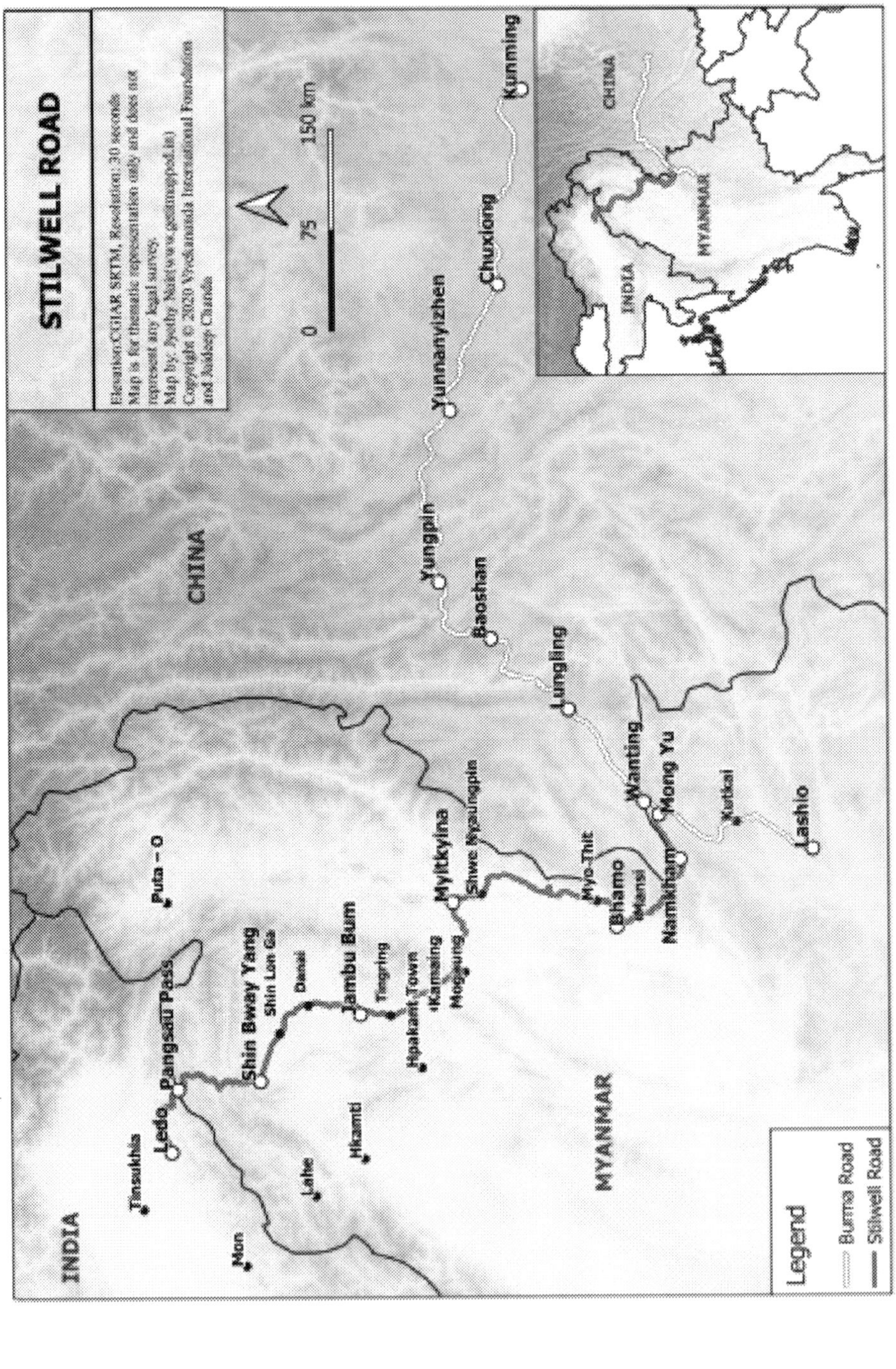
STILWELL ROAD
0
75
150 km
INDIA
CHINA
MYANMAR
Ledo
Pangsau Pass
Shin Bway Yang
Jambu Bum
Myitkyina
Bhamo
Namkham
Mong Yu
Wanting
Lashio
Lungling
Baoshan
Yungpin
Yunnanyizhen
Chuxiong
Kunming
Legend
Burma Road
Stilwell Road

Paletwa (under construction) axes in Mizoram are the only available road communication links. The construction of the Stilwell Road (see Figure 14.4) from India to China (through Myanmar) is an imperative and a low-hanging fruit to be harvested for improving India-Myanmar connectivity. The bulk of the portion from India to Myitkyina has been overrun by vegetation and is disused. However, closer to the Chinese border, the road is used and maintained. It was constructed during World War II for the Allies to be able to maintain the Chinese nationalist forces in Kunming from the railhead at Ledo in Assam.[17]

For a brief history of the Stilwell Road, **see Appendix Q**. Reconstructing the Stilwell Road is considered a low-hanging fruit ready to be harvested since the road formation already exists and, less a few diversions, the available alignment can be used for construction after clearing the foliage and the debris due to landslides and rock falls. However, the traditional security mindset of the Indian Government stakeholders based on the experience of insurgency in the Northeast holds back construction of this link between Arunachal Pradesh and the NSAZ, Sagaing and Kachin provinces. The concerns, all of which are valid, include the possibility of exposing Arunachal Pradesh to a glut of Chinese products; increasing the possibility of contraband smuggling; the lack of any major commercial benefit due to paucity of traffic and the lack of any strategic (read: utility to security forces) advantage to India.

However, this argument intrinsically seems defeatist and hinges on the fear of failure rather than the hope of success. Nation building needs bold decisions and road construction is one activity which does wonders for remote locations and trans-border people-to-people contact. Hence, to measure the utility of a road against the narrow template of commercial viability and strategic utility solely from a security perspective would be to deny the region and its locals an opportunity to pull themselves out of poverty. It would be a positive political statement and a display of national confidence in the region. A road is a route to security and a symbol of hope. In the fringes of the Northeast, a road is a means for national and regional integration. The region here is the India-Myanmar border region. Even from the security perspective, a road is a capability, which needs to be developed during peace time, for eventualities which may not even be perceived at this stage. The valid apprehensions of Chinese products and contraband entering the markets needs to be addressed directly, not by avoiding building the road. Adequate intermediate options are available to address security concerns. One option is to build the road partly and not connect it to Myitkyina in the first phase. This provides our mutual traders access to each other's territory while denying Chinese access to this sector, at least, initially. This would provide our business sector the first mover advantage into the region. Thus, the road could be built up to Kamaing thereby touching two townships and then, instead of continuing along the original alignment of the Stilwell Road, could swing west to Hpakant Town and possibly further west back into India, thereby creating a circuit. This would enable traders from India to drive across Pangsau Pass, to access Kachin, Sagaing and then re-enter India from the south at Mon (terrain permitting) or it can also connect with the Moreh-Tamu axis and enter at Manipur, and *vice versa.* Secondly, the need for strict border control including customs and immigration cannot be stressed enough. The common refrain of paucity of immigration and customs staff can easily be overcome by deputing CAPF troops to these entities to enable them to meet the requirements of 100 per cent security checking, especially of vehicles. These troops can operate under the overall authority of the responsible immigration and customs staff to ensure compliance.[18]

Departmental inefficiencies cannot hold the development of the nation and its borderlands to ransom. Where required, crises and *fait accompli* will need to be created to push the development. For long, we have scoffed at our predecessors for not building roads in the Northeast for fear of a Chinese invasion. The question is now that we have come to the same crossroads, will we make the same mistakes and be cursed by our successors for eternity; or do we seize the opportunity, take the risk and push for creating history in the region.[19]

Presently, air connectivity to Myanmar is limited to three cities (Kolkata, daily; Gaya, weekly; Imphal to Mandalay, chartered flight only) and three airlines (including one from Myanmar). In comparison, China has 14 airlines connecting 22 Chinese cities to Myanmar, including Mandalay, pre-COVID-19 figures. The recently-opened flight from Imphal to Mandalay is still not approved to be a scheduled flight and is only a chartered flight which operates infrequently. This is apparently because the Ministry of Civil Aviation has not approved scheduled flights from Imphal, although it appears there is adequate demand for this, especially from the Myanmar side to access Bodh Gaya. Secondly, for unknown reasons, the flight goes from Imphal through Aizwal to Mandalay. This is 1 hour 45 minute–flight, when compared to the direct route from Imphal to Mandalay which is just one hour, would be cheaper and faster. This too can be achieved by pushing the respective agencies to expedite activity.

The Third Space and Small Businesses

The Third Space is that space beyond government-to-government relations where residents of the two countries can conduct informal and heart-to-heart exchanges between peoples of different disciplines and backgrounds, ranging from people of eminence to the individual stakeholder on the ground, from across the region and beyond. This leads to the ability to ideate, share thoughts, concepts, differences and solutions to lead to people-to-people connect and collaboration. The Asian Confluence,[20] a Shillong-based think tank which works on the Third Space, writes:

> *Governments provide political and policy structures and businesses complement with the economic and commercial counterparts. There is however a "Third Space" beyond such efforts which needs to be nurtured. The Third Space is essentially the human and spiritual connect. As a network of individuals, institutions and communities, it builds bridges of trust and creates votaries for win-win solutions beyond and across borders of states, identities and ideologies.*[21]
>
> *In a rapidly evolving space of ideas, cultures, politics and commerce, there has been a renewed vigour in engagement among the nation states in forging cooperation and connect. A lot of action to this end has been happening in two spaces: one, led by Governments and two, initiated by Big Businesses. Governments can put in political structures. Big Businesses with government together can take a step forward by putting in economic structures. There is however a Third Space beyond such efforts which needs to be nurtured: that of a Civil Society driven network of individuals and communities across the nation states and regions who are votaries for win-win solutions that promote overall balanced economic growth, and ensure security and stability.*[22]

Thus, two distinctions emerge in this quest to improve people-to-people relations. One is that governments have a role to play, as do the 'Big Businesses'. Ambassador Rajiv Bhatia contextualises this when he writes[23] that governments and corporates are key players in forging and sustaining relations among states, but between two neighbouring democracies, the role of 'Third Space'—media, academics, think tanks, civil society, etc.—is beginning to be appreciated widely and this applies specifically to the development of relations between India and Myanmar now.

I take this perspective forward with a rider in which I include 'Small Businesses' in the realm of the third space, as distinct from 'Big Businesses'. Since this discussion is not about businesses *per se*, I deign to define small businesses and only elaborate that these are businesses that will be able to address the requirement of meeting the 'hearts and minds' needs of investments articulated above. Herein, lies the crux of the argument that Ambassador Saurabh Kumar put forward during a video conference on *India-Myanmar Business Promotion Challenges and*

Opportunities—Post COVID-19, on 9 June 2020. It is these small businesses and small scale industries, which probably fall into the category of Micro, Small and Medium Enterprises (MSMEs),[24] that will provide the critical mass and tip the scale towards better India-Myanmar people-to-people relations, if they can be catalysed. Thus, a large part of the focus of governmental and quasi-governmental organisations, chambers of commerce, civil society organisations and media would be to inspire this category of businesses to invest in Myanmar. Investment in businesses in Myanmar would essentially amount to investments in India-Myanmar relations.

The India-Myanmar Chamber of Commerce (IMCC) with over 114 member companies works closely with the Embassy of India, Yangon. During the visit of the VIF delegation to Myanmar, a programme on 'Understanding Business Climate in Myanmar' was organised and a presentation was made by Shri Sunil Seth, President IMCC. A few aspects which emerged were, firstly, Myanmar does not have a middle class as yet. The bulk of the population is either upper or lower income segment. There is a major misconception that companies have in India that Myanmar is still under sanctions as hithertofore. Mr. Seth explained that Myanmar is a country with high business potential but one has to enter with a marathon mentality and not a sprint mentality. Finally, there is a need for more road shows, interactions, discussions and education of businessmen in India so that they invest in Myanmar.

An Assessment of India-Myanmar Relations in 2020

Possibly, the best dividends accrued by India in the India-Myanmar calculus lies in the security domain. The latest feather in the cap is the handing over of 22 wanted Indian insurgents apprehended by Myanmar to Indian authorities. A Myanmar military special aircraft flew in from Hkamti, Sagaing Region, to Imphal, Manipur, and thence to Guwahati, Assam, and delivered the 22 fugitives. They included 12 Manipuri insurgents of the United National Liberation Front (UNLF), People's Revolutionary Party of Kangleipak (PREPAK Pro), Kanglei Yawaol Kanna Lup (KYKL) and People's Liberation Army of Manipur (PLA). The remaining 10 were from the National Democratic Front of Bodoland (NDFB) and Kamtapur Liberation Organisation (KLO).[25] This is a significant development and symbolises a massive improvement in India-Myanmar relations from the time that 192 insurgents apprehended by the Myanmar Army were allowed to escape, ostensibly in return for pecuniary considerations, for the Regional Commanders.[26]

The other major success was in the conduct of the two operations, 'Operation

Sunrise I & II'. Both succeeded in hitting at the respective insurgent groups of both countries. For India, it was a game-changer in that the major headquarters of the insurgent groups in Myanmar, i.e., at Taga was hit and hit hard. 'Operation Sunrise I' broke the back of insurgency in the Northeast as it wiped out the last bastion of refuge the insurgents had in Myanmar. If that broke the back, the repatriation of the captured 22 insurgents was effectively the last nail in the coffin of insurgency as it prevailed in the Northeast as per common knowledge. Does that mean that all is well in the Seven Sisters and that there will be no more insurgent attacks? Far from it, unless this present security improvement is quickly followed up with requisite administrative and developmental work. Further, notwithstanding the military successes, the easy availability of money, motivation and military equipment (read: weapons) in the Northeast, rules out the chances of a totally secure environment for a long time. The security forces can only do so much in curbing insurgency. If not followed up by prompt action to redress the circumstances that gave rise to the insurgency, the situation can slide back into the abyss of violence.

The India-Myanmar Joint Statement issued during the visit of President U Win Myint to India in February 2020 is the most recent bilateral document available in the public domain which provides a comprehensive idea about India's engagements with Myanmar. This author, in a VIF web article[27] brought out that the sheer scale, scope and spread of the engagement between the two countries suggests that as far as reach goes, India's quiet diplomacy strategy using soft power is fulfilling the needs of Myanmar in those aspects in which it needs help the most. These projects, if implemented in a timely manner by the Indian Government, will have a far greater positive impact on the Myanmar economy and people than the Chinese economic blitzkrieg and high-profile optics during Xi Jinping's January 2020 visit.

The author, in the same article, has highlighted that this joint statement reveals a rare efficiency and energy in India-Myanmar relations and speaks volumes for the governments on both sides. Rather than trying to match the Chinese largesse dollar for dollar, India seems to have skilfully used its strengths and capabilities to genuinely assist Myanmar and incidentally counter the Chinese influence as an added bonus. The joint statement surprisingly did not touch upon the recently started Imphal–Mandalay chartered flight, the proposed film festival and the state level interactions that have commenced.

Addressing the Delivery Gap

The success and future of Indian foreign policy hinges on a major caveat, the ability to deliver on commitments of all international projects. This author has brought out[28] that:

> *India is fighting a running battle on two fronts, one internally and the other externally. The internal battle is to improve its implementation of these projects. Till the time the Indian Government machinery does not deliver the projects, the initiative taken our diplomats all across the world, will not fructify. Secondly, externally, it has to jettison the dubious perception it has acquired over non-delivery of bilateral projects Hence the era of large projects going over decades with innumerable cost and time overruns should be shunned and the Government should ensure guaranteed execution of the projects agreed upon bilaterally.*

This is as true in the case of Myanmar as it is in the case of the rest of the world. Amara Thiha from the Myanmar Institute of Peace and Security, a Yangon-based think tank, writes that '*...the strategic military-to-military partnership between New Delhi and the Tatmadaw creates space for Myanmar to adhere to a core principle, an independent and active foreign policy, by giving an alternative to China for Myanmar to engage with.*' This rests on the hope that India lives up to its promise and makes it possible for Myanmar to retain its' independence in matters external and be the preferred and trusted alternative to China that Myanmar is looking for.[29]

That said, the question arises, why is it that the nation falls short on delivery? An interaction with Dr. Arvind Gupta, former Deputy National Security Advisor; Secretary, National Security Council Secretariat (NSCS); Director General, Institute of Defence Studies and Analyses and presently, Director, VIF, during the course of the Fellowship in this regard, was insightful. He explained that while a deliverable negotiated by an Ambassador and the MEA in consultation with the PMO and sometimes even with the NSCS, was a high-priority agenda at the national level, the same was often not the case from the perspective of the ministry responsible for delivery. For this ministry, the domestic compulsions were so high and pressing and likely to have political compulsions that the MEA-driven agenda became lower in its priority. Plus, the External Affairs Minister and the Minister in the other ministry would often have political differences which spilled over into the working of the ministries. In an article,[30] he specifies that:

> *The foreign policy agenda cuts across several ministries and departments of the government. A comprehensive government approach to foreign policy needs to be*

devised. The ministries of external affairs, finance and commerce need to work together to identify and implement winning strategies. At the same time, other departments like that of industry will have to take steps to improve India's productivity. International trade negotiations are affairs (in which the) ministry is a facilitator at best. The government should set up a multi-ministry task force, duly empowered, to deal with international negotiations on trade issues. There is a need for creating effective mechanisms within the government to implement the foreign policy agenda.

Kanti Bajpai and Byron Chong of the Centre on Asia and Globalisation, Lee Kuan Yew School of Public Policy, National University of Singapore, have carried out[31] a study of the strengths and weaknesses of the Indian Foreign Service (IFS) and the MEA. Their paper examines India's Foreign Service at three levels—the individual, organizational, and systemic in relation to its analytical, operational and political competencies. It has identified nine elements of policy capacity which have been assessed for the Indian foreign policy system and reveals that despite being staffed by skilled and talented individuals, the institution suffers from considerable weaknesses at the organizational level.

The study finds that foreign policy capacity in India is relatively strong at the level of individual competence and relatively weak at the organizational and systemic levels, and this may provide an answer. Talented and skilled individuals think imaginatively and creatively in response to India's external challenges; but organizational and systemic constraints lead to watered-down implementation. This is a familiar lament in public policy studies—the gap between conceptualization and implementation and may well be the story of Indian foreign policy capacity and effectiveness.

The study by Bajpai and Chong brings out a number of aspects, out of which only those relevant to this argument of the delivery gap are brought out below:

Individual Level

- *The IFS is thought to live in its own "bubble" by the other services, and IFS officers themselves admit to not knowing the administrative byways of India as intimately or shrewdly as the officers of the various domestic services. However, even if they are not as politically knowledgeable as their domestic service counterparts, they are by no means naïve.*

Organisational Level

- *The MEA is not involved in the daily business of Indian administration and therefore has a certain "distance" from politics and politicization and is the least politicised of all the services. The flip side of this positive distancing, though, is that it is not greatly influential in domestic administration and does not have strong links to India's political institutions except the Prime Minister's Office (PMO).*

- *The MEA increasingly deals with state governments and has a dedicated section, the States' Division, for coordinating with state capitals. However, at the organisational level, the MEA is largely divorced from domestic governance.*
- *Those from the domestic services often feel that they are simply better qualified and trained and could do a better job at protecting and advancing Indian interests abroad. IFS officers are seen as generalists who do not know very much about Indian administration or technical matters, as superficial minded and divorced from the "realities" of Indian life, and as operating at the margins of policy decisions.*

Systemic Level

- *The knowledge of and specialization in foreign policy and international relations in India is quite limited. The media, which is the greatest disseminator of information, has failed to develop expertise in foreign policy and International Relations. It has turned to increasingly superficial analysis and reporting of the news including foreign policy. This impacts appreciation of foreign policy matters by other agencies as a whole. This is reflected in the very limited number of international relations courses offered and also the very few IR oriented think tanks in India.*
- *Another major systemic limit on foreign policy capacity is the rather poor coordination between the MEA and other parts and sections of the government, and even worse with the private sector and civil society. The MEA and the embassies do collaborate with Indian business associations like the CII which is particularly active abroad, with 11 offices outside India, and cooperates with the MEA and other Indian departments. The MEA also works with private sector organizations that have a foreign policy function such as the Ananta Aspen Centre which is backed by the Avantha Group. However, the quality of interaction is not high. While industry usually aligns itself closely with the government's foreign policy stances, the ministry remains rather suspicious of any role for it in foreign policy.*
- *MEA's interactions with NGOs have been even less fructuous. In short, the MEA has a rather imperial and exclusivist view of foreign policy and does not trust entities outside the government, indeed, outside the IFS. At the same time, the private and people sectors find the MEA rather heavy-footed and old-fashioned as well as ill-informed in their areas of operation.*

To pile all the blame on the MEA alone is unfair. The foreign policy system includes a larger pool of decision makers and institutions: the Prime Minister and his office (the PMO); the Cabinet and its Committee on Security in particular; the Ministry of Defence; the Ministry of Home Affairs; various economic ministries; the foreign affairs committee of Parliament; even the media must take responsibility. The visit of the Myanmar President to India in February 2020 not being covered in most mainstream media is a case in point.

Ambassador K.S. Rana[32] informs us[33] that though the MEA is headed by four civil servants of the highest rank, the, Secretary, the Foreign Secretary, their equal and the uncontested leader, bears an impossibly disproportionate burden. He is the head of the IFS cadre and also looks after four major roles, viz., head of the foreign policy machinery; administrative head of the IFS; supervisor of relations with key countries; and the adviser who accompanies the PM and EAM to regional and global summits and major bilateral meets. Ambassasor Rana highlights that in contrast, though heading sizable MEA divisions, the other secretaries are relatively underworked.

Ambassador Rana adds that the Foreign Secretary is the only one with the necessary clout to engage the economic ministries and other official stakeholders in such domestic diplomacy along multiple tracks. He maintains that a *de novo* approach is needed to bring Indian states into the foreign policy process, within the ambit of the Central Government as mandated by the Indian Constitution. He suggests that a whole-of-government policy is needed to overcome turf battles. Finally, he recommends setting up a permanent machinery for inspections of embassies and enforcement of procedures, development of annual plans, incorporating the practice of 'handing over notes' by ambassadors at the end of their term. Under the MEA's "Development Partnership Administration" process[34] embassies also manage aid and have responded well to the new responsibilities.

Turf battles are another bane of the Indian bureaucracy. India-Myanmar relations allegedly paid the price of one such battle between the ministries of External Affairs and Petroleum. In 2005, India, Bangladesh and Myanmar were to sign a tripartite agreement for laying of a US$ 1 billion Myanmar-India gas pipeline running 290 km from the gas reserves at Shwe field in Block A-1 in offshore Myanmar Arakan (Rakhine) state in Myanmar, through the Indian states of Mizoram and Tripura before crossing Bangladesh to Kolkata (Figure 14.5). It was perceived that it would get the volumes that were expected to be discovered in its adjacent Block A-3. In both the blocks, the ONGC Videsh Ltd. had a 20 per cent stake and GAIL (India) had10 per cent while South Korea's Daewoo was the operator of both the blocks.[35] The project would help Myanmar sell its gas found in the Bay of Bengal while allowing Bangladesh to earn transit fee and realise value for the stranded gas in north-eastern Bangladesh. For India, the project would help feed its growing economy while also helping tap the stranded gas in the northeastern states.[36]

Figure 14.5: India-Bangladesh-Myanmar Gas Pipeline (IBM)

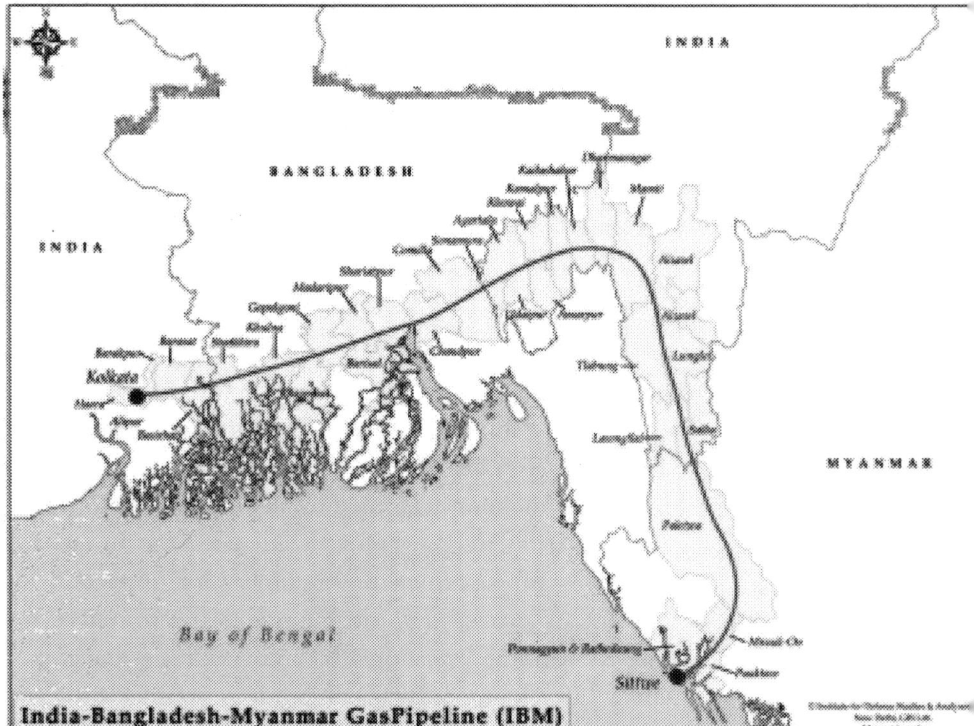

Source: Sanket Sudhir Kulkarni (2016), *India's Decision Making on Cross-Border Natural Gas Pipelines* (1989–2012), Strategic Analysis, 40:5, 405-424, DOI:10.1080/09700161.2016.1209907© IDSA

As per former IFS officer and Indian Petroleum Minister, Mr. Mani Shankar Aiyar,[37] the MEA scuttled the project on the grounds that since the Indian Government was anti-Khaleda Zia, who was in power at that time, it did not want the project to fructify. He rants about an '*awful joint secretary who was only interested in turf. He said foreign policy would be decided by MEA and not by me* (i.e., Mr. Aiyar). *Besides, they were desperately sucking up to the Americans.*' He further added:

They knew nothing about petroleum and gas and petroleum (and) knew nothing about foreign affairs. Therefore, when I came in, I immediately set up an oil advisory committee consisting of all my foreign service colleagues who had just retired and come back to Delhi. So we had people who knew Bangladesh, who knew the Arab world, who knew Latin America. It was called the Oil Advisory Committee and my last chairperson was a person called Mohammad Hamid Ansari (current Vice President of India). The day after I was sacked, he was curtly informed by some section officer that "you have been terminated, the committee doesn't exist".

The conversation had taken place in an interview with *Down to Earth*,[38] which seemed to infer that he had rattled the global energy markets by vigorously promoting a compact of Asian countries to ensure their energy security. However, he was stripped of his portfolio well before completion of his tenure. Even if one were to discount the vitriolic version by the former minister, the accusation of turf battles is plausible. However, a more balanced account[39] of the events suggests that the MEA stance, however debatable, was a more considered position based on the management of geopolitical risks and the political and social stability of the transit countries rather than the outcome of the decision of 'an awful joint secretary'.

Engaging the Tatmadaw

(This section has been taken from an article by this author written on the occasion of the Tatmadaw National Day on 27 March 2020.) [40]

The Tatmadaw has been found wanting in working towards delivery of national-level aspirations. This is a mismatch between capability and aspirations which the military leadership does not publicly acknowledge, either because they do not realise it, or they are do now want to highlight it at the peril of losing face and space in the national narrative.

So what then is the way forward for the Tatmadaw to recover lost ground, reputation and relevance today? To begin with, acknowledging the problem is half the battle. Senior commanders in Tatmadaw need to start with identifying and acknowledging the problem that besets the organisation. There seems to be a total lack of honest introspection in the organisation fuelled by an overbearing sedition law which threatens everyone even constructively critical of the organisation. *Prima facie*, the lucre of high office, the comfortable bogey of national security and the need to secure one's position and status in the national leadership spectrum, drives all higher level military motivation. Honest introspection will naturally lead the decision makers to the correct path for reviving the Tatmadaw.

Secondly, politics has been the bane for militaries the world over. So it is for the Tatmadaw. Truly, the Tatmadaw is in an unenviable position. Having to extricate itself from a system where it has been ruling the roost for decades, while securing itself from prosecution, it is in itself a difficult and vulnerable situation. If it lets go of the power, it makes itself vulnerable to prosecution by civilian law makers. Thus, it has no option really but to hold on to the power. Militarily, unless it is able to let go of the politics, there is unlikely to be any improvement in the quality of soldiering that it can produce. When commanders in the chain are involved in politicking, it is at the cost of military efficiency. Politics has become an expensive distraction for a force which is paying the price in blood. The question is, with elections looming and with the hold that Aung San Suu Kyi has over the military, can she convince them to take a step back in exchange for a degree of immunity which they would desperately need, in order to step back? In an article[41] in *The Economist* titled 'General Myopia: Why Myanmar's army is wrong to reject limits on its power', the author argues that:

> *Amending the Constitution to provide more of a semblance of civilian supremacy over the armed forces would be a good start. The army could cede control of the various security ministries, for example, or give up its voting majority on the special government committee empowered to declare a state of emergency. At one level, it would be merely a token gesture: Miss Suu Kyi surely knows that the army would not hesitate to stage another coup if it felt truly threatened. But over time, the new rules might evolve from polite fictions into institutional norms.*[2]

Thirdly, once the military has been able to move away from the politics, it has to undergo major internal reforms to convert into the much touted and sought after Standard Army. This means it needs to withdraw, introspect, go back to the basics, re-equip and train, before it can be re-launched into operations. Further, the strategy of launching operations on all fronts against a large number of Ethnic Armed Organisations (EAOs) goes against the basic military principle of concentration of force. This is especially true against evolved EAOs who collaborate under the moniker, Brotherhood Alliance. Observers often note that the battlefield turnout and body language of the EAOs is far better than that of the Myanmar Armed Forces...which reflects better confidence, a product of better competence, which eventually translates into better military successes for the EAOs.

Fourth, it has to reconnect with its troops. The route to a Standard Army has to jettison the feudal connect and develop and sustain a professional officer-man relationship where professional dissent is not seen as seditious. The rampage that the Tatmadaw troops have inflicted in their areas of operations in North Rakhine on the Rohingya populated areas as also the AA, is simply a result of undisciplined and unprofessional troops operating without any effective supervision by officers. The unspoken concept of 'living off the land' has to be replaced with accountability at the lowest levels.

Fifthly, a back-to-the-basics approach to counter insurgency operations which involves shunning over-reliance on artillery and air power, needs to be followed.

It has to develop HUMINT for which it has to operate like a responsible and disciplined force. The Tatmadaw needs to start getting small successes before it can even dream of trying to eradicate insurgent groups of the scale, motivation and cunning of the AA.

Finally, it needs strategic guidance, either from the Myanmar civilian government, or from within. The irony of fighting a bitter insurgency with an insurgent organisation which is not even seeking separation from Myanmar is hard to fathom. Where peace has a sliver of a chance, the Tatmadaw must exploit it. It has a historical precedent. Post the 1988 Revolution, the Tatmadaw had made a large number of concessions to EAOs and narcotics-based armies to placate them and make them amenable to the Tatmadaw. This worked, though only partially. But it bought time to the Tatmadaw to recover and focus. It must see federalism as a viable structure existing all over the world without any dilution of national solidarity and sovereignty.

The Tatmadaw must conserve its strength for more meaningful nation building activities. Only if these brave and drastic actions are taken can the Tatmadaw ensure that history remembers it kindly as an organisation which lived up to national causes.[42] Without course correction, it may go down as the organisation which, in the process of trying to uphold national causes, in effect caused the exact opposite.

The Tatmadaw has to realistically assess its strengths and weaknesses before it applies itself to combat. It must take into consideration the power of the EAOs. In cases where it falls short, the deficit in power has to be compensated by negotiation, politics and diplomacy. Presently, what is lacking is the benefit of higher military leadership.[43]

Resolving the Rakhine Conflict

The AA and Tatmadaw are inextricably involved in the conflict with no conclusive and decisive victory in sight for either side. Both are facing casualties and are in danger of getting embroiled in a long, expensive and dirty fight with a large amount of human rights violations by both sides. Stands have hardened on both sides even as both grudgingly realise the futility of military options. The AA has faced major casualties, far in excess of the Tatmadaw, but the casualties of Tatmadaw are increasing by the day. Conversely, the Tatmadaw conduct in the region alienates locals and hence they are losing local support totally and even neutrals are likely to tilt towards the AA. The local polity of Rakhine State is also sympathetic to the AA, though covertly, since any overt association with the AA will invite action by the Myanmar Army under the strict sedition laws.

India needs to stimulate and initiate the peace process in this region which, being in the close vicinity of the Bangladesh, India and Myanmar trijunction, affects all the three countries. If allowed to spread, this could effectively drag on and hinder development and the Act East Policy with Myanmar and therefore the connect with ASEAN markets. The appointment of a special envoy or a similarly empowered and experienced person (e.g., an ex-ambassador) to oversee the overall process would be required. Ice-breaker meetings would need to be hosted with AA representatives at Thailand, Kolkata or Delhi under a Track 2 organisation, e.g., a think tank along with other think tanks from Myanmar. Depending on the progress and response from the AA, the Tatmadaw could then be incorporated into the negotiations. The overall aim would be to reduce hostilities to enable the Kaladan Project road from Paletwa to Zorinpui to be constructed and traffic commences to connect Mizoram with the Northeast to this alternate mode of connectivity and effectively create the redundancy to offset the Chicken's Neck vulnerability. The spin offs to the locals in Myanmar would be substantial.

Social Media

Ending decades of technological isolation, Myanmar in 2019, changed over to Unicode, the most common computer script with characters from most of the world's languages. Aung San Suu Kyi officially launched it calling for Myanmar to catch up with its neighbour, Cambodia, which embraced Unicode in 2010. Till 2019, Internet users in Myanmar had no option but to use the local Zawgyi script and the adoption of Unicode is expected to make a huge difference to the digital aspirations of the population there.

Radhika Daga writes[44] that Myanmar's phone ownership rates skyrocketed in just a span of half a decade, equipping people from cities and rural areas with an Internet-enabled smartphone. Notably, despite having access to the Internet, most of this population used it for Facebook, which took up "*over 85 per cent of all Internet traffic*".

> *From the start, Facebook presented itself as a one-stop-shop for the long-awaited connectivity that eluded the citizens of this country. In his/her maiden spell, the average user turned to Facebook for socialising, news, entertainment, and even e-commerce. Typically pre-installed on their smartphone, this application provided instant updates from the pages of their preferred political parties, organisations or companies. This tendency led to an over-reliance on Facebook as a content provider, also reflective of Myanmar's stunted levels of digital literacy. Because Facebook became the common man's go-to online platform, there was little incentive for its users to learn how to use or explore the wider world web to search for information. The act of curating one's own content through Internet browsing develops one's ability to analyze whether information found on the Internet is accurate and true. But because most users did not engage in such an activity, they were not able to accurately discern fake information from real information on Facebook.*

This is what fuelled inter-ethnic clashes in Myanmar in 2014 in Mandalay. In 2018, Reuters found more than 1,000 examples of posts, comments and pornographic images attacking the Rohingya and other Muslims on Facebook. The military too has resorted to Facebook as a powerful means of psychological warfare.

This provides India with another opportunity to engage Myanmar in keeping with the 'hearts and minds' principle. India has massive software skills and the opening up of Myanmar to Unicode simply opens up the world of social media over and beyond Facebook. Sarah Kreps of Cornell University explains[45] that democracies have advantages such as good governance largely because the freedom of expression and the Press which provides a platform for honest debate about the pros and cons of different policies that educate the public, enable accountability, and produce better policy implementation. However, social media undermines these democratic advantages by creating misinformation, '*often strategically deployed by foreign actors seeking to exploit polarization in the political landscape and undermine trust in domestic institutions*'. Hence, the importance of engaging in India consciousness in Myanmar using social media is a key element to successful India-Myanmar relations.

Interaction between Think Tanks

There is need for Indian and Myanmar think tanks to interact more frequently on a plethora of issues. Interaction between think tanks enables the exchange of ideas and opinions and generates the possibility of coming out with viable policy recommendations. The culture of think tanks in Myanmar started with the Myanmar Institute of Strategic and International Studies (MISIS) which was established in 1992 by the SLORC with the then Minister for Foreign Affairs as its Chairman. More recently, the Myanmar Institute of Peace and Security (MIPS) is a think tank which has been functioning since 2017. It maintains one of the most comprehensive conflict-management databases which form the basis for its much sought after monthly and annual reviews. The Institute of Strategy and Policy—Myanmar (ISP Myanmar) is another independent think tank which opened around the same time and seeks to promote democratic leadership and strengthening civic participation by conducting policy-oriented research, analysis, public outreach, training and through leadership-level dialogue. The Thay Ninga Institute of Strategic Studies (TISS), is a Tatmadaw-driven think tank run by a former Tatmadaw hepatologist which started operations in 2015. In addition, the Tampadipa Institute and the Tagaung Institute of Political Studies are smaller think tanks which have a security-related focus.

Figure 14.6: The VIF Delegation at MISIS in December 2019

Development versus Security and the Over-Securitisation Trap

Dr. Wolfgang-Peter Zingel, Associate Member, South Asia Institute (SAI), University of Heidelberg, Germany, states[46] that '*national security is a precondition for economic and social development as much as economic and social development is a precondition for national security. The question then arises: Is there a trade-off between national security and economic development? Is economic and social development possible without national security and how much security does development need?*' The Northeast is militarised and security is foremost in the mind space of most policy makers. This is a natural fallout of the legacy of seven decades of insurgency and violence in various parts of the region. The overall situation has improved drastically in the past few years and more so in 2019 post the 'Op Sunrise'-

coordinated operations between India and Myanmar. The situation is now ripe for administrative initiatives to take the lead and work towards transition of the region into the 'developmental pull' cycle. The push involves taking calculated risks since all risks will not manifest into threats and all threats do not lead to catastrophes. Further, the Indian Government today has the capability and the political will to contain threats and prevent catastrophes in national security, but it does not have the luxury of holding back development in its farthest regions.

In this context, the security establishments need to undertake a shift in their approach to over-securitisation of all potential risk situations. Rather than applying knee-jerk and reactive actions which are typically indiscriminately preventive, prohibitive or overly restrictive in nature, they need to view implications of such security aspects from a nation-building perspective. A typical example would be proposals for opening up border areas for tourism, mountaineering and trade, which would normally have been turned down on simply 'security concerns' and that are now slowly being viewed from a nation-building perspective. This needs to be mainstreamed and as such enhancements in trade and tourism provide an opportunity to locals to benefit thereby indirectly enhancing human security. The need for taking up the gun or indulging in illegal activities proportionately decreases. These initiatives should increase the stakes beyond the level where the locals feel tempted to compromise security as a community. In any society there will always be some individuals who will want to indulge in illegal activities, but as a whole the community should not feel it a right to indulge in activities counter to security considerations.

Finally, the over-securitisation trap holds valid even in the India-Myanmar context. The dangers of losing out on people-to-people relations in fear of security concerns needs to be balanced with the opportunities available to increase contact between the peoples of the two nations to promote a developed IMB region.[47]

The Irrawaddy Imperatives

India-Myanmar relations have moved far ahead from the lows of the early 1990s, when there was no Indian Ambassador in Myanmar for over a year from 1988 when Ambassador I.P. Singh relinquished office and till August 1990 when Ambassador P.M.S. Malik took charge. On the security front, they have reached a high level of confidence and mutual understanding. However much more is required to be done in the fields of trade and commerce and to increase people-to people contact. Sir Girija Shankar Bajpai's postulation of the three circles of security with the inner-most circle being from Hindukush Mountains to the Irrawaddy, provides us the key to the most crucial requirement for security and development of the Northeast and India-Myanmar relations. The need is for good Indian initiatives and good investments to reach the Irrawaddy and populate the vacuum between the IMB and the Irrawaddy. These are the Irrawaddy Imperatives required to generate good will and create the momentum to develop the region and the necessary insulation required to keep at bay the Chinese negative influence.

I conclude with a statement by the External Affairs Minister, Mr. S. Jaishankar who, in July 2020, articulated[48] sentiments which sum up the arguments I have tried to present in this project:

> *The era of great caution, and greater dependence on multilateralism, is behind us. We have to step out more. We have to be more confident, we have to articulate our interests better. We need to take risks. Without taking risks, you can't get ahead. Those are choices we have to make.*

NOTES

1. During an Interactive video conference on *India-Myanmar Business Promotion Challenges and Opportunities—post Covid-19,* on 9 June 2020, organised by the Punjab Haryana & Delhi (PHD) Chamber of Commerce and Industry along with the India-Myanmar Chamber of Commerce.
2. Government of India, Ministry of External Affairs, *India-Myanmar Bilateral Relations,* https://mea.gov.in/Portal/ForeignRelation/India_Myanmar_Bilateral_Brief_Website_jan_2019.pdf (Accessed on 1 February 2021).
3. Book discussion on *'The Borderlands and Boundaries of the Indian Subcontinent: Baluchistan to the Patkai Range and Arakan Yoma'* by Shri Dilip K. Chakrabarti, Professor Emeritus, University of Cambridge & Distinguished Fellow, VIF, on 18 March 2020. https://www.youtube.com/watch?v=8e8_6abcxZ8 (Accessed on 20 April 2020). Amb Bajpai speaks at 49:27 mins.
4. Kenbo is a Chinese scooter brand, popular in the Northeast border towns as taxis or private transport. The term 'Kenbo effect' alludes to the uncontrolled influx of Chinese goods into the economy and unregulated trade of these good leads to a Kenbo economy.
5. See https://www.dailypioneer.com/2019/columnists/time-to-up—the-game.html; https://www.firstpost.com/india/indias-foreign-policy-for-next-5-years-new-delhi-must-stave- off-chinese-influence-on-myanmar-through-trade-development-assistance-6846731.html; http://eleventhcolumn.com/2019/06/26/what-india-must-focus-on-in-myanmar/ and https://timesofindia.indiatimes.com/india/why-chinese-president-xi-jinpings-myanmar-visit- may-worry-india/articleshow/73324878.cms
6. https://www.dica.gov.mm/sites/dica.gov.mm/files/news-files/mig_final_2018final26-4-19_1.pdf
7. Jaideep Chanda, Xi Hajoor! Old wine in the 'New Era' for Myanmar, New Delhi, 20 January 2020, https://www.vifindia.org/article/2020/january/22/xi-hajoor-old-wine-in-the-new-era-for-myanmar (Accessed on 5 May 2020).
8. Myanmar-China Oil & Gas Pipeline Project (Myanmar Section) "Special Report on Social Responsibility": http://csr.cnpc.com.cn/cnpccsr/xhtml/PageAssets/mdbg2016-en.pdf (Accessed on 3 November 2019).
9. Darshana Barua's "India's Answer to the Belt and Road: A Road Map for South Asia", Carnegie

India Working Paper, August 2018: https://carnegieendowment.org/files/WP_Darshana_Baruah_Belt_Road_FINAL.pdf (Accessed on 1 December 2019).

10. Ambassador T.P. Sreenivasan, A mysterious country that has baffled the world, Rediff.com, 28 November 2015, https://www.rediff.com/news/column/a-mysterious-country-that-has-baffled-the-world/20151128.htm (Accessed on 18 May 2020).
11. Ashley J. Tellis, Troubles Aplenty: Foreign Policy Challenges for the Next Indian Government, Carnegie Endowment for International Peace, Article, 20 May 2020, https://carnegieendowment.org/2019/05/20/troubles-aplenty-foreign-policy-challenges-for-next-indian-government-pub-79161(Accessed on 28 May 2020).
12. Jaideep Chanda, *Raising 'Myanmar Consciousness': Visit of the President of Myanmar to India (26-29 February 2020),* Vivekananda International Foundation Web Article, 28 February 2020: https://www.vifindia.org/article/2020/february/28/raising-myanmar-consciousness-visit-of-the-president-of-myanmar-to-india (Accessed on 30 June 2020).
13. Manipur University website http://www.manipuruniv.ac.in/department/center-for-myanmar-studies-2 (Accessed on 29 April 2020).
14. Manipur University website, List of Students, http://www.manipuruniv.ac.in/department/center-for-myanmar-studies-2/students-2-2-2-2-2-2-2-3-2-2-3 (Accessed on 29 April 2020).
15. HQ Integrated Defence Staff Website, https://www.ids.nic.in/sfl.php (Accessed on 29 April 2020).
16. R. Lee Hadden, "*The Geology of Burma (Myanmar): An Annotated Bibliography of Burma's Geology, Geography and Earth Science*", Topographic Engineering Centre, US Army Corps of Engineers, September 2008, Virginia, pg. 17. https://www.pdfdrive.com/the-geology-of-burma-myanmar-an-annotated-bibliography-of-burmas-geology-geography-and-e40832598.html (Accessed on 9 May 2020).
17. For a comprehensive history of the Stilwell Road, see Donovan Webster, "*The Burma Road: The Epic Story of One of World War II's Most Remarkable Endeavours*", London, 2003; Lipi Ghosh, "*The Lost Trail: The Stilwell Road in Historical and Contemporary Scenarios*" in Rakhee Bhattacharyya and Binoda K. Mishra edited *A Journey through the Stillwell Road*, MAKAIAS, 2011; Leslie Anders, *Ledo Road: General Joseph W. Stilwell's Highway to China,* University of Oklahoma Press, 1965.
18. As a reference, it may be noted that on the 105 Mile Border Crossing at Muse/Jiagaong China-Myanmar border there were 16 officers and 275 staff from nine different departments including Myanmar Trade Department, Customs, Inland Police, Inland Revenue, Myanmar Economic Bank, Immigration, Agriculture, Food & Drug and Livestock departments. Ram Upendra Das, *Enhancing India-Myanmar Border Trade: Policy and Implementation Measures,* Ministry of Commerce and Industry GOI and RIS, 2016, https://www.ris.org.in/enhancing-india-myanmar-border-trade-policy-and-implementation-measures-ministry-commerce-and (Accessed on 28 May 2020).
19. For more on this, see Rakhee Bhattacharya and Binoda K. Mishra, *A Journey through the Stilwell Road,* Maulana Abul Kalam Azad Institute of Asian Studies, Anshah Publishing House, Kolkata, 2011.
20. Asian Confluence was conceived in 2010 as a self-sustaining, independent civil society initiative with a permanent centre in Shillong.
21. The Asian Confluence, Vision and Mission, https://www.asianconfluence.org/about/vision-mission (Accessed on 28 May 2020).
22. The Asian Confluence, Third Space Conversations, https://www.asianconfluence.org/initiatives/third-space (Accessed on 28 May 2020).
23. Rajiv Bhatia, India-Myanmar: 'Third Space' as driver in new era, Observer Research Foundation, Commentaries, 30 April 2016, https://www.orfonline.org/research/india-myanmar-third-space-as-driver-in-new-era/ (Accessed on 28 May 2020).

24. The Gazette of India, Extraordinary, Part II, Section 3, Sub-section (ii), Ministry of Micro, Small and Medium Enterprises Notification, 1 June 2020, https://msme.gov.in/sites/default/files/MSME_gazette_of_india.pdf vide the latest (June 2020) regulation, the criteria for the industries is:

Scale	*Investment in Plant, Machinery & Equipment*	*Turnover*
Micro	Does not exceed 1 crore	Does not exceed 5 crore
Small	Does not exceed 10 crore	Does not exceed 50 crore
Medium	Does not exceed 50 crore	Does not exceed 250 crore

25. Cchavi Vasisht, *Myanmar Round Up: May 2020*, Vivekananda International Foundation Web Article, https://www.vifindia.org/article/2020/june/10/myanmar-round-up-may-2020 (Accessed on 30 July 2020).
26. Wasbir Hussain, *Insurgency in India's Northeast Cross-border Links and Strategic Alliances*, South Asia Terrorism Portal Website, https://www.satp.org/satporgtp/publication/faultlines/volume17/wasbir.htm (Accessed on 30 July 2020).
27. Chanda, Footnote 12.
28. Keshava Parthasarthy and Vriti Vankani, Myanmar President's visit: What does it mean to India? The Kootneeti Web Editorial, 3 March 2020, https://thekootneeti.in/2020/03/03/myanmar-presidents-visit-what-it-brings/ (Accessed on 10 March 2020).
29. Chanda, Footnote 27.
30. Dr. Arvind Gupta, *New govt's foreign policy needs comprehensive approach*, The Economic Times ePaper,3 June 2019, https://economictimes.indiatimes.com/news/politics-and-nation/new-govts-foreign-policy-agenda-needs-comprehensive-approach/articleshow/69626240.cms?utm_source=contentofinterest&utm_medium=text&utm_campaign=cppst (Accessed on 10 March 2020).
31. Kanti Bajpai & Byron Chong (2019) India's Foreign Policy Capacity, Policy Design and Practice, 2:2, 137-162, DOI: 10.1080/25741292.2019.1615164
32. Kishan S. Rana was a member of the Indian Foreign Service from1960 to 1995, serving as ambassador to Algeria, Czechoslovakia, Kenya, Mauritius and Germany. He was also joint secretary in Prime Minister Indira Gandhi's office from 1981 to 1982, and later headed personnel administration in the Ministry of External Affairs. Ambassador Rana now teaches, writes and advises other governments on diplomatic practice. He is the author of *21st Century Diplomacy: A Practitioner's Guide* (Bloomsbury Academic, 2011) and *The Contemporary Embassy: Paths to Diplomatic Success* (Palgrave Macmillan, 2013).
33. http://www.afsa.org/sites/default/files/flipping_book/0614/files/assets/basic-html/index.html#24
34. Ambassador Rana describes this as an umbrella unit established in 2012 to implement an expanded aid program that takes India's external aid contribution to around 0.2 per cent of gross domestic product.
35. PTI, *India, Bangladesh, Myanmar to sign MOU*, The Economic Times ePaper, 27 February 2005, https://economictimes.indiatimes.com/india-bangladesh-myanmar-to-sign-mou/articleshow/1034489.cms?from=mdr (Accessed on 21 May 2020).
36. The News Wire, Political differences hindering Myanmar pipeline dream: Aiyar, 6 January 2006, https://www.outlookindia.com/newswire/story/political-differences-hindering-myanmar-pipeline-dream-aiyar/346762 (Accessed on 21 May 2020).
37. *How MEA torpedoed the Bangladesh India gas pipeline*, Down to Earth, https://www.downtoearth.org.in/interviews/how-mea-torpedoed-the-bangladeshindia-gas-pipeline-43066 (Accessed on 20 June 2020).
38. A fortnightly magazine focused on politics of environment and development, published in New Delhi, India. The Centre for Science and Environment assists in the production of the magazine.

39. https://shodhganga.inflibnet.ac.in/bitstream/10603/250533/10/10_chapter%202.pdf
40. Jaideep Chanda, *Tatmadaw Day 27 March 2020: Things that the Myanmar Armed Forces must do to remain credible and relevant,* Vivekananda International Foundation Web Article, 27 March 2020: https://www.vifindia.org/2020/march/27/tatmadaw-day-27-march-2020-things-that-the-myanmar-armed-forces (Accessed on 30 June 2020).
41. *The Economist*, 'General Myopia: Why Myanmar's army is wrong to reject limits on its power', 10 March 2020. https://www.economist.com/leaders/2020/03/10/why-myanmars-army-is-wrong-to-reject-limits-on-its-power (Accessed on 27 March 2020).
42. The Three National Causes are the non-disintegration of the Union, The non-disintegration of national solidarity and the perpetuation of national sovereignty.
The Four Solemn Vows are Loyalty to the State and the People; Loyalty to the Fallen Soldiers; Pledge to dutifully perform the tasks and orders given by the superiors and Pledge to sacrifice our lives for our State, our people and our Tatmadaw.
43. Aakriti Vinayak, Alakh Ranjan & Jaideep Chanda, *Myanmar Monthly Round Up: October 2019,* Vivekananda International Foundation Web Article, 21 November 2019: https://www.vifindia.org/article/2019/november/21/myanmar-round-up-october-2019(Accessed on 30 June 2020).
44. https://www.vifindia.org/article/2019/december/30/digital-empowerment-of-myanmar
45. Sarah Kreps, *Social Media and International Relations,* Cambridge University Press, Cambridge, 2020. http://dx.doi.org/10.1017/9781108920377 (Accessed on 22 July 2020).
46. https://www.bundesheer.at/pdf_pool/publikationen/eco_impacts_02_national_security_zingel.pdf
47. https://theprint.in/opinion/for-a-place-in-new-world-order-india-must-reverse-over-securitisation-of-its-foreign-policy/342489/ and https://www.newsecuritybeat.org/2011/09/development-or-security-which-comes-first/
48. *Times of India, Era of great caution in foreign policy is behind us: Jaishankar,* 21 July 2020, https://timesofindia.indiatimes.com/india/era-of-great-caution-in-foreign-policy-is-behind-us-jaishankar/articleshow/77075012.cms (Accessed on 21 July 2020).

Postscript

Two events of strategic importance have necessitated this postscript. One, the COVID-19 outbreak has changed the world and also India and Myanmar. However, India-Myanmar relations endure and if anything, India's steadfast support to Myanmar has only strengthened in this adverse hour. Barring an economic jolt, Myanmar is expected to recover from the pandemic better than India, since its economy was relatively less globalised as compared to India. The second event was the one which has impacted this book and the outlook of the author. This was the major clash on 15 June 2020 with Chinese troops in Galwan Valley which led to the demise 20 Indian soldiers and apparently over double the number of Chinese soldiers. This event has been a game-changer for the present and subsequent generations of Indians.

The India-China relationship of cooperation and competition had always been a reality, and one would take comfort in the fact that since no shots had been fired since the mid-1960s, it was assumed that both sides would prefer to retain the *status quo*. This assumption hinged on the premise that both countries would not want to rock the boat of economic growth. Galwan changed this equation. By indulging in such thoughtless violence, China reduced itself to the level of Pakistan and is henceforth doomed to be treated in the same way that Indians treat Pakistan. To understand what this implies, one needs to understand the relationship between India and Pakistan. The one defining feature of this relationship is the lack of trust. Hence in this relationship, there are no concessions made or sought. It is understood that any dealings with Pakistan will take place at a zero-trust level, and hence all actions will manifest with this premise. China is the new Pakistan in the post-Galwan scenario. Henceforth, all actions by Chinese troops, diplomats, government officials, NGOs, PSUs, universities, think tanks and even private companies will face a zero-trust environment in India and from Indians.

The zero-trust environment is a regrettable outcome of a situation foisted on the nation by a belligerent neighbour pursuing an archaic expansionist policy. Conflict in this age transcends conventional silos of traditional and non-traditional security. It is but natural, given this all pervasive nature of conflict, that both sides will end up competing more than cooperating with each other. This competition will spill over across the borders of both India and China, into Asia and beyond. However much India desires a pragmatic and cooperative relationship with China, the reality will be that India and Indians will see China and the Chinese as threats which need to be countered in India and in its immediate and extended neighbourhood. In this context, the Irrawaddy Imperatives become even more relevant. The need to insulate the India-Myanmar borderlands from Chinese influence and to develop this border region for its own intrinsic strength is indisputable. A whole-of-nation approach to these problems is the way forward with especially business communities coming forward to invest in businesses in the India-Myanmar borderland regions.

APPENDICES

APPENDIX A

Agreement on International Boundary with India 10 March 1967

BOUNDARY AGREEMENT BETWEEN THE GOVERNMENT OF INDIA AND THE GOVERNMENT OF THE UNION OF BURMA

Rangoon

The Government of the Republic of India and the Government of the Union of Burma, BEARING in mind the friendly relations existing between the two countries, FIRMLY believing that the formal delimitation and demarcation of the entire traditional boundary between the Republic of India and the Union of Burma will further strengthen the friendly relations between the two countries, HAVE agreed as follows:

ARTICLE I

The Contracting Parties agree that the following shall be the description of the boundary between the Republic of India and the Union of Burma beginning from its southern extremity and ending at its northern extremity:

The southern extremity of the India-Burma boundary is about 1/2 mile south of the triangulation station Reng Tlang. From this point the boundary runs in a general northeasterly direction along the divide separating the waters of the Tuichong from those of the Kola Chaung or Sekul Lui to a point just west of the source of a nameless feeder of the Varang Lui; thence in as easterly direction down the midstream of this nameless feeder to its junction with the Varang Lui, thence down the midstream of the Varang lui to its junction with the Kola Chaung or Sekul Lui, thence up the midstream of the Kola Chaung or Sekul Lui to its junction with the Zocha Lui; thence up the midstream of the Zocha Lui to its source on the Samang Tlang range; thence across the range to the source of the Samak of Kwiman Lui, thence down the midstream of the Samak or Kwiman Lui to the Kaladan River, thence across the Kalandan River to the mouth of the Khangza lui and up the midstream of the Khangza Lui to its source in the Tlang to the source of the Rale (Shweleik) Lui; thence down the midstream of the Rale (Shweleik) Lui to its junction with the Sala Lui; thence up to the midstream of the Sala Lui to its junction with the Khenkhontg (Kaikheu) Lui;

thence up the midstream of the Khenkhong (Kaikheu) Lui to a point on the Pathian Klang range approximately 700 yards north of height 4146; thence generally northwards along this range to the source of the Para Lui and down the midstream of the Para Lui to its junction with the Tisi Va or Mi Chaung; thence up the midstream of this river to its junction with the Kimung Va of Kheimu Lui; thence up the midstream of the Kimung Va or Kheimu Lui to its source on the Kashia Klang to the source of the Raphu Va; thence down the midstream of the Raphu Va to its junction with the Boinu or Tuipui river; thence down the midstream of the Boinu or Tuipui river to its junction with the Tyao or Tio Va river; thence up the midstream of the Tyao or Tio Va river to its source on a saddle marked by Boundary Pillar No. 3 L/CH; thence across that saddle to the source of the Bapi Va and down the midstream of the Bapi Va to its junction with the Timang Va or Tuimang river; thence down the midstream of the Timang Va or Tuimang river to its junction with the Tuisa river; thence down the midstream of the Tuisa river to its junction with the Tuivai river; thence up the stream; thence up the midstream of the Tuikui stream to its source below Boundary Pillar No. 8 situated on a saddle about 4-$^{1}/_{2}$ miles east of Lunglen Hill. From Boundary Pillar No. 8, the boundary runs down the midstream of a nameless feeder of the Tuimong Lui to its junction with the Tuimong Lui, thence down the midstream of the Tuimong Luito its junction with the Tuivel river; thence up the midstream of the Tuivel river to its junction with the Tuinuam Lui; thence up the midstream of the Tuinuam Lui to a saddle where Boundary Pillar No. 7 is located; thence down the midstream of Paiphum Lui; thence up a ridge; thence to its junction with the Tuivai Lui and thence down the midstream of a nameless stream to its junction with the Tuivai Lui and thence down the midstream of the Tuivai Lui to its junction with the Sumtui Lui; thence up the midstream of the Sumtui Lui to its source on Leng Tang range where Boundary Pillar No. 6 is located; thence in an easterly direction down to a neless feeder of the (Tuita) Tuitha or (Kuga) Khuga river; thence down the midstream of this feeder to its junction with the (Tuita) Tuitha or (Kuga) Khuga river; thence up the midstream of the (Tuita) Tuitha or (Kuga) Khuga river to its junction with the Chalao Loam or Chika stream; thence along the midstream of this stream up a ravine to Boundary Pillar No. 5; thence down the midstream of the Yangkau Lokto its junction with the Manipur River; thence northwards up the left bank of the Manipur River to its junction with the Yangdung Lui; thence up the midstream of this stream to its source marked by Boundary Pillar No. 3; thence generally northeastwards to height 7582; thence generally eastwards along the watershed between the tributaries of the Manipur River on the one hand and the tributaries of the Chindwin River on the other hand to the source of the Khengyoi Dung and marked by Boundary Pillar 2 and 1; thence down the midstream of the Khengyoi Dung and the Tuisa Dung to Boundary Pillar No. 39 on the left bank of the Tuisa Dung; thence generally eastwards for approximately 400 yards along the left bank of the Tuisa Dung; thence northwards up the midstream of a nameless feeder to Boundary Pillar No. 38 on Nat Taung Hill; thence generally northwards down the slope of the hill to a ravine; thence generally eastwards along the bed of the stream to where Boundary Pillar No. 37 is located; thence in a general northerly direction to Boundary Pillar No. 36 and thence in the same direction to Boundary Pillar No. 35 located on the right bank of the Auktaung Chaung; thence down the midstream of the Auktaung Chaung to Boundary Pillar No. 34 on the left bank of the Auktaung Chaung; thence in a northerly direction to Boundary Pillar No. 33 located on the left bank of the Tiwan Lam or Tuiwang Dung; thence in a north-northeasterly direction to Boundary Pillar No. 32 located on the right bank of the Tiddim Dung or Naneka Chaung; thence in a north-northeasterly direction to Boundary Pillar No. 31; thence in a north-northwesterly direction to Boundary Pillar No. 30; thence in a northeasterly direction to Boundary Pillar No. 29 located on the left bank of the Rangkep Lok; thence down the midstream of the same stream for a distance of approximately 1 mile to Boundary Pillar No. 28 also located on the left bank of the Rangkep Lok; thence in a north-northeasterly direction to Boundary Pillar No. 27; thence in a northerly direction to Boundary Pillar No. 26 located about 500 yards from the right bank of the Pantha Chaung; thence in a northerly direction to Boundary Pillar No. 25 located on the left bank of the Nanpalaung Chaung; thence in a northeasterly direction to Boundary Pillar No. 24 located about 400 yards from the left bank of the Chaungngyinaung Chaung; thence in a northerly direction to Boundary Pillar No. 23 located on the right bank of the Lokehao River or Chaunggyi Chaung; thence down the midstream of this river for about a mile to Boundary Pillar No. 22; thence in a north-northeasterly direction to Boundary Pillar No. 21; thence in the same direction to Boundary Pillar No. 20; located on the right bank of a tributary of the Chaunggyi Chaung; thence in the same direction to Boundary Pillar No. 19 located approximately 1 mile southeast of Laiching peak trigonometrical station; thence in a northerly direction to Boundary Pillar No. 18 located on the right bank of the Manjet Lok; thence in an easterly direction to Boundary Pillar No.17; thence in a northeasterly direction to Boundary Pillar No. 16 located about 700 yards from the South bank of the Waksu Lok or Wetyu Chaung; thence in a northwesterly direction to Boundary Pillar No. 15 on the left bank of the Waksu Lok or Wetyu Chaung; thence in a northeasterly direction to Boundary Pillar No. 14; thence in a northerly direction to Boundary Pillar No. 13 located about half a mile south of the Tuiyang or Nantisin Chaung; thence in a northwesterly direction to Boundary Pillar No. 12 located on the left bank of the Tuiyang or Nantisin Chaung; thence in a northeasterly direction to Boundary Pillar No. 11, thence in a northerly direction to Boundary Pillar No. 10 located on the right bank of the Taret River or Nantalet Chaung; thence due east to Boundary Pillar No. 9; thence in a north-northeasterly direction to Boundary Pillar No. 8 located on the right bank of the Yu river; thence across the Yu river to Boundary Pillar No. 7 which is located on the left bank of the Yu river opposite Boundary Pillar No. 8, thence in a northeasterly direction to Boundary Pillar No. 6; thence in the same direction to Boundary Pillar No. 5 which is located almost north of height 1192; thence in a north-northeasterly direction to Boundary Pillar No. 4 located on height 1226; thence in a northerly direction to Boundary Pillar No. 3; thence in a north northwesterly direction to Boundary Pillar No. 2 located on the right bank of a tributary of the Saga Chaung; thence in the same direction to Boundary Pillar No. 1 located on the left bank of the Saga Chaung. Thence in a northeasterly direction for a distance of approximately 2500 yards; thence in a southeasterly direction for approximately 1100 yards; thence in a northeasterly direction for approximately 700 yards; thence in a northerly direction for approximately 1000 yards; thence in a northeasterly direction of approximately 1200 yards to a point on the right bank of a tributary of the Nam A-ya; thence down the midstream of this stream for about one mile; thence in a southeasterly direction for approximately 1000 yards; thence in a northeasterly direction for approximately 700 yards; thence in a an easterly direction for approximately 1000 yards to a point on the right bank of the Tinaing Chaung; thence up the midstream of the Tinaing Chaung to its source; thence across the ridge, where it crosses a track going from Manipur to Burma, thence to the source of the Pangero for Hpinnge Chaung starting from the north face of the ridge, thence down the midstream of this Chaung to its junction with the Khunou Khong; thence down the midstream of this stream to its junction with the Sana Lok and thence along the midstream of the Nam Pangato the point where the main spur of the Kassom range (Lahinpi Taung) meets this river.

From the above point where the main spur of the Kassom range (Lahinpi Taung) meets the Nam Panga, the boundary proceeds along this spur generally in a north-northeasterly direction till it meets the trigonometrical station Mawlashin Taung; thence generally northwestwards, then northeastwards and then northwards along the watershed between the Sana Lok in the West and the Nam Panga, Nam Tagin, Nam Mawnghkam and Nam Hka streams in the east, passing through trigonometrical station Thyoliching (Kampal Mol) and peak Hting Hting Bum (Kassom) to trigonometrical station Hkacha Bum; thence in a general northwesterly direction along the same watershed to trigonometrical station Hkayam Bum; thence in a general northwesterly direction along the watershed between the Tuikang stream and the Tizu river in the west and the Nam Hka and the Nam We or Shwezalong Chaung in the east to height 7870; thence in a general north northeasterly direction along the same watershed to a point approximately 1000 yards southeast of height 8256; thence in a general northeasterly direction to peak Mol Len (Kasulum Bum); thence generally southeastwards, then eastwards and then northeastwards along the same watershed to peak Dazipfu (shiloi Mol); then down the midstream of the Petamtsi Ti to its junction with the Ti-Ho or Nantaleik or Tizu river; thence up the midstream of this river for about two miles to its junction with a nemeless tributary of the Ti-Ho or Nantaleik or Tizu river flowing from the northeast; thence up the midstream of this nameless tributary to its source near peak Chaku Mol; thence in a northeasterly direction along the watershed between the Ti-Ho or Nantaleik or Tizu river and the Zungki river in the west and the Chilachi Chaung, a tributary of the Latnyu He or Nantaleik or Sawmalin Chaung the Kundwin He-mu or Mya Chaung, and the Nam Salein or Charing Hka in the east to peak Saramati (Nwemauktaung or Kaiwanya Kyein); thence in a general northerly direction along the same watershed to height 10003; thence in a general northeasterly direction along the same watershed passing through peak Mataungse Kyein to height 11029; thence in a general northwesterly direction along the watershed between the Chokla Lu, the Langnyu river and the tributaries of the Brahmaputra River in the west and the tributaries of the Chindwin River in the east to height 8790; thence in a general northerly direction along the same watershed to height 8650; thence in a general northeasterly direction along the same watershed to height 9840; thence generally northwestwards and then northwards and then northeastwards along the same watershed which is known as Patkai Range, passing through trigonometrical stations 7912 and 5268 to trigonometrical station 8511; thence generally northeastwards, then northwards, then northeastwards and then southeastwards along the same watershed to height 8203; thence in a general northeasterly direction following the watershed between the Brahmaputra and the Chindwin river systems along the Patkai Bum, passing through height 8029 and peak Pungkang to height 7489; thence generally southeastwards along the same watershed to peak Longsip; thence generally northeastwards along the same watershed passing through heights 7578, 7041 and 7340 to peak Ranglung Kan; thence generally eastwards along the same watershed to peak Okhutohap; thence generally northeastwards along the same watershed passing through heights 6257 and 5959 to trigonometrical station Maium (Patkai Bum); thence generally northeastwards, then eastwards and then southeastwards following the watershed between the Brahmaputra and the Chindwin river systems along the Patkai Bum to peak Shawngshan Bum; thence along the watershed between the Irrawaddy and the Brahmaputra river system to its northern extremity, the exact location of which northern extremity will remain provisional pending to its final determination.

ARTICLE II

The boundary between the Republic of India and the Union of Burma has been delineated in the maps attached to this Agreement in accordance with the description given in Article I above.

ARTICLE III

The Contracting Parties agree to establish a Joint Boundary Commission composed of officials representing the two countries who will be charged with the task of planning and carrying out demarcation of the boundary between the two countries, with the preparation of boundary maps and with drafting a boundary treaty.

ARTICLE IV

The Contracting Parties agree that should any dispute arise concerning the interpretation of the application of this Agreement, it shall be settled by negotiations between them.

ARTICLE V

1. This Agreement is subject to ratification and the instruments of ratification will be exchanged in New Delhi within three months of the signature of the Agreement.

2. This Agreement will come into force immediately on the exchange of the instruments of ratification and shall automatically cease to be in force when the boundary treaty between the Republic of India and the Union of Burma to be signed by the Contracting Parties comes into force.

DONE in duplicate in Rangoon on the Tenth Day of March Nineteen hundred and sixty-seven in the English language.

Sd/-	Sd/-
K M KANNAMPILLY	KYI MAUNG
Plenipotentiary of the Government of the Republic of India	Government of the Union of Burma

APPENDIX B

Detailed State-wise Physical and Demographic Description of the India-Myanmar Border

The IMB starts from south to north at the triangular tri-junction Border Pillar (BP) No. 1 in the Parva Salient of Mizoram. Since a detailed description of the IMB *per se,* has already been given in Page 10 in Chapter 1, we move directly to the state-wise description, from the South to the North in deference to the alignment of the BPs.

Mizoram Border[1] with Chin State

The terrain in this region comprises low hills, dense forests and numerous ridgelines running north to south making east-west movement difficult. The IMB here runs 510 km and can be studied in three different segments based on the cardinal directions, i.e., the southern, central and northern segments. The IMB in the southern segment (BP 1 24) traverses rivers and ridge lines. The areas astride this segment of the IMB are underdeveloped and poverty stricken on both sides. The development has now accelerated (2019-2020) with the advent of mobile towers and road construction. The local population in this region comprises of Lais, Maras and Chakmas on both sides of the IMB. Even within this southern segment, the northern part on the Indian side is better developed than the southern part in Myanmar. Subsistence agriculture sustains the population which is isolated from mainstream development due to the lack of connectivity. On the Myanmar side, insurgency adds to the woes and due to the absence of the writ of the Myanmar Government in these regions, this area is described as the Wild South of the IMB.

The central segment of the IMB in Mizoram runs from BP 24 to 27 and is the more developed segment of the IMB in this state with roads and major towns located here. These include the border trading towns of Zokhawthar (India) and Rikhawdhar (Myanmar); Aizwal, Champai and Lunglei in India and Tiddim and Falam in Myanmar. The presence of these towns ensures relative economic development and prosperity in the region since by virtue of being on the main axes, they provide trade and employment opportunities to the residents. The Tyao River demarcates the IMB clearly. This rain-fed river remains in spate from May to November. BP 27 is also the location for the India-Myanmar Post Level Meetings (IMPLM)[2] between sub-unit level representatives of the Indian Army and the Myanmar Army. Demographically, the Lushai tribes inhabit this segment on both sides of the border with less numbers of the Lai tribe.

The northern segment of the IMB from BP 27 to 32 runs through a mix of riverine and hilly terrain. The Tuivai River flowing East to West is the interstate border between Mizoram and Manipur. Compared with the central segment, the northern segment too is underdeveloped and poverty stricken. Demographically, the Paites and Mizos inhabit both sides including Falam district in Chin. Christianity and the linguistic commonality binds the communities on both sides. As in the other segments, the Indian side has a better road network and therefore is in a better economic condition compared to Myanmar. The ethnologue map below shows the linguistic commonalities on both sides of the border.

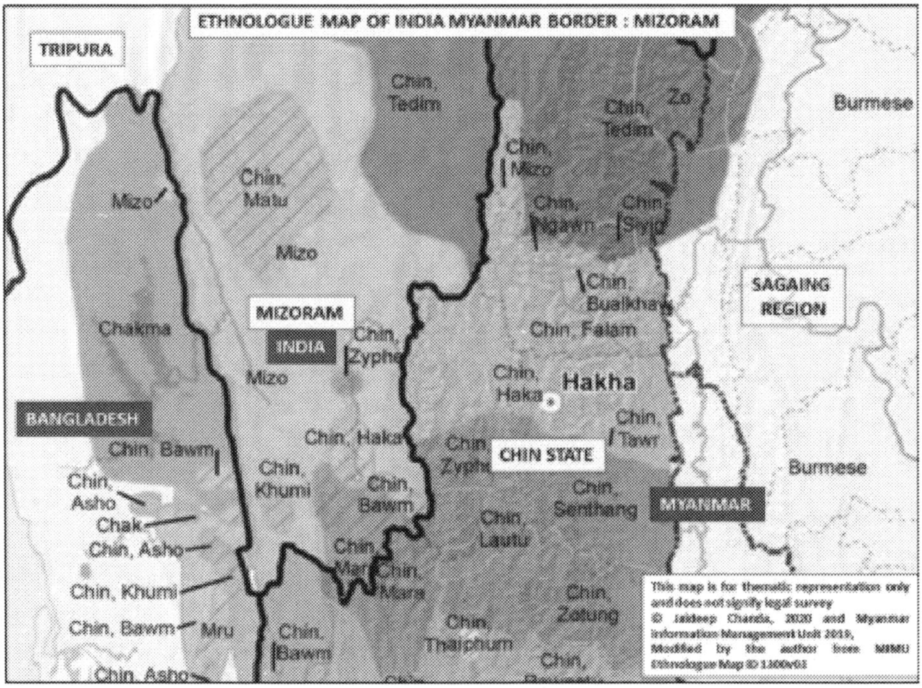

Manipur Border with Chin State and Sagaing Administrative Division

Manipur borders Chin State and Sagaing Administrative Division, running 398 km from BP 33 to 130. The southern portion of the Manipur-Myanmar IMB runs west to east and then turns 90 degrees north near Khampat (in Myanmar) to commence its long run from south to north till the IMB concludes at BP 186 in Arunachal Pradesh. Overall, the IMB in Manipur is sparsely populated and under developed with rampant drug smuggling and cultivation. The IMB in this state is also divided into three segments with a South Manipur segment (BP 32 to 60); a Moreh segment (BP 60 to 88) in the centre and to the north lies the Ukhrul Sector (BP 88 to BP 130). From south to north, the IMB passes through Churachandpur, Chandel, Tegnoupal, Kamjang and Ukhrul districts. On the Myanmar side, the important towns are Homalin, Tamu, Mawliak and Sittang.

In South Manipur, the terrain astride the IMB is mountainous and interspersed with rivers and nallahs except for a 10 km stretch on the watershed between BP 51 to 54 and an 11 km stretch in the plains of Kabaw Valley (BP 60 to 64). Demographically, the population is Kuki/Zou having ethnic linkages with Chins. The trading point is at Beheng/Chikka where the monthly IMPLM is held with the Myanmar Army.

Moreh Segment

In the Moreh segment, the IMB generally runs along the west of the Kabaw Valley. The population density is comparatively high, especially opposite the Kabaw Valley with limited ethnic affiliations. Trading occurs at Moreh/Tamu which is also the location where the IMPLM is held. The demographic cocktail in the trading region comprises Kuki, Tamil, Nepali, Meitei, Punjabi, Telegu, Bihari, Marwari and Muslim Pangals. In contrast, in the hill regions (in south Manipur) Paites and Kukis dominate the population. Expectedly, the plains are economically well off due to the commercial hub of Moreh-Tamu. In the hills on the Indian side, people are better connected by roads and hence economically better off even if they are primarily dependent on agriculture.

The Kabaw Valley is a highland valley in Myanmar which spreads 150 km by 60 km and since all the major rivers of the region drain through it, it is one of the most fertile pieces of real estate in the area. It is an emotive and sensitive issue both historically and geographically. Historically, since it has changed hands a number of times between Burmese and Manipuri kings before finally being delineated to Burma vide the Treaty of Yandabo in 1826, and geographically because of the productivity value of the land. It connects Manipur and Mizoram in India with Mandalay in the east and hence effectively is *the* gateway between South Asia and South East Asia. It is a key geographic feature in India's Act East policy and almost all Indian connectivity projects pass through this location. The important places in the valley are Moreh (India) and Tamu, Kaley and Kalewa in Myanmar. Moreh and Tamu are referred to as the twin border towns of trade in the border region. Places like Imphal, Mandalay and Monywa are provided connectivity through this valley. The valley is home to a number of ethnic minorities including the Meitei (Kathe and Paona), the Mizo, the Kadu and the Kanan. At the north end of the valley, lies the Manipuri town of Humine, with the first Burmese town being Zedi.

Ukhrul Segment

In this segment, the IMB runs along the watershed with rocky cliffs and primary jungles of the Ukhrul and Kamjong districts of Manipur. Across the corresponding district in Myanmar is the Hkamti district of Sagaing Administrative Division.

Population is also restricted to a limited number of pockets and trans-border routes are comparatively less. The trading points are at Somra and BP 98, and both the locations host the monthly IMPLMs. Demographically, Ukhrul, Kamjong and Hkamti districts are inhabited by Tangkhul Nagas. This complete area was Tangkhul territory before being split up by the Treaty of Yandaboo in 1826.

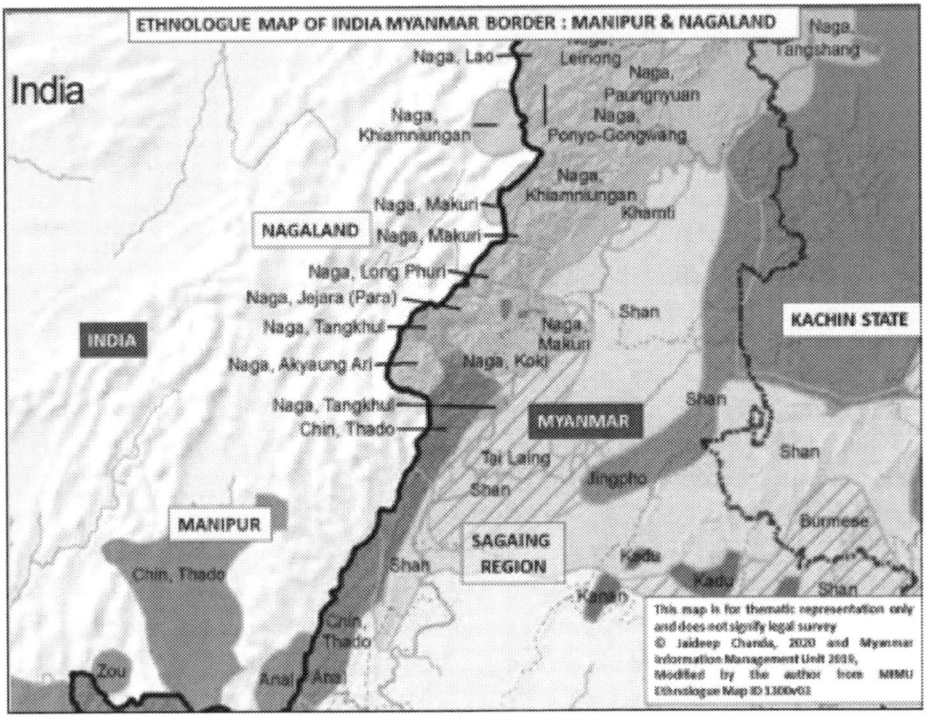

Nagaland Border with Sagaing Administrative Division

In Nagaland, the IMB runs from BP 131 to 156 for a total distance of 215 km along the ridge lines of Naga Hills and Paktai Range which range from approximately 1,500 to 3,350 m. Here, the southern segment covers the Phek and Kiphire districts while the northern segment covers Tuensang and Mon districts.

Phek and Kiphire Districts Segment

This segment is comparatively more rugged with heights ranging from 1,500 to 3,350 m. Sparse population, poor connectivity in terms of roads and tracks and consequent limited infrastructure development characterise this segment. From the demographic perspective, the Naga tribes of Sangtam and Sema, both Christian tribes, inhabit this segment. Unlike their counterparts across the border, these tribes have forsaken their animistic and tribal rituals and practices under the influence of the Church. The Khianmungan, Yimchunger and Pochury tribes also inhabit these areas and they, unlike the other tribes, have limited landholdings in Myanmar. The Chokesang and Pochury tribes are predominant in Phek District.

Tuensang and Mon Districts Segment

This segment has hills which are lower in height compared to the southern (Phek and Kiphire) segment with heights ranging from 1,200 to 2,400 m. Two International Trade Centres have been proposed in Lungwa and Dan. Both these places also host the monthly IMPLMs. The areas in Mon district are Konyak-inhabited. Konyaks are the largest Naga tribe and known for their craft, artisanship and fighting skills. They were the last of the tribes to succumb to Christianity and hence head hunting remained a common practice till the middle of the 20th century. It has remained isolated and has been the least developed for long. Tuensang is inhabited by Changs, Sangtams, Yimchungers and Khiamingans with Aos and Sema tribes forming a small pocket across the border in Myanmar. Subsistence agriculture predominates the economic activity in the area.

Arunachal Pradesh Border with Sagaing Administrative Division and Kachin State

The IMB in Arunachal Pradesh is restricted to the southern portion of Arunachal Pradesh and runs from BP 157 to 186 for 520 km. The area north of BP 186 up to 136 km till the China India-Myanmar trijunction, falls in the Lohit sub-sector and remains undemarcated.[3] The accessibility to IMB is severely restricted by the presence of many rivers and a limited road network. The IMB in this region can be divided into segments east and west of the Pangsau Pass since the IMB runs from southwest to northeast, with Vijaynagar Salient being a unique segment by itself.

West of Pangsau Pass Segment

This area has comparatively well-developed infrastructure with the population spread over the three Naga predominant districts of Tirap, Changlang and Longding. Pangsau Pass is the designated trading and transit point from where movement across the IMB takes place. The important towns in this area are Jairampur, Nampong and Khonsa facing the Nanyun area of Sagaing Division. The altitudes here rise from 200 m adjoining the Assam–Arunachal border, up to 4,000 m along the IMB as part of the Patkai Hills. Demographically, this region is inhabited by the Nocte, Konyak, Wancho, Tutsa and Tangsa Naga tribes. In this region, both Buddhism and Christianity are practiced by the tribes.

East of Pangsau Pass Segment

The IMB in Arunachal and Kachin states have hostile and inhospitable terrain covered with snow covered peaks. This region is characterised by lack of population with altitudes from 1,150 m to 2,400 m. The absolute lack of roads and tracks in the area affects the mobility of the people including Free Move Regime (FMR) with absence of both regulated and unregulated movement. The Myanmar area is equally desolate.

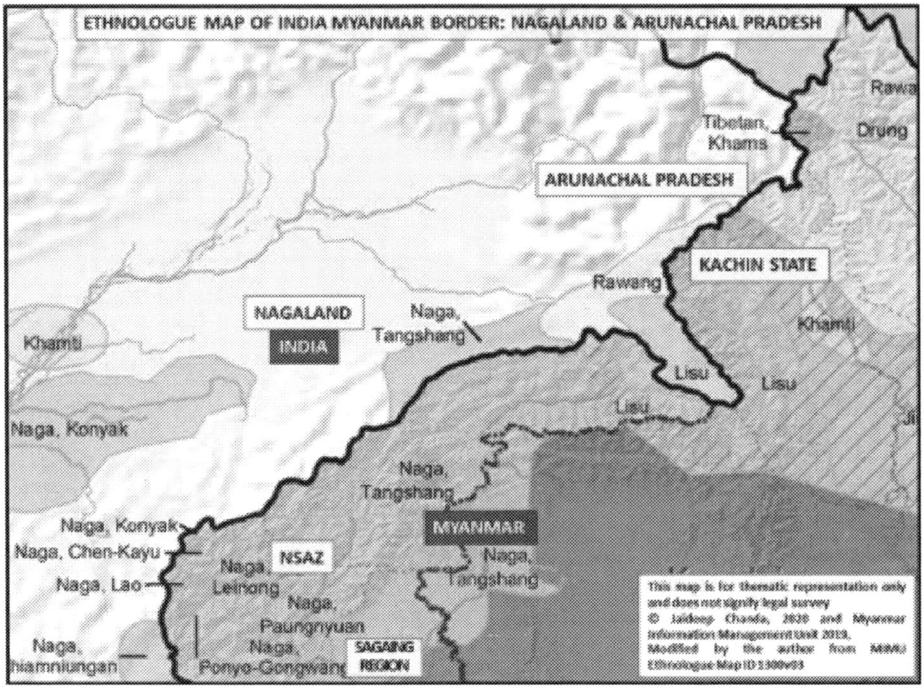

Vijaynagar Salient Segment

The Vijaynagar salient, which includes Gandhidham, is a finger-like projection of the IMB into Myanmar, technically coming under the east of Pangsau Pass segment. This deserves a special mention in view of the peculiarities of this place. Vijaynagar is surrounded on three sides by Myanmar, while the remaining side abuts the thick forest of the Namdapha National Park. The nearby cities are Miao (157 km, 7 to 10 days' walk), Hayuliang and Tezu in India. Putao (40 km) is the nearest city in Myanmar. Being the remotest tehsil of Changlang District of Arunachal Pradesh, it has no motorable road connectivity and hence is connected and maintained only by air supply. It is inhabited by retired soldiers of Indian Army and the Assam Rifles and their families and a few Chakma families. The Chakmas are employed as porters to ferry provisions from the nearest town, i.e., Miao which takes approximately six to 10 days on foot. Vijaynagar comprises 16 villages having a population of 4,438 people. The villagers depend on wetland and jhoom cultivation for their livelihood, and depend on rainfall for irrigation. The day-to-day requirement of groceries is met by a few shops which bring the stores from Dibrugarh by air or from Miao on foot. Fifty-five per cent of the population belong to retired Assam Rifles personnel and 45 per cent is of civilians comprising mainly Lisu (Yobin) people. The settlement of the Assam Rifles personnel began from 7 May 1961 onwards. Prior to 1961, this place was little known to the outside world. The villages have a number of primary schools and an Arunachal Pradesh Government-run secondary school up to the tenth standard.[4] The tribes of Khamti and Singhpho are also there, but they are few in number. On the Myanmar side, the Rawangs and Lisus inhabit the area and are regarded part of the Kachin nationalities. The Hta Lone tribe located to the west of Putao has an average height of four feet and are referred to as Myanmar Pygmies.

A Pradhan Mantri Gram Sadak Yojana road of 156 km length costing ₹ 225 crore commenced in February 2013 and approximately 57 per cent of the work has been completed. The construction has been delayed due to the realignment of the road to skirt the Namadhapa Wildlife Sanctuary.[5] In September 2019, the Governor of Arunachal Pradesh ordered expedited construction by first completing the central bridge pier.[6] There are plans to extend this road to Putao Airport in Myanmar under the Look East policy, thus connecting it to both India's and Myanmar's national highway networks. Vijaynagar would be the eastern terminus of the Arunachal Pradesh Frontier Highway, a proposed 2,000-km road following the McMahon Line to Mago and Thingbu in the west.

Map Shows the Proposed 2,000 km Highway

Map Not to Scale

Source: https://www.tribuneindia.com/2014/20141016/nat7.jpg

The Vijaynagar Airport, also called the Vijaynagar Advanced Landing Ground (ALG) is the eighth ALG in Arunachal Pradesh. It was upgraded by the Indian Air Force (IAF) and Indian Army (IA) in September 2019 to allow the landing of fighter jets and large transport planes.[7,8]

NOTES

1. The author was fortunate to have visited Mizoram State from the Vivekananda International Foundation as part of the Fellowship. Details of the visit are covered in a chapter dedicated to it.
2. These meetings have been institutionalised vide the *Memorandum of Understanding on Border Cooperation* signed by Amb Gautam Mukhopadhaya and Maj Gen Kyaw Nyunt, Deputy Defence Minister of Myanmar on 10 May 2014. https://mea.gov.in/press-releases.htm?dtl/23315/india+and+myanmar+sign+memorandum+of+understanding+on+border+cooperation (Accessed on 11 May 2020).
3. Ministry of Home Affairs, *Annual Report, 2017-18,* Para 3.19 https://www.mha.gov.in/sites/default/files/MINISTRY%20OF%20HOME%20AFFAIR%20AR%202017-18%20FOR%20WEB.pdf (Accessed on 21 May 2020).
4. Government of Arunachal Pradesh, Changlang District Website, Vijoynagar, https://changlang.nic.in/tourist-place/vijoynagar/ (Accessed on 21 May 2020).
5. Damien Lepcha, Miao-Vijaynagar road review meeting in Arunachal Pradesh, The Telegraph India ePaper, 20 March 2019, https://www.telegraphindia.com/states/north-east/miao-vijaynagar-road-review-meeting-in-arunachal-pradesh/cid/1755874 (Accessed on 20 May 2020).
6. Damien Lepcha, Expedite Miao-Vijaynagar road: Arunachal Governor, Northeast Now, 2 September 2019, https://nenow.in/north-east-news/expedite-miao-vijaynagar-road-arunachal-governor.html(Accessed on 20 May 2020).
7. Rahul Karmakar, New IAF 'airport' in Arunachal provides an alternative to walking 157 km, The Hindu, Web Edition, Guwahati, 18 September 2019, https://www.thehindu.com/news/national/other-states/new-iaf-airport-in-arunachal-is-alternative-to-walking-157-km/article29448790.ece (Accessed on 20 May 2020).
8. India Sets up Military Landing Ground for Fighter Jets near Chinese Border, Sputnik News, 18 September 2019, https://sputniknews.com/military/201909181076830159-india-sets-up-military-landing-ground-for-fighter-jets-near-chinese-border/ (Accessed on 20 May 2020).

APPENDIX C

Detailed Description of Chin State[1]

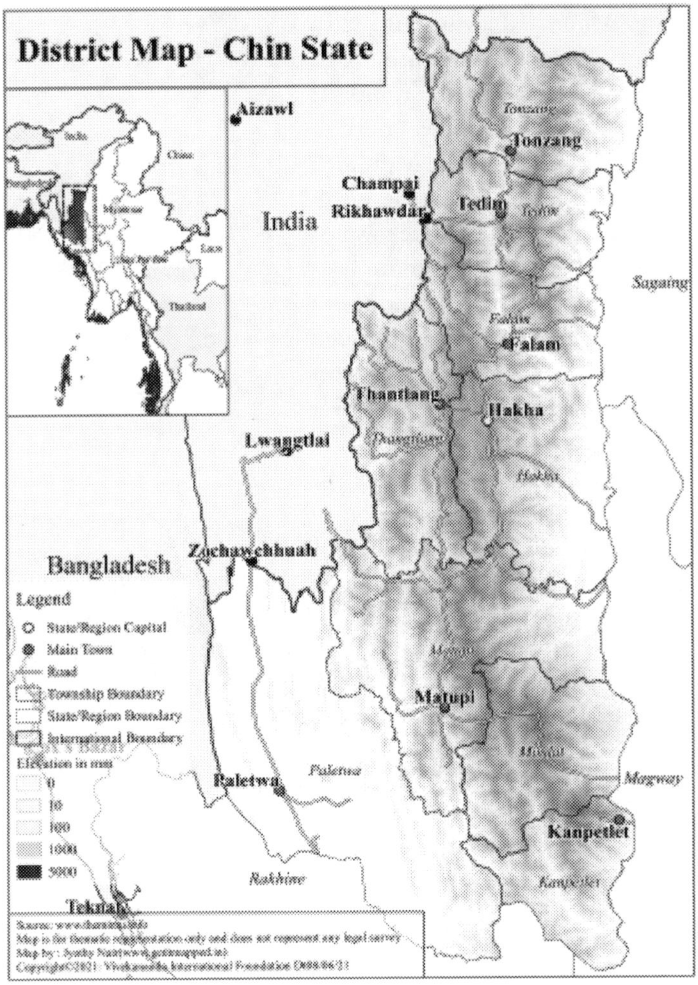

The 36,019 sq km Chin State (capital, Hakhar) is located in Northwest Myanmar between 20° 40′ N and 24° 06′ N latitudes and 92° 37′ E and 94° 09′ E longitudes.

The total area of Chin State within the Myanmar Union amounts to 4.4 per cent of Myanmar's total area (678,500 sq km). To the north and east of the State lies the Sagaing Division, to the south are Magway Division and Rakhine State, and to the west are Bangladesh and the Indian state of Mizoram while Manipur lies in the north

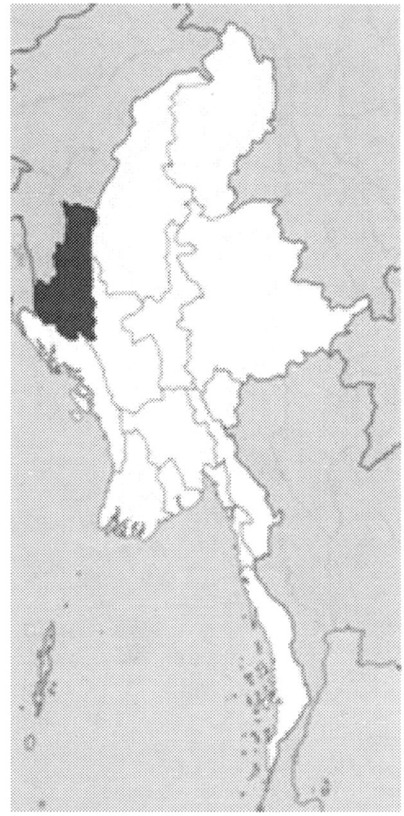

Source: Wikipedia

The state is mountainous and has limited transportation links. It is sparsely populated and remains one of the least developed areas of the country. Many natural water bodies flow along the mountain ranges from north to south forming a number of valleys and gorges. Bungtla waterfall in Matupi is the longest water fall in the state. Mount Khawnusoum (also known as Mount Victoria, Khonumthung or Khonuamtung and even Nat Ma Tong), at 10,500 feet (3,200 m) is the highest peak in Chin State and the second highest in Myanmar. The mountainous region starts in the north where steep peaks and valleys continue towards the south. The State has a lot of rivers and the Manipura River flows through its northern territory. The river Meitei Gun flows through northern Chin. The Tio River forms the border with India in the north. The Kaladan River (aka. Bawinu/Beino/Chhimtuipui River upstream from its confluence with Tiau), is the border with India for the central portion of the state. In the southwestern part of the state, the Kaladan River leaves India and flows down past Sinletwa/Salyutlana and Paletwa and enters Rakhine State. Rivers in the southeast area of Chin such as River Yaw Creek, Salin Creek and Mon Creek run towards the east. In recent years, due to heavy rains, deforestation and farming a lot of mud pours into the stream, causing frequent floods.[2]

As per the 2014 Census, the population of Chin State is about 478,801 and the overall density of population is approximately 13 persons per sq km with a sex ratio of 92 males per 100 females.[3] This makes it the second-least populated province in Myanmar after Kayah. Chin State has the highest poverty rate of 73 per cent and the official radio broadcasting dialect in Chin is Falam. Chins, though less than two per cent of the population of Myanmar are also found in Mizoram State in India and in the upland areas to the east of the port city of Chittagong in Bangladesh.

Evolution of the Chin State and Chin National Day

In 1896, the Chin Hills became a part of the Pakokku Hill Tracts Districts of British Burma until 4 January 1948. Chin Hills Special Division was carved out of the Chin Hills. Its capital was established at Falam. Post Burma's independence from the United Kingdom in 1948. The status of Chinland was discussed at the Constituent Assembly where it was decided that Chin Hills would be a 'division' with a special status, leading to the name of Chin Hills Special Division.[4] On 4 January 1974, it was granted state status and became Chin State. However, the State has little infrastructure and remains extremely poor and undeveloped. Chin National Day is celebrated on 20 February since 1951 (the first celebration) to commemorate the formation of the General Assembly of Chinland held in 1948. The first event was attended by the then President, U Nu. Nevertheless, later, this event was not well recognized by the Myanmar Government until the 2010s. In fact, in 1994, the military junta imposed a complete ban on Chin National Day celebrations. Instead, the Chins were made to celebrate 20th February as Chin State Day, with more of a geographic bias rather than Chin National Day. Rather than forestalling Chin ethnic nationalism, the ban on Chin National Day backfired by inflaming public sentiment. In open defiance of the orders, Chin university students throughout the country held separate private celebrations under the Chin National Day banner.[5]

In 2020, the 72nd Chin National Day was held at Thantlang[6] and attended even by the Myanmar State Counsellor, Daw Aung San Suu Kyi, who addressed the gathering in her capacity as the Chairperson of the Central Committee for Development of Border Areas and National Races.[7]

Figure 1: Participants at the 72nd Chin National Day 2020

Figure 2: Daw Aung San Suu Kyi at the 72nd Chin National Day 2020

Administrative Divisions

Chin State has four districts, namely, from south to north, Mindat, Matupi, Hakha and Falam districts.[8] These are further divided into nine townships, namely, (south to north) Kanpetlet and Mindat under Mindat District; Paletwa and Matupi under Matupi District; Thantlang and Hakha under Hakha District and finally, Falam, Tedim and Tonzang under Falam District. The Matupi District has three smaller sub-townships, namely, Rezua, Samee and Lailenpi. Similarly, the Mindat District has Kanpetlet and Makui Innu sub-townships under it. Falam District also has several smaller sub-townships, namely, Cikha, Rihkhawdar (bordering the Indian town of Zokhawthar which is the designated Land Crossing Point), Khai Kam and Webulah. In addition, there are a number of smaller towns.

Demography and Language

There are eight main ethnic groups and their languages in Chin State: Laimi; Matu; Zomi; Mizo; Asho; Khumi and Daai. These are further divided into 53 different sub-tribes and languages. The term *Laimi* is a collective name for the population in Falam, Hakha, Thantlang and Lawngtlai districts. The Tedim language is commonly used among the Zomi/Zo people and spoken widely in Kalay township (of Sagaing Region) where they have been in abundance since pre-Independence times. The population of Tedim language-speaking people is calculated to be more than 100,000. Lai is the main language in Falam, Hakha and Thantlang townships and it is used and understood by most of the Chin people. As the dialects in the areas of Hakha and Falam are of Tibeto-Burman origin and 85 per cent of the phonetics and accents are the same, people from Falam can easily communicate with Hakha and vice versa. The Chin have an understanding of the Mizo language, except for those who live in very remote areas speaking dialects. The Chins are called by names such as Laimi and the Zos are called K'Cho, Lusei (later Mizo), Kuki and others based on the names they were designated by the Burmese in the surrounding areas or the British. The tribes in India united under the Zomi Council are Paite, Simte, Vaiphei, Zou, Komrem, Mate and Tedim. These tribes under the Zomi Council and the Thadous speak different dialects that are close to those of the Tedims. They migrated to Manipur State in India about 800 years ago. The population of Laimi is the second-largest after the Zomis in Chin state. Laimi may be divided in two groups—Hakha and Falam—as the two dialects differ a bit but the Hakha Lai Language is understood by more people.

In Chin State, as per the 2014 Census, 85 per cent of the population is Christian, 13 per cent Buddhist (Theravada), 0.4 per cent follow the tribal religion (animism) while 0.1 per cent is Islamic. Chin State is currently the only one in Myanmar with a Christian majority. Benedict Rogers, in his book *Burma: A Nation at the Crossroads,* writes that the reason the Chins converted to Christianity almost *en masse*, was that they were monotheistic and the belief was based around a Supreme Being, souls and reincarnation.[9]

Connectivity

An official report from the Department of Urban Housing and Development under the Ministry of Construction stated that as on March 2019, the total length of roads in Chin State was 10,770 km. The *Global New Light of Myanmar* listed 404 wooden, suspension, Bailey and concrete bridges and box culverts in Chin State.[10, 11] All road networks in Chin State were repaired by the local government in cooperation with the Ministry of Construction by spending over K 91,669 million in the fiscal year 2018-2019. Maintenance work for road networks in Chin State will also be undertaken with the use of nearly K 75,000 million in the current financial year, according to a senior official from the local government. Construction of a new road financed by the World Bank is scheduled to begin in October 2019. The new road would link Kalay in Sagaing Region with Falam and Haka in Chin State. The 185 km Kalay-Falam-Haka road is already complete. Bituminous roads include the Gangaw-Haka Road; Mindat-Matupi-Rezua Road; Haka-Rezua-Matupi Road; Kalay-Falam-Haka Road. The Haka-Hmandaw Road is under construction and is almost complete with donations of Chin (Laimis) communities from around the world. The Kyaukhtu-Mindat road linking Chin State and Magway Division has been built. The ASEAN Highway crosses through the centre of Chinland settling areas of Madalay-Kalay-Tamu-Lamka/Behiang. Vehicles can reach Kanpetlet from Magway via Saw and from Kyautthu, Mindat and Matupi in southern Chin State from Pakukku via Kyaukhtu.

Kyaukhtu Airport, built by the Military Engineers of the Defence Ministry of in Kyaukhtu, Saw Township, Gangaw District, Magway Division, was commissioned on July 10, 2004. The airport has connected southern Chin State, with Yaw and Pakokku in Magway Division.

The Concept of Chinram[12]

Chinram is the land of the Chin as referred to by the Chins. Lian H. Sakhong, an exiled former Secretary General of the Chin National League for Democracy, writes that "*Chinram was once an independent land ruled by Chin chiefs and where the people followed traditional Chin religion. By the turn of the twentieth century, however, it had been abruptly transformed by British annexation and the arrival of Christian missionaries. As the Chin became increasingly related to Burmese independence movements, they began to articulate their own Christian traditions of democracy and assert a burgeoning self-awareness of their own national identity. In short, Christianity provided the Chin people*

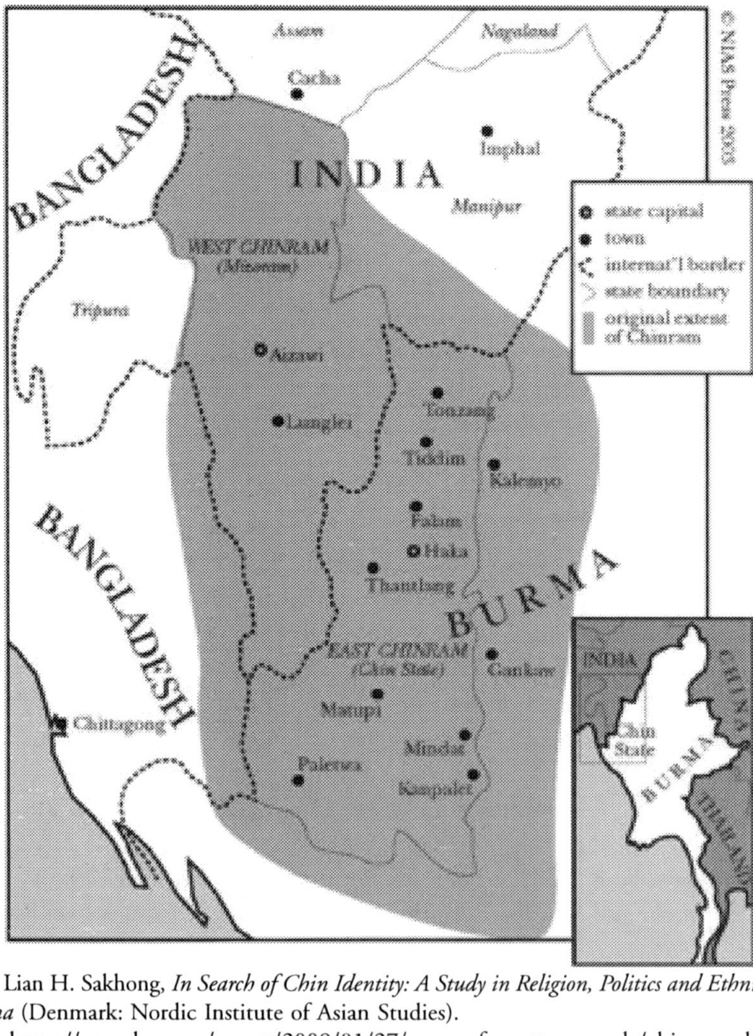

© 2003 Lian H. Sakhong, *In Search of Chin Identity: A Study in Religion, Politics and Ethnic Identity in Burma* (Denmark: Nordic Institute of Asian Studies).

Source: https://www.hrw.org/report/2009/01/27/we-are-forgotten-people/chin-people-burma-unsafe-burma-unprotected-india

with a means of preserving their national identity in the midst of multiracial and multi-religious environments."[13] Chinram included East Chinram (present day Chin State) and West Chinram which was basically the Indian state of Mizoram and the Chittagong Hill Districts. Chinram also is used to refer to the ancient home of the Chins in the valley of the Chindwin River. The word 'Chindwin' means the 'the cave of the Chins'. The map opposite presents a graphic indication of Chin aspirations.

Importance for India

Chin State holds critical importance for Indian interests in Myanmar. Firstly, it borders Mizoram which has an intense relationship with Chin. It is said that the biggest lake of Mizoram is the Rhi-Dil which is incidentally in Chin State in Myanmar.[14] The present political dispensation in Mizoram has a distinctly pro-Chin orientation which was evidenced by the release of the Chin NLD MP held hostage by the Arakan Army at the behest of the Chief Minister of Mizoram, Pu Zoramthanga, in January 2020. This affinity for the AA, though not Chin in ethnicity, harks back to the ages when the Mizo National Party was an insurgent Mizo National Force. This is covered in detail in the chapter on the Rakhine Conflict.

Secondly, a critical aspect is the success of the Kaladan Project which runs through the Paletwa Township of Chin State and is currently held up due to violence between the AA and the Tatmadaw. This project has the potential to have a huge positive impact on Northeast India, specifically Mizoram and the Chin and Rakhine states. A MEA-commissioned Environmental Impact Assessment Report of the Detailed Project Report of the Two Laned Road from Paletwa to Zorinpui prepared by IRCON Infrastructure Services Limited mentions specifics worthy of study. The details are covered in Chapter 5 on the Kaladan Project.

Thirdly, Mizoram has two established border crossing points, one at Zokhawthar and the second one at Zorinpui (as and when it comes up). Both are important from the connectivity aspect and impact Mizoram and Chin directly and India and Myanmar overall.

From the perspective of the Indian investor, Chin State holds promise. As per the brochure of the Chin State division of the Directorate of Investment and Company Administration (DICA), the State welcomes local and international investors to invest in 10 projects in the Hotel and Tourism Sector and 28 projects in the Electricity & Energy Generation and Distribution Sector. To incentivise and facilitate this, the State will provide land, water and skilled and unskilled labour and tax benefits to the investor.[15]

NOTES

1. Due to paucity of sources, parts of this section has been collated from Wikipedia and Ministry of External Affairs documents.

2. Chin State - Wikipedia. https://en.wikipedia.org/wiki/Chin_State (Accessed on 20 May 2020).
3. Myanmar Department of Population, Ministry of Immigration and Population, with technical support from UNFPA, 2014 Myanmar Population and Housing Census, *A Changing Population: Chin State Figures at a Glance, May 2015,* https://myanmar.unfpa.org/sites/default/files/pub-pdf/3D_Chin_Figures_ENG.pdf (Accessed on 20 May 2020).
4. Salai Van Cung Lian, *Chin National Day,* BNI Online, 18 February 2020, https://www.bnionline.net/en/news/chin-national-day (Accessed on 20 May 2020).
5. Salai Za Uk Ling, *Chin National Day: collateral damage*, Frontier Myanmar, 18 February 2020, https://frontiermyanmar.net/en/chin-national-day-collateral-damage and Zing Cung, Chin Identity and Chin National Day, 21 February 2005, http://www.norwaychin.no/chin-identity-and-chin-national-day/ (Both accessed on 20 May 2020).
6. This year the event was scheduled at Paletwa but due to the violence, it could not be held there for the second consecutive year.
7. Myanmar News Service, State Counsellor hails celebrations of 72nd Chin National Day in Thantlang, Chin State, 21 February 2020, https://www.globalnewlightofmyanmar.com/state-counsellor-hails-celebrations-of-72nd-chin-national-day-in-thantlang-chin-state/ (Accessed on 20 May 2020).
8. Hakha District was formed by the first Chin State Hluttaw emergency meeting No. 2/2012 on 1 June and Matupi District was formed by the second Pyidaungsu Hluttaw regular meeting on 28 June 2017.
9. Benedict Rogers, *Burma: A Nation at the Crossroads,* Rider Books, UK, 2012, pg. 105.
10. Kyaw Htike Soe, *Transport infrastructure upgrades take shape in Chin State,* Global New Light of Myanmar, 2 February 2020, https://www.globalnewlightofmyanmar.com/transport-infrastructure-upgrades-take-shape-in-chin-state/ (Accessed on 20 May 2020).
11. For a detailed analysis of the development plans of Chin State, please see the brochure at Appendix. It also gives out the potential investment areas in Chin. https://www.dica.gov.mm/sites/dica.gov.mm/files/news-files/03_infrastructure_and_urban_development_plans_in_chin_state.pdf (Accessed on 20 May 2020).
12. Donald M. Seekins, *The Historical Dictionary of Burma (Myanmar)*, Rowman & Littlefield, London, 2017, pg. 151.
13. Lian H. Sakhong, *In Search of Chin Identity in Burma: A Study in Religion, Politics and Ethnic Identity*, NIAS Press, 2003, http://www.ubcpress.ca/in-search-of-chin-identity-in-burma (Accessed on 20 May 2020).
14. State Portal of Mizoram, Rih Dil (Rih Lake), https://mizoram.gov.in/page/rih-dil-rih-lake (Accessed on 20 May 2020).
15. Invest Myanmar Summit 2019 Brochure, *Chin,* Nay Pyi Taw, Myanmar, 28-29 January 2019 https://investmyanmar2019.com/regions/chin/ (Accessed on 2 June 2020).

APPENDIX D

Detailed Description of Sagaing Region

Sagaing Region lies in the northwestern part of Myanmar between latitude 21° 30' north and longitude 94° 97' east. It is geographically Myanmar's second largest state after Shan State. On its western borders lie the Indian states of Nagaland, Manipur, and Arunachal Pradesh; Kachin State, Shan State (North) and Mandalay Region lie to the east; Mandalay and Magway Regions cover the south; with the Irrawaddy River flowing astride most part of its eastern and also southern boundary while the Chin State sits to the southwest.[1] The capital of Sagaing Region is Sagaing town, 20 km south west of Mandalay on the banks of the Irrawaddy. The Naga New Year Festival held in January is popular amongst the locals of Sagaing. This festival is well-known worldwide and many tourists visit Myanmar to experience it. Across the Irrawaddy are the Mingun Pahtodawgyi (an incomplete monument) and the largest ringing bell known as Mingun Bell. Sagaing Hill is a well-known destination for meditation while Thanboddhay Pagoda in Monywa is another popular destination for tourists.[2]

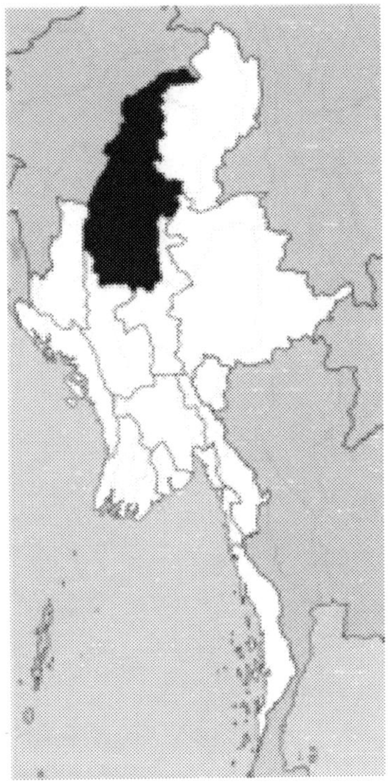

Source: Wikipedia

Sagaing covers 93,527 sq km with a population of 5,325,347 persons and a population density of 56.8 per sq km and a sex ratio of 89.6 males per 100 females. The total population of Sagaing Region represents 10.3 per cent of the total population of Myanmar and makes it the fifth-most populous province in Myanmar. Approximately, 15 per cent of the population lives in urban areas and the remaining 83 per cent in rural areas.

The region is geographically diverse as it includes flat alluvial plains in the south and centre and hills and mountains in its north. The southern plains belong to the

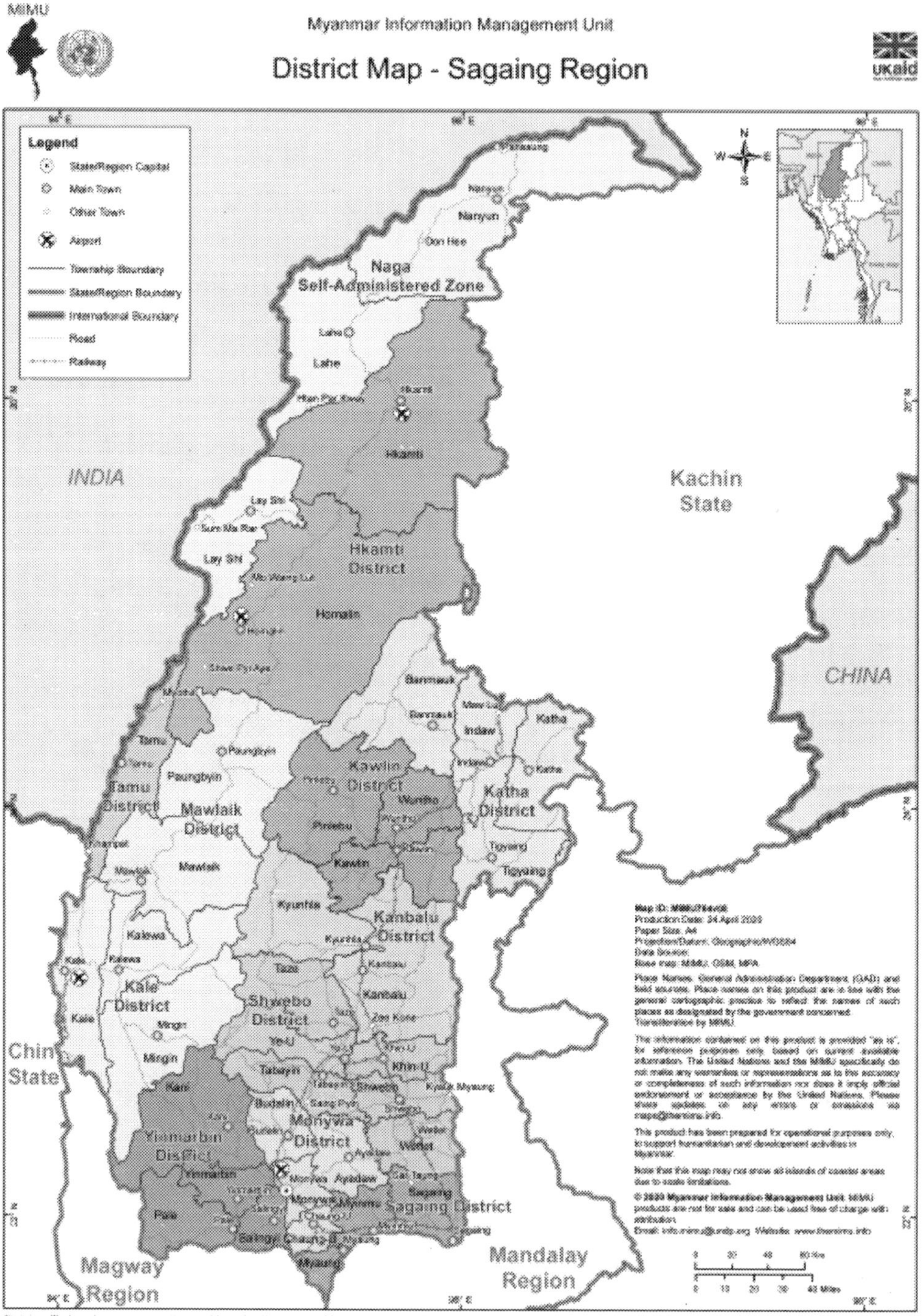

Disclaimer: The boundaries and names shown and the designations used on this map do not imply official endorsement or acceptance by the United Nations.

major Myanmar eco-region known as the "Dry Zone", for its relatively low rainfall patterns, which distinguishes it from the southern coastal monsoon climate. The Patkoi mountain range and Naga Hills form the border with the states of Northeast India. With a height of 3,826 m, Nwemauk (Saramati) is one of the highest peaks of Myanmar. Two main rivers, the Irrawaddy and the Chindwin River, form its main economic arteries and have played a significant role for the region's history and culture. The Irrawaddy is Myanmar's largest river and most important commercial waterway. Its tributary, the Chindwin River, can be used by regular river-going vessels up to the town of Homalin, about 640 km from its confluence with the Irrawaddy.[3]

Administrative Divisions

Sagaing Region consists of nine districts divided into 34 townships, 11 sub-townships with 198 wards and villages. However, only two districts, namely, Tamu and Hkamti (including the NSAZ) border India. The major cities are Hkamti, Katha, Kale, Monywa, Mawlaik, Shwebo, Sagaing, Tamu and Ye U. Mingun with its famous bell is located near Sagaing but can be accessed by crossing the Irrawaddy at Mandalay. The districts are Monywa, Shwebo, Sagaing, Katha, Kale (Kalemyo), Tamu, Mawlaik, Yinmarpin and Hkamti. In August 2010, three former townships of Sagaing Region were transferred in accordance with the 2008 constitution, to a new administrative unit, the NSAZ, which is no longer part of Sagaing Region. Those townships were Lahe, Leshi and Nanyun. Agriculture is the chief occupation. The leading crop is rice, which occupies most of the arable ground. Sagaing is Myanmar's leading producer of wheat, contributing more than 80 per cent of the country's total production.

After independence in 1947, Sagaing was integrated as a division into the directly administered areas under central government control, while the system of local administration was largely left intact from the colonial era. However, the government now attempted to expand direct control to all the areas which had previously enjoyed a large degree of autonomy and self-governance. Sagaing Division was reorganized territorially with the establishment of Kachin as a separate State as per the 1947 Constitution (thus ceding its northernmost Kachin-inhabited territories to the new State but gaining Katha District) which gave it roughly the shape it has today. Following the 1962 military coup, Security and Administration Committees (SACs) were set up across Sagaing Division at the local level, which were chaired by the regional military commander, and by the (military) Minister of Home Affairs at the centre. The 1974 Constitution introduced the concept that States and Divisions had the same status. Sagaing Region then became one of the 'constituent units' of the 'Socialist Republic of the Union of Burma', made up of 7 States and 7 Divisions. This Constitution did not foresee any particular form of autonomy or self-governance for the Naga areas. People's Councils were introduced at all levels of government administration where the central government had control. The basic units of villages/village tracts and wards, towns and townships were established in Sagaing Region along the lines of how they had been set up in Ministerial Burma in the 1920s.

The mining sector in Sagaing Region received considerable attention following protests at the Letpadaung copper mine, near Monywa, in November 2012 when police cracked down on demonstrators protesting against the seizure of land. The use of force led to questioning by the local people of the sincerity of the government's democratic reforms. A high-profile Pyidaungsu Hluttaw Committee, led by the NLD leader Aung San Suu Kyi, investigated the events and made a series of recommendations. The incidents of shooting in December 2014 further galvanised opposition to the project. What the incidents and their aftermath demonstrated was that there continues to be considerable issues of mistrust between the state and the people as well as communication and coordination challenges when it comes to resource extraction. In 2012, anti-Muslim riots demonstrated that Sagaing Region is not free from the challenge of inter-communal tensions, which represents a challenge for the Region Government and local authorities. Equitable local development policies and inclusive local governance institutions are no doubt among the essential ingredients for successfully addressing these underlying social challenges and threats to peace in Sagaing Region.

Demography and Language

The Bamar are the major ethnic group in the arid regions, along the Mandalay-Myitkyina Railroad and along the Irrawaddy River. Shwebo, Monywa and Sagaing districts belong to the core areas of traditional Bamar culture and historical settlements. The Shans live in the upper Chindwin River valley in Hkamti district (especially in Kawlin, Wuntho and Pinlebu townships). A sizable minority of Nagas resides in the north of the north-west mountain ranges and the Kuki which includes the Thadou in the south. Smaller ethnic groups native to the region include the Kadu and Ganang, who live in the upper Mu River valley and Meza River valley. In the south, there are pockets of Chin settlements. Population density differs starkly between its populous southern plains areas (in the lower regions of the Chindwin and Mu rivers, and alongside the Ayeyarwady, and its sparsely populated northern hill and mountain areas. Approximately 3,000 Catholic Bayingyi people of 16th and 17th century Portuguese stock who were adventurers and mercenaries, live in their ancestral villages on the Mu River valley.

Connectivity

Inland water transport is the common mode of transport for people and cargo in a country blessed with great rivers, the Irrawaddy and the Chindwin. Sagaing Region otherwise relies on road and rail networks, which are in poor condition. The Chindwin river originates in the Hugawng Valley and flows through mountain ranges and forests, passing through Sagaing, until it reaches the disgorges into the Irrawaddy. People from different ethnic groups (Burmese, Chin, Kuki, Kachin, Naga and Shan) depend for their livelihoods and culture on the unique and bio-diverse river ecosystem. In 2004, the Tamanthi dam had been proposed by the India and Myanmar governments, which would have changed the Chindwin River irreversibly. The dam projected provoked strong civil society opposition over the large social and environmental impacts and was eventually cancelled in 2013.[4]

Both countries have agreed to set up border *haats* (markets) for trade in locally produced products in an MoU signed during the visit of the then Indian PM, Dr. Manmohan Singh, in May 2012. Consequently, India identified eight points for building border haats. As a pilot, the two countries agreed that one border haat would first be opened at Pangsau Pass (Nampong) in Chaglang district of Arunachal Pradesh, corresponding to Pangsu in Sagaing Region of Myanmar. Other locations would be agreed upon by both countries based, *inter alia*, on historical aspects, interaction, and convenience of access, the interdependence of the population on both sides of the border, and availability of suitable locations.

The border trade agreement between India and Myanmar, signed on 21 October 1994 in New Delhi, provides for three Land Customs Stations (LCS) on the Indian side of the border; Moreh in Manipur; Zokhawthar (Champai) in Mizoram and Nampong in Arunachal Pradesh. The first two are now functional. The Nagas and Kachins across the border in Myanmar are heavily dependent on markets in the small Arunachali hamlet of Nampong as the nearest towns from Pangsau village on the Myanmar side are over a hundred kilometres away with poor road connectivity. Every Friday (known as Burma Day) Myanmar citizens are allowed to come into Nampong to trade and conversely on the 15th and 30th of every month (called India Day) Indians are allowed to visit Myanmar for a brief period and with permission from the civilian authorities in Nampong, guarded by a contingent of the Assam Rifles.[5]

Importance for India

Out of the three provinces of Myanmar located on the IMB, Sagaing provides the maximum opportunity for Indian investors to invest in. It has a complete blend of all types of terrain, urban and rural mix of population and availability of labour and material especially for agro based industries. Agriculture is the predominant occupation with the major crop being rice, which occupies most of the cultivable ground. Other crops include peanut, wheat, sesame, pulses, cotton, and tobacco. Sagaing is the gateway to India for Myanmar. Sagaing is Myanmar's leading producer of wheat, contributing more than 80 per cent of the country's total production.[6] Forestry is important in the wetter upper regions along the Chindwin River, with teak and other hardwoods extracted. The Region is flush with gold, coal, salt and some petroleum. Industrially textiles, copper refining, gold smelting and a diesel engine plant are prevalent. The region has several rice, edible oil, saw and cotton mills, and some mechanized weaving factories. Local industry includes earthen pots, silverware, bronze-ware, iron-ware and lacquer ware. The controversial Letpadaung copper mine in southern Sagaing Division, Monywa Township, where the project is located, and issues of resource governance more broadly could come to the fore in a region where large-scale illegal logging is reportedly a major problem.[7]

Nationally controlled mining and forestry interests are found throughout Sagaing. Kalewa Township hosts several coalmines, and there is a large copper mine located outside Monywa that has been the site of several serious incidents relating to land and resource rights. Forestry products have played an important role in the economy since ancient times, especially in the northern areas, where teak and other hardwoods are extracted.[8]

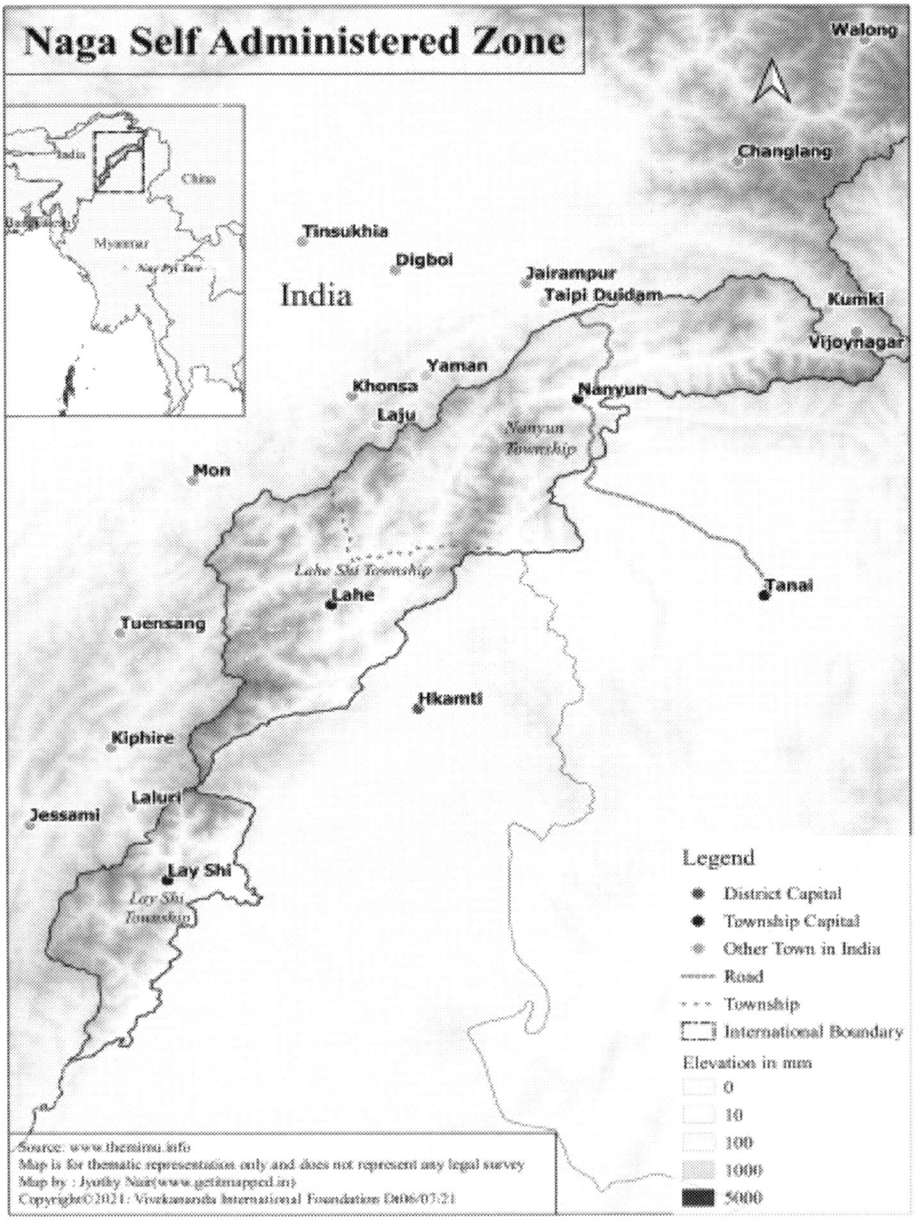

Secondly, from the security perspective, the Sagaing Region used to be home to the bulk of the IIGs till January 2019 when, in a coordinated operation named Operation Sunrise 1, the Indian and Myanmar armies went for an offensive against the IIGs in their respective sides, thereby denying space to the IIGs who till then had simply been moving across the porous border whenever one army operated against it. This effectively destroyed the back of the insurgent movement which was surviving on criminal intent rather than on ideology. However, the risk of the IIGs reviving in Sagaing again remains and it is for this reason that Sagaing will remain a top security concern for India. Further, being a gateway to India, this is the preferred smuggling route for trade and contraband items. The Moreh-Tamu trade link is badly compromised by ineffective checks and balances and is a well known source for prohibited items including arms and weapons.

Naga Self-Administered Zone (NSAZ)

The NSAZ is one of Myanmar's self-administered areas and it is located in the Naga Hills area of Sagaing Region adjoining the IMB near Nagaland and Arunachal Pradesh. It is the only self-administered zone outside Shan State. Its administrative seat is the town of Lahe. The NSAZ is a hilly region in northwestern Myanmar's Sagaing Region, consisting of three townships; Lahe Township, Leshi Township, and Nanyun Township. As has been brought out earlier in this book, the NSAZ was created under the terms of the 2008 Constitution of Myanmar and its official name was announced by decree on 20 August 2010. The NSAZ is "*administered by a leading body, which consists of at least ten members and includes Regional Hluttaw (Assembly) members elected from the Zone and members nominated by the Armed Forces. The Leading Body performs both executive and legislative functions and is led by a Chairperson, currently Kay Hsai. The Leading Body has competence in ten areas of policy, including urban and rural development, road construction and maintenance, and public health*". In 2015, it was proposed that Hkamti and Homalin townships be added to the NSAZ. This was welcomed by ethnic Nagas but came against opposition from other ethnic groups in the townships. Two-thirds of the Naga people in Myanmar are Christian and one-third practice Theravada Buddhism.8 On the Myanmar side, there are 10 Naga tribes living in and around three townships that comprise the NSAZ.

Remoteness, isolation, high poverty, malnutrition and food insecurity prevent the development of this region where ethnic Nagas live their indigenous way of life. According to a 2018 report by HARP and MIMU titled *Vulnerability In Myanmar*, townships in NSAZ are "extreme outliers in terms of development needs and exposure to conflict", making them some of the most vulnerable townships in Myanmar. NSAZ is also one of the regions in Myanmar that receives the least external aid and has one of the lowest numbers of civil society organizations. The region is highly prone to natural disasters and diseases, such as malaria, which is easily preventable. A measles outbreak in 2016 caused the death of over 40 children across NSAZ. This area has not been mapped for data and very few studies have been conducted in the region. Data availability would help all stakeholders in coordinating, planning and implementing suitable response strategies for entire NSAZ.[10]

Rather than forming a single homogenous ethnic community, the Nagas, who are known for their strong martial traditions and their fierce sense of independence, are actually a conglomeration of many tribes inhabiting the northeastern part of India (where they form the majority ethnic group in the Indian state of Nagaland) and north-western Myanmar. Their total number is estimated at around 2 million, although precise figures are not available. The tribes have similar but distinct cultures and traditions, and speak various distinct Tibeto-Burman languages. The Nagas had neglible contact with the world outside, including that of central India, until the nineteenth century British colonization of the region.. It was during the colonial period that many Naga tribes adopted Christianity, and began to develop more of a 'Naga' identity. Nowadays, more than 95 per cent of the Nagas in Nagaland are said to be Christians, mostly Baptist. In more recent times, the Naga have undergone similar drastic social changes as other traditional hills people in South East Asia, which threaten their traditional social cohesion and customs. Such changes have challenged the inherited forms of social organization of Naga society, such as the traditional relations between elders and the young and the subordinate role of women who are traditionally not included in the decision-making process of the clan or the village. The clan and the village have been eroded as agents of social control. As can be seen in an analysis of the efforts to institute contemporary forms of local governance in these communities, this process has affected the way in which the state has interacted with communities and the manner in which communities participate in public affairs.[11]

The elections in the Naga SAZ took place in 2010 wherein each of the three townships sent two representatives to the Region Hluttaw, with each township a constituency for one seat in the Pyithu Hluttaw, and all three townships together formed a constituency for the Amyotha Hluttaw. Naga SAZ therefore has 10 elected representatives, all of which were won by the USDP. In Lahe, the USDP won the two seats for the Region Hluttaw as well as the Pyithu Hluttaw seat unopposed. The Leading Body is vested with legislative powers relating to the matters listed in the Schedule Three of the Constitution.[12] Laws adopted by the Leading Body of the SAZ must only be within these areas, and must otherwise comply with the Constitution, Union Law or Region Law. As these areas are also included in the Union or State and Region list, or both, in reality the legislative function of Leading Bodies is marginal. It is more useful to think of them as special administrative areas within the region that have additional arrangements available for development programmes for the townships concerned.

The administration of the SAZ is carried out by the Leading Body under the leadership of the Chairperson (Oak-Ka-Hta). The Leading Body of the SAZ is formed by (i) the Region Hluttaw representatives elected from townships in the SAZ; (ii) military representatives nominated by the Commander-in-Chief of the Defence Services (1/4) who will be assigned duties relating to security or border affairs; (iii) additional representatives selected by persons stated in (i) and (ii). Members of the Leading Body thus constituted shall "co-ordinate among themselves" and "select a suitable person as the Chairperson" of the SAZ from among the Region Hluttaw representatives elected from the townships in the SAZ.[13]

Importance for India

The Naga insurgency is one of the oldest and most expensive insurgencies for the nation. It envisages a Nagalim or Greater Nagaland encompassing the Indian and Myanmar portions of the Naga Hills, i.e., the NSAZ, in effect, in addition to the Naga areas of Manipur and Arunachal Pradesh. Now though with the ceasefire in effect, the NSAZ continues to be relevant since the Naga aspiration of a Nagaland without an artificial IMB in between continues to be espoused by the Nagas.

NOTES

1. Sagaing Region - Wikipedia. https://en.wikipedia.org/wiki/Sagaing_Region (Accessed on 20 May 2020).
2. Myanmar Travel Information, *Sagaing Region,* https://myanmartravelinformation.com/sagaing-region.html and Sagaing Region. https://myanmars.net/travel/sagaing-region.html (Both accessed on 20 May 2020)
3. United National Development Program, Local Governance Mapping, The State of Local Governance: Trends in Sagaing, Myanmar, 2015, https://themimu.info/sites/themimu.info/files/documents/Report_Local_Governance_Mapping_Sagaing_UNDP_Feb2015.pdf (Accessed on 24 May 2020).
4. Tamanthi dam on Chindwin River, Sagaing Division, Myanmar, https://ejatlas.org/print/tamanthi-dam-cancelled-following-devastating-impacts-chindwin-river-sagaing-division-myanmar (Accessed on 21 May 2020).
5. Anasua Basu Ray Chaudhury and Pratnashree Basu, *India-Myanmar Connectivity: Possibilities and Challenges,* ORF, Kolkata, 2015, https://www.orfonline.org/wp-content/uploads/2015/12/IndiaMyanmar.pdf pg 85, 96 & 94 (Accessed on 26 May 2020).
6. Invest Myanmar Summit 2019, *Sagaing Region,* Nya Pyi Taw, Myanmar 28-29 January 2019, https://investmyanmar2019.com/regions/sagaing/ (Accessed on 2 June 2020).
7. The Irrawaddy, Region, *Sagaing Division,* https://www.irrawaddy.com/election/region/sagaing-division (Accessed on 20 May 2020).
8. UNDP, note 2.
9. Wikipedia, *Naga Self-Administered Zone,* NAGA Self-Administered Zone WFP Myanmar, https://en.wikipedia.org/wiki/Naga_Self-Administered_Zone#cite_note-4 (Accessed on 21 May 2020).
10. NAGA Self-Administered Zone WFP Myanmar, https://docs.wfp.org/api/documents/WFP-0000107116/download/ (Accessed on 21 May 2020).
11. UNDP, note 2, pg 15.
12. Schedule Three of the Constitution includes: 1. Urban and Rural Projects, 2. Construction and Maintenance of Roads and Bridges, 3. Public Health, 4. (Municipal) Development Affairs, 5. Prevention of Fire Hazard, 6. Maintenance of Pasture, 7. Conservation and Preservation of Forest, 8. Preservation of Natural Environment in Accord with Law Promulgated by the Union, 9. Water and Electricity Matters in Towns and Villages, and 10. Market Matters of Towns and Villages.
13. UNDP, note 2, pp 21–24.

APPENDIX E

Detailed Description of Kachin State

The northernmost province in Myanmar is the Kachin State. Hemmed in by Arunachal Pradesh to the northwest and west; Tibet to the northern apex; Yunnan to the northeast and east; Shan State to the south and Sagaing Region to the southwest, Kachin holds 89,041 sq km area with a population of 1,689,441 and density of 19 persons per sq km making it the 10th most populous of the 14 provinces of Myanmar.

Myitkyina is the capital, and the other important towns are Bhamo, Mohnyin and Putao. Mt. Hkakabo Razi, 5,889 m (19,321 ft), Myanmar's tallest mountain, adorns the apex and is effectively the southern tip of the Himalayas. The Indawgyi Lake is another notable feature in the state, being the largest in the country at 209 sq km.[1] Land wise, Kachin has the third largest area of the 14 states and regions in Myanmar. It also has the highest mountain ranges with the snow line at 4,500 m, beyond which the peaks are perennially snow-clad. The glaciers in the region feed the Nmai Hka and Mali Hka which merge to create the Irrawaddy. The climate in Kachin varies from sub-tropical monsoon in the plains to tundra-highland climate in the mountainous north. The lack of connectivity in the region and the altitude has preserved the states pristine virgin environment but illegal logging and poaching are known to be rampant.

The rain forests in Kachin are biodiversity hotspots and include the Hukawng Valley Tiger Reserve in Tanai Township, which covers 22,000 sq km, one of the world's largest tiger reserves. The residents of Kachin State comprise ethnic groups, including Kachins, Bamars and Shans. The economy is mainly agricultural, though it includes timber production, the famous jade mines and other mineral products.[2]

Under British colonial administration, much of what constitutes Kachin State today was designated as the "Kachin Hills" and governed indirectly as part of the Frontier Areas. The turbulence of the Second World War extended its reach into the Kachin Hills and many Kachins fought on the British side, against the Burmese Independence Army (BIA). Members of the Kachin community were victims of atrocities committed by the BIA. The experience of the war years produced anti-Bamar sentiments within the Kachin community and shaped the development of modern, nationalist Kachin politics. With the end of the war, and with Burman nationalists seeking independence from Britain, Kachin leaders took part in the 1947

Panglong Conference. During the course of the negotiations, a vision for the creation of Kachin State was articulated, including the lowland areas of Myitkyina and Bhamo. Myitkyina and Bhamo were ceded to Kachin State in exchange for Kachin representatives abandoning the ability to invoke the right of secession, claimed by the Karenni and Shan representatives at Panglong. However, many in the Kachin community, like members of other ethnic nationality communities, found themselves disappointed and frustrated that the promise of federalism, which had led groups to sign the Panglong Agreement, was never fulfilled. Growing frustration and a sense of vulnerability was provoked by a combination of actions taken by the central government in Rangoon. These included the decision to adjust the boundary line between Kachin State and China, handing over three Kachin villages to China; the prospect of road construction and displacement; and a growing sense that Kachin politicians were not able to influence developments in their own state or control the state budget. The outbreak of the Kachin armed struggle came in early 1961, ushering in an extended period of conflict from 1961 to 1994. The Kachin uprising would come to be part of what South and others have described as the "second wave" of ethnic insurgencies that emerged during the Ne Win era and involved many of the groups that had taken part in the Panglong Conference. In 1991, Tatmadaw pressure resulted in the defection of a large part of the KIA's Fourth Brigade in northern Shan State. This group went on to form the Kachin Defence Army (KDA), which agreed to a ceasefire in 1991, and was granted control of an area north of Lashio, Shan State, that was designated Shan State Special Region. Following the upheaval surrounding the student-led demonstrations in 1988 and the NLD's electoral win in 1990, KIO Chairman Brang Seng, called upon the authorities to hold a national convention to draft a new Constitution. Through mediation efforts undertaken by Rev. Saboi Jum of the Kachin Baptist Convention (KBC) in 1993 and 1994, a dialogue was successful in establishing a ceasefire between the KIO and the Tatmadaw. The Kachin ceasefire period, from 1994-2011, saw the emergence of civil society actors. Kachin State saw the establishment of Myanmar's first two official NGOs, with the creation of the Metta Development Foundation in 1998 and the Shalom (Nyein) Foundation in 2000. The most recent resurgence of violence in Kachin took place in June 2011 when the KIA and the Tatmadaw broke the ceasefire and clashed near the Taping hydroelectric plant along the Taping River east of Bhamo, Fighting occurred throughout Kachin State, as well as the north-western parts of Shan State. Since then, till date, numerous rounds of ceasefire have taken place, interspersed with fighting. The latest ceasefire in vogue is 112-day from 10 May till 31 August 2020, ostensibly to fight the COVID-19 menace.[3]

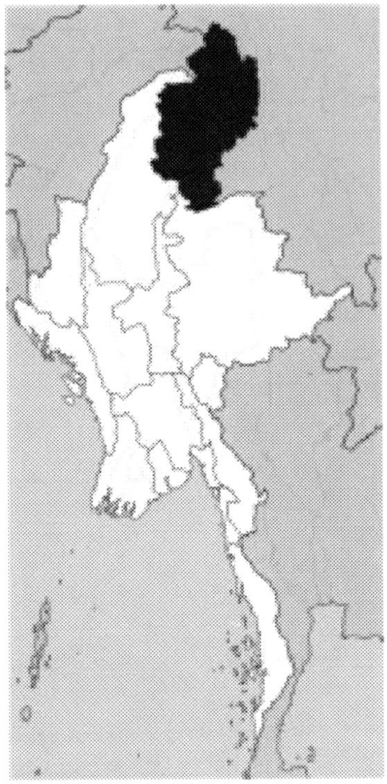

Source: Wikipedia

Administrative Divisions

Kachin State has four districts, namely, Putao, Myitkyina, Mohnyin and Bhamo. Putao is the district which borders India with a very small portion of Myitkyina district (Tanai Township) which also touches the Vijaynagar salient of India. These four districts are composed of 18 townships, three of which border India, i.e., Tanai, Putao and Nawgnmun. Putao district has five townships, namely, Putao, Nawngmun, Machanbaw, Khaunglanhpu and Sumprabum of which Putao and Nawngmun border India. The Myitkyina district has six townships and includes Tanai, Myitkyina, Injangyang, Tsawlaw, Chipwi and Waingmaw. Mohnyin has three townships, namely, Hpakant, Mohnyin and Mogaung while Bhamo includes four townships, viz., Mansi, Momauk, Bhamo and Shwego.

Demography and Language

The state's name and ethnic association refer to a complex set of ethnic identities that began to emerge in the late nineteenth century. The term 'Kachin' was formalised by British colonialists as they came into contact with the variety of communities living in the borderlands of Burma, China, and India. As such, 'Kachin' was used as a catch-all designation that referred to the larger Jingphaw group and its smaller clans, as well as other groups. Community leaders also found the term useful in building unity across a diverse range of communities.[4] The ethnicities and religions include Kachin (including Zaiwa), Lisu, Han-Chinese, Shan, Naga, Bamar, Nu, Tibetan and Burmese Gorkha. The Kachin group has six tribes or subdivisions: Lisu, Rawang, Lachid (Lachid and Ngaw Chang), Zaiwa (Ah Zi), Lhaovo (Maru) and Jinghpaw Hkahku (Jinghpaw), Gauri (Jinghpaw), Majimala (Jinghpaw), Wunla (Jinghpaw), Duleng (Jinghpaw), Manmaw (Jinghpaw), Sammung (Sinli) (Jinghpaw) and Hting Nai (Jinghpaw)). The word 'Wunpong', which means 'Strong and United Human Beings',[5] also represents the six Kachin tribes. The region is also home to a number of Shans and a small number of Tibetans. The religious distribution is Theravada Buddhism 64 per cent, Christianity 33.8 per cent, Islam 1.6 per cent, Hinduism 0.1 per cent and Mahayana Buddhism 0.1 per cent.

The Jingpho language is the traditional language of the area, and is the state's *lingua franca*. The Bamars were a minority in Kachin State before the independence of Burma from the British, but after 1948, groups of Bamars came to Kachin State to settle so that offices could be run in the Burmese language, which has caused a language shift and commenced the decline of the Kachin language. Many later Kachin generations did not have a chance to speak or learn their language properly at school. Some Kachin tribes speak and write their own language: the Zaiwa, the Rawang, and the Lisu, who speak both the Lisu language and the Lipo language.[6]

Connectivity

Kachin State is served by three airports, namely, Bhamo Airport, Myitkyina Airport and the Putao Airport. There is a railroad between Myitkyina and Mandalay (through Sagaing) which takes 21–30 hours from Mandalay to Myitkyina. This province has very poor connectivity with India and no official crossing places.

Importance for India

The links between Kachin and India are marginally developed and have the most potential for mutual benefit. The Putao Single Runway Airfield (7,000 × 100 feet) is the closest to India, being just 40 km away from the Vijaynagar salient. There is a proposal for the revival and development of the Ledo road, also known as the Stilwell Road. The Ledo road connects Assam, in India, with Kunming, in China, through Myanmar. Named after Gen. Joseph Stilwell of the US Army, it was built during World War II for the Allied powers to transport supplies to China. The major part of this road lies in Myanmar territory, passing through Shingbwiyang, Myitkyina and Bhamo in Kachin State and although it is no longer in use, upgrading the road will make it useful for Myanmar. The Indian Government is wary that the road may be used by anti-India insurgents and rebels.[7]

State linkages remain unexploited unlike in Manipur where the state interacts with the Sagaing Region frequently with friendly football matches and other cultural or people-to-people interactions. Similar interaction is required between Arunachal Pradesh and the Kachin Government to enable trade and other opportunities to be exploited.

NOTES

1. Wikipedia contributors, "Kachin State," *Wikipedia, The Free Encyclopedia,* https://en.wikipedia.org/w/index.php?title=Kachin_State&oldid=1014719672 (accessed 20 May 2020).
2. United Nations Development Programme, *Local Governance Mapping: The State of Local Governance: Trends in Kachin,* February 2015, https://www.mm.undp.org/content/myanmar/en/home/library/poverty/TheStateofLocalGovernanceChin/LocalGovmappingKachin.html (Accessed on 22 May 2020).
3. Outlook, The News Scroll, *Myanmar military starts ceasefire, with conditions,* https://www.outlookindia.com/newsscroll/myanmar-military-starts-ceasefire-with-conditions/1829825 (Accessed on 22 May 2020).
4. Infogalactic, The Planetary Knowledge Core, *Kachin State,* https://infogalactic.com/info/Kachin_State (Accessed on 22 May 2020).
5. Sarah L Clarke, Seng Aung Sein Myint and Zabra Yu Siwa, *Re-examining Ethnic Identity in Myanmar*, 31 May 2019, https://themimu.info/sites/themimu.info/files/documents/Report_Re-Examining_Ethnic_Identity_in_Myanmar_CPCS_2019.pdf (Accessed on 25 May 2020).
6. Intriguing Myanmar, *Kachin State,* https://intriguingmyanmar.com/kachin-state/ (Accessed on 20 July 2020).
7. Anasua Basu Ray Chaudhury and Pratnashree Basu, *India-Myanmar Connectivity: Possibilities and Challenges*, ORF, Kolkata, 2015, https://www.orfonline.org/wp-content/uploads/2015/12/IndiaMyanmar.pdf pg 85, 96 & 94 (Accessed on 26 May 2020).

APPENDIX F

Detailed Description of Rakhine State

Rakhine State is a crescent shaped coastal region on the western seaboard of Myanmar adjoining Bangladesh. On the north it is bounded by Chin State; Magway, Bago and Ayeyarwady regions border it on the eastern side; the Bay of Bengal lies to its west and the Chattogram Division of Bangladesh to the northwest. The Rakhine Yoma mountains run through the state and separate it from the Myanmar mainland from north to south. The Rakhine coastline reputedly has the world's best natural deep sea harbour. The large islands of Ramree, Munaung and Kyaukphyu dominate the coastline. It extends from the Naf River estuary near Bangladesh till the Gwa River in the south.

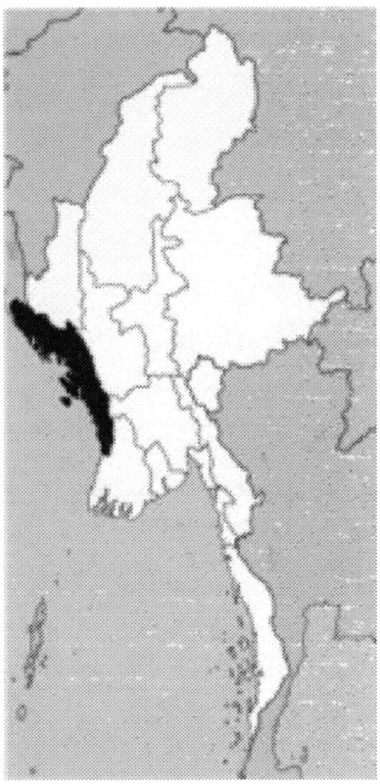

Source: Wikipedia

Rakhine State is an estuarine territory and has an area of 36,762 square kilometres with its capital at Sittwe. Official Burmese figures state the population of Rakhine State as 3,118,963. Ethnic Rakhine Theravada Buddhists make up the majority, followed by a considerable population of Bengali Muslims, commonly referred to as Rohingya Muslims. The Rakhines reside mainly in the lowland valleys as well as on the islands. The other ethnic minorities like the Thet, Kaman Muslims, Chin, Mro, Chakma, Khami, Dainet, Bengali Hindus and the Maramagri also inhabit the higher reaches of the state. Muslims constitute more than 80–96 per cent of the population near the border with Bangladesh and the coastal areas. Martin Smith writes[1] that the borders of Rakhine mark three geo-political meeting-points: between Myanmar, Bangladesh and India; South and Southeast Asia; and the Buddhist and Muslim worlds. As such, it has often been referred to as Myanmar's "Western Gate". But due to its singular geography, its peoples and politics were historically

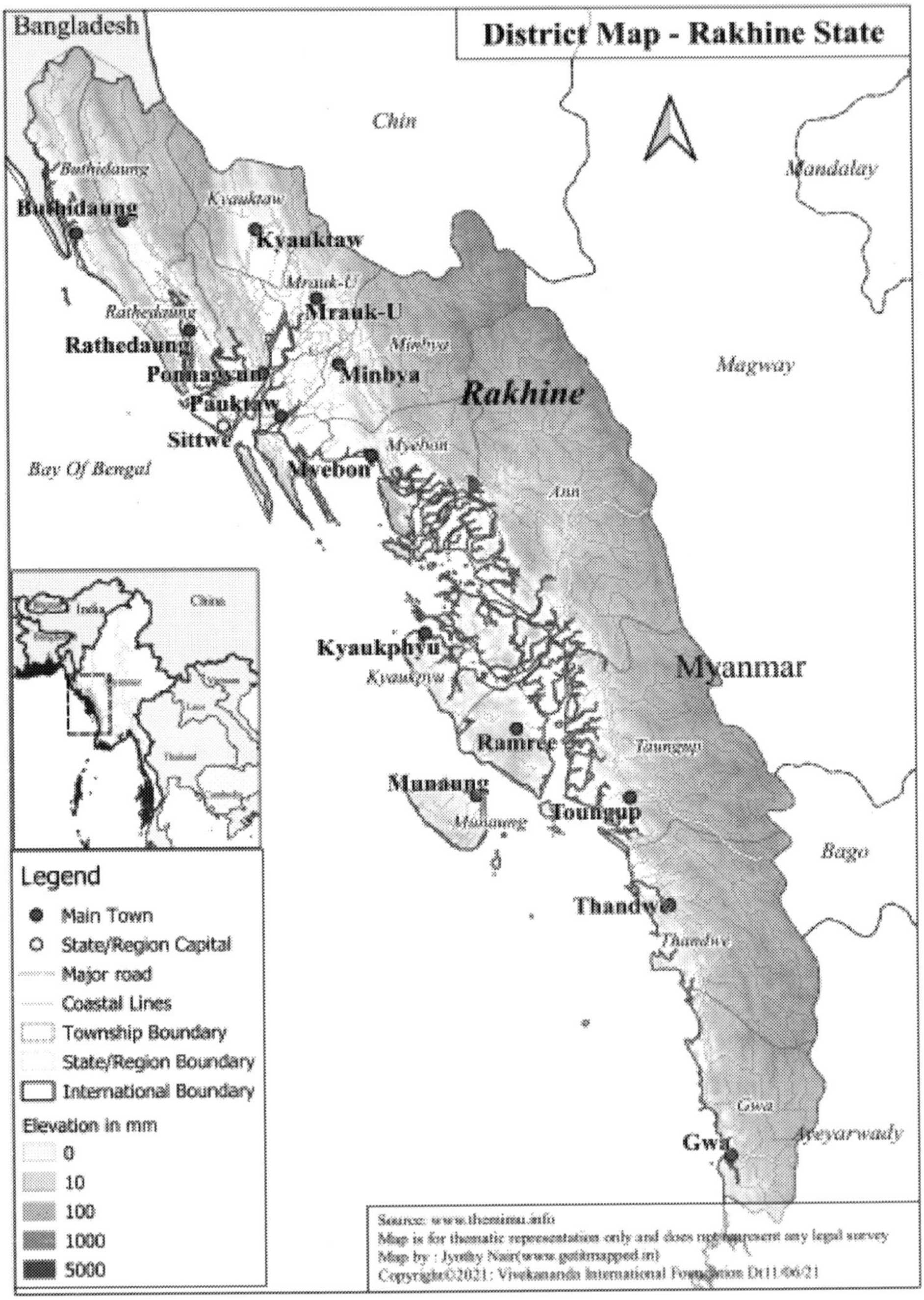
District Map - Rakhine State
Bangladesh
Chin
Mandalay
Magway
Bago
Myanmar
Rakhine
Bay Of Bengal
Kyauktaw
Mrauk-U
Rathedaung
Minbya
Sittwe
Myebon
Kyaukphyu
Ramree
Munaung
Toungup
Thandwe
Gwa
Legend
Main Town
State/Region Capital
Major road
Coastal Lines
Township Boundary
State/Region Boundary
International Boundary
Elevation in mm
0
10
100
1000
5000

isolated from the kingdoms of the Bamar and Mon people who lived in the plains of the Irrawaddy and Sittoung river valleys to the south and east. Rather, protected by the forests and mountains of the Arakan Yoma, most human habitation developed along a coastal strip of muddy creeks and winding rivers that run down to the Bay of Bengal. The natural hillside vegetation of evergreen forests has been replaced over wide areas by jhum cultivation (slashing and burning to clear land) and has been overrun by wild bamboo groves. Due to conflict, however, progress on international investments has been slow. Tourism has also been adversely affected at the two main sites: the ancient capital of Mrauk-U in the north and beaches at Ngapali near Thandwe in the south. Rakhine State also remains closely inter-linked with the politics and economy of the former Arakan Hill Tracts. This is a thinly-populated highland region of 9,176 square kilometres in the tri-border area with Bangladesh and India. At independence in 1948, these territories were conjoined with the neighbouring Chin Hills because of their Chin-majority people. Social and political inter-relations, however, have continued on both sides of the borders.[2]

Administrative Divisions

Rakhine State consists of five districts (Sittwe, Mrauk-U, Maungdaw, Kyaukphyu and Thandwe), 17 townships, 1,164 village-tracts and 3,861 villages. The State extends approximately 640 km long to 145 km at its widest. The region's principal rivers are the Nâf estuary and the Mayu, Kaladan and Lemro rivers. Up to 10 per cent of Rakhine's hilly landscape is cultivated. Rice is the dominant crop in the delta areas, where the bulk of the population resides. Other crops include fruits, chillies, *dhani* (thatch) and tobacco.[3] The main towns are coastal and include Sittwe, Sandoway, Kyaukpyu and Taungup.

The etymology of the word 'Rakhine' is believed to be the Pali word '*Rakkhapura*', closely linked to the Sanskrit word '*Raksapura*', meaning a land of *rakshasas* (demons).[4]

Demography and Language

The Rakhine conflict around the Bengali Muslim population, who the world refers to as the Rohingya population, is all about demography. Ethnic Buddhist Rakhines constituted about 60 per cent of the population and Muslim communities, including Rohingya and Kaman (Kamein), around 30 per cent. The remaining 10 per cent were estimated to consist of Chin and smaller nationality groups, including Mro, Khami, Daingnet and Maramagyi. There are also Hindus and other people of Indian heritage living in Rakhine State. The 2014 Myanmar Population and Housing Census, the official census document, very cryptically states[5] that '*Some populations in three areas of the country were not enumerated. This included an estimate of 1,090,000 persons residing in Rakhine State.*' Thus, as per this document, while the Rakhine State population is estimated at 3,188,807, it excludes the above figure which is about 33 per cent of the total population of the State. The Census goes on to state that:

> *It is worth noting that in Rakhine State an estimated 34 per cent of the population were not enumerated, as members of some communities were not counted because they were not allowed to self-identify using a name that was not recognized by the Government. The Government made the decision in the interest of security and to avoid the possibility of violence occurring due to inter-communal tension. Consequently, data for Rakhine State, as well as for several Districts and Townships within it, are incomplete, and only represent about two-thirds of the estimated population.*

The majority of the population in Rakhine State which was left out were the Rohingyas and also some Kaman Muslims. Presently around 128,000 people (mostly Muslims) remain in displacement camps in central Rakhine State after the 2012 violence and over 90,000 civilians of Rakhine, Chin and Mro ethnicity were displaced in fighting during 2019 between the security services and the United League of Arakan (ULA) in the northern part of the state.

Connectivity

The Rakhine road network includes roads that traverse the length of the state from Gwa in the far south to Mrauk-U and further north into Chin State. Laterals from this central road peel off to the east towards the neighbouring states. An all-weather road running through a pass in the Arakan Yoma connects Taungup with Pyè on the Irrawaddy River. Myanmar Railways has announced a 480 km rail line to Sittwe from Pathein via Ponnagyun-Kyauttaw-Mrauk-U-Minbya-Ann which will be the first railway connection in the state. Air travel remains the usual mode of travel from Yangon and Mandalay to Sittwe and Ngapali, the popular beach resort, with the major airports being Sittwe, Kyaukphyu, Thandwe, Ann and Manaung airports. A deep sea port is proposed to be constructed in Kyaukphyu to facilitate the transport of natural gas and crude oil from the Indian Ocean to China, bypassing the Malacca Straits.

Importance for India

Rakhine State holds significance for India for a number of reasons. For one, the Kaladan Project commences here at Sittwe Port and the success of the project depends on the security situation here. This is the closest state to the Indian mainland from the sea route with Kolkata Port being just over 500 km away. Rakhine is well endowed with mineral resources such as gas. The State also produces a large amount of food items such as rice which is relevant for food security in the COVID-19 scenario. It provides access to Chin state which is contiguous with Mizoram and critical for India. A Kanyin Chaung Economic Zone and Ponnagyun Industrial Zone are being developed with Bangladesh. As these projects go ahead, Rakhine State is likely to witness its greatest social and economic changes since the British departure. The Kaladan valley that connects Sittwe in Rakhine State, Paletwa Township in Chin State and Mizoram in Northeast India is the focus of much economic and geo-political interest today. A large population faces relocation in Rakhine and Chin states over plans to build two hydropower dams on the Lemro (Laymyo) River that flows into Rakhine State. During the past year, several thousand villagers have been displaced and hundreds of schools have been closed due to the fighting and the refugee flow may eventually subsume parts of Mizoram. From a more geopolitical and security angle, the Chinese interest in the Kyaukphyu deep sea port and the Shwe gas fields necessitates India's countervailing presence there. It is indeed a matter of time before China decides to securitise the port and place its military presence in the region and in the Bay of Bengal. Thus, despite the fact that the State has no border contiguous with India, it holds its importance for India.[6]

NOTES

1. Martin Smith, *Arakan (Rakhine State): A Land in Conflict on Myanmar's Western Frontier,* Transnational Institute (TNI), Amsterdam, December 2019, pg. 14. https://www.tni.org/en/publication/arakan-rakhine-state-a-land-in-conflict-on-myanmars-western-frontier (Accessed on 19 July 2020).
2. Ibid.
3. Britannica, The Editors of Encyclopaedia. "*Arakan*". Encyclopedia Britannica, 24 Feb. 2015, https://www.britannica.com/place/Arakan. Accessed 2 March 2020.
4. For an exhaustive work on etymology, see Mohamed Ashraf Alam, *The etymology of Arakan, Rohingya and Rakhine,* Kaladan Press Network, 29 June 2007, https://www.kaladanpress.org/index.php/scholar-column-mainmenu-36/36-rohingya/696-the-etymology-of-arakan-rohingya-and-rakhine.html (Accessed on 19 July 2020).
5. The Republic of the Union of Myanmar 2014 Myanmar Population and Housing Census, *Thematic Report on Population Projections for The Union Of Myanmar, States/Regions, Rural and Urban Areas, 2014–2050 Census Report* Volume 4-F, Department of Population, Ministry of Labour, Immigration and Population with technical assistance from UNFPA, March 2017.
6. Ashrafuzzaman Khan, *The Asian Voice, The strategic importance of Rakhine State: Daily Star contributor*, 3 September 2018, https://www.straitstimes.com/asia/south-asia/the-strategic-importance-of-rakhine-state-daily-star-contributor and Annabelle Heugas, *The Geopolitics of Rakhine,* Mizzima, 6 November 2017, https://www.bnionline.net/en/news/geopolitics-rakhine (Both accessed on 26 June 2020).

APPENDIX G

Passport (Entry into India) Rules, 1950

THE GAZETTE OF INDIA

EXTRAORDINARY

PART II—Section 3—Sub-section (i)

PUBLISHED BY AUTHORITY

No. 403

NEW DELHI, WEDNESDAY, JULY 21, 2010/ASADHA 30, 1932

MINISTRY OF HOME AFFAIRS

NOTIFICATION

G.S.R. 611(E).—In pursuance of clause (i) of sub-rule (1) and sub-rule (2) of rule 4 of the Passport (Entry into India) Rules, 1950 and of all other powers thereto enabling and in supersession of the notification of the Government of India, in the Ministry of Home Affairs number G.S.R. 1265, dated the 28th June, 1968, the Central Government being of the opinion that it is necessary and expedient in the public interest so to do, hereby exempts from the provisions of rule 3 of the said rules, every member of the hill tribes, who is either a citizen of India or a citizen of the Union of Myanmar and who is ordinarily resident of any area within sixteen kilometers on either side of the India-Myanmar Border, entering India across the said border, subject to the following conditions, namely:

(a) If he/she is a citizen of India,—

(i) who has departed to Myanmar on the basis of permit issued in accordance with the notification of the Government of India, in the Ministry of External Affairs No. SI/108/1/66, dated the 28th June, 1968 he/she shall be in possession of such permit which is valid and effective at the time of re-entry, and

(ii) in any other case in possession of a permit (which is in the form given in the Schedule thereto annexed and valid and effective at the time of re-entry) issued by the Government of India or the State Government or by such authority as the Government of India or the State Government may specify in this behalf.

(b) If he/she is a citizen of Union of Myanmar, he/she shall be in possession of—

(i) a permit or other like document issued by any authority empowered under the law for the time being in force in Myanmar, or by such other authority in Myanmar as the Government of Myanmar may specify for the purpose, or

(ii) a permit (which is in the form given in the Schedule hereto annexed and valid and effective at the time of re-entry) issued by the Government of India or the State Government or by such authority in India as the Government of India or the State Government may specify for the purpose, and he/she shall not, on the basis of that permit move into area in India which is beyond sixteen kilometers from the aforesaid frontier.

2. This notification shall come into force one month after the date of its publication.

SCHEDULE

PERMIT

(See notification of Government of India, Ministry of Home Affairs, No. 25022/14/2007-Imm., dated 21st July, 2010)

1. Name (in full)
2. Father's/husband's Name
3. Age/date of birth
4. Place of birth
5. Sex
6. Nationality
7. Permanent Address
8. Tribe and Occupation
9. Marks of identification
10. Places intended to be visited
11. Purpose of visit
12. The amount of cash and merchandise being carried across the international border
13. Route
    (a) for inward journey
    (b) for return journey

Photograph of the permit holder

14. Signature of thumb impression of holder This permit is valid for 24 hours/48 hours/72 hours (strike off whichever is not applicable) from the date and time of issue.

Date .... (Issuing Authority)

Time ....

Seal Signature

Place ....

(Name in block letters)

Designation

[F. No. 25022/14/2007-Imm.]

G.V.V. SARMA, Jt. Secy.

APPENDIX H

Land Border Crossing Agreement, 2018

AGREEMENT BETWEEN
THE GOVERNMENT OF THE REPUBLIC OF INDIA
AND
THE GOVERNMENT OF THE REPUBLIC OF THE UNION OF MYANMAR
ON LAND BORDER CROSSING

The Government of the Republic of India and the Government of the Republic of the Union of Myanmar (hereinafter collectively referred to as the "Contracting Parties" and separately as the "Contracting Party")

CONSIDERING the existing friendly relations between the Republic of India and the Republic of the Union of Myanmar,

DESIRING to further strengthen such relations by facilitating the entry and exit of the nationals of the two countries as well as to promote economic activities in the borders,

HAVE AGREED as follows;

ARTICLE 1
SCOPE OF AGREEMENT

This Agreement shall apply to the facilitation of entry into and exit from the territory of India and Myanmar across the International Boundary of nationals of the Contracting Parties and third countries.

ARTICLE 2
DEFINITION

1. For the purpose of this Agreement—

"Border Area" means the Myanmar Border Area ox the India Border Area up-to 16 km from the International Boundary in each of the border districts in Myanmar and India respectively.

"Local residents" mean persons permanently residing in the Border Areas.

"Travel Document" means a valid passport or border pass issued by either Contracting Party to its own nationals.

ARTICLE 3
PURPOSE

Under this Agreement, nationals of both countries would be allowed to cross the borders into the territory of the other Contracting Party with valid travel document.

2. The holder of a passport with valid Indian or Myanmar visa shall be entitled to travel within the entire territory of the country issuing the visa. The holder of a Border Pass shall be entitled to enter into and travel within the Border Areas of the Contracting Parties.

ARTICLE 4
ENTRY AND EXIT OF NATIONALS OF INDIA AND MYANMAR AND THIRD COUNTRIES

1. Nationals of the Contracting Parties and any third country holding a valid passport with valid visa/e-visa may be granted entry and exit through the authorized entry/exit points for this purpose on the land border, namely Tamu (Myanmar) - Moreh (India) and Rihkhawdar (Myanmar) - Zowkhawthar (India). The Contracting Parties may, through diplomatic channels, establish additional authorized points of entry/exit for passport/visa holders as may be mutually agreed upon in future.

2. Such nationals shall be permitted to stay in the territory of the other Contracting Party for the duration of stay specified in the visa, which can be extended to any longer period permitted by laws, rules and regulations of the receiving country. They shall also be allowed to depart at any designated international entry/exit points.

3. The holder of a Border Pass shall be entitled to enter into and travel within the respective Border Areas of the Contracting Parties. Holders of Border Pass who are permanently residing in the Tamu-Moreh and Rihkhawdar-Zowkhawthar border area may also be permitted to cross the land border through the respective authorized entry/ exit points.

4. The Indian personnel working on the Kaladan Multi Modal Transit Transport Project will be enabled to enter and exit through Zorinpui (India) -Paletwa (Myanmar) for a mutually agreed duration on the basis of a work permit to be issued by the Myanmar authorities at the request of the Indian authorities. This agreement shall be valid until the completion of the Project.

5. Procedures and privileges under the existing Agreement on Visa Exemption for Official and Diplomatic Passport Holders between the Contracting Parties will be extended at the authorized entry/exit points.

ARTICLE 5
BORDER PASS ARRANGEMENTS

1. A Border Pass is a restricted travel document issued under this Agreement by the relevant authorities of India and Myanmar to their own nationals who are Local Residents to enable them to enter the Border Area of the other Contracting Party. The Contracting Parties shall inform the other of changes in the security features or amendments regarding their border pass, if any.

2. A Border Pass shall be valid for a period of one (1) year from the date of issue and its validity may be extended upon renewal, for a subsequent period of one (1) year at a time. It shall be valid for multiple entries, with the holder permitted to stay in the Border Area of the other Contracting Party for up to two (2) weeks per visit.

3. An applicant for a Border Pass may apply for inclusion therein of the name(s) of his/her child (children) accompanying him/her subject to the child not having attained the age of twelve (12) years.

4. The Contracting Party shall make available to the other Contracting Party through diplomatic channels the names and specimen signatures of the persons who are authorized to issue a Border Pass.

5. Each Contracting Party shall endeavor to make available the data of all the Border Passes issued to the other Contracting Party, so as to prevent forgeries and misuse.

6. The format and contents of the border pass is at Appendix A, which is an integral part of this Agreement.

ARTICLE 6
REFUSAL OF ENTRY

1. Each Contracting Party reserves the right to refuse the entry into its territory of any holder of a travel document if its relevant authorities have reasonable grounds to believe that:

(i) The visa has been issued in contravention of its rules and regulations;
(ii) The holder of the visa is an undesirable person according to its laws;
(iii) The Border Pass has been issued in contravention of the provisions of this Agreement; and
(iv) The holder of the travel document is an undesirable person under its laws.

ARTICLE 7
REMOVAL

Each Contacting Party may remove from its territory any holder of a travel document who violates any of the terms or conditions under which he/she has been admitted or any of the laws, rules and regulations in force in its territory. Any person so removed shall be accepted immediately into the territory of the Contracting Party issuing the travel document.

ARTICLE 8
APPLICATION OF LAWS

A holder of a valid Passport with Visa or a Border Pass who enters the territory of the other Contracting Party shall be subject to the laws, rules and regulations in force in the territory of the Contracting Party.

ARTICLE 9
SUSPENSION OF ENTRY

In circumstances where a Contracting Party deems it justified for reasons of security, it may suspend entry into its Border Area for a specified period provided that suspension of entry and the specified duration shall have been notified to the other Contracting Party in advance of the suspension.

ARTICLE 10
REVISION OR AMENDMENT

Either Contracting Party may request in writing through diplomatic channels any revision or amendment of this Agreement. Any revision or amendment which has been agreed to by the Contracting Parties shall come into effect on a date to be mutually agreed upon and shall accordingly form part of this Agreement.

ARTICLE 11
SETTLEMENT OF DISPUTES

Any difference or dispute arising out of the interpretation, application or implementation of this Agreement shall be settled amicably by consultation or negotiation between the Contracting Parties.

ARTICLE 12
ENTRY INTO FORCE AND TERMINATION

This Agreement shall enter into Force ninety (90) days after signing by the Contracting Parties and thereafter shall remain in force until terminated by either Contracting Party by giving to the other six (6) months prior notice in writing through diplomatic channels of its intention to terminate the Agreement.

IN WITNESS WHEREOF, the undersigned, being duly authorized by their respective Governments have signed this Agreement.

DONE at Nay Pyi Taw on this 11th day of May 2018, in two originals in Hindi, Myanmar and English languages, all texts being equally authentic. In case of any divergence, the English text shall prevail.

For and on behalf of the Government of the Republic of India
(Sushma Swaraj)
Minister of External Affairs

For and on behalf of the Government of the Republic of the Union of Myanmar
(Thein Swe)
Minister of Labour, Immigration and Population

APPENDIX A
DETAILS OF BORDER PASS

1. Holders of Border Pass will be permitted to enter the Border Areas for the following purposes—
   (a) Visiting relatives
   (b) Tourism
   (c) Business
   (d) Sports
   (e) Official duty
   (f) Medical Treatment
   (g) Border Trade Affairs
   (h) Attending seminars, meetings or conferences
   (i) Cultural Exchange Programmes
   (j) Any other purposes that may be later agreed upon by the contracting parties.

2. The Border Pass shall contain particulars of the holder as follows;
   (a) Name
   (b) Name of father/mother
   (c) Sex
   (d) Identity card
   (e) Date of birth
   (f) Occupation
   (g) Nationality
   (h) Height
   (i) Place of birth
   (j) Address
   (k) Visible distinguishing mark
   (l) Photograph
   (m) Signature or right thumb print

3. A Border Pass which includes the name(s) of the child (children) of the holder, shall contain particulars of the child (children) as follows;
   (a) Name
   (b) Name of father/mother
   (c) Sex
   (d) Date of birth
   (e) Place of birth
   (f) Photograph

4. These particulars shall appear in the Indian Border Pass in English Hindi and local language and in the Myanmar Border Pass in Myanmar and English.

APPENDIX I
List of Books on Myanmar and India-Myanmar Relations by Indian Authors

Sl.No.	*Year*	*Author*	*Name of Book*	*Publisher*	*Remarks*
1	1960	Usha Mahajani	The Role of Indian Minorities in Burma & Malay	Vora & Co, Bombay	
2	1961	Walter Sadgun Desai	A pageant of Burmese history	Orient Longman	
3	1967	Walter Sadgun Desai	Deposed King Thibaw of Burma in India, 1885-1916	Bharatiya Vidya Bhavan, Bombay	
4	1971	S. B. Mukherjee	Burma and the West	Ranjan Prakash	
5	1971	Nalini Ranjan Chakravarti	The Indian Minority in Burma	OUP, London	
6	1979	Uma Shankar Singh	Burma and India: 1948 – 1962	Oxford and IBH Publishing, New Delhi	
7	1980	Surendra Pratap Singh	Growth of nationalism in Burma 1900-1942	Firma KLM,Calcutta	
8	1981	D. P. Singhal	British Diplomacy and the Annexation of Upper Burma	South Asia Publishers	
9	1983	P. Sharan	Government and Politics of Burma	Metropolitan, New Delhi	
10	1983	Kalyani Bandhopadhaya	Burma and Indonesia	South Asia Publishers	
11	1989	Kumar Badri Narain Singh	Freedom Struggle in Burma	Commonwealth Publishers	
12	1990	AmbIndu Prakash Singh	Aborted Revolution	Vikas Publishing House	Ambassador to Myanmar from 1985-88
13	1992	B. Pakem	India-Burma Relations	Omsons Publication	
14	1993	Balwant Singh	Independence and Democracy in Burma, 1945-1952: The Turbulent Years	CSSEAS Publications, Ann Arbor	
15	2000	Verinder Grover	Myanmar : Government and Politics	NK	Hardcover ISBN-10: 8171009360 ISBN-13: 978-8171009367
16	2000	Amitav Ghosh	The Glass Palace	Harper Collins, New Delhi	Historical fiction
17	2000	Swatanter K. Pradhan	New Dimensions in Indo-Burmese Relations	Rajat Publications, New Delhi	
18	2005	Gurudas Das (ed.)	Indo-Myanmar Border Trade: Status, Problems and Potentials	Akansha Publishing House, New Delhi	

Sl.No.	Year	Author	Name of Book	Publisher	Remarks
19	2006	Langpoklakpam Suraj Singh	Movement for Democracy in Myanmar	Akansha Publishing House, New Delhi	
20	2006	Rajshekhar	Myanmar's Nationalist Movement (1906-1948) and India	South Asian Publishers, New Delhi	https://shodhganga.inflibnet.ac.in/handle/10603/18129
21	2007	Swapna Bhattacharya (Chakraborti)	India-Myanmar Relations 1886-1948	K.P Bagchi & Co. Publication, Kolkata	
22	2008	K. Yhome	Can the Generals Resist?	Rupa, New Delhi	Senior Fellow, ORF
23	2009	Nandita Haksar	Rogue Agent: How India's Military Intelligence Betrayed the Burmese Resistance	Penguin India	Daughter of P. N. Haksar and Human Rights Lawyer
24	2009	K. Robin	Chin : History, Culture and Identity	Dominant Publishers & Distributors, New Delhi	
25	2012	Sudha Shah	The King in Exile: The Fall of the Royal Family of Burma	Harper Collins, Noida, India	
26	2014	Rajiv Bhatia, Vijay Sakhuja & Vikash Ranjan (ed.)	Change in Myanmar	Shipra Publications, ICWA Delhi	Proceedings of the Conference Change in Myanmar: Impact on India-Myanmar Relations', held at Rangoon on 6 March 2013.
27	2015	Rajiv Bhatia	Myanmar main Parivartan	ICWA	Hindi translation
28	2015	Swapna Bhattacharya	Rakhine State of Myanmar: Interrogating History, Culture and Conflict	Manohar Publishers, New Delhi	
29	2015	Sonu Trivedi	Transition from Authoritarianism to Democracy: A Comparative Study of Indonesia and Myanmar	Atlantic Publication	
30	2015	Preet Malik	My Myanmar Years: A Diplomat's Account of India's Relations with the Region	Sage	Ambassador from 1990 to 1991
31	2016	Rajiv Bhatia	India-Myanmar Relations: Changing Contours	Routledge, New Delhi	Ambassador from 2002 to 2005
32	2016	N. Kipgen	Myanmar: A Political History	OUP	Prof at Jindal University
33	2016	N. Kipgen	Democratization of Myanmar	Routledge, New Delhi	

(Contd.)

Sl.No.	*Year*	*Author*	*Name of Book*	*Publisher*	*Remarks*
34	2016	Lipi Ghosh	India Myanmar Relations: Historical Links to Contemporary Convergence	Paragon International, New Delhi, 2015	She has also authored a book *Burma: Myth of French Intrigue*, published by Naya Udyog, Kolkata, 1994. Since it is not about India-Myanmar Relations, it has not been included in this list.
35	2018	Sonu Trivedi	Democratization in Myanmar: Progress and Prospects	Gyan Publishers, New Delhi	Former Fellow at NMML
36	2018	TS Letkhosei Haokip	Ethnicity and Insurgency in Myanmar /Burma: A Comparative Study of Kuki-Chin and Karen Insurgencies	Educreation Publishing	
37	2018	Col Mohinder Pal Singh	Myanmar and its Strategic Dilemma	Pentagon Press, New Delhi	

APPENDIX J
Dramatis Personae

Year	Ambassador	Foreign Minister	Prime Minister	Foreign Secretary	Defence Attache	Defence Secretary	Chief of Army Staff	Eastern Army Commander	Myanmar Defacto Head of State
1946									
1947						1. GS Bhalija (21 Jul- 6 Oct) 2. H.M Patel (7 Oct 1947-)	Gen Sir Rob Lockhart (15 Aug -31 Dec)		
1948							Gen Sir Roy Butcher (1 Jan 1948)		
1949				KPS Menon (16Apr 1948-)	Col. Omkar Deva (4 Apr 1949-)		1. Gen Sir Roy Butcher (15 Jan 1949) 2. Gen KM Cariappa (16 Jan 1949)	Lt Gen TN Singh (Mar 1947-)	
1950						HM Patel			
1951	Dr M.A. Rauf (8 Nov 1946-1953)				1. Col Omkar Deva (-30 Sep 1951) 2. Col SN Thakar (3 Oct 1951-)		Gen KM Cariappa		
1952				1.KPS Menon (21 Sep 1952) 2.RK Nehru (22 Sep 1952-)					
1953				RK Nehru	Col SN Thakar	1. HM Patel (20 Jul 1953) 2. BB Ghosh (21 Jul- 12 Nov) 3. MK Vellodi (13 Nov 1953-)	1. Gen KM Cariappa (14 Jan 1953) 2. Gen Rajendrasinhji Jadeja (14 Jan 1953-)	1. Lt Gen TN Singh (- Feb 1953) 2. Lt Gen Sant Singh (Feb 1953-)	
1954					1. Col SN Thakar (31 Aug 1954) 2. Col. R Sawhny (1 Sep 1954-)		Gen Rajendrasinjhi Jadeja		U Nu
1955	Sh. RR Saxena (19 Dec 1954-1955)	Pt. Jawahar Lal Nehru (2 Sep 1946- 27 May 1964)	Pt. Jawahar Lal Nehru (15 Aug 1947- 27May 1964)	1. RK Nehru (10 Oct 1955) 2. Subimal Dutt (11 Oct 1955-)	Col. R Sawhny	MK Vellodi	1. Gen Maharaj Rajendra Singhi (-14 May 1955) 2. Gen SM Srinagesh (15 May 1955-)	Lt Gen Sant Singh	
1956	Sh. Lalji Mehrotra (17 Sep 1956-1958)				1. Col. R Sawhny (27 Oct 1956) 2. Col HL Sodhi (28 Oct 1956-)		Gen SM Srinagesh	1. Lt Gen Sant Singh (Sep 1956) 2. Lt Gen KS Thimayya (Oct 1956-)	
1957				Subimal Dutt	Col HL Sodhi	1. MK Vellodi (- 13 Jun 1957) 2. OP Raddy (14 Jun 1957-)	1. Gen SM Srinagesh (- 7 May 1957) 2. Gen KS Thimayya (8 May 1957-)	1. Lt Gen KS Thimayya (- Mar 1957) 2. Lt Gen SPP Thorat (Mar 1957-)	

Year	Ambassador	Foreign Minister	Prime Minister	Foreign Secretary	Defence Attache	Defence Secretary	Chief of Army Staff	Eastern Army Commander	Myanmar Defacto Head of State
1958						OP Reddy	Gen KS Thimayya	Lt Gen SPP Thorat	
1959									
1960	Sh. RS Mani (4 Nov 1960-1963)				1. Col HL Sodhi (10 Apr 1960) 2. Col N Bose (11Apr 1960-)				
1961				1. Subimal Dutt (- 17 Jan 1961) 2. MJ Desai (11Apr 1961-)	Col N Bose		1. Gen KS Thimayya (7 May 1961) 2. Gen RN Thapar (8 May 1961-)	1. Lt Gen SPP Thorat (May 1961) 2. Lt Gen LP Sen (May 1961-)	
1962				MJ Desai		1. OP Reddy (- 21 Nov 1962) 2. PVR Rao (21 Nov 1962-)	1.Gen GN Thapar (-19Nov 1962) 2. Gen JN Chaudhuri (20 Nov 1962-)	Lt Gen LP Sen	1. U Nu (- 2 Mar 1962) 2. Ne Win (2 Mar 1962-)
1963				1. MJ Desai (- 4 Dec 1963) 2. YD Gundevia (5 Dec 1963-)		PVR Rao	Gen JN Chaudhuri	1. Lt Gen LP Sen (-Apr 1963) 2. Lt Gen PP Kumaramangalam (May - Nov) 3. Lt Gen TB Henderson Brooks (Nov 1963-)	
1964	Vice Admiral RD Katari (1 Jun 1964-1969)	1. Gulzarilal Nanda (27 May-9 Jun) 2. Lal Bahadur Shastri (9 Jun-17 July) 3. Swaran Singh (18 July 1964-)	1.Gulzarilal Nanda (27 May-9 Jun) 2. Lal Bahdur Shastri (9 Jun 1964-)	YD Gundevia	1. Col N Bose (- 2 Apr 1964) 2. Col AK Mitra (3 Apr 1964-)			1. Lt Gen TB Henderson Brooks (-Mar 1964) 2. Lt Gen Sam Manekshaw (Nov 1964-)	
1965		1.Swaran Singh (18 July 1964-14 Nov 1966) 2. MC Chagla (14 Nov 1966-)	Lal Bahadur Shastri	1. YD Gundevia (- 18 Feb 1965) 2. CS Jha (19 Feb 1965-)	Col AK Mitra	1. PVR Rao (- 3 Apr 1965) 2. AD Pandit (4 Apr - 4 Aug) 3. PVR Rao (5 Aug 1965-)		Lt Gen Sam Manekshaw	
1966			1.Shastri (-11 Jan 1966) 2.Gulzari Lal Nanda (11 Jan -24Jan) 3.Indira Gandhi (24 Jan 1966-)	CS Jha		PVR Rao (-31 Dec 1966)	1. Gen JN Chaudhuri (7 Jun 1966) 2. Gen PP Kumaramangalam (8 Jun 1966-)		

Year	Ambassador	Foreign Minister	Prime Minister	Foreign Secretary	Defence Attache	Defence Secretary	Chief of Army Staff	Eastern Army Commander	Myanmar Defacto Head of State
1967		1. MC Chagla (14 Nov 1966-5 Sep 1967) 2. Indira Gandhi (6 Sep 1967-)	Indira Gandhi	1. CS Jha (- 13 Aug 1967) 2. Rajeshwar Dayal (19 Aug 1967-)		V Shankar (1 Jan 1967-)	Gen PP Kumaramangalam		Ne Win
1968		1. Indira Gandhi (6 Sep 1967-13 Feb 1969) 2. Dinesh Singh (14 Feb 1969-)		1. Rajeshwar Dayal (- 6 Nov 1968) 2. TN Kaul (7 Nov 1968-)	1. Col AK Mitra (-11 Jun 1968) 2. Col MCS Menon (12 Jun 1968-)	1. V Shankar (- 2 Nov 1968) 2. HC Sarin (3 Nov 1968-			
1969				TN Kaul	Col MCS Menon	HC Sarin	1. Gen PP Kumaramangalam (-7 Jun 1969) 2. Gen SHFJ Manekshaw (8 Jun 1969-)	1. Lt Gen Sam Manekshaw (Jun 1969) 2. Lt Gen JS Arora (Jun 1969-)	
1970	Sh. Baleshwar Prasad (9 Feb 1970-1971)	1. Dinesh Singh (14 Feb 1969-27 June 1970) 2. Swaran Singh (27June 1970-)				1. HC Sarin (- 7 Dec 1970) 2. KB Lall (8 Dec 1970-)	Gen SHFJ Manekshaw	Lt Gen JS Arora	
1971		Swaran Singh			1. Col MCS Menon (- 28 Jun 1971) 2. Col V Badhwar (29 Jun 1971-	KB Lall			
1972	Sh. Ralengnao Khathing (10 Jan 1972 - 1974)			1. TN Kaul (- 3 Dec 1972) 2. Kewal Singh (4 Dec 1972-)	Col V Badhwar				
1973				Kewal Singh		1. KB Lall (- 18 May1973) 2. Govind Narain (19 May 1973-)	1. Field Marshall Manekshaw (- 14 Jan) 2. Gen GG Bewoor (15 Jan 1973-)	1. Lt Gen JS Arora (-Feb 1973) 2. Lt Gen NC Rawley (Feb 1973-)	
1974		1. Swaran Singh (- 10 Oct 1974) 2. Yashwantrao Chavan (10 Oct 1974-)			1. Col V Badhwar (- 30 Jul 1974) 2. Col Suresh C (31 Jul 1974-)	Govind Narain	Gen GG Bewoor	1. Lt Gen NC Rawley (-Jul 1974) 2. Lt Gen JFR Jacob (Aug 1974-)	

Year	Ambassador	Foreign Minister	Prime Minister	Foreign Secretary	Defence Attache	Defence Secretary	Chief of Army Staff	Eastern Army Commander	Myanmar Defacto Head of State
1975	Sh. NP Alexander (26 Feb 1975-1977)	Yashwantrao Chavan			Col Suresh C	1. Govind Narain (- 31 May 1975) 2. DR Kohli (1 Jun 1975-)	1. Gen GG Bewoor (-31 May 1975) 2. Gen TN Raina (1 Jun 1975-)	Lt Gen JFR Jacob	Ne Win
1976				1. Kewal Singh (-31 Mar 1976) 2. JS Mehta (1 Apr 1976-)		DR Kohli	Gen TN Raina		
1977		1. Yashwantrao Chavan (-24 Mar 1977) 2. Atal Bihari Vajpayee (26 Mar 1977-)	1. Indira Gandhi (-24 May 1977) 2. Morarji Desai (24 Mar 1977-)	JS Mehta	1. Col Suresh C (-8 Aug 1977) 2. Col JC Pendse (9 Aug 1977-)	1. DR Kohli (- 31 Mar 1977) 2. Gian Prakash (4 Apr 1977-)			
1978	Sh. AN Bose (27 Jun 1978-1979)	AB Vajpayee	Morarji Desai		Col JC Pendse	1. Gian Prakash (- 26 Mar 1978) 2. S Banerjee (27 Mar 1978-)	1. Gen TN Raina (- 31 May 1978) 2. Gen OP Malhotra (1 Jun 1978-)	1. Lt Gen JFR Jacob (-Jul 1978) 2. Lt Gen EA Vas (Aug 1978-)	
1979		1. AB Vajpayee (- 28 July 1979) 2. Shyam Nandan Mishra (28 July 1979-1980)	1. Morarji Desai (-28 July 1979) 2. Charan Singh (28 July 1979-)	1. JS Mehta (- 18 Nov 1979) 2. RD Sathe (19 Nov 1979-)		1. S Banerjee (- 3 Jul 1979) 2. JA Dave (9 Jul 1979-)	Gen OP Malhotra	Lt Gen EA Vas	
1980	Sh. GG Swell (11Nov 1980-1984)	PV Narasimha Rao (14 Jan 1980-)	1. Charan Singh (- 14 Jan 1980) 2. Indira Gandhi (14 Jan 1980-)	RD Sathe	1. Col JC Pendse (- 20 Dec 1980) 2. Col PK Puri (21 Dec 1980)	1. JA Dave (- 10 Apr 1980) 2. KPA Menon (5 May 1980-			
1981			Indira Gandhi		Col PK Puri	1. KPA Menon (- 11 Aug 1981) 2. PK Kaul (12 Aug 1981-)	1. Gen OP Malhotra (- 31 May 1981) 2. Gen KV Krishna Rao (1 Jun 1981-)	1. Lt Gen EA Vas (-May 1981) 2. Lt Gen AS Vaidya (Jun 1981-)	
1982				1. RD Sathe (- 30 Apr 1982) 2. MK Rasgotra (1 May 1982-)		PK Kaul	Gen KV Krishna Rao	Lt Gen AS Vaidya	
1983						1. PK Kaul (-30 Jun 1983) 2. SM Ghosh (26 Jul 1983-)	1. Gen KV Krishna Rao (-31 Jul 1983) 2. Gen AS Vaidya (1 Aug 1983-)	1. Lt Gen AS Vaidya (-Aug 1983) 2. Lt Gen Chiman Singh (Aug 1983-)	

Year	Ambassador	Foreign Minister	Prime Minister	Foreign Secretary	Defence Attache	Defence Secretary	Chief of Army Staff	Eastern Army Commander	Myanmar Defacto Head of State
1984		1. PV Narasimha Rao (-19 Jul 1984) 2. Indira Gandhi (19 July- 31 Oct) 3. Rajiv Gandhi (31 Oct 1984-)	1. Indira Gandhi (-31 Oct 1984) 2. Rajiv Gandhi (31 Oct 1984-)	MK Rasgotra	1. Col PK Puri (-9 Jul 1984) 2. Col CM Mehta (10 Jul 1984-)	1. SM Gosh (- 25 Jun 1984) 2. SK Bhatnagar (6 Jul 1984-)	Gen AS Vaidya	Lt Gen Chiman Singh	
1985		1. Rajiv Gandhi (-24 Sep 1985) 2. Bali Ram Bhagat (25 Sep 1985-)		1. MK Rasgotra (- 31 Jan 1985) 2. Romesh Bhandari (1 Feb 1985-)					
1986	Dr. IP Singh (12 Aug 1985-1988)	1. Bali Ram Bhagat (-12 May 1986) 2. P Shiv Shankar (12 May1986- 22 Oct 1986) 3. ND Tiwari (22 Oct 1986-)	Rajiv Gandhi	1. Romesh Bhandari (-31 Mar 1986) 2. AP Venkateswaran (1 Apr 1986-)	Col CM Mehta	SK Bhatnagar	1. Gen AS Vaidya (-31 Jan 1986) 2. Gen K Sunderji (1 Feb 1986-)	1. Lt Gen Chiman Singh (-Jan 1986) 2. Lt Gen JK Puri (Feb 1986-)	
1987		1. ND Tiwari (-25 Jul 1987) 2. Rajiv Gandhi (25 July 1987-)		1. AP Venkateswaran (- 20 Jan 1987) 2. KPS Menon Jr (Jan 1987-)	1. Col CM Mehta (-30 Dec 1987) 2. Col CS Brar (31 Dec 1987-)		Gen K Sunderji	1. Lt Gen JK Puri (- May 1987) 2. Lt Gen VN Sharma (Jun 1987-)	
1988		1. Rajiv Gandhi (-25 Jun 1988) 2. PV Narasimha Rao (25 Jun 1988-)		KPS Menon Jr		1. SK Bhatnagar (-31 May 1988) 2. TH Seshan (1 Jun 1988-)	1. Gen K Sunderji (- 30 Apr 1988) 2. Gen VN Sharma (1 May 1988)	1. Lt Gen VN Sharma (-Apr 1988) 2. Lt Gen RM Vohra (May 1988-)	1. Ne Win (-23 Jul 1988) 2. Saw Murg (18 Sep 1988)
1989		1. PV Narasimha Rao (-2 Dec 1989) 2. VP Singh (2 Dec 1989- 5 Dec 1989) 3. IK Gujral (5 Dec 1989-)	1. Rajiv Gandhi (-2 Dec 1989) 2. VP Singh (2 Dec 1989-)	1. KPS Menon Jr (- Feb 1989) 2. SK Singh (16 Feb 1989-)	Col CS Brar	1. TH Seshan (-22 Feb 1989) 2. Naresh Chandra (22 Feb 1989-)	Gen VN Sharma	Lt Gen RM Vohra	

Year	Ambassador	Foreign Minister	Prime Minister	Foreign Secretary	Defence Attache	Defence Secretary	Chief of Army Staff	Eastern Army Commander	Myanmar Defacto Head of State
1990	Sh. PMS Malik (25 Aug 1990-1991)	1. IK Gujral (-10 Nov 1990) 2. VC Shukla (21 Nov 1990-)	1. VP Singh (-10 Nov 1990) 2. Chandra Shekhar (10 Nov 1990-)	1. SK Singh (- 19 Apr 1990) 2. Muchukund Dubey (20 Apr 1990-)		1. Naresh Chandra (-21 Mar 1990) 2. NN Vohra (21 Mar 1990-)	1. Gen VN Sharma (-30 Jun 1990) 2. Gen SF Rodrigues (1 Jul 1990-)	1. Lt Gen RM Vohra (-May 1990) 2. Lt Gen KS Brar (Jun 1990-)	Saw Mung
1991		1. VC Shukla (-20 Feb 1991) 2. Madhavsinh Solanki (21 Jun 1991-)	1. Chandra Shekhar (-21 Jun 1991) 2. PV Narasimha Rao (21 Jun 1991-)	1. Muchkund Dubey (- 30 Nov 1991) 2. JN Dixit (1 Dec 1991-)	1. Col CS Brar (-17 Jan 1991) 2. Col AK Chopra (18 Jan 1991-)	NN Vohra	Gen SF Rodrigues	Lt Gen KS Brar	
1992	Sh. G. Parthasarathy (12 Nov 1992-1995)	1. Madhavsinh Solanki (-31 Mar 1992) 2. PV Narasimha Rao (31 Mar 1992-)	PV Narasimha Rao	JN Dixit	Col AK Chopra			1. Lt Gen KS Brar (-Sep 1992) 2. Lt Gen Jameel Mahmood (Oct 1992-)	
1993		1. PV Narasimha Rao (-18 Jan 1993) 2. Dinesh Singh (18 Jan 1993-)				1. NN Vohra (- 6 Apr 1993) 2. KA Nambiar (6 Jun 1993-)	1. Gen SF Rodrigues (- 30 Jun 1993) 2. Gen BC Joshi (1 Jul 1993-)	1. Lt Gen Jameel Mahmood (-May 1993) 2. Lt Gen RN Batra (Jun 1993-)	1. Saw Mung (- 23 Apr 1992) 2. Than Shwe (23 Apr 1992-)
1994		Dinesh Singh		1. JN Dixit (- 31 Jan 1994) 2. Krishnan Srinivasan (1 Feb 1994-)	1. Col AK Chopra (-2 Mar 1994) 2. Col PC Bhardwaj (3 Mar 1994-)	KA Nambiar	1. Gen BC Joshi (-18 Nov 1994) 2. Gen S Roychowdhury (22 Nov 1994-)	Lt Gen RN Batra	
1995		1. Dinesh Singh (- 10 Feb 1995) 2. Pranab Mukherjee (10 Feb 1995-)		1. Krishnan Srinivasan (- 28 Feb 1995) 2. Salman Haidar (1 Mar 1995-)	Col PC Bhardwaj		Gen S Roychowdhury		
1996	Sh. LT Pudaite (22 Sep 1995-1996)	1. Pranab Mukherjee (- 16 May 1966) 2. Sikander Bakht (21 May-1 June) 3. IK Gujral (1 Jun 1996-)	1. PV Narasimha Rao (-16 May 1996) 2. AB Vajpayee (16 May-1 Jun) 3. HD Deve Gowda (1 Jun 1996-	Salman Haidar		1. KA Nambiar (-6 Jun 1996) 2. TK Banerjee (5 Aug 1996-)		1. Lt Gen RN Batra (-Feb 1996) 2. Lt Gen Ravi Eipe (Jun 1996-)	

Year	Ambassador	Foreign Minister	Prime Minister	Foreign Secretary	Defence Attache	Defence Secretary	Chief of Army Staff	Eastern Army Commander	Myanmar Defacto Head of State
1997		IK Gujral	1. HD Gowda (-21 Apr 1997) 2. IK Gujral (21 Apr 1997-	1. Salman Haidar (- 30 Jun 1997) 2. K Raghunath (1 Jul 1997-)	1. Col PC Bhardwaj (-14 May 1997) 2. Col Jasbir Singh (15 May 1997-)	1. TK Banerjee (- 31 May 1997) 2. Ajit Kumar (31 May 1997-)	1. Gen S Roychowdhury (-30 Sep 1997) 2. Gen VP Malik (1 Oct 1997-)	Lt Gen Ravi Eipe	
1998	Sh. Shyam Saran (20 Apr 1997- 2001)	1. IK Gujral (-18 Mar 1998) 2. Vajpayee (19 Mar-5 Dec) 3. Jaswant Singh (5 Dec 1998-)	1. IK Gujral (- 19 May 1998) 2. AB Vajpayee (19 May 1998-)	K Raghunath	Col Jasbir Singh	Ajit Kumar	Gen VP Malik	1. Lt Gen Ravi Eipe (-Feb 1998) 2. Lt Gen HRS Kalkat (Apr 1998-)	
1999				1. K Raghunath (- 1 Dec 1999) 2. Lalit Mansingh (1 Dec 1999-)		1. Ajit Kumar (- 1 Jan 1999) 2. TR Prasad (1 Jan 1999-)			
2000		Jaswant Singh		Lalit Mansingh	1. Col Jasbir Singh (- 28 May 2000) 2. Col Shakti Gurung (29 May 2000-)	1. TR Prasad (- 20 Oct 2000) 2. Yogendra Narain (20 Oct 2000-)	1. Gen VP Malik (-30 Sep 2000) 2. Gen S Padmanabhan (30 Sep 2000-)	Lt Gen HRS Kalkat	Than Shwe
2001			AB Vajpayee	1. Lalit Mansingh (- 11 Mar 2001) 2. Chokila Iyer (12 Mar 2001-)	Col Shakti Gurung	Yogendra Narain	Gen S Padmanabhan		
2002	Sh. Vivek Katju (8 Aug 2001-2002)	1. Jaswant Singh (-23 Jun 2002) 2. Yashwant Sinha (1 July 2002-)		1. Chokila Iyer (- 29 Jun 2002) 2. Kanwal Sibal (1 Jul 2002-)		1. Yogendra Narain (-30 Jun 2002) 2. Subir Dutta (20 Jun 2002-)	Gen S Padmanabhan (-31 Dec 2002)	1. Lt Gen HRS Kalkat (-Jul 2002) 2. Lt Gen JS Verma (Aug 2002-)	
2003		Yashwant Sinha		1. Kanwal Sibal (- 30 Nov 2003) 2. Shashank (19 Nov 2003-)	1. Col Shakti Gurung (- 4 Dec 2003) 2. Col JS Chopra (5 Dec 2003-)	1. Subir Dutta (- 4 Jul 2003) 2. Ajay Prasad (14 Jul 2003-)	Gen NC Vij	Lt Gen JS Verma	

Year	Ambassador	Foreign Minister	Prime Minister	Foreign Secretary	Defence Attache	Defence Secretary	Chief of Army Staff	Eastern Army Commander	Myanmar Defacto Head of State
2004	Sh. RK Bhatia (28 Jun 2002-2005)	1. Yashwant Sinha (-22 May 2004) 2. Natwar Singh (22 May 2004-)	1. AB Vajpayee (-22 May 2004) 2. Dr. Manmohan Singh (22 May 2004-)	1. Shashank (- 31 Jul 2004) 2. Shyam Saran (31 Jul 2004-)	Col JS Chopra	1. Ajay Prasad (- 30 Jun 2004) 2. Ajai Vikram Singh (1 Jul 2004-)	Gen NC Vij (1 Jan 2003-)	Lt Gen JS Verma (- Dec 2004)	Than Shwe
2005		1. Natwar Singh (-6 Nov 2005) 2. Dr. Manmohan Singh (6 Nov 2005-)	Dr. Manmohan Singh	Shyam Saran		1. Ajai Vikram Singh (- 31 Jul 2005) 2. Shekhar Dutt (1 Aug 2005-)	1. Gen NC Vij (-31 Jan 2005) 2. Gen JJ Singh (1 Feb 2005-)	Lt Gen Arvind Sharma (Jan 2005- Dec 2006)	
2006	Sh. Bhaskar K Mitra (1 Sep 2005- 2008)	1. Dr. Manmohan Singh (- 24 Oct 2006) 2. Pranab Mukherjee (24 Oct 2006-)		1. Shyam Saran (- 1 Sep 2006) 2. Shivshankar Menon (1 Sep 2006-)		Shekhar Dutt	Gen JJ Singh		
2007		Pranab Mukherjee		Shivshankar Menon	1. Col JS Chopra (-28 May 2007) 2. Col MM Naravane (29 May 2007-)	1. Shekhar Dutt (- 31 Jul 2007) 2. Vijay Singh (1 Aug 2007-)	1. Gen JJ Singh (-30 Sep 2007) 2. Gen Deepak Kapoor (1 Oct 2007-)	Lt Gen KS Jamwal (Jan 2007-)	
2008					Col MM Naravane	Vijay Singh	Gen Deepak Kapoor	1. Lt Gen KS Jamwal (-Feb 2008) 2. Lt Gen VK Singh (Mar 2008-)	
2009	Sh. Aloke Sen (6 Oct 2008-2010)	1. Pranab Mukherjee (-22 May 2009) 2. SM Krishna (22 May 2009-)		1. Shivshankar Menon (- 31 Jul 2009) 2. Nirupama Rao (31 Jul 2009-)		1. Vijay Singh (- 31 Jul 2009) 2. Pradeep Kumar (1 Aug 2009-)		Lt Gen VK Singh	
2010		SM Krishna		Nirupama Rao	1. Col MM Naravane (-21 Jul 2010) 2. Col Rajesh Kumar (22 Jul 2010-)	Pradeep Kumar	1. Gen Deepak Kapoor (- 31 Mar 2010) 2. Gen VK Singh (1 Apr 2010-)	1. Lt Gen VK Singh (-Mar 2010) 2. Lt Gen Bikram Singh (1 Apr 2010-)	

Year	Ambassador	Foreign Minister	Prime Minister	Foreign Secretary	Defence Attache	Defence Secretary	Chief of Army Staff	Eastern Army Commander	Myanmar Defacto Head of State
2011		S M Krishna		1. Nirupama Rao (- 31 Jul 2011) 2. Ranjan Mathai (1 Aug 2011)	Col Rajesh Kumar	1. Pradeep Kumar (- 14 Jul 2011) 2. Shashi Kant Sharma (14 Jul 2011-)	Gen VK Singh	Lt Gen Bikram Singh	1. Than Shwe (30 Mar 2011) 2. Thein Sein (30 Mar 2011)
2012	Dr. VS Seshadri (5 Jul 2010-2013)	1. SM Krishna (-26 Oct 2012) 2. Salman Khurshid (28 Oct 2012-)		Ranjan Mathai		Shashi Kant Sharma	1. Gen VK Singh (-31 May 2012) 2. Gen Bikram Singh (1 Jun 2012-)	1. Lt Gen Bikram Singh (-30 Apr 2012) 2. Lt Gen Dalbir Singh Suhag (16 Jun 2012-)	
2013		Salman Khurshid		1. Ranjan Mathai (- 1 Aug 2013) 2. Sujatha Singh (1 Aug 2013-)	1. Col Rajesh Kumar (- 27 May 2013) 2. Col Gaurav Sharma (28 May 2013-)	1. Shashi Kant Sharma (-22 May 2013) 2. RK Mathur (25 May 2013-)	Gen Bikram Singh	Lt Gen Dalbir Singh Suhag (-31 Dec 2013)	Thein Sein
2014		1. Salman Khurshid (-26 May 2014) 2. Sushma Swaraj (30 May 2014-)	1.Dr. Manmohan Singh (-26 May 2014) 2.Narendra Modi (26 May 2014-)	Sujatha Singh	Col Gaurav Sharma	RK Mathur	1. Gen Bikram Singh Jul (-31 Jul 2014) 2. Gen Dalbir Singh Suhag (1 Aug 2014-)	Lt Gen MMS Rai (1 Jun 2014-)	
2015	Sh. G Mukhopadhaya (14 Jun 2013-2016)			1. Sujatha Singh (- 28 Jan 2015) 2. S Jaishankar (28 Jan 2015-)		1. RK Mathur (- 24 May 2015) 2. G Mohan Kumar (25 May 2015-)	Gen Dalbir Singh Suhag	1. Lt Gen MMS Rai (-31 Jul 2015) 2. Lt Gen Praveen Bakshi (1 Aug 2015-)	
2016		Sushma Swaraj		S Jaishankar	1. Col Gaurav Sharma (-30 Jul 2016) 2. Col Naveen Mahajan (31 Jul 2016-)	G Mohan Kumar	1. Gen Dalbir Singh Suhag (-31 Dec 2016) 2. Gen Bipin Rawat (31 Dec 2016-)	Lt Gen Praveen Bakshi	1. Thein Sein (-30 Mar 2016) 2. Htin Kyaw (30 Mar 2016 -) Daw Aung San Suu Kyi (16 Apr 2016 -)
2017	Sh. Vikram Misri (31 Aug 2016-2018)		Narendra Modi		Col Naveen Mahajan	1. G Mohan Kumar (- 24 May 2017) 2. Sanjay Mitra (25 May 2017-)	Gen Bipin Rawat	1. Lt Gen Praveen Bakshi (- 31 Jul 2017) 2. Lt Gen Abhay Krishna (1 Aug 2017-)	Htin Kyaw
2018				1. S Jaishankar (- 28 Jan 2018) 2. Vijay Keshav Gokhale (29 Jan 2018-)		Sanjay Mitra		1. Lt Gen Abhay Krishna (- 25 Sep 2018) 2. Lt Gen MM Naravane (25 Sep 2018-)	1. Htin Kyaw (- 21 Mar 2018) 2. Win Myint (30 Mar 2018-)

Year	Ambassador	Foreign Minister	Prime Minister	Foreign Secretary	Defence Attache	Defence Secretary	Chief of Army Staff	Eastern Army Commander	Myanmar Defacto Head of State
2019	Sh. Saurabh Kumar (30 Jan 2019-till date)	1. Sushma Swaraj (-30 May 2019) 2. S Jaishankar (30 May 2019-)		Vijay Keshav Gokhale	1. Col Naveen Mahajan (- 4 Sep 2019) 2. Col Ketan Arun Mohite (5 Sep 2019-)	1. Sanjay Mitra (-23 Aug 2019) 2. Ajay Kumar (23 Aug 2019-)	1. Gen Bipin Rawat (- 31 Dec 2019) 2. Gen MM Naravane (31 Dec 2019-)	1. Lt Gen MM Naravane (-31 Aug 2019) 2. Lt Gen Anil Chauhan (31 Aug 2019-)	Win Myint Apr 2016 -)
2020		S Jaishankar			Col Ketan Arun Mohite	Ajay Kumar	Gen MM Naravane	Lt Gen Anil Chauhan	

APPENDIX K

Treaty of Peace and Friendship, 1951

TREATY OF FRIENDSHIP BETWEEN INDIA AND THE UNION OF BURMA

Rangoon, 7 July 1951

The President of India and the President of the Union of Burma being desirous of strengthening and developing the many ties that have bound the two countries for centuries and being urged by mutual recognition of the need for maintaining the peace and friendship that have always existed between the two States, have resolved to conclude this Treaty for the common benefit of their peoples and in furtherance of the objectives of their respective countries, and have, to this end, appointed as their Plenipotentiaries the following persons, namely,

1. The President of India:
2. His Excellency Dr. M.A. RAUF, Ambassador Extraordinary and Plenipotentiary.
3. The President of the Union of Burma:
4. The Hon'ble SAO HKUN HKIO, K.S.M., Minister for Foreign Affairs.

Who, having examined each other's credentials and found them good and in due form, have agreed to and signed the following Articles:

ARTICLE I

The two States recognize and respect the independence and rights of each other.

ARTICLE II

There shall be everlasting peace and unalterable friendship between the two States who shall ever strive to strengthen and develop further the cordial relations existing between the peoples of the two countries.

ARTICLE III

The two States agree to continue diplomatic and consular relations with each other by means of representatives of either party in the territory of the other and agree that such representatives and their agreed staff shall have, on a reciprocal basis, such privileges and immunities as are customarily granted by recognized international principles.

ARTICLE IV

The two States agree that their representatives shall meet from time to time and as often as occasion requires to exchange views on matters of common interest and to consider ways and means for mutual co-operation in such matters.

ARTICLE V

The two States agree to start negotiations for the conclusion of agreements, on a reciprocal basis, relating to trade, customs, cultural relations, communications, extradition of criminals, immigration or repatriation of nationals of each country resident in the other, or of dual nationals of the two countries, and all other matters of common interest to the two countries.

ARTICLE VI

Any difference or dispute arising out of the interpretation or application of this Treaty or one or more of its Articles shall be settled by negotiations through the ordinary diplomatic channels and if no settlement is reached by that method within a reasonable time, the matter shall be referred to arbitration in such manner as may be mutually determined by a general or special arrangement between the two parties.

ARTICLE VII

The treaty shall be subject to ratification and shall come into force from the date of exchange of the instruments of ratification, which shall take place as soon as possible at Rangoon.

ARTICLE VIII

This Treaty shall continue in force for five years from the date of its coming into force and shall thereafter remain in force: Provided that after the termination of the said period of five years either party may give to the other party a notice of not less than six months intimating its intention to terminate the Treaty and on the expiry of the period of such notice the Treaty shall cease to be in force.

IN FAITH WHEREOF, the said Plenipotentiaries have signed the present Treaty in the Hindi, Burmese and English languages (the English text shall prevail in case of conflict between the three texts) and have affixed hereto their seals.

DONE in duplicate in Rangoon on the seventh day of July 1951.

For the President of the Union of Burma:

(Sd.) S.H. HKIO. In the presence of— (Sd.) TUN SHETN.

For the President of India:

(Sd.) M.A. RAUF. In the presence of— (Sd.) K.M. KANNAMPTLTY.

APPENDIX L

MoUs Exchanged during visit of President U Win Myint of Myanmar: 26-29 Feb 2020

Sl.No.	*Nature of Document*	*For*	*Remarks*
		Pertaining to Rakhine State	
1.	Project Agreement	• Construction of incinerator in Mrauk Oo township hospital • Construction of seed storage houses and water supply systems in Gwa township	Project Agreements between Rakhine State Government and Embassy of India, Yangon under Rakhine State Development Programme
2.	Project Agreement	• Distribution of electricity by solar power in five townships of Rakhine State	
3.	Project Agreement	Construction of • Kyawlyaung-Ohlphyu road, • Kyaung Taung Kyaw Paung road, both in Buthedaung Township	
4.	Project Agreement	Construction of preschools in Rakhine State	Project Agreement between Ministry of Social Welfare, Relief & Resettlement and Embassy of India, Yangon
		Other Projects	
5.	MoU	Cooperation for Prevention of Trafficking in Persons; Rescue, Recovery, Repatriation and Re-Integration of Victims of Trafficking	
6.	Agreement	Indian Grant Assistance for Implementation of Quick Impact Projects (QIP)	Agreement between the Government of the Republic of India and the Government of the Republic of the Union of Myanmar
7.	MoU	Cooperation on Combating Timber Trafficking, and Conservation of Tigers and other Wildlife	
8.	MoU	Cooperation in the field of Petroleum Products	MoU between India (MoPNG) and Myanmar (Ministry of Electricity & Energy)

Sl.No.	*Nature of Document*	*For*	*Remarks*
9	MoU	Cooperation in the field of Communication	MoU between the Ministry of Communications of the Republic of India and the Ministry of Transport & Communications of Myanmar
10	MoU	Cooperation in the field of Health Research	MoU between Indian Council of Medical Research (ICMR) and Department of Medical Research (DMR), M/o Health & Sports of Myanmar

Source: MEA: Statements: Bilateral/Multilateral Documents (n.d.). Retrieved June 06, 2020, from https://www.mea.gov.in/bilateral-documents.htm?dtl%2F32433%2FMoUs_Exchanged_during

APPENDIX M

List of Agreements, Joint Statements, Memoranda of Understanding and other Selected Documents pertaining to India-Myanmar Relations (2014–2020)*

Sl.No.	*Date of Document*	*Name of Agreement/Declaration/Statement*	*Remarks*
		2014	
1	8th May, 2014	MoU Between the Government of the Republic of India and the Republic of the Union of Myanmar on **Border Cooperation**	The objective of the MoU was to ensure **peace, tranquility, security and stability** along the International Border, crucial for overall development and prosperity. Both sides decided to **designate Nodal Officers, establish channels of communication and conduct coordinated patrols** to achieve the same. (Treaty Detail. (n.d.). Retrieved June 06, 2020, from https://www.mea.gov.in/TreatyDetail.htm?1884)
2	8th May, 2014	MoU Between the Government of the Republic of India and the Republic of the Union of Myanmar For **Setting up of Language Laboratories and E-Resource Centre in Myanmar**	The objective of the MoU was to support development of Information and Communication Technology (ICT) in Myanmar through setting up of Language Laboratories and E-Resource Centre at Yangon and Nay Pyi Taw. (Treaty Detail. (n.d.). Retrieved June 06, 2020, from https://www.mea.gov.in/TreatyDetail.htm?1883)
3	11th August, 2014	The **ASEAN PMC+1 Session with India** at Nay Pyi Taw, Myanmar.	1) The Meeting expressed satisfaction with the overall progress of the ASEAN-India **Strategic Partnership** and reaffirmed its contribution to regional growth and prosperity and global peace and security. 2) The Meeting agreed to promote maritime cooperation including through engagement in the ASEAN Maritime Forum (AMF) and its expanded format **to address common challenges on maritime issues, sea piracy, search and rescue at sea, maritime environment, maritime security, maritime connectivity, freedom of navigation, fisheries and other areas of cooperation.** 3) The Meeting **welcomed India's commitment to support the Master Plan on ASEAN Connectivity** (MPAC) through both hard and soft infrastructure linkages. The Meeting encouraged both sides to look into the possibility of **taking**

*Compiled by the author from MEA and other official sources. List is updated till 30 Jun 2020. Details prior to 2014 are available in Amb Bhatia's book, India-Myanmar Relations: Changing Contours

Sl.No.	*Date of Document*	*Name of Agreement/Declaration/Statement*	*Remarks*
			concrete steps towards the development of the Mekong-India Economic Corridor. 4) The Meeting encouraged the ongoing **development of the India-Myanmar-Thailand Trilateral Highway and its extension to Laos and Cambodia as an initiative to increase greater ASEAN-India physical connectivity.** (*MEA: Statements:* Bilateral/Multilateral Documents. (n.d.). Retrieved June 06, 2020, from https://www.mea.gov.in/bilateral-documents.htm?dtl%2F23891% 2FExtract_from_Chairman s_stat eme nt_on_the_Post_Ministerial _Conference_PMC _10_43_1_Sessions_ 910_August_2014_ Nay_Pyi_ Taw_Myanmar)
4	12th Nov, 2014	The **12th ASEAN India Summit** at Nay Pyi Taw, Myanmar.	It was agreed to— 1) **strengthen maritime cooperation** through existing mechanisms in order to maintain peace and stability in the region 2) recognize the importance of the **Regional Comprehensive Economic Partnership (RCEP)** as a key instrument in realizing the ASEAN Economic Community 3) enhance **people-to people connectivity** through exchange of culture, education, media and tourism. The ASEAN Leaders expressed appreciation for India's support for **the Master Plan on ASEAN Connectivity (MPAC) and highlighted the importance of building physical, institutional and people-to-people connectivity between ASEAN and India.** In this regard, the parties welcomed the commencement of **direct shipping services from India to Myanmar since October 2014.** ASEAN Leaders also **welcomed India's proposed special facility for easing project financing on connectivity** that would further contribute towards narrowing the development gap in ASEAN. (*MEA: Statements:* Bilateral/Multilateral Documents. (n.d.). Retrieved June 06, 2020, from https://www.mea.gov.in/bilateral-documents.htm?dtl%2F24 243%2FC hairmans_statement_of_the_12th_ASEANIndia_Summit_in_Nay_Pyi _Taw_ Myanmar)
5	13th Nov, 2014	Declaration of the 9th East Asia Summit on **Regional Response to Outbreak of Ebola Virus Disease,** Nay Pyi Taw, Myanmar	The parties agreed to fully support the establishment of **United Nations Mission for EVD Emergency Response,** or UNMEER to stem the crisis, treat the infected, ensure essential services, preserve stability and prevent further outbreaks. Further they agreed to **increase public awareness, implement effective health surveillance and coordinate efforts with all relevant United Nations System entities.** (*MEA: Statements:* Bilateral/Multilateral Documents. (n.d.). Retrieved June 06, 2020, from https://www.mea.gov.in/bilateral-documents.htm?dtl%2F24256%2FJoint_StatementDeclaration_of_the_9th_ East_Asia_Summit_on_Re gional_Response_to_Outbreak_of_Ebola_Virus_Disease_ Nay_ Pyi_Taw_ Myanmar_November_13__2014)

Sl.No.	*Date of Document*	*Name of Agreement/Declaration/Statement*	*Remarks*
6	13th Nov, 2014	East Asia Summit (EAS) Statement on **Rapid Disaster Response**, Nay Pyi Taw, Myanmar	The parties recognized the need for a **coordinated and planned regional approach for responding rapidly to a request from, or offer assistance to, a disaster affected country**; and that the quality and efficiency of rapid disaster response requires constant preparedness, planning, capacity building and testing of response plans, systems and mechanisms at national and regional levels. (*MEA: Statements:* Bilateral/Multilateral Documents. (n.d.). Retrieved June 06, 2020, from https://www.mea.gov.in/bilateral-documents.htm?dtl%2F24255%2FEast_Asia_Summit_ EAS_Statem ent_on_Rapid_Disaster_Response_Nay_Pyi_Taw_M yanmar_November_13__2014)
7	13th Nov, 2014	East Asia Summit Statement on the **Rise of Violence and Brutality Committed by Terrorist/Extremist Organisations** in Iraq And Syria, Nay Pyi Taw, Myanmar	The parties expressed deep concern over **the rise of violence and brutality committed by the self-declared ISIL and other terrorist/extremist organisations** and radical groups in Iraq and Syria, noting that these individuals not only pose a **threat to the people of Iraq and Syria, but to their home countries as well as third countries around the world.** (MEA: Statements: Bilateral/Multilateral Documents. (n.d.). Retrieved June 06, 2020, from https://www.mea.gov.in/bilateral-documents.htm?dtl%2F24254%2FEast_Asia_Summit_Sta tement_on_the_rise_of_violence_and_brutality_committed_by_t erroristextremist_organisations_in_Iraq_and_Syria_Nay_Pyi _Taw_Myanmar_N)
8	13th Nov, 2014	East Asia Summit Declaration on **Combating Wildlife Trafficking**, Nay Pyi Taw, Myanmar	The parties agreed to **promote action to further strengthen regional and international cooperation on combating wildlife trafficking**. They agreed to support the **ASEAN Regional Action Plan in CITES Trade in Wild Fauna and Flora which aims at effective regional cooperation** on improved **implementation of CITES, including law enforcement collaboration through ASEAN-WEN**. (*MEA: Statements:* Bilateral/Multilateral Documents. (n.d.). Retrieved June 06, 2020, from https://www.mea.gov.in/bilateral-documents.htm?dtl%2F24253%2FEast_Asia_S ummit_ Declaration_on_combating_wildlife_trafficking_Nay_Pyi_Taw_Myanmar_ November_13__2014)
		2015	
9	16th July, 2015	Joint Statement by India and Myanmar on First Meeting of the **India-Myanmar Joint Consultative Commission**	The parties reaffirmed their shared commitment to fight the scourge **of terrorism and insurgent activity** in all its forms and manifestations. They also emphasized the importance of enhancing **connectivity between the two countries as a means of promoting commercial, cultural, touristic and other exchanges**. The need for **cooperation to further energy security** was also acknowledged. (*MEA: Statements:* Bilateral/Multilateral Documents. (n.d.). Retrieved June 06, 2020, from https://www.mea.gov.in/bilateral-documents.htm?dtl%2F25485%2FJoint_Statem ent_by _India_and_Myanmar_on_First_Meeting_of_the_IndiaMyanmar_J oint_Consultative_Commission)

Sl.No.	*Date of Document*	*Name of Agreement/Declaration/Statement*	*Remarks*
		2016	
10	25th July, 2016	Joint Statement on **the 7th Mekong-Ganga Cooperation Ministerial Meeting**, Vientiane	The parties welcomed the completion of construction by India of the **MGC Textiles Museum** in Siem Reap, Cambodia, thanked all partner countries on its operationalisation and decided to jointly collaborate on the promotion of the Museum as a popular tourist attraction through effective ways. They also appreciated **India's contribution to capacity building and human resource development in the CLMV countries, including over 900 annual scholarships under the Indian Technical and Economic Cooperation** (ITEC) **programme**. Further, the **maritime connectivity** between the parties was deemed to be of importance. (*MEA: Statements:* Bilateral/Multilateral Documents. (n.d.). Retrieved June 06, 2020, from https://www.mea.gov.in/bilateral-documents.htm?dtl%2F27138%2FJoint_ Statement _on_the_7th_MekongGanga_Cooperation_Ministerial_Meeting_ Vientiane)
11	29th August, 2016	India-Myanmar **Joint Statement during the Visit of the President of Myanmar to India**	The Indian leadership expressed support to the national reconciliation and peace process of the Government of Myanmar under the "21st Century Panglong Conference". The two sides reviewed ongoing development cooperation initiatives being undertaken with technical and financial assistance from the Government of India, including in the areas of connectivity and capacity building, health and education infrastructure, agriculture, information technology, industrial training, and various training programme. They expressed satisfaction at the progress made in the implementation of Kaladan Multi Modal Transit Transport Project. The Indian side also invited Myanmar to participate in the International Solar Alliance Initiative. (MEA: Statements: Bilateral/Multilateral Documents. (n.d.). Retrieved June 06, 2020, from https://www.mea.gov.in/bilateral-documents.htm?dtl%2F27343%2FIndia+Myanmar+Join t+Statement+during+the+visit+of+the+President+of+Myanmar+to+India+29+August+2016)
12	29th August, 2016	MoU on **Cooperation in the Construction of 69 Bridges including AP Aproach Roads in the Tamu-Kyigone-Kalewa Road Section of the Trilateral Highway in Myanmar**	(*MEA: Statements:* Bilateral/Multilateral Documents. (n.d.). Retrieved June 06, 2020, from https://www.mea.gov.in/bilateral-documents.htm?dtl%2F27342%2FList_of _MoUsAgreement_signed_during_the_visit_of_President_ of_Myanmar_to_India_29_August_2016)
13	29th August, 2016	MoU on **Cooperation in the Construction/Upgradation of the Kalewa–Yagyi Road Section**	(MEA: Statements: Bilateral/Multilateral Documents. (n.d.). Retrieved June 06, 2020, from https://www.mea.gov.in/bilateral-documents.htm?dtl%2 F27342%2FList_of_MoUs Agreement_signed_during_the_visit_of_President_of_Myanmar_to_India_ 29_ August_2016)
14	29th August, 2016	MoU on **Cooperation in the Field of Renewable Energy**	(MEA: Statements: Bilateral/Multilateral Documents. (n.d.). Retrieved June 06, 2020, from https://www.mea.gov.in/bilateral-documents.htm?dtl%2F27342%2FList_of _MoUsA greement_signed_during_the_visit_of_President_of_Myanmar_to_India_ 29_August_2016)

Sl.No.	*Date of Document*	*Name of Agreement/Declaration/Statement*	*Remarks*
15	29th August, 2016	MoU on **Cooperation in the Field of Traditional Systems of Medicine**	(MEA: Statements: Bilateral/Multilateral Documents. (n.d.). Retrieved June 06, 2020, from https://www.mea.gov.in/bilateral-documents.htm?dtl%2F27342%2FList_of_MoUs Agreement_signed_during_the_visit_of_President_of_Myanmar_to_India_29_August_2016)
16	17th Oct, 2016	**BIMSTEC Leader's Retreat** 2016 Outcome Document	The parties agreed **to cooperate on climate change, terrorism, trade and development of connectivity to ensure overall peace and stability in the region.** (MEA: Statements: Bilateral/Multilateral Documents. (n.d.). Retrieved June 06, 2020, from https://www.mea.gov.in/bilateral-documents.htm?dtl%2F27501%2F BIMSTEC_Leaders_Retreat_2016_Outcome_Document)
17	19th Oct, 2016	India-Myanmar **Joint Statement during the Visit of State Counsellor of Myanmar to India**	Both parties agreed to cooperate on fight against **terrorism, infrastructure development, connectivity and development of ocean based Blue economy** among various other areas. They also expressed that maintaining **security along border** was essential for overall socio-economic development. (*MEA: Statements:* Bilateral/Multilateral Documents. (n.d.). Retrieved June 06, 2020, from https://www.mea.gov.in/bilateral-documents.htm?dtl%2F27513%2FIndia Myanmar_Joint_ Statement_during_the_visit_of_State_Counsellor_of_Myanmar_to_India)
18	19th Oct, 2016	MoU Between **Financial Regulatory Department of Myanmar and Insurance Institute of India for Designing an Academic and Professional Building Programme for Insurance Industry of Myanmar**	(MEA: Statements: Bilateral/Multilateral Documents. (n.d.). Retrieved June 06, 2020, from https://www.mea.gov.in/bilateral-documents.htm?dtl%2F27508%2FList_of_agreementsMOUs_signed_between_Government_of_India_and_Government_of_Myanmar)
19	19th Oct, 2016	MoU on **Cooperation in the Field of Power Sector**	(MEA: Statements: Bilateral/Multilateral Documents. (n.d.). Retrieved June 06, 2020, from https://www.mea.gov.in/bilateral-documents.htm?dtl%2F27508%2FList_of_agreementsMOUs_signed_ between_Government_of_India_and_Government_of_Myanmar)
20	19th Oct, 2016	MoU on **Banking Supervision Between RBI and Central Bank of Myanmar**	(MEA: Statements: Bilateral/Multilateral Documents. (n.d.). Retrieved June 06, 2020, from https://www.mea.gov.in/bilateral-documents.htm?dtl%2F27508%2FList_of_agreementsMOUs_signed_between_Government_of_India_and_Government_of_Myanmar)
		2017	
21	9th August, 2017	Joint Ministerial Statement for the **8th Mekong-Ganga Cooperation Ministerial Meeting** in Manila, Philippines	The parties appreciated the ongoing activities of the **MGC Textiles Museum** in Siam Reap, Cambodia, and thanked all partner countries on the efforts towards making the Museum operational and functional. Further, the parties welcomed the progress made towards strengthening **cooperation in agriculture, food security, tourism and connectivity. India's contribution towards capacity building and human resource development** in the CLMV countries was also acknowledged. (*MEA: Statements:* Bilateral/Multilateral Documents. (n.d.).

Sl.No.	*Date of Document*	*Name of Agreement/Declaration/Statement*	*Remarks*
			Retrieved June 06, 2020, from https://www.mea.gov.in/bilateral-documents.htm?dtl%2F28815%2FJoint)
22	11th August, 2017	Joint Statement of the **15th BIMSTEC Ministerial Meeting**	The parties called for greater cooperation in **trade, investment, public health, counter terrorism, energy and agriculture**. They also noted the urgency for cooperation in the **fight against climate change**. (MEA: Statements: Bilateral/Multilateral Documents. (n.d.). Retrieved June 06, 2020, from https://www.mea.gov.in/bilateral-documents.htm?dtl%2F28862%2FJoint_Statement_of_the_15th_BIMSTEC_Ministerial_Meeting_August_11_2017)
23	6th Sept, 2017	MoU on **Maritime Security Cooperation** Between the Government of the Republic of India and the Government of the Republic of the Union of Myanmar	(MEA: Statements: Bilateral/Multilateral Documents. (n.d.). Retrieved June 06, 2020, from https://www.mea.gov.in/bilateral-documents.htm?dtl%2F28921%2FLi st_of_MoUs Agreements_signed_during_State_visit_of_Prime_Minister_to_Myanmar)
24	6th Sept, 2017	**Cultural Exchange Programme** Between the Government of the Republic of India and the Government of the Republic of the Union of Myanmar for the Year 2017-2020	(*MEA: Statements:* Bilateral/Multilateral Documents. (n.d.). Retrieved June 06, 2020, from https://www.mea.gov.in/bilateral-documents.htm?dtl%2F28921%2FList_of_MoUs Agreements_signed_during_State_visit_of_Prime_Minister_to_Myanmar)
25	6th Sept, 2017	MoU Between the Government of the Republic of the Union of Myanmar and the Government of the Republic of India on Enhancing the Cooperation of the **Upgradation of the Women's Police Training Centre at Yamethin, Myanmar**	(*MEA: Statements:* Bilateral/Multilateral Documents. (n.d.). Retrieved June 06, 2020, from https://www.mea.gov.in/bilateral-documents.htm?dtl%2F28921%2FList_of_MoUs Agreements_signed_during_State_visit_of_Prime_Minister_to_Myanmar)
26	6th Sept, 2017	MoU for **Sharing White Shipping Information** Between the Indian Navy and Myanmar Navy	(*MEA: Statements:* Bilateral/Multilateral Documents. (n.d.). Retrieved June 06, 2020, from https://www.mea.gov.in/bilateral-documents.htm?dtl%2F28921%2FList_of_MoUs Agreements_signed_during_State_visit_of_Prime_Minister_to_Myanmar)
27	6th Sept, 2017	Technical Agreement Between the Government of the Republic of India and the Government of the Republic of the Union of Myanmar for Providing **Coastal Surveillance System**	(*MEA: Statements:* Bilateral/Multilateral Documents. (n.d.). Retrieved June 06, 2020, from https://www.mea.gov.in/bilateral-documents.htm?dtl%2F28921%2FList_of_MoUs Agreements_signed_during_State_visit_of_Prime_Minister_to_Myanmar)
28	6th Sept, 2017	MoU Between the **Central Drugs Standard Control Organization (CDSCO), Ministry of Health and Family Welfare of the Republic of India and Food and Drugs (FDA), Ministry of Health and Sports of Myanmar on Cooperation in Medical Products Regulation**	(*MEA: Statements:* Bilateral/Multilateral Documents. (n.d.). Retrieved June 06, 2020, from https://www.mea.gov.in/bilateral-documents.htm?dtl%2F28921%2FList_of_MoUs Agreements_signed_during_State_visit_of_Prime_Minister_to_Myanmar)
29	6th Sept, 2017	MoU Between the **Ministry of Health and Family Welfare of the Republic of India and the Ministry of Health and Sports of the Republic of the Union of**	(*MEA: Statements:* Bilateral/Multilateral Documents. (n.d.). Retrieved June 06, 2020, from https://www.mea.gov.in/bilateral-documents.htm?dtl%2F28921%2FList_of_MoUs Agreements_signed_during_State_visit_of_Prime_Minister

Sl.No.	*Date of Document*	*Name of Agreement/Declaration/Statement*	*Remarks*
		Myanmar on Cooperation in the Field of Health and Medicine	_to_Myanmar)
30	6th Sept, 2017	Exchange of Letter for Extension of MoU on the **Establishment of MIIT**	(*MEA: Statements:* Bilateral/Multilateral Documents. (n.d.). Retrieved June 06, 2020, from https://www.mea.gov.in/bilateral-documents.htm?dtl%2F28921%2FList_of_MoUs Agreements_signed_during_State_visit_of_Prime_Minister_to_Myanmar)
31	6th Sept, 2017	Exchange of Letter for Extension of MoU on the Establishment of **India-Myanmar Center for Enhancement of it-Skill**	(*MEA: Statements:* Bilateral/Multilateral Documents. (n.d.). Retrieved June 06, 2020, from https://www.mea.gov.in/bilateral-documents.htm?dtl%2F28921%2FList_of_MoUs Agreements_signed_during_State_visit_of_Prime_Minister_to_Myanmar)
32	6th Sept, 2017	MoU in the Field of Elections Between **the Election Commission of India and the Union Election Commission of Myanmar**	(*MEA: Statements:* Bilateral/Multilateral Documents. (n.d.). Retrieved June 06, 2020, from https://www.mea.gov.in/bilateral-documents.htm?dtl%2F28921%2FList_of_MoUs Agreements_signed_during_State_visit_of_Prime_Minister_to_Myanmar)
33	6th Sept, 2017	MoU on **Cooperation Between Myanmar Press Council and the Press Council of India**	(*MEA: Statements:* Bilateral/Multilateral Documents. (n.d.). Retrieved June 06, 2020, from https://www.mea.gov.in/bilateral-documents.htm?dtl%2F28921%2FList_of_MoUs Agreements_signed_during_State_visit_of_Prime_Minister_to_Myanmar)
		2018	
34	25th January, 2018	**Delhi Declaration** of the ASEAN-India Commemorative Summit to Mark the **25th Anniversary of ASEAN-India Dialogue Relations**	The parties agreed to strengthen and deepen the ASEAN-India Strategic Partnership for mutual benefit, across the whole spectrum of **political-security, economic, socio-cultural and development cooperation, through further strengthening of relevant institutional mechanisms and broadening of the network Between government institutions, parliamentarians, business circles, scientists, academicians, think-tanks, media, youth and other stakeholders**, for the building of a peaceful, harmonious, caring and sharing community in the region. (*MEA: Statements:* Bilateral/Multilateral Documents. (n.d.). Retrieved June 06, 2020, from https://www.mea.gov.in/bilateral-documents.htm?dtl%2F29386%2FDelhi_ Declaration_ of_ the_ ASEANIndia_ Commemorative_ Summit _to_mark_the_25th_Anniversary_of_ASEANIndia_ Dialogue_Relations)
35	10th May, 2018	MoU Between **Foreign Service Institute, Ministry of External Affairs**, Republic of India and **Strategic Studies and Training Department, Ministry of Foreign Affairs**, Republic of the Union of Myanmar	The objective of the MoU was to cooperate **in setting up of customized training and capacity building programmes** by Foreign Service institute for the officers of Myanmar Foreign Service. The parties also agreed to **exchange information about training programmes, trainees, students, faculty members and experts**. (Treaty Detail. (n.d.). Retrieved June 06, 2020, from https://www.mea.gov.in/TreatyDetail.htm?3298)
36	31st August, 2018	**Fourth BIMSTEC Summit** Declaration, Kathmandu, Nepal	The parties agreed to intensify efforts to realize the objectives and purposes of BIMSTEC as embodied in the **1997 Bangkok Declaration**, and reiterated their pledge to work

Sl.No.	Date of Document	Name of Agreement/Declaration/Statement	Remarks
			collectively towards making BIMSTEC a stronger, more effective and result-oriented organization for achieving a peaceful, prosperous and sustainable Bay of Bengal Region. (*MEA: Statements:* Bilateral/Multilateral Documents. (n.d.). Retrieved June 06, 2020, from https://www.mea.gov.in/bilateral-documents.htm?dtl%2F30335%2FFourth_BIMSTEC_Summit_Declaration_Kathmandu_Nepal_August_3031_2018)
37	22nd Oct, 2018	MoU Between the Government of the Republic of India and the Government of the Republic of the Union of Myanmar	The objective of the MoU was to agree on **appointment of a private operator for operation and maintenance of Sittwe Port, Paletwa Inland Water Transport (IWT) Terminal and associated facilities during the period until the completion of road component or five years**, whichever is earlier. It was agreed that the private **operator shall be jointly selected by GOI and GOM. Only Indian firms or Joint Venture (JV) Between Indian and Myanmar firms, with the Indian firm as a lead partner, shall be allowed to participate in the tender.** (Treaty Detail. (n.d.). Retrieved June 06, 2020, from https://www.mea.gov.in/TreatyDetail.htm?3471)
38	11th Dec, 2018	**Programme of Cooperation in Science and Technology** Between the Government of the Republic of India and the Government of the Republic of the Union of Myanmar for the Period 2018-2021	The objective of the MoU was to **establish India-Myanmar Joint Working Group For Scientific and Technological Cooperation**. The Working Group is responsible for the following: **(a) Determining the areas of mutual interest and fields of cooperation; (b) Exchanging opinions on the overall perspectives of the bilateral scientific and technical cooperation; (c) Consideration of new proposals for the development of the cooperation; (d) Approving the implementation of joint activities; (e) Monitoring and review of the on-going cooperation activities** (Treaty Detail. (n.d.). Retrieved June 06, 2020, from https://www.mea.gov.in/TreatyDetail.htm?3523)
39	11th Dec, 2018	MoU Between the **National Judicial Academy of India and the Office of Union Chief Justice on Training and Capacity Building Programme for Myanmar Judges and Judicial Officers in India**	(*MEA: Statements:* Bilateral/Multilateral Documents. (n.d.). Retrieved June 06, 2020, from https://www.mea.gov.in/bilateral-documents.htm?dtl%2F30692%2FList_of_Documents_signed_during_the_State_Visit_of_President_to_Myanmar)
		2019	
40	2nd August, 2019	Joint Ministerial Statement of the 10th Mekong-Ganga Cooperation Ministerial Meeting	The parties adopted the new MGC Plan of Action 2019-2022 that envisages project-based cooperation in the **seven areas of MGC cooperation, namely tourism and culture, education, public health and traditional medicine, agriculture and allied sectors, transport and communication, MSMEs as well as three new areas of cooperation, i.e. water resources management, science and technology, skill development and capacity building.** They also welcomed **India's assistance to Cambodia, Lao PDR, Myanmar and Viet Nam under the MGC Quick Impact Projects (QIP) Scheme and in the educational sector.** (MEA: Statements: Bilateral/Multilateral Documents. (n.d.). Retrieved June 06, 2020, from https://www.mea.gov.in/

Sl.No.	*Date of Document*	*Name of Agreement/Declaration/Statement*	*Remarks*
			bilateral-documents.htm?dtl%2F31713%2FJoint_Ministerial_Statement_of_the_10th_MekongGanga_Cooperation_Ministerial_ Meeting)
		2020	
41	20th Feb, 2020	MoU Between the Government of the Republic of India and the Government of the Republic of the Union of Myanmar on Cooperation for **Prevention of Trafficking in Persons, Rescue, Recovery, Repatriation and Re-Integration of Victims of Trafficking**	The objective of the MoU was to establish a working group that would enable cooperation for the prevention of trafficking in persons. The parties agreed to put in **place preventive measures and mechanisms that would allow for repatriation of victims.** (Treaty Detail. (n.d.). Retrieved June 06, 2020, from https://www.mea.gov.in/TreatyDetail.htm?3687)
42	27th Feb, 2020	MoU Between the **Ministry of Communications** of the Republic of India and **The Ministry of Transport and Communications** of the Republic of the Union of Myanmar	The objective of the MoU was to ensure **cooperation between the two parties in telecommunications, spectrum management, wireless communications, network security and development and application of Telecommunication technologies.** The parties agreed to **establish a joint working group that would prepare the required plan of action.** (Treaty Detail. (n.d.). Retrieved June 06, 2020, from https://www.mea.gov.in/TreatyDetail.htm?3688)
43	27th Feb, 2020	MoU Between the **Ministry of Petroleum and Natural Gas**, The Republic of India and **Ministry of Electricity and Energy**, The Republic of the Union of Myanmar for Cooperation in the Field of Petroleum Products	The objective of the MoU was to establish a framework for cooperation in the petroleum sector between the Parties on the basis of equality and mutual benefit. The parties agreed to **exchange information pertaining to technology and scientific research and organize seminars to promote business opportunities and draw investments.** (Treaty Detail. (n.d.). Retrieved June 06, 2020, from https://www.mea.gov.in/TreatyDetail.htm?3686)
44	27th Feb, 2020	MoU Between the Government of the Republic of India and the Government of the Republic of the Union of Myanmar for **Cooperation on Combating Timber Trafficking and Conservation of Tigers and other Wildlife**	The objective of the MoU was to ensure **Forest Officers of the Parties along the border have periodic meetings to discuss area of concern and formulate transboundary managerial strategies.** Further, they agreed to **have high level ministry meetings group to review measures. A working group** was constituted **to share viable data with focus on protection of habitat, tigers and other wildlife.** (Treaty Detail. (n.d.). Retrieved June 06, 2020, from https://www.mea.gov.in/TreatyDetail.htm?3685)
45	27th Feb, 2020	Agreement Between the Government of the Republic of India and the Government of the Republic of the Union of Myanmar Regarding Indian Grant Assistance for **Implementation of Quick Impact Projects (QIP)**	(*MEA: Statements:* Bilateral/Multilateral Documents. (n.d.). Retrieved June 06, 2020, from https://www.mea.gov.in/bilateral-documents.htm?dtl%2F32433%2FMoUs_Exchanged_during_the_State_Visit_of_President_of_Myanmar)
46	27th Feb, 2020	Project Agreement Between Rakhine State Government and Embassy of India, Yangon for **Construction of Incinerator in Mrauk Oo Township Hospital, Construction of Seed Storage Houses and Water Supply Systems in Gwa Township under Rakhine State Development Programme**	(MEA: Statements: Bilateral/Multilateral Documents. (n.d.). Retrieved June 06, 2020, from https://www.mea.gov.in/bilateral-documents.htm?dtl%2F32433%2FMoUs_Exchanged_during_the_State_Visit_of_President_of_Myanmar)

Sl.No.	*Date of Document*	*Name of Agreement/Declaration/Statement*	*Remarks*
47	27th Feb, 2020	Project Agreement Between Rakhine State Government and Embassy of India, Yangon for **Distribution of Electricity by Solar Power in Five Townships of Rakhine State under Rakhine State Development Programme**	(*MEA: Statements:* Bilateral/Multilateral Documents. (n.d.). Retrieved June 06, 2020, from https://www.mea.gov.in/bilateral-documents.htm?dtl%2F32433%2FMoUs_Exchanged_during_the_State_Visit_of_President_of_Myanmar)
48	27th Feb, 2020	Project Agreement Between Rakhine State Government and Embassy of India, Yangon **for Construction of Kyawlyaung-Ohlphyu Road, Construction of Kyaung Taung Kyaw Paung Road in Buthedaung Township under Rakhine State Development Programme**	(MEA: Statements: Bilateral/Multilateral Documents. (n.d.). Retrieved June 06, 2020, from https://www.mea.gov.in/bilateral-documents.htm?dtl%2F32433%2FMoUs_Exchanged_during_the_State_Visit_of_President_of_Myanmar)
49	27th Feb, 2020	Project Agreement Between **Ministry of Social Welfare, Relief and Resettlement and Embassy of India, Yangon for Construction of Pre-Schools under Rakhine State Development Programme**	(*MEA: Statements:* Bilateral/Multilateral Documents. (n.d.). Retrieved June 06, 2020, from https://www.mea.gov.in/bilateral-documents.htm?dtl%2F32433%2FMoUs_Exchanged_during_the_State_Visit_of_President_of_Myanmar)
50	27th Feb, 2020	MoU for **Cooperation in the Field of Health Research Between Indian Council of Medical Research (ICMR) and Department of Medical Research (DMR), M/O Health & Sports of Myanmar**	(*MEA: Statements:* Bilateral/Multilateral Documents. (n.d.). Retrieved June 06, 2020, from https://www.mea.gov.in/bilateral-documents.htm?dtl%2F32433%2FMoUs_Exchanged_during_the_State_Visit_of_President_of_Myanmar)
51	27th Feb, 2020	**India-Myanmar Joint Statement during the State Visit of the President of Myanmar to India (26–29 February 2020).**	(*MEA: Statements:* Bilateral/Multilateral Documents. (n.d.). Retrieved June 06, 2020, from https://www.mea.gov.in/bilateral-documents.htm?dtl%2F32433%2FMoUs_Exchanged_during_the_State_Visit_of_President_of_Myanmar)

APPENDIX N

Framework Agreement Between India and Myanmar on Kaladan Multi-Modal Transit Transport Project, 2008

FRAMEWORK AGREEMENT BETWEEN
THE GOVERNMENT OF THE REPUBLIC OF INDIA
AND
THE GOVERNMENT OF THE UNION OF MYANMAR
FOR THE CONSTRUCTION AND OPERATION OF A MULTI-MODAL
TRANSIT TRANSPORT FACILITY ON KALADAN RIVER
CONNECTING THE SITTWE PORT IN MYANMAR
WITH THE STATE OF MIZORAM IN INDIA

The **Government of the Republic of India** and the **Government of the Union of Myanmar** hereinafter referred to as the Contracting Parties:

BEING desirous of further developing and strengthening friendly and good neighbourly relations;

HAVING agreed to cooperate bilaterally to promote greater economic cooperation for mutual benefit and for the well being of their people;

CONSIDERING development of infrastructural projects including transport facilities as important for facilitating greater economic integration and people-to-people contact:

DESIROUS of exploring the possibility of constructing a multi-modal transit transport facility connecting the port of Sittwe in Myanmar with the State of Mizoram in India combining a system of inland waterway and highways;

HAVING examined the Detailed Project Report (DPR) prepared and submitted by RITES Ltd. in April and December 2003;

BEING aware of environmental considerations and in this connection, noting that the DPR prepared by RITES does not reflect any adverse impact.

BEARING in mind the principles of sovereignty, equality and mutual benefit; Have agreed as follows:

ARTICLE 1: DEFINITIONS

For the purposes of this Agreement:

"Multi-modal Transit Transport Facility" means an inland waterway link connecting the port of Sittwe and Setpyitpyin (Kaletwa) along the Kaladan River and a highway linking Setpyitpyin (Kaletwa) to the India-Myanmar border in the State of Mizoram.

"Protocol on Facilitation of Transit Transport" means a mutually agreed document defining the operational aspects of the project, which shall be annexed to and form an integral part of this Agreement.

"Protocol on Maintenance and Administration" means a mutually agreed document to define the operation, maintenance, and administration of the Kaladan Multi-Modal Transit Transport Facility for mutual benefit which shall be annexed to and form an integral part of this Agreement.

ARTICLE 2

For the purpose of implementation of this Agreement, the Contracting Parties shall appoint respective nodal agencies. The Ministry of External Affairs shall represent the Government of the Republic of India and the Ministry of Foreign Affairs shall represent the Government of the Union of Myanmar.

With a view to advising and supervising the overall progress of work on the project the respective nodal agencies shall appoint a Multi-Sectoral group. The group shall hold periodic meetings to review progress.

ARTICLE 3

The Contracting Parties agree to construct the Kaladan multi-modal transit transport facility with the following key components:

(a) The land required for the Project will be provided gratis by the Government of the Union of Myanmar.

(b) Construction of a port/Inland Water Transport (IWT) terminal and related infrastructure facilities at the port of Sittwe in Myanmar for trans-shipment from ships to inland vessels and vice versa, including development of the navigation channels.

(c) Development of Kaladan waterway from Sittwe to Setpyitpyin (Kaletwa) - about 225 km by undertaking river engineering works such as dredging, removal of rock out-crops/rapids, navigation aids, etc.

(d) Construction of an IWT/Highway trans-shipment terminal and related facilities at Setpyitpyin (Kaletwa).

(e) Construction of a highway from Setpyitpyin (Kaletwa) to India-Myanmar border.

(f) Maintenance and management of the above facility components.

The details of these project components including alignment have been examined in the Detailed Project Report already submitted to the Parties by M/s RITES Ltd. in 2003 and accepted by the respective Parties.

The Detailed Project Report estimates the cost of construction of the Project as under: Upgradation of Sittwe port and Kaladan waterway: US $ 68.24 million.

Construction of a road from Setpyitpyin (Kaletwa) to India-Myanmar border: US $49.14 million

The details of the project components have been examined and accepted by the Contracting Parties.

ARTICLE 4

(a) The Government of India shall appoint the Project Development Consultant from India. The Project Development Consultant shall be responsible for the following in the execution of the project.

- (i) Preparation for selection of the construction contractors for development of various project facilities as indicated in Article 3.
- (ii) Coordination/liaison between the nodal agencies and the construction contractors; and
- (iii) Supervision of construction and project management of various works.

(b) The Government of India shall appoint the main contractor from India. If required different sub contractors from both the contracting parties may be appointed for implementing various components of the project.

ARTICLE 5

For proper implementation of the project, the Government of the Union of Myanmar during the period of construction, which commences from the date mutually agreed by the Parties, after the entry into force of the Agreement shall:

- (A) Extend the following facilities free of charge:
  - (i) Allocation of waterfront area for construction of port terminal structures.
  - (ii) Allocation of adequate land for construction of onshore facilities.
  - (iii) Provision of adequate security for the machinery, materials and personnel or any other clearance required under local laws;
  - (iv) Permissions from the local authorities on account of environment or any other clearance required under local laws and;
  - (v) Any other facility in connection with the project as mutually agreed.
- (B) Provide the following at appropriate charges:
  - (i) Use of the existing Sittwe Port terminal facilities for berthing
  - (ii) Facilities such as provision of fuel, boats and barges for transportation of personnel/equipment/material along the project corridor including on river Kaladan;

(iii) Communication facilities including telephone/ fax connections;
(iv) A suitable number of interpreters to facilitate discussion amongst personnel using Myanmar, English and Hindi languages and;
(v) Any other facility in connection with the project as mutually agreed.

ARTICLE 6

The concerned agencies of the Government of the Republic of India shall be permitted to bring in equipment, material and personnel including technicians required for the execution of the project free of impediments and costs. The nodal agency in Myanmar shall be responsible for facilitating these activities.

ARTICLE 7

For any machinery/equipment/construction material, etc. required to be procured locally, the Government of the Union of Myanmar shall permit its procurement and use without impediment and free of local taxes and duties.

ARTICLE 8

The equipment/machinery imported for the project by the Indian side shall be allowed, to be taken into and out of Myanmar and the Project site, by India without impediments or taxes in accordance with the internal procedures of Myanmar.

ARTICLE 9

The Government of the Union of Myanmar shall facilitate entry and exit of personnel including technicians involved in the execution of the project on production of a passport or travelling document issued by the Government of the Republic of India.

The concerned authorities of the Government of the Union of Myanmar shall provide temporary stay permits to Indian nationals employed for implementation of the project upon receipt of information (with complete bio-data) thereto from the Embassy of India in Yangon. Such temporary stay permits, if necessary, will be renewed in accordance with the rules and regulations of stay extension procedures of the Government of the Union of Myanmar against a certificate of identity issued by the project consultant.

ARTICLE 10

The Government of the Union of Myanmar shall facilitate duty free import, as mutually agreed upon, of personal effects of the personnel deputed from India for the implementation of the project.

ARTICLE 11

The personnel including technicians brought in from India for the execution of the project shall not be subject to local income tax of Myanmar. They will also be exempt from other taxes and duties as mutually agreed upon, during their entire stay in Myanmar.

ARTICLE 12

The Government of the Union of Myanmar shall provide necessary security to the project personnel including technicians. The Government of the Union of Myanmar shall make available medical facilities to project personnel including technicians as provided to Myanmar nationals at the nearest medical centre/ hospital.

ARTICLE 13

The Government of the Union of Myanmar shall permit and assist the internal travel of project personnel including technicians and transport of equipment and materials. It shall also provide space for accommodation for project personnel including technicians and site offices without cost within the project area.

ARTICLE 14

The cost of the construction of the project shall be borne by the Government of the Republic of India.

ARTICLE 15

On completion, the Project will be handed over to the Government of the Union of Myanmar on terms and conditions mutually agreed upon. It shall be operated and maintained by the Government of the Union of Myanmar in accordance with the provisions contained in the Protocol on Facilitation of Transit Transport and Protocol on Maintenance and Administration.

ARTICLE 16

Both parties shall provide all support and facilities for meeting genuine requirements in terms of communication facilities, use of materials including explosives, hiring of labour, etc. These details shall be worked out by the nodal agencies through mutual agreement and in accordance with their laws.

ARTICLE 17

Indian personnel including technicians shall abide by the laws of the Union of Myanmar and shall not interfere in the internal affairs of the Union of Myanmar during their stay in that country. Disciplinary action against Indian personnel including technicians shall be taken by the relevant Indian authorities and the guilty personnel could be repatriated, if necessary. Criminal cases will be dealt with as per the laws of the Union of Myanmar.

Indian labour laws, including rates of payment and compensation, will apply to Indian personnel including technicians, in case of injury/death. The Myanmar workers shall be subject to Myanmar labour laws.

ARTICLE 18

The Indian nodal agency shall establish and operate a liaison office at Sittwe for coordinating the project works. The Myanmar side shall facilitate the establishment of such an office.

ARTICLE 19

Any dispute arising out of the interpretation or application of this Agreement shall be settled through mutual consultations between the Contracting Parties.

ARTICLE 20

This Agreement may be amended or supplemented by mutual agreement in writing between the Contracting Parties.

ARTICLE 21

This Agreement shall enter into force on the date of its signature. The Agreement shall remain in force until it is terminated by mutual agreement in writing between the Contracting Parties.

In witness whereof, the undersigned being duly authorized by their respective Governments, have signed this Agreement:

Done at New Delhi on the 2nd day of April, in the year 2008 in three originals each in Hindi, Myanmar and English languages, all the texts being equally authentic. In case of any difference or doubt, the English text shall prevail.

For the Government of the
Republic of India

(Pranab Mukherjee)
Minister of External Affairs

For the Government of the
Union of Myanmar

(Nyan Win)
Minister for Foreign Affairs

APPENDIX O

Arakan Rohingya Salvation Army

(Sections of this Appendix have taken from a VIF Paper written by this author, titled, *Counterproductive Effects of Sanctions – The Myanmar Case Study,* published on 28 October 2019)[1]

Background

The present state of affairs w.r.t. Rohingyas, germinated from a British Second World War strategy to arm pro-British Muslims in Arakan to create a rear-guard cum intelligence gathering guerrilla force called the 'V' Force to slow down the Japanese during the retreat from Burma in 1942.[2] In return, they were apparently promised a '*Muslim National Area*'[3] in northwest Arakan but the British eventually reneged on their promise. This strategy effectively pitched the Arakan Muslim Rohingyas against their Buddhist brethren who had sided with the Japanese against the colonial British.[4,5] These Arakan Buddhists were armed by Aung San's Burma Independence Army and ended up clashing with this same 'V' Force. It was under these circumstances in 1942 that the first large scale massacre of Rohingyas by Arakan Buddhists took place claiming over one lakh lives.[6]

In continuation of the pursuit for the promised Muslim National Area, in May 1946, a leading Rohingya-led Muslim organisation, *Jami-atul Ulema-e Islam* apparently even approached Jinnah to consider amalgamation of two Muslim-majority townships of Northwest Arakan viz. Buthidaung and Maungdaw with the new state of East Pakistan, but failed. The aggregate of these actions forged a sense of betrayal in the Bamar psyche which has acquired its own momentum over time. Out of the eight main groups of Muslims in Myanmar, none face the extreme Buddhist animosity that is exclusively reserved for Rohingyas.[7]

Expectedly, over time and driven to the wall, the Rohingyas have tried to fight back for recognition and self-determination which has resulted in a series of violent clashes and bloodletting in Northern Rakhine State. In summary, successive regimes in Myanmar had carried out major armed operations against the Rohingyas in 1975, 1978 (Operation Naga Amin), 1989, 1991-92, 2002, and 2012. Each of these operations has led to mass exodus of Rohingyas into neighbouring Bangladesh. Currently the broad figures stand at 7.5 lakhs Rohingyas in camps in Bangladesh with a balance of 6 lakh Rohingyas remaining in Arakan.

The Current Crisis and Pakistan's involvement in it

The current crisis was precipitated by the actions publicly claimed by the Rohingya militant group *Harakah al-Yaqin*[8] [subsequently renamed as the Arakan Rohingya Solidarity Army (ARSA)] which launched four attacks since 2012. The attacks on 9 October 2016 and on 25 Aug 2017 were the ones which triggered the Myanmar military's response. The International Crisis Group investigated the attack and reported that the *Harakah al-Yaqin* was funded by Rohingyas émigrés in Saudi Arabia and commanded on the ground by Rohingyas with international training and experience in modern guerrilla war tactics.

The 9 October 2016 attack was launched by 250 militants armed with knives and hand-made guns and killed nine police officers and injured five in Maungday and Rathedaung Townships. The attackers stole 50 guns and 10,000 bullets but lost eight members while two were captured alive by the Myanmar forces. They disclosed that they were members of the terrorist group called Aqa Mul Mujahid (AMM) led by Ataullah Abu Ammar Junjuni@ Hafiz Tohar[9] which subsequently merged with ARSA.

The 25 Aug 2017 attack broke new ground in scale, coordination, brutality and symbolism. The attack took place near *simultaneously* on 30 police posts and one army base in the townships of Maungdaw, Buthidaung and Rathedaung in North Rakhine killing ten police officers, one soldier and an immigration official against 77 insurgents killed and one captured as per reports of the International Crisis Group.[10] It is also coordinated because *on the same date* the ARSA conducted a brutal massacre of 99 Hindu children, women and men of Ah Nauk Kha Maung Seik and Ye Bauk Kyar villages in north Maungdaw Township as reported by Amnesty International.[11] This was followed up the next day on 26 August 2017 when ARSA members killed another six Hindus – two women, a man, and three children near Myo Thu Gyi village outside Maungdaw town. ARSA animosity for Hindus has been documented in a number of incidents and is expected given its lineage as covered below.[12]

The *symbolism* of the timing of the attack was significant since the previous evening i.e. on 24 Aug 2019,[13] former UN Secretary-General Kofi Annan had released the final report of the Advisory Commission on Rakhine State[14] at Ballroom II of the glitzy Hotel Sule Shangrila in Yangon. This Commission had been tasked with identifying solutions for peace and development for all stakeholders in Rakhine State. The Commission had been established based on a request from Daw Aung San Suu Kyi, the State Counsellor of Myanmar to the Kofi Annan Foundation and the timing of the attacks by ARSA symbolised their disdain and contempt for the process and the person who initiated it.[15]

It was subsequently reported that the 25 Aug 2017 attacks had been in effect coordinated by the Pakistan's notorious Inter Services Intelligence (ISI). Investigations revealed that Hafiz Tohar, commander of the ARSA Military Wing was recruited by Abdul Qadoos Burmi, the chief of Harkat ul Jihad al Islami -Arakan (HUJI-A) from

Kyauk Pyin Siek village of Maungdaw in 2014. He was, along with a few others, trained in Pakistan with the terrorist group Lashkar e Tayyaba (LET) after which he set up the AMM which he eventually merged with the ARSA after it was formed in the summer of 2016. Interrogation of top Jamaat-ul-Mujahideen Bangladesh (JMB) leader Abul Kashem by Bangladesh intelligence officials revealed that new Rohingya recruits from Rakhine and the refugee camps in Bangladesh were trained in camps astride the Bangladesh-Myanmar border at Naikhongcherri in the Chittagong Hill Tracts under a Major Salamat of Pakistan ISI on under cover deputation with the LET during Apr – May 2016. He further disclosed that totally 88 ARSA recruits and 63 JMB cadres had trained here during this period.

During raids by Bangladesh security forces on this camp, contact number of one Brigadier Ashfaq was also found and he was later identified as the head of the ISI's Eastern Operations Wing who had then recently interacted with Bangladesh Nationalist Party (BNP) leader and former Bangladesh PM Khaleda Zia and Vice Chairman Tarique Rahman in London to plot the downfall of the ruling Awami League and Sheikh Hasina government.

In this connection, three calls intercepted simultaneously by intelligence agencies in two countries are revealing. On 23 August 2017 at 11.32 a.m. Bangladesh time, a 37 min call from Brig Ashfaq's number was made to a Bangladesh Grameenphone mobile used by Hafiz Tohar whereby Ashfaq told Hafiz that ARSA had to hit multiple targets within the next 48 hours. Tohar replied that though his squads were already in a position to strike, suggesting long planning and mobilisation, it would not be possible to strike the multiple targets before midnight of 24th August. "***Kala Admi*** *report detehi hamla ho,*" said Ashfaq and Tohar replied in chaste Urdu, "*Ji Janaab, jo hukum, par 24 rat se pahle nahi hoga.*" The 'Kala Admi' or 'Black Man' was assessed to be Kofi Annan and the ISI officer was asking for the attacks to be timed immediately after Annan submitted his report the evening itself. Tohar said it would not be possible before midnight of 24th Aug.

The second 28 minute call was intercepted on 24th Aug at 2.13 p.m. Bangladesh time where Brig Ashfaq enquired when the 'Kala Admi" (Annan) was making his report public to which Hafiz Tohar informed him that this was scheduled shortly at 3 p.m. that day itself. Ashfaq pleaded for launching the attacks as quickly as possible, soon after dark. Tohar said ' runners' have been sent to all the ARSA squads with instructions to launch the attacks at midnight. "*Der kyon kar rahe ho*" (Why are you taking so much time?) enquired Ashfaq to which Tohar replied that "*Message paunchaneme time lagta hai Sir*" (Sir it takes time to deliver the message). Evidently,

ARSA was communicating through physical runners and maintaining complete radio silence to avoid detection.

The last 14 minute call to Tohar was intercepted at 6.02 p.m. from an Iraqi number of purportedly the "***Al-Amin of Daesh***". He on behalf of the ISIS wished ARSA the best in its jihad against the Burmese colonialists, Buddhist and Hindu fanatics.

ISI's Great Game, it was assessed, was to create a new theatre of jihad to adversely affect Bangladesh, India and Myanmar, all of which had governments in power which were not conducive to Islamic radicalism[16], the leitmotif of the ISI and Pakistan. And geographically there was no better common ground than a place closest to the Bangladesh-India-Myanmar trijunction, to execute this Great Game.

ARSA has since been declared a terrorist organisation by the Republic of the Union of Myanmar Anti-terrorism Central Committee Order No. 1/2017 dated 25 August 2017.[17]

Myanmar Response

The Myanmar response to the ARSA attacks of Aug 2017 have as always, been violent, brutal and disproportionate to the scale of the violence perpetrated by ARSA. However on this occasion, the Tatmadaw acted to a plan to evict the Rohingya for good under the euphemism of '*clearance operations*', duly funded by Tatmadaw-solicited donations. Effectively what has been alleged by the UN delegated International Independent Fact-Finding Mission on Myanmar (IIFFMM) on clearance operations[18] falls into a typical pattern Tatmadaw troops attacking villages, indiscriminate firing leading up to deaths, looting, targeted killing of civilians, arson, murder and rape.

Resurgence of ARSA in 2020

In a series of incidents which could signify the resurgence of the ARSA, the organisation ambushed a group of ethnic Rakhine nationals at Maungtaw Township, Rakhine State, on 30 March 2020, killing two using improvised explosive devices (IEDs) and injuring nine others.[19] This was followed up by a number of incidents including on 8 April, 15 April and 30 April 2020.

In the incident on 8 April, Myanmar security forces seized a suspected encampment of ARSA fighters and recovered ammunition, food and uniforms. It consisted of two tents, and was located 2500 metres from Khamaungseik Village, in Maungdaw township in Rakhine State. Troops also recovered one Islamic holy book in one of the tents, as well as an identity card issued by the United Nations High Commissioner for Refugees in temporary shelters in Cox's Bazar in Bangladesh where thousands of Rohingyas have sought refuge. It was noted that the wrappers of food recovered in the encampment had logos of the World Food Programme. Last year, troops seized three ARSA camps in the area. The latest encampment was discovered following tip-off from nearby residents who expressed concern the predominantly Islamic armed group might be planning a big attack in the coming months.[20]

On 15 April, the terrorists ambushed a police party and killed one police officer of Aungzu area office, two km northwest of Khamaungseik Village. On 29 April, two ARSA terrorists were arrested with narcotic drugs, local-made mine and related accessories at the place, about 1,500 metres north of BP 41. In the latest attack on 2 May 2020, ARSA terrorists ambushed members of Myanmar Border Guard Police Force patrolling along the Bangladesh-Myanmar Border from across the fence in Bangladesh, near BP 41. In the incident, two police members were injured.[21] The Myawaddy (Army owned media outlet) suggests that as Myanmar needs to submit a report on Myanmar-Gambia legal issue in May 2020, ARSA terrorists are continuously triggering violence to provoke a response.

ARSA and AA Connivance?

While the AA indignantly denies any alliance with the ARSA, unconfirmed reports suggest a quid-pro-quo between the two is likely since AA relies on Bangladesh territory for arms and ammunition. Allegedly two camps comprising a brigade worth of AA troops are also stationed at Bangladesh. As far as the Bangladesh government and security agencies are concerned, they are looking the other way either due to lack of resources to take on the AA or due to the fact that they are tacitly encouraging the AA as a payback for the Rohingya crisis. There is strong suspicion that the Bangladesh Border Guards are hand in glove with the AA which is indulging in drug smuggling for funding and the BGB officials are benefitting financially. The recent Eastern Link expose on the induction of a large amount of arms and ammunition by the AA through the Chittagong Hill Tracts (CHT) is evidence of the same.[22] The route of induction of the weapons is shown in Fig. 1.

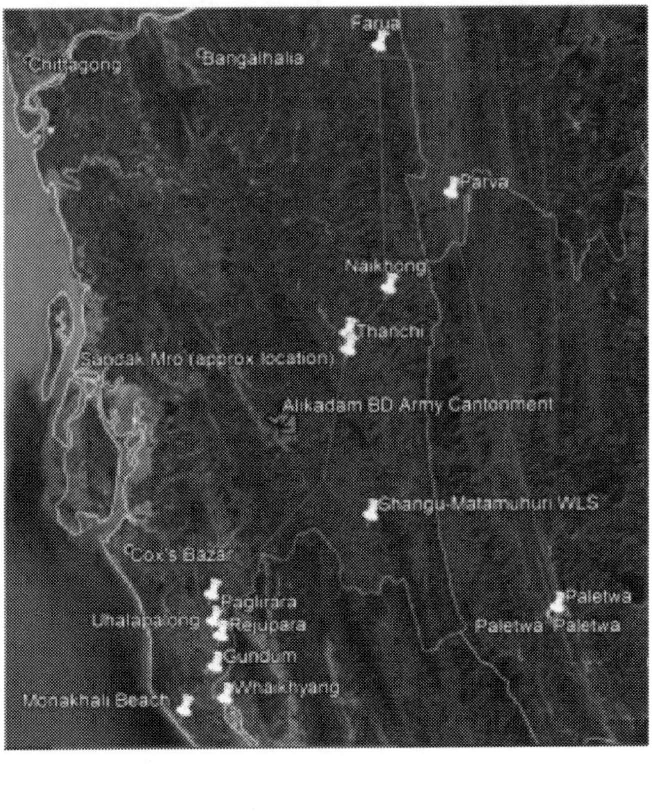

A recent (June 2020) Youtube Video by Rick Heizman, a San Francisco based American ethnomusicologist[23] and Myanmar enthusiast reveals interesting details of the activities of the ARSA. One such nuggest is the claim by the cadres of the ARSA on camera, claiming to have worked together with the AA. Authenticity of the video could not be verified, however, prima facie it seems to be convincing.[24,25]

India's Options

The ARSA and the AA are ideologically opposed but share a common battleground. ARSA operates in the three northern most townships of Rakhine State viz. Buthedaung, Rathedaung and Maungdaw. AA has a wider reach and also operates in these three townships. Ideologically AA has declared that it will establish its HQ at Mrauk-U in Mrauk-U township by end 2020. Its operations have extended upto Ann township which is also the HQ of the Tatmadaw Western Command and close to the Chinese port location of Kyauk Phyru.

India's approach to these two organisations operating against the Myanmar Government has to be nuanced and different. The ARSA with its LeT lineage has to be eradicated and all unfettered assistance to the Myanmar Government has to be provided including technical intelligence. Pressure on Bangladesh Government must also be exerted to act against the ARSA, while supporting its efforts to repatriate Rohingyas to Myanmar.

With AA, the situation is more complex. Currently, as things stand, the Tatmadaw is in no position to eradicate the AA. Like the other EAGs the AA is not asking for independence from Myanmar. However, where most of the others are asking for federalism, AA is gunning for confederalism. Federalism refers to a system of government in which power is split between the national or federal government and state or regional governments, with the national government having more power over the state. However, it is important to note that the regional governments have independent powers and responsibilities. In fact, federalism allows the regional governments to have their own legislative, executive, and judiciary branches through which laws can be passed, interpreted, and enforced as long as they do not contravene the constitution. The system is advantageous because it not only enables the state governments to respond more effectively to the needs of the citizens in their jurisdictions but also provides a mechanism to check the activities of the national government. Even though the national government reserves the rights to make foreign policy, control imports and exports, and declare war, it works together with the state governments in such matters as civil rights, taxation, and environmental protection, among others.

On the other hand, confederalism is a system of government in which sovereign power is held by the regional governments, to which the national government is accountable. The member states are independent and separate but give certain powers to a central authority for reasons of mutual security, convenience, and efficiency.

Member states are the ones that appoint the central authority, which can make rules that will pass as laws only after all constituent states have passed them. Currently Belgium is a confederacy.

Now while confederacy is not acceptable to the Myanmar Government, federalism may be an option.

India's Kaladan Project is doomed unless the AA and Myanmar Government bring peace to the region. Currently the passions are high and the fighting is at its peak. However within a year or so, the battle weariness will set in. India now needs to start overtly and covertly acting for peace and acknowledging the presence of AA, even at the cost of antagonising the Myanmar Government. China has already acknowledged the presence of AA and it (AA) is craving the same from India. India has to drive the two parties to the table for two reasons. First, for the success of the Kaladan Project; and secondly for overall peace in the region. The violence in the region will not subside on its own and its fallout can actually spill over into Mizoram where the population and the State Government is pro-AA.

NOTES

1. Jaideep Chanda, 'Counterproductive Effects of Sanctions - The Myanmar Case Study', VIF Paper, 28 October 2019, https://www.vifindia.org/paper/2019/october/28/counterproductive-effects-of-sanctions-the-myanmar-case-study (Accessed on 9 May 2021).
2. Jayita Sarkar, "Rohingyas and the Unfinished Business of Partition", The Diplomat, 16 January 2018, https://thediplomat.com/2018/01/rohingyas-and-the-unfinished-business-of-partition/ (Accessed on 11 September 2019)
3. https://www.theaustralian.com.au/world/the-times/britains-role-in-the-rohingya-tragedy/news-story/d84285fbc330b4615997b3e4e62d9933
4. Tathagata Dutta, "The Rohingya Crisis Is Another Colonial Legacy", *The Wire,* 16 September 2019: https://thewire.in/south-asia/rohingya-crisis-colonoialsm-second-world-war (Accessed on 16 September 2019).
5. Jayita Sarkar writes '*By late 1944, the pro-Japanese Burmese military units had grown disillusioned with the Japanese and Tokyo's promise of Burmese independence. Aung San, the military leader of the Burma National Army and father of Aung San Suu Kyi, decided to switch loyalty to the British, leading to the 1945 Kandy Conference at the Allied headquarters of the South East Asia Command in present-day Sri Lanka.*' https://thediplomat.com/2018/01/rohingyas-and-the-unfinished-business-of-partition/. (Accessed on 11 September 2019)
6. https://www.thestateless.com/2016/09/the-muslim-massacre-of-arakan-in-1942.html
7. The India Muslims of South Asian origin; the Zerbadees (Muslim fathers and Burmese mothers); Panthays or Chinese Muslims; Kamans or Arakan Muslims; Tambukias of Southern Arakan; Turks and Pathans; Myay Du Muslims in Arakan and the Burmese Muslims who have converted from Buddhism and the Rohingyas.
8. The Faith Movement.
9. For a complete picture of the involvement of ARSA with Islamic terrorist organisations, a study of the Background Paper on Rakhine State by the Myanmar Institute of Strategic and International Studies, May 2018 is highly recommended.
10. International Crisis Group Statement, "Myanmar Tips into New Crisis after Rakhine State Attacks", 27 August 2017: https://d2071andvip0wj.cloudfront.net/Myanmar%20statement%2027viii17.pdf (Accessed on 10 September 2019).

11. Amnesty International, "Myanmar: New evidence reveals Rohingya armed group massacred scores in Rakhine State", 22 May 2018 : https://www.amnesty.org/en/latest/news/2018/05/myanmar-new-evidence-reveals-rohingya-armed-group-massacred-scores-in-rakhine-state/ (Accessed on 1 September 2019)
12. https://blogs.lse.ac.uk/wps/2020/04/21/can-we-take-you-as-a-bride-the-stories-of-eight-hindu-women/
13. Advisory Commission on Rakhine State, "Towards a Peaceful, Fair and Prosperous Future for the People of Rakhine", *Final Report,* 24 August 2017: www.rakhinecommission.org/app/uploads/2017/08/final_report-20170822-news-release_For-Web.pdf (Accessed on 15 August 2019)
14. In September 2016, following a request from Daw Aung San Suu Kyi, the State Counsellor of Myanmar, the Kofi Annan Foundation and the Office of the State Counsellor established an Advisory Commission on Rakhine State. The Rakhine Commission is a national entity and the majority of its members are from Myanmar. It was mandated to examine the complex challenges facing Rakhine State and to propose answers to those challenges. Its final report was an outcome of over 150 consultations and meetings held since its launch in September 2016 and was presented on 24 August 2017. Commission members travelled extensively throughout Rakhine State, and held meetings in Yangon and Naypyitaw, Indonesia, Thailand, Bangladesh, and Geneva.
15. Article on news website "Pakistan, ISIS allegedly behind Rakhine imbroglio", *Mizzima,* 5 September 2016: http://mizzima.com/news-regional/pakistan-isis-allegedly-behind-rakhine-imbroglio (Accessed on 30 August 2019).
16. Article on news website "Pakistan links to Rohingya militants 'deep-rooted'", *Mizzima,* 19 October 2016: http://www.mizzima.com/news-domestic-regional/pakistan-links-rohingya-militants-%25E2%2580%2598deep-rooted%25E2%2580%2599 (Accessed on 30 August 2019).
17. https://web.archive.org/web/20180213022345/http://www.statecounsellor.gov.mm/nrpcen/node/124
18. Human Rights Council, "Report of the detailed findings of the Independent International Fact-Finding Mission on Myanmar" *United Nations,* September 2018, Pp 177 : https://www.ohchr.org/Documents/HRBodies/HRCouncil/FFM-Myanmar/A_HRC_39_CRP.2.pdf (Accessed on 19 September 2019).
19. https://www.globalnewlightofmyanmar.com/arsa-explosive-kills-two-in-maungtaw/
20. https://www.mmtimes.com/news/myanmar-troops-seize-arsa-encampment-northern-rakhine.html
21. http://www.myawady.net.mm/englishnews/item/59427-2020-05-03-08-55-52
22. https://nenow.in/neighbour/bangladesh/chinese-weapons-for-arakan-army-through-bangladesh.html
23. Ethnomusicology is the study of music in its social and cultural contexts. It examines music as a social process in order to understand not only what music is but what it means to its practitioners and audiences. https://www.ethnomusicology.org/page/AboutEthnomusicol#:~:text= Ethnomusicology%20is%20the%20study%20of,Ethnomusicology%20is%20highly%20interdisciplinary. (Accessed 2 Aug 2020).
24. See http://thingsasian.com/story/strings-and-things-burmese-interview-musicologist-rick-heizman, https://www.frontiermyanmar.net/en/yangon-region-minister-hosts-american-anti-rohingya-activist/, https://www.lowyinstitute.org/the-interpreter/myanmar-press-freedom-mirage and https://www.achtzaamheid.nl/en/rakhine-arakan-2/ (Accessed 2 Aug 2020).
25. https://www.youtube.com/watch?v=PhfrCKXZHa4&t=181s (Accessed 2 Aug 2020).

APPENDIX P

First Person Account of Indian Abducted by the Arakan Army

My company won the bid for the road construction from km 60 to km 109 on 21 Oct 2019. We immediately went to Sittwe and Paletwa and opened small offices at both the places. By 2 Nov 2019 I along with my team reached Paletwa and the next morning, 3 Nov 2019 (Sunday), we were returning from Paletwa by speed boat. The team comprised six of us, two boat men and one interpreter. At around 11:00 AM right in between Paletwa and Kyauktaw, our speed boat was flanked on both sides by armed men with AK-47 rifles. They were also on boats. Very tactically they steered us to the river bank. There was another speed boat travelling ahead of us which too had been intercepted and taken aside. I saw the passenger and recognised him as the MP of Paletwa since he had met us and introduced him to us at the jetty site. So we were all asked to disembark and they took everything including the engines of the boat. Thereafter they towed the boats to the other side of the river. Once disembarked, they took away our passports, mobiles and whatever we had on person. By now we had understood that they were Arakan rebels. They slowly they started talking to us and then realised that we were Indians. They were actually after the MP and since our boats were following, they thought we were part of his entourage. They apparently wanted to exchange him for the wife of the Arakan Army Chief who had been kidnapped (arrested) in Thailand.

Anyways, they had tied the MP and taken him away. We were offered tea and then asked to walk along a track away from the river into the jungles. We had walked for about a kilometre when we were asked to turn back and move to the river. When we reached the river, we were placed in a country boat and made to cross the river. All our luggage was also placed in this boat, including the engines of original boats. On the other bank we could see our original boats tied to the river bank. When we asked where we were being taken, our captors now seemed apologetic and indicated that they had made a mistake but they were unable to release us here so they were taking us to their Chief and after that they would release us in some secure place and manner. On the other side they started to make us walk. We must have walked for about three to four hours through agricultural fields and up and down through hills. At this stage, one of our colleagues, who unfortunately was not keeping well, showed signs of fatigue from the strain. By now we were approaching sunset and the time was approximately 5:30 or 6 PM. Now I decided to tell them that I could no longer go forward and even our unwell colleague was lagging behind me a some distance. I came to a stream and sat down and said that I would not go any further since I was too fatigued. One of our team was a local who was interpreting. The captors now insisted angrily that I would have to keep on going since they had orders to take us to meet the leader. By this time I had also had enough. I simply told them that you are 15-20 people and are carrying weapons, please shoot me and take my dead body to your leader. You treat me as if I am gone. My other team mate is also not well, he also can't walk anymore. At this, the captors were now confused as to what to do. It was evident that they were worried and annoyed with us at the same time. One of them had a walkie talkie and he started communicating with his leader. I kept on lying down and told them that I was not feeling well at all and I am 64 years old and not young like you. All of them were in range of 18 to 20 years. They kept giving me water to drink. They also kept telling me that 'no no we will do something...you have to meet our chief', but I would not budge. After about half an hour I could make out a number of people coming from down from the top. The gradient was almost 70 degrees. They had got something like a 'palqui' with them. They asked me to get into the palqui and in about 45 minutes they carried me to the top, which was the destination. The rest of my team had already reached there. Then they rushed down to get our unwell colleague as well.

At the top they kept inspecting my passport and going onto the internet and checking my details. They asked me about my job profile after going through my internet profile. My other team mate had not carried his passport so they could not verify his details. By this time the team carrying my unwell colleague also reached. However since he was a rather bulky person, they had a tough time carrying him up. Plus the ride up would have been a very traumatic experience for him. By the time he reached, he was severely ill. They tried to revive him by applying drip and injecting him. Unfortunately, at around 8 PM he passed away in front of us. They immediately evacuated his mortal remains back to the boat, via the palqui. My other colleague and I raised serious objections and protested about the death and said that our Hindu philosophy prohibits us from leaving the body of a deceased, we have to be with his mortal remains. At this they said that they were very sorry about the incident and that he was in their custody and will be sent to his family. They kept profusely apologising about the death. This interaction kept on going between the two sides for about an hour. In the meanwhile they kept communicating with some people through the several types of communication devices kept there. By now even the Indian authorities had come to know of our situation and activated the channels for our release. We continued to tell them that look we are physically very exhausted and we have to go next to our deceased friend at all costs. Then they quickly prepared a simple dinner comprising noodles. Immediately after that they again brought the palqui and I got on it and we started down. The entire contingent was about 25 strong including our younger team members who walked down. The journey down took just about less than two hours since we took some alternative route. But now they did not take us to our boats. Rather they took us to the outskirts of some village by the river. There was a thatched hut there where they had put a few beds and food was placed for us. Then they told us to take rest since it was 11:30 PM and that they would release us next morning at 5:30 AM when the sun rises since at night if they released us, Myanmar Army might intercept us since boats do not ply on the river at night. But before they left, they gathered their entire team which was over thirty people now, and we met and shook hands with each one of them. Then they told us that they were leaving and four of their local men in plain clothes armed with sticks, would remain with us and escort us in the morning. In front of us they showed us our passports and mobile phones and handed them over to those four men. Then they left. We were very tired and fell asleep right away. They woke us up at 4:00 AM and served us tea. Overall they had been very courteous with us throughout. Then we walked to the boats which were about half an hour walk from there. We boarded the boats and were relieved to find the mortal remains of our colleague placed in the boat properly. Thereafter we set off for Sittwe and reached without any further incident.

APPENDIX Q

Selected Extracts of the Republic of the Union of Myanmar Defence White Paper (2015)

Layout of the White Paper

Chapter	*Subject*	*Sections*
	Introduction	
I	International and Regional Security (Situation)	1. International Security Arena 2. Regional Security
II	Security of Myanmar	1. Geography 2. Challenges on the Security of the Union
III	National Policy and National Defence Policy	1. National Interests 2. National Policy 3. National Objectives 4. Foreign Policy 5. National Defence Policy 6. Defence Missions 7. Defence Strategy
IV	The Establishment of National Defence	1. National Defence and Security Council 2. The Responsibility of Myanmar Tatmadaw 3. Army 4. Navy 5. Air Force 6. Corps and Services 7. Defence Reserve Elements 8. Myanmar Police Force 9. People's Militia
V	Serving Defence Duties	1. Protecting Land Territories 2. Protection of Territorial Waters 3. Protection of Airspace 4. Demarcation of Boundaries 5. System of Military Services 6. Training 7. Organizing Activities 8. Military Equipment 9. Defence Research and Development

Chapter	*Subject*	*Sections*
		10. Defence Expenditure
VI	State Building	1. Background History 2. National Politics & the Role of the Myanmar Tatmadaw 3. State Development Activities under the Leadership of the Tatmadaw 4. Participation of the Tatmadaw in HADR Activities 5. The Contribution of Tatmadaw to the Peace and Stability of the State and Prevalence of Law and Order
VII	Security Cooperation with International Organizations	1. Security Cooperation with United Nations 2. Security Cooperation with International Community 3. Security Cooperation with Regional Organizations and States
	Conclusion	

SELECTED EXTRACTS

Introduction

Para 3. Myanmar lays down her cardinal principles that "**The Union practices independent, active and non-aligned foreign policy aimed at world peace and friendly relations with nations and upholds the principles of Peaceful Co-existence among them**".[1] She also upholds that "**The Union shall not commence aggression against any other nation**"[2] and that "**No foreign troops shall be permitted to be deployed in the territory of the Union**".[3] Myanmar will persevere to build the Myanmar Tatmadaw emerging as a modern fighting force, only for the national defence and security the very existence of the Union. Even though the Union never has any intention to commence any military adventure, aggression, military intervention and coercion, responses and protective measures will be taken in case the State's sovereignty and national interests are threatened.

(*Note:* The bold parts are as marked in the original text).

CHAPTER III

NATIONAL POLICY AND NATIONAL DEFENCE POLICY

National Policy

Para 25. The following "Three Main National Causes"[4] are the National Policy of Myanmar:

(a) Non-Disintegration of the Union;
(b) Non-Disintegration of the National Solidarity; and
(c) Perpetuation of the Union Sovereignty.

National Objectives

Para 26. National objectives are laid down for perpetuation and development of national interests. In accordance with the current political, economic, social and international situations, our national objective is to build a peaceful, modern developed and well disciplined democratic state.

Foreign Policy

Para 28. ...Furthermore, the Union always adheres to the following Five Principles of Peaceful Co-existence:

(a) Mutual respect for each other's territorial integrity and sovereignty;
(b) Mutual non-aggression;
(c) Mutual non-interference in each other's internal affairs;
(d) Equality and cooperation for mutual benefit; and
(e) Peaceful co-existence.

Para 29. The basic principles of the Foreign Policy of the Republic of the Union of Myanmar are as follows:

(a) Respect of and adherence to the principle of equality among peoples and among nations in accordance to the Five Principles of Peaceful Co-existence;
(b) Taking a non-aligned, independent and just stand in international issues;
(c) Maintaining friendly relations with all nations, and good-neighbourly relations with neighbouring countries.
(d) Continued support of, and active participation in United Nations and its affiliated organizations;
(e) Pursuance of mutually beneficial bilateral and multilateral cooperation programmes;
(f) Consultation and beneficial cooperations in regional economic and social affairs;
(g) Active participation in the maintenance of international peace and security and opposition to the creation of an inequitable economic order and imperialism, neo-colonialism, intervention, aggression and hegemonism; and
(h) Acceptance of foreign assistance which is beneficial to national development, provided there are no strings attached.

National Defence Policy

Para 31. The Republic of the Union of Myanmar lays down and practices the National Defence Policies to safeguard the national interests of the Union and it's citizens. Taking into consideration the aspects of historical background, socio-economic conditions and geographical location of the Union, overall situation of the region and the historical tradition of the Tatmadaw, the following National Defence Policies are laid down:

(a) To prevent all acts detrimental to the Three Main National Causes which are non-disintegration of the Union, non-disintegration of the national solidarity and perpetuation of sovereignty;
(b) To formulate National Defence with the People's War Strategy pivoting on Tatmadaw while relying on the synergy of the internal resources of the entire people;
(c) To boldly and effectively prevent any foreign aggression and various ways and means of interference in the internal affairs of the Union, while avoiding interference in the internal affairs of other nations;
(d) To build a defence system that leads towards friendly relations with other nations in accord with the Five Principles of Peaceful Co-existence;
(e) To deter from forming and participating in any military alliance with any other nations and the deployment of any foreign troops in the territory of the Union; and
(f) To cooperate with international community in non-traditional security issues and anti-terrorist matters and to render assistance when natural disasters hit the Union.

Defence Missions

Para 32. To fully safeguard the independence and perpetuation of sovereignty, the defence missions are laid down as follows:

(a) To build a strong, capable and modern patriotic Tatmadaw, combining with the reserve elements in order to dutifully carry out the materialization of our Three Main National Causes: non-disintegration of the Union, non-disintegration of the national solidarity and perpetuation of sovereignty;
(b) To form a modern people's defence system for national defence comprising the entire people based on internal elements without depending on foreign assistance;
(c) To abide by the provisions of the State Constitution and to safeguard the new nation that will emerge according to that constitution for sustained development;
(d) To train and develop a strong defence force which is instilled with military, political, economic and administrative outlooks and competent with the Three Capabilities – Military Capability, Administrative Capability and Organizational Capability – in order to be capable of participating in the national political leadership role in the future state; and
(e) To safeguard the Twelve objectives of the state in order to see the flourishing of the noblest and worthiest of worldly values such as justice, liberty and

equality to ensure the security of national economic interests as well as freedom and security of citizens.

Defence Strategy

Para 33. The National Defence Strategy of the Republic of the Union of Myanmar is the People's War Strategy. The strategy is to deter, contain, repel and annihilate any aggressor trespassing the territory of land, air and sea of the Union by employing the People's War Strategy pivoting on Tatmadaw (Army, Navy and Air Force) and comprising the entire people.

Para 34. The Union has been promoting the balanced development of the political, economic, social and military might to repel the threats of internal and external destructive elements.

CHAPTER IV
THE ESTABLISHMENT OF NATIONAL DEFENCE

The Responsibility of Myanmar Tatmadaw

Para 42. Furthermore, it is also stated in Article 20 (f)[5] that the Tatmadaw is principally responsible for safeguarding the Constitution.

Para 43. Myanmar Tatmadaw lays down the following three principal duties in priority for the successful accomplishment of its core responsibility:

(a) Duty to defend the nation;
(b) Duty to undergo training;
(c) Duty to serve the interests of the people.

Para 44. For the successful accomplishment of national defence duty, Myanmar Tatmadaw lays down the following strategies:

(a) Tatmadaw is principally formulating plans to build strong, competent, modern and patriotic Armed Forces and to implement the People's War Strategy to protect the nation from external military threat.
(b) Since armed conflicts among ethnic groups also pose a threat to internal security and hinder national development, Tatmadaw places specific emphasis on ending the conflicts through peaceful means, aiming at national reconciliation.
(c) Tatmadaw is providing assistance to the respective organizations for the internal security, stability and rule of law which are vital pre-conditions for the development of a nation.
(d) Tatmadaw is taking part enthusiastically in rendering social services, prevention from natural disasters, relief and reconstruction tasks.
(e) Tatmadaw is participating in eradication of narcotics drugs as a national

duty and cooperating with international community for protecting the nation from non-traditional security threats.

(f) Tatmadaw undergoes regular training in order to implement its defence duty anywhere and anytime with alertness and readiness as well.

Army

Para 45. Objective. The Army is to safeguard the National Policy of the State by taking a leading role of the entire Armed Forces – Army, Navy and Air Force. In this regard, Tatmadaw will conduct conventional warfare, unconventional warfare and people's war strategy if necessary in time of external aggression and follow the policies laid down by the State in facing internal insurgencies with prowess.

Para 46. During peace time, the Army has adopted the following objectives to carry out:

(a) To build the Army with the aim of being a strong, competent, modern and patriotic one;

(b) To execute plans for the military operation missions, security and area dominance;

(c) To assist rule of law on land territory, national development and government administrative mechanisms;

(d) To serve the interests of the people including measures of natural disaster prevention;

(e) To safeguard the interests of the Union and the citizens;

(f) To foresee and prepare for foreign aggression; and

(g) To undergo training for combined operations of Army, Navy and Air Force.

Para 47. In times of war, the Army has adopted the following objectives to carry out:

(a) To execute conventional and unconventional warfare in time of external aggression;

(b) To fully launch people's war strategy with nation wide mobilization when facing overwhelming foreign aggression;

(c) To successfully deter, defend and counteract the foreign aggression by taking advantages of natural geography, assets and resources;

(d) To launch combined operations of Army, Navy and Air Force; and

(e) To launch military operations other than war (MOOTW).

Para 48. Formation and Structure. Battalions are organised to be capable of operating independently to a certain extent. Based on battalions, Tactical Operation Command, Light Infantry Divisions and respective Regional Military Commands are formed as follows:

(a) Tactical Operation Commands are formed to command and control battalions.

(b) Light Infantry Divisions are formed to conduct independent operations.

(c) The whole country is divided into 14 regions under command Regional Military Commands, which are assigned to carry out the missions of military operations, security and area dominance in their respective regions.

Navy

Para 49. Objective. Navy is part of the Tatmadaw in maintaining and upholding the defence and security of the Republic of the Union of Myanmar. Myanmar is a coastal country adjacent to the Bay of Bengal and Andaman Sea, Indian Ocean and Myanmar possesses territorial waters as well as area of interests comprising internal waters, territorial sea, contiguous zone and Exclusive Economic Zone (EEZ). For the perpetuation of national sovereignty and territory, the Navy is serving with the following objectives within these sea territories:

(a) To protect Myanmar territorial waters from any form of aggressions;

(b) To protect and safeguard the maritime interests within Myanmar territorial waters;

(c) To launch combined military operations of Army, Navy and Air Force.

Para 50. Formation and Structure. For the successful accomplishment of the objective, the Navy is organised into Naval Regional Commands, naval fleets and operation support units. To be able to build a modern Navy which can effectively protect territorial waters of the Union, the Navy is operating in accordance with the two fundamental principles of being a balanced navy and a combat ready one. Against this backdrop, the Navy is implementing the following activities to form a balanced Navy:

(a) To build an efficient and modern Navy where functions are being regulated for the balanced development of three main pillars; naval fleets, logistics and training; and

(b) Naval fleets are being upgraded to acquire the operational efficiency.

Air Force

Para 51. Air Force is one of the Defence Services arms that can promptly reach out to any remote places and operate. For the defence and security of the Republic of the Union of Myanmar, Air Force lays down objectives to accomplish the following missions:

(a) To assist in implementing the National Policy and National Objectives with the use of aerospace capabilities;

(b) To provide fulltime protection for the security of the Union's airspace and air dominance;

(c) To form a leaner and capable Air Force which possesses effective airpower and aerospace capabilities;

(d) To provide effective support to conventional and unconventional warfare and military operations other than war (MOOTW) by utilizing aerospace capabilities; and

(e) To provide air support to Army and Navy.

Para 52. Formation and Structure. In order to fully implement the objectives of the Air Force with the aim to form a lean and capable one, the Air Force prepares to fulfil its needs and undergoes training to utilize the full power of modern aircrafts, helicopters and weapons, to apply developing military tactics and strategies and to successfully execute the modern warfare.

CHAPTER V
SERVING DEFENCE DUTIES

System of Military Services

Para 73. As every citizen has the duty to protect the Union and serve in armed forces, the Tatmadaw, with the approval of the National Defence and Security Council, has the authority to administer the participation of the entire people in the security and defence of the Union and the People's War Strategy shall be implemented under the leadership of the Tatmandaw.

Military Equipment

Para 77. In modernizing Myanmar Tatmadaw, Army, Navy, and Air Force units are equipped as follows:

(a) **Infantry Regiments and Light Infantry Regiments.** Equipped with modern weaponry, mobilization and training are being carried out for combat efficiency and for coping with any contingency for infantry regiments and light infantry regiments to be credible and flexible forces. Basically, at the regimental level, apart from regimental level assault weapons, fire support weapons, anti-tank weapons and air defence weapons are equipped. Furthermore, equipped with more capable weapons at the levels of Tactical Operation Command, Divisional Command and Regional Military Command are still in the process. For the army as a whole, three levels of fire support, battalion level fire support, and tactical level fire support and pistols, light machine guns, assault rifles, and machine guns as small arms in addition to heavy machine guns, anti-tank weapons and mortars, are equipped to the infantry units.

(b) **Corps of Artillery.** Myanmar Tatmadaw is building the Artillery Corps to be a modernized and a highly capable one. Artillery divisions are organized to annihilate the enemy by fire power as demanded by the tactical objectives. Corps of Artillery is composed with field artillery, mountain guns, anti-aircraft guns, self-propelled guns and multiple rocket launchers.

(c) **Corps of Armour.** Myanmar Armour Corps is equipped with armoured personnel carriers, armoured fighting vehicles, light tanks and main battle tanks.

(d) **Corps of Air Defence.** As the air operations play a vital role in modern warfare, improvement of air defence systems becomes imperative in national defence sector. As for Myanmar Tatmadaw, depending on the area to be covered and capabilities of airborne weapon platforms by the potential adversaries, applicable defence radar systems, air defence artillery systems and air defence missile systems are positioned for air defence.

(e) **Navy.** Myanmar navy is being modernised to take responsibilities of safeguarding the Myanmar coastlines, territorial waters and contiguous zones, exclusive economic zones, delta region and ports and of conducting maritime evacuation, maritime law enforcement, anti-piracy, etc. Myanmar Navy is formed with frigates, corvettes, fast attack crafts (missile), fast attack craft (gun), submarine chasers, torpedo boats, mine warfare vessels, offshore vessels, supply ships, landing crafts and survey vessels.

(f) **Air Force.** Myanmar Air Force is undertaking the duty of defending airspace of the Union and safeguarding the national defence and security jointly with Army and Navy. The Air Force is equipped with multi-role and air superiority fighters, interceptors, ground attack fighters and bomber aircraft, jet and propeller trainers, reconnaissance aircraft, transport aircraft, attack helicopters and transport helicopters.

NOTES

1. This has been enshrined in Article 41 of the Constitution of the Republic of the Union of Myanmar, 2008. The Defence White Paper (2015) reproduces a number of such phrases from the Constitution.
2. Article 42(a) of the Constitution of the Republic of the Union of Myanmar, 2008.
3. Article 42(b) of the Constitution of the Republic of the Union of Myanmar, 2008.
4. Article 20(e) of the Constitution of the Republic of the Union of Myanmar, 2008.
5. Article 20(f) of the Constitution of the Republic of the Union of Myanmar, 2008.

APPENDIX R

Summary of Current Resolutions and Reports of the UN in Relation to Myanmar

Document No (Date)	*Name*	*Gist of Contents*
A/HRC/RES/34/22 (3 Apr 2017)	Resolution adopted by the Human Rights Council on 24 March 2017	This Resolution, vide Para 11 decides to despatch an **Independent International Fact Finding Mission on Myanmar.**
A/HRC/39/64 (12 Sep 2018)	Report of the **Independent International Fact-Finding Mission on Myanmar**	A 21 pg document which gives out the gist of the detailed report submitted subsequently.
A/HRC/39/CRP.2 (17 Sep 2018)	Report of the detailed findings of the Independent International Fact-Finding Mission on Myanmar	A 441 pg document which should be read in conjunction with the report of the Independent International Fact-Finding Mission on Myanmar (A/HRC/39/64) above.
A/HRC/RES/39/2 (3 Oct 2018)	Resolution adopted by the Human Rights Council on 27 September 2018 on ***Situation of human rights of Rohingya Muslims and other minorities in Myanmar***	The Resolution, vide Para 3, **calls** for a full and ***independent investigation*** of the reports of systematic and widespread human rights violations **AND** vide Para 22, **decides** to establish an ongoing independent mechanism to collect, consolidate, preserve and analyse evidence of the most serious international crimes and violations of international law committed in Myanmar since 2011, and to prepare files in order to facilitate and expedite fair and independent criminal proceedings **AND** vide Para 30, **decides** to extend the mandate of the independent international fact-finding mission, established by the Human Rights Council in its resolution 34/22, until the new mechanism is operational to ensure that the large and continually increasing amount of evidence of human rights violations and abuses it has collected is fully documented, verified, consolidated and preserved in order for the material to be effectively shared, accessed and used by the mechanism, and requests the fact-finding mission to submit a final report on its main activities to the Council at its forty-second session.
A/HRC/40/L.19 (19 Mar 2019)	Human rights situations that require the Council's attention	Decides to extend the mandate of the Special Rapporteur on the situation of human rights in Myanmar for a further

Document No (Date)	*Name*	*Gist of Contents*
		period of one year, requests the Special Rapporteur to present an oral progress report to the Human Rights Council at its forty-first and forty second sessions and to submit a report to the Third Committee of the General Assembly at its seventy-fourth session and to the Council at its forty-third session, in accordance with its annual programme of work, and invites the Special Rapporteur to continue to monitor the situation of human rights and to measure progress in the implementation of the recommendations made by the Special Rapporteur
A/HRC/42/50 (8 Aug 2019)	Report of the independent international fact-finding mission on Myanmar*	A 20 pg document which contains the findings of the Independent International Fact-Finding Mission on Myanmar since its previous report (A/HRC/39/64).
A/HRC/42/CRP.3 (5 Aug 2019)	The economic interests of the Myanmar military	A 111 pg thematic supplementary report.
A/HRC/42/66 (7 Aug 2019)	Report of the **Independent Investigative Mechanism for Myanmar**	A 10 pg first report of the Independent Investigative Mechanism for Myanmar on the progress of its work since the Head of the Mechanism officially commenced his functions on 1 July 2019
A/HRC/42/CRP.4 (22 Aug 2019)	Sexual and gender-based violence in Myanmar and the gendered impact of its ethnic conflicts	A 61 pg thematic supplementary report.
A/HRC/42/CRP.5 (16 Sep 2019)	Detailed findings of the Independent International Fact-Finding Mission on Myanmar	A 190 pg document which contains information complementary to that contained in the official report (A/HRC/42/50), submitted to the Human Rights Council pursuant to resolution 39/2.
A/HRC/42/CRP.6 (16 Sep 2019)	Compilation of all recommendations made by the Independent International Fact-Finding Mission on Myanmar, to the Government of Myanmar, armed organizations, the UN Security Council, Member States, UN agencies, the business community and others	A 20 pg summary of recommendations that have appeared in most of the above mentioned documents.

APPENDIX S

Summary of Sanctions Imposed on Myanmar by Various Entities

(Compiled from Open Source English Media. List is not exhaustive)

Imposed By	*Nature of Sanction*	*Start Date*	*Lifted On*	*Remark*
USA	Visa Restrictions	03-10-1996	19-09-2012	Sanctions prohibited the issuing of visas to selected Burmese officials. Waiver lifted the visa ban for President Thein Sein and Speaker Shwe Mann.
	Restrictions on Financial Services	28-07-2003	11-07-2012	Sanctions limited the export or re-export of financial services to Burma. Waiver, allowed the provision of financial services to Burma.
	Frozen Assets	18-10-2007	–	Prohibition on the transfer or utilization of assets of selected Burmese officials held by U.S. financial institutions.
	Import Restrictions	–	–	Ban on the import of products of Burmese origin.
	Investment Restrictions	20-05-1997	11-07-2012	Sanctions banned the new U.S. investments in Burma. Waiver, allowed new U.S. investments in Burma.
	Assistance Ban	28-02-1990	14-09-2012	Sanctions added limitations on the provision for certain types of assistance to Burma by the U.S. government and international financial institutions. Waiver, allowed U.S. assistance, which were previously prohibited due to Burma's poor performance on illegal drug trafficking and production.
EU	Arms Trade Restriction	28-10-2002	30-04-2020	Sanctions were extended in 2007. It is prohibited to export arms and related materiel to Myanmar (Burma). Related technical or financial assistance and services are also prohibited.
	Visa Restrictions	28-10-1996	22-04-2013	Member States shall enforce travel restrictions on persons listed in the Annex of Council Decision 2013/184/CFSP
	Frozen Assets	28-10-1996	22-04-2013	All assets of the persons and entities listed in Annexes IV of Council Regulation (EU) 401/2013 should be frozen. It is also prohibited to make any funds or assets directly or indirectly available to them. The list of persons and entities concerned is included in the Financial Sanctions Database (linked).

Imposed By	*Nature of Sanction*	*Start Date*	*Lifted On*	*Remark*
	Dual-use goods exports restrictions	28-10-1996	22-04-2013	The export of dual-use goods and technology to Myanmar (Burma) is prohibited if those items are or may be intended for military use, military end-user or the Border Guard Police. Any provision of related technical assistance, financing or financial assistance, brokering services or other services are also prohibited.
	Restriction on equipment used for internal repression	28-10-1996	30-04-2020	It is prohibited to export equipment which might be used for internal repression to Myanmar/Burma. Related technical or financial assistance and services are also prohibited.
	Telecommunication equipment restriction	28-10-1996	30-04-2020	It is prohibited to export telecommunications monitoring and interception equipment, technology or software as listed in Annex III of Council Regulation (EU) No 401/2013 to Myanmar (Burma). Related technical assistance or brokering services are also prohibited, unless the competent authority of the relevant Member State has given prior authorisation.
	Restrictions on Military Training and Cooperation	28-10-1996	30-04-2020	The provision of military training to or military cooperation with the Myanmar Armed Forces (Tatmadaw) and the Border Guard Police shall be prohibited. The prohibition shall not apply to training or cooperation aimed at strengthening democratic principles, the rule of law or respect for international law.
Canada	Exports Restrictions	13-12-2007	24-04-2012	Following seemingly positive developments in Myanmar in 2010, including progress towards democracy and improvements to the human rights situation, Canada eased its economic sanctions against Myanmar on April 24, 2012. Most prohibitions under the Special Economic Measures Act were suspended, including most of those pertaining to exports, imports, financial services and investment.
	Restrictions on Aid and Assistance	13-12-2007	24-04-2012	
	Frozen Assets	13-12-2007	–	Canada maintained sanctions against certain listed individuals and entities, which are still in place today. A trade embargo on arms and related material, as well as on related technical and financial assistance, also remains in place.
	Restrictions on Financial Services	13-12-2007	–	
	Restrictions on Technical Assistance	13-12-2007	–	
Australia	Restrictions on the export of supply of goods	26-05-2011	–	Australia continues to maintain an arms embargo and restrictions on the export or provision of services to Myanmar, due to ongoing concerns about armed conflict, weapons proliferation and human rights.

Imposed By	*Nature of Sanction*	*Start Date*	*Lifted On*	*Remark*
	Restrictions on the Export or Provision of Services	26-05-2011	–	
	Targeted Financial Sanctions	26-05-2011	01-07-2012	In October 2018, the Minister for Foreign Affairs imposed new targeted financial sanctions and travel bans on members of the Myanmar military (Tatmadaw), in response to the release of the full report of the UN Fact-Finding Mission on Myanmar, which documented human rights abuses committed primarily by Myanmar's military against ethnic minorities.
	Travel Bans	26-11-2011	01-07-2012	
Japan	Restricted Aid and Assistance	1996	2008	In the absence of progress toward democratization and human rights improvements, however, in fiscal 1996 no grant aid or yen loans for new projects were provided other than small-scale, grass-roots assistance through non-governmental organizations. Outlined below is Japan's economic cooperation with Myanmar in fiscal 1995 when Suu Kyi was released from house arrest, and in fiscal 1996. Resumed aid and assistance, following cyclone Nargis in May 2008.

Source: Compiled by Anjali Gupta, Young Professional, Vivekananda Foundation, from the UN Website.

APPENDIX T

Department of Investment and Company Affairs: Investment Opportunities in Myanmar[1]

Directorate of Investment and Company Administration (DICA)

DICA is the primary interface between businesses and the government and is mandated to promote private sector development and boost domestic and foreign investment by creating a conducive investment climate. It is a key agency within the Government of the Republic of the Union of Myanmar's Ministry of Investment and Foreign Economic Relations (MIFER).

DICA has several functions as:

- A regulator on investment and companies
- A company registrar
- An investment promotion agency
- The secretariat of the Myanmar Investment Commission

Furthermore, it is also responsible for drafting, negotiating and approving bilateral investment promotion and protection agreements and serves as a focal department for all ASEAN investment related affairs.

One of the key roles of DICA is to encourage and facilitate both foreign and local investment by providing information, fostering coordination and networks between investors and continually exploring new opportunities in Myanmar that would benefit both the nation and the business community. To promote business in all areas that benefit Myanmar's ongoing development, DICA acts to explore and evaluate new investment opportunities: to seek land space and capital for investment: to facilitate mutually-beneficial coordination between investors: to prioritise Myanmar and its growth and development and to promote investment services and products in Myanmar.

New Legislation to Promote Investment in Myanmar[2]

Myanmar has created a modern and accessible environment in which to do business by abolishing a 100-year old Companies Act and replacing the restrictive investment laws of the past. The new Myanmar Investment Law (MIL) and the new Myanmar

Companies Law are the regulatory foundations that engender confidence in Myanmar as an investment destination. Investment, in turn, will generate the sustainable development, jobs and economic growth. The new MIL creates a business-friendly environment for foreign and domestic investors by simplifying procedures and making it easier to invest in Myanmar. Three key elements of the MIL are that most investment proposals no longer need to be screened or approved by the Myanmar Investment Commission; now tax 'holidays' of up to seven years are available for promoted sectors in certain geographic areas and funds can now be transferred overseas by foreign and domestic investors.

A new Companies Law, which was enacted in December, 2017 offers world-best practice corporate regulation. Key elements of the Companies Law provide for:

- Foreign investors to own up to 35% of a Myanmar company before it is considered a foreign company,
- Replacement of the inflexible Articles of Association and Memorandum of Association with a corporate Constitution,
- Companies to have at least one resident director who need **not** be a Myanmar citizen,
- New protections for minority shareholders.

Investment Prioritisation[3]

Myanmar Investment Commission (MIC) prioritises the following areas when the investors submit their proposals:

(1) Agriculture and its related services, value-added production of agricultural products
(2) Livestock production, breeding and production of fishery products
(3) Export promotion industries
(4) Import substitution industries
(5) Power sector
(6) Logistics industries
(7) Education services
(8) Health care industry
(9) Construction of affordable housing
(10) Establishment of industrial estate

Agriculture

Myanmar is an agro-based country with fertile land and abundant water resources. It is the backbone of Myanmar's economy, with approximately 50% of its population engaged in agricultural work. It accounts for approximately 20% of GDP. Given the landscape profile, topographic dimensions and different climatic areas of Myanmar – not only perennial plants, but also crops such as rice, pulses and beans, fruits and vegetables can be easily grown. The Myanmar government aims to transform it's mostly traditional agricultural economy into a productive and sustainable agro-economy. To achieve this goal, increases in agricultural productivity and quality are required, for which it has identified certain sub-sectors for investment including:

- Distribution of low-cost irrigation systems to rural communities (e.g. solar-powered, with instruction)
- Leasing of agricultural tools and machinery
- Distribution of high-quality seeds for higher yields (e.g. rice unification in cooperation with the Myanmar Agricultural Bank to incentivise conversion of communities to agriculture with higher productivity levels)
- Establishment of the production of fertilisers, crop protection chemicals etc.
- Contract farming (i.e. direct sourcing from rural communities – based on partnership agreements)
- Introducing value-added production/processing based on local agricultural produce (e.g. groundnut, sesame)
- Establish packaging/canning industry for agricultural produce
- Establishment of research and training institutions or demonstration farms on integrated agriculture, crop sequencing, fertiliser use, organic agriculture and agriculture-related business skill development
- Construction of warehouses and cold storage facilities
- Microfinance, microinsurance and trade finance services for farmers

Aquaculture and Fisheries

Given Myanmar's 2,832 kilometers of coastline along the Bay of Bengal and in the Andaman Sea, fisheries represent an important opportunity for communities and businesses in the coastal areas of Myanmar (**particularly in Rakhine State**). Myanmar's continental shelf covers 228,781 sq km and the country has a Maximum Sustainable Yield (MSY) of approximately 1.05 million metric tonnes annually. In addition to processing abundant reserves of marine produce, Myanmar's inland waters are home to more than 300 different species of fish. The livestock and fishery sector has significantly improved in recent years, with approximately 15% of the population engaged in livestock and fishery work. It accounts for approximately 8% of GDP. Fishing grounds in Myanmar's waters are relatively less exploited than elsewhere. The aquaculture sector is operating almost 50,000 hectares of freshwater ponds. Opportunities in the sector exist inshore (e.g. fish ponds, inland river systems and aquaculture), offshore, and in deep sea locations. The identified sub-sectors for investment include:

- Capture and aquaculture of different types of fish, shrimp and prawn
- Fish and seafood processing facilities,

- Fish food production,
- Cooling, canning and packaging facilities,
- Establishment of education and research institutions to broaden knowledge and enhance human resources available to the fisheries sector

Urbanisation

Myanmar is experiencing a gradual migration process of people moving from rural to urban areas. This is driven by a diverse set of educational, professional and income opportunities. Along with the challenges of urbanisation, there are also opportunities for local and foreign businesses to help develop better, smarter and more liveable cities in the country. Changing demand patterns of the rapidly growing middle class opens up new opportunities for the distribution of a larger spectrum of consumer goods, as well as an emergence of new service industries (e.g. restaurants, entertainment, education). Investment opportunities include:

- Realisation of projects for affordable housing in Yangon, Mandalay and second-tier cities in **all states and regions**
- Restoration of colonial heritage buildings in Downtown Yangon
- Investments into systems for the improvement of public transport in urban agglomerations
- Establishment of parks and facilities for recreation and entertainment
- Provision of private healthcare facilities
- Establishment of private education institutions (e.g. private universities, business schools, certified vocational training)
- Smart traffic management and road safety solutions
- Urban waste management
- Water treatment facilities
- Production and distribution of consumer goods and lifestyle articles

Tourism and Hospitality

The tourism and hospitality sector in Myanmar has been rapidly evolving following the political and economic opening of the country. At the moment, foreign tourists (on their first short-term visit to Myanmar) mostly visit Yangon, Bagan, Inle Lake, Nyaung Shwe and Mandalay. However, Myanmar offers many additional unexplored treasures of natural beauty – from Kawthaung in the tropical South-East, to Putao[4] in the Himalaya. Investment opportunities include:

- Exploring new high-potential investment locations in hospitality and tourism
- Developing eco-tourism (e.g. sustainable hotels and lodges, along with respective activities such as trekking routes or tours)
- Building cultural and community-based tourism (e.g. development of shops for the sale of locally produced cultural goods)

Power

There are many opportunities for investors to help Myanmar reach the objective of full national electrification by 2030. The installation of considerable additional capacity to the current 4,422 MW and the rapid construction of transmission lines are national priorities. In the medium run, Myanmar may even be able to develop into a net exporter of electricity to neighbouring countries. Investment opportunities include:

- Construction of medium to large-scale hydro and gas-fired power plants in Public-Private Partnerships (PPPs)
- Investments into the transmission system (e.g. high-voltage transmission lines between the North of Myanmar and Yangon)
- Realisation of small-scale hydro-power projects (e.g. to supply a village tract)
- Establishment of solar energy farms and wind power farms
- Provision of efficient and practical solar-power kits to communities currently off-grid, as well as of solar-power based solutions (e.g. solar-powered pumps, solar lighting)
- Upgrading of the current power infrastructure in urban centres and industrial zones

Manufacturing

The manufacturing sector opens up opportunities due to the significant domestic market of Myanmar, direct access to the strategic markets of Southeast Asia (ASEAN Economic Community) as well as to China. Myanmar also has comparatively low labour costs, rich natural resource endowments, and a diverse agricultural base for further value-added production to help encourage growth of the manufacturing sector. The investment opportunities in manufacturing include:

- Labour-intensive industries in second-tier cities (e.g. Pathein,[5] Bago, Hpa An) in areas such as production of garments and shoes, or assembling of toys and stationery articles
- Agro-processing industries
- Production of building materials strongly demanded by the national construction industry (e.g. cement, bricks, steel, glass, paints, doors, windows)
- Gemstone processing industries (e.g. jade, sapphires, rubies) to establish value-adding production such as design, cutting and polishing
- Capital-intensive industries (e.g. automotive, land machinery) particularly at locations with good access to international and national markets (e.g. SEZs)

- Wood-processing industry particularly based on hardwood and bamboo (e.g. furniture production)
- Developing the paper and cardboard industry
- High-tech industries (e.g. in Yangon, Nay Pyi Taw, Bago and Mandalay) based on local, regional and global demand and the opportunities through the proximity of international airports
- Chemical industries (e.g. pharmaceutical and plastic articles) based on local and regional demand
- Industrial services (e.g. waste water management, recycling, training)

Infrastructure

The development of better infrastructure is an important requirement to be able to physically carry industrial and agricultural growth in Myanmar. The Government prioritises infrastructural and economic development along certain major trade paths through the country, in order to facilitate the integration of Myanmar into production networks of the Greater Mekong Subregion and Myanmar's Western neighbours. The Government of Myanmar has experience in conducting infrastructural projects under Build-Operate-Transfer (BOT) and other PPP agreements (e.g. in the railway and highway sector), and welcomes investors for infrastructural improvement projects. Investment opportunities include:

- Road, bridge and railway construction
- Construction and operation of airports
- Construction of ports
- Establishment and retrofitting of industrial parks and supportive infrastructure
- Logistics infrastructure

Extractive Industries (Minerals/Oil and Gas)

Myanmar possesses natural resources in abundance, including the following minerals: Alum, Amber, Antimony, Barite, Bauxite, Beryl, Bismuth, Cadmium, Chromite, Cinnebar, Coal, Cobalt, Columbite, Copper, Corundum, Gemstones, Gold, Graphite, Gypsum, Iridium, Iron Ore, Jadeite, Kaolin, Lead, Manganese, Mica, Molybdenum, Natural Gas, Nickel, Ochre, Oil, Oil Shale, Phosphates, Platinum, Salt, Saltpetre, Silver, Soda, Steatite, Sulphates, Sulphides, Sulphur, Tin, Titanium, Tungsten and Zinc. Investors may support the responsible exploration and extraction of natural resources according to international best practices. Myanmar is a candidate of the Extractive Industries Transparency Initiative. Investment opportunities include:

- Exploration and feasibility studies for projects in mining, as well as oil and gas
- Medium to large-scale operation of mines and wells

- Offshore and onshore opportunities for the exploration and extraction of oil and gas
- Establishment of petroleum-based industrial, processing and supportive facilities (e.g. refineries, fertilizers, LPG, LNG)
- Value-added production based on natural resources
- Supporting industries, such as machinery, maintenance, consulting services
- Establishment of education and research institutions to broaden knowledge and enhance human resources available to the extractive industries sector

Forestry-based Industries

Myanmar is one of the leading producers of teak and hardwood (particularly Pyinkadoe and Padauk). In order to prevent unsustainable forestry practices and large-scale log harvesting, the Government of Myanmar strictly and effectively abandoned the export of unprocessed teak and hardwood in April 2014. This structural change offers opportunities to foreign and local investors to support the emergence of value-added and sustainable forestry (e.g. by establishing new wood-processing industries in Myanmar). Furthermore, stronger engagement of the private sector to help restore forests in an environmentally and economically sustainable way is desired. Investment opportunities include:

- Establishment of wood-processing industries (e.g. furniture production)
- Expansion of bamboo forests and bamboo-based production (i.e. handicrafts)
- Rubber-based industries (e.g. tyre production in Mon and Karen State)
- Teak and hardwood plantations
- Sandalwood-processing industries
- Community-based forestry

IMB PROVINCE WISE FOCUS AREAS

Rakhine

With a land area of 36,778 sq km and a population of 31 lakhs, Rakhine attracts much attention due to the two conflicts currently underway there i.e. the Rohingya conflict and the one with the ethnic Buddhist Arakan Army. Rakhine's Mrauk U City is a major archaeological and tourist destination, and the second largest producer of rice in Myanmar after Ayeyarwady Region. Thandwe City is a major seaport in Rakhine State, and only 7km away from Ngapali Beach, one of Myanmar's famous beaches. Rakhine State holds unexplored potential for petroleum and natural gas production. Agriculture, fishery, forestry and tourism hold potential here. Only one-tenth of the state's generally hilly land is cultivated. Rice is the dominant crop in the delta areas, where most of the population is concentrated. Other crops include fruits, chilies, dhani (thatch), and tobacco. The natural hillside vegetation of evergreen forest has been destroyed over wide areas by shifting cultivation (slashing and burning to clear land for cultivation) and has been replaced by a useless tangle of bamboo. An all-weather road running through a pass in the Arakan Yoma connects Taungup with Pyè on the Irrawaddy River. Road infrastructure is critical to facilitate Rakhine State's connection to the rest of Myanmar. The State also needs improvements to its power and communication infrastructure. The Rakhine division of DICA welcomes local and international investment in land development and construction and infrastructure development including urban city, airport and industrial zone development.

Chin

With a land area of 36,019 sq km and a population of 4.78 lakhs, from the perspective of the Indian investor Chin State holds promise. As per the brochure of the Chin State division of the DICA, the state welcomes local and international investors to invest in 10 projects of the Hotel and Tourism Sector and 28 projects of the Electricity & Energy Generation and Distribution Sector. To incentivise and facilitate this, the state will provide land, water and skilled and unskilled labour and tax benefits to the investor.[6] Government efforts with road upgrades in mountainous areas, and renewable energy infrastructure are ongoing but more needs to be done to support agribusinesses and cottage industries like weaving.

The Kaladan Project Two Laned Road from Paletwa to Zorinpui which runs through the Paletwa Township of Chin State and is currently held up due to violence between the Arakan Army and the Tatmadaw. This project has the potential to have a huge positive impact on North East India, Mizoram in specific and Chin and Rakhine States. The potential activity in the wake of the road will provide major benefits for investors.

Sagaing

With a land area of 93,704.5 sq km and a population of 53 lakhs, Sagaing is one of the most important regions on the IMB for Indian investors. Agriculture is the chief occupation. The leading crop is rice, which occupies most of the arable ground. Sagaing is Myanmar's leading producer of wheat, contributing more than 80% of the country's total production. The Region has many rice mills, edible oil mills, saw mills, cotton mills, and mechanized weaving factories. Local industry includes earthen pots, silverware, bronze-wares, iron-wares and lacquerware. Forestry is important in the wetter upper regions along the Chindwin River, with teak and other hardwoods extracted. Important minerals include gold, coal, salt and small amounts of petroleum. Industry includes textiles, copper refining, gold smelting, and a diesel engine plant. The Region has many rice mills, edible oil mills, saw mills, cotton mills, and mechanized weaving factories. Local industry includes earthen pots, silverware, bronze-wares, iron-wares and lacquerware. The controversial Letpadaung copper mine in southern Sagaing

Division, Monywa Township where the project is located, and issues of resource governance more broadly could take the fore in a region where large-scale illegal logging is reportedly a major problem.[7]

Nationally controlled mining and forestry interests are found throughout Sagaing. Kalewa Township hosts several coalmines, and there is a large copper mine located outside of Monywa that has been the site of several serious incidents relating the land and resource rights. Forestry products have played an important role in the economy since ancient times, especially in the northern areas, where teak and other hardwoods are extracted.[8]

Kachin

The Arunachal Pradesh and Kachin link remains the weakest in the entire IMB. In fact Kachin State does not find mention on the Invest Myanmar 2019 website. State linkages remain unexploited unlike in Manipur where the state interacts with the Sagaing Region frequently with friendly football matches and other cultural/people to people interactions. Similar interaction is required between Arunachal Pradesh and the Kachin Government to enable trade and other opportunities to be exploited.

There is a proposal for the revival and development of the Ledo road, also known as the Stilwell Road.[9] See **Appendix U** for a detailed study of the Stilwell Road.

NOTES

1. Culled out from various websites including, https://www.dica.gov.mm/en/investment-opportunities; https://www.dica.gov.mm/sites/dica.gov.mm/files/news-files/mig_final_2018 final26-4-19_1.pdf; https://investmyanmar2019.com/ and the Socio-Economic Atlas of Myanmar (https://elibrary.steiner-verlag.de/book/99.105010/9783515116251).
2. https://www.dica.gov.mm/sites/dica.gov.mm/files/news-files/mig_final_2018final26-4-19_1.pdf, pg 1 and 2
3. Ibid, pg 10.
4. Putao in Kachin State is 40 km from Vijaynagar Salient and lends itself to road connectivity from Arunachal Pradesh in India. A border crossing in the vicinity would enable Myanmar and Indian nationals to connect and use the Putao Airport for further travel into Myanmar. Eventually a scheduled flight from Tezu or Dibrugarh in India to Putao would be the natural logical step forward.
5. Hindi is an important language spoken in Pathein
6. https://investmyanmar2019.com/regions/chin/ (Accessed on 2 June 2020).
7. https://www.irrawaddy.com/election/region/sagaing-division (Accessed on 20 May 2020).
8. https://themimu.info/sites/themimu.info/files/documents/Report_Local_Governance_Mapping_Sagaing_UNDP_Feb2015.pdf (Accessed on 24 May 2020).
9. https://www.orfonline.org/wp-content/uploads/2015/12/IndiaMyanmar.pdf, pg 85, 96 & 94 (Accessed on 26 May 2020).

APPENDIX U

A Brief History of the Stilwell Road

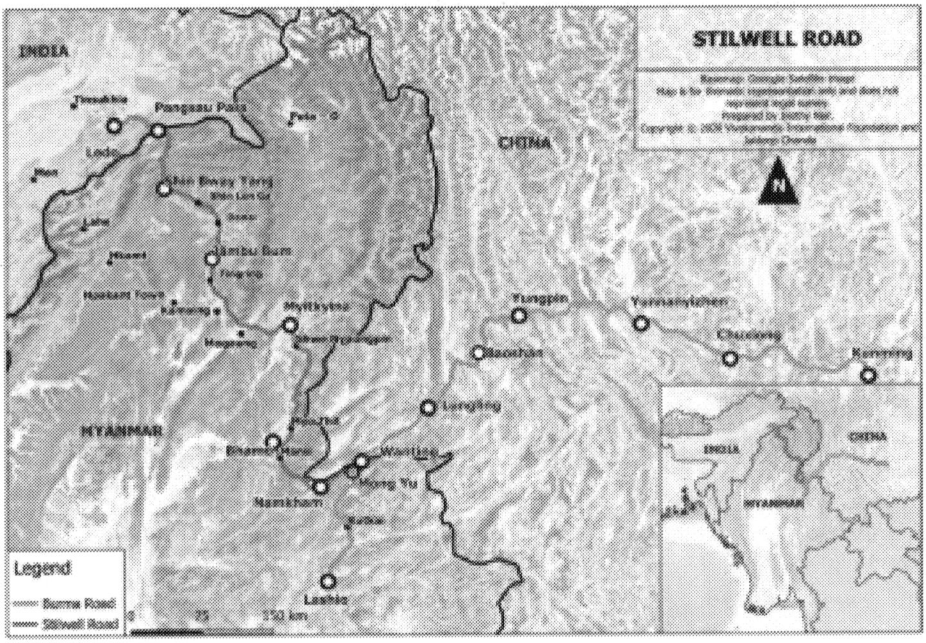

Stilwell Road Alignment[1]

Sl.No.	*Location*	*Distance from Ledo*	
		Km	*Miles*
1	**Ledo (India)**	0	0
2	**Pangsau Pass (India Myanmar Border)**	61	38
3	Tagap Hill (not on map)	127	79
4	**Shin Bway Yang**	165	103
5	**Jambu-Bum**	287	178
6	Warazup (not on map)	304	189
7	**Myitkyina**	403	250
8	**Bhamo**	595	372
9	**Namkham**	707	439
10	**Mong-Yu** (Ledo-Burma Road junction) 10 miles south of Wanting	749	465
11	**Wanting*** (in China)	811	507

Sl.No.	Location	Distance from Ledo	
		Km	Miles
12	**Lungling*** (in China)	896	560
13	**Baoshan*** (in China)	1,043	652
14	**Yungpin*** (in China)	1,208	755
15	**Yunnanyi*** (in China)	1,402	876
16	**Tsuyung*** (in China)	1,543	959
17	**Kunming*** (in China)	1,726	1,079
	Length of Road Lies within	**Km**	**Miles**
	INDIA	61	38
	MYANMAR (BURMA)	1,033	646
	CHINA	632	395

*Part of Burma Road. (Lashio-Kunming)

History of Stilwell Road[2]

Stilwell road is a famous tourist spot in Tinsukia district, Assam State in India. It was constructed in the year 1942 and since then it has been attracting a lot of tourists from places far and wide. In the early part of 1942, Japan occupied Burma during the World War II and the British troops retreated to Assam. The Japanese had cut all communications to China and gradually moves towards the north. And it was during this time that the road was constructed in order to continue with all the supplies to China by the British troops since the Japanese had cut all communications with the Chinese.

General Stilwell was a special representative of American President Roosevelt whose headquarters were at Taipha in Hukawang valley of Myanmar beyond the Patkai. General Stilwell was entrusted with the responsibility of attending to the supplies of the Chinese nationalist forces and hence the construction of the Stilwell road we see today. The sole reason was the maintenance of the supply line to China from the Ledo rail head in Assam, the Stilwell road was planned in the year 1942 in February initially from Moguang on the Myitkyina Railway on the Irrawaddy river in the Kachin State of Burma. The project was however, initially named as the Ledo Road.

The responsibility for the strict supervision during the construction of the Stilwell road was endowed on Mr. Lambert IPS, who was posted in February, 1942. Mr. Lambert was actively involved in the planning, construction of the Stilwell Road. He was on special duty here in the area for six long months. The work on the road started in April, 1942 with an initial length of 1079 miles which is about 1736 kms and then finally completed in the year 1944 in October making a record of completing it in two and a half years. The road successfully connected all important places between Ledo and Kunming. The long road fell in not only one country but in three different countries. Of the entire length of the road, 36 miles (57 kms) fall in India, 646 miles (1,040 kms) fall in Myanmar and 397 miles (639 kms) in China.

Though the Stilwell Road was started initially by the Civil authority, under the direct supervision of the Political Officer, yet later on it was taken over by the American engineers for speedy progress. After the construction of the road was completed, its name was changed to Stilwell road to dedicate it to General Stilwell for his dedication towards the construction of the Road.[3]

Soon after the construction of the road and after the war, it was to be maintained by the political officer. It was also kept open for civilian usage such as for tourists and general use. However, it was soon abandoned by the Myanmar government and gradually the road became impossible for vehicular traffic due to landslides. The portion between Jairampur and Zero mile that falls under Assam jurisdiction was handed over to the Assam Government for maintenance who in turn handed it over to NEC who again did not pay any attention to it leading to the total devastation of the road. However, the Arunachal Pradesh portion up to the border, which covers around 36 kms. is still however maintained from the administrative and security point of view. But owing to insurgent activities the border was sealed by the Government several years back except movement of civilians including the tribals living on the border causing obstruction in their cultural relations and village economy by way of better system of trade with their counterparts.

Present Status[4]

The border between Assam and Arunachal Pradesh has 14 km of the road section repaired and the construction of international trade route is underway to link Myanmar at Pangsau Pass. In India side, the road is being repaired and renovated up to Nampong under this scheme and extension of the renovation work up to Pangsau Pass, Indo-Myanmar border is underway. The section of road which lies within Arunachal Pradesh has been maintained by the Government of Arunachal Pradesh and the road section which lies within the area of Assam out of 14 km has been in maintained by the Government of Assam respectively. The Indian government has proposed this road for reopening as International Highway for trade route to link Myanmar, China and other Southeast Asian countries in its Act East Policy. The reopening of this road as trade route will increase the interaction between the people of neighbouring countries and maintain good relationship among the member countries. It will also boost trades and attracts inland and foreign tourists as the road itself is historically famous and significant due to Second World War, which in turn will boost socio-economic development of this most backward border area and will benefit the local people.

NOTES

1. https://changlang.nic.in/stilwell-road-ledo-road/
2. www.tinsukiaonline.in, 'city-guide' stilwell-road
3. For further reading see *A Surgeon with Stilwell: Dr. John H. Grindlay and Combat Medicine in the China-Burma-India Theater of World War II (https://www.pdfdrive.com/a-surgeon-with-stilwell-dr-john-h-grindlay-and-combat-medicine-in-the-china-burma-india-theater-of-world-war-ii-d196870206.html)*; Images of War: Stilwell and the Chindits - The Allied Campaign in Northern Burma 1941-1944 (https://www.pdfdrive.com/images-of-war-stilwell-and-the-chindits-the-allied-campaign-in-northern-burma-1941-1944-d194942623.html); Stilwell's Mission to China (https://www.pdfdrive.com/stilwells-mission-to-china-d165024784.html); and Burma Road, 1943-1944: Stilwell's Assault on Myitkyina (https://www.pdfdrive.com/burma-road-19431944-stilwells-assault-on-myitkyina-d184710002.html) (All accessed on 2 August 2020).
4. https://changlang.nic.in/stilwell-road-ledo-road/

Index

Advanced Centre for Agricultural Research and Education (ACARE), 52, 278
Aiyar, Mani Shankar, former IFS officer and Indian Petroleum Minister, 328
Ajmani, Manmeet, 222
Al Jazeera, 235
All India Radio (AIR), 301
All Tripura Tiger Force (ATTF), 194
Amara Thiha, 324
Amb Gautam Mukhopadhyaya, 75, 79
Amb K.S. Rana, 327
Amb Mukhopadhyaya, 81, 84
Amb Preet Malik, 33, 51
Amb Rajiv Bhatia,
  India-Myanmar Relations: Changing Contours, 45
Amb Rajiv Sikri, 310
Amb Saurabh Kumar, 96
Amb Shyam Saran, 80-81, 197
Amb T.P. Sreenivasan, 85
Annual Army Day Reception, 196
anti-Muslim, 235
anti-Rohingya, 235
Aqa Mul Mujahid (AMM), 57
Arakan Army (AA), 14, 136, 144-45, 153, 158-60, 177, 365, 432, 435, 458-59
  Aspirations, 134
  Declaration, 142
  First Person Account of Indian Abducted, 435-37
  Funding, 156
  Kingdom, 134
  Leadership, 154
  Motivation, 154
  Operations, Strategic Clarity, 144
Arakan National Congress (ANC), 57
Arakan National Party (ANP), 137
Arakan Rohingya Salvation Army (ARSA), 57, 59, 132-33, 147, 184, 207-8, 232, 235-36, 428-32
  Current Crisis and Pakistan's Involvement, 428
  Myanmar Response, 430
  and AA Connivance, 431
  India's Options, 432
ASEAN, 83, 117, 195, 222, 225-26, 283-84, 309, 332
ASEAN+, 225, 227
ASEAN+6, 223
Asia Pacific, 166
Assam Rifles, 104, 125-26, 198, 356-57, 371
Ataullah Abu Ammar Junjuni@ Hafiz Tohar Aqa Mul Mujahid (AMM), 207
Aung San Suu Kyi, 59
Autonomous District Councils (ADC), 127

Bangladesh, 10, 157, 225-26, 429
Bangladesh-China-India-Myanmar Economic Corridor (BCIM-EC), 255
Belt and Road Initiative (BRI), 59, 254-55
  Projects in Myanmar, 266
Bhabhatron-2, 278
Bhagwan Mahaveer Viklang Sahayata Samity (BMVSS), 61
Bharat Dynamics Limited (BDL), 200
Bhaumik, Subir, 123, 125
  Insurgent Crossfire, 121
  The Troubled Periphery, 121
Big Businesses, 321
BIMSTEC MILEX 2018, 61
BIMSTEC, 79, 82-84, 195, 225, 227, 283, 314
Border Pillar (BP), 10

Brig K.A. Muthanna, 190
Brig Rumel Dahiya, 195
BROUK, 235
Burma-China Boundary, 18
Burmese Rohingya Organisation of UK (BROUK), 234

Centre for International Private Enterprise (CIPE), 270
Chander, Rajiv, 226
Chattopadhyay, Sarat Chandra
    Pather Dabi (*Demands of the Road*), 298
Chaudhury, Dipanjan Roy, Journalist, 269
Chettiars, 302
Chin National Day, Evolution, 361
Chin State, 153, 361
    Administrative Divisions, 362
    Demography and Language, 362
    Connectivity, 363
    Importance for India, 365
China, 2, 16, 31, 58, 85-86, 110, 116-17, 146, 195, 214, 223-24, 249, 279-80, 310, 314, 317, 324, 340-41, 462-63
China Communications Construction Company Ltd. (CCCC), 271
China's Engagement in Myanmar's Internal Affairs, 58
China-India 'Power Rivalry', 166
China-India-Myanmar, 2, 18
China-Indochina-Peninsula Economic Corridor (CIPEC), 255-56
China-Myanmar Economic Corridor (CMEC), 59, 254, 283-84
    Current Status, 268-71
    Deciphering, 261-66
    Evolution, 258-59
    Hambantota Effect, 272
Chinese Involvement, 156
Chinram Concept, 364
Christian Socialism, 125
Citizenship Amendment Bill 2019, 119
Cohen, David, 222
Col Arvind Dutta, 191
Coomaraswamy, Radhika, 210
Coordinated Operations, 190
Corr, Anders, 158
Counter-Insurgency (CI) operations, 137
COVID-19, 16-17, 118, 144, 246, 279, 310, 340
Cultural Connects, 297
Cyclone Nargis, 48

Daulat Qazi, 293
Davis, Anthony, 172, 176
Daw Aung San Suu Kyi, 73, 232, 247
    Visited India, 59
Defence Attaches (DAs), 191
Defence Cooperation, 190, 200
Defence Diplomacy, 50, 190-91, 203
    Criticisms, 201
    Foreign Policy, 193
    Genesis, 189
Defence Services Council Order, 173
Democratic Voice of Burma, 235
Detailed Project Report (DPR), 94
Development of North Eastern Region (DoNER), 79
Development Pillar, 213
Development versus Security, 334
Directorate of Defence Services Intelligence (DDSI), 195-96
Directorate of Investment and Company Administration (DICA), 15, 452
Down to Earth, 329
Dr. Arpita Mitra, 292, 297-98, 303
Dr. Arvind Gupta, 189
Dr. Manmohan Singh, former Indian Prime Minister, 52, 53
Dr. Maung Aung Myoe
    Building the Tatmadaw: Myanmar Armed Forces since 1948, 163
Dr. Min Zaw Oo, 174
Dr. Myint Zaw, 274
Dr. Naing Swe Oo, 182
Dr. Prashanth Parameshwaran, 171
Dramatis Personae, 397-401

East Coast Rail Link (ECRL), 256
Emperor Bahadur Shah Zafar, 291, 293-95
Engagement Present Levels, 199
Engineering Projects India Limited (EPIL), 103
Ethnic Armed Organisations (EAO), 136
EU, 166

Fast Moving Consumer Goods (FMCG), 100
Federal Political Negotiations and Consultative Committee (FPNCC), 136
Foreign Office Consultations, 19
Free Movement Regime (FMR), 17

G2G, 314
Gandhi, Rajiv, 32, 35
  visited Myanmar, 47
Gas Authority of India Limited (GAIL), 267, 283, 314
Gates, Robert, former US Secretary of State, 190
Gen Ne Win, 29, 32, 35-36, 38, 40-41, 315
Gen V.P. Malik, 178-79, 197-98, 201, 312
Genesis Blind Spot, 74
Greater South Asia, 82-83
Guanxi versus *Ah nar de*, 274-75
Gujral Doctrine, 74-75

Harakah al-Yaqin, Rohingya Militant Group, 207
Hearts and Mind Investments, 283, 313
Huffington Post, 235
Human Rights Pillar, 213
HUMINT, 151

Independent Investigative Mechanism in Myanmar (IIMM), 209
India, 2, 10, 16, 19, 24, 26, 32-35, 38, 41, 46-53, 61, 64, 66-68, 100, 109, 118, 129, 159, 192, 201, 223-24, 226-27, 254-55, 284, 292, 310, 314-16, 319-20, 323, 332, 340-41, 432
India-Myanmar
  Agreements, Joint Statements, MoU and other Selected Documents, 411-20
  Assessment, 322
  Bilateral Relations, 203
  BIMSTEC, 68
  Books on Myanmar by Indian Authors, 394-96
  Commerce, 66
  Connectivity, 317
  Cultural Exchange, 68
  Defence Cooperation, 65
  Development Cooperation, 64
  History, 31
  Kaladan Multi-Modal Transit Transport Project, 421
  Language, 315
  Project Preparation Facility, 69
  Space and Small Businesses, 320
  Training & Capacity Building, 67
  Visit of Business Delegations, 67
India-Myanmar Border (IMB), 1-2, 7-8, 10-12, 15, 17-19, 117, 119, 173, 312-13, 317, 351-56, 371, 458
  Evolution, 6
  Political and Demographic Description, 10
  Terrain, 8
  Trijunction to Trijunction, 11
India-Myanmar Chamber of Commerce (IMCC), 322
India-Myanmar Coordinated Patrol (CORPAT), 199
India-Myanmar International Boundary Agreement, 345-50
India-Myanmar Naval Exercise (IMNEX-18), 199
India-Myanmar Post Level Meeting (IMPLM), 173
Indian Insurgent Groups (IIGs), 15, 194
Indian National Army (INA), 194
Indian Technical and Economic Cooperation (ITEC) Programme, 49
Indira Gandhi-Ne Win, 192
Indonesia, 225
Inland Water Transport (IWT), 94, 96, 98-99, 138, 422
  Layout Plan, 101
Inland Waterways Authority of India (IWAI), 95
INS *Sindhuvir*, 200
Institute for Training and Technical Co-operation (ITTC), 220
International Court of Justice (ICJ), 232, 239
  Gambian Application, 240
  Judgement, 245
  Lady Leads Myanmar Defence, 243
  Reactions, 246
  Next Steps, 246
  Why The Gambia?, 240
International Criminal Court (ICC), 232, 237
International Criminal Tribunal for Rwanda (ICTR), 237
International Independent Fact-Finding Mission on Myanmar (IIFFMM), 208-11
  Recommendations Quality, 217-19
Internet, 151
IRCON Infrastructure Services Limited, 103
Irrawaddy Imperatives, 335-36

Joint Operations, 190
Joint Trade Committee (JTC), 20
Joint Working Group (JWG), 19
Joshi, P.K., 222

Judge Xue Hanqin, 246

K. Yhome, 225
Kabaw Valley Border, 19
Kachin Independence Army (KIA), 137
Kachin State, 6, 11, 268, 312-13, 355, 376, 461
    Administrative Divisions, 378
    Connectivity, 379
    Demography and Language, 379
    Importance for India, 380
Kaladan Multi Modal Transit Transport Project (KMMTTP), 14, 90-110
    Impact on Mizoram, 123
Kalinga International Foundation, 149
Kamtapur Liberation Organisation (KLO), 322
Kanglei Yawaol Kanna Lup (KYKL), 322
Kaplan, Robert D., 1, 254
    Monsoon: The Indian Ocean and the Future of American Power, 31
Karen National Union (KNU), 63
Kennedy, John F., 203
Kensuke Yamaguchi, 248
Khaing Thukha, 147
Khazani, Sohel, M/s A to Z Exim, 98, 100, 102
Khin Khin Kyaw Kyee, Executive Director, Institute for Strategy and Policy, Myanmar, 274
Khine Thukha, 146
King Thibaw, 295
Kishore, Avinash, 222
Korea Gas Corporation (KOGAS), 267, 283, 314
Kovind, Ram Nath, President of India, 61
Kumar, Saurabh, Indian Amb in Myanmar, 308

Lalbiakmawia, Ricky, 119
Land Border Crossing Agreement (LBCA), 18
Land Border Crossing Agreement, 2018, 389-93
Laos, 2, 223
Least Developed Countries (LDC), 56
Liberation Tigers of Tamil Eelam (LTTE), 123
Light Infantry Battalion (LIB), 138
Light Infantry Divisions (LIDs), 137
Lord Mountbatten, 32
Lt Gen Moe Myint Tun, 182, 185

Manipur Border with Chin State, 352
Marston, Hunter, 248
Martin, Michael F.
    Sanctions on Burma, 224
Maung Aung Myoe, 165, 181
Menon, V.K. Krishna, 23
Mere Pia Gaye Rangoon, 291
Micro, Small and Medium Enterprises (MSMEs), 322
Ministry of Development of North East Region (MDONER), 95, 110
Mizo Accord, 124
Mizo Insurgency, Arakan Connect, 120
Mizo National Famine Front (MNFF), 120
Mizo National Force, 14
Mizo National Front, 120
Mizo National Party (MNP), 14
Mizoram, 126, 127
    Border with Chin State, 351
    Field Visit, 118
    Politics, Church Importance, 125
Mizzima, 235
Modi, Narendra, Indian Prime Minister, 55, 58
Moreh Segment, 353
Murphy, Erin, 220
Muslim National Area, 207
Myanmar
    Absent Discipline, 82
    Banned Wagon, 219
    Borders, 3
    Consciousness, 73, 280
        Absence, 77
    Elevation and Major Rivers, 4
    Genuine Development, 310
    Geographic Subdivisions, 5
    India's Support, 224-27
    Investment Opportunities, 452-60
        Agriculture, 453
        Aquaculture and Fisheries, 454
        Chin, 459
        Minerals/Oil and Gas, 457
        Forestry-based Industries, 458
        Infrastructure, 457
        Investment Prioritisation, 453
        Manufacturing, 456
        New Legislation to Promote Investment, 452
        Power, 456
        Tourism and Hospitality, 455
        Urbanisation, 455
    Response, 208
    Sanctions Imposed, 449

Self-Administered Zones and Divisions, 13
State Structures, 14
Myanmar Defence White Paper, 166, 438-46
Air Force, 444
Army, 443
Defence Missions, 441
Defence Strategy, 442
Foreign Policy, 440
Military Equipment, 445
National Defence Policy, 440
National Objectives, 440
National Policy, 439
Navy, 444
System of Military Services, 445
Tatmadaw Responsibility, 442
Myanmar Economic Corporation (MEC), 215
Myanmar Economic Holdings Limited (MEHL), 215
Myanmar Institute of Information and Technology (MIIT), 278
Myanmar Institute of Peace and Security (MIPS), 62, 169
Myanmar National Democratic Alliance Army (MNDAA), 143, 246
Myanmar Oil and Gas Enterprise (MOGE), 267, 283, 314
Myanmar's Border, Importance for India, 12
Myanmar's International Purchases, 222
Myanmar-China Border Economic Cooperation Zones (BECZ), 263-64
Myanmar-China Gas Pipeline Project, 267
Myanmar-China Oil Pipelines, 267
Myawady Daily, 141
Myitkyina Economic Development Zone (MEDZ), 268, 270

Naga Self-Administered Zone (NSAZ), 11-12, 55, 121, 129, 319, 369, 373-75
Importance for India, 375
Nagaland Border, 354
Nan Lwin, 268
National Company Law Tribunal (NCLT), 103
National Defence and Security Council, 167
National Democratic Front of Bodoland (NDFB), 322
National Development and Reform Commission (NDRC), 255
National Ideology and the Role of Defence Services (NIRDS), 182
National Knowledge Network (NKN), 279
National League for Democracy (NLD), 14
National Level Meetings (NLM), 19
National Policy and National Defence Policy, 167
Nationwide Ceasefire Agreement (NCA), 54
NATO, 166
Nehru Memorial Museum and Library, 24, 32, 36, 75, 192
Nehru, Jawaharlal, former Indian Prime Minister, 24, 26-27, 32-36, 85-86, 301, 315
Netaji Subhash Chandra Bose, 296
New Democratic Army-Kachin (NDA-K) militia, 269
New Yangon Development Company (NYDC), 271
No Construction Zone, 19
Nobel Laureate Guru Rabindranath Thakur, 296
Non-Governmental Organisations (NGOs), 143
Northern Rakhine Victims, 239

ONGC CASPIAN E&P B.V. (OCEBV), 267, 283, 314
OODA loop, 282
Operation All Clear, 121
Operation Golden Bird, 193, 194
Operation Jericho, 120
Operation Naga Amin, 422
Operation Parakram, 79
Operation Sunrise, 15, 117, 123, 134, 154, 159, 177, 200, 226, 322-23, 373
Organisation of Islamic Cooperation, 232
Outspoken Advocacy, 213

Panda, Ankit, 91
Pandit Kabi Syed Alaol, 293
Pandit Ram Niwas, 298
Pangsau Pass Segment, 355
Parameswaran, Prashanth, 142
Passport (Entry into India) Rules, 1950, 386-88
Peace and Security Pillar, 213
Peace-talk Creation Group (PCG), 143
People's Daily, 280
People's Liberation Army (PLA), 194
People's Liberation Army of Manipur, 322
People's Revolutionary Party of Kangleipak (PREPAK Pro), 322

People's War Strategy, 167
Phek and Kiphire Segment, 354
Political Tradition of the Tatmadaw, 181
Politics and Prisoners, 295
Port & Inland Water Transport (PIWT), 94
POSCO DAEWOO, 267, 283, 314
Prasad, Baleshwar, 30, 192
Prof. Daw Kyi Kyi Hla, 232
Prof. Dilip K. Chakravarti, 9, 291-92
Prof. L.K. Choudary, 36
Project Development Consultant (PDC), 94
Pu Zoramthanga, 121

Quantity towards Quality, 173
Quiet Diplomacy, 212-13

Rakhine State, 12, 16, 61-62, 64, 102, 132-33, 137-39, 152, 267, 275, 313, 360, 381, 458
    Administrative Divisions, 383
    Conflict Resolving, 331-32
    Connectivity, 384
    Demography and Language, 383
    Importance for India, 384
    Operations Area, 152
Raschid, Bilal,
    The Invisible Patriot: Reminiscences of Burma's Freedom Movement, 301
Rau, Benegal Narsing, 34
Rauf, Mohammed Abdul, 26-29, 301
Reciprocal Exiles, 293
Recruitment, 173
Regional Border Committee (RBC), 20, 201
Regional Conflict Complex, 133
Relatively Speaking, 301
Renaud, Egretau, 47
Restoration Council of Shan State (RCSS), 63
Rice-Killing Day, 60
Riverine Warfare, 149
Road Components, 103
Robust Advocacy, 213
Rosenthal, 212-13
Roy, Devesh, 222

SAARC, 75, 78, 83-85
Sagaing Region, 11, 17, 313, 367, 459
    Administrative Divisions, 369
    Demography and Language, 370
    Connectivity, 370
    Importance for India, 371
Sasanavamsa, 297
Sectoral Level Meetings (SLM), 19
Security Diplomacy, 190
Security Sector Reform, 218
Self-Administered Division, 116
Self-Administered Zones, 116
Selth, Andrew
    Secrets and Power in Myanmar: Intelligence and the fall of General Khin Nyunt, 176
Senior Gen Ming Aung Hlaing, 185
Serving Defence Duties, 168
Seth, Sunil, President IMCC, 322
SGBV30 Victims, 239
Shah, Sudha
    The King in Exile: The Fall of the Royal Family of Burma, 295
Shwe Nadi, 146
Sidoti, Christopher, 210
Siliguri Corridor, 90, 110
Singapore, 225
Sittwe Port, 94-96, 99-100, 106-7, 110
    Layout Plan, 97
Small Businesses, 321
Smeets, Maarten, 221
Smith, Martin, 57, 132
Social Media, 155, 332
Soe Myint Aung, 248
South East Asia Pipeline (SEAP) Company, 267, 283, 314
South-East Asia Gas Pipeline Company Limited (SEAGP), 267, 283
South-East Asia Gas Pipeline Company Limited, 314
Standard Army, 165, 169, 171, 172
State Building, 168
State Development Activities, 168
Stilwell Road, 456-58
Sweeney, John, 221

Ta'ang National Liberation Army (TNLA), 58, 60, 62, 143, 246
Tactical Innovation, 146
Tatmadaw, 165, 173, 296
    Counter-Insurgency Operations, 183
    Day 2020, 177
    Engaging, 329-31
    Intelligence, 150, 176
    Professional Ethos, 177
    Senior General and Succession Plans, 184
Tatmadaw's Attempts to Isolate AA, 143
TECHINT, 151

Thailand, 2, 6, 223, 225
Thant Myint-U, 1, 206
The Diplomat, 91, 142, 171
The Gambia, 240, 244, 245
The House of Memories, 296
The Irrawaddy, 143-44, 147, 171, 268
The Pioneer, 196
Thematic Report: Myanmar Military Economic Interests, 214
Think Tanks Interaction, 333
Third Space, 321
Thomson, Andrew, 223-24
Three Brotherhood Alliance, 136
Tim Mbiti, 136
Tin Mukh Pillar, 10
Treaty of Peace and Friendship, 1951, 407-08
Tri-junction Border Pillar, 10
Tuensang and Mon Segment, 355
Tula Toli Victims, 239
Turnell, Sean, 302-3
Turner, Carl, 133
Tyabji, S.A.S., 25-26

U Htin Kyaw, Myanmar President visited India, 56
U Hwei Ting, 147
U Win Myint, President of Myanmar MoUs Exchanged, 277-78, 409
Ukhrul Segment, 353
UMFCCI, 47
UN Role in Myanmar, Independent Inquiry, 211
Union Election Commission (UEC), 50
Union Solidarity and Development Party (USDP), 185
United League of Arakan (ULA), 56
United Liberation Front of Assam (ULFA), 117, 194, 198
United National Liberation Front (UNLF), 322
United Nationalities Federation Council (UNFC), 57
United Nations (UN), 166, 206, 211
    Initiatives, 208
    Resolutions and Reports, 442-43
United Nations Human Rights Council (UNHRC), 208
    Resolution No. 39/2, 209-10
Unlawful Association, 142
Unmanned Combat Aerial Vehicles (UCAVs), 139
Unresolved Border Alignment Issues, 18

Valley of Rubies, 6
Vasisht, Cchavi, 134, 137
Verghese, B.G., 90
Vice Admiral Ram Dass Katari, India's first Indian Naval Chief & Amb to Burma, 7, 39, 192
Victims, Participation and Reparations Section (VPRS), 238
Vijaynagar Salient Segment, 356
Vipassana, 298
Voice of Myanmar, 144

Way of Rakhita, 144
Winger, Gregory, 190
WTO, 166, 221

Xi Jinping, 59, 63, 156, 254-55, 261-63, 266, 270, 274-75, 314, 323

Yahya A.J.J. Jammeh, 241
Yan Pai, 171
Yezdezard (Yezdi) Dinshaw Gundevia, 24-25
    Outside the Archives, 24
Yhome, 226
Yun Sun, 151-52, 282
Yunnan Tengchong Heng Yong Investment Company (YTHIC), 268

Zoramthanga, 122

*